T0229207

Computational Intelligence

Critical acclaim for
Computational Intelligence

Russ Eberhart and Yuhui Shi have succeeded in integrating various natural and engineering disciplines to establish computational intelligence. This is the first comprehensive textbook, including lots of practical examples.

– Professor Shun-ichi Amari
RIKEN Brain Science Institute
Japan

Computational Intelligence *describes a large, diverse, and evolving field of theories and techniques, all inspired in one way or the other by nature. The three pillars of CI—neural networks, fuzzy systems, and evolutionary computation—along with their many variants, interact in meaningful ways to solve very complex problems. This book is an excellent introduction to the field, greatly suited for an advanced undergraduate/beginning graduate student course, or for an interested scientist or engineer. The authors guide the reader in an easy-flowing way through the history and foundational mathematics toward practical implementation of a few fundamental problem-solving systems in each area. In the fuzzy set chapters, they picked the most common application tool, fuzzy rule-based systems, even mixing evolutionary design into the implementation. This book is an excellent choice on its own but, as in my case, will form the foundation for our advanced graduate courses in the CI disciplines.*

– Professor James M. Keller
University of Missouri–Columbia

This excellent new book by Eberhart and Shi asserts that computational intelligence rests on a foundation of evolutionary computation. This refreshing view has set the book apart from other books on CI. It has an emphasis on practical applications and computational tools, which are very useful and important for further development of the computational intelligence field. I am delighted that I have a copy of this book.

– Professor Xin Yao
The Centre of Excellence for Research in
Computational Intelligence and Applications
The University of Birmingham, Edgbaston
Birmingham, United Kingdom

Computational Intelligence Concepts to Implementations

Russell C. Eberhart

Yuhui Shi

AMSTERDAM • BOSTON • HEIDELBERG • LONDON
NEW YORK • OXFORD • PARIS • SAN DIEGO
SAN FRANCISCO • SINGAPORE • SYDNEY • TOKYO

Morgan Kaufmann Publishers is an imprint of Elsevier

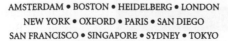
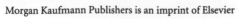

Publisher	Denise E. M. Penrose
Publishing Services Manager	George Morrison
Project Manager	Marilyn E. Rash
Assistant Editor	Mary E. James
Copyeditor	Joan Flaherty
Proofreader	Dianne Wood
Indexer	Keith Shostak
Cover Design	Chen Design
Typesetting/Illustrations	diacriTech
Interior Printer	The Maple-Vail Book Manufacturing Group
Cover Printer	Phoenix Color Corp.

Morgan Kaufmann Publishers is an imprint of Elsevier.
30 Corporate Drive, Suite 400, Burlington, MA 01803

This book is printed on acid-free paper.

Copyright © 2007 by Elsevier Inc. All rights reserved.

Designations used by companies to distinguish their products are often claimed as trademarks or registered trademarks. In all instances in which Morgan Kaufmann Publishers is aware of a claim, the product names appear in initial capital or all capital letters. Readers, however, should contact the appropriate companies for more complete information regarding trademarks and registration.

No part of this publication may be reproduced, stored in a retrieval system, or transmitted in any form or by any means—electronic, mechanical, photocopying, scanning, or otherwise—without prior written permission of the publisher.

Permissions may be sought directly from Elsevier's Science & Technology Rights Department in Oxford, UK: phone: (+44) 1865 843830, fax: (+44) 1865 853333, e-mail: permissions@elsevier.com. You may also complete your request on-line via the Elsevier homepage (*http://elsevier.com*), by selecting "Support & Contact" then "Copyright and Permission" and then "Obtaining Permissions."

Library of Congress Cataloging-in-Publication Data
Eberhart, Russell C.
   Computational intelligence: concepts to implementations/Russell C. Eberhart, Yuhui Shi.
     p. cm.
   Includes bibliographical references and index.
   ISBN 978-1-55860-759-0 (alk. paper)
   1. Computational intelligence. 2. Neural networks (neurobiology)   I. Shi, Yuhui. II. Title.
   Q342.E34 2007
   006.3–dc22   2007021459

For information on all Morgan Kaufmann publications,
visit our Web site at *www.mkp.com* or *www.books.elsevier.com*

Printed and bound by CPI Group (UK) Ltd, Croydon, CR0 4YY

Transferred to Digital Print 2011

Working together to grow libraries in developing countries

www.elsevier.com | www.bookaid.org | www.sabre.org

ELSEVIER   BOOK AID International   Sabre Foundation

Contents

chapter five

Neural Network Concepts and Paradigms 145

chapter six
Neural Network Implementations   197

chapter nine

Computational Intelligence Implementations

chapter ten

Performance Metrics

Preface

Several computational analytic tools have matured in the last 10 to 15 years that facilitate solving problems that were previously difficult or impossible to solve. These new analytical tools, known collectively as *computational intelligence tools*, include artificial neural networks, fuzzy systems, and evolutionary computation. They have recently been combined among themselves as well as with more traditional approaches, such as statistical analysis, to solve extremely challenging problems. Diagnostic systems, for example, are being developed that include Bayesian, neural network, and rule-based diagnostic modules, evolutionary algorithm-based explanation facilities, and expert system shells. All of these components work together in a "seamless" way that is transparent to the user, and they deliver results that significantly exceed what is available with any single approach.

At a system prototype level, computational intelligence (CI) tools are capable of yielding results in a relatively short time. For instance, the implementation of a conventional expert system often takes one to three years and requires the active participation of a "knowledge engineer" to build the knowledge and rule bases. In contrast, computational intelligence system solutions can often be prototyped in a few weeks to a few months and are implemented using available engineering and computational resources. Indeed, computational intelligence tools are capable of being applied in many instances by "domain experts" rather than solely by "computer gurus."

This means that biomedical engineers, for example, can solve problems in biomedical engineering without relying on outside computer science expertise such as that required to build knowledge bases for classical expert systems. Furthermore, innovative ways to combine CI tools are cropping up every day. For example, tools have been developed that incorporate knowledge elements with neural networks, fuzzy logic, and evolutionary computing theory. Such tools are able to solve quickly classification and clustering problems that would be extremely time consuming using other techniques.

The concepts, paradigms, algorithms, and implementation of computational intelligence and its constituent methodologies—evolutionary computation, neural networks, and fuzzy logic—are the focus of this book. In addition, we emphasize practical applications throughout, that is, how to apply the concepts, paradigms, algorithms, and implementations discussed to practical problems in engineering and computer science. This emphasis culminates in the real-world case studies in a final chapter, which are available on this book's web site at *http:// www.computelligence.org/issue/CICI/CICI.html*.

Computational intelligence is closely related to the field called "soft computing." There is, in fact, a significant overlap. According to Lotfi Zadeh (1998), the inventor of fuzzy logic and one of the leading proponents of soft computing:

> Soft computing is not a single methodology. Rather, it is a consortium of computing methodologies which collectively provide a foundation for the conception, design and deployment of intelligent systems. At this juncture, the principal members of soft computing are fuzzy logic (FL), neurocomputing (NC), genetic computing (GC), and probabilistic computing (PC), with the last subsuming evidential reasoning, belief networks, chaotic systems, and parts of machine learning theory. In contrast to traditional hard computing, soft computing is tolerant of imprecision, uncertainty and partial truth. The guiding principle of soft computing is: "exploit the tolerance for imprecision, uncertainty and partial truth to achieve tractability, robustness, low solution cost and better rapport with reality."

Zadeh also believes that soft computing is serving as the foundation for the emerging field of computational intelligence, and that "In this perspective, the difference between traditional AI [artificial intelligence] and computational intelligence is that AI is based on hard computing whereas CI is based on soft computing" (Zadeh 1994). We believe that soft computing is a large subset of computational intelligence. We heartily agree with him when he says, "Hybrid intelligent systems are definitely the wave of the future" (Zadeh 1994).

Some of the material in this book is adapted from *Computational Intelligence PC Tools* by Eberhart, Dobbins, and Simpson (Academic Press 1996). The extensive rewrite and reorganization of that material reflect the change in our perception of computational intelligence that has occurred over the years. That change is reflected in an increased emphasis on evolutionary computation as providing a foundation for CI. It also features significant recent developments in particle swarm optimization and other evolutionary computation tools.

The primary intended audience for *Computational Intelligence: Concepts to Implementations* comprises researchers and graduate students with engineering or computer science backgrounds and those with a special interest in computational intelligence and/or system adaptation. One of the authors [RE] has taught a CI introductory course for several years; the material in this book was developed to support that course. Other audiences include researchers in fields such as cognitive science and the physical sciences and those who are motivated to learn about computational intelligence via self-study. We assume this book's users understand the basic concepts of classical (two-valued) logic, classical set theory, and elementary probability theory. We also assume that readers have a familiarity with computers and a very basic familiarity with calculus. Knowledge of a computer language such as Java, C, or Visual BASIC is very helpful but not required.

The implementation chapters frequently refer to and list portions of computer code. In Chapters 4 and 6 we use the most common general-purpose, procedural programming language, C, to implement the evolutionary algorithms and the artificial neural networks. Data structures, routines, and finite state machines are used extensively in the C programming. In Chapters 8 and 9, reflecting programming language evolution trends, we use an object-oriented programming language instead of the procedural programming language C to implement the fuzzy systems and evolutionary fuzzy systems. There are a variety of object-oriented languages, such as C++, Java, and C#. We use C++ here primarily because it can be looked at as an extension of the C language.

Organization of the Book

This book is divided into twelve chapters. Chapters 1 and 2 lay the groundwork for the topic, introducing computational intelligence and its foundations. The next portion of the book includes the "backbone" chapters on the three main constituents of CI: evolutionary computation, neural networks, and fuzzy logic, in that order. This order provides an initial focus on evolutionary computation, which is presented as providing a foundation for development of computational intelligence tools involving neural networks and fuzzy logic. For instance, when we discuss neural networks, we see how evolutionary computation can be used to evolve the weights and structure of feedforward neural networks, and with fuzzy logic, we examine evolutionary computation applications to tools built using fuzzy logic. In other words, the evolutionary computation theme pervades this book. Within each backbone chapter, we discuss the histories of computational intelligence, evolutionary computation, neural networks, and fuzzy logic.

We follow each backbone chapter with a chapter discussing implementation and examples. Each one contains a section on implementation considerations that addresses features frequently incorporated into these implementations, which features we chose and why we chose them, and the guidelines to using them, as well as interactions among them. The implementation chapters are intended to provide readers with the insight to clearly understand "canned," commercially packaged software applications and to enable a more thorough understanding of software and hardware implementation issues for CI paradigms.

Each chapter ends with exercises.

Chapters' Contents

Chapter 1, Foundations, defines terms used throughout the book and briefly reviews biological and behavioral motivations for the constituent methodologies of computational intelligence. This is followed by a brief review of the major application areas for each methodology, as well as of CI. The chapter concludes with a review of major computational intelligence application areas.

Chapter 2, Computational Intelligence, launches directly into the core subject of this book. We first review the concepts of adaptation and self-organization, key to our view of computational intelligence. Then we summarize the brief history of the CI field, viewing it from the perspectives of other researchers. This leads us into a discussion of the relationships among the three major components and how they cooperate and/or are integrated into a computational intelligence system. We present our definition of computational intelligence, supported by diagrams that place it into context.

Chapter 3, Evolutionary Computation: Concepts and Paradigms, has been adapted from the Evolutionary Computation Theory and Paradigms chapter in *Swarm Intelligence* (Kennedy, Eberhart, and Shi 2001) with updates and augmentations, including recent developments in particle swarm optimization and other evolutionary computation approaches. After reviewing the history of evolutionary computation and giving an overview of the field, we discuss its main paradigms: genetic algorithms, evolutionary programming, evolution strategies, genetic programming, and particle swarm optimization.

Chapter 4, Evolutionary Computation Implementations, discusses factors to consider when implementing evolutionary computation paradigms and presents two implementation examples: a canonical genetic algorithm and a real-valued particle swarm that can be run in single-swarm or multiswarm configurations.

Chapter 5, Neural Network Concepts and Paradigms, first briefly presents an overview of the history of neural networks, then examines what they are and why they are useful. A discussion of neural network components and terminology follows, with a review of neural network topologies. A more detailed look at neural network learning and recall comes next, focusing on three of the most common neural network paradigms: back-propagation, learning vector quantization, and self-organizing feature map networks. These networks represent the two basic learning types: supervised learning (back-propagation) and unsupervised learning (learning vector quantization and self-organizing feature maps). We also briefly discuss hybrid networks and recurrent networks. Finally, considerations of preprocessing and post-processing are evaluated.

Chapter 6, Neural Network Implementations, discusses factors to consider when implementing artificial neural networks and presents four implementation examples: back-propagation, learning vector quantization, self-organizing feature maps, and evolutionary neural networks.

Chapter 7, Fuzzy Systems Concepts and Paradigms, leads off with a brief review of the history of the field, followed by an examination of fuzzy sets and fuzzy logic, the concepts of fuzzy sets, and approximate reasoning. We stress the differences between fuzzy logic and probability, and we present both Mamdani and Takagi–Sugeno–Kang approaches to the design and analysis of fuzzy systems. The chapter concludes with a look at some design considerations and special topics related to fuzzy systems.

Chapter 8, Fuzzy System Implementations, discusses factors to consider when implementing fuzzy systems and presents two implementation examples: a traditional fuzzy rule system and an evolutionary fuzzy rule system. The evolutionary fuzzy rule system provides a transition into computational intelligence systems.

Chapter 9, Computational Intelligence Implementations, reflects recent developments in the field, including evolutionary fuzzy systems and approaches to system adaptation using computational intelligence. We expand the discussion of the interaction and cooperation among the three basic components of CI and include a section on adaptive evolutionary computation using fuzzy systems.

Chapter 10, Performance Metrics, includes a number of system performance measures not generally used in other disciplines. Included are percent correct, sum-squared error, absolute error, normalized error, receiver operating characteristic curves, recall and precision, confusion matrices, and the chi-squared test.

Chapter 11, Analysis and Explanation, presents several tools that are helpful in assessing and explaining how well a computational intelligence tool is doing its job. Included are sensitivity analyses, Hinton diagrams for neural networks, and the use of evolutionary computing tools for analysis. An example of using particle swarm to develop an explanation facility is included in this chapter.

The book concludes with Chapter 12, Case Study Summaries, which provides examples of practical applications. This "virtual" chapter is located on the book's web site. Having it there makes it a "living" chapter that can be updated periodically. We will add new case studies from time to time and delete older ones as they become obsolete. We invite you, the reader, to submit case studies you would like to have considered for inclusion. (Please see the web site for more information about this.) Among the initial case studies posted are two based on recent work by us, the authors, including one on human EEG analysis and another on optimization of logistics operations. Other case studies discussed in detail are schedule optimization and control system design. Several other case study examples are briefly reviewed.

A bibliography concludes the book. The glossary is a "virtual" one that is located, with Chapter 12, on this book's web site *http://www.computelligence.org/issue/CICI/ CICI.html.*

Our Approach: What This Book Is, and Is Not, About

This book asserts that computational intelligence rests on a foundation of evolutionary computation. This is certainly not the only way to view computational intelligence, but so far in the authors' experience, it has proved useful and effective.

It is about *computational tools* that you can use in practical applications. Although the authors have backgrounds in engineering and computer science, CI tools are just as applicable to problems in other fields such as cognitive science and business.

This book is about self-organization, which is closely related to *emergent computation*. *Self-organization* involves simple processes that lead to complex results, and the whole being greater than the sum of its parts. As Stephen Wolfram (1994) said, "It is possible to make things of great complexity out of things that are very simple. There is no conservation of simplicity."

It is about *complex adaptive systems*, a term that describes nonlinear systems comprising the interaction of numerous adaptive elements, or entities. The concepts of self-organization and complexity are related, as we discuss later.

This book is not an exhaustive treatise on all permutations and variations of computational intelligence and its constituent methodologies. If you want an exhaustive discussion of artificial neural network paradigms, for instance, you'll need to turn to another book. We present only those paradigms we believe provide the most useful tools for someone solving practical problems.

It is not a compendium of mathematical derivations and proofs. We present only those few we believe are essential to gaining a working-level understanding of how and why the computational tools work.

This book is not about agents. Most of our computational intelligence tools do not qualify as "agents" because they lack the required autonomy and specialization. They can, however, be incorporated into intelligent agents and agent systems.

It is not about life. We nip around the edges of artificial life in a few places, but we don't address the question "What is alive?" (We do, however, share some preliminary thoughts on that subject.) We also do not address the search for artificial intelligence (whatever that is) or even for a computational intelligence tool from which intelligent behavior will emerge. Our focus is on solving problems.

Throughout the text, additional aspects of our approach and philosophy should become evident, perhaps a little bit at a time. First, when considering computational intelligence tools and systems, traditional distinctions between hardware and software get a bit blurred; distinctions between data and program are often almost nonexistent. Second, our emphasis is on problem solving and applications rather than physiological, biological, or behavioral plausibility. We do not pay too much attention to whether the CI tools reflect what actually goes on in the brain or any other part of a biological organism. Third, we believe that the activities of a computational intelligence application developer and user are often somewhat different from those in other technical areas.

Developing computational intelligence applications requires the developer to play two roles. The first is the hands-on active design, develop, test, and debug role that is fairly common in other technical areas. The second, as important as the first, is a more passive observation and analytical thinking role. Results from a computational intelligence tool are often not what was expected. Most of the time, if the developer takes the time to observe and think, rather than "bash to fit and paint to match," something very useful can be learned.

Web Site Details

The authors' web site for this book is *http://www.computelligence.org/issue/CICI/ CICI.html.* (There is a link to this site from the publisher's web site.) Software implementations are written for the Windows and/or Java environment, and executable versions of software described in the implementation chapters are located and maintained on the web site. Included as part of each implementation are the ancillary files—a run file and a data file—needed to run the implementation. In addition, output (results) files, obtained by the authors using the executable and ancillary files, are provided. You may want to rename these output files, or move them to another directory, so that you can compare your results with those of the authors.

We'd like to emphasize that the software is not just for demonstration; you can use it for many real-world applications. The C and C++ source code has been written using the Borland C++ 4.5 development environment. The Java code will run on any computer that supports the Java Virtual Machine; this includes machines running Windows, Unix, and Macintosh operating systems.

Of special note are the recent variations of particle swarm optimization that have been integrated into the EC theory and paradigms chapter and the EC implementations chapter. Source code is provided on the web site for some of the implementations so that you can modify the software for specific applications.

Some of our software can be run using a web browser. Other software, including source code, is useful only after downloading it from the book's web site. Approximately 600 slides that cover the material in this book are available to instructors (or anyone else) at no cost. These slides, configured as Word files, are downloadable from the web site. The site also contains hyperlinks to other resource information on the Internet related to subjects in this book.

A significant amount of source code is also on the web site. A total of eight software modules are available, both as executables and as source code:

- Genetic algorithm
- Particle swarm optimization (including multiple swarms)
- Back-propagation neural network
- Learning vector quantization neural network
- Self-organizing feature map neural network
- Evolutionary back-propagation neural network
- Fuzzy rule system
- Evolutionary fuzzy rule system

We ask that you send the authors a payment of US $25 per software module of source code ($150 for all of the source code) if you find it useful. We are relying on your honesty. (The address is on the web site with the software.)

Finally, as described previously, Chapter 12, Case Studies, is available on the web site.

Acknowledgments

Each of us has numerous people who should be acknowledged; we mention only a few.

Russ Eberhart: First, I want to acknowledge my wife Francie and son Sean who put up with a higher than usual absence rate of their spouse and father, respectively. I also want to acknowledge my son Mark, a three-time cancer survivor, who has taught me what courage is. Special thanks go to my students in ECE 536, Introduction to Computational Intelligence. They were the guinea pigs. Sometimes, just from their eyes glazing over, I knew that a section needed to be rewritten (or deleted). Their patience is appreciated, and their input has been invaluable.

Yuhui Shi: I would like to thank my parents and parents-in-law for taking good care of my daughter Melissa Xueyin Shi and my son Nicholas Yuge Shi so that I had plenty of quality time to work on this book. My thanks also go to professors Zhenya He of Southeast University, M. N. S. Swamy and M. Omair Ahmad of Concordia University, Xin Yao of the University of Birmingham, Jinhyung Kim of the Korean Advanced Institute of Science and Technology, and to Russell C. Eberhart, who are my mentors and have paved the way for me in my career development.

Both of us acknowledge the contributions of our technical reviewers. Their insights resulted in improvements in both the organization and content of this book. Finally, we are grateful to the team at Morgan Kaufmann Publishers who worked diligently with us throughout the process of writing, editing, and production. Working with Denise Penrose, Diane Cerra, Emilia Thiuri, Marilyn Rash, and Mary James has been a pleasure and a learning experience.

chapter
one

Foundations

This chapter introduces general terms used to discuss computational intelligence as well as component methodologies—computational intelligence (CI), including *artificial neural networks*, *fuzzy logic*, and *evolutionary computation*—as they are used in this text. We review the biological bases for artificial neural network and evolutionary computation analysis tools, including the differences between biological structures and these analysis tools, and we discuss the behavioral motivations for fuzzy systems. The chapter ends with a review of myths related to implementations and applications of CI and its component technologies, and a review of major application areas for each of the three main computational intelligence methodologies. ▪

Definitions

This section defines some of the most important terms used in this book. These definitions set the stage for more detailed analyses; more comprehensive definitions appear in subsequent chapters. Often, the first time a term is used in the book, it is in *italics*. In addition, whenever a term is italicized, you can find its definition in the glossary.

We begin with a general definition of intelligence and then focus on the issues relevant to computational intelligence. A standard dictionary (*Webster's New Collegiate Dictionary*, 1975) definition of intelligence is: "**1 a** (1): The ability to learn or understand or to deal with new or trying situations : REASON; *also* : the skilled use of reason (2): the ability to apply knowledge to manipulate one's environment or to think abstractly as measured by objective criteria (as tests)."

"*Intelligence* is the capability of a system to adapt its behavior to meet its goals in a range of environments. It is a property of all purpose-driven decision-makers." This definition, perhaps more relevant to the subject matter of this book, was published by David Fogel (1995).

An *artificial neural network* (ANN) is an analysis paradigm that is roughly modeled after the massively parallel structure of the brain. It simulates a highly interconnected, parallel computational structure with many relatively simple individual *processing elements* (PEs). Henceforth in this text the terms *artificial neural network* and *neural network* are used interchangeably.

As used in this text, *fuzziness* refers to nonstatistical imprecision and vagueness in information and data. Most concepts dealt with or described in the "real world" are fuzzy. For example, "It is kind of foggy outside now, but it should be fairly sunny before too long" is an example of a statement that incorporates three fuzzy concepts: "kind of," "fairly," and "before too long." (It could even be argued that the word "now" is imprecise and vague enough to be fuzzy.)

Fuzzy sets model the properties of imprecision, approximation, or vagueness. In conventional logic, known as *crisp logic*, an element either is or is not a member of the set. It can be said, therefore, that each element has a membership value of either 1 or 0 in the set. In a fuzzy set, fuzzy membership values reflect the membership extents (or grades) of the elements in the set. It will be shown that a membership function is the basic idea in fuzzy set theory; a fuzzy membership function is identical to a fuzzy set.

Fuzzy logic is the logic of "approximate reasoning." It comprises operations on fuzzy sets including equality, containment, complementation, intersection, and union; it is a generalization of conventional (two-valued, or crisp) logic.

Evolutionary computation comprises machine learning optimization and classification paradigms roughly based on mechanisms of evolution such as biological genetics and natural selection. The evolutionary computation field includes genetic algorithms, evolutionary programming, genetic programming, evolution strategies, and particle swarm optimization. All of these paradigms use populations of individuals (potential solutions), rather than single data points or vectors.

Genetic algorithms are search algorithms that incorporate natural evolution mechanisms, including *crossover, mutation*, and survival of the fittest. They are more often used for optimization, but also are used for classification. *Evolutionary programming* algorithms are similar to genetic algorithms, but do not incorporate crossover. Rather, they rely on survival of the fittest and mutation. *Evolution strategies* are similar to genetic algorithms but use *recombination* to exchange information between population members instead of crossover, and often use a different type of mutation as well. *Genetic programming* is a methodology used to evolve computer programs. The structures being manipulated are usually *hierarchical tree structures.* *Particle swarm optimization* flies potential solutions, called particles, through the problem space. The particles are accelerated toward selected points in the problem space where previous fitness values have been high.

Computational intelligence is a methodology involving computing that provides a system with an ability to learn and/or to deal with new situations, such that the system is perceived to possess one or more attributes of reason, such as generalization, discovery, association, and abstraction. Computational intelligence systems usually incorporate hybrids of paradigms such as artificial neural networks, fuzzy systems, and evolutionary computation systems, augmented with knowledge elements. They are often designed to mimic one or more aspects of biologiacal intelligence. Computational intelligence is also closely related to *adaptation*. In fact, another definition of CI is that it comprises practical *adaptation* concepts, paradigms, algorithms, and implementations that enable or facilitate appropriate actions (intelligent behavior) by systems in complex and changing environments. We discuss adaptation in more detail in the next chapter.

A paradigm is a particular example of computational intelligence attributes—in the case of a neural network, the architecture, activation and learning rules, update procedure, and so on—that exhibits a certain type of behavior. Put another way, it is a clear and specific example of a concept. *Back-propagation* is one example of a neural network paradigm because it implies a certain set of attributes, for example, the architecture and the learning rule. A paradigm is a particular set of choices for all attributes. Development of a new paradigm involves assembling a set of attributes that define the intended behavior of the CI tool.

An implementation is a computer program written and compiled for a specific computer or class of computers that implements a paradigm. The back-propagation neural network application on the book's web site (described in Chapter 4) is an implementation of the back-propagation paradigm.

The discussion in this book deals with semantics, as well as with concepts. To an extent, we are the prisoners of our terminology. For example, consider the term *artificial intelligence*. It is the authors' opinion that labeling some subset of intelligence artificial is somewhat analogous to calling what an airplane does "artificial flight."

There are also terms that require careful usage. One example is *neural networks*, for which it is necessary to specify whether we are referring to biological wetware or artificial neural network analytical tools. We must also be aware of what Bezdek (1994) calls "seductive semantics," which are words and phrases that are often interpreted too literally, resulting in meanings being inferred that are more profound and important than are warranted. Examples are *cognitive* and *genetic*. With that caveat, and having presented the basic definitions we use, let us now review the theory and technology foundations of computational intelligence tools and component methodologies.

Biological Basis for Neural Networks

Every day of our lives, each of us carries out thousands of tasks that require us to keep track of many things at once and to process and act on these things. Relatively simple actions, such as picking up a glass of water or dialing a telephone number, involve many individual components requiring memory, learning, and physical coordination. The complexity of such "simple" tasks, which most of us do all the time without consciously "thinking" about them, is underscored by the difficulty involved in teaching robots to perform them. Performance of these tasks is facilitated by our complex adaptive biological structure.

Neurons

Studies in fields such as biology and biophysics over the past few decades have shed some light on the construction and operation of our brains and nervous systems, which helps us understand how these tasks are performed. Living organisms are made up of cells, and the basic building blocks of the nervous system are nerve cells called *neurons*. The major components of a neuron include a central cell body, dendrites, and an axon.

Figure 1.1 is a conceptual diagram of a neuron.[1] The signal flow goes from left to right, from the dendrites, through the cell body, and out through the axon. The signal from one neuron is passed on to others by means of connections between the axon of the first and dendrites of the others. These connections are called *synapses*. Axons often synapse onto the trunk of a dendrite, but they can also synapse directly onto the cell body.

The human brain has a large number of neurons, or processing elements (PEs). Typical estimates of the total number are on the order of 10 to 500 billion (Rumelhart and McClelland 1986). According to one estimate by Stubbs (1988), neurons are

---

[1] There are many kinds of neuron; for detailed information on their configuration and functioning, refer to a book on neuroanatomy or neurology, such as Kandel, Schwartz, and Jessell (2000).

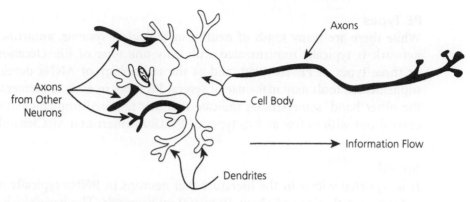

Figure 1.1 Conceptual diagram of a neuron.

arranged into about 1,000 main modules, each with about 500 neural networks. Each network has on the order of 100,000 neurons. The axon of each neuron connects to anywhere from hundreds to thousands of other neurons; the value varies greatly from neuron to neuron and from neuron type to neuron type. According to a rule called Eccles's law, each neuron either excites or inhibits all neurons to which it is connected.

Biological versus Artificial Neural Networks

While the processing element in an artificial neural network (ANN) is generally considered to be very roughly analogous to a biological neuron, there are significant differences between a neural biological structure (as it is currently understood) and the implementation or representation of this structure in artificial neural networks. We summarize the most important differences here, recognizing there are many others.

Eccles's Law

In a typical implementation of an ANN, connections among PEs can have either positive or negative weights. These weights correspond to excitatory and inhibitory neural connections, so Eccles' law is not usually implemented in ANNs.

AC versus DC

Information about the state of activation, or excitation, of a PE generally is passed to other PEs to which it is connected as a value that roughly corresponds to a direct current (DC) level. In biological neural networks (BNNs), a train of pulses across a synapse carries the information, and higher absolute values of activation result in higher pulse rates, so that something analogous to alternating current (AC) frequency, or pulse repetition rate, generally corresponds to activation level. There are exceptions to the pulse rate carrying information in biological networks, but they are relatively unimportant for our discussion.

PE Types

While there are many kinds of neuron in biological systems, an artificial neural network is typically implemented with only one type of PE. Occasionally, two or three types of PE are used, and as the technology of ANNs develops, more sophisticated tools may make use of several PE types in each implementation. On the other hand, some studies indicate that any required implementation can be carried out with as few as two types of PE (Rumelhart and McClelland 1986).

Speed

It is reported widely in the literature that neurons in BNNs typically operate on individual cycle times of about 10 to 100 milliseconds. The basic clock frequency in a personal computer is a few gigahertz, which results in a basic cycle time for the computer of less than a nanosecond. Even taking into account the number of multiply–accumulate operations needed to calculate and propagate a new value for a PE (typically 10–100), the basic cycle time for an individual PE is still only about 10 to 100 nanoseconds. In some ways, however, speed is deceptive. Despite its slower cycle, the brain is still able to perform some tasks orders of magnitude faster than today's fastest digital computer. This, most likely, is because of the brain's massively parallel architecture. (Recent research related to neural processing in echo-locating bats, however, indicates that these creatures are physiologically processing signals in a time span of a few hundred nanoseconds, so it seems obvious that we still have much to learn about how the brain functions.)

Quantity of PEs

There is a significant difference between the number of PEs in the typical ANN and the number of biological neurons involved in any task in a BNN. Typical ANNs are implemented with something like a few dozen to several hundred PEs. Each of the 1,000 main modules in the human brain described by Stubbs (1988) contains about 500 million neurons, and it is almost certain that several (perhaps many) of these main modules are involved in any simple task. Of course, for any practical application, most engineers and computer scientists might be hard pressed to figure out how to effectively use a neural network tool (NNT) with 500 million PEs!

Some biologically oriented scientists have criticized artificial neural networks because they don't model all the activities of the brain sufficiently well. Our primary goal as engineers and computer scientists, however, is to solve complex problems, not to model the brain. Our interest, then, is in adapting relevant concepts to solve difficult problems. As an oft-quoted saying (oft-quoted in engineering circles, anyway) puts it, "Scientists study what is. Engineers create what has never been." This statement is not meant to be antagonistic toward scientists. What scientists do is just as noble and worthwhile as what engineers do; they just have a different mission and a different perspective.

Biological Basis for Evolutionary Computation

Whereas individuals adapt and learn over their lifetimes using their neural networks to accomplish tasks, species survive by reproducing and evolving over time by passing on new information through their genes. In a manner somewhat analogous to neural networks' ties with biology, the field of evolutionary computation has roots in biological genetics. The concept of chromosomes is central to both genetics and evolutionary computation.[2]

Chromosomes

All living organisms are made up of cells such as neurons, as described earlier. *Chromosomes* are structures in cell nuclei (cell bodies) that transmit genetic information. Each representative of a given species has a characteristic number of chromosomes. Humans normally have 46, occurring as 23 homologous (corresponding) pairs in the female and 22 homologous pairs and one nonidentical pair in the male. One of each pair is derived from the father, one from the mother. A sketch of three pairs of human chromosomes appears in Figure 1.2.

Individual *patterns*, or strings, in evolutionary computation systems are basically analogous to chromosomes in biological systems. In fact, the term *chromosome* is commonly used in most genetic algorithm and evolutionary programming systems. In genetics, the collection of chromosomes required to completely specify

Figure 1.2 Sketch of three pairs of human chromosomes. The patterns of bands along the chromosomes are the result of a staining technique and allow identification of the individuals of chromosome pairs. *Source*: Drawing by Mark C. Eberhart.

---

[2] In this text, the term *genetics* refers to biological genetics, which is "a branch of biology that deals with the heredity and variation of organisms" (*Webster's New Collegiate Dictionary*, 1975).

an organism is called the *genotype*. In evolutionary computation, the collection of patterns or strings needed to completely specify a system is known as a *structure*. Most of the systems considered in this text are specified by one pattern, or string, or state vector; the terms *chromosome* and *structure* are thus generally interchangeable.

In the biological world, chromosomes are made up of *genes*, each of which is identified by its location (*locus*) and its function, such as a person's hair color gene. In other words, genes are specific segments of chromosomes associated with specific functions. Individual values a gene may assume are called *alleles*; a hair color allele value may be "brown hair." In the artificial chromosomes of evolutionary computation systems, the chromosome patterns or strings are made up of parameters, or features, that can vary over a specified range of values. A given parameter or feature occupies a fixed location in the artificial chromosome. The chromosome therefore is encoded to represent a set of parameters.

Biological versus Artificial Chromosomes

Just as artificial neural networks are only roughly analogous to collections of biological neurons, so artificial chromosomes are only approximately modeled after biological ones.

Composition
Biological chromosomes contain linear threads of DNA, nucleic acids that make up an extremely complex double helix structure. Artificial chromosomes are typically strings of binary and/or real values. Each occurrence of the string typically represents a system state vector.

Length
The biological chromosomes that define an organism vary in length, although a specific chromosome is generally the same length from one organism to another. Each artificial chromosome in a population is the same length, that is, contains the same number of bits.

Reproduction
Biological chromosomes duplicate themselves during cell division, which occurs during a normal cell's lifetime. Many cell divisions (duplications) occur within an organism for every event of sexual reproduction. During reproduction, the egg and the sperm each contribute one chromosome for each homologous pair. In evolutionary computation, the duplication of chromosomes analogous to what occurs during biological cell division is generally called "reproduction." Also, the synthesis of new chromosomes from two "parents" is called crossover, or recombination, in evolutionary computation. Furthermore, during crossover (or recombination), any number of bits or real values can be exchanged between two parent artificial

chromosomes, as compared with the fixed 50 percent contribution of chromosomes by each parent in human reproduction.[3]

This section has primarily discussed the biological basis of evolutionary computation from a genetics point of view. Concepts such as survival of the fittest, associated with Darwinian evolution, also play an important role in CI and are discussed in Chapter 3.

Behavioral Motivations for Fuzzy Logic

The biological motivation or basis for fuzzy logic does not originate at the cellular and subcellular level, as is the case with neural networks and evolutionary computation, respectively. It is reflected at the behavioral level of the organism, that is, in the ways the organism interacts with its environment. While the previous two methods are deeply rooted in biology, fuzzy logic deals mainly with uncertainty and vagueness. We do not live in a world of ones and zeros, black and white, true and false, or other absolutes. Our observations, communications, and experiences almost always include a large measure of uncertainty. For example, a statement such as "Next year I will visit Hawaii" cannot be categorized in terms of truth and falsehood. It is uncertain.

Two main types of uncertainty exist. One is *statistical*, based on the laws of probability. An example of statistical uncertainty is the outcome of the toss of a coin. Observations or measurements can be used to resolve statistical uncertainty. For example, once the coin is tossed, no statistical uncertainty remains. The other type of uncertainty is nonstatistical and is based on vagueness, imprecision, and/or ambiguity. Nonstatistical uncertainty is illustrated by statements such as "Go to bed *pretty soon*" and "Jim is *very tall*" and "That car is going *around* 75 kilometers per hour." The concept of fuzziness is associated with nonstatistical uncertainty.

Those of you who are experts in the English language may have noticed that, particularly in the first statement, the imperative state does not mesh very well with the vague qualifier "pretty soon." This, however, is exactly the kind of vague, messy English we often use for communication. One of the primary attributes of fuzzy logic is its ability to efficiently capture and manipulate these vague, messy concepts.

Fuzziness is an inherent property of a system. It is not resolved or altered by observation or measurement. Allowing uncertainty in the description of a complex system makes it more tractable to analysis. Fuzzy logic thus provides a framework within which nonstatistical uncertainty can be defined, described, and analyzed. A similar perspective on fuzzy logic is articulated by George Klir (Klir and Folger 1988), who refers to fuzziness as arising from what he calls "linguistic imprecision."

---

[3] For more information on natural genetics, refer to a genetics text. A good choice is one written by Mange and Mange (1998).

Myths about Computational Intelligence

There are a number of myths regarding computational intelligence. First, it is a myth that the only way to achieve results with CI tools is with a vast sum of money, a supercomputer, and an interdisciplinary team of Nobel laureates, as some commercial vendors imply. Having a supercomputer or a parallel processing machine isn't required to do something useful with CI tools. It's not even necessary to have a Sun workstation. A personal computer is a perfectly adequate hardware base for most implementation and application projects. So, with relatively simple hardware and software tools, it is possible to solve problems that are otherwise impossible or impractical. Computational intelligence tools *do* offer solutions to some problems that aren't feasible to solve in any other way known to the authors. That isn't a myth!

What *is* a myth is that some combination of CI tools can solve all difficult engineering or computer science problems faster and cheaper than anything previously available. It is also a myth that CI tools can solve most problems single-handedly. They are often inappropriate for problems requiring precise calculations. For example, it is unlikely that anyone will ever successfully balance a checkbook with a neural network.

Another statement that qualifies as *mostly* myth is that no programming is needed to use artificial neural networks. This is at best misleading. It is true that a neural network trains (adapts) and runs on input data and according to a set of rules that update the weights that connect the processing elements, or nodes, and that the learning of the network is not, strictly speaking, programmed. It is also true that computer-aided software engineering (CASE) tools are becoming more available and that little or no programming expertise may be required to use these tools to generate executable neural network code.

It is also true, however, that in the real world of neural network applications, some programming is required to get from the specification of the problem to a solution. Neural network applications significantly reduce the requirement for *re*programming. Once the problem is specified, it is not unusual to reuse the network code repeatedly, making changes in data preprocessing and network runtime parameters.

Furthermore, although it is accurate to say that computational intelligence tools such as neural networks can play a key role in the solution of several classes of problems that are difficult if not impossible to solve any other way currently known, it is almost always true that the CI portion of the solution is only a relatively small part of the overall system. For example, in terms of the total amount of computer code in a neural network-based solution, the network often accounts for only about 10 percent of the total solution. It is an absolutely indispensable 10 percent, and success would not be possible without it, but it is important to keep it in perspective. Preprocessing and further manipulation of the data to form pattern files for presentation to the network typically involve much of the code (although we'll show you a way to develop a neural network that eliminates much of the preprocessing). Interpreting and displaying the results often account for another large portion.[4]

Another myth about neural network and evolutionary computation applications is that it is necessary to know something about neural biology or biological genetics, respectively, to understand them. Nothing could be further from the truth. In fact, for most engineers and computer scientists, neural network and evolutionary computation tools can be considered just another (powerful) set of resources in the CI analysis toolkit. Furthermore, a good case can be made for the argument that neural networks are technical descendants of analog computing just as much as they are descended from biology or neurology.

A myth about fuzzy logic is that it is really fuzzy, or imprecise. It is not. The inputs to a fuzzy system are precise values for input parameters. Likewise, outputs from a fuzzy system are "crisp" (exact) values, capable, for instance, of being used as precise inputs to control systems.

Another myth about fuzzy logic is that it is just another version of probability. It isn't. Probability deals with statistical uncertainty, whereas fuzzy logic is related to nonstatistical uncertainty, as we discussed previously.

Finally, it is a myth that optimization exists. This is being said somewhat with tongue in cheek, but it is important to realize that very seldom does a real-world CI implementation find the absolute optimum of anything. It is almost always sufficient to get within a specified region of the optimum, if it is known. Often, in fact, the optimum value is not even known. Note that we use the term *optimization* in its pure "dictionary definition" sense: Optimization is the identification of the very best solution, or, in the case in which multiple optima exist, the identification of all of the multiple optima.

Computational Intelligence Application Areas

Each component methodology of computational intelligence has application areas for which it is particularly well suited. We briefly review these areas in this section. Keep in mind that application areas may overlap; that is, a given problem may be solvable by either a neural network or a fuzzy system, albeit with different levels of performance. In later chapters we examine combinations of the methodologies that can produce different results. This compilation of application areas is not meant

---

[4] The 10 percent of the code typically represented by the neural network often takes a disproportionately large percentage of the development effort, perhaps 20 percent, but that effort associated directly with neural network application development is usually still a relatively small portion of the total project.

to be complete. It is not necessarily even representative of all of the major areas of applications. It *is* meant to convey some sense of the range of problems to which CI's component methodologies have been applied.

Neural Networks

There are five application areas for which neural networks are generally considered to be best suited. The first three are related.

Classification

This area analyzes which of several predefined classes best reflects an input pattern. The number of classes is typically small compared with the number of inputs. One example is a decision whether or not a given segment of EEG data represents an epileptiform spike waveform. Neural networks' ability to construct nonlinear mappings between high-dimensional spaces is another type of classification analysis. Some types of video image processing by neural networks (such as diagnoses of tumors) are examples of this application area.

Content Addressable Memory or Associative Memory

A typical example is obtaining the complete version of a pattern at the output of the network by providing a partial version at the input. (The input and output nodes of the network may sometimes be the same nodes.) This process is sometimes described as obtaining an exemplar pattern from a noisy and/or incomplete one.

Clustering or Compression

This area involves classification but can also be considered a form of encoding. An example is the significant reduction of the dimensionality of an input, as in the case of speech recognition. Another is the reduction of the number of bits that must be stored or transmitted to represent, within some allowed error margin, a block of data; in other words, the original block of data can be reconstructed within the allowed error with fewer bits than were in the original data.

Generation of Sequences or Patterns

This fourth area is somewhat different from the first three in that no classification is involved. This generation of patterns is done by a network trained to examples. For instance, if a network is trained to reproduce a certain style of musical sequence, then it is possible for the network to compose "original" versions of that type of music. Or a neural network may be trained to model, or simulate, something. Growing numbers of applications in the financial world, becoming known as "financial engineering" applications, are being reported. Because of inherent randomness in the process being simulated, there may be no "right" answers, but the system can perhaps be described statistically. The network simulation may then be designed to reproduce these statistical qualities. This area can be extended to many areas of application and represents the ability of a neural network system to be "creative."

Control Systems

The use of neural networks in control systems is one of the fastest-growing application areas. It is enjoying widespread implementation for several reasons. First, a neural network-based control system can deal with all of the nonlinearities of a system. (The system doesn't have to be approximated as linear.) Second, a network can be used to model the nonlinear system in the process of designing the control system. Third, the development time for a neural network control system is typically much shorter than it is for other more traditional techniques.

The number of specific neural network applications for each of the five areas grows, it seems, daily. Some applications are specific to a discipline. For example, applications in medicine include EEG waveform classification and appendicitis diagnosis. In business and finance, neural networks are part of systems for trading options on commodity futures contracts and finance company credit application processing. Military-related applications include target tracking and recognition, fault diagnoses in aircraft, and the detection of trace amounts of explosives. In the automotive industry, neural networks can determine the battery pack state-of-charge in an electric vehicle, help determine the proper distance a car should follow another, and, in fact, simultaneously control the positions of a number of cars on an expressway. Artistic endeavors are supported as well, with neural networks that can compose music. Other applications cut across disciplines, such as networks for speech recognition, text-to-speech conversion, and image processing.

Evolutionary Computation

The two main areas of application for evolutionary algorithms are optimization and classification. Most of the discussion in this text focuses on optimization, since most engineering applications of evolutionary computation are related to optimization.

Optimization

One of the early applications that popularized genetic algorithms was the control of gas pipeline transmission (Goldberg 1989). Evolutionary algorithms have also been applied to multiple-fault diagnosis, robot track determination, schedule optimization, conformal analysis of DNA, load distribution by an electric utility, neural network explanation facilities, and product ingredient mix optimization. (In some of these cases, other CI paradigms have been used, too.)

Classification

A use of evolutionary computation that has applications across many fields, including both classification and optimization, is the evolution of neural networks. This computational intelligence-based methodology is discussed in detail in

Chapter 6. Other classification applications include rule-based machine learning systems, such as that used to learn control of pipeline operations by Goldberg (1989) (which also had an optimization element) and classifier systems for high-level semantic networks.

Fuzzy Logic

Fuzzy logic is being applied in a wide range of applications in engineering areas ranging from robotics and control to architecture and environmental engineering. Other areas of application include medicine, management, decision analysis, and computer science. As with neural networks, new applications appear almost daily. Two of the major application areas are fuzzy control and fuzzy expert systems.

Control Systems

Fuzzy control systems have been applied to subway systems, cement kilns, traffic signal systems, home appliances, video cameras, and various subsystems of automobiles including the transmission and brake systems. One application familiar to many is the circuitry inside a video camera that stabilizes the image in spite of the unsteady holding of the camera.

Expert Systems

Fuzzy expert systems have been applied in the areas of medical diagnostics, foreign exchange trading, robot navigation, scheduling, automobile diagnostics, and the selection of business strategies, just to name a few. We present an example of the role of fuzzy logic in a scheduling system in Chapter 12.

Summary

This chapter provides background information from which to learn about CI and its implementation. We introduce the definitions and component methodologies of CI, and we debunk some of the myths you may have heard. Having understood the biological basis for the component methodologies, you will be able to better conceptualize how these systems work. Briefly reviewing some application areas offers an idea of the types of problem that computational intelligence tools can be used to solve.

Exercises

1. What are some alternative terms for *processing element*? Discuss the choices, listing advantages and disadvantages for each.

2. State a myth relative to neural networks, fuzzy systems, or evolutionary computation, in addition to those discussed in this chapter. Why is it a myth?

3. How do you think adaptation and self-organization are interrelated?

4. Survey recent technical publications and the Internet for these additional areas to which one of the component technologies of CI has been successfully applied: face recognition, health screening, creating art.

   a. What motivated the use of the technology in these applications?
   b. What technical tools, in addition to CI, were required to solve the problems?
   c. What was the role of the CI component technology in each case?

5. What is the difference between fuzziness and probability? Provide an example to illustrate the difference.

6. What is the definition of artificial intelligence? List some differences between computational intelligence and artificial intelligence.

chapter
two

Computational Intelligence

This chapter covers the key elements of computational intelligence and how computational intelligence fits into the larger picture comprising machine intelligence and biological intelligence. We examine adaptation and learning, how they differ, and what that means for computational intelligence (CI). We build from the bottom up, identifying each element in turn. First we discuss three main types of adaptation that are incorporated into a variety of computational models: supervised, unsupervised, and reinforcement adaptation. Next we briefly examine the concept of self-organization, which we believe plays an important role in evolution. We then look at how computational intelligence has been perceived and defined by various researchers. Finally, we discuss our view of computational intelligence and how it fits into a model of intelligent systems.

Despite the relatively widespread use of the term *computational intelligence*, there is no commonly accepted definition of the term. The definitions offered in Chapter 1 include assumptions about the nature of what are called the "constituent methodologies" of computational intelligence. As will be seen, other researchers make different assumptions and arrive at different perspectives.

As is true for researchers in any developing, maturing field, we are standing on the shoulders of those who have preceded us. Of particular influence has been work published by Marks (1993) and Bezdek (1981, 1992, 1994, 1998). An extension of their work presented in this chapter is a new model of biological and machine intelligence that defines the context for computational intelligence.

This chapter is not meant to be the final word on any aspect of computational intelligence. It is intended only to be a snapshot in time, and a relatively subjective snapshot at that. If it stimulates discussion and further development, it will accomplish our objective.

With those caveats, the chapter is initiated by discussing adaptation and presenting several definitions. None of these definitions is meant to be particularly controversial. Rather, they are intended to provide the framework for the remainder of the book. ▪

Adaptation

We discuss adaptation and, later, self-organization because they play an important role in our view of computational intelligence. The concept of adaptation is central to computational intelligence. One definition stated in Chapter 1 is that computational intelligence comprises practical *adaptation* concepts, paradigms, algorithms, and implementations that enable or facilitate appropriate actions (intelligent behavior) in complex and changing environments.

Webster's New Collegiate Dictionary's (1991) definition of adaptation provides a useful beginning to our discussion:

> **1:** the act or process of adapting: the state of being adapted **2:** adjustment to environmental conditions: as **a:** adjustment of a sense organ to the intensity or quality of stimulation **b:** modification of an organism or its parts that makes it more fit for existence under the conditions of its environment.

The same source defines the word *adapt* as follows: "to make fit (as for a specific or new use or situation) often by modification." To be fit is to be suitable, that is, adapted so as to be capable of surviving and acceptable from a particular viewpoint.

Thus, we define *adaptation* as the ability of a system to change, or evolve, its parameters in order to better meet its goal. Dynamic adaptation is the ability of a system to adapt "online," that is, in essentially real time, in a changing environment. In dynamic adaptation, the system adapts while it is running (online), rather than being taken offline to be retrained. For a system to exhibit adaptation, its trajectory through the problem space must depend on the state of its environment.

Accordingly, a number of factors can make adaptation difficult (Holland 1992):

1. A large problem space (the hyperspace comprising the dynamic ranges of all problem variables), which contains many alternative (candidate) solutions, called structures.

2. A large number of variables in each structure, making difficult the determination of which variables, and which combinations of variables, contribute to good solutions.

3. The function used to measure the performance of the system (which we call the fitness function) is very complex and nonlinear, having many local optima and/or discontinuities.

4. The fitness function landscape of global and local optima varies with time and over the problem space.

5. A complex and changing environment in which the system exists.

We are making certain assumptions when we say that a system is adaptive. First, we assume that the system is converging to a sufficiently good solution. Second, we assume that adaptive processes drastically shorten the time required to arrive at a solution when compared with enumerative methods that must explore significant portions of the problem space (Kennedy, Eberhart, and Shi 2001).

We believe that most engineering and computer science applications are driven by what we call the *law of sufficiency*: If a solution is good enough, fast enough, and cheap enough, it is sufficient. (Being good enough simply means it meets specifications.) We believe that for most "optimization" applications, it is more appropriate to use the term "adaptation" because we generally do not actually find the optimum solution and often do not even know where it is.

In the remainder of this section, we look at adaptation from three perspectives. First, we examine and compare the concepts of *adaptation* and *learning*. Next, we review the three main types of adaptation paradigm: supervised adaptation, unsupervised adaptation, and reinforcement adaptation. Finally, we consider the three spaces with which we must deal when working with adaptive systems: problem space, function space, and fitness space.

Adaptation versus Learning

The preceding definitions of adaptation describe and apply to computational intelligence systems extremely well. Too often, the process of altering structures such as neural networks, evolutionary computation tools, and fuzzy systems is described as learning. The word *learning*, in fact, appears throughout this book. This usage is in accordance with that of many researchers.

Learning, however, is defined as "knowledge or skill acquired by instruction or study," and the synonym listed for learning is *knowledge*. Likewise, to learn is defined as "to gain knowledge or understanding of or skill in by study, instruction or experience" (Mish 2001).

Instead, learning is what an entire intelligent system does. All of the main components of an intelligent system participate in the learning process; all exchange information with the component of the system that is the repository of the system knowledge. *Learning* thus applies to the entire intelligent system, while *adaptation* mainly applies to the portion of the system we address in this book—the portion where computational intelligence exists.

Adaptation must overcome numerous barriers, including local optima and nonlinearities. The problem hyperspace landscape (topography, environment) is constantly changing. The adaptive systems with which we are dealing are complex, and the fitness or performance measure is often complicated and varying over time.

Adaptive systems answer this challenge by progressively modifying population structures, using a set of operators that themselves evolve (adapt) over time. These adaptive processes drastically shorten the time required to arrive at a solution when compared with enumerative methods that must explore significant portions of the problem space.

As you continue through this chapter, you will see that we assert that adaptation is arguably the most appropriate term for what computational intelligence systems do. In fact, it is not too much of a stretch to say that *computational intelligence and adaptation (with self-organization) are synonymous*. Adaptation, thus, is the leitmotif of this book.

Three Types of Adaptation

There are various ways to categorize adaptation.[1] Each of the following sections discusses one of three categories pertinent to computational intelligence: supervised adaptation, reinforcement adaptation, and unsupervised adaptation.[2]

Note that in all three cases we separate the adaptation algorithm from the adaptive system. Usually, the algorithm is used to adapt (tune) the system and is then removed. The adaptive system (with its parameters frozen) then responds to input vectors from the environment. This is traditionally called *offline adaptation*. Sometimes the adaptation algorithm, or a portion of it, remains active as the system is used. This is traditionally called *online adaptation*. Unlike offline adaptation, there are various degrees of online adaptation.

Supervised Adaptation

Compared to the other two categories of adaptation, *supervised adaptation* is well defined. A "teacher" that provides relevant input/output (I/O) examples is always present. In addition, it has a number of characteristics, including:

- Adaptation is often carried out one step (iteration) at a time. The system adapts so that it emulates the training I/O examples while acquiring the ability to generalize.

---

[1] In many textbooks, the title of this section would be "Three Types of Learning." Based, however, on the reasoning earlier in this section, we generally use the term *adaptation* in this book to describe what computational intelligence systems do. We realize that this is somewhat unconventional, but we believe that the reasoning is sound, and that "adaptation," more accurately than "learning," describes what is going on in a computationally intelligent system.

[2] Other authors might call these supervised learning, reinforcement learning, and unsupervised learning.

- The system's performance metric is often inversely proportional to some function of the sum of errors over the I/O examples. Examples include sum-squared error, mean-squared error, and sum of absolute error. The supervised adaptation algorithm often uses information about the gradient of the error with respect to an error surface that is averaged over all I/O examples to adapt the current point.

An example of supervised adaptation appears in Figure 2.1. In Figures 2.1 through 2.3, an arrow going through the adaptive system box indicates the ability to adjust the parameters of the system. Supervised adaptation often results in an adaptive system that is used for what is, or amounts to, function approximation. The system is good at mapping input vectors to output vectors over its domain.

One example of supervised adaptation that we examine in this book is a neural network adapted by the back-propagation algorithm. Input patterns for which the output patterns are known are presented to the network. The difference between what was expected at each output and what was actually there (defined as the error) is calculated for each output and each pattern. Some function of the error at each output is then used to adjust system parameters. In the case of a neural network, the weights of the network are adjusted in an attempt to minimize the error.

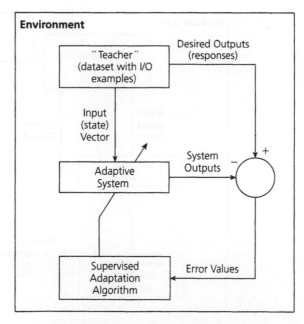

Figure 2.1 Supervised adaptation example. An arrow going through the adaptive system box indicates the ability to adjust the parameters of the system.

Reinforcement Adaptation

Reinforcement adaptation of a system is achieved through its interaction with a "critic" that provides heuristic reinforcement information. An illustration of reinforcement adaptation appears in Figure 2.2. The input variable information often includes the dynamic range of each variable and perhaps other variable information such as the precision required. Some sort of goal or fitness metric is also necessary. For example, in a multiple-city delivery-scheduling problem (e.g., the traveling salesman problem), the goal may be to minimize the total distance traveled to visit all of the cities. The critic provides some fitness measure based on the goal—for example, a scaled number inversely proportional to the total distance traveled. So, although some kind of goal or fitness metric is required, the fitness cannot be obtained directly, but only a suggestion on how good the solution is relative to other solutions. (A direct fitness metric is possible only with supervised adaptation.)

Of the three types of adaptation, reinforcement adaptation is most closely related to biological systems. One very simple illustration is that animals (including humans) tend to avoid behavior that causes us discomfort and tend to seek or repeat behavior that brings us comfort. Reinforcement adaptation has roots in the optimal control theory area called *dynamic programming* (Bellman 1957). Sequential decision making obtains much of its mathematical foundation from dynamic programming.

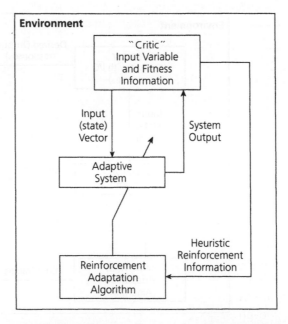

Figure 2.2 Reinforcement adaptation example. An arrow going through the adaptive system box indicates the ability to adjust the parameters of the system.

Characteristics of reinforcement adaptation often (but not always) include

- The system often deals with a time series of input (state) vectors, waiting until the sequence is complete to judge the fitness of the system.

- The critic looks at only the outcomes (the results), not at some error measure due to each input.

An example of a paradigm using reinforcement adaptation is particle swarm optimization, which is introduced in Chapter 3. A particle swarm explores the problem space, keeping track of the fitness of its particles and also remembering where in the problem space the best solutions have so far been found. We probably do not know where the optimal solution is. We may not even know whether a single optimal solution exists (there may be multiple optima). There may be a number of constraints, making the problem very complex. All we can tell the system is whether one solution is better than another; sometimes, as in the case of particle swarm optimization, we can calculate how much better it is. But that's about the extent of it.

Unsupervised Adaptation

In the case of *unsupervised adaptation*, no external teacher or critic is involved in system adaptation. Instead, a dataset comprising example vectors of the system's variable parameters is provided. That is operated on by the unsupervised learning algorithm. A representation of unsupervised adaptation appears in Figure 2.3. Characteristics of unsupervised adaptation algorithms include:

- There is no indication of fitness whatsoever incorporated into the unsupervised adaptation algorithm. It just plods along with blinders on, executing its job, which may involve clustering or "competitive learning."

- The interpretation of what the unsupervised algorithm did, and how well it did it, and whether it is even appropriate and/or usable, is done after the algorithm stops running. This offline evaluation is typically done by a human or other intelligent system.

Clustering aggregates similar input patterns into distinct, mutually exclusive subsets referred to as clusters. As stated by Anderberg (1973), "the objective is to group either the data units or the variables into clusters such that elements within a cluster have a high degree of 'natural association' among themselves while the clusters are 'relatively distinct' from one another." Clustering is generally considered a two-phase process. In the first phase, the number of clusters in the data is determined or assumed. The second phase assigns each data point (pattern) to a single cluster.

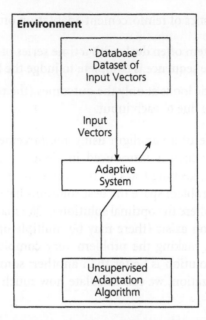

Figure 2.3   Unsupervised adaptation example. An arrow going through the adaptive system box indicates the ability to adjust the parameters of the system.

Examples of unsupervised adaptation are two types of neural network we discuss in this book, *self-organizing feature maps* and *learning vector quantization neural networks*, which we examine in Chapter 6, Neural Network Implementations. When a set of patterns is presented to either of these types of network, the adaptation algorithm clusters patterns that are similar, perhaps subject to some constraints. With the proper algorithm and constraints, the output distribution will accurately represent the probability distribution of the input patterns, but there is no hint of a "teacher" telling the network what the answer is pattern by pattern, or even a "critic" giving the network qualitative fitness hints.

Summary

In summary, what are the differences, and the implications of these differences, among the three types of adaptation? Our thoughts on this comprise a thread that runs through the book. For now, we confine our comments to a few relatively straightforward observations.

What does it mean to use a "teacher," a "critic," or a "dataset"? A teacher has detailed input/output information, which consists of a number of specific examples. Typically, the more of these examples that are available, the better a system will be able to adapt to emulate the structure underlying them. This is not always true, of course. For instance, it is impossible to build a multiclass classifier if all of your examples are from one class. (A multiclass classifier specifies which of several output classes represents an input pattern best. For example, a medical diagnostic classifier decides which disease in its inventory best represents a given a set of medical symptoms comprising an input pattern.) So the distribution of the input/output patterns over the problem space is important.

A critic has some notion that one solution is qualitatively better than another, but can't calculate a fitness metric specific to the problem. Furthermore, a critic doesn't inherently know where an optimum is, or even if there is one; a teacher may know the optimum location of a solution in the problem space.

The dataset is just that: a dataset. There is no fitness information, qualitative or quantitative, within it.

Does that make one kind of adaptation, say supervised, better than another, say unsupervised? We believe that one kind can be better than another only when considered from the perspective of a specific application. If all we have is a dataset with no fitness information, then we will use unsupervised adaptation to find features, or clusters, in the data. We can then apply other analytic techniques to these clusters or features. Even if we have output information with our input vectors, we may use unsupervised adaptation to find new ways to look at the data or as a sort of preprocessing step to reduce the problem's dimensionality to facilitate a supervised adaptation application.

Now that we've looked at the three main types of adaptation, we look at the spaces in which these adaptation methods operate.

Three Spaces of Adaptation

No matter which type of adaptation is implemented, we typically refer to three kinds of space when we work with adaptive systems. We call them input parameter space, system output space, and fitness space. As there is no standard terminology, however, other authors call our input parameter space *problem space*, and our system output space *function space*.

The *input parameter space* is defined by the dynamic ranges of the input variables. In general, these dynamic ranges are specified. However, sometimes all we have to work with are example patterns, and we may not have a valid basis for constraining the input parameters to the ranges represented by the example vectors.

The *system output space* is defined by the dynamic range(s) of the output variable(s). It is not unusual for the output dynamic ranges to be specified as either a hard or a soft constraint. (A hard constraint is one that cannot be violated; a soft constraint can be violated, but a penalty is applied to the system performance measure.) We prefer to name this space system "output" rather than "function" since it is common not to know what function, if any, is represented by the data. Often, we aren't interested in finding the function, at least not as our first objective.

The *fitness space* is the space we use to define the "goodness" of the solutions (in the output space) generated by the adaptive system. It is common practice to scale the fitness to values between 0 and 1, with the optimal value being 0 or 1 depending on whether the goal is to minimize or maximize the fitness value. Sometimes the fitness space and the system output space are the same. A simple example of this is maximizing the function $\sin(\pi x/256)$ for integer values of x between 0 and 255 (the input parameter space). This is the example we use in Chapter 3 to illustrate the step-by-step process of a genetic algorithm. In this case, the output values vary between 0 and 1, and the maximum fitness value of 1 occurs at an input value of 128.

In general, however, the system output and fitness values do not coincide. Consider another simple example of minimizing $\sum_{i=1}^{3} x_i^2$ given a dynamic range for x_i of $[-10, 10]$. In this case, the system output space is $[0, 300]$. We often transform the output space to a better representation for the purposes of calculating fitness, frequently in the range of $[0, 1]$. One possible simple fitness function is just $1/(\text{abs}(\text{output}))$, which ranges from $1/300$ (fairly close to 0) to 1.0 for a perfect answer.

Always keep these three spaces of adaptation in mind. And always know which one you are dealing with!

Now that you have some understanding of the concept of adaptation, with its three main types and three spaces, we'll discuss another concept central to computational intelligence: self-organization.

Self-organization and Evolution

Although self-organization's inclusion as a key concept in computational intelligence is, for the authors, relatively recent, the term *self-organization* was apparently used for the first time in the literature relevant to computational intelligence by W. Ross Ashby (Ashby 1945, 1947). He first used the term "self-organization" in his 1947 paper, but he was writing about the same concept in 1945. He cited the nervous system as an example of self-organization. He wrote that the nervous system, when in contact with a new environment, tends to develop an internal organization that leads to behavior that is adapted to that environment. (Note the reference to adaptation!)

Ashby maintained that self-organization has two methods of implementation (Dyson 1997). The first is illustrated by a system that starts with its parts separate (so that the behavior of each is independent of the others' states) and whose parts then act so that they change in order to form connections. An example of the second is where a system's interconnected components become organized in a productive or meaningful way. An example is an infant's brain, where self-organization is achieved less by the growth of new connections and more by allowing meaningless connections to die out.

Farley was an early contributor to the investigation of self-organizing systems. In Farley and Clark (1954), the subject is the simulation of self-organizing systems by digital computer. In Farley (1960), he said that self-organizing systems "automatically organize themselves to classify environmental inputs into recognizable percepts or 'patterns,'" and that "this self-organizing ability is called 'learned perception.'" Kleyn (1963), another early contributor, wrote: "A system is said to be self-organizing if, after observing the input and output of an unknown phenomenon (transfer relation), the system organizes itself into a simulation of the unknown phenomenon."

Today, there are almost as many ways to define self-organization as there are writers on the subject, but summaries of attributes and descriptions of self-organization often include the following points (Kennedy, Eberhart, and Shi 2001):

- Self-organizing systems usually exhibit what appears to be spontaneous order.

- Self-organization can be viewed as a system's incessant attempts to organize itself into ever more complex structures, even in the face of the incessant forces of dissolution described by the second law of thermodynamics.

- The overall system state of a self-organizing system is an emergent property of the system.

- Interconnected system components become organized in a productive or meaningful way based on local information; global dynamics emerge from local rules.

- Complex systems can self-organize.

- The self-organization process works near the "edge of chaos."

Bonabeau et al. (1999) define self-organization as "a set of dynamical mechanisms whereby structures appear at the global level of a system from interactions among its lower-level components. The rules specifying the interactions among the system's constituent units are executed on the basis of purely local information, without reference to the global pattern, which is an emergent property of the system rather than a property imposed on the system by an external ordering influence." This definition illustrates the close ties between self-organization and the emergent property of a system.

Examples of self-organization are all around us. A simple example is the formation of ice crystals on the surface of water as it begins to freeze. Another simple example happens in a salt solution when the water is dried and crystals are observed forming. Yet another example is the often complex and beautiful patterns generated by cellular automata (CAs), which are specified by very simple mathematical functions. These CAs are not programmed to produce these patterns; rather, the patterns are an emergent feature of the system.

As a more complex example, the evolution of the human brain has been described as a self-organizing process (McKee 2000). McKee uses the term *auto-catalysis* to describe how the design of an organism's features at one point in time affects or even determines the kinds of designs it can change into later. Thus the evolution of the organism is determined not only by selection pressures but by the constraints and opportunities offered by the structures that have evolved so far (Kennedy, Eberhart, and Shi 2001).

The concept of self-organization has had a profound effect on how the authors view evolution, and the way evolution is viewed has had a profound effect on how we perceive computational intelligence. The following section reviews this new per-spective of evolution and illustrates why we believe that evolutionary computation provides the foundation of computational intelligence.

Evolution beyond Darwin

What is usually described as the Darwinian view of evolution is perhaps bet-ter described as the neo-Darwinian view. For example, chromosomes weren't even known in Darwin's time, so the prevailing view is a sort of amalgam of Darwinian and Mendelian ideas. (In 1865 Gregor Johann Mendel, an Augustinian priest in the Brno Monastery in the Czech Republic, described to the Brno Nat-ural Science Society the transfer of genetic material in pea plants. Unfortunately, the fundamental importance of Mendel's finding was not understood by the Soci-ety. Until about 1900 it was not recognized that Mendel had discovered the "law of heredity.")

The neo-Darwinian view of evolution reflects three main observations. First is that chromosome composition is determined by the parents (at least in animals and humans). Second is that random mutation expands the search space of the species, providing the desirable attribute of diversity. Third is that fitter individuals have a higher probability of surviving to the next generation.

According to modern researchers, including Kauffman (1993, 1995), there are two fundamental shortcomings of the existing theory. The first is that the ori-gin of life by "chance" or mutation is highly improbable in the time frame of earth's history. The second is that evolution of complex life forms solely through mutation is also highly improbable. A detailed discussion of these points is beyond the scope of this book, but Kauffman (1993, 1995) offers compelling arguments.

This leads to a new view of evolution, in which, due primarily to self-organization, complex systems can "appear" over a relatively short time frame compared with

Darwinian evolution. In this new perception of evolution, it appears that natural selection and self-organization work hand-in-hand. That is,

evolution = natural selection + self-organization

It is the authors' opinion that the neo-Darwinian view of evolution tends to constrain evolutionary computation to a supporting role in computational intelligence, while the incorporation of self-organization facilitates the viewpoint that evolutionary computation is computational intelligence's foundation.

Self-organization remains an active area of inquiry. See, for example, the works of Stuart Kauffman (1993, 1995).

It should be evident to you by now that adaptation and self-organization are intertwined, an idea that we return to at various points in this book. It should also be evident that we consider adaptation and self-organization to play important roles in computational intelligence. With our discussions of adaptation and self-organization complete, it is time to look at computational intelligence, starting with early work in the field.

Historical Views of Computational Intelligence

As is the case with adaptation and self-organization, there is no universally accepted definition of computational intelligence. In this section, we present views of computational intelligence by other researchers. As you will see, these views are not the same. In the next section, we present our view of computational intelligence. It is somewhat different from the views presented in this section.

In an editorial in *IEEE Transactions on Neural Networks*, then editor-in-chief Robert Marks wrote, "Neural networks, genetic algorithms, fuzzy systems, evolutionary programming, and artificial life are the building blocks of CI." He further stated, "Although seeking similar goals, CI has emerged as a sovereign field whose research community is virtually distinct from AI" (Marks 1993).

David Fogel said in 1995 that CI generally describes "methods of computation that can be used to adapt solutions to new problems and do not rely on explicit human knowledge."

Walter Karplus of the University of California at Los Angeles, who was then president of the IEEE Neural Networks Council (NNC), offered the following comment at the June 2, 1996, meeting of the ADCOM of the NNC: "CI substitutes intensive computation for insight into how the system works. NNs, FSs, and EC were all shunned by classical system and control theorists. CI umbrellas and unifies these and other revolutionary methods."

Bezdek (1998), who has probably thought about computational intelligence more than most other researchers, asserts that computational intelligence is a proper subset of artificial intelligence but that artificial intelligence is not a subset of the much more complex biological intelligence. Rather, he believes that biological intelligence is used to guide artificial intelligence (and thus computational intelligence) models of it. He also views computational pattern recognition as one of many subsets of computational intelligence. In Bezdek's scheme, biological intelligence is organic (carbon-based), while computational intelligence (and its subsets) and artificial intelligence are examples of machine intelligence and are thus silicon-based. He believes that some computational models lack biological equivalents.

Now that we've briefly toured the historical views of computational intelligence, let's see how the concepts we discussed previously, adaptation and self-organization, fit into it.

Computational Intelligence as Adaptation and Self-organization

This section discusses the authors' view of computational intelligence, in which adaptation and self-organization play key roles. The authors have a different view with respect to several aspects of computational intelligence presented above.

We assert that intelligence is manifested both in carbon-based and silicon-based systems, and sometimes in hybrids of the two. In fact, intelligence need not be limited to systems based on carbon and silicon: Other substances are the active subjects of inquiry in fields such as molecular computing. It does not matter what kind of system produces the intelligence for it to exist.

It follows that the statement that some computational models do not have biological equivalents is irrelevant to this discussion. (It could be argued that computational models implemented by humans have biological analogies since humans conceived of, designed, developed, and tested them. The validity of this statement, however, is also irrelevant.) What is relevant is that no distinction should be made between biological and nonbiological intelligence. Thus, we assert that statements arguing biological equivalency, one way or the other, are not relevant to the discussion of intelligence or computational intelligence.

In this book, computational intelligence is defined as a methodology involving computing that provides a system with an ability to learn and/or to deal with new situations, such that the system is perceived to possess one or more attributes of reason, such as generalization, discovery, association, and abstraction. The output of a computationally intelligent system often includes predictions and/or decisions. Put another way, CI comprises practical adaptation and self-organization concepts, paradigms, algorithms, and implementations that enable or facilitate appropriate actions (intelligent behavior) in complex and changing environments.

Computational intelligence systems in silicon often comprise hybrids of paradigms such as artificial neural networks, fuzzy systems, and evolutionary computation systems, augmented with knowledge elements. Silicon-based computational

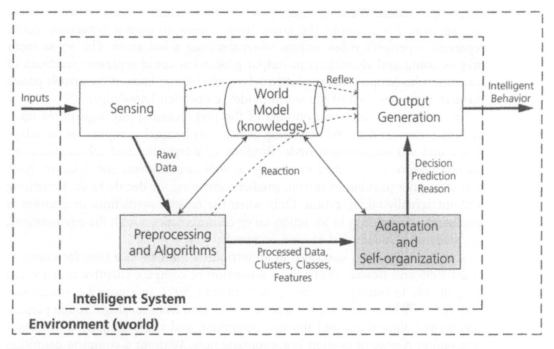

Figure 2.4 Relationships among components of intelligent systems. Thick arrows represent the main pathway through the system.

intelligence systems are often designed to mimic one or more aspects of carbon-based biological intelligence.

The relationships among the components of intelligent systems are represented very approximately by Figure 2.4. To make the figure easier to understand, we have emphasized pattern recognition, a common computational function. Many additional functions would be needed to make the figure more complete. Examples include function approximation, pattern association, filtering, and control.

The inputs to the intelligent system from the environment can be sensory in the case of biological systems or they can be via a computer keyboard, in the case of a silicon-based system. The output of an intelligent system via the output generation node is intelligent behavior. (The main pathway through the system is represented by the thick arrows.)

What is intelligent behavior? In the movie named after him, Forest Gump says, "Stupid is as stupid does." We believe that *intelligence is as intelligence does*. Intelligent behavior has an effect on the system's environment, perhaps via communication or action. If there is no action or communication that affects the environment, then there is no intelligent behavior. In Figure 2.4, one arrow goes directly from sensing to output generation; another goes from preprocessing and algorithms to output generation. These represent processes that include actions related to safety and survival. For example, the arrow from sensing to output generation could represent a person's reflex actions when touching a hot stove. The arrow from preprocessing and algorithms to output generation could represent reactions of someone who happens upon a rattlesnake while hiking. Each of the arrows passes through the outer shell of the world model (embedded knowledge).

In addition to reactions, outputs of the preprocessing and algorithms node include processed data and clustering, which may be used as inputs for the adaptation and self-organization node. Products of adaptation and self-organization include reason, as described previously, as well as prediction and decision. Note that it is quite possible to reason, predict something, or decide to do something without actually taking action. Only when the reason, prediction, or decision is implemented, resulting in an action on or communication with the environment, is intelligent behavior said to have occurred.

Complexity is often described as an attribute of intelligence (see, for example, Fogel 1995 and Bezdek 1994); for a discussion of complex adaptive systems that is applicable to intelligent systems, see Holland (1992). In Figure 2.4, complexity may generally be considered to increase as we move from sensing through preprocessing and algorithms, and through adaptation and self-organization to output generation. A note of caution is appropriate here. Without a complete definition and characterization of complexity, and subsequent application to intelligent systems, which is beyond the scope of this book, it may be premature to characterize systems that effect intelligent behavior as more complex than, say, sensing systems such as human sight.

Stochasticity, or randomness, is also sometimes listed as an attribute of intelligent systems. It is somewhat uncertain whether the attribute should be represented as randomness, pseudorandomness, or chaos. (Note that computer systems cannot generate randomness, just pseudorandomness.) However it is represented, it seems to permeate many aspects of carbon-based intelligent systems, from basic biology to behavioral intelligence, as well as most silicon-based intelligent processes and systems.

In the representation in Figure 2.4, nodes at the tails of arrows need not be subsets of those at the heads, and any node can provide input to the output generation node. For example, sensing is not necessarily a subset of preprocessing and algorithms. Furthermore, sensing can provide an input to output generation via reflex.

The world model at the top center of the diagram (which includes data and knowledge) and the arrows going to and from it require additional explanation. For each of the four nodes (sensing, preprocessing and algorithms, adaptation and self-organization, and output generation) arrows run both to and from the world model, signifying a flow of "information" in both directions.

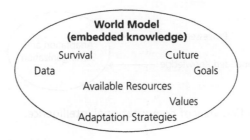

Figure 2.5 An expanded view of the world model.

The sizes of the arrowheads are meant to very roughly reflect the relative quantities of the flows. For example, the flow *from* sensing *to* the world model is much greater than the flow *to* sensing *from* the world model. And, as we move from the sensing node through preprocessing and algorithms, and then through adaptation and self-organization to output generation, a greater proportion of the flow comes *from* the world model *to* the node.

Figure 2.5 is an expanded view of the world model, within which some of the categories of "information" are stored. Note that the world model is dynamic, constantly being revised and updated. In Figure 2.5, the knowledge complexity generally increases moving from left to right (keeping in mind the previous note of caution about complexity). Only a few components of the model are given.

The diagrams in Figures 2.4 and 2.5 are simplistic, but they are meant to convey the authors' belief that there should be no distinction between carbon- and silicon-based intelligence. A system simply possesses one or more of the attributes shown in the figures, and the actions on and communications to the environment are intelligent to some degree, depending on the system attributes.

So, where's the computational intelligence? In accordance with our earlier definitions, it resides primarily in the adaptation and self-organization node. We also believe that elements of computational intelligence can be found in the preprocessing and algorithm node and in the output generation node. As represented, computational intelligence is buried deeply in the core of the system, be it biological or machine, perhaps the furthest from the interface with the environment. It is an area in which developments are occurring that will lead to exciting new analytical tools.

At the risk of oversimplifying the concept of computational intelligence as illustrated in Figure 2.4, we extract the portion of the figure most closely associated with computational intelligence and depict it with Figure 2.6. This prompts another definition, as follows: Computational intelligence comprises adaptation and self-organization using processed data and embedded knowledge as input and producing predictions, decisions, generalizations, and reason as output. The embedded knowledge resides within the system, while the processed data originates outside the system.

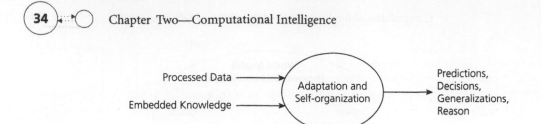

Figure 2.6 A simplified view of computational intelligence.

We have presented our view of computational intelligence in this section. We hope you now understand something about our model of CI and the important roles played by adaptation and self-organization. We discuss one capability of a CI system, the ability to generalize, in more detail in the next section.

The Ability to Generalize

One key capability of a computational intelligence system is the ability to generalize. This ability is one of the aspects of computational intelligence that distinguishes it from hard computing. This section briefly reviews what is meant by the term *generalization* and some of its implications.

Often, when developing a computational intelligence implementation, we are provided with, or obtain ourselves, a dataset comprising a number of input/output patterns. Usually, these pattern pairs comprise only a very small portion of all possible pattern pairs in the problem space. For the sake of this discussion, assume that there is only one input and one output in each pattern pair; more inputs and/or outputs do not change what we are discussing, and the single input/output version makes the representation easier.

We generally assume that there is some (probably nonlinear) function $f(x)$ that maps each input to an output in the problem space: $y = f(x)$ for the input space X and the output space Y. We can represent our dataset as $S = \{(x_i, y_i) \in X \times Y\}$, $i = 1, K, n$, where n is the number of pattern pairs.

The goal of the computational intelligence system, then, is to build a model f^* that will map other values of x into Y such that $f^*(x) \approx f(x)$ for $x^* \notin S$. This is usually what we mean by generalization. It is the ability to correctly map examples in the problem space to which the system was not exposed during training.

What the generalization metric is, however, can vary from problem to problem. Most of the time it is assumed that, for a "perfect" system, $y = f(x) \ \forall \ x \in S$ and $f^*(x) = f(x) \ \forall \ x \in S$. The first assumption may not be valid because of errors and/or noise that almost inevitably appear in even the most "gold-plated" datasets.

The second assumption can be troublesome if we split our dataset S into training and test datasets, as is usually done. The dataset is usually split because we don't have any values of $x^* \notin S$ for which we know the correct $f(x^*)$. So we use some of the dataset for training and some for testing.

We usually assume that the ability of a model to generalize is best measured by the system performance on the test set. It is quite possible that the best test set performance does not coincide with the best performance on the training set. A neural network, for example, can be overtrained on the training set (it is said to "memorize" it) so that it performs relatively poorly on the test set.

In summary, it is important to define what you mean when you use the term *generalization* and what metric you will use to measure it. Remember that the size n of the dataset S has to be large enough to have sufficient input/output patterns for both training and testing. It is impossible to say anything about generalization if you can't train the system (build the model) in the first place; it is difficult to say much about generalization with insufficient testing patterns.

With definitions of computational intelligence under our belts and having discussed a key concept of computational intelligence, generalization, we now consider where computational intelligence fits in the overall picture, which includes artificial intelligence and hard computing.

Computational Intelligence and Soft Computing versus Artificial Intelligence and Hard Computing

This section summarizes where computational intelligence belongs in the overall scheme of computing and its relationship to artificial intelligence (AI). We concur with Lotfi Zadeh's assertion (1998) that soft computing is the basis of computational intelligence and that hard computing is the basis of artificial intelligence. (We discuss Zadeh's considerable contributions to computational intelligence in Chapter 7, Fuzzy Systems Concepts and Paradigms.)

Where, then, does "traditional AI" fit? The authors' perception is that some of it is at the outer level, or near the interface surface, of the adaptation and self-organization node in Figure 2.4, where arrows depart for the output generation node and the world model. Some of it resides in the world model. At the heart of the adaptation and self-organization node are (in silicon-based systems) such computational intelligence tools as the hybrid neural network/genetic algorithm/fuzzy logic tools described in the definition of computational intelligence near the beginning of this chapter. These tools have access to, and use, embedded knowledge. There is, therefore, a difference between artificial intelligence and computational intelligence, albeit a somewhat "fuzzy" one.

And what about hard computing? If truth be told, the authors don't consider very much of what is defined as hard computing to be eligible for inclusion in an intelligent system, and Figure 2.4 is our concept of an intelligent system.

So what is the bottom line with respect to hard computing versus soft computing, traditional AI versus computational intelligence? Which attributes of a CI system do not hold for traditional AI and hard computing? We believe that four important ones are

- The ability to generalize, as discussed previously
- The ability to deal successfully with partial truths and uncertainty
- Tolerance for errors and noise, which results in graceful degradation of system performance
- The ability to perform well in changing and complex environments

Which attributes of a hard computing system do not hold for a computational intelligence (soft computing) system? We believe that two important ones are

- Precision
- Certainty

It is unlikely that any of us will ever use a computational intelligence system to balance our checkbook or calculate our taxes. So there is definitely a place for hard computing.

On the other hand, real life and real systems are replete with imprecision, uncertainty, partial truths, and nonlinearity. We are finding that many very difficult jobs, such as developing optimization and diagnostics systems in complex and changing environments, can be accomplished with computational intelligence implementations. Hard computing doesn't stand a chance in these arenas.

Summary

This chapter presents basic information on computational intelligence. It discusses adaptation and self-organization and examines their roles in computational intelligence.

We look at adaptation from three perspectives. We first examine and compare the concepts of adaptation and learning. As defined in this book, *learning* applies to the entire intelligent system, while *adaptation* mainly applies to the portion of the system where computational intelligence is relevant.

Next we review the three main types of adaptation paradigms: supervised adaptation, reinforcement adaptation, and unsupervised adaptation. The three types of adaptation use a "teacher," a "critic," or an algorithm operating on the dataset with no feedback, respectively.

A teacher has detailed input/output information comprising a number of specific examples. Typically, the more of these examples that are available, the better a system will be able to adapt to emulate the structure underlying them. This is not always true, of course. For instance, it is impossible to build a multiclass classifier if all of your examples are from one class. So the distribution of the input/output patterns over the problem space is important.

A critic has some notion that one solution is qualitatively better than another but can't calculate a fitness metric specific to the problem. Furthermore, a critic doesn't inherently know where an optimum is or even if there is one; a teacher may know the location of an optimum solution in the problem space.

The algorithm operating on a dataset with no fitness feedback is just that. There is no fitness information, qualitative or quantitative, that results from running the unsupervised algorithm.

How, then, do we decide which type of adaptation to use? We believe that the choice should be made from the perspective of a specific application. If all we have is a dataset with no fitness information, then we will use unsupervised adaptation to find features, or clusters, in the data. We can then apply other analytic techniques to these clusters or features. Even if we have output information with our input vectors, we may use unsupervised adaptation to find new ways to look at the data or as a preprocessing step to reduce the problem's dimensionality to facilitate a supervised adaptation application.

Additionally in this chapter, we consider the three spaces with which we must deal when working with adaptive systems: problem space, function space, and fitness space. Always be aware which space you're in at any given time.

There is no universally accepted definition of computational intelligence (CI). Several views of computational intelligence are presented, followed by the authors' view of computational intelligence. That is, computational intelligence comprises practical adaptation and self-organization concepts, paradigms, algorithms, and implementations that enable or facilitate appropriate actions (intelligent behavior) in complex and changing environments. The inclusion of self-organization in our definition of computational intelligence is a relatively recent development; inspiration and insight came from the current views of evolution as natural selection plus self-organization by researchers such as Kaufmann.

In the next chapter, we look at the methodology we believe provides the foundation of computational intelligence: evolutionary computation. We explore genetic algorithms, evolutionary programming, evolution strategies, genetic programming, and particle swarm optimization.

Exercises

1. What other elements might be appropriate for inclusion in the world model of Figure 2.5?

2. Read other discussions of computational intelligence, including Bezdek (1998). Develop your own one-paragraph definition of computational intelligence.

3. Find an article or a chapter in another book on emergent computing. Compare the concept of emergent computing as presented there with the concept of self-organization presented in this chapter.

4. Find another source of information on cellular automata. Discuss the relationship between cellular automata and self-organization.

5. Randomness is sometimes listed as an attribute of intelligent systems. Why?

6. Give a real-world example of each type of adaptation: supervised, reinforcement, and unsupervised.

chapter
three

Evolutionary Computation Concepts and Paradigms

One of the component methodologies of computational intelligence, and the one we believe provides its foundation, is evolutionary computation. This chapter goes into some detail in reviewing the field of evolutionary computation, which consists of machine learning optimization and classification paradigms that are roughly based on evolution mechanisms such as biological genetics, natural selection, and emergent adaptive behavior. Evolutionary computation paradigms provide tools to build intelligent systems that model intelligent behavior.

This chapter also provides basic information needed to use evolutionary computation tools to solve practical problems. The terminology and key concepts are presented, followed by paradigms that are developed from and illustrate the key concepts. The chapter is written largely from the perspective of an engineer or computer scientist, emphasizing the application potential of evolutionary computation tools and drawing comparisons with other applied problem-solving techniques. ■

History of Evolutionary Computation

There are a number of ways to address the history of almost any subject, evolutionary computation included. We choose to focus on people rather than theory or technology for two main reasons. First, it seems a more interesting way to look at history. History is, after all, just a record of people doing things. Second, the evolutionary computation field, particularly in the early days, revolved around a few key individuals. These individuals and their followers seem to us to have sometimes resembled minicultures.

Having said that, the selection of individuals is somewhat arbitrary because the intent is to provide a broad sample of people, rather than an exhaustive list, who contributed to current technology. Some well-known researchers are mentioned only briefly, and others are omitted. The fact that someone is discussed only briefly, or even omitted altogether, is not meant to reflect the authors' opinion of that person's contribution. The selected people and their contributions are discussed roughly in chronological order. We organize our history according to the main evolutionary computation areas.

The evolutionary computation field considered in this book includes the following five areas[1]:

- Genetic algorithms
- Evolutionary programming
- Evolution strategies
- Genetic programming
- Particle swarm optimization

Of the five methodologies, more work has been done in genetic algorithms than in any other area, and so we focus on that field. (We realize that the emphasis on genetic algorithms is fading somewhat. In fact, hybrids of the five methodologies are becoming increasingly popular.) Contributors to the other four areas are also discussed but in somewhat less detail. Although it might be argued that work in the early twentieth century on Darwinian synthesis by Haldane (1990) and others is the place to start, what is now known as evolutionary computation really began to take shape about 50 years later. We begin our journey looking at the roots of genetic algorithms in the 1950s.

Genetic Algorithms

The development of genetic algorithms (GA) has its origins in work done in the 1950s by biologists using computers to simulate natural genetic systems. One of

---

[1] There are other ways to look at the field, such as considering genetic programming as a branch of genetic algorithms, but we choose this approach.

those doing work most closely related to our current concepts of genetic algorithms was A. S. Fraser, an Australian who began publishing in the field in the late 1950s (Fraser 1957). Our history of evolutionary computation thus (arbitrarily) begins with him.

Fraser was working in the area of epistasis (suppression of the effect of a gene) and represented each of three parameters of an epistatic function as 5 bits in a 15-bit string. He then based his selection of "parents" by choosing those strings whose variable values produced function values between −1 and +1. Fraser was working with natural systems, and although his work somewhat resembles function optimization as currently done by genetic algorithms, he apparently did not consider the possibilities of applying his methodology to artificial systems (Fraser 1960, 1962).

Also beginning to publish in the early 1960s was the man who, together with his students, has probably had more influence on the field of genetic algorithms than any others: John H. Holland of The University of Michigan. Holland attended MIT as an undergraduate, where he was influenced by such luminaries as Norbert Weiner and John McCarthy. He was part of a team that programmed the prototype of the IBM 701 to "learn" something about running a maze, prompting Holland to regard the computer as a sort of "simulated lab rat." After working at IBM, Holland went to the University of Michigan, where, under Arthur Burks, he obtained the first Ph.D. in the United States in computer science (Levy 1992).

Davis (1991) stated:

> John Holland . . . created the genetic algorithm field. The field would not exist if he had not decided to harness the power inherent in genetic processes in the early 1970s and functioned as the technical and political leader of the genetic algorithm field from its inception to the present time. Our understanding of the unique features of genetic algorithms has been shaped by the careful and insightful work of Holland and his students from the field's critical first years to the present time. (p. vi)

Holland's interest is in machine intelligence, and he and his students developed and applied the capabilities of genetic algorithms to artificial systems. He taught courses in adaptive systems in the early 1960s while laying the groundwork for applications to artificial systems with his publications on adaptive systems theory (Holland 1962). Holland's systems were adaptive because of their robustness in spite of changes and uncertainty in the environment. Further, they were self-adaptive in that they could make adjustments based on their interaction with the environment over time.

The GA metaphor is genetic inheritance at the level of the individual. A problem solution is considered as an individual's chromosome, or pattern of genetic alleles, and low-level operations such as those in the nuclei of cells are proposed for developing new solutions.

One of Holland's many contributions was his use of a population of individuals, conceptualized as chromosomes, in the search process, rather than single individuals, as was common at the time. (Fraser used populations but, as stated previously, didn't apply his methodology to artificial systems.) He also derived the schema theorem, which shows that schema (fundamental building blocks of individual chromosomes) that are more "fit" with respect to a defined fitness function are more likely to reproduce in successive generations of the population of chromosomes. We go into more detail about the schema theorem later in this chapter.

Chromosomes in nature are formed of twisted strands of DNA, composed of the four proteins adenine, cytosine, guanine, and thymine. These strands are presently understood as a kind of computer program that gives instructions to the cells that comprise the organism; the DNA sequence contains instructions about how to develop and what to do. While our digital computers use the base-2, or binary, number system to encode program instructions and data, chromosomes use a base-4 method, encoded in the ordering of the four proteins. Genetic algorithms usually use base-2 chromosomes, though the methods developed by Holland and his followers can be applied to any base number system, including floating-point decimals.

Beginning in the 1960s Holland's students routinely used selection, crossover, and mutation in their applications. Several of Holland's students made significant contributions to the genetic algorithm field, often starting with their Ph.D. dissertations. We mention only a few.

The term *genetic algorithm* was used first by Bagley (1967) in his dissertation, which utilized genetic algorithms to find parameter sets in evaluation functions for playing the game of Hexapawn, which is played on a 3 × 3 chessboard on which each player starts with three pawns. Bagley's genetic algorithm resembled many used today, with selection, crossover, and mutation.

In 1975, Holland published one of the field's most important books, entitled *Adaptation in Natural and Artificial Systems.* In the first five years after it was published, the book sold 100 to 200 copies per year and seemed to be fading into oblivion. Instead, between 1985 and 1990, the number of people working on genetic algorithms—and interest in Holland's book—increased sufficiently to persuade Holland to update and reissue it (Holland 1992).

Also in 1975, K. A. De Jong, one of Holland's students, published his Ph.D. dissertation entitled, "An Analysis of the Behavior of a Class of Genetic Adaptive Systems." As part of his work, De Jong put forward a set of five test functions designed to measure the performance of any genetic algorithm. Two metrics were devised, one to measure the convergence of the algorithm, the other to measure the ongoing performance. De Jong examined the effects of varying four parameters (population size, crossover probability, mutation probability, and generation gap) on the performance of six main kinds of genetic algorithm paradigm (De Jong 1975). Although a number of other benchmark functions have emerged, De Jong's five-function test bed and two performance metrics are still among frequently referenced criteria for genetic algorithm performance.

From Michigan De Jong went to the University of Pittsburgh, where he taught genetic algorithms to a number of students, among them Steve Smith and John Grefenstette. Smith published a significant dissertation on machine learning involving a classifier system that became known as "Smith's Poker Player" (Smith 1980). After graduation, Grefenstette began teaching yet another generation of students at Vanderbilt University, including J. David Schaffer, who was the first to develop a multiobjective algorithm (Schaffer 1984), work that has enjoyed a revival in popularity.

Grefenstette developed a genetic algorithm implementation called GENESIS that, in its various incarnations and reincarnations, became perhaps the most widely used genetic algorithm implementation in the late 1980s (Grefenstette 1984a, 1984b). He also was instrumental in founding and editing the proceedings of the first International Conference on Genetic Algorithms, a premier conference in the field (Grefenstette 1985).

David E. Goldberg, another of Holland's students, has concentrated on engineering applications of genetic algorithms. He is a former gas pipeline worker whose Ph.D. dissertation considered a 10-compressor, 10-pipe, steady-state, serial gas pipeline problem (Goldberg 1983). The goal was to provide a strategy that minimizes the power consumed in the pumping stations, subject to pressure-related constraints. He summarized the power the genetic algorithm brought to the pipeline problem when he wrote, "If we were, for example, to search for the best person among the world's 4.5 billion people as rapidly as the GA, we would only need to talk to four or five people before making our near optimal selection" (Goldberg 1987). Goldberg's 1989 volume is one of the most influential books on genetic algorithms: *Genetic Algorithms in Search, Optimization and Machine Learning* (Goldberg 1989). He continues to be an important contributor to the field.

The author of another significant genetic algorithm book is self-taught in genetic algorithms. Lawrence (Dave) Davis got interested in them while working at Texas Instruments, where he obtained support to evaluate genetic algorithms for 2D bin packing in a chip layout application. He published the *Handbook of Genetic Algorithms* after moving to the Boston area, where he worked for BBN. His book comprises two main parts. The first is a tutorial on genetic algorithms; the second is a collection of case studies contributed by a number of researchers (Davis 1991). In the mid-1990s, two of the most widely read books by people wanting to learn about genetic algorithms were those by Goldberg and Davis.

At approximately the same time that Holland and his students were developing genetic algorithms, two groups were working on opposite sides of the Atlantic on different approaches that do not use *crossover*, a main feature of genetic algorithm implementations. These approaches are evolutionary programming and evolution strategies. We begin with evolutionary programming.

Evolutionary Programming

In the United States, Larry J. Fogel and his colleagues developed what they named *evolutionary programming*. Evolutionary programming uses the selection of the fittest, but the only structure-modifying operation allowed is mutation—there is no crossover. Fogel and his colleagues mainly worked with finite state machines and were interested in machine intelligence; they were able to solve some problems that were quite difficult for genetic algorithms.

Fogel (1994) described evolutionary programming as taking a fundamentally different approach from that of genetic algorithms:

> The procedure abstracts evolution as a top-down process of adaptive behavior, rather than a bottom-up process of adaptive genetics. It is argued that this approach is more appropriate because natural selection does not act on individual components in isolation, but rather on the complete set of expressed behaviors of an organism in light of its interaction with its environment.

Philosophically, then, evolutionary programming researchers consider each point in the population to represent an entire species, with species competing to fill environmental niches.

Fogel summarizes evolutionary programming as implementing "survival of the more skillful" rather than the "survival of the fittest" emphasized by genetic algorithm developers. In the mid-1960s a book documenting this approach proved to be quite controversial (Fogel et al. 1966). Misunderstandings and misinterpretations related to the book have been identified as a contributing factor to problems experienced by researchers in obtaining funding for evolutionary computation in the late 1960s and 1970s (Goldberg 1989). It is probable, however, that another significant factor was the well-known symbolics versus numerics controversy (temporarily won by Minsky and the symbolics researchers). One of the leading evolutionary programming researchers during the 1970s was at New Mexico State University. Don Dearholt and his students were responsible for a significant number of publications on evolutionary programming during this decade.

Evolution Strategies

At the same time that Fogel and his group were working on evolutionary programming, across the Atlantic Ocean Ingo Rechenberg and Hans-Paul Schwefel were experimenting with mutation in their attempts to find optimal physical configurations for a series of hinged plates in a wind tunnel and a tube that delivered liquid—the usual gradient-descent techniques were unable to solve the sets of equations for reducing wind resistance. They began experimenting with mutation, slightly perturbing their best problem solutions to search randomly in the nearby regions of the problem space.

Rechenberg and Schwefel used the first computer available at the Technical University of Berlin to simulate various versions of the approach that became known as *evolution strategies* (Rechenberg 1965; Schwefel 1965). In the early 1970s, Rechenberg published a book that is considered the foundation for this approach (Rechenberg 1973), and evolution strategies continue to experience significant activity, especially in Europe. Research developments in Germany and the United States continued in parallel, with each group unaware of the other's findings until the 1980s (although they may have known about each other [Fogel 2000]).

Genetic Programming

The fourth major area of evolutionary computation is genetic programming. Some of the earliest related work (Friedberg 1958; Friedberg et al. 1959) dealt with fixed-length computer programs that were coded by another program designed to optimize their performance. Their programs, dubbed "Herman" and "Ramsey," each comprised a set of 64 instructions, with each instruction being 14 bits long. The programs were defined such that every arrangement of the 14 bits was a valid instruction, and each set of 64 instructions was a valid program. Unfortunately, the results of the efforts did not live up to expectations; and, in retrospect, there were probably three main reasons for this. First, the programs were limited in length to 64 instructions: A "failure" was tallied if the program did not terminate successfully by the end of the 64th instruction (even if there was a loop). Second, there was only one program; thus, there was a population of just one that evolved. Third, it is not clear that the fitness function used was appropriate.

These limitations were successfully dealt with by Stanford's John Koza (yet another former student of Holland), who developed genetic programming in its current form in the late 1980s. Whereas the other three evolutionary computation approaches use string-shaped chromosomes, Koza evolved computer programs in a population of tree-shaped ones. The units used for crossover were LISP symbolic expressions that are essentially subroutines. Koza has been a prolific producer of documentation, including books (Koza 1992) and videotapes related to genetic programming, which is one of the fastest-growing and most fascinating areas of evolutionary computation. The idea of evolving computer programs has been around for decades; it is now becoming a reality.

Particle Swarm Optimization

The fifth major area of evolutionary computation is the "new kid on the block," particle swarm optimization, which has roots in three main component areas.

Perhaps most obvious are its ties to artificial life (A-life) in general and to bird flocking, fish schooling, and swarming theory in particular. It is also related to evolutionary computation, with ties to both genetic algorithms and evolution strategies (Bäck 1995). The third component area is social psychology. This brief history focuses on three of the main contributing paradigms from social psychology. The A-life and evolutionary computation roots are reviewed in the introduction to the section on particle swarm optimization later in this chapter.[2]

The first social psychology paradigm is Latané's dynamic social impact theory (Latané 1981). Summarized, this theory states that the behaviors of individuals can be explained in terms of the self-organizing properties of their social system, that clusters of individuals develop similar beliefs, and that subpopulations diverge from one another (polarize). There are four major characteristics of social impact theory: consolidation, clustering, correlation, and continuing diversity. Consolidation means that opinion diversity is reduced as individuals are exposed to majority arguments. Clustering means that individuals become more like their neighbors in social space. Correlation means that attitudes that were originally independent tend to become associated. Finally, continuing diversity means that clustering prevents minority views from complete consolidation. In summary, individuals influence one another and, in doing so, become more similar, and patterns of belief held by individuals tend to correlate within regions of a population. This theory is consistent with findings in the fields of social psychology, economics, and anthropology.

The second paradigm is Axelrod's culture model (Axelrod 1984). In this model, populations of individuals are represented as strings of symbols, or "features." The probability of interaction between two individuals is a function of their similarity, and individuals become more similar as a result of their interactions. The observed dynamic is polarization, that is, homogeneous subpopulations that differ from one another.

The third paradigm is Kennedy's adaptive culture model (Kennedy 1998). In this model, there is no effect of similarity of individuals on the probability of their interaction. In fact, the effect of similarity is negative in that it is *dis*similarity that creates boundaries between cultural regions. Interactions between individuals occur if their fitnesses are different. Kennedy's work in culture and cognition can be summarized as follows:

- Individuals searching for solutions learn from the experiences of others (individuals learn from their neighbors).

- An observer of the population perceives phenomena of which the individuals are the parts (individuals that interact frequently become similar).

---

[2] For a more detailed account of all three component areas, see Kennedy, Eberhart, and Shi (2001).

- Culture affects the performance of individuals that comprise it (individuals gain benefit by imitating their neighbors).

Jim Kennedy and Russ Eberhart both worked at Research Triangle Institute in North Carolina in the early 1990s. Kennedy was interested in exploring the possibility that an evolutionary computation paradigm might play a role in his modeling of social systems. The two continued to collaborate even after Kennedy moved to Washington, D.C., and Eberhart moved to Indianapolis (both moved in 1994). The first two papers were published in 1995 (Kennedy and Eberhart 1995, Eberhart and Kennedy 1995). One was delivered in Nagoya, Japan; the other, in Perth, Australia. The international flavor of the work in the field continues. As of the writing of this book, the authors are aware of work being done in over 30 countries on particle swarm optimization.

Toward Unification

As the 1980s came to a close, the first four areas of evolutionary computation continued to develop relatively independently, with little cooperation or communication among them. In 1994, however, an important meeting was held that brought together researchers from all four evolutionary computation areas: the IEEE World Congress on Computational Intelligence, held at Walt Disney World, Florida. The World Congress comprised a mini-symposium on computational intelligence and three conferences: The International Conference on Neural Networks; the fuzzy logic conference (FUZZ/IEEE 1994); and the First IEEE Conference on Evolutionary Computation (ICEC), chaired by Zbigniew Michalewicz of the University of North Carolina at Charlotte. A total of 96 papers were presented orally in ICEC and 63 in poster sessions, representing authors from 23 countries worldwide. The two volumes of proceedings from this evolutionary computation conference are a landmark in the field (Michalewicz et al. 1994).

At the second World Congress, held in Anchorage, Alaska, in 1998, particle swarm optimization joined the program. The third World Congress, held in Honolulu, Hawaii, featured a significant number of papers from each of the five main areas, as well as interesting and promising hybrids. Researchers in the five areas of evolutionary computation are now communicating and working significantly more with each other.

Now that we've looked at the history of evolutionary computation, let's look at what it is and how to use it.

Evolutionary Computation Overview

The five areas of evolutionary computation (EC) share attributes and implementation procedures, which we now discuss before moving on to separate overviews of each area. EC paradigms generally differ from traditional search and optimization paradigms in three main ways:

1. EC paradigms utilize a population of points (potential solutions) in their search.

2. EC paradigms use direct "fitness" information instead of function derivatives or other related knowledge.

3. EC paradigms use stochastic, rather than deterministic, transition rules.

In addition, EC implementations sometimes encode the parameters in binary or other symbols, rather than working with the parameters themselves. We now examine these differences in more detail, beginning with the attributes of EC paradigms.

EC Paradigm Attributes

How do traditional optimization methods differ from EC paradigms? Most traditional optimization paradigms move from one point in the decision hyperspace to another, using some deterministic rule. One of the drawbacks of this approach is the likelihood of getting stuck at a local optimum. For example, if the fitness landscape resembles some hills surrounding a mountain that represents the optimum, it is likely that a traditional paradigm will get stuck at the top of a hill and never find the mountain (global optimum). EC paradigms, on the other hand, start with a population of points (hyperspace vectors). They typically generate a new population with the same number of members each epoch, or generation. Thus, many maxima or minima can be explored simultaneously, lowering the probability of getting stuck. Operators such as crossover and mutation effectively enhance this parallel search capability, allowing the search to directly "tunnel through" from one promising hyperspace region to another. (An operator is a rule for changing a proposed problem solution.)

Evolutionary computation paradigms do not require information that is auxiliary to the problem, such as function derivatives. Many hill-climbing search paradigms, for example, require the calculation of derivatives in order to explore the local maximum. In EC optimization paradigms the fitness of each member of the population is calculated from the value of the function being optimized, and it is common to use the function output as the measure of fitness. Fitness is a direct metric of the individual population member's performance on the function being optimized.

The fact that EC paradigms use probabilistic transition rules certainly does not mean that a strictly random search is being carried out. Rather, stochastic operators are applied to operations that direct the search toward regions of the hyperspace that are likely to have higher values of fitness. Thus, for example, reproduction (selection) is often carried out with a probability that is proportional to the individual's fitness value.

Some EC paradigms, particularly genetic algorithms, use special encodings for the parameters of the problem being solved. In genetic algorithms, the parameters are often encoded as binary strings, but any finite alphabet can be used. These strings are almost always of fixed length, with a fixed total number of 1s and 0s, in the case of a binary string, being assigned to each parameter. By "fixed length" it is meant that the string length does not vary during the running of the EC paradigm. The string length (number of bits for a binary string) assigned to each parameter depends on its maximum range for the problem being solved and on the precision required.

Now that we've discussed the attributes of the paradigms, let's see how to implement them.

Implementation

Regardless of the paradigm implemented, evolutionary computation applications often follow a similar procedure:

1. Initialize the population.
2. Calculate the fitness for each individual in the population.
3. Reproduce selected individuals to form a new population.
4. Perform evolutionary operations, such as crossover and mutation, on the population.
5. Loop to step 2 until some condition is met.

Initialization is commonly done by seeding the population with random values. When the parameters are represented by binary strings, this simply means generating random strings of 1s and 0s (with a uniform probability for each value) of the fixed length described earlier. It is sometimes feasible to seed the population with "promising" values that are known to be in the hyperspace region relatively close to the optimum. (Based on our experience, however, we caution you against using this approach. Randomly generated populations tend to be more reliable.) The number of individuals chosen to make up the population is both problem and paradigm dependent, but it is often in the range of a few dozen to a few hundred.

The fitness value is often proportional to the output value of the function being optimized, though it may also be derived from some combination of a number of function outputs. The fitness function takes as its inputs the outputs of one or more functions, and then it outputs some probability of reproduction. Sometimes it is necessary to transform the function outputs to produce an appropriate fitness metric; sometimes it is not.

Selection of individuals for reproduction to constitute a new population (often called a new generation) is usually based on fitness values. The higher the fitness, the more likely it is that the individual will be selected for the new generation. Some paradigms that are considered evolutionary, however, such as particle swarm optimization, can retain all population members from epoch to epoch.

Now that we've discussed the step-by-step process, let's consider the process as a whole. In many, if not most, cases, a global optimum exists at one point in the decision hyperspace. (Sometimes multiple optima exist.) Furthermore, stochastic or chaotic noise might be present. Occasionally the global optimum changes dynamically because of external influences; frequently there are very good local optima as well. For these and other reasons, the bottom line is that it is often unreasonable to expect any optimization method to find a global optimum (even if it exists) within a finite time. The best that can be hoped for is to find near-optimum solutions and that the time it takes to find them increases less than exponentially with the number of variables. We agree with one leading EC researcher who suggests that the focus should be on "meliorization" (improvement) rather than on optimization (Schwefel 1994).

Put another way, evolutionary computation is often the second-best way to solve a problem. Classical methods such as linear programming should often be tried first, as should customized approaches that take full advantage of knowledge about the problem. (It is also possible that a hybrid approach that uses elements from classical methods with elements of evolutionary computation will work well.)

Why should we be satisfied with second best? For one thing, classical and customized approaches are frequently not feasible, while EC paradigms are feasible in a vast number of situations. Also, a real strength of EC paradigms is that they are generally quite robust. In this field, robustness means that an algorithm can be used to solve many problems, and even many kinds of problems, with a minimum amount of special adjustments to account for special qualities of a particular problem. Typically an evolutionary algorithm requires specification of the length of the problem solution vectors, some details of their encoding, and an evaluation function; the rest of the program does not need to be changed. Finally, robust methodologies are generally fast and easy to implement. This is especially true of EC paradigms, which are often one or more orders of magnitude faster than other approaches (if other approaches exist).

We've completed our overview of evolutionary computation. The next sections review five areas of evolutionary computation: genetic algorithms, evolutionary programming, evolution strategies, genetic programming, and particle swarm optimization. Genetic algorithms, discussed in the next section, receive a majority of the attention, as they currently account for most of the successful applications in the literature (although this is changing).

Genetic Algorithms

It seems that every technology has its jargon, and genetic algorithms are no exception. Therefore, we begin by reviewing some of the basic terminology that is needed to understand the genetic algorithm (GA) literature. A sample problem is then presented to illustrate how GAs work; a step-by-step analysis illustrates a GA application, with options discussed for some of the individual operations. The section concludes with a more detailed look at the fundamental Schema theorem and at approaches for improving GA performance in some situations.

In this book, unless otherwise specified, we deal with canonical genetic algorithms, a basic version of GAs that feature binary parameter encoding, one- or two-point crossover, and bit-by-bit mutation. (We discuss these attributes later in this section.)

Details of implementing GAs are discussed in Chapter 4, where a specific GA implementation is summarized. We begin here by looking at the general features of GAs.

Overview of Genetic Algorithms

One perspective of genetic algorithms is that they are search algorithms that reflect in a very primitive way some of the processes of natural evolution. (As such, they are analogous to artificial neural networks' status as primitive approximations of biological neural processing.) Engineers and computer scientists do not care as much about the biological foundations of GAs as about their utility as analysis tools (another parallel with neural networks). GAs often provide very effective search mechanisms that can be used in optimization or classification applications.

EC paradigms work with a population of points rather than a single point; each "point" is actually a vector in hyperspace representing one potential, or candidate, solution to the optimization problem. A population is thus just an ensemble, or set, of hyperspace vectors. Each vector is called an individual in the population; sometimes an individual in a GA is referred to as a chromosome because of the analogy to genetic evolution of organisms.

Because real numbers are often encoded in GAs using binary numbers, the dimensionality of the problem vector might be different from the dimensionality of the bitstring chromosome. The number of elements in each vector (individual) equals the number of real parameters in the optimization problem. A vector "element" generally corresponds to one parameter, or dimension, of the numeric vector. Each element can be encoded in any number of bits, depending on the representation of each parameter. The total number of bits defines the dimension of hyperspace being searched. If a GA is being used to find "optimum" weights for a neural network, for example, the number of vector elements equals the number of weights in the network. If there are w weights, and it is desired to calculate each weight to a precision of b bits, then each individual will consist of $w \cdot b$ bits, and the dimension of the binary hyperspace being searched is 2^{wb}. Thus we can see that even for a fairly modest problem involving the optimization of three variables to a resolution of three decimal places each (10 bits), the search space is 2^{30}. The variables being optimized comprise what is called the phenotype space, and the behavior of the system given certain values of the variables is the *phenotype*. The binary strings on which operators such as crossover and mutation work comprise what is called the *genotype space*, and the strings themselves are the *genotypes*.

The series of operations carried out when implementing a canonical (basic) GA paradigm is:

1. Initialize the population.
2. Calculate fitness for each individual in the population.
3. Reproduce selected individuals to form a new population.
4. Perform crossover and mutation on the population.
5. Loop to step 2 until some condition is met.

In some GA implementations, operations other than crossover and mutation are carried out in step 4. We will further explore GAs by applying a basic GA to a simple problem.

A Sample GA Problem

Because implementing a canonical (basic) GA paradigm is so simple, a sample problem (also simple) seems to be the best way to introduce most of the basic GA concepts and methods. As will be seen, implementing a basic GA involves only copying strings, exchanging portions of strings, and flipping bits in strings.

Our sample problem is to find the value of x that maximizes the function $f(x) = \sin(\pi x / 256)$ over the range $0 \leq x \leq 255$, where values of x are restricted to integers. This is just the sine function from zero to π radians, as illustrated in Figure 3.1. Its maximum value of 1 occurs at $\pi / 2$, or $x = 128$. The function value and the fitness value are thus defined to be identical for the sample problem.

There is only one variable in our sample problem: x. We assume for the sample problem that the GA paradigm uses a binary alphabet. The first decision to be made is how to represent the variable. It is easy in this case because the variable can only take on integer values between 0 and 255. It is therefore logical to represent each individual in our population with an 8-bit binary string. Using standard binary encoding, the binary string 00000000 will evaluate to 0; 11111111, to 255.

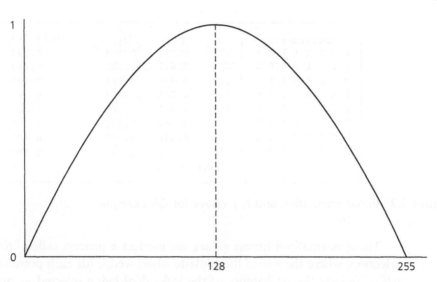

Figure 3.1 Function to be optimized in example problem.

The determination of the number of bits needed is usually more complex than this case. There is generally more than one variable, and the number of bits for each variable must be chosen to yield the desired precision. For example, a real variable that varies between 0 and 1 and has a precision of three decimal places (one part in a thousand) can be represented by a string of 10 bits (one part in 1,024).

We must decide next how many individuals will make up the population. In an actual application, it is common to have between a few dozen and a few hundred individuals. For the purposes of this illustrative example, however, the population consists of eight individuals.

The next step is to initialize the population, which is usually done randomly. A random number generator is thus used to assign a 1 or 0 to each of the eight positions in each of the eight individuals, resulting in the initial population in Figure 3.2. Also shown in the figure are the values of x and $f(x)$ for each binary string.

After fitness calculation, the next step is reproduction. Reproduction consists of forming a new population with the same number of individuals by selecting from members of the current population with a stochastic process that is weighted by each of their fitness values. In the sample problem, the sum of all fitness values for the initial population is 5.083. Dividing each fitness value by 5.083, then, yields a *normalized fitness* value f_{norm} for each individual. The sum of the normalized values is, of course, 1. The normalized values are shown in an accumulated fashion in the *cumulative f_{norm}* column in Figure 3.2.

Individuals	x	f(x)	f_{norm}	cumulative f_{norm}
1 0 1 1 1 1 0 1	189	0.733	0.144	0.144
1 1 0 1 1 0 0 0	216	0.471	0.093	0.237
0 1 1 0 0 0 1 1	99	0.937	0.184	0.421
1 1 1 0 1 1 0 0	236	0.243	0.048	0.469
1 0 1 0 1 1 1 0	174	0.845	0.166	0.635
0 1 0 0 1 0 1 0	74	0.788	0.155	0.790
0 0 1 0 0 0 1 1	35	0.416	0.082	0.872
0 0 1 1 0 1 0 1	53	0.650	0.128	1.000

$$\Sigma f(x) = 5.083$$

Figure 3.2 Initial population and *f(x)* values for GA example.

These normalized fitness values are used in a process called "roulette wheel" selection, where the size of the roulette wheel wedge for each population member, which reflects the probability of the individual being selected, is proportional to its normalized fitness value.

The roulette wheel is "spun" by generating eight random numbers between 0 and 1. If a random number is between 0 and 0.144, the first individual in the existing population is selected for the next population. If it is between 0.144 and $(0.144 + 0.093) = 0.237$, the second individual is selected, and so on. Finally, if the random number is between $(1 - 0.128) = 0.872$ and 1.0, the last individual is selected. The probability that an individual is selected is thus proportional to that individual's fitness value. It is possible, though highly improbable, that the individual with the lowest fitness value could be selected eight times in a row and make up the entire next population. It is more likely that individuals with high fitness values are picked more than once for the new population. (Note that roulette wheel selection works as described here only when all fitness values are positive. Modifications must be made to accommodate negative fitness values.)

The eight random numbers generated (presented in random order) are 0.293, 0.971, 0.160, 0.469, 0.664, 0.568, 0.371, and 0.109. As shown in Figure 3.3, this results in initial population member numbers 3, 8, 2, 5, 6, 5, 3, and 1 being chosen to make up the population after reproduction.

The next operation is crossover. To many evolutionary computation practitioners, crossover of binary encoded substrings is what makes a genetic algorithm a genetic algorithm. Crossover is the process of exchanging portions of the strings of two "parent" individuals. An overall probability is assigned to the crossover process, which is the probability that, given two parents, the crossover process will occur. This *crossover rate* is often in the range of 0.65 to 0.80; a value of 0.75 is selected for the sample problem.

First, the population is divided randomly into pairs of parents. Because the order of the population after reproduction in Figure 3.3 is already randomized,

```
0 1 1 0 0 0 1 1
0 0 1 1 0 1 0 1
1 1 0 1 1 0 0 0
1 0 1 0 1 1 1 0
0 1 0 0 1 0 1 0
1 0 1 0 1 1 1 0
0 1 1 0 0 0 1 1
1 0 1 1 1 1 0 1
```

Figure 3.3 Population after reproduction.

		Individuals	x	f(x)
1	2			
0 1 1|0 0 0|1 1		0 1 1 1 0 1 1 1	119	0.994
0 0 1|1 0 1|0 1		0 0 1 0 0 0 0 1	33	0.394
1	2			
1|1 0 1 1|0 0 0		1 0 1 0 1 0 0 0	168	0.882
1|0 1 0 1|1 1 0		1 1 0 1 1 1 1 0	222	0.405
2	1			
0 1|0 0 1 0 1|0		1 0 0 0 1 0 1 0	138	0.992
1 0|1 0 1 1 1|0		0 1 1 0 1 1 1 0	110	0.976
0 1 1 0 0 0 1 1		0 1 1 0 0 0 1 1	99	0.937
1 0 1 1 1 1 0 1		1 0 1 1 1 1 0 1	189	0.733
(a)		**(b)**	**(c)**	**(d)**

Figure 3.4 Population before crossover showing crossover points (a); after crossover (b); and values of *x* (c) and *f(x)* (d) after crossover.

parents will be paired as they appear there. For each pair, a random number is generated to determine whether crossover will occur. It is thus determined that three of the four pairs will undergo crossover.

Next, for the pairs undergoing crossover, two crossover points are selected at random. (Other crossover techniques are discussed later in this chapter.) The portions of the strings between the first and second crossover points (moving from left to right in the string) will be exchanged. The paired population, with the first and second crossover points labeled for the three pairs of individuals undergoing crossover, is illustrated in Figure 3.4(a) before the crossover operation. The portions of the strings to be exchanged are in bold. Figure 3.4(b) illustrates the population after crossover is performed.

Note that, for the third pair from the top, the first crossover point is to the right of the second. The crossover operation thus "wraps around" the end of the string, exchanging the portion between the first and the second, moving from left to right. For two-point crossover, then, it is as if the head (left end) of each individual string is joined to the tail (right end), thus forming a ring structure. The section exchanged starts at the first crossover point, moving to the right along the binary ring, and ends at the second crossover point. The values of x and $f(x)$ for the population following crossover appear in Figure 3.4(c) and (d), respectively.

The final operation in this plain vanilla genetic algorithm is mutation. Mutation consists of flipping bits at random, generally with a constant probability for each bit in the population. As is the case with the probability of crossover, the probability of mutation can vary widely according to the application and the preference of the researcher. Values between 0.001 and 0.01 are not unusual for the mutation probability. This means that the bit at each site on the bitstring is flipped, on average, between 0.1 and 1.0 percent of the time. One fixed value is used for each generation and is often maintained for an entire run.

As there are 64 bits in the sample problem's population (8 bits × 8 individuals), it is quite possible that none will be altered as a result of mutation, so the population of Figure 3.4(b) will be taken as the "final" population after one iteration of the GA procedure. Going through the entire GA procedure one time is said to produce a new generation. The population of Figure 3.4(b) therefore represents the first generation of the initial randomized population.

Note that the fitness values now total 6.313, up from 5.083 in the initial random population, and that there are now two members of the population with fitness values higher than 0.99. The average and maximum fitness values have thus both increased. It is important to note that in most GA applications the fitnesses don't monotonically increase. There are times when the children have lower fitnesses than their parents. If this situation continues, however, the individuals with lower fitness will probably be eliminated through the selection process.

The population of Figure 3.4(b) and the corresponding fitness values in Figure 3.4(d) are now ready for another round of reproduction, crossover, and mutation, producing yet another generation. More generations are produced until some stopping condition is met. The researcher may simply set a maximum number of generations for the algorithm to search, may let it run until a performance criterion has been met, or may stop it after some number of generations with no improvement.

This completes our simple application of the basic GA. It's time to back up and review the GA's operations.

Review of GA Operations in the Simple Example

Now that one iteration of the GA operations (one generation) for the sample problem has been completed, each operation is reviewed in more detail. Various approaches, and reasons for each, are examined.

but at a higher computational cost. The authors have generally used populations of between 20 and 200 individuals, depending primarily, it seems, on the string length of the individuals. It also seems (in the authors' experience) that the sizes of populations tend to increase approximately linearly with individual string length rather than exponentially, but "optimal" population size (if an optimal size exists) depends on the problem as well.

The initialization of the population is usually done stochastically, though it is sometimes appropriate to start with one or more individuals that are selected heuristically. The GA is thereby initially aimed in promising directions, or given hints. It is not uncommon to seed the population with a few members selected heuristically and to complete it with randomly chosen members. Regardless of the process used, the population should represent a wide assortment of individuals. The urge to skew the population significantly should generally be avoided if the limited experience of the authors is generalizable.

The calculation of fitness values is conceptually simple, though it can be quite complex to implement in a way that optimizes the efficiency of the GA's search of the problem space. In the sample problem, the value of $f(x)$ varies (quite conveniently) from 0 to 1. Lurking within the problem, however, are two drawbacks to using the "raw" function output as a fitness function: one that is common to many implementations, the other arising from the nature of the sample problem.

The first drawback common to many implementations is that after the GA has been run for a number of generations it is not unusual for most (if not all) of the individuals' fitness values, after, say, a few dozen generations, to be quite high. In cases where the fitness value can range from 0 to 1, for example (as in the sample problem), most or all of the fitness values may be 0.9 or higher. This lowers the fitness differences among individuals that provide the impetus for effective roulette wheel selection; relatively higher fitness values should have a higher probability of reproduction.

One way around this problem is to space the fitness values equally. For example, in the sample problem the fitness values used for reproduction could be equally spaced from 0 to 1, assigning a fitness value of 1 to the most fit population member, 0.875 to the second, and 0.125 to the least fit of the eight. In this case the population members are ranked on the basis of fitness and then their ranks are divided by the number of individuals to provide a probability threshold for selection. Note that the value of 0 is often not assigned, since that would result in one population member being made ineligible for reproduction. Also note that $f(x)$, the function result, is now not equal to the fitness and that, in order to evaluate actual performance of the GA, the function value should be monitored as well as the spaced fitness.

Another way around the problem is to use what is called *scaling*. Scaling takes into account the recent history of the population and assigns fitness values on the basis of comparison of individuals' performance to the population's recent average performance. When the GA optimization is maximizing some function, scaling involves keeping a record of the minimum fitness value obtained in the last w generations, where w is the size of the scaling window. If, for example, $w = 5$, the minimum fitness value in the last five generations is kept and used, instead of 0, as the "floor" of fitness values. Fitness values can be assigned a value based on their actual distance from the floor value, or they can be equally spaced, as described earlier.

The second drawback is that the sample problem exacerbates the compression of fitness values situation described earlier because near the global optimum fitness value of 1, $f(x)$ (which is also the fitness) is relatively flat. There is thus relatively little selection advantage for population members near the optimum value $x = 128$. If this situation is known to exist, a different representation scheme might be selected, such as defining a new fitness function, which is the function output raised to some power.

What we have been talking about with respect to both drawbacks is *selection pressure*, or how much reproduction advantage is given to population members with higher fitness values. Too much pressure (advantage) can result in premature convergence, and not enough may allow the population to wander aimlessly.

Note that the shape of some functions "assists" discrimination near the optimum value. For example, consider maximizing the function $f(x) = x^2$ over the range 0 to 10; there is a higher differential in values of $f(x)$ between adjacent values of x near 10 than near 0. Thus a slight change in the independent variable results in great improvement or deterioration of performance—which is equally informative—near the optimum.

In the discussion thus far, we have assumed that optimization implies finding a maximum value. Sometimes, of course, optimization requires finding a minimum value. Many versions of GA implementations allow for this possibility. Often, it is required that the user specify the maximum value f_{max} of the function being optimized, $f(x)$, over the range of the search. The GA can then be programmed to maximize the fitness function $f_{max} - f(x)$. In this case, scaling, described previously, keeps track of f_{max} over the past w generations and uses it as a "roof" value from which to calculate fitness.

We now consider roulette wheel selection. In genetic algorithms, the expected number of times each individual in the current population is selected for the new population is proportional to the fitness of that individual relative to the average fitness of the entire population. Thus, in the initial population of the sample problem, where the average fitness was $5.083/8 = 0.635$, the third population member had a fitness value of 0.937, so it could be expected to appear about 1.5 times in the next population; it appeared twice.

The conceptualization is that of a wheel whose surface is divided into wedges representing the probabilities for each individual (see Figure 3.5). For instance, one point on the edge is determined to be the zero point and each arc around the circle corresponds to an area on the number line between 0 and 1. A random number

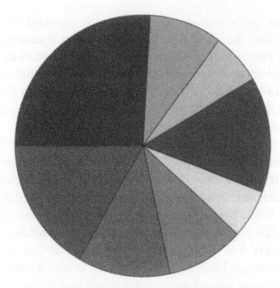

Figure 3.5 Roulette wheel selection, in which the probability of an individual being selected is proportional to its fitness.

is generated, between 0.0 and 1.0, and the individual whose wedge contains that number is chosen. In this way, individuals with greater fitness are more likely to be chosen. The selection algorithm can be repeated until the desired number of individuals has been selected. There are a number of variations to the roulette wheel procedure. A few of them are reviewed next.

One variation on the basic roulette wheel procedure is a process developed by Baker (1987) in which the portion of the roulette wheel is assigned based on each unique string's relative fitness. One spin of the roulette wheel then determines the number of times each string will appear in the next generation. To illustrate how this is done, assume that the fitness values are normalized (sum of all equals 1). Each string is assigned a portion of the roulette wheel proportional to its normalized fitness. Instead of one "pointer" on the roulette wheel spun n times, there are n pointers spaced $1/n$ apart; the n-pointer assembly is spun only once. Each of the n pointers now points to a string; each place one of the n pointers points determines one population member in the next generation. If a string has a normalized fitness greater than $1/n$ (corresponding to an expected value greater than 1), it is guaranteed at least one occurrence in the next generation.

In the discussion thus far, we have assumed that all of the population members are replaced each generation. Although this is usually the case, sometimes it is desirable to replace only a portion of the population—for example, the 80 percent with the worst fitness values. The percentage of the population replaced each generation is sometimes called the *generation gap*.

Unless some provision is made, with standard roulette wheel selection it is possible that the individual with the highest fitness value in a given generation may not survive reproduction, crossover, and mutation to appear unaltered in the new generation. It is frequently helpful to use what is called the *elitist strategy*, which ensures that the individual with the highest fitness is always copied into the next generation. Most GA applications with which the authors are familiar implement elitist strategy.

The most important operator in GAs is crossover, based on the metaphor of sexual combination. Its purpose is to pass on information from population member to population member. If a solution is encoded as a bitstring, then mutation may be implemented by setting a probability threshold and flipping bits when a random number is less than the threshold. As a matter of fact, mutation is not considered by most GA practitioners to be an especially important operator in GA; it is usually set at a very low rate and sometimes omitted. Crossover is generally considered more important because it is considered to play a more important role in guiding the population toward an acceptable solution.

Crossover is a term for the recombination of genetic information during sexual reproduction. In GAs, offspring have equal probabilities of receiving any gene from either parent because the parents' chromosomes are combined randomly. In nature, chromosomal combination leaves sections intact—that is, contiguous sections of chromosomes from one parent are combined with sections from the other, rather than simply shuffling randomly. In GAs there are many ways to implement crossover.

The two main attributes of crossover that can be varied are the type of crossover that is implemented and the probability that it occurs. The following paragraphs examine variations of each.

A crossover probability of 0.75 was used in the sample problem, and two-point crossover was implemented. Two-point crossover with a probability of 0.60 to 0.80 is a relatively common choice, especially when Gray coding is used.

The most basic crossover type is *one-point crossover*, as described by Holland (1992) and others, for example, Goldberg (1989), and Davis (1991). It is inspired by natural evolution processes. One-point crossover involves selecting a single crossover point at random and exchanging the portions of the individual strings to the right of the crossover point. Figure 3.6 illustrates one-point crossover; portions to be exchanged are in bold in Figure 3.6(a).

```
1 0 1 1 0|0 1 0     1 0 1 1 0 1 0 0
0 1 0 0 1|1 0 0     0 1 0 0 1 0 1 0
        (a)                (b)
```

Figure 3.6 One-point crossover before (a) and after (b) crossover.

Another type of crossover that has been found useful is *uniform crossover*, described by Syswerda (1989). A random decision is made at each bit position in the string as to whether or not to exchange (cross over) bits between the parent strings. If a 0.50 probability at each bit position is implemented, an average of about 50 percent of the bits in the parent strings are exchanged. Note that a 50 percent rate will result in the maximum disruption due to uniform crossover. Higher rates just mirror rates lower than 50 percent. For example, a 0.60 probability uniform crossover rate produces results identical to a 0.40 probability rate. If the rate were 100 percent, the two strings would simply switch places, and if it were 0 percent neither would change.

Values for the probability of crossover vary with the problem. In general, values between 60 and 80 percent are common for one-point and two-point crossover. Uniform crossover sometimes works better with slightly lower crossover probability. It is also common to start out running the GA with a relatively higher value for crossover, then taper off the value linearly to the end of the run, ending with a value of, say, one-half the initial value.

Inversion is a GA operation that is not generally used today. It is functionally related to crossover, but involves a single parent producing a single child. Figure 3.7 illustrates the process, which consists of switching end for end a portion of the parent structure, shown between the cut points in bold in Figure 3.7(a), in the child. One reason it is not in general use is that it is perceived to destroy the basic building blocks, or schemata, by inverting them. The term *schemata* usually refers to substrings of an individual population member string; a more detailed description appears in the next section, Schemata and the schema theorem.

In GAs, mutation is the stochastic flipping of bits that occurs in each generation. Its purpose is to introduce diversity into the population and is generally done bit by bit on the entire population. It is often done with a probability of something like 0.001, but higher probabilities are not unusual. For example, Liepins and Potter (1991) used a mutation probability of 0.033 in a multiple-fault diagnosis application.

If the population comprises real-valued parameters, mutation can be implemented in different ways. For instance, in an image classification application, Montana (1991) used strings of real-valued parameters that represented thresholds of event detection rules as the individuals. Each parameter in the string was range-limited and quantized (i.e., could take on only a certain finite number of values). If chosen for mutation, a parameter was randomly assigned any allowed value in the range of values valid for that parameter.

```
1 0|0 1 1 0 1|0    1 0 1 0 1 1 0 0
     (a)                (b)
```

Figure 3.7 Example of string before (a) and after (b) inversion operation.

The probability of mutation is often held constant for the entire run of the GA, although this approach does not produce optimal results in many cases. It can be varied during the run and, if varied, usually is increased. For example, mutation rate may start at 0.001 and end at approximately 0.01 when the specified number of generations has been completed. In the software implementation described on this book's web site, a flag in the run file can be set that increases the mutation rate significantly when the variability in fitness values becomes low, as is often the case late in the run.

Selecting the number of generations for which the GA is run is often a trial-and-error process. In general, given enough computing time, the number of generations is adjusted until the desired response is obtained. Other factors, such as population diversity and fitness improvement of the best population member, can enter into the decision to end the GA run. For example, if the best fitness has not changed for, say, 100 generations, we may choose to terminate the run.

The optimum number of generations is often a function of the problem. For instance, if the GA is being used to train a neural network, the same caveats apply as would apply if any neural network paradigm such as back-propagation were being used. What is desired is optimum results with a test set, so conditions such as overtraining must be avoided.

Whatever the application, given the stochastic nature of a GA, multiple runs will probably be desirable. Then the best-performing individuals from each run can be tested.

This completes our review of basic GA operations. In the next section, we consider a theorem that provides some insight into how GAs work.

Schemata and the Schema Theorem

Exactly how do GAs do what they do? How is it possible to develop new population members that, on average, are fitter than the previous generation while searching new regions of the problem space? Since all that GAs have to work with are (often binary) strings, there must be features related to the fitness inherent in the strings that are used.

The string features that are relevant to the optimization process are called *schemata* (singular: *schema*). The *schema theorem* describes why the canonical GA paradigm is able to efficiently direct an optimization process. (This theorem also applies to other proportional selection methodologies.)

First described for the GA field by Holland (1975, 1992), schemata are similarity templates for strings. Each schema defines a subset of strings with identical values at specified string locations. As used here, the word *string* usually refers to substrings of an individual population member string, but it can refer to the entire string. Schemata provide a means by which relevant similarities among the individual population members can be described and exploited.

To define schemata, the alphabet of the strings is used to define values at specified locations, and an additional character is used as a "don't care" symbol in locations where the value doesn't matter. As is common in the GA literature, the pound symbol (#) is used in this book as the "don't care" symbol. Schemata can thus generally be thought of as comprising an alphabet of $a_o + 1$ characters, where a_o is the number of characters in the GA representation. In most cases, as in the example, the GA strings have a binary representation, so the schemata comprise the characters $\{0, 1, \#\}$.

As an example, consider the schemata of length 4 that may appear in, say, the leftmost four positions of the population strings of the sample problem. One such schema is #000, which has two member strings. That is, two strings match the schema: 1000 and 0000. The schema 1##0 has four matching strings: 1000, 1010, 1100, and 1110.

Holland argues that adaptation can be thought of in terms of schemata. Genetic optimization increases the likelihood that the schemata that most improve the species' fitness will persist to the next generation. He also argues that crossover among the fittest members of a population will result in the discovery and survival of better schemata.

It should be noted that some researchers have recently found errors in Holland's argument, and the issue is currently controversial. Even if the proof is shaky, it can be observed empirically, simply by running GA programs, that crossover is quite effective, if not always fast, for finding good solutions to highly complex problems.

How many schemata are possible for a string length of l and an alphabet of a_o characters? In the previous example, for $a_o = 2$, there can be a 0, 1, or # at each string position, resulting in a total possible number of schemata of $3 \times 3 \times 3 \times 3 = 81$. Generalizing, there are $(a_o + 1)^l$ total possible schemata for any representation of length l.

Another informative measure is the total number of unique schemata possible in a population. Consider a specific string of length 8, taken from the example problem: 01110111. Since each string position can assume the value it has or the wild-card value, the string belongs to $2^8 = 256$ schemata. Any binary string of length l thus belongs to 2^l schemata. In a population of n individuals, then, there are between 2^l (if all members are identical) and $n2^l$ (if no two individuals are the same) schemata. Populations with higher diversity have a greater number of schemata.

Schemata that are part of an individual with high fitness have a higher than average probability of reproducing. Therefore, highly fit schemata benefit from differential reproduction relative to fitness. If selection were the only operator used, though, no new regions of the search hyperspace would ever be explored. Crossover and mutation provide new schemata to guide the search into new regions.

Crossover is a slightly more complicated matter than reproduction. Consider two schemata: ##1####0 and ###10###. If both are part of strings of equal fitness, which is more likely to be passed on to the new population? Either one- or two-point crossover is more likely to disrupt the first, since it is quite likely that a crossover point will occur between the two string endpoints. The second is more compact and less likely to be disrupted by a one- or two-point crossover operation.

Mutation is not likely to disrupt either schema, since it typically occurs at a very low rate. And since it is considered on a bit-by-bit basis, if it does occur it is just as likely to disrupt one as the other.

Although crossover and mutation are potentially disruptive, they facilitate an efficient search by introducing innovations. Furthermore, compact (short) schemata that are part of highly fit individuals will, with high probability, appear in ever-increasing numbers in future generations. The schemata are the elements from which future generations are built; Holland (1992) named them "building blocks." The schema theorem sums up all of this and provides a quantitative estimation of one aspect of GA performance.

The schema theorem predicts the number of times a specific schema will appear in the next generation of a GA, given the fitness of the population member(s) containing the schema, the average fitness of the population, and other parameters. The GA can be thought of as effectively working with a large number of schemata simultaneously, ranging from very short schemata to schemata as long as the individual population members. This has been named "intrinsic parallelism" by Holland. The schema theorem provides a quantitative prediction for all schemata, regardless of length. It should be noted that the theorem applies only to "plain vanilla" GAs. As soon as you do anything special, including something as simple as implementing elitism, where the fittest population member is automatically copied into the next generation, the schema theorem no longer applies.

The schema theorem appears as equation 3.1.[3]

$$n_{t+1}(S) \geq n_t(S)\frac{f(S)}{f_{\text{avg}}}\left[1 - p_c\frac{\delta(S)}{l-1} - o(S)p_m\right] \tag{3.1}$$

In equation 3.1, n is the total number of examples of a particular schema S. The subscripts $t+1$ and t refer to time steps, or generations. The parameter $f(S)$ is the average fitness of the individual population members that contain the schema S, while f_{avg} is the average fitness of the entire population. The probabilities of crossover and mutation are p_c and p_m, respectively.

The parameter $\delta(S)$ is called the "defining length" of the schema; it is the distance between the first and last specific string positions. For example, for the schema #01#11#, the defining length is 4. The total length of the string is l, while $o(S)$ is the "order" of the schema, or the number of fixed positions (1s and 0s) in

---

[3] The derivation of the theorem is beyond the scope of this book. The reader is referred to the derivation in Goldberg (1989).

the schema. In the preceding example, the order of the schema is 4. The defining length of a schema is just the number of potential "cut" points within the schema that could be affected by crossover.

Summarized, equation 3.1 states that the expected number of occurrences of schema S in generation $t + 1$ is the number in the current generation multiplied by the average schema fitness divided by the average population fitness, less the disruptive effects caused by crossover and mutation. Schemata with above-average fitness values will be represented an increasing number of times as generations proceed. Those with below-average values will be represented less and less; they will "die out," just as happens in nature.

The schemata with small values for defining length are disrupted least by crossover, so the most rapidly increasing representation in any population will be of highly fit, short schemata, called building blocks, which will experience exponential growth. Building blocks illustrate that it is often beneficial to keep some parts of a solution intact. This is the most important consequence of the schema theorem.

Note that the schema theorem, by itself, does not specify how well a GA will solve a particular problem. It should also be noted that there is controversy in the EC community with respect to the usefulness and validity of the theorem. We include it, as have other recent books dealing with GAs such as (Mitchell 1996), (Pedrycz 1998), and (Haupt and Haupt 1998), because we believe it provides useful insights into GA processes.

We've now told you what we think you need to know about GAs, how they work, and how to apply them to practical problems. All that is left are a few final observations.

Comments on Genetic Algorithms

In sum, a genetic algorithm operates by evaluating a population of bitstrings (there are real-numbered GAs, but binary implementations are more common) and selecting survivors stochastically based on their fitness; thus, fitter members of the population are more likely to survive. Survivors are paired for crossover, and often some mutation is performed on chromosomes. Other operations might be performed as well, but crossover and mutation are the most important ones. Sexual recombination of genetic material is a powerful method for adaptation.

In Chapter 2, we discussed three spaces of adaptation: the parameter space, the function space, and the fitness space. Much of the literature in evolutionary computation treats the function space as if it were identical to the fitness space; that is, the function output provides a number that indicates how close to the global optimum the search algorithm is. There are, however, dangerous ambiguities in the confusion of these two quantities. The fitness landscape can be very different depending on the fitness function utilized. The fitness measure should probably be scaled between 0 and 1 when possible, making it easy to understand as well as an indication of the probability of a population member's survival.

The material on genetic algorithms in this chapter provides only an introduction to the subject. We suggest that you explore GAs further by sampling the references cited in this section. With further study and application, it will become apparent why GAs have such a devoted following. In the words of Davis (1991):

> [T]here is something profoundly moving about linking a genetic algorithm to a difficult problem and returning later to find that the algorithm has evolved a solution that is better than the one a human found. With genetic algorithms we are not optimizing; we are creating conditions in which optimization occurs, as it may have occurred in the natural world. One feels a kind of resonance at such times that is uncommon and profound.

This feeling, of course, is not unique to experiences with GAs; using other evolutionary algorithms can result in similar feelings. An implementation of a genetic algorithm is presented in Chapter 4. The software for the GA implementation is on the book's web site.

That's it for genetic algorithms. Let's now turn our attention to an evolutionary computation paradigm that eschews crossover—evolutionary programming.

Evolutionary Programming

Evolutionary programming (EP) is similar to genetic algorithms in its use of a population of candidate solutions to evolve an answer to a specific problem; it differs in its concentration on top-down processes of adaptive behavior. The emphasis in evolutionary programming is on developing behavioral models, that is, models of observable system interactions with the environment. Theories of natural evolution heavily influence the development of evolutionary programming concepts and paradigms.

Evolutionary programming is derived from the simulation of adaptive behavior in evolution: GAs are derived from the simulation of genetics. The difference is perhaps subtle but important. Genetic algorithms work in the genotype space of the information codings, while evolutionary programming (EP) emphasizes the phenotype space of observable behaviors (Fogel 1990). EP is therefore directed at evolving "behavior" that solves the problem at hand; it mimics "phenotypic evolution."

Evolutionary programming is a more flexible approach to evolution than some of the other paradigms. Operators are freely adapted to fit the problem at hand. Generally, the paradigm relies on mutation—not sexual recombination—to produce offspring. Whereas evolution strategies systems usually generate many more offspring than parents (a ratio of seven to one is common, as we will see in the next section), EP usually generates the same number of children as parents. Parents are selected to reproduce using a tournament method; their features are mutated to produce children who are added to the population. When the population has doubled, the members—parents and offspring together—are ranked, and the best half are kept for the next generation.

Now that we have a rough idea of what EP entails, let's see how to implement it in an application. After that, we'll look at examples of specific application areas.

Evolutionary Programming Procedure

The process for implementing EP will look familiar to you; the process itself is similar to the one we used for GAs. The procedure generally followed when implementing EP appears in the following list:

1. Initialize the population.
2. Expose the population to the environment.
3. Calculate fitness for each member.
4. Randomly mutate each "parent" population member.
5. Evaluate parents and children.
6. Select members of the new population.
7. Go to step 2 until some condition is met.

The population is randomly initialized. For problems in real (computable) space, each component variable of each individual's vector is generally a real value that is constrained to some dynamic range. In the two EP examples that follow, the variables (vector elements) represent finite state machine parameters and function variables, respectively. The number of population members is problem dependent, but is often a few dozen to a few hundred, as in to GA populations.

To better understand the remaining steps in the EP procedure, two examples are examined. These two examples are representative of two main types of problem to which EP paradigms are often applied. The first involves time series prediction using a finite state machine. The second is the optimization of a mathematical function.

Finite State Machine Evolution for Prediction

Remember that prediction is one of the attributes of computational intelligence systems we discussed in Chapter 2. Evolutionary programming paradigms are sometimes used for problems involving prediction. One way to represent prediction of the environment is with a sequence of symbols. As with GAs, the symbols must be members of a finite alphabet. A system comprising a finite state machine, for example, can be used to analyze a symbol sequence and to generate an output that optimizes a fitness function, which often involves predicting the next symbol in the sequence. In other words, a prediction is used to calculate a system response that seeks to achieve some specified goal.

A *finite state machine* is defined as "a transducer that can be stimulated by a finite alphabet of input symbols, can respond in a finite alphabet of output signals, and possesses some finite number of different internal states" (Fogel 1991). The input and output symbol alphabets need not be identical. The initial state of the machine must be specified. It is also necessary to specify, for each state and input symbol combination, the output symbol and next state. Table 3.2 specifies a three-state finite state machine with an input alphabet of two characters and three possible output symbols.

Finite state machines are essentially a subset of Turing machines, developed by the English mathematician and computer science pioneer Alan Turing (1937). Turing machines are capable, in principle, of solving all mathematical problems (of a defined general class) in sequence. Finite state machines, as used in EP, can model, or represent, an organism or system.

Unlike GAs, where crossover is an important component of producing a new generation, mutation is the only operator used in EP systems. Each member of the current population typically undergoes mutation to produce a "child." Given the specification of the finite state machine, and its operation, five main types of mutation can occur: As long as more than one state exists, the initial state can be changed and/or a state can be deleted. A state can be added. A state transition can be changed. Finally, an output symbol for a given state-input symbol can be changed.

Although the number of children produced by each parent is a system parameter, each "parent" typically produces one "child," and the population becomes twice its original size after mutation. After measuring the fitness of each structure, the best half are kept, maintaining the population size at a constant value from

Table 3.2 Specification Table for a Three-State Finite State Machine

Existing state	A	A	B	B	C	C
Input symbol	1	0	1	0	1	0
Output symbol	Y	Y	X	Z	Z	Y
Next state	A	B	C	B	A	B

Source: Fogel (1991).

generation to generation. At some point in some applications, it is necessary to predict the next symbol in a sequence. The structure with the highest fitness is chosen to generate this new symbol, which is then added to the sequence. (It is also possible to specify the problem so that the symbol predicted is farther in the future than one time step.)

Unlike other evolutionary paradigms, in EP systems mutation can change the size of structures (states can be added and deleted). This fact and the potential for changing state transitions lead to another consideration: The specification table for a finite state machine can have unfilled blanks. There can be mutations that add states that are never utilized in a given problem; Fogel (1991) calls these "neutral mutations." It is also possible to create the situation via mutation where a specified state transition is not possible because the new state has been deleted. These mutations and others, such as changing output symbols, tend to have less effect the more states the machine has, but can still cause fatal errors in the finite state machine if they are not handled properly.

Although Fogel (1995) usually allows a variable-length structure, it is also possible to evolve a finite state machine with EP using a fixed structure. First, the maximum number of states must be determined. For purposes of illustration, using the three-state machine defined earlier as an example, we will assume that no more than four states are allowed.

Each state can then be represented by a fixed 5-bit binary element as follows. The first bit could represent the "activation" of the state: if it is 1, the state is active; if 0, the state is inactive (that is, it does not exist). The next two bits can represent the output symbol (X, Y, or Z) for an input of 0, and the final two bits can represent the output symbol for an input of 1. (Note that our example above has only three output symbols. With binary representation, we have to allow for four and handle a nonexistent symbol the way nonexistent states are handled.) We thus require a total element length of $(1 + n_i * b_o)$ bits, where n_i is the number of possible inputs and b_o is the number of bits needed to represent the output symbols.

The population in our example is thus initialized with individuals 20 bits long. For the example it may be a good idea to specify that only individuals with at least two active states can be allowed in the initial population.

A child is now generated for each parent. Given the five possible kinds of mutation outlined earlier, one possible mutation procedure is:

1. For each individual, generate a random number from 0 to 1.

2. If the number is between 0.0 and 0.2, change the initial state; if between 0.2 and 0.4, delete a state, etc.

3. The mutation selected in step 2 is done with a flat probability across all possibilities. For example, if the initial state is to be changed and there

are *a* active states, then one active state is selected to be the initial state; each active state has the probability of 1/*a* of being selected.

4. Infeasible state transitions are modified to be feasible. If a state transition to an inactive state has been specified, one of the active states is selected to be the object of the transition. As above, each active state has the probability of 1/*a* of being selected.

5. Evaluate fitnesses and keep the best 50 percent, resulting in a new population of the same size.

This scenario is only one of many possibilities. For example, it might be desirable to lower the probability ranges (the ranges between 0 and 1 in step 2) for adding and deleting states and correspondingly increase the mutation probability ranges for changing input symbols and/or output symbols. It is also possible to *evolve* the ranges, number of states, and so on.

One example of finite state machines is the development by Fogel (1995) using evolutionary programming of finite state machines that do very well at playing Axelrod's prisoner's dilemma game. As described in Kennedy, Eberhart, and Shi (2001):

> The prisoner's dilemma is a situation where two interacting players have opposite, symmetrical motives. Each player has the choice to cooperate or compete with the opponent: if both cooperate, their payoffs are high, and if both compete payoffs are low. If one competes (the technical term is defecting) while the other cooperates, the defector receives a very high reward while the cooperator's payoff is very low—the lowest in the game, called the "sucker's payoff." When the game is played just one time, the most reasonable thing to do is to defect, as there is no basis for trusting the other player, and there is nothing to gain by being a sucker.
>
> Usually though, the game is iterated, a series of games is played. A player would score the highest if he always defected while his partner always cooperated—but of course no sensible player would continue to cooperate while being hammered repeatedly by a competitive opponent. Repeated trials require some consideration of strategy, for instance, a player might end up with the highest score if he lulled his opponent into cooperating, then struck with a defection, then lulled and defected, and so on. It might be that the best approach would be just to cooperate from the start—except that nothing then prevents the opponent from taking advantage. The simple game then produces opportunities for many kinds of strategies. Axelrod roughly grouped these into two kinds: "nice" strategies, which rely on cooperation to keep the level of payoffs high for both parties, and strategies he refers to as "mean" (specifically that includes only the all-defect strategy) or "not nice." Strategies that are not nice include ones that might try to use cooperation as a way to make the opponent vulnerable, then defect for the higher payoff.

The payoff function is that used by Axelrod (1980): If both cooperate, each player gets 3 points; if both defect, each player gets 1 point; if one defects and one cooperates, the cooperating player gets no points while the defecting player gets 5 points.

Fogel allowed the finite state machines to have up to eight states. This doesn't represent all possible behaviors *à la* Axelrod, but it does allow a dependence on sequences of greater than third-order. Fogel was able to evolve finite state machines that had average scores slightly greater than 3.0, which is the score that is achieved through mutual cooperation alone.

Figure 3.8 is the diagram for a seven-state finite state machine (one of many evolved by Fogel) to play prisoner's dilemma. The start state is state 6, and play is begun by cooperating. In the table, "C" denotes cooperate and "D" denotes defect.

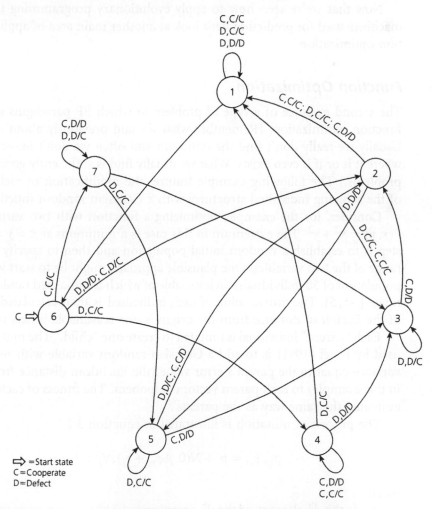

Figure 3.8 A seven-state finite state machine to play prisoner's dilemma. *Source:* Fogel 1995; © IEEE. Used with permission.

The input alphabet comprises [(C,C), (C,D), (D,C), (D,D)], where the first letter represents the finite state machine's previous move and the second the opponent's. So, for example, a label of C,D/C on the arrow leading from state X to state Y means that if the system is in state X and on the previous move the finite state machine cooperated and the opponent defected, then cooperate and transition to state Y. Sometimes, more than one situation can result in the same state transition. For example, in Figure 3.8, assume the machine is in state 6, in which case if the machine and opponent both defected on the previous move, the machine defects (D,D/D) and transitions to state 2. Likewise, a transition from state 6 to state 2 occurs if the machine cooperated and the opponent defected on the previous move; the machine cooperates in this case (C,D/C) as it moves into state 2.

Now that we've seen how to apply evolutionary programming to finite state machines used for prediction, let's look at another main area of application, function optimization.

Function Optimization

The second example of a type of problem to which EP paradigms are applied is function optimization. (Remember what we said previously about optimization: Usually we really don't find the optimum and often we don't know much about where it is or if it even exists. What we usually find is sufficiently good solutions to problems.) The following example features the modification of each component of the evolving individual structures with a Gaussian random function.

Consider, for the example, optimizing a function with two variables such as $F(x, y) = x^2 + y^2$. The extremum in this case is a minimum at $x = y = 0$. The first step is to establish a random initial population and then to specify the dynamic range of the two variables. One plausible approach might be to start with an initial population of 50 individuals, each variable of which is initialized randomly over the range $[-5, 5]$. The fitness value of each individual is then calculated. The inverse of the Euclidean distance from the origin is one reasonable fitness measure.

Each "parent" individual is mutated to create one "child." The mutation method used by Fogel (1991) is to add a Gaussian random variable with zero mean and variance equal to the parent's error value (the Euclidean distance from the origin in this example) to each parent vector component. The fitness of each child is then evaluated the same way as the parents'.

The process of mutation is illustrated in equation 3.2:

$$p_{i+k, j} = p_i + N(0, \beta_j \phi_{p_i} + z_j), \forall_j = 1..., n, \tag{3.2}$$

where

$p_{i,j}$ is the jth element of the ith organism

$N(\mu, \sigma^2)$ is a Gaussian random variable with mean μ and variance σ^2

ϕ_{p_i} is the fitness score for p_i

β_j is a constant of proportinality to scale ϕ_{p_i}

z_j represents an offset

For the function used in the example, it has been shown that the optimum rate of convergence is represented by $\sigma = \frac{1.224\sqrt{f(x)}}{n}$, where n is the number of dimensions (Bäck and Schwefel 1993).

Another way to perform mutation involves a process known as self-adaptation. In this variation, the standard deviations (and rotation angles, if used) are modified based on their current values. As a result, the search adapts to the error surface contours (Fogel 1995).

Fitness, however, is sometimes not used directly by itself to decide which half of the augmented population will survive to the next generation. Tournament selection is used, with each individual competing with a number, say 10, of other individuals in the following way.

For each of the 10 competitions with other individuals, a probability of "scoring a point" is set equal to the error score of the opponent divided by the sum of the individual and opponent errors. For instance, if the error of the individual is 2 and that of the opponent (one of 10 opponents) is 3, the probability of scoring a point is 3/5, or 60 percent. The total score is tallied over the 10 competitions for each individual, and the one-half of the population with the highest total scores is selected for the next generation.

This concludes our discussion of using evolutionary programming for optimization. (Keep in mind that, as we discussed previously, we believe that it really isn't optimization most of the time.)

Comments on Evolutionary Programming

The implementation of evolutionary programming concepts seems to vary more from application to application than GA implementations. A number of factors contribute to the differences in approach, but the most important factor seems to be the top-down emphasis of EP. Another is the fact that selection is a probabilistic function of fitness rather than being tied directly to it. One developer of EP (Fogel 1991) stated that EP is at its best when it is used to optimize overall system behavior.

Evolution Strategies

We begin our look at evolution strategies (ES) with the concept of the *evolution of evolution*. As a biological analogy, evolution strategies model problem solutions as species rather as they have been described earlier, as populations of normally distributed multivariate points scattered around a fitness landscape. The aspect of these populations that permits them to adapt to their environment (in research this is often simulated by a test function or hard optimization problem) is their ability to evolve their own evolvability.

If evolutionary programming is based on evolution, then, reasons Rechenberg (1994), the field of evolution strategies is based on the evolution of evolution. Since biological processes have been optimized by evolution, and evolution is a biological process, then evolution must have optimized itself. Evolution strategies, although utilizing forms of both mutation and crossover (usually called "recombination" in the evolution strategies literature), have a slightly different view of both operations than either evolutionary programming or genetic algorithms.

There are many similarities between evolution strategies and evolutionary programming, and in fact the two paradigms are moving closer together as researchers exchange techniques across the Atlantic. Evolution strategies, like evolutionary programming, take a top-down view. They also stress the phenotypic behavior as opposed to the genotypic. This means, for example, that the phenotypic behavior ramifications of recombination are of importance, rather than what happens to the genotypes. ES paradigms also usually use real values for the variables rather than the binary coding favored in genetic algorithm implementations.

In evolution strategies the goal is to move the mass of the population toward the best region of the landscape. Through application of the simple rule, "survival of the fittest," the best individuals in any generation are allowed to reproduce; their offspring resemble them but with some differences introduced through mutation. An individual is a potential problem solution characterized by a vector of numbers representing phenotypic features. Mutation is performed by adding normally distributed random numbers to the parents' phenotypic coordinates, their position in the search space, so that the next generation of children explores around the area in the landscape that has proven good for their parents.

The amount of mutation—the evolvability of the population—is controlled in an interesting way in ES. An individual is typified by a set of features and by a corresponding set of strategy parameters. These are usually variances or standard deviations (the square root of the variance), though other statistics are sometimes used. The strategy parameters are used to mutate the feature vectors for the individual's offspring; for instance, standard deviations can be used to define the variability of the normal distribution used to perturb the parent's features. Random numbers can be generated from a probability distribution with a mean of zero and a standard deviation defined by the strategy parameters; adding these random numbers to the values in the parent's feature vector simulates mutation in the offspring. They resemble the parents but differ from them to some controlled extent. Since the evolutionary process is applied to the strategy parameters themselves, the range of mutation, or the variability of the changes introduced in the next generation, evolves along with the features that are being optimized.

Intuitively it can be seen that increasing the variance is like increasing the step-size taken by population members on the landscape. High variance equals exploration and wide-ranging search for good regions of the landscape, and it corresponds to a high rate of mutation; low variance is exploitation, focused search within regions. The strategy parameters stochastically determine the size of the steps taken when generating offspring of the individual; a large variance means that large steps are likely to be taken, that the children are likely to differ greatly from their parents. As the children are randomly generated from a normal distribution, though, a large variance *can* produce a small step size, and vice versa. It is known that 68.26 percent of random normal numbers generated fall within one standard deviation, 95 percent will fall within 1.96 standard deviations of the mean, and so on. So widening the standard deviation widens the dispersion of randomly generated points.

Evolution strategies' unique view of mutation includes the concept of an *evolution window*. The theory behind the concept is that mutation operations result in fitness improvement only if they land within a defined step-size band, or window (Rechenberg 1994). Crossover and mutation operations that land outside the evolution window are not helpful. A theoretical derivation of Rechenberg states that if mutations are carried out with an optimal standard deviation, the probability of a "successful" (helpful) mutation is about one-fifth. Evolution strategies carry the idea of the evolution window still further. They assert that dynamic adjustment of the mutation size to a dynamic evolution window can provide benefits called "meta-evolution," or evolution of the second kind (Rechenberg 1994).

Like evolutionary programming, ES employs Gaussian noise functions with zero mean to determine mutation magnitudes for the variables. For the strategic parameters, log normal distributions are sometimes used as mutation standard deviations.

Evolution strategies theory states that mutation rates should be inversely proportional to the number of variables in the individual population member and should be proportional to the distance from the function optimum. In real-world applications, of course, the exact value of the optimum is usually unknown. However, some knowledge often exists about the optimum. It is often known within an order of magnitude, sometimes to within a factor of two or three. Even limited knowledge such as this can be helpful in guiding the evolution strategy search.

In ES, *recombination* manipulates entire variable values. This is usually done using one of two methods. The first and more common method (the local method) involves forming one new individual using components (variables) from two randomly selected parents. The second method, the global method, uses the entire population of individuals as potential sources from which individual components for the new individual can be obtained.

Each of the two methods, local and global, is generally implemented in one of two ways. The first is called *discrete recombination*, which consists of selecting the parameter value from either parent. In other words, the parameter value in the child equals the value of one parent. The second way, called *intermediate recombination*, involves setting each parameter value for a child at a point between the values for the two parents; typically, the value is set midway between those values. If the parents are denoted by A and B, and the ith parameter is being determined, then the value established using intermediate recombination is $x_i^{\text{new}} = x_{A,i} + C(x_{B,i} - x_{A,i})$, where C is a constant, usually set to 0.5 to yield the midpoint between the two parent values.

Thus we see that evolution strategies contain a component representing sexual combination of features. In intermediate recombination, for instance, the children's features are computed as a kind of average of the two parents' features; in discrete recombination, individual features may come intact or mutated from one parent or the other.

In the experience of ES practitioners, the best results often seem to be obtained by using the local version of discrete recombination for the parameter values and the local version of intermediate recombination for the strategy parameter(s). In fact, Bäck and Schwefel (1993) report that implementation of strategy parameter recombination is mandatory for the success of any ES paradigm.

All of this is well and good; we know now how to transform individual population members using recombination and mutation. How, then, do we select the members of the next generation? How do we accomplish selection?

Selection

In evolution strategies, as in all Darwinian models, an individual's fitness determines the probability that it will reproduce in the next generation. There can be many ways to decide this; for instance, we could rank all the individuals from best to worst, chop off the bottom of the list, and save only the proportion that we want to survive. This proportion depends on how many offspring they will have, assuming the population size remains constant from one generation to the next.

In nature, of course, there is no ranking of individuals; the survival of each depends on the environment and that individual's chance encounters. Imagine a snowshoe hare that has a mutation that makes its fur turn black in the winter. In the snow this hare is more visible than its camouflaged cousins. It might just happen, though, that no predators come into the area where this hare lives, so they don't see it and it subsequently reproduces, passing on the mutation. It can happen; it is just that the likelihood is reduced relative to the alternative, which is that a predator that comes into the area immediately notices this contrastive morsel and eats him rather than his harder-to-see littermates. In nature, the measure of fitness has a great amount of error in it; possible improvements are commonly lost.

This suggests that selection needs to be probabilistic—you can't just propagate the best so-many individuals to the next generation. A lesson learned from *simulated annealing* is that sometimes a step backward is productive in the long run. In the same way, natural evolution lets some less-fit individuals reproduce, and it is quite likely that eventual improvement is transmitted through the less obvious route. Evolutionary computation researchers have come up with a number of techniques for stochastically selecting survivors for the next generation. In order to better model the stochastic aspect of natural selection—what could be called survival of the luckiest—several computational methods of selection have been devised. Common methods include ranking, roulette wheel selection, and tournament selection.

Ranking is the simplest procedure, though it does not have the advantage of allowing selection of less-fit individuals. The population is sorted from best to worst, and individuals above the cutoff in the list are chosen. One salient objection to this method is that it requires global information. Knowledge of all fitness values is needed in order to determine the rank of any individual. Obviously, nature does not work this way; only local information is used in natural selection, and errors in ranking—occasions where more-fit members fail to reproduce or less-fit members succeed—contribute to the adaptation of the population. This might be a weaker argument than it seems, though; there are plenty of times when a computer needs to use global information in order to accomplish things that nature does without it. For instance, to detect collisions in virtual worlds requires computation of the relative positions of all objects in the world, but in the physical world things behave appropriately without any such computations. Running into a brick wall stops you, period. So evolution in a computer program might be acceptable even if it required global information as a way to accomplish an end.

Roulette wheel selection was discussed in the section on genetic algorithms. Recall that, in roulette wheel selection, each individual is given a probability of selection proportional to its fitness. Tournament selection was discussed in the section on evolutionary programming.

Tournament selection uses local competitions to determine survivors. In its simplest form, individuals are paired at random and the better member of each pair is selected to reproduce. This can be repeated until the next generation is sufficiently populated. Other tournament methods pair up individuals in some number of competitions, adding a point to their score each time they win, and then keep individuals with more than a critical number of points; other methods select subgroups at random from the population and allow the one with the highest fitness to survive to the next generation.

The results of tournament selection correlate with the results of ranking—that is, fitter individuals survive in general. One-on-one, winner-take-all tournaments allow the most error in terms of less-fit individuals being selected; while the very best individual is guaranteed to survive and the very worst is guaranteed not to, it is entirely possible that the next-to-worse individual is paired with the worst one and thus is selected. Repetitive and subgroup tournaments decrease the amount of error while increasing the correlation with ranking results, until an algorithm where each individual engages in n-1 unique tournaments, where n is the population size, is exactly equivalent to ranking.

Differences exist between evolution strategies and other paradigms of evolutionary computation with respect to selection. ESs generally operate with a surplus of descendants. Schwefel (1994) describes the most common versions of ES selection, known as the (μ, λ) and $(\mu + \lambda)$ ES. In both versions, the number of children generated from μ parents is $\lambda > \mu$. Commonly used is a λ/μ ratio of 7. In the original $(1 + 1)$ ES, one parent produces one offspring, with only the fitter of the two surviving. This version is seldom used now.

The difference between the "plus" and "comma" versions comes in the next step. In the (μ, λ) version, the μ individuals with the highest fitness values out of the λ children are selected. Note that the μ parents are not eligible for selection in this scheme, only the children. In the $(\mu + \lambda)$ version, the best μ individuals are selected from a pool of candidates that includes both the μ parents and the λ children—that is, the union of the two groups of individuals. Whichever method is used, the μ individuals that are left have thus been selected completely deterministically and have equal probabilities to mate and have descendants in the next generation.

The discussion of genetic algorithms mentioned the elitist strategy, in which the individual in each generation with the highest fitness is guaranteed to survive to the next generation. This individual may be carried over from the previous generation or may appear as a result of operations in the current one. As can be seen from the preceding discussion, the $(\mu + \lambda)$ version implements elitism, as the most-fit parent will be retained, while the (μ, λ) version does not. Elitism is generally considered helpful in GA applications. With evolution strategies, however, the (μ, λ) version is generally observed to yield better performance (Bäck and Schwefel 1993).

The following list summarizes the procedure used in most evolution strategies.

1. Initialize population.

2. Perform recombination using the μ parents to form λ children.

3. Perform mutation on all children.

4. Evaluate λ or $\mu + \lambda$ population members.

5. Select μ individuals for the new population.

6. If the termination criterion is not met, go to step 2; otherwise, terminate.

Key Issues in Evolution Strategies

In sum, in evolution strategies mutation is applied to the parent's features to generate children that resemble the parent but differ stochastically from it. Each survivor's positional coordinates are entered as the mean of a normal distribution, and the corresponding strategy parameter is entered as the variance or standard deviation, and a child vector of numbers is generated for both positions and strategy parameters. These are evaluated, selection is applied, and the cycle repeats. The evolution of strategy parameters suggests the evolution of evolvability, adaptation of the mutability of a species as it searches for, then settles into, a niche.

This completes our review of evolution strategies. Recall that evolutionary programming, the area we discussed just prior to evolution strategies, does not use crossover, only mutation. The area we discuss next, genetic programming, emphasizes crossover, relegating mutation to a minor supporting role. Genetic programming also uses a somewhat different structure than we've seen up to now.

Genetic Programming

The three areas of evolutionary computation discussed thus far have involved individual structures that are defined as strings. Some are strings of binary values and some include real-valued variables, but all are strings, or vectors. The genetic programming (GP) paradigm deals with evolving hierarchical computer programs that are generally represented as tree structures. Furthermore, while individual structures used up to this point have generally been of fixed length, programs being evolved by genetic programming generally vary in size, shape, and complexity.

One perspective is that GPs are a subset of GAs that evolve executable programs. Differences between GPs and generic GAs include:

- Population members are executable structures (generally computer programs) rather than strings of bits and/or variables.

- The fitness of an individual population member in a GP is measured by executing it. (Generic GAs' measure of fitness depends on the problem being solved.)

The goal of a genetic programming implementation is to "discover" a computer program within the space of potential computer programs being searched that gives a desired output for a given set of inputs. In other words, a computer is figuring out how to write its own code.

Each program is represented as a parse tree, where the functions defined for the problem appear at the internal tree points and the variables and constants are located at the external points (leaves). The nature of the computer programs generated makes genetic programming inherently hierarchical.

In preparation for running a genetic programming implementation, five steps are carried out.

1. Specify the terminal set.
2. Specify the function set.
3. Specify the fitness measure.
4. Select the system control parameters.
5. Specify termination conditions.

The terminal set comprises the variables (the system state variables) and constants associated with the problem being solved. For example, consider a "cart centering" problem, where the goal is to center a cart in the least amount of time on a one-dimensional frictionless track by imparting fixed-magnitude forces that accelerate the cart left or right. The variables are the cart's position x and velocity v. A constant such as -1 is also an appropriate terminal for this problem (see Koza 1992, Chapter 6).

The functions selected for the function set are limited only by the programming language implementation used to run the programs evolved by the GP implementation. They can thus include mathematical functions (cos, exp, etc.), arithmetic operations ($+$, $*$, etc.), Boolean operators (AND, NOT, etc.), conditional operators such as *if–then–else*, and iterative and recursive functions. Each function in the function set requires a certain (fixed) number of arguments, known as the function's *arity*. (Terminals are functions with arity 0.) One task of specifying the function set is to select a minimal set that is capable of accomplishing the task.

This leads to two properties that are desirable in any GP application: *closure* and *sufficiency*. For the closure property to be satisfied, each function must be able to successfully operate on any function in the function set and on any value of any data type assumable by a member of the terminal set.

This occasionally requires definition of special cases for functions. For example, in arithmetic functions division by 0 can be defined for the purposes of a problem as being equal to some constant value such as 1. If Boolean values returned by conditional operators are not acceptable, the conditional operator can be redefined in one of two ways: (1) Numerical values (such as 0 and 1) can be returned rather than Boolean values (such as F and T), or (2) conditional branching and conditional comparative operators can be defined to execute one of their arguments depending on the evaluation of the test involving an external state or condition or on the comparison test outcome. Functions that are redefined so as to return acceptable values are called protected functions. If the closure property is not satisfied, some method must be specified for dealing with infeasible population members and with members whose fitness is not acceptable.

For the sufficiency property to be satisfied, the set of functions and set of terminals must be sufficiently extensive to allow a solution to be evolved. In other words, some combination of functions and terminals must be capable of producing a solution. Some knowledge of the problem is generally required to be able to judge when the sufficiency property is met. In some problem domains, sufficiency is relatively easy to determine. For example, if Boolean functions are being used, it is well known that the function set comprising AND, OR, NOT is sufficient for any problem. For other problems, it can be relatively difficult to establish sufficiency.

Having more than the minimally sufficient number of functions has been found to degrade performance somewhat in some cases and to significantly improve it in others. Having too many terminals, however, usually degrades performance (Koza 1992).

The fitness measure often is selected to be inversely proportional to the error produced by program output. Other fitness measures are also common, such as the score a program achieves in the game.

The two main control parameters are the population size and the maximum number of generations that will be run. Other parameters used include reproduction probability, crossover probability, and the maximum size allowed (as measured by the depth, or number of hierarchical levels) in the initial and final program populations.

The termination condition is usually determined by the maximum number of generations specified. The winning program is usually the best program (in terms of the fitness measure) created thus far in any generation.

After the five preparatory steps for running a GP are completed, the GP process can be implemented as follows:

1. Initialize the population of computer programs.

2. Determine the fitness of each individual program.

3. Carry out reproduction according to fitness values and reproduction probability.

4. Perform crossover of subexpressions.

5. Go to step 2 unless termination condition is met.

The population is initialized with randomly generated computer programs comprising functions and terminals from the selected sets. In other words, each program in the initial population is created by building a rooted tree structure with randomly selected functions and terminals from the defined sets. No restrictions are placed on the size or shape (configuration) of acceptable programs, other than the maximum depth, or number of hierarchical levels, allowed. Each structure created is a hierarchically structured executable program. A population of 500 has been reported to be sufficient for most problems solved with GP implementations (Koza 1992).

Figure 3.9 Example of root of randomly created program in initial population. Other functions continue down from the two branches.

The root of each program tree is a function randomly selected from the function set. The root of a randomly created program appears at the top of Figure 3.9. The number of lines, or branches, emanating from the function is equal to its arity. In the figure, the multiplication function "*" takes two arguments.

Once the root function is selected, program population can be created in a number of ways. Following is a description of what Koza (1992) calls the *ramped half-and-half* method. It makes use of two approaches to building program trees: the "grow" method and the "full" method.

In the grow approach, a random selection is made from the combined set of functions *and* terminals for placement at the end of each line emanating from the root function. If a function is selected, program creation continues recursively with selections from the combined set. Whenever a terminal is selected, a leaf, or endpoint, of the tree is established. Program creation along that line is thus terminated. Except for the root function, therefore, all functions are at internal tree locations. The leaves of the tree are all terminals. Any time the maximum depth (number of hierarchical levels) is reached, the random selection is limited to the terminal set. When the grow method is used, the program tree configuration is guided by the ratio of the number of functions to the number of terminals. When the ratio is higher, the average depth of each limb is higher.

In the full approach, each limb of the program tree extends for the full depth. Only functions are selected for placement at the end of each line until the maximum depth is reached, at which time only terminals are selected. All programs created using the full approach thus have identical fully developed structures.

The ramped half-and-half approach produces a population of diverse sizes and shapes. Koza (1992) reports using this method for almost all problems except those involving Boolean functions. The method consists of creating programs with evenly distributed depth parameters ranging from 2 to the maximum depth. For example, if the maximum depth is 5, 25 percent of the population will have depth 2; 25 percent, depth 3, and so on. Within each subpopulation of a given depth, one-half of the programs are created using the grow approach, one-half using the full approach.

The fitness of each program is generally calculated for a number of cases, with the average fitness value over the cases being defined as a program's fitness. For example, if a program were being evolved to calculate *y* as some function of *x*, each program might be tested over 50 or 100 cases, each representing a value of *x* in the domain. It is important to use a sufficient number of cases to represent this domain. Although it is possible to use different cases in different generations, the same fitness cases are usually used across all generations.

Fitness can be calculated in a number of ways. Koza (1992) defines four fitness metrics: raw, standardized, adjusted, and normalized. Raw fitness can be calculated in one of several ways, according to the problem being solved. For example, if the objective is to maximize the score of a game, or a profit margin, the raw fitness can be the score or the profit margin, respectively. Likewise, if the objective is to minimize costs or miles traveled, raw fitness could be the cost or number of miles, respectively. Another, more common, raw fitness metric is the sum over all cases of the absolute value of error. The error can be calculated as the sum of the linear differences between the correct values and the program values, or as the sum of the squares of the differences. For programs that output Boolean or symbolic values, the error can be calculated as the number of incorrect outputs for the test cases. Note that desirable raw fitness values can be either larger or smaller, depending on how the fitness calculation is formulated.

Standardized fitness is configured so that lower values are more desirable. In fact, the fitness value is often mathematically adjusted such that the optimum standardized fitness value is 0. In some problems, such as when cost or error values are being minimized, raw fitness and standardized fitness are identical. If raw fitness is calculated such that better values are greater, then standardized fitness is calculated by subtracting the raw fitness from the maximum possible value of raw fitness.

Adjusted fitness is calculated using standardized fitness: adjusted fitness $f_a = 1/(1 - f_s)$, where f_s is standardized fitness. Values of adjusted fitness thus range between 0 and 1, where 1 is the optimum value. Koza prefers adjusted fitness for most of his applications (Koza 1992). One reason for this is its behavior as its value approaches 1. Near the optimum, small changes in standardized fitnesses have relatively more effect on adjusted fitness than similar changes that are distant from the optimum. For example, consider a problem where standardized fitness values can vary between 0 (optimum) and 20. A change in standardized fitness from 20 to 19 only moves the adjusted fitness from 0.0476 to 0.0500, while changing standardized fitness from 3 to 2 results in an adjusted fitness increment from 0.25 to 0.33. The calculation of adjusted fitness is somewhat analogous to spacing and scaling, discussed in the Genetic Algorithm subsection on fitness calculation.

Normalized fitness is the same as the normalized fitness used in GA applications. It is the adjusted fitness value (for an individual program) divided by the sum of adjusted fitness values for all programs that make up the population. As in GAs, normalized fitness is used in roulette wheel selection.

Steps 3 and 4 of the GP process are often carried out in parallel. A probability is assigned to reproduction, and another to crossover, so that the two sum to 1. If, for example, the probability of reproduction is 10 percent (a typical value in

Koza's problems), then the probability of crossover is 90 percent. This means that once fitness calculations have been made, and it is time to build the new program population, a decision is made based on these probabilities whether to perform reproduction or crossover.

If reproduction is selected, it is often carried out in a similar fashion to the roulette wheel selection used in GAs. A candidate program is selected for reproduction with a probability proportional to its fitness divided by the sum of all of the programs' fitnesses (its normalized fitness). For very large populations of 1,000 or more, highly fit individuals are sometimes given an even greater probability of selection than their normalized fitness. This is called *overselection*.

If crossover is selected, it is accomplished by first selecting two parents using a method based on normalized fitness similar to that used for reproduction. Then, one point is randomly selected in each parent as the crossover point. The point can be anywhere in each program, including the root and internal functions, or the terminals. The entire substructure consisting of the crossover point root and everything below it is exchanged between the two programs.

Note that the parent programs, as well as the exchanged substructures, are usually of different sizes and configurations. Note also that the results of some operations may not be what is usually expected of crossover. An example is when the roots of the two programs are selected as crossover points, in which case the results are identical to the two programs being selected for reproduction into the new population.

When a crossover operation results in a program that exceeds the maximum defined depth, the program that would exceed the depth limit as a result of crossover is copied unaltered into the new population, while the crossover operation is carried out for the other program. In other words, the subtree at and below the crossover point in the unaltered program replaces the program portion at and below the crossover point in the other program.

Preprocessing and postprocessing as typically done when working with other computational intelligence tools, such as artificial neural networks and genetic algorithms, play a relatively minor role in GP implementations. The selection of the function and terminal sets significantly depends on the problem domain, however, so this selection could be thought of as preprocessing.

Formulating the approach to solving a problem with a GP implementation can be difficult. Discovering what other people have done in similar circumstances is often helpful. Chapter 26 of Koza's 1992 book presents tables to guide a user in selection of terminal sets, function sets, population size, and so on. Koza's videotapes are also useful sources of information.

Now that we've explored genetic programming, we turn to the youngest of the evolutionary computation areas, particle swarm optimization. It has a number of attributes in common with the areas discussed previously but is also different in several ways.

Particle Swarm Optimization

Particle swarm optimization (PSO) is an evolutionary computation technique developed by Kennedy and Eberhart in 1995 (Kennedy and Eberhart 1995; Eberhart and Kennedy, 1995; Eberhart, Simpson, and Dobbins 1996). Thus, at the time of the writing of this book PSO has been around for just over 10 years. Already, it is being researched and used in more than 30 countries. This section reviews developments related to PSO since its origin in 1995, along with resources available to help you learn more about it. It is written from an engineering and computer science perspective, and it is not meant to be comprehensive in areas such as the social sciences.

Following the introduction, major developments in the particle swarm algorithm since its origin in 1995 are reviewed. The original algorithm is presented first. Following are brief discussions of constriction factors, inertia weights, and tracking dynamic systems. (Applications, both those already developed and promising future application areas, are presented in Chapter 12. Those already developed include human tremor analysis, power system load stabilization, and product mix optimization.) Finally, particle swarm optimization resources are listed. Most of them can be accessed via the book's web site.

Developments

The story of particle swarm optimization is still unfolding. We can report on only the developments that have occurred as of the publication of this book. For now, let's start at the beginning. The particle swarm concept originated as a simulation of a simplified social system. The original intent was to graphically simulate the graceful but unpredictable choreography of a bird flock. Initial simulations were modified to incorporate nearest-neighbor velocity matching, eliminate ancillary variables, and incorporate multidimensional search and acceleration by distance (Eberhart and Kennedy 1995; Kennedy and Eberhart 1995). At some point in the evolution of the algorithm, it was realized that the conceptual model was, in fact, an optimizer. Through a process of trial and error, a number of parameters extraneous to optimization were eliminated from the algorithm, resulting in the very simple original implementation (Eberhart, Simpson, and Dobbins 1996).

Partical swarm optimization is similar to a genetic algorithm in that the system is initialized with a population of random solutions. It is unlike a GA, however, in that each potential solution is also assigned a randomized velocity and the potential solutions, called *particles*, are then "flown" through the problem space.

Each particle keeps track of its coordinates in the problem space that are associated with the best solution (fitness) it has achieved so far. (The fitness value is also stored.) This value is called "pbest." Another "best" value that is tracked by the global version of the particle swarm optimizer is the overall best value, and its location, obtained so far by any particle in the population. This location is called "gbest."

The PSO concept consists of, at each time step, changing the velocity (accelerating) each particle toward its pbest and gbest locations (in the global version of PSO). Acceleration is weighted by a random term, with separate random numbers being generated for acceleration toward pbest and gbest locations.

There is also a local version of PSO in which, in addition to pbest, each particle keeps track of the best solution, called "lbest," attained within a local topological neighborhood of particles.

The (original) process for implementing the global version of PSO is as follows:

1. Initialize a population (array) of particles with random positions and velocities on d dimensions in the problem space.

2. For each particle, evaluate the desired optimization fitness function in d variables.

3. Compare each particle's fitness evaluation with its pbest. If current value is better than pbest, set the pbest value equal to the current value and the pbest location equal to the current location in d-dimensional space.

4. Compare fitness evaluation with the population's overall previous best. If the current value is better than gbest, reset gbest to the current particle's array index and value.

5. Change the velocity and position of the particle according to equations 3.3 and 3.4, respectively:

$$v_{id} = v_{id} + c_1 * \text{rand}() * (p_{id} - x_{id})$$
$$+ c_2 * \text{Rand}() * (p_{gd} - x_{id}) \tag{3.3}$$

$$x_{id} = x_{id} + v_{id} \tag{3.4}$$

6. Loop to step 2 until a criterion is met, usually a sufficiently good fitness or a maximum number of iteration generations.

Note that in equation 3.4 we appear to be adding a velocity to a position. However, we are really adding a velocity occurring over a single time increment (iteration), so the equation is valid.

Particles' velocities on each dimension are clamped to a maximum velocity Vmax. If the sum of accelerations causes the velocity on that dimension to exceed Vmax, which is a parameter specified by the user, then the velocity on that dimension is limited to Vmax.

Vmax is therefore an important parameter. It determines the resolution, or fineness, with which regions between the present position and the target (best so far) position are searched. If Vmax is too high, particles might fly past good solutions. If Vmax is too small, on the other hand, particles may not explore sufficiently beyond locally good regions. In fact, they could become trapped in local optima, unable to move far enough to reach a better position in the problem space.

The acceleration constants c_1 and c_2 in equation 3.3 represent the weighting of the stochastic acceleration terms that pull each particle toward pbest and gbest positions. Thus, adjustment of these constants changes the amount of "tension" in the system. Low values allow particles to roam far from target regions before being tugged back, while high values result in abrupt movement toward, or past, target regions.

Early experience with particle swarm optimization (trial and error mostly) led us to set each the acceleration constant c_1 and c_2 equal to 2.0 for almost all applications. Vmax was thus the only parameter we routinely adjusted, and we often set it at about 10 to 20 percent of the dynamic range of the variable on each dimension.

Based on, among other things, findings from social simulations, it was decided to design a "local" version of the particle swarm. In this version, particles have information only of their own and their neighbors' bests, rather than that of the entire group. Instead of moving toward a kind of stochastic average of pbest and gbest (the best location of the entire group), particles move toward points defined by pbest and lbest, which is the index of the particle with the best evaluation in the particle's *neighborhood*.

If the neighborhood size is defined as two, for instance, particle(i) compares its fitness value with particle($i - 1$) and particle($i + 1$). Neighbors are defined as topological neighbors; neighbors and neighborhoods do not change during a run. For the neighborhood version, the only change to the process defined in the six steps given earlier is the substitution of p_{ld}, the location of the *neighborhood best*, for p_{gd}, the *global best*, in equation 3.4. Early experience (again, mainly trial and error) led to neighborhood sizes of about 15 percent of the population being used for many applications. So, for a population of 40 particles, a neighborhood of six, or three topological neighbors on each side, was not unusual.

The population size selected is problem-dependent. Population sizes of 20 to 50 are probably most common. It was learned early on that smaller populations than were common for other evolutionary algorithms (such as GAs and evolutionary programming) were optimal for PSO in terms of minimizing the total number of evaluations (population size times the number of generations) needed to obtain a sufficient solution.

We now look at the development of the *inertia weight*. The maximum velocity, Vmax, serves as a constraint to control the global exploration ability of a particle swarm. As stated earlier, a larger Vmax facilitates global exploration, while a smaller Vmax encourages local exploitation. The concept of an inertia weight was developed to better control exploration and exploitation. The motivation was to be able to eliminate the need for Vmax. The inclusion of an inertia weight in the particle swarm optimization algorithm was first reported in the literature in 1998 (Shi and Eberhart 1998a, 1998b).

Equations 3.5 and 3.6 describe the velocity and position update equations with an inertia weight included. It can be seen that these equations are identical to equations 3.3 and 3.4 with the addition of the inertia weight w as a multiplying factor of v_{id} in equation 3.3.

$$v_{id} = w * v_{id} + c_1 * \text{rand}() * (p_{id} - x_{id})$$
$$+ c_2 * \text{Rand}() * (p_{gd} - x_{id}) \tag{3.5}$$

$$x_{id} = x_{id} + v_{id} \tag{3.6}$$

The use of the inertia weight w has provided improved performance in a number of applications. As originally developed, w often is decreased linearly from about 0.9 to 0.4 during a run. Suitable selection of the inertia weight provides a balance between global and local exploration and exploitation and results in fewer iterations on average to find a sufficiently optimal solution. (A different form of w, explained later, is currently being used by one of the authors, RE.)

After some experience with the inertia weight, it was found that although the maximum velocity factor, Vmax, couldn't always be eliminated, the particle swarm algorithm works well if Vmax is set to the value of the dynamic range of each variable (on each dimension). Thus, you don't need to think about how to set Vmax each time the particle swarm algorithm is used.

Another approach to using an inertia weight is to adapt it using a fuzzy system. The first paper published reporting this approach used the Rosenbrock function with asymmetric initialization as the benchmark function (Shi and Eberhart 2000). The fuzzy system comprised nine rules, with two inputs and one output. Each input and the output had three fuzzy sets defined. One input was the global best fitness for the current generation; the other was the current inertia weight. The output was the change in intertia weight. The results reported show that by using a fuzzy adaptive inertia weight, the performance of particle swarm optimization can be significantly improved in terms of the mean best fitness achieved in a given number of iterations. We discuss fuzzy systems in Chapter 7.

The next major development we consider is the constriction factor. Because particle swarm optimization originated from efforts to model social systems, a thorough mathematical foundation for the methodology was not developed at the same time as the algorithm. Within the last few years, a few attempts have been made to begin to build this foundation.

Recent work done by Clerc (1999) indicates that use of a constriction factor may be necessary to ensure convergence of the particle swarm algorithm. A detailed discussion of the constriction factor is beyond the scope of this book, but a simplified method of incorporating it appears in equation 3.7, where K is a function of c_1 and c_2 as reflected in equation 3.8.

$$v_{id} = K^* [v_{id} + c_1 \,{}^*\text{rand}(\ ) \,{}^*(p_{id} - x_{id})$$
$$+ \ c_2 \,{}^*\text{Rand}(\ ) \,{}^*(p_{gd} - x_{id})] \tag{3.7}$$

$$K = \frac{2}{\left|2 - \varphi - \sqrt{\varphi^2 - 4\varphi}\right|}, \text{ where } \varphi = c_1 + c_2, \ \varphi > 4 \tag{3.8}$$

Typically, when Clerc's constriction method is used, φ is set to 4.1 and the constant multiplier K is thus 0.729. This results in the previous velocity being multiplied by 0.729 and each of the two $(p - x)$ terms being multiplied by $0.729 * 2.05 = 1.49445$ (times a random number between 0 and 1).

In initial experiments and applications, Vmax was set to 100,000, because it was believed that Vmax isn't necessary when Clerc's constriction approach is used. However, from subsequent experiments and applications (Eberhart and Shi 2000), it has been concluded that a better approach is to limit Vmax to Xmax, the dynamic range of each variable on each dimension, while selecting w, c_1, and c_2 according to equations 3.7 and 3.8.

What we've discussed so far is fine as long as we're dealing with static systems. Most applications of evolutionary algorithms are to the solution of static problems. Many real-world systems, however, change state frequently (or continuously). These system state changes result in a requirement for frequent, sometimes almost continuous, reoptimization.

It has been demonstrated that particle swarm optimization can be successfully applied to tracking and optimizing dynamic systems (Eberhart and Shi 2001). A slight adjustment was made to the inertia weight for this purpose. The inertia weight w in equation 3.5 was set equal to [0.5 + (Rand()/2.0)]. This produces a number randomly varying between 0.5 and 1.0, with a mean of 0.75. This was selected in the spirit of Clerc's constriction factor described above, which sets w to 0.729. Constants c_1 and c_2 in equation 3.5 were set to 1.494, also according to Clerc's constriction factor.

The random component of the inertia weight is important because when tracking a dynamic system, it cannot be predicted whether exploration (a larger inertia weight) or exploitation (a smaller inertia weight) will be better at any given time. An inertia weight that varies roughly within our previous range addresses this.

For the limited testing done (Eberhart and Shi 2001) using the parabolic function, the performance of particle swarm optimization was shown to compare favorably (faster to converge, higher fitness) with other evolutionary algorithms for all conditions tested. The ability to track a 10-dimensional function was demonstrated.

Now that we've seen how particle swarm optimization works and some of the exciting developments that have occurred recently, let's look at how to get more information about it.

Resources

Three main categories of resources are available with respect to particle swarm optimization: books, web sites, and technical papers. The first book to include a section on particle swarm optimization was Eberhart, Simpson and Dobbins (1996). See Kennedy and Eberhart (1999) for a book chapter on PSO. An entire book is now available, however, on the subject of swarms: *Swarm Intelligence* (Kennedy, Eberhart, and Shi 2001) discusses both the social and psychological as well as the engineering and computer science aspects of swarm intelligence. The web site for the book, *www.Computelligence.org*, is a guide to a variety of resources related to particle swarm optimization. Included are Java applets that can be run online illustrating the optimization of a variety of benchmark functions. The user can select a variety of parameters. Also on the web site is PSO software written in C++, Visual BASIC, and Java that can be downloaded. A variety of links to other web sites are also provided. The web site for this book is, obviously, another major source of PSO information and pointers to other sites. With respect to conferences, those related to evolutionary computation (such as the Congress on Evolutionary Computation) sponsored or cosponsored by the IEEE provide the richest source of publications on PSO. A special issue of the *IEEE Transactions on Evolutionary Computation* devoted to particle swarm optimization was published in June 2004.

Summary

In this chapter, we first present a brief history of evolutionary computation, followed by an overview of the evolutionary computation field. Five main evolutionary algorithms are then discussed in detail in their own sections, respectively. The five areas are genetic algorithms, evolutionary programming, evolution strategies, genetic programming, and particle swarm optimization. Among the five, the genetic algorithm is emphasized, with more detailed discussion on subjects such as schemata and the schema theorem.

The five evolutionary algorithms share many features. First, all are population-based search algorithms. The cooperation and/or competition among the population move the potential solutions toward the better search areas. Second, all are motivated by nature. Particle swarm optimization is motivated by social behavior, and the other four main evolutionary algorithms are motivated by the survival of the fittest and/or evolution. Third, the five evolutionary algorithms employ direct "fitness" information instead of function derivatives or other related knowledge. Therefore, evolutionary algorithms can solve problems that are not continuous, not differentiable, and multimodal. Fourth, randomness plays roles in all of the algorithms. The search process is not deterministic. It is this randomness and the "fitness" information that gives evolutionary algorithms the ability to enable individuals to move to anywhere and escape from local optima.

Finally, they all generate the next generation from the previous generation. In particle swarm optimization, the individuals (particles) "fly" through the search space with dynamically changing velocities. That is, the individuals "fly" to the next generation from the current generation. In the other four evolutionary algorithms, the next generation is obtained by applying so-called evolution operators to the current generation: In genetic algorithms and evolution strategies, the selection, mutation, and crossover (recombination) operators are applied; in genetic programming, selection and crossover operators are used; and in evolutionary programming, selection and mutation operators are utilized.

Comparisons of evolutionary computation tools (in these five areas) and other processing methods are also discussed in each section, respectively. Evolutionary algorithms are recommended to solve nonlinear problems for which the traditional approaches are hard, if not impossible, to apply. It is usual and reasonable to expect evolutionary algorithms to find near optimal solutions within a limited period of time—a solution that is good enough to be acceptable.

Exercises

1. Convert the following binary coded strings to Gray coding: 10101010, 10011100, 01100110.

2. How many schemata are possible for a 6-bit binary string?

3. According to the schema theorem, what happens to highly fit schemata in successive generations? What are the effects of crossover and mutation according to the theorem? Why use crossover and mutation?

4. Assume standard binary encoding of parameters is used for a genetic algorithm implementation. Briefly discuss how the effects of uniform crossover and two-point crossover change as the number of bits representing a parameter is increased.

5. After running a genetic algorithm for a fairly long time, the fitness values tend to cluster at the high end of the scale. For example, on a scale of 0 to 1, they might cluster from 0.90 to 0.98. What is the main problem with this? How can it be alleviated?

6. Assume that the average fitness of strings containing a particular schema S is 20 percent less than the average fitness of all schemata, and the schema appears in 50 percent of the initial population. Assume that the probability of disruption of this schema by crossover or mutation is negligible. Calculate when S will disappear from a population with 50 members. Repeat for a 100-member population.

7. Assume each population member in a GA consists of 8 binary coded bits (as in the GA example in the chapter), representing the integers 0 to 255. Briefly describe or sketch the portion of the problem space covered by the following schemata: 0*******, *******1, 10******, ******10, ***11***.

8. What is the main difference between evolutionary programming and evolution strategies?

9. Assume you are going to use genetic programming to evolve a program to classify the Iris dataset (pp. 197–198). Specify a function set and a terminal set that are appropriate to solve the problem.

10. Sketch out a genetic programming representation of the best possible *approximate* solution to $v = \pi r^2 h$, (v is the volume of a right cylinder, r is its radius, and h is its height) given that the maximum depth of the program is five layers and you may only use the constant values 0, 1, and 10. If you were going to evolve programs to do this calculation using genetic programming, what would you propose to use as a function set?

11. How is a particle swarm optimizer similar to a genetic algorithm? How is it different? How does it resemble an evolution strategies implementation?

chapter
four

Evolutionary Computation Implementations

In the last chapter, we reviewed the concept of evolutionary computation, seeing how it can provide a foundation for computational intelligence. We examined five main areas of evolutionary computation: genetic algorithms, evolutionary programming, evolution strategies, genetic programming, and particle swarm optimization.

In this chapter, we discuss the common issues related to the implementation of evolutionary algorithms. We present two implementations of evolutionary computation: a genetic algorithm implementation and a particle swarm optimization implementation.

The genetic algorithm (GA) implementation is basically a "plain vanilla" GA, but with a few interesting options. It implements one-point, two-point, or uniform crossover, and roulette wheel, tournament, or ranking selection. It has an interesting

set of options for mutation, one of which is reminiscent of evolution strategies.

Five benchmark functions are included with the GA implementation: the parabolic function (sometimes referred to as the spherical function), the Rosenbrock function, the Rastrigin function, the Griewank function, and Schaffer's F6 function.

The function equations appear in Table 4.1. All have optimal function (output) values of 0 ($f^*(x) = 0$) except for Schaffer's F6 function, for which the function value at the optimum is 1.0. The parameter values (x^*) at the optimum are all $(0, 0, \ldots, 0)^T$ except for the Rosenbrock function, for which $x^* = (1, 1, \ldots, 1)^T$.

Table 4.2 lists the dynamic range and error criterion for each function. The dynamic range is the range within which the variables are initialized. Each dynamic range is symmetrical; that is, for the

Table 4.1 Functions Used in GA and PSO Implementations

Function	Formula
Parabolic	$f_0(x) = \sum_{i=1}^{n} x_i^2$
Rosenbrock	$f_1(x) = \sum_{i=1}^{n} (100(x_{i+1} - x_i^2)^2 + (x_i - 1)^2)$
Rastrigin	$f_2(x) = \sum_{i=1}^{n} (x_1^2 - 10\cos(2\pi x_i) + 10)$
Griewank	$f_3(x) = \dfrac{1}{4000} \sum_{i=1}^{n} x_i^2 - \prod_{i=1}^{n} \cos\left(\dfrac{x_i}{\sqrt{i}}\right) + 1$
Shaffer's F6	$f_6(x) = 0{:}5 - \dfrac{\left(\sin\sqrt{x^2 + y^2}\right)^2 - 0{:}5}{\left(1{:}0 + 0{:}001\,(x^2 + y^2)\right)^2}$

Table 4.2 Functions, with Their Typical Initialization Ranges
and Error Criteria

Function	Dyanamic range (X_{max})	Error criterion
Parabolic	10	0.01
Rosenbrock	100	100
Rastrigin	5.12	100
Griewank	600	0.05
Shaffer's F6	10	0.00001

parabolic function the dynamic range is [–10, 10]. The error criterion is the maximum error value generally acceptable (in the literature) as a stopping criterion, if error value is used as a stopping criterion. The error value column gives you a metric for how well the algorithm performed.

The particle swarm optimizer (PSO) is implemented to run multi-PSOs simultaneously. By doing so, it can be used both for the optimization of nonlinear functions and for optimization problems that require multi-PSOs running simultaneously. An implementation of a co-evolutionary PSO is described that solves min-max problems.

The PSO implementation includes the same five benchmark functions, listed in Table 4.1, as the GA implementation. In addition, for the multiple-swarm version of the PSO implementation, functions have been added that require simultaneous minimize/maximize operations (constraint satisfaction). These functions are listed and described in the section on multi-PSOs near the end of the chapter.

Implementation Issues

Before we get into specific evolutionary computation implementations, it is important to understand some of the issues common to the implementations of all evolutionary algorithms. These issues include chromosome representation methods, learning strategies, programming strategies, and memory handling.

In this section, when the term "learning" is used, it is in accordance with what is commonly found in the literature. However, our perspective is that "adaptation" often describes what a computational intelligence system does better than "learning" (see Chapter 2), so please consider mentally inserting the word "adaptation" when you see "learning."

Homogeneous versus Heterogeneous Representation

Let's first look at homogeneous versus heterogeneous representation. Representation is an important factor that requires careful consideration. Traditionally, homogeneous representations have been adopted; that is, all individuals are strings of binary bits, integers, or real values. One advantage of homogeneous representations is that they are simple, and existing evolutionary operators can therefore be employed (under the assumption that the same dynamic integer ranges are used for each element when integer representation is utilized). But they may result in inaccuracy and even difficulties in mapping from genotypes to phenotypes. For example, using binary representation to represent the optimization functions' real-valued parameters can result in inaccuracy, and using real-valued representation to represent discrete parameters can result in difficulties. (If you are trying to build a rule-based system, it is difficult to decode the real valued–based chromosomes into rules.) One way to overcome the inaccuracies and difficulties is by using heterogeneous representations—for example, using real values to represent real value parameters and using integers or binary bits to represent discrete parameters. The principal feature of the heterogeneous representations is that they are intuitive and natural. But representation-specific evolutionary operators have to be designed for each different representation, and the complexity of the algorithm is increased.

Genetic algorithms originally used binary representations, on which the theoretical foundation of genetic algorithms is based. Binary representations are still popular. It is natural and intuitive to represent everything using binary strings because computer computation is based on 0s and 1s. A disadvantage of this kind of representation is that the length of the chromosome will be extremely long when the numbers or precision of variables is large. Also, inaccuracy is introduced when binary strings are used to represent real-valued parameters. The advantage of the binary representation is its simplicity and generality.

For the representation of multivalue discrete parameters, a more natural and intuitive way is to use integer representation. Also, binary representation can be easily transformed into integer representation. The advantage of integer representation is that the length of the chromosome is reduced compared with that of binary representation. The disadvantage is that special evolutionary operators have to be designed. Special care has to be taken in designing evolutionary operators, especially when a different dynamic integer range is used for each element.

To overcome the inaccuracy problems introduced by using binary representations for encoding real values, a more natural and intuitive way is to use real-valued representations to encode real value parameters. The use of real-valued representations makes it possible to use large domains (even unknown domains) for the variables, which is difficult to achieve with binary and integer representations. The disadvantage of this representation is that discrete parameters can't be represented easily.

Even though every parameter can be represented by binary strings, integer strings, or real-valued strings, it is hard to say, generally, which representation is the best. It depends on the problem to be solved and your objectives. The advantage to using uniform representation is that it is simple, and existing evolutionary operators can be employed directly except in the case of integer representation. For integer representation, each element may have a different dynamic integer range since different variables may have different multivalue discrete parameters. In this case, the mutation operator should be position dependent and specially designed.

Generally speaking, it will be more natural to represent the problem to be solved in a chromosome in the way it appears in the system implementation. In this way, the problem can be more finely adjusted. Certainly this may increase the complexity of the evolutionary operators. There is a trade-off between representation and complexity of the evolutionary operators. Now that we've considered the subject of representation, let's look at adaptation.

Population Adaptation versus Individual Adaptation

One of the main questions with respect to adaptation is whether to use individual or population adaptation. Evolutionary algorithms have been commonly implemented as population adaptation algorithms, as in the Pittsburgh approach (Smith 1980), where a set of samples is available to be used as training examples. This is the scenario for most function optimization and classification system designs where the training examples can be obtained before training. For other cases, individual adaptation approaches may have to be adopted. The best-known individual adaptation approach is the so-called Michigan approach (Holland 1978).

In the Pittsburgh approach, each chromosome represents the problem to be solved, and a set of samples is available to be used as training examples. Since the training is often offline, some complicated and large systems can be evolutionarily designed by using fast computers, or even a group of computers, where each one evaluates only a small portion of the chromosomes and all of them communicate. The most important feature of the Pittsburgh approach is that the performance of each candidate solution is directly proportional to the fitness of its chromosome representation, which makes evolutionary search more effective and efficient since the search is guided by fitness.

In nature, not all components in a system behave in the same way; some may have a "good" contribution while others have a "bad" contribution to the performance of the system. All the components both cooperate and compete among themselves, and, in theory, the "good" components should have more chance to survive than the "bad" ones. In the Pittsburgh approach, all the components of a system are represented in a chromosome and treated the same regardless of their contributions. This may bring difficulties into the search since the search process only reflects the competition among chromosomes.

These are situations where the Michigan approach may be appropriate. In the Michigan approach, each chromosome represents only a single component of the system and the whole population represents the complete system. So there is both cooperation and competition among all the components of the system, and therefore the strongest potential components have more of a chance to appear and survive. Since the whole population represents only one system, only that single system needs to be evaluated in each generation, which makes it possible to evaluate the chromosomes online. Since in the Michigan approach only one system is evaluated for each generation, only a single fitness from the environment is obtained. Therefore, special techniques have to be used to distribute the payback among all the chromosomes.

The evolutionary computation implementations described in this chapter all use the Pittsburgh approach.

Static versus Dynamic Adaptation

In addition to the population versus individual adaptation question, the choice of static versus dynamic adaptation exists. The most common evolutionary algorithms take a static adaptation approach; that is, the algorithms have fixed parameters through the course of the running of the algorithm. For example, the probabilities of the crossover and mutation operators, the population size, and so on, are kept constant through the run. But even though evolutionary algorithms with static adaptation approaches have been applied to successfully solve problems, when solving complicated and large problems, in order for evolutionary algorithms to have sufficiently good performance to successfully evolve the systems, the relationship between exploration and exploitation abilities should be kept balanced during the run.

One way to maintain the balance is through the dynamic adaptation of the algorithm parameters. Different levels of adaptation can be implemented, such as environment-level adaptation, population-level adaptation, individual-level adaptation, and component-level adaptation. Which level of adaptation to use depends on the problem and your objective, but population-level adaptation is the most commonly used among the four. For instance, if an operator such as the mutation operator is adapted during a run, the adapted mutation rate is most often applied to the entire population.

Flowcharts versus Finite State Machines

Two of the primary ways to represent evolutionary computation (and other computational intelligence) systems are as flowcharts and finite state machines. Flowcharts are straightforward and easy to understand. They have been used frequently in programming systems, especially simple systems. Finite state machines have been very useful for programming systems that require frequent interaction with the environment (the user). An example is pressing the Pause button through a graphic user interface to pause the running of a system. In state machine implementations, a task (or a system with a single task) is divided into several states, with each state performing only a simple action. The system is actually a transition process from one state to another, and the system can be interrupted at each state transition. Since, for each state, only simple action is performed, it can enable the system to have real-time interaction. It is also very useful when multitasking is involved. Also, finite state machines are often more suited to the structured (object-oriented) approach to systems development.

Handling Multiple Similar Cases

How do we handler situations where several possible cases exist? Each case has its associated function to handler the corresponding situation, and so which of the functions to call depends on the situation or the case. In the C language, a common method is to use the switch statement. First, a new enumeration data type is defined to index the cases. For example, there are several ways to do the crossover operation: one-point crossover, two-point crossover, uniform crossover, and so on. The new enumeration data type can be defined as that shown in Listing 4.1.

Listing 4.1 Enumeration data type for crossover operators.

```
Typedef enum crossover_type_tag
{
    ONE_POINT_CROSSOVER,
    TWO_POINT_CROSSOVER,
    UNIFORM_CROSSOVER,
    NUM_CROSSOVER
}   crossover_type;
```

A new data type to record the index of the current crossover operator to be used can be declared as

```
crossover_type   crossover_index;
```

Which crossover operator to use, then, depends on the `crossover_index` as shown in Listing 4.2.

Listing 4.2 Example of a crossover index.

```
static void crossover_handler(int crossover_index)
{
    switch (crossover_index)
    {
        case ONE_POINT_CROSSOVER:
                one_point_crossover(); break;
        case TWO_POINT_CROSSOVER:
                two_point_crossover(); break;
        case UNIFORM_CROSSOVER:
                uniform_crossover();    break;
    }
}
```

In Listing 4.2, `one_point_crossover()`, `two_point_crossover()`, and `uniform_crossover()` are the routines actually handling the crossover operations. In the above implementation, if the `NUM_CROSSOVER` is less than 3, an if–then statement in the C language would generally be used instead of a switch statement.

Another way to handler the multicase situation is to use a function pointer. Corresponding to the enumeration data type `crossover_type`, an array of function pointers is defined as that shown in Listing 4.3.

Listing 4.3 An array of function pointers for crossover handlers.

```
static constant fptr crossover_handler[NUM_CROSSOVER] =
{
    one_point_crossover,
```

```
        two_point_crossover,
        uniform_crossover,
};
```

In Listing 4.3, `fptr` is the function pointer data type. To invoke the crossover routine now is as simple as passing the case index to the array of function pointers to point to the right function. One disadvantage of using this is that the order of the function pointers is critical, and it has to be in exactly the same order as in the definition of the enumeration data type. Otherwise, a different function will be called. Cautions thus have to be taken when deleting and/or adding cases.

Allocating and Freeing Memory Space

Handling memory is always a challenge when using the C language. In programming a computational intelligence system, numerous arrays and vectors are typically used. In order for the source code to be reusable and suitable for general use, these arrays and vectors should be dynamically configured. The sizes of these arrays and vectors are dynamically read in when the program is running, and the memory space can't be reserved for them before runtime or during compile time. The memory space has to be allocated to them during the run and freed after finishing the program run. Listing 4.4 is an example of memory allocation and cleanup for a two-dimensional integer array.

Listing 4.4 An example of memory allocation and cleanup.

```
/* declare an integer array */
int      **population;

/* allocate memory space for the array */
population = (int **)calloc(number_of_row, sizeof(int *));
for (idx_i = 0; idx_i < number_of_row ; idx_i++)
        population[idx_i] = (int *)calloc(number_of_column, sizeof(int));

/* release the allocated space */
for (idx_i = 0; idx_i < number_of_row; idx_i++)
        free(population[idx_i]);
free(population);
```

Error Checking

In any application, it is a good habit to add error checking into your source code for debugging. Generally, most runtime errors can be detected by doing this. From an error message, you can (usually) easily locate the source of the error and fix it. For example, when accessing an element in a vector, you should first check whether the index is valid. You should also check whether the system has enough memory space to be allocated to the array every time you are allocating memory space. You can use the `assert()` routine defined in `ASSERT.H` or write your own error checking. If `assert()` is used in your source code, it is recommended that you remove the `assert` statements from the source code once your program has been debugged. Listing 4.5 is an example of error checking for memory allocation.

Listing 4.5 An example of error checking for memory allocation.

```
/* allocate memory space for the array */
population = (int **)calloc(number_of_row, sizeof(int *));
assert(population != NULL);
for (idx_i = 0; idx_i < number_of_row ; idx_i++)
{
    population[idx_i] = (int *)calloc(number_of_column, sizeof(int));
    if (population[idx_i] == NULL)
    {
        printf("file name: %s\t line number = %d\n",__FILE__, __LINE__);
        exit(1);
    }
}
```

Genetic Algorithm Implementation

Now that we've looked at issues common to the implementations of all evolutionary algorithms, let's get down to some specifics. This section discusses the genetic algorithm implementation. The implementation is essentially a canonical genetic algorithm that uses mutation and crossover operators. It closely resembles the basic genetic algorithm described in the previous chapter, so material discussed there is not repeated. Please refer to Chapter 3 for the basics of genetic algorithms. We begin by examining some issues related to programming GAs.

Programming Genetic Algorithms

In genetic algorithm implementations, the evaluation/fitness function is an integral part of the algorithm. The selection of representation methods depends heavily on the problem to be solved. The genetic algorithm implemented here is applied to search for optima of several benchmark functions with real-valued parameters. A good way to encode the problem is to use real-valued representation, but we choose to use a binary representation instead, since binary representation is the original type that has been studied and implemented in the literature and the genetic operators have been thoroughly studied and are mature. It is also the original fundamental version of the genetic algorithm on which the schema theorem (discussed in Chapter 3) is based.

Figure 4.1 shows the flowchart of the GA implementation in this book.

Definition of Enumeration and Structure Data Types

Since C is not an object-oriented language, it's a good habit to define some enumeration and structure data types at the beginning of the GA implementation. (It can be argued that C is "object-based" since new objects and data types can be created via enumerated types and structures.) This can make the implementation more closely

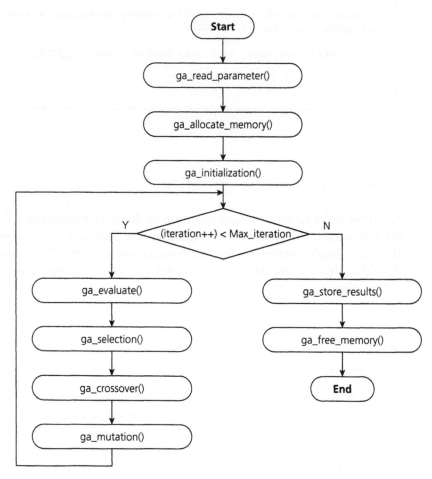

Figure 4.1 Flowchart of the binary genetic algorithm implementation. Routines in this figure are discussed in the text.

resemble an object-oriented one, and make it more reusable. In Listing 4.6 are the new enumeration data types used in the implementation.

Listing 4.6 Enumeration data type in the GA implementation.

```
typedef enum selection_type_tag
{
    ROULETTE_WHEEL_SCALING,
    BINARY_TOURNAMENT,
    RANKING,
    NUM_SELECTION
} selection_type;

typedef enum  crossover_type_tag
{
    ONE_POINT_CROSSOVER,
    UNIFORM_CROSSOVER,
    TWO_POINT_CROSSOVER,
    NUM_CROSSOVER
} crossover_type;

typedef enum Evaluate_Function_Tag
{
    F6,                         // 0 :F6: min
    PARABOLIC,                  // 1 :Parabolic: min
    ROSENBROCK,                 // 2 :Rosenbrock: min
    RASTRIGRIN,                 // 3 :Rastrigrin: min
    GRIEWANK,                   // 4 :Griewank: min
    NUM_EVALUATE_FUNCTIONS      // Total no. of eval. functions
} Evaluate_Function_Type;
```

Listing 4.7 Structure data type in the GA implementation.

```
typedef struct ga_binary_data_type_tag
{
    unsigned char  **population;
            // double pointer to the population of binary GA
    double    *fit;         // pointer to the fitness vector
    int       popu_size;    // population size:  popsize
    int       indi_length;  // length of chromosome: length
    int       iter_max;     // iter: maximum number of iterations
    double    crossover_rate;       // crossover rate
    double    mutation_rate;        // mutation rate
    double    termination_criterion;  // criterion
    int       best_index;
            // index of best individual of current population
    unsigned char  bits_per_para;
            // each weight represented by bits_per_para bits
    unsigned char  mutation_flag;
            // flag for mutation, 1, variable, 0 constant
    crossover_type  c_type;
            // crossover type: 0: one, 1: uniform, 2: two
```

```
    selection_type      s_type;       // selection method
    double            *gau;   // store gaussian function value for each bit
    int       gene_index; // index of current generation
    double    fit_variance;
              // variance of fitness of the current generation
    double    fit_mean;    // average of fitness of the current generation
} ga_binary_data_type;

typedef struct ga_env_data_type_tag
{
    char      resultFile[NAME_MAX];           // result file name
    int       dimension;                      // N:
    Evaluate_Function_Type    function;       // function to be solved
} ga_env_data_type;
```

The enumeration data types `selection_type`, `crossover_type`, and `Evaluate_Function_Type` are defined to specify which types of selection operators, crossover operators, and optimization functions will be implemented in the software run, respectively.

Listing 4.7 shows the new structure data types in the GA implementation. In the `ga_binary_data_type` definition, `unsigned char **population` is a double `unsigned char` pointer pointing to the population. The `unsigned char` is used to represent a bit, which is a waste of memory space. The `unsigned char` type occupies 1 byte, which consists of 8 bits. To save memory, a bit should be used to represent a bit in the population member string. Since there is no data type in the C language for bit, an `unsigned char` should be used to represent 8 bits in a binary representation. For example, a binary representation with individual length 160 can be stored in 160/8 = 20 bytes, that is, an array of 20 `unsigned chars`.

```
unsigned  char *binary_individual;
binary_individual = (unsigned char*)calloc(20, sizeof(unsigned char));
```

The disadvantage of using a byte to represent eight elements in binary representation is that the genetic operations involve bit manipulations, which makes the computation more complex and generally consume more computation time. There are thus trade-offs between required memory space and computation time/complexity and between code simplicity and complexity and a programmer's time to write and test extra code. For generality, we use the `unsigned char` type here.

The `unsigned char` variable `bits_per_para` is the number of bits used to represent a real-valued parameter. The variable `fit` is a double pointer pointing to fitness values of the population; `gau` is a double pointer pointing to the vector `bits_per_para` number of real values, which are used to store the probability of mutating each bit. These probabilities are used for implementation of bit-position–based mutation.

The integer type variables `popu_size`, `indi_length`, and `iter_max` are the population size, the length of the individual, and the maximum number of generations. The double variables `crossover_rate`, `mutation_rate`, and `termination_criterion` are the crossover rate, the baseline mutation rate at the population level, and the criterion for terminating the run, respectively. (The only termination method implemented in the software on the book's Internet site is reaching the maximum number of generations.) The integer type variables `best_index` and `gene_index` are the index of the best individual among the population at the current generation and the index of the current generation, respectively. The unsigned char `mutation_flag` specifies which kind of mutation is going to be performed (explained later). The `crossover_type` and `selection_type` variables `c_type` and `s_type` specify which types of crossover operator and selection operator are going to be used. The double types `fit_variance` and `fit_mean` are the variance and mean of the fitness values of the current generation.

Another defined `struct` data type is `ga_env_data_type`, which includes three data types: the first is a file name in which the results of the run are to be stored; the second is the dimension of the problem (function). The length of each individual is calculated by multiplying it with `bits_per_para`. The last one is the function to be solved.

Two global data variables `ga_data` and `ga_env_data` are defined, as shown below, so the GA and its environment-related parameters are not required to be passed from one routine to another within the GA module.

```
ga_binary_data_type ga_data;
ga_env_data_type    ga_env_data;
```

The GA `main()` Routine

Listing 4.8 is the `main()` routine, which is the entry point of the program. It is a good habit to keep `main()` routines simple. In the `GA_Start_Up(datFile)` routine, shown in Listing 4.8, all the GA problem-related parameters are read in from the input file. For example, the variable "bits per parameter" `bits_per_para` is read in from the input file. This variable tells how many bits are used to encode one parameter to be evolved. The larger `bits_per_para` is, the higher the resolution is and the longer the individual population member length is, and therefore the more computation time it consumes. Also, memory space is allocated to the dynamic data, and the population is initialized. In the `GA_Clean_Up()` routine, the results are stored to an output file and the previously allocated memory space is de-allocated.

Listing 4.8 The main() routine of the binary GA implementation.

```c
void main(int argc,char *argv[])
{
    if (argc != 2)
    {
        printf("usage: ga  [datFile]\n");
        exit(1);
    }
    GA_Start_Up(dataFile);
    GA_Main_Loop();
    GA_Clean_Up();
}

void GA_Start_Up (char *datFile)
{
    int idx_i;
    ga_read_parameter(datFile);
    ga_data.indi_length = ga_env_data.dimension  * ga_data.bits_per_para;
    ga_allocate_memory();
    ga_initialization();
    for (idx_i = 0; idx_i < ga_data.bits_per_para; idx_i++)
        ga_data.gau[idx_i] = gaussian(sqrt(idx_i));
}

void GA_Clean_Up (void)
{
    ga_store_results();
    ga_free_memory();
}

void GA_Main_Loop (void)
{
    while ((++(ga_data.gene_index)) < ga_data.iter_max)
    {
        ga_evaluate();
        ga_selection();
        ga_crossover();
        ga_mutate();
    }
}
```

The GA_Main_Loop() routine is the main loop of the GA implementation. All the genetic operations are performed here. These operations form the core of the search process.

For each cycle (generation), first the population of solutions is evaluated, then the next generation of solutions is selected using the selection operator according to the fitness values obtained in the last step. The newly formed solutions then go through crossover and mutation operations. This process is repeated until either the specified maximum number of generations is reached or a termination criterion is met. We didn't implement a termination criterion but left it as an exercise for the student (see Exercise 6 at the end of this chapter).

The `ga_evaluate()` Routine

In the `ga_evaluate()` routine, shown in Listing 4.9, each individual is evaluated. First the binary representation is decoded into the real-valued parameters by calling the `get_parameter()` routine, then the evaluation function specified in ga_env_data (`ga_env_data.function`) is called. We have implemented five benchmark functions: Shaffer's F6, Parabolic, Rosenbrock, the generalized Rastrigin, and the generalized Griewank functions. They all are minimum optimization problems except Shaffer's F6 and have been transformed to the maximum optimization problems by multiplying by –1 in the implementation.

Listing 4.9 The `ga_evaluate()` routine.

```
void ga_evaluate (void)
{
    int      idx_i;
    double *para;          /* pointer to the parameters */

    /* allocate memory space for the parameter matrix */
    para = (double *)calloc(ga_env_data.dimension,sizeof(double));

    /* fitness calculation */
    for (idx_i = 0; idx_i < ga_data.popu_size; idx_i++)
    {
        /* convert binary vector to real valued parameters */
        get_parameter(idx_i,para);
        /* get fitness  */
        ga_data.fit[idx_i] =
    OPT_Function_Routines(ga_env_data.function,ga_env_data.dimension,para);
    }

    free(para);
    ga_data.best_index = maximum(ga_data.fit,ga_data.popu_size);
    ga_data.fit_mean = average(ga_data.fit, ga_data.popu_size);
    ga_data.fit_variance = variance(ga_data.fit,ga_data.fit_mean,
                                    ga_data.popu_size);
}


double OPT_Function_Routines (int fun_idx,int dim, double *para)
{
    double result;
    switch (fun_idx)
    {
        case F6:
          result = f6(para);              break;
        case PARABOLIC:
          result = parabolic(dim,para);  break;
        case ROSENBROCK:
          result = rosenbrock(dim,para); break;
        case RASTRIGIN:
          result = rastrigin(dim,para); break;
        case GRIEWANK:
```

```
            result = griewank(dim,para);   break;
        default:                           break;
    }
    return(result);
}
```

The `ga_selection()` Routine

The main objective of the selection operator in a GA is to give the candidate solutions having better performance (higher fitness value) more chances to survive and reproduce more copies into the next generation.

In the `ga_selection()` routine, shown in Listing 4.10, several selection mechanisms are implemented. They are proportionate selection, binary tournament selection, and ranking selection. All of them are combined with the elitist strategy; that is, at least one copy of the best candidate solution will be reproduced into the next generation.

For the proportionate selection operator, the quantity of each candidate solution copied into the next generation is proportional to its fitness value. The simplest one is called roulette wheel selection, with each solution occupying an area on the wheel proportionate to its fitness value. (Roulette wheel selection is discussed in Chapter 3.) The wheel is spun as many times as the size of the population. Each time, a solution is selected according to where the pointer points. The advantage of this selection is that the concept is simple and easy to implement. The disadvantage is that the fitness value has to be positive, which generally can't be guaranteed, especially when there is no a priori knowledge about the problem to be solved. A way to overcome this problem is to shift the fitness values of the population. In our implementation, we shift the raw (original) fitness values by moving the minimal fitness value to about 10 percent of the dynamic fitness range (`max_fitness - min_fitness`):

```
new_fitness[i] = old_fitness - min_fitness + 0.1 * (max_fitness -
                                                    min_fitness)
```

Another disadvantage of the roulette wheel selection operator is that this approach can't be directly used for a minimization optimization problem. The problem has to be converted to a maximization problem. If the original fitness value is positive, then the fitness value of the converted problem is negative. The shifting approach then has to be applied to the fitness value of the converted problem in order to use a roulette wheel selection operator. This shift approach is also useful for relatively flat fitness surfaces and/or near the end of a run.

For the binary tournament selection operator, two individuals are randomly picked and their fitness values are compared. The individual with the better fitness is copied into the next generation. The advantages of this approach are that it is easy to implement, there are no restrictions on fitness values, it is suitable for parallel implementation and thus runs fast, and it can be applied to solve both minimization and maximization optimization problems directly.

The ranking selection operator is similar to that for roulette wheel selection. First the solutions are ranked, then each solution is assigned a predetermined ranked fitness value based on its rank in the population. These values are usually evenly spaced, often between 0 and 1. After that the operations are similar to that in roulette wheel selection, so we don't repeat them here. This process is most useful when the fitnesses have become bunched together late in the run. As a simple example, consider a ranked population of four individuals with fitnesses of 0.95, 0.96, 0.97, and 0.98. As is, they have very similar probabilities of selection into the next generation. Now evenly space their fitness values between 0 and 1, so that their ranked fitness values are now 0.25, 0.50, 0.75, and 1.0. Now the probabilities of selection are 10 percent, 20 percent, 30 percent, and 40 percent, respectively, and the selection pressure has been substantially increased.

Which selection operator to choose and how to implement it is critical since it impacts the selection pressure and, therefore, the performance of the GA. In Listing 4.11, the source code of the implementation of a binary tournament selection operator is shown. In this implementation, an integer pointer flag is defined and a `popu_size` quantity of integer type memory space is allocated to it. `Flag[i]` is used to record the copies of the individual i that have been selected for the next generation. At the beginning, no copies are selected for each individual; that is, $flag[i] = 0, \forall i \in \{0, \ldots, popu\_size - 1\}$. Each time an individual i is selected into the next generation, `flag[i]` increases by 1. This process is repeated until total `popu_size` copies of individuals have been selected. Then the new population is formed by checking each `flag[i]`. If `flag[i]` = 0, it means individual i has not been selected for the next generation. It is then replaced by an individual j with `flag[j]` > 1, and `flag[i]` increases by 1 and `flag[j]` decreases by 1. This process is repeated until $flag[j] = 1, \forall j \in \{0, \ldots, popu\_size - 1\}$.

Listing 4.10 The `ga_selection()` routine.

```
void ga_selection (void)
{
    switch (ga_data.s_type)
    {
        case ROULETTE_WHEEL_SCALING:
            roulette_wheel_scaling(); break;
        case BINARY_TOURNAMENT:
            binary_tournament();        break;
        case RANKING:
            ranking();                  break;
        default:
            binary_tournament();        break;
    }
}
```

Listing 4.11 The Binary tournament selection operator.

```c
static void binary_tournament (void)
{
    int idx_i,idx_j,idx_k;
    int kid_1,kid_2;
    int *flag;                /* information for selected times */
    int no;

    flag = (int *)calloc(ga_data.popu_size,sizeof(int));

    /* set all flags to be zero, means no one has been selected */
    for (idx_i = 0; idx_i < ga_data.popu_size; idx_i++)
        flag[idx_i] = 0;

    flag[ga_data.best_index] = 1;  /* keep the best */

    /* set the flags for all individuals */
    for (idx_i = 0; idx_i < (ga_data.popu_size - 1); idx_i++)
    {
        kid_1 = rand()%(ga_data.popu_size);
        kid_2 = rand()%(ga_data.popu_size);

        if ((ga_data.fit[kid_1]) > (ga_data.fit[kid_2]))
            flag[kid_1] +=1;
        else
            flag[kid_2] += 1;
    }

    /* form the new population */
    for (idx_i = 0; idx_i < ga_data.popu_size; idx_i++)
    {
        if (flag[idx_i] == 0)
        {
            no = 0;
            for (idx_j = 0; idx_j < ga_data.popu_size; idx_j++)
            {
                if (flag[idx_j] > 1)
                {
                    idx_k = idx_j;
                    no = no + 1;
                    break;
                }
            }
            if (no == 0)
            {
                printf("something wrong in selection \n");
                exit(1);
            }
            flag[idx_k] = flag[idx_k] - 1;

            /* copy the selected individual to new individual */
            for (idx_j = 0; idx_j < ga_data.indi_length; idx_j++)
                ga_data.population[idx_i][idx_j] = ga_data.population
                                                 [idx_k][idx_j];
            flag[idx_i] += 1;
```

```
        }
    }

    /* check the selection */
    for (idx_i = 0; idx_i < ga_data.popu_size; idx_i++)
    {
        if (flag[idx_i] != 1)
        {
            printf("something wrong with selection \n");
            exit(1);
        }
    }
    free(flag);
}
```

The ga_crossover() Routine

In the ga_crossover() routine, as shown in Listing 4.12, three types of crossover operator are implemented. Which one to use is specified in the input file. First, (population size)/2 pairs of individuals are randomly picked. Which pair of individuals is going to experience the crossover operation is randomly determined, with crossover occurring with a probability of crossover_rate. In the implementation, all the individuals have one chance to be selected to undergo the crossover operation. An integer pointer store_index is defined and allocated popu_size quantity of integer type memory space. Each element of store_index stores an index of an individual that has not been selected to go through the crossover operation. Another integer data variable remain_number is defined to store the number of individuals that have not been selected. At the beginning, store_index[j] = j and remain_number = popu_size since no individuals have been selected yet.

Each time an individual j is selected through calling the search() routine, store_index[j], j = j,..., remain_number is replaced by its next element through calling the reorder() routine, that is, store_index[j] = store_index[j+1]. Then remain_number decreases by 1. Each pair of individuals selected has a chance (crossover_rate) to undergo the crossover operation. This process is repeated until remain_number < 2. To facilitate fast computation, store_index may be better defined as a linked list data type.

Listing 4.12 The ga_crossover() routine.

```
void ga_crossover(void)
{
    int idx_i,idx_j;
    int *store_index;
    int remain_number,kid1,kid2;
    double prob;

    store_index = (int *)calloc(ga_data.popu_size,sizeof(int));
```

```
        for (idx_i = 0; idx_i < ga_data.popu_size; idx_i++)
            store_index[idx_i] = idx_i;
    remain_number = ga_data.popu_size;

    /* begin crossover among population */
    for (idx_i = 0; idx_i < (ga_data.popu_size/2 + 1); idx_i++)
    {   /* two kids are chosen each time */
        if (remain_number >= 2)
                            /* at least two individuals remain unchosen */
        {
            idx_j = search(remain_number); /* find the first kid */
            kid1 = store_index[idx_j];     /* index to the first kid */
            remain_number--;      /* update number of remaining unchosen */
            reorder(store_index,remain_number,idx_j);
                            /* reorder the sign vector */
            idx_j = search(remain_number); /* find the second kid2
            kid2 = store_index[idx_j];     /* index to the second kid */
            remain_number--;     /* update number of remaining unchosen */
            reorder(store_index,remain_number,idx_j);
                            /* reorder the sign vector */
            prob = (rand()%1000)/1000.0;
            if (prob <= ga_data.crossover_rate)
                            /* probability for crossover */
            {
                if ((kid1 != ga_data.best_index) && (kid2 !=
                            ga_data.best_index))
                {   /* keep  the best */
                switch(ga_data.c_type)
                    {
                        case ONE_POINT_CROSSOVER:
                            onecross(kid1,kid2); break;
                        case UNIFORM_CROSSOVER:
                            unicross(kid1,kid2); break;
                        default:
                            twocross(kid1,kid2); break;
                    }
                }
            }
        }
    }
    free(store_index);
}

static int search (int si)
{
    int re;
    re = rand()%(si);
    return(re);
}

static void reorder (int *vec,int si,int ind)
{
    int i;
    if (ind<si)
        for (i=ind;i<si;i++)
                *(vec+i)=*(vec+i+1);
}
```

The `ga_mutation()` Routine

For a GA with binary representation, the mutation operation is generally performed by independently, randomly, uniformly flipping bits with a small probability. In the `ga_mutation()` routine, shown in Listing 4.13, two mutation methods are implemented. Which one to use depends on a "mutation according to bit position" flag, `mutation_flag`, which is read from the input file. When this flag is 0 (disabled), mutation is carried out in the normal way: mutation is done bit by bit with a fixed probability of mutation read in from the input file. When it is 1 (enabled), the probability of mutation m_b varies with the bit position in each variable.

The variation in mutation across each variable is an exponential function; that is, it is much more probable that the least significant bit will be mutated than it is that the most significant bit will be. It is implemented according to equation 4.1, where b is the bit position ($b = 0$ for the least significant bit, $b = 1$ for the next-to-least significant bit, etc.) and m_0 is the probability of mutation used when `mutation_flag = 0`.

$$m_b = m_0 \frac{1}{\sqrt{2\pi}} e^{-b^2/2} \qquad (4.1)$$

Note that the calculation is done across each variable. So, for a variable represented by 16 bits, the resulting probability of mutation is $m_0(1/2\pi)^{1/2}$, or about $(m_0)(0.40)$ for the least significant bit and about $(m_0)(0.40)exp(-7.5) = (m_0)(0.40)$ (0.00055) for the most significant bit. The variance for the quasi-Gaussian function can thus be seen to depend on the variables' dynamic range and how each variable is represented by the binary string.

This mutation by bit position can be seen to be similar in concept to the Gaussian mutation carried out in the evolutionary programming function optimization example and to the mutation scheme employed in evolutionary strategies, both described in Chapter 3. We therefore implement a hybrid GA/EP/ES algorithm with this mutation option. Listing 4.13 lists the `ga_mutation()` C source code, where `gau[idx_i]` records the bit-position–dependent probability for the *i*th bit, which is obtained by equation 4.1.

Listing 4.13 GA mutation operation C source code.

```
void ga_mutate (void)
{
    int idx_i,idx_j;
    double prob,rate_m;

    for (idx_j = 0; idx_j < ga_data.popu_size; idx_j++)
        if (idx_j != (ga_data.best_index))
            for (idx_i = 0; idx_i < ga_data.indi_length; idx_i++)
            {
```

```
                prob = (rand()%1000)/1000.0;
                if ((ga_data.mutation_flag == 1))
                    rate_m = ga_data.mutation_rate *
                        ga_data.gau[idx_i%(ga_data.bits_per_para)];
                else
                    rate_m = ga_data.mutation_rate;

            if (prob <= rate_m)
                if ((ga_data.population[idx_j][idx_i]) == 0)
                    ga_data.population[idx_j][idx_i] = 1;
                else
                    ga_data.population[idx_j][idx_i] = 0;
        }
    }
```

Generally, values of mutation rate within [0.001, 0.01] are recommended for the canonical binary genetic algorithm discussed in this section, especially when a fixed mutation rate is used. The mutation operation, generally speaking, has a disruptive impact on the population and therefore brings new information into the population. It facilitates exploration of the search space.

Running the GA Implementation

Now that we've looked at the individual components of the GA implementation, let's put them all together. To run the genetic algorithm implementation (the code for which is on the book's web site) requires the executable file ga.exe and an associated run file, for example, ga.run. To run the implementation from within the directory containing ga.exe and ga.run, at the system prompt type ga ga.run.

One way to present the genetic algorithm implementation is to examine and discuss the contents of a typical run file, as shown in Listing 4.14, that can be invoked with the executable file.

Listing 4.14 An example of a GA run file.

```
results.out
10
4
10000
16
20
0.75
0.005
0.02
0
2
1
```

The first entry, `results.out`, is the name of the data file where the results are stored. The next two numbers are the dimension of the problem (10) and the function type (4—Griewank). These inputs are related to the GA's working environment; that is, the function to be solved is the 10-dimensional generalized Griewank function. The results of the run will be stored in a file named `results.out`.

Following the environment inputs are numbers: the maximum number of generations (10,000), the number of bits per variable (16), the population size (20), the percent probability of crossover divided by 100 (0.75), the probability of mutation (0.005), the acceptable fitness values to which the problem is to be evolved (0.02), the "mutate according to bit position" flag (0), the crossover type (2), and the selection type (1).

The maximum number of generations is the maximum number of epochs, that is, the maximum number of times the problem will be evaluated for the fitness of all individuals in the population.

The number of bits per variable allows the user to set the resolution for each vector element; in this case, each element represents one function parameter. The trade-off here is that a relatively high number of bits provides the resolution needed to successfully adjust parameters on a complex fitness surface, but it also increases computational complexity significantly. This GA implementation provides a tool to investigate this question with a variety of datasets representing various problems.

The number of population members (20 in this case) can be varied according to the problem. A higher number allows a more thorough exploration of the problem domain, but increases computing time. Typically, the value should be set between 20 and 200, but values outside the range may be appropriate for relatively simple problems that involve relatively short individuals (< 20) or for highly complex problems that involve very large chromosomes (> 200).

The probability of crossover should be set between 60 and 80 percent for many problems. The straightforward two-point crossover operator (as described in Chapter 3) can be implemented, as can one-point and uniform crossover.

The next value (0.005 in the list) is the probability of mutation. Options for mutation implemented in this GA were explained previously. The value listed here is a sort of baseline value; it can be implemented in one of two ways. If not modified, however, the value represents the chance that mutation will occur determined bit by bit.

The next value, 0.02, is the fitness target for the performance of the "evolved" solution. The GA will terminate when this fitness level is achieved or when the maximum number of generations have been calculated, whichever occurs first. In either case, the results are written to the specified output file. In this implementation, this value is not used. We terminate the run only when the maximum number of generations is reached.

The next value (0) is the "mutation according to bit position" flag. The meaning of this flag was explained in the previous section.

The next-to-last value in the list (2) is the crossover type. The GA implementation allows the user to choose one of three kinds of crossover. If the crossover type is set to 0, one-point crossover is implemented. If it is set to 1, uniform crossover is implemented, and a value of 2 implements two-point crossover.

The last value in the list (1) is the selection type. The GA implementation allows the user to choose any of three kinds of selection mechanisms. If the selection type is set to 0, the roulette wheel selection operator is implemented; if it is set to 1, the binary tournament selection operator is implemented; and a value of 2 implements the ranking selection operator.

The output file lists the input parameters specified in the run file. It then lists the fitness value for each population member at the end of the run. Last, the parameter values for the population member with the highest fitness are listed.

It is important to experiment with the GA implementation. Be aware that because of its stochastic nature, a GA may converge to a different point each time it is run. Researchers rely on computational experimentation to compare the effectiveness of evolutionary algorithms. You are encouraged to use accepted statistical tests such as t-tests and Tukey's method when you are reporting your results.

You now know everything you need to know about running the GA implementation. We suggest you take the application for a trial run.

Particle Swarm Optimization Implementation

Now that we've reviewed the GA software, we discuss PSO implementation. The PSO implementation is essentially an asynchronous version of particle swarm optimization that uses global best and pbest (see Chapter 3). The basic particle swarm optimization discussed in the previous chapter is implemented first, then the implementation is expanded to provide the capability of running multi-PSOs, particularly co-evolutionary particle swarm optimization. We begin by looking at some programming issues.

Programming the PSO Implementation

In contrast to the implementation of the genetic algorithm discussed in the last section, the implementation of PSO is based on a state machine (SM) instead of a flowchart. Figure 4.2 shows the state machine of this PSO implementation. The arrow leading from one state to another state is called a transition. It describes how the SM transitions from state to state. The label of a transition describes the condition that triggers the transition.

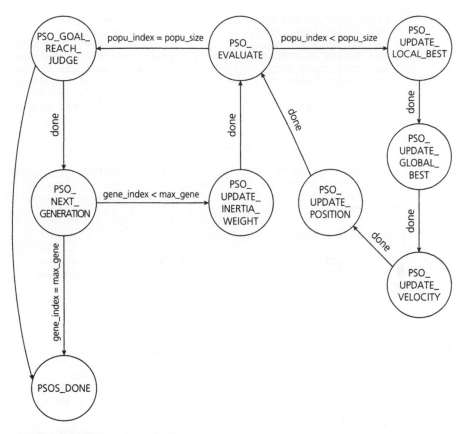

Figure 4.2   A state diagram of an asynchronous particle swarm optimization implementation.

As in the GA implementation, some new data types are defined initially. Listings 4.15 and 4.16 show these definitions.

Listing 4.15   Definition of some new data types in the PSO implementation.

```
typedef float      *P_FLOAT;
typedef P_FLOAT    FVECTOR;
typedef P_FLOAT    *FMATRIX;

/*****************************************/
/* Enumerations                         */
/*****************************************/
typedef enum PSO_State_Tag
{
    PSO_UPDATE_INERTIA_WEIGHT,    // Update inertia weight
    PSO_EVALUATE,                 // Evaluate particles
```

```
    PSO_UPDATE_GLOBAL_BEST,        // Update global best
    PSO_UPDATE_LOCAL_BEST,         // Update local best
    PSO_UPDATE_VELOCITY,           // Update particle's velocity
    PSO_UPDATE_POSITION,           // Update particle's position
    PSO_GOAL_REACH_JUDGE,          // Judge whether reach the goal
    PSO_NEXT_GENERATION,           // Move to the next generation
    PSOS_DONE,                     // Finish one cycle of PSOs
    NUM_PSO_STATES                 // Total number of PSO states
} PSO_State_Type;

typedef enum PSO_Initialize_Tag
{
    PSO_RANDOM_SYMMETRY_INITIALIZE,    // 0 :Symmetry Initialization
    PSO_RANDOM_ASYMMETRY_INITIALIZE,   // 1 :Asymmetry Initialization
    NUM_PSO_INITIALIZE                 // Number of initialization methods
} PSO_Initialize_Type;

typedef enum MINMAX_Tag
{
    MINIMIZATION,              // 0 :Minimization problem
    MAXIMIZATION               // 1 :Maximization problem
} MINMAX_Type;

typedef enum Evaluate_Function_Tag
{
    F6,                        // 0 :F6: min
    PARABOLIC,                 // 1 :Parabolic: min
    ROSENBROCK,                // 2 :Rosenbrock: min
    RASTRIGRIN,                // 3 :Rastrigrin: min
    GRIEWANK,                  // 4 :Griewank: min
    NUM_EVALUATE_FUNCTIONS     // Total number of evaluation functions
} Evaluate_Function_Type;


typedef enum Inertia_Weight_Update_Method_Tag
{
    CONSTANT_IW,         // 0 :Constant inertia weight
    LINEAR_IW,           // 1 :Linearly decreasing inertia weight
    NOISE_ADDITION_IW,   // 2 :Adding noise to the constant inertia weight
    NUM_IW_UPDATE_METHODS  // Number of inertia weight update methods
} IW_Update_Type;
```

Listing 4.16 Structure data type definitions for PSO.

```
/***************************************/
/* Structures                          */
/***************************************/
typedef struct PSO_Initialize_Range_Type_Tag
{
    float  left;
    float  right;
} PSO_Initialize_Range_Type;
```

```
typedef struct PSO_Environment_Type_Tag
{
  MINMAX_Type              opti_type;
  Evaluate_Function_Type   function_type;
  IW_Update_Type           iw_method;
  PSO_Initialize_Type      init_type;
  PSO_Initizlize_Range_Type  init_range;
  float                    max_velocity;
  float                    max_position;
  int                      max_generation;
  int                      boundary_flag;
  FVECTOR                  low_boundaries;
  FVECTOR                  up_boundaries;
} PSO_Environment_Type;

typedef struct PSO_Type_Tag          // PSO parameters
{
  PSO_Environment_Type     env_data;
  int                      popu_size;
  int                      dimension;
  float                    inertia_weight;
  float                    init_inertia_weight;
  int                      global_best_index;
  FVECTOR                  pbest_values;
  FMATRIX                  velocity_values;
  FMATRIX                  position_values;
  FMATRIX                  pbest_position_values;
  float                    eva_fun_value;
  int                      popu_index;
  int                      gene_index;

} PSO_Type;
```

In Listing 4.15 the enumeration data type PSO_State_Type defines all the states in the PSO state machine. There are nine states, with each state having a handling routine corresponding to it. The PSO_Initialize_Type defines the methods to initialize the population. There are two methods: symmetrical and asymmetrical initialization. The MINMAX_Type defines the types of optimization problems the PSO is going to solve: either a maximization problem or a minimization problem.

Evaluate_Function_Type defines the optimization functions to be solved as in the GA implementation. The IW_Update_Type defines methods to update the inertia weight dynamically. Three ways to deal with the inertia weight are implemented. The inertia weight can be kept constant, decreased linearly, or added as random noise through the course of the run.

In Listing 4.16 the struct data type PSO_Initialize_Range_Type defines the data range within which the initialization is performed. The PSO_Environment_Type defines a struct data type that includes parameters related to the PSO environment. Included are optimization type (opti_type), optimization function (`function_type`), inertia weight updating method (`iw_method`), PSO initialization method (`init_type`), PSO initialization range (`init_range`), maximum velocity allowed (`max_velocity`), maximum position allowed (`max_position`), maximum number of generations (`max_generation`), a flag telling whether there are boundaries for the parameters to be evolved (`boundary_flag`), and the upper and lower boundaries if the `boundary_flag` is TRUE (`low_boundaries` and `up_boundaries`).

The `PSO_Type` defines a `struct` data type that includes all PSO parameters. Included are PSO environment data (`env_data`), population size (`popu_size`), dimension of the problem or length of the individual (`dimension`), current inertia weight (`inertia_weight`), initial inertia weight (`init_inertia_weight`), index of the global best at the current generation (`global_best_index`), vector of pbest values (`pbest_values`), matrix of velocity values (`velocity_values`), matrix of position values (`position_values`), matrix of pbest position values (`pbest_position_values`), fitness value of the current individual of the current generation (`eva_fun_value`), population index (`popu_index`), and index of the current generation (`gene_index`).

A `PSO_Type` variable `pso`, shown below, is defined at the PSO module scope so it is unnecessary to pass the PSO-related parameters and variables from one routine to another within the PSO module.

```
static PSO_Type pso;
```

The `main()` Routine

The `main()` routine is shown in Listing 4.17. As in the GA implementation, it is kept as simple as possible to make the PSO module as independent as possible. In the `PSO_Start_Up()` routine, as shown in Listing 4.17, all the necessary parameters for running the PSO implementation are read from the input file, then the dynamic data storage variables are allocated memory space and initialized. In the `PSO_Clean_Up()` routine, the results are stored in an output file and the previously allocated memory space is de-allocated. The `PSO_Main_Loop()` routine is the core of the PSO implementation, where the state machine is run.

Listing 4.17 The PSO `main()` routine.

```
void main (int argc, char *argv[])
{
    if (argc>=2)
    {
        printf("Too many command line parameters");
        exit(1);
    }
    PSO_Start_Up();
    PSO_Main_Loop();
```

```
    PSO_Clean_Up();
}

void PSO_Start_Up (void)
{
    read_pso_parameters();
    allocate_pso_memory();          // allocate memory for particles
    pso_initialize();               // initialize particles
}

void PSO_Clean_Up (void)
{
    pso_store_results();            // output results
    free_pso_memory();              // free memory space of particles
}
```

The `PSO_Main_Loop()` Routine

Before running the `PSO_Main_Loop()` routine, as shown in Listing 4.18, a PSO module scope variable is defined as

```
static PSO_State_Type PSO_current_state;
```

This variable records the current state of the PSO state machine and is defined as `static` to prevent the state from being changed by an outside module accidentally. When running the state machine, the current state calls its handling routine through `pso_state_handler(PSO_current_state)`, where the state performs its action until a transition to another state occurs. The state machine keeps running until it reaches the state `PSOS_DONE`.

Listing 4.18 The `PSO_Main_Loop()` routine.

```
void PSO_Main_Loop (void)
{
    BOOLEAN running;
    running = TRUE;
    while (running)
    {
        if (PSO_current_state == PSOS_DONE)
            running = FALSE;
        pso_state_handler(PSO_current_state);
    }
}
```

State Handling Routines

The main part of the PSO state machine is its state handler, which is shown in Listing 4.19. The state handler routine called is based on the current PSO state.

For example, if the current state is PSO_EVALUATE, then the PSO_evaluate() handler routine, shown in Listing 4.20, is called. Within this routine, if the current population index is less than the population size, the evaluation function is called to evaluate the fitness of the current individual, and the state transitions to PSO_UPDATE_LOCAL_BEST; otherwise, the current state transitions to the state PSO_GOAL_REACH_JUDGE and the current population index is assigned the value of 0.

Listing 4.19 The PSO state handling routine.

```
static void pso_state_handler (int state_index)
{
    switch (state_index)
    {
        case PSO_UPDATE_INERTIA_WEIGHT:
          PSO_update_inertia_weight();      break;
        case PSO_EVALUATE:
          PSO_evaluate();                    break;
        case PSO_UPDATE_GLOBAL_BEST:
          PSO_update_global_best();          break;
        case PSO_UPDATE_LOCAL_BEST:
          PSO_update_local_best();           break;
        case PSO_UPDTAE_VELOCITY:
          PSO_update_velocity();             break;
        case PSO_UPDATE_POSITION:
          PSO_update_position();             break;
        case PSO_GOAL_REACH_JUDGE:
          PSO_goal_reach_judge();            break;
        case PSO_NEXT_GENERATION:
          PSO_next_generation();             break;
        case PSOS_DONE:
          PSOs_done();                       break;
        default:                             break;
    }
}
```

Listing 4.20 The PSO_evaluate() routine.

```
static void PSO_evaluate (void)
{
    if ((pso.popu_index) < (pso.popu_size))
    {
        evaluate_functions(pso.env_data.function_type);
        PSO_current_state = PSO_UPDATE_LOCAL_BEST;
    }
    else
    {
        PSO_current_state = PSO_GOAL_REACH_JUDGE;
        pso.popu_index = 0;
    }
}
```

Programming the Co-evolutionary PSO

In the previous section, we described the implementation of a basic PSO. In this section, we expand it to provide the capability of running multi-PSOs. As we know, evolutionary algorithms have been successfully applied to solve many optimization problems. They have also been used to solve optimization problems with constraints by converting the constrained problems into unconstrained problems, which are what the evolutionary algorithms are good at. The most commonly employed conversion method adds penalty functions to punish the infeasible individuals.

Another, potentially better, approach is to employ the augmented Lagrangian method to convert the constrained problem into min–max problems (Tahk and Sun 2000). Then two evolutionary algorithm populations are used to solve the min–max problems. One is used to solve the minimization problem, with the maximization problem treated as a fixed environment of the minimization problem; the other is used to solve the maximization problem, with the minimization problem treated as the fixed environment of the maximization problem. The only interaction between these two algorithms is the fitness evaluations; that is, each is treated as an environment of the other.

Procedure for Running the Co-PSO

The procedure for running the co-PSO is (Shi and Krohling 2002):

1. Initialize two PSOs.
2. Run the first PSO for `max_gen_1` generations.
3. Reevaluate the `pbest` values for the second PSO if it is not the first cycle.
4. Run the second PSO for `max_gen_2` generations.
5. Re-evaluate the `pbest` values for the first PSO.
6. Loop to step 2 until a termination condition is met.

Each member of the first population is a vector of variables (elements), the values of which we are trying to optimize, and each element is randomly initialized within the range given for that variable when the problem is stated. Each member of the second population represents a λ vector, each element of which is initialized in the range [0,1]. It is important to note that for both PSOs, the *function* that is evaluated is the augmented Lagrangian. The first PSO is run as a minimization problem, and the second as a maximization problem. The population sizes of the two populations do not have to be the same (but they may be).

After initialization, the first PSO is run for `max_gen_1` generations, as follows: The fitness of each population member vector of variables is evaluated with each λ vector in the second PSO population. The highest fitness (lowest function value) thus obtained among all of the member/λ combinations is defined as the fitness of that population member. Note that the λ values are fixed during this step; they are part of the "environment" within which the evaluation occurs.

In the first iteration, called a cycle, we then go to step 4 of the procedure. If it is not the first cycle, the pbest values for the second PSO population are recalculated.

In step 4, we run the second PSO for max_gen_2 generations. This time, we are optimizing with respect to the λ values in the second population. We evaluate the fitness of each population member vector of λ values with each vector of variables (population member) in the first population. The highest fitness (highest function value) thus obtained among all of the λ/member combinations is defined as the fitness of that λ population member. Note that all variable values are fixed during this step; they are part of the environment.

In step 5, the pbest values for the first PSO population are recalculated. This is the completion of one *cycle* of the procedure.

Benchmark Problems Selected for Implementation

Three benchmark-constrained optimization problems reported in (Michalewicz and Schoenauer 1996), (Tahk and Sun 2000) and (Shi and Krohling 2002) were selected for implementation in this book. The first optimization problem G1 consists of minimizing:

$$f(x) = 5x_1 + 5x_2 + 5x_3 + 5x_4 - 5\sum_{i=1}^{4} x_i^2 - \sum_{i=5}^{13} x_i$$

subject to

$$2x_1 + 2x_2 + x_{10} + x_{11} \leq 10$$
$$2x_1 + 2x_3 + x_{10} + x_{12} \leq 10$$
$$2x_2 + 2x_3 + x_{11} + x_{12} \leq 10$$
$$-8x_1 + x_{10} \leq 0$$
$$-8x_2 + x_{11} \leq 0$$
$$-8x_3 + x_{12} \leq 0$$
$$-2x_4 - x_5 + x_{10} \leq 0$$
$$-2x_6 - x_7 + x_{11} \leq 0$$
$$-2x_8 - x_9 + x_{12} \leq 0$$

where

$$0 \leq x_i \leq 1, \qquad i = 1, \ldots, 9$$
$$0 \leq x_i \leq 100, \quad i = 10, 11, 12$$
$$0 \leq x_i \leq 1, \qquad i = 13$$

The global minimum is known to be

$$x^* = (1,1,1,1,1,1,1,1,1,3,3,3,1)$$

with $f(x^*) = -15$.

The second optimization problem G7 consists of minimizing:

$$
\begin{aligned}
f(x) = {}& x_1^2 + x_2^2 + x_1 x_2 - 14x_1 - 16x_2 + (x_3 - 10)^2 \\
& + 4(x_4 - 5)^2 + (x_5 - 3)^2 + 2(x_6 - 1)^2 + 5x_7^2 \\
& + 7(x_8 - 11)^2 + 2(x_9 - 10)^2 + (x_{10} - 7)^2 + 45
\end{aligned}
$$

subject to

$$105 - 4x_1 - 5x_2 + 3x_7 - 9x_9 \geq 0$$
$$-3(x_1 - 2)^2 - 4(x_2 - 3)^2 - 2x_3^2 + 7x_4 + 120 \geq 0$$
$$-10x_1 + 8x_2 + 17x_7 - 2x_8 \geq 0$$
$$-x_1^2 - 2x(x_2 - 2)^2 + 2x_1 x_2 - 14x_5 + 6x_6 \geq 0$$
$$8x_1 - 2x_2 - 5x_9 + 2x_{10} + 12 \geq 0$$
$$-5x_1^2 - 8x_2 - (x_3 - 6)^2 + 2x_4 + 40 \geq 0$$
$$3x_1 - 6x_2 - 12(x_9 - 8)^2 + 7x_{10} \geq 0$$
$$-0.5(x_1 - 8)^2 - 2(x_2 - 4) - 3x_5^2 + x_6 + 30 \geq 0$$

where

$$-10 \leq x_i \leq 10, \quad i = 1, \ldots, 10$$

The global minimum is known to be

$$x^* = (2.171996, 2.363683, 8.773926, 5.095984$$
$$0.9906548, 1.430574, 1.321644, 9.828726$$
$$8.280092, 8.375927)$$

with $f(x^*) = 24.3062091$.

The last optimization problem G9 consists of minimizing:

$$f(x) = (x_1 - 10)^2 + 5(x_2 - 12)^2 + x_3^4 + 3(x_4 - 11)^2$$
$$+ 10x_5^6 + 7x_6^2 - 4x_6x_7 - 10x_6 - 8x_7$$

subject to

$$127 - 2x_1^2 - 3x_2^4 - x_3 - 4x_4^2 - 5x_5 \geq 0$$
$$282 - 7x_1 - 3x_2 - 10x_3^2 - x_4 + x_5 \geq 0$$
$$196 - 23x_1 - x_2^2 - 6x_6^2 + 8x_7 \geq 0$$
$$-4x_1^2 - x_2^2 + 3x_1x_2 - 2x_3^2 - 5x_6 + 11x_7 \geq 0$$

where

$$-10 \leq x_i \leq 10; \quad i = 1, \ldots, 7$$

The global minimum is known to be

$$x^* = (2.330499, 1.951372, -0.4775414, 4.365726,$$
$$-0.6244870, 1.038131, 1.594227)$$

with $f(x^*) = 680.6300573$.

For all three benchmark problems, the population sizes can be set to 40 and 30, respectively. The maximum number of generations for each PSO of one cycle is generally chosen to be 10. To test the convergence speed of the co-evolutionary PSO, three maximum numbers of cycles can be tested, such as 40, 80, and 120. The particles are randomly initialized within the boundaries for each run. The inertia weight of each PSO can be linearly decreased over the course of each run, starting from 0.9 and ending at 0.4. Each different parameter setting can be tested by running multiple times, such as 50 times. Each run is terminated only when the maximum number of cycles has been reached.

Modification of Data Types and Routines of PSO Implementation

To implement the co-evolutionary PSO, the PSO implementation in the previous section is expanded so that multi-PSOs can co-exist. New states have been included into the enumeration data type PSO_State_Type since there is now transition between different PSOs. The new PSO_State_Type is defined as that shown in Listing 4.21.

Listing 4.21 The PSO_State_Type for multi-PSOs.

```
typedef enum PSO_State_Tag
{
    PSO_UPDATE_INERTIA_WEIGHT,    // Update inertia weight
    PSO_EVALUATE,                 // Evaluate particles
```

```
    PSO_UPDATE_GLOBAL_BEST,          // Update global best
    PSO_UPDATE_LOCAL_BEST,           // Update local best
    PSO_UPDATE_VELOCITY,             // Update particle's velocity
    PSO_UPDATE_POSITION,             // Update particle's position
    PSO_GOAL_REACH_JUDGE,            // Judge whether reach the goal
    PSO_NEXT_GENERATION,             // Move to the next generation
    PSO_UPDATE_PBEST_EACH_CYCLE,     // Update pbest each cycle for co-pso
                                     // due to the environment changed
    PSO_NEXT_PSO,            // Move to the next PSO in the same cycle or
                            // the first pso in the next cycle
    PSOS_DONE,                       // Finish one cycle of PSOs
    NUM_PSO_STATES                   // Total number of PSO states
} PSO_State_Type;
```

The new added states are `PSO_UPDATE_PBEST_EACH_CYCLE` and `PSO_NEXT_PSO`. The state `PSO_UPDATE_PBEST_EACH_CYCLE` is used to adjust the `pbest` fitness value since the environment in which the `pbest` positions are evaluated was changed when the multi-PSO's algorithm was transitioned from one PSO to the other PSO; the state `PSO_NEXT_PSO` is used to start the new PSO evaluation. The state machine is shown in Figure 4.3.

The `PSO_Type pso` has also been replaced by

```
static int NUM_PSO;
static PSO_Type *psos;
```

where `NUM_PSO` is read in from the input file at the beginning and tells how many PSOs co-exist in the implementation. The variable `psos` is a `PSO_Type` pointer pointing to the array of the `NUM_PSO` number of PSOs.

The `PSO_Main_Loop()` also has to be modified to allow multi-PSOs to coexist, as shown in Listing 4.22.

Listing 4.22 The `PSO_Main_Loop()` routine in multi-PSOs.

```
void PSO_Main_Loop (void)
  {
    BOOLEAN running;
    while ((pso_cycle_index++) < total_cycle_of_PSOs)
    {
        running = TRUE;
        while (running)
        {
            if (PSO_current_state == PSOS_DONE)
                running = FALSE;
            pso_state_handler(PSO_current_state);
        }
    }
  }
```

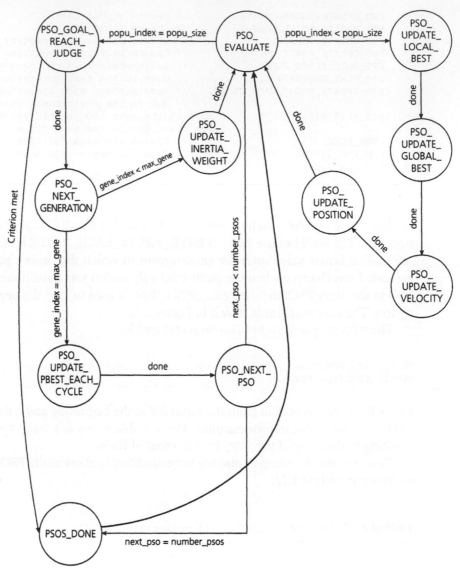

Figure 4.3 State diagram of asynchronous version of multi-PSOs.

In Listing 4.22 the integer variable `total_cycle_of_PSOs` keeps track of the number of cycles the multi-PSOs have run, with each running for the maximum number of generations specified in its corresponding `PSO_Type` variable; the integer `pso_cycle_index` is the index of the PSO that is running. The variable `total_cycle_of_PSOs` is specified in an input file and is read in at the beginning of the run.

The `Evaluate_Function_Type` has also been expanded to include constrained problems, and it is shown in Listing 4.23. Each constrained problem is associated with two evaluation functions corresponding to the two PSOs in the co-evolutionary PSO algorithms, respectively. For example, for the G1-constrained problem, `G1_MIN` is the case index corresponding to the evaluation function of the PSO that is responsible for the minimum part of the min–max problem transformed from the G1 problem; `G1_MAX` is that for the maximum part of the min–max problem.

Listing 4.23 Expanded `Evaluate_Function_Type`.

```
typedef enum Evaluate_Function_Tag
{
    G1_MIN,                  //  0: G1, min part
    G1_MAX,                  //  1: G1, max part
    G7_MIN,                  //  2: G7, min part
    G7_MAX,                  //  3: G7, max part
    G9_MIN,                  //  4: G9, min part
    G9_MAX,                  //  5: G9, max part
    F6,                      //  6: F6: min
    PARABOLIC,               //  7: Parabolic: min
    ROSENBROCK,              //  8: Rosenbrock: min
    RASTRIGRIN,              //  9: Rastrigrin: min
    GRIEWANK,                // 10: Griewank: min
    NUM_EVALUATE_FUNCTIONS   // Total number of evaluation functions
} Evaluate_Function_Type;
```

The `pso_state_handler(int state_index)` also has to be modified to include new cases for handling the new states, which is shown in Listing 4.24.

Listing 4.24 Modified `pso_state_handler`.

```
static void pso_state_handler (int state_index)
{
    switch (state_index)
    {
        case PSO_UPDATE_INERTIA_WEIGHT:
          PSO_update_inertia_weight();    break;
        case PSO_EVALUATE:
          PSO_evaluate();                 break;
        case PSO_UPDATE_GLOBAL_BEST:
          PSO_update_global_best();       break;
        case PSO_UPDATE_LOCAL_BEST:
          PSO_update_local_best();        break;
        case PSO_UPDATE_VELOCITY:
          PSO_update_velocity();          break;
        case PSO_UPDATE_POSITION:
          PSO_update_position();          break;
```

```
        case PSO_GOAL_REACH_JUDGE:
          PSO_goal_reach_judge();        break;
        case PSO_NEXT_GENERATION:
          PSO_next_generation();         break;
        case PSO_UPDATE_PBEST_EACH_CYCLE:
          PSO_update_pbest_each_cycle(); break;
        case PSO_NEXT_PSO:
          PSO_next_pso();                break;
        case PSOS_DONE:
          PSOs_done();                   break;
        default:                         break;
    }
}
```

The PSO_EVALUATE State

As in the single PSO implementation, if all the individuals have been evaluated, the state transitions to state PSO_GOAL_REACH_JUDGE, and the index of population is set to 0. Otherwise, the current individual is evaluated and the state transitions to state PSO_UPDATE_LOCAL_BEST since this is an asynchronous version of multi-PSO implementation. For a synchronous version of PSO implementation, the state stays at its current state PSO_EVALUATE until all the individuals have been evaluated, at which time it transitions to state PSO_UPDATE_LOCAL_BEST. For the co-evolutionary PSO, each PSO passes its function type to the evaluate_functions() routine to call its corresponding function to evaluate the PSO's performance. For example, if the problem to be solved is G7, one PSO for solving the minimization problem calls G7_MIN(), and the other PSO for solving the maximization problem calls G7_MAX(). The evaluate_functions() routine is shown in Listing 4.25.

Listing 4.25 The evaluate_functions() routine.

```
static void PSO_evaluate (void)
{
    if ((psos[cur_pso].popu_index) < (psos[cur_pso].popu_size))
    {
        evaluate_functions(psos[cur_pso].env_data.function_type);
        PSO_current_state = PSO_UPDATE_LOCAL_BEST;
    }
    else
    {
        PSO_current_state = PSO_GOAL_REACH_JUDGE;
        psos[cur_pso].popu_index = 0;
    }
}

static void evaluate_functions (int fun_type)
{
```

```
        switch (fun_type)
        {
            case G1_MIN:
                g1_min();      break;
            case G1_MAX:
                g1_max();      break;
            case G7_MIN:
                g7_min();      break;
            case G7_MAX:
                g7_max();      break;
            case G9_MIN:
                g9_min();      break;
            case G9_MAX:
                g9_max();      break;
            case F6:
                f6();          break;
            case PARABOLIC:
                parabolic();   break;
            case ROSENBROCK:
                rosenbrock();  break;
            case RASTRIGRIN:
                rastrigrin();  break;
            case GRIEWANK:
                griewank();    break;
            default:           break;
        }
    }
```

The PSO_UPDATE_LOCAL_BEST State

In this state, the handler routine, as shown in Listing 4.26, first checks whether it's a minimization or a maximization problem according to the current PSO's optimization type so that the implementation can be applied to solve both the minimization and maximization problems. If the implementation is run as a co-evolutionary PSO, one PSO is run to solve the minimization problem; the other is run to solve the maximization problem.

If the optimization type of the current PSO is minimization, it first checks whether it is the first generation of the first cycle. If it is, it assigns 0 as the global best index and the evaluation value as the current individual's pbest value. It then checks whether the current individual's evaluation value is less than its pbest value. If it is, the current position values are assigned to pbest position values, and the pbest value is assigned to be the evaluation value of the current individual's evaluation value. Finally, the state transitions to state PSO_UPDATE_GLOBAL_BEST.

Listing 4.26 The PSO_UPDATE_LOCAL_BEST state handler routine.

```
static void PSO_update_local_best (void)
{
    int idx_i;
```

```
            if ((psos[cur_pso].env_data.opti_type) == MINIMIZATION)
            {   // minimization problem
                if ((pso_cycle_index == 1) && ((psos[cur_pso].gene_index) == 0))
                {
                    psos[cur_pso].global_best_index = 0;
                    psos[cur_pso].pbest_values[psos[cur_pso].popu_index] =
                            psos[cur_pso].eva_fun_value;
                }
                if ((psos[cur_pso].eva_fun_value) <
                        (psos[cur_pso].pbest_values[psos[cur_pso].popu_index]))
                {
                    psos[cur_pso].pbest_values[psos[cur_pso].popu_index] =
                            psos[cur_pso].eva_fun_value;
                    for (idx_i = 0; idx_i < (psos[cur_pso].dimension) ;idx_i++)
                    {
(psos[cur_pso].pbest_position_values[psos[cur_pso].popu_index][idx_i]) =
(psos[cur_pso].position_values[psos[cur_pso].popu_index] [idx_i]);
                    }
                }
            }
            else
            {   // maximization problem
                if ((pso_cycle_index == 1) && ((psos[cur_pso].gene_index) == 0))
                {
                    psos[cur_pso].global_best_index = 0;
                    psos[cur_pso].pbest_values[psos[cur_pso].popu_index] =
                            psos[cur_pso].eva_fun_value;
                }
                if ((psos[cur_pso].eva_fun_value) >
                        (psos[cur_pso].pbest_values[psos[cur_pso].popu_index]))
                {
                        psos[cur_pso].pbest_values[psos[cur_pso].popu_index] =
                                psos[cur_pso].eva_fun_value;
                        for (idx_i = 0; idx_i < (psos[cur_pso].dimension) ;idx_i++)
                        {
(psos[cur_pso].pbest_position_values[psos[cur_pso].popu_index][idx_i])=
(psos[cur_pso].position_values[psos[cur_pso].popu_index][idx_i]);
                        }
                }

            }
            PSO_current_state = PSO_UPDATE_GLOBAL_BEST;
        }
```

The PSO_UPDATE_GLOBAL_BEST State

Similar to the state PSO_UPDATE_LOCAL_BEST, this state first checks the optimization type, then updates the global best index if the current individual of the current PSO performs better than the global best. The state handler routine is shown in Listing 4.27.

Listing 4.27 The `PSO_UPDATE_GLOBAL_BEST` state handler routine.

```
static void PSO_update_global_best (void)
{
   if ((psos[cur_pso].env_data.opti_type) == MINIMIZATION)
   {   // minimization problem
      if ((psos[cur_pso].eva_fun_value) <
          (psos[cur_pso].pbest_values[psos[cur_pso].global_best_index]))
      {
         psos[cur_pso].global_best_index  =  psos[cur_pso].popu_index;
      }
   }
   else
   {   // maximization problem
      if ((psos[cur_pso].eva_fun_value) >
          (psos[cur_pso].pbest_values[psos[cur_pso].global_best_index]))
      {
         psos[cur_pso].global_best_index  =  psos[cur_pso].popu_index;
      }
   }
   PSO_current_state =  PSO_UPDATE_VELOCITY;
}
```

The `PSO_UPDATE_VELOCITY` State

In this state, the velocity values of the current individual of the current PSO are updated according to equations 3.5 and 3.6 (in Chapter 3) and are checked with the maximum velocity to keep the velocity values within the boundary. The state is then transitioned to state `PSO_UPDATE_POSITION`.

Listing 4.28 The `PSO_UPDATE_VELOCITY` state handler routine.

```
static void PSO_update_velocity (void)
{
   int idx_i;
   for (idx_i = 0; idx_i < (psos[cur_pso].dimension) ;idx_i++)
   {
       psos[cur_pso].velocity_values[psos[cur_pso].popu_index][idx_i] =
             psos[cur_pso].inertia_weight) *
(psos[cur_pso].velocity_values[psos[cur_pso].popu_index][idx_i]) +
             2*(rand()/32767.0) *
(psos[cur_pso].pbest_position_values[psos[cur_pso]. popu_index][idx_i] -
 psos[cur_pso].position_values[psos[cur_pso].popu_index][idx_i]) +
             2*(rand()/32767.0) *
(psos[cur_pso].pbest_position_values[psos[cur_pso].global_best_index]
[idx_i] - psos[cur_pso].position_values[psos[cur_pso].popu_index][idx_i]);
       if ((psos[cur_pso].velocity_values[psos[cur_pso].popu_index]
             [idx_i]) > (psos[cur_pso].env_data.max_velocity))
       {
             psos[cur_pso].velocity_values[psos[cur_pso].popu_index]
                  [idx_i] = psos[cur_pso].env_data.max_velocity;
       }
```

```
        else if ((psos[cur_pso].velocity_values[psos[cur_pso].popu_index]
                [idx_i]) < (-(psos[cur_pso].env_data.max_velocity)))
        {
         psos[cur_pso].velocity_values[psos[cur_pso].popu_index][idx_i] =
                -(psos[cur_pso].env_data.max_velocity);
            }
        }
    PSO_current_state = PSO_UPDATE_POSITION;
}
```

The PSO_UPDATE_POSITION State

As in the previous state, the position values are updated according to equations 3.5 and 3.6. The position values are then checked to see whether they are within the boundaries. If they exceed a boundary, they are assigned to the boundary value plus a random value to force them to be within the boundary. The state transitions back to the state PSO_EVALUATE to complete the remainder of the PSO operations for one individual. The index of the population is increased by 1. The state handler routine is shown in Listing 4.29.

Listing 4.29 The PSO_UPDATE_POSITION state handler routine.

```
static void PSO_update_position (void)
{
    int idx_i;
    for (idx_i = 0; idx_i < (psos[cur_pso].dimension) ;idx_i++)
    {
        psos[cur_pso].position_values[psos[cur_pso].popu_index][idx_i] +=
            psos[cur_pso].velocity_values[psos[cur_pso].popu_index][idx_i];
        if (psos[cur_pso].env_data.boundary_flag)
        {
            if ((psos[cur_pso].position_values[psos[cur_pso].popu_index]
                    [idx_i]) < (psos[cur_pso].env_data.low_boundaries[idx_i]))
            {
             psos[cur_pso].position_values[psos[cur_pso].popu_index][idx_i] =
                psos[cur_pso].env_data.low_boundaries[idx_i] +
                    ((psos[cur_pso].env_data.up_boundaries[idx_i] -
psos[cur_pso].env_data.low_boundaries[idx_i]) * rand()/(2 * 32767.0));
            }
            else if ((psos[cur_pso].position_values[psos[cur_pso].popu_index]
                    [idx_i]) > (psos[cur_pso].env_data.up_boundaries[idx_i]))
            {
             psos[cur_pso].position_values[psos[cur_pso].popu_index][idx_i] =
                psos[cur_pso].env_data.up_boundaries[idx_i] -
                    ((psos[cur_pso].env_data.up_boundaries[idx_i] -
psos[cur_pso].env_data.low_boundaries[idx_i]) * rand()/(2 * 32767.0));
            }
        }
    }
```

```
    PSO_current_state =  PSO_EVALUATE;
    psos[cur_pso].popu_index)++;
}
```

The `PSO_GOAL_REACH_JUDGE` State

In this state, all the criteria are checked. If the termination criteria are satisfied, the state transitions to state `PSOS_DONE`; otherwise, it transitions to state `PSO_NEXT_GENERATION`. Since we have not implemented criterion checking in this implementation, it transitions to state `PSO_NEXT_GENERATION` unconditionally. The state handler routine is shown in Listing 4.30.

Listing 4.30 The `PSO_GOAL_REACH_JUDGE` state handler routine.

```
static void PSO_goal_reach_judge (void)
{
    PSO_current_state = PSO_NEXT_GENERATION;
}
```

The `PSO_NEXT_GENERATION` State

In this state, the handler routine, as shown in Listing 4.31, first checks whether the generation index of the current PSO has reached its maximum number of generations. If it hasn't, the generation index increases by 1 to start the next generation of the current PSO, and the state transitions to state `PSO_UPDATE_INERTIA_WEIGHT`. Otherwise, it moves to the next PSO by increasing the PSO's index by 1. If all the PSOs have completed their runs within this cycle, the PSO's index is assigned to 0 to start from the first PSO for the next cycle. The state transitions to state `PSO_UPDATE_PBEST_EACH_CYCLE`.

Listing 4.31 The `PSO_NEXT_GENERATION` state handler routine.

```
static void PSO_next_generation (void)
{
    if ((++(psos[cur_pso].gene_index)) <
            (psos[cur_pso].env_data.max_generation))
    { // next generation of the same population of PSO
        PSO_current_state = PSO_UPDATE_INERTIA_WEIGHT;
    }
    else
    {
        if ((++cur_pso) >= NUM_PSO)
```

```
    {   // end of the cycle
        cur_pso = 0;              // move to the first pso
    }
    PSO_current_state = PSO_UPDATE_PBEST_EACH_CYCLE;
                                  // move to the next state
    psos[cur_pso].popu_index = 0;
  }
}
```

The `PSO_UPDATE_INERTIA_WEIGHT` State

In this state, the current PSO updates its inertia weight according to its inertia weight updating method. The state transitions to the state `PSO_EVALUATE`. The index of the population is set to 0 to start from the first individual. The state handler routine is shown in Listing 4.32.

Listing 4.32 The `PSO_UPDATE_INERTIA_WEIGHT` state handler routine.

```
static void PSO_update_inertia_weight (void)
{
    iw_update_methods(psos[cur_pso].env_data.iw_method);
    PSO_current_state = PSO_EVALUATE;   // move to the next state
    psos[cur_pso].popu_index = 0;       // start with the first particle

}
```

The `PSO_UPDATE_PBEST_EACH_CYCLE` State

In this state, if the `PSO_UPDATE_PBEST_EACH_CYCLE_FLAG` flag is disabled, it transitions to the state `PSO_NEXT_PSO` by doing nothing. If the `PSO_UPDATE_PBEST_EACH_CYCLE_FLAG` is enabled, it calls the evaluation function to evaluate the current individual's `pbest` position. This state is maintained until all the individuals' `pbest` positions have been reevaluated. The reason to do this is that when a new PSO is running, the environment of the new PSO may have been changed after the last time it was run. The `pbest` values don't reflect the true values within the current environment. For example, in the co-evolutionary PSO, evaluating the current PSO will treat the other PSO's parameters as fixed values (environment), which have been changed since the last time the current PSO was run. The state handler routine is shown in Listing 4.33.

Listing 4.33 The `PSO_UPDATE_PBEST_EACH_CYCLE` state handler routine.

```
static void PSO_update_pbest_each_cycle (void)
{
    if (PSO_UPDATE_PBEST_EACH_CYCLE_FLAG)
```

```
    {
        pso_update_pbest_each_cycle_pending = TRUE;
        if ((psos[cur_pso].popu_index) < (psos[cur_pso].popu_size))
        {
            evaluate_functions(psos[cur_pso].env_data.function_type);
            psos[cur_pso].pbest_values[psos[cur_pso].popu_index] =
                psos[cur_pso].eva_fun_value;
            psos[cur_pso].popu_index++;
        }
        else      // done with evaluation, move to the next state
        {
            PSO_current_state =  PSO_NEXT_PSO;
            pso_update_pbest_each_cycle_pending = FALSE;
        }
    }
    else
    {
        PSO_current_state =  PSO_NEXT_PSO;
    }
}
```

The PSO_NEXT_PSO State

In this state, the handler routine, as shown in Listing 4.34, first checks whether all PSOs have been run in this cycle. If they have, the state transitions to state PSOS_DONE to end the current cycle. Otherwise, the state transitions to state PSO_EVALUATE to start running the new PSO.

Listing 4.34 The PSO_NEXT_PSO state handler routine.

```
static void PSO_next_pso (void)
{
    if (cur_pso > 0)
       PSO_current_state = PSO_EVALUATE;
    else
       PSO_current_state = PSOS_DONE;         // end of the cycle
    psos[cur_pso].popu_index = 0;             // start with the first particle
    psos[cur_pso].gene_index = 0;             // start with the first particle
}
```

The PSOS_DONE State

In this handler routine, as shown in Listing 4.35, the postprocessing is performed. For example, the results for this cycle can be saved to an output file for later view. Here we simply transition the state to PSO_EVALUATE, which makes the first PSO start with the state PSO_EVALUATE if the maximum number of cycles has not been reached, as shown in the PSO_Main_Loop() routine.

Listing 4.35 The PSOS_DONE state handler routine.

```
Static void PSOs_done (void)
{
    PSO_current_state = PSO_EVALUATE;
}
```

Running the PSO Implementation

Running the particle swarm optimization implementation requires the executable file psos.exe and an input file psos.run. To run the implementation from within the directory containing psos.exe and psos.run, at the system prompt type psos psos.run.

The parameters required for running psos are read in from the input file psos.run. One way to demonstrate how to run the PSO implementation is to present and discuss the contents of a run file, as shown in Listing 4.36, that can be invoked with the executable.

Listing 4.36 An example of a multi-PSOs run file.

```
2
1
300

0
6
1
1
0.0
50.0
10
100
100
30
13
0.9
1
0      1.0
0      1.0
0      1.0
0      1.0
0      1.0
0      1.0
0      1.0
0      1.0
0      1.0
0.0    100.0
0.0    100.0
0.0    100.0
0.0    1.0
```

```
1
7
1
1
0.0
1.0
0.5
1
70
20
9
0.9
1
0.0      1.0
0.0      1.0
0.0      1.0
0.0      1.0
0.0      1.0
0.0      1.0
0.0      1.0
0.0      1.0
0.0      1.0
```

The first entry (2) specifies that two PSOs are included in this run. If it is 1, only one PSO will be run. Any number of PSOs can be specified here to make multi-PSOs co-exist. The next number (1) is the `pso_update_pbest_each_cycle_flag` flag. When it is enabled, it means that before starting to run the next PSO, its `pbest` positions will be re-evaluated first, as in the co-evolutionary PSO algorithm discussed previously. Following this is the number that specifies the total number of cycles to run the PSOs (300), which means the PSOs will be run for 300 cycles. These three inputs relate to all PSOs (here two PSOs). Following them are inputs specifying parameters for each PSO, starting with the first PSO, then the next, until all the PSOs have been specified.

The fourth to fifteenth inputs are numbers for the first PSO: the optimization type (0—minimization), the function type (0—(G1_MIN), the inertia weight update method (1—linearly decreasing), the initialization type (1—asymmetry), left initialization range (0.0), right initialization range (50.0), maximum velocity (10.0), maximum position (100.0), maximum number of generations for each cycle (100), the population size (30), the dimension of the individual (13), and the initial inertia weight (0.9).

The next value (in the list) is the boundary flag (1). If it is disabled (0), it means no boundary values are required to be read from the input file. It is then the end of the input for the first PSO. If it is enabled (1) as in the list, then the boundaries must be provided in the input file. The first line after the boundary flag specifies the upper and lower boundary values for the first parameter to be evolved, followed by the second, and so on. Since the dimension in this example is 13, a total 13 lines of boundaries values must be provided.

Following the numbers for the first PSO are the numbers for the second PSO. All of the numbers have similar meanings to those for the first PSO, so we don't repeat the explanation here. Three points, however, should be noted. First, the optimization type is 1 (maximization problem) instead of 0 (minimization problem) and the corresponding function type is 1 (G1_MAX) instead of 0 (G1_MIN). Through this kind of specification, the two PSOs work as two swarms in a co-evolutionary PSO algorithm. Second, the number of dimensions (9) corresponds to the number of constraints. Third, the upper and lower boundaries for all of the parameters to be evolved are the same (0.0, 1.0) since they are the Lagrangian multipliers.

Summary

In this chapter, we first discuss the common issues related to the implementation of evolutionary algorithms. These issues include chromosome representation methods, learning strategies, programming strategies, and memory handling.

We then present two implementations of evolutionary computation: genetic algorithm implementation and a particle swarm optimization implementation. The genetic algorithm implementation is basically a "plain vanilla" genetic algorithm. The particle swarm optimization is implemented to be able to run either a single PSO or multi-PSOs simultaneously. An implementation of co-evolutionary PSO is described that solves min–max problems.

The genetic algorithm is implemented based on flowchart programming strategy, and the particle swarm optimization is implemented based on the finite state machine programming strategy. The strength and weakness of each strategy, therefore, are illustrated through the two implementations.

Five benchmark functions are included with both the GA implementation and the PSO implementation. Also, additional constrained optimization problems are included for the (co-evolutionary) PSO implementation.

Finally, how to run the implementations is specified in detail. Remember that output (results) files are provided on the book's Internet site; they were obtained by the authors using the executable and ancillary files provided. You may want to rename these output files, or move them to another directory, so that you can compare your results with the authors'. If you forget to do that, just go back to the Internet site and download them again.

Exercises

1. In the implementation of mutation operator, a "mutation according to bit position" flag is used to tell whether or not a mutation by bit position is implemented.

Define an enumeration data type to replace the flag and make corresponding changes in the implementation of the mutation operator.

2. Draw a state machine diagram for the GA implementation.

3. Draw a flowchart for the implementation of PSO.

4. Draw a state diagram for the synchronous version of PSO and compare it with the asynchronous version.

5. Five benchmark functions are identified in Table 4.2. Identify an additional benchmark function appropriate for evolutionary algorithms. Justify your choice. Modify the source code for the GA to implement this benchmark function so that it becomes an additional choice for the user.

6. Add the capability for specifying a termination criterion (acceptable error, for example) to the GA source code.

7. Implement the benchmark function you identified in exercise 5 into the PSO source code.

8. Run the GA implementation, optimizing the Griewank function. Try two different crossover types and two different selection types (four combinations of parameters). For each combination of parameters, how many total generations are required to achieve a fitness of -1.3 or better? Turn in and discuss your results. Based on your results, which combination of parameters would you select?

9. Run the PSO implementation as a single swarm, optimizing the F6 function. Note that the run file example in Listing 4.36 is for two swarms, so make sure you have an appropriate run file for a single swarm. Try two population sizes. Turn in and discuss your results.

10. Run the PSO implementation using two swarms to optimize the G1 function. Try two different population sizes for each of the two swarms (four combinations total). Turn in and discuss your results.

chapter
five

Neural Network Concepts and Paradigms

In the previous two chapters, we reviewed concepts, paradigms, and implementations of evolutionary computation. Chapters 3 and 4 provide a foundation on which we build our computational intelligence structure. Now we examine the second main component of computational intelligence, artificial neural networks.

Building intelligent systems that can model human behavior has captured the attention of the world for decades. So it is not surprising that a technology such as neural networks has generated great interest. This chapter first discusses the history of neural networks. It next provides an evolutionary introduction to neural networks beginning with the key elements and terminology of neural networks and then developing the topologies, adaptation methods, and recall dynamics from this infrastructure.

The perspective taken in this chapter is largely that of an engineer or computer scientist, emphasizing the application potential of neural networks and drawing comparisons with other techniques that have similar motivations. As such, we rely on mathematics in some of the discussions to make points more precisely.

The chapter includes a review of what neural networks are and why they are so appealing. We introduce a typical neural network to illustrate several key features. Using this network as a reference, we describe fundamental elements of a neural network such as input and output patterns, processing elements, connections, and activation calculations, and then we describe neural network topologies, adaptation algorithms, and recall dynamics. Finally, we present a comparison of neural networks and similar non-neural information processing methods. Let's get started by traveling back to the roots of neural networks and looking at their history.　　■

Neural Network History

As is the case with the other history sections in this book, the focus is on people rather than just on theory or technology. Again, the selection of individuals is somewhat arbitrary because the intent is to provide a broad sample, rather than an exhaustive list, of people who contributed to current technology. We mention some well-known researchers only briefly and omit others. The fact that someone is discussed only briefly, or even omitted, is not meant to reflect the authors' opinion of that person's contribution. We discuss the selected people and their contributions roughly in chronological order.

We address neural network history first by examining how neural networks got their name. Then we discuss the history of neural network development in five time segments, which we call *ages*. The first age begins at the time of William James, just over a century ago (1890). This is called the Age of Camelot. It ends in 1969 with the publication of Minsky and Papert's book on perceptrons. Next is the Dark Age, beginning in 1969 and ending in 1982 with Hopfield's landmark paper on neural networks and physical systems. The third age, the Renaissance, begins with Hopfield's paper and ends with the publication of *Parallel Distributed Processing, Volumes 1 and 2*, by Rumelhart and McClelland, in 1986. The fourth age, called the Age of Neoconnectionism after a review article on neural nets and artificial intelligence (Cowan and Sharp 1988), runs from 1987 until 1998. The final age, the Age of Computational Intelligence, runs from the second IEEE World Congress on Computational Intelligence in 1998 until the present.

Where Did Neural Networks Get Their Name?

If artificial neural networks are so different from biological ones, why are they even called *neural networks* instead of something else? The answer is that the background and training of the people who first developed useful neural network implementations were generally in the biological, physiological, and psychological areas rather than in engineering and computer science.

One of the most important publications that opened up neural network analysis by presenting it in a useful and clear way was a three-volume set of books entitled *Parallel Distributed Processing* (Rumelhart and McClelland 1986; McClelland and Rumelhart 1986; McClelland and Rumelhart 1988). The chapters in the first two volumes were authored by members of the interdisciplinary Parallel Distributed Processing (PDP) research group, who were from a variety of educational institutions. Several members of the PDP research group are cognitive scientists. Others are psychologists. Computer scientists are definitely in the minority, and judging from the professional titles and affiliations of the PDP authors, none is an engineer.

Had the concept of massively parallel processing initially been developed and made practical by electrical or computer engineers, we could be using "massively parallel adaptive filter" implementations instead of neural network implementations, or they might be called something that has no reference to the word *neural*. Neural networks do have technical roots in the fields of analog computing and signal processing that date back five or six decades and that rival in importance their roots in biology and cognitive science. This engineering heritage is reviewed in this section.

Much of the neural network effort in biology, cognitive science, and related fields resulted from efforts to explain experimental results and observations in behavior and in brain construction. Why should engineers and computer scientists care about experimental results in brain research and cognitive science? For one thing, as Anderson and Rosenfeld (1988) point out, if we can find out what kind of "wetware" runs well in our brains, we may gain insight into what kind of software to write for neural network applications. In other words, cognitive scientists and psychologists may provide some important information for reverse-engineering artificial neural network software.

The Age of Camelot

We begin our look at neural network history in the Age of Camelot with a person considered by many to be the greatest American psychologist who ever lived, William James. James also taught, and thoroughly understood, physiology. It has been over a century since James published his *Principles of Psychology,* and its condensed version *Psychology (Briefer Course)* (James 1890).

James was the first to publish a number of facts related to brain structure and function. He first stated, for example, some of the basic principles of correlational learning and associative memory. In stating what he called his Elementary Principle, James (1890) wrote: "Let us then assume as the basis of all our subsequent reasoning this law: when two elementary brain processes have been active together or in immediate succession, one of them, on re-occurring, tends to propagate its excitement into the other." This is closely related to the concepts of associative memory and correlational learning.

He seemed to foretell the notion of a neuron's activity being a function of the sum of its inputs, with correlation history contributing to the weight of interconnections:

The amount of activity at any given point in the brain-cortex is the sum of the tendencies of all other points to discharge into it, such tendencies being proportionate (1) to the number of times the excitement of each other point may have accompanied that of the point in question; (2) to the intensity of such excitements; and (3) to the absence of any rival point functionally disconnected with the first point, into which the discharges might be diverted. (James 1890)

Over half a century later, McCulloch and Pitts (1943) published one of the most famous neural network papers, in which they derived theorems related to models of neuronal systems based on what was known about biological structures in the 1940s. In coming to their conclusions, they stated five physical assumptions:

> 1. The activity of the neuron is an "all-or-none" process. 2. A certain fixed number of synapses must be excited within the period of latent addition in order to excite a neuron at any time, and this number is independent of previous activity and position on the neuron. 3. The only significant delay within the nervous system is synaptic delay. 4. The activity of any inhibitory synapse absolutely prevents excitation of the neuron at that time. 5. The structure of the net does not change with time.

The period of *latent addition* is the time during which the neuron is able to detect the values present on its inputs, the synapses. This time was described by McCulloch and Pitts as typically less than 0.25 milliseconds. The *synaptic delay* is the time between sensing inputs and acting on them by transmitting an outgoing pulse, stated by McCulloch and Pitts to be on the order of half a millisecond.

The neuron described by the five preceding assumptions is known as the McCulloch–Pitts neuron. The theories they developed were important for a number of reasons, including the fact that any finite logical expression can be realized by networks of their neurons. They also appear to be the first authors since William James to describe a massively parallel neural model.

Although the paper was very important, it is quite difficult to read. In particular, the theorem proofs presented by McCulloch and Pitts have stopped more than a few engineers in their tracks. Furthermore, not all of the concepts presented in the paper are being implemented in today's neural networks. In this book, comparisons are not made between the theories and conclusions of McCulloch and Pitts (or anyone else) and the current theories of neural biology. The focus is strictly on the implementation (or nonimplementation) of their ideas in current neural network tools.

One concept that is not generally being implemented is their all-or-none neuron. A binary, on or off, neuron is used as the processing element (PE) in neural networks such as the Boltzmann machine (Rumelhart and McClelland 1986), but it is not generally used in most neural network paradigms today. Much more common is a PE whose output value can vary continuously over some range, such as [0, 1] or [−1, 1].

Another example of an unused concept involves the signal required to "excite" a PE. First, because the output of a PE generally varies continuously with the input, there is no "threshold" at which an output appears. The PEs used in some neural networks activate at some threshold, but not in most of the network implementations discussed in this text. For PEs with either continuous outputs or thresholds, no "fixed number of connections" (synapses) must be excited. The net input to a PE is generally a function of the outputs of the PEs connected to it upstream (presynaptically) and of the connection strengths to those presynaptic PEs.

A third example is that there is generally no delay associated with the connection (synapse) in a neural network implementation. Typically, the output states (activation levels) of the PEs are updated synchronously, one layer at a time. Sometimes, as in Boltzmann machines, they are updated asynchronously, with the update order determined stochastically. There is almost never, however, a delay built into a connection from one PE to another.

A fourth example is that the activation of a single inhibitory connection does not usually disable or deactivate the PE to which it is connected. Any inhibitory connection (a connection with a negative weight) has the same absolute magnitude effect, albeit subtractive, as the additive effect of a positive connection with the same absolute weight.

With regard to the fifth assumption of McCulloch and Pitts, it is true that the structure of a neural network implementation does not change with time, with a couple of caveats. First, it is usual to "train" neural networks prior to their use. During the training process, the structure doesn't usually change but the interconnecting weights do. In addition, it is not uncommon, once training is complete, for PEs and/or interconnecting weights that aren't contributing significantly to be removed. This certainly can be considered a change to the structure of the network.

Given these examples, what are we left with of McCulloch and Pitts' five assumptions? If truth be told, when referring to today's neural network implementations, we are in most cases left with perhaps one assumption, the fifth.

Then why is their 1943 paper so important? First, they proved that networks of their neurons could represent any finite logical expression. Second, they used a massively parallel architecture. And, third, they provided the stepping stones for the development of the network models and adaptation techniques that followed.

Just because neural network implementations don't conform to McCulloch and Pitts' work doesn't imply in any way that their work was bad. Current artificial neural networks don't always reflect what we understand about biological neural networks, either. For instance, it appears that a biological neuron acts somewhat like a voltage-controlled oscillator, with the output frequency a function of the input level (input voltage): The higher the input, the more pulses per second the neuron puts out. Neural network implementations usually work with basically steady-state values of the PE from one update to the next.

The next personality along our journey through the Age of Camelot is Donald O. Hebb, whose 1949 book *The Organization of Behavior* (Hebb 1949) was the first to define the method of updating synaptic weights that we now refer to as *Hebbian*. He is also among the first to use the term *connectionism*. Hebb presented his method as a "neurophysiological postulate" in his chapter entitled "The First Stage of Perception: Growth of the Assembly" as follows: "When an axon of cell A is near enough to excite a cell B and repeatedly or persistently takes part in firing it, some growth process or metabolic change takes place in one or both cells such that A's efficiency as one of the cells firing B, is increased."

Hebb made four primary contributions to neural network theory:

1. He stated that in a neural network, information is stored in the weights of the synapses (connections).

2. He postulated a connection weight training rate that is proportional to the product of the activation values of the neurons. Note that his postulate assumed that the activation values are positive. Because he didn't provide a means for the weights to be decreased, they could theoretically go infinitely high. Adaptation that involves neurons with negative activation values has also been labeled Hebbian. This is not included in Hebb's original formulation but is a logical extension of it.

3. He assumed that weights are symmetric. That is, the weight of a connection from neuron A to neuron B is the same as that from B to A. Although this may or may not be true in biological neural networks, it is often applied to neural network implementations.

4. He postulated a cell assembly theory, which states that as adaptation occurs, strengths and patterns of synapse connections (weights) change, and assemblies of cells are created by these changes. Stated another way, if simultaneous activation of a group of weakly connected cells occurs repeatedly, these cells tend to coalesce into a more strongly connected assembly.

All four of Hebb's contributions are generally implemented in today's neural networks, at least to some degree. We often refer to adaptation schemes implemented in some networks as Hebbian.

In the late 1950s, a landmark paper by Frank Rosenblatt (1958) defined a neural network structure called the *perceptron*. The perceptron was probably the first valid neural network *implementation* because it was simulated in detail on an IBM 704 computer at the Cornell Aeronautical Laboratory. This computer-oriented paper caught the imaginations of engineers and physicists, despite the fact that its mathematical proofs, analyses, and descriptions contained tortuous twists and turns. Anyone capable of wading through the variety of systems and modes of organization in the paper will see that the perceptron is capable of "learning" to classify certain pattern sets as similar or distinct by modifying its connections. It can therefore be described as a "learning machine," or as we prefer to call it, an "adaptation machine."

Rosenblatt used biological vision as his network model. Input node groups consisted of random sets of cells in a region of the retina, each group being connected to a single association unit (AU) in the next higher layer. AUs were connected bidirectionally to response units (RUs) in the third (highest) layer. The perceptron's objective was to activate the correct RU for each particular input pattern class. Each RU typically had a large number of connections to AUs.

He devised two ways to implement the feedback from RUs to AUs. In the first, activation of an RU would tend to excite the AUs that sent the RU excitation (positive feedback). In the second, inhibitory connections existed between the RU and the *complement* of the set of AUs that excited it (negative feedback), therefore inhibiting activity in AUs that did not transmit to it. Rosenblatt used the second option for most of his systems. In addition, for both options, he assumed that all RUs were interconnected with inhibitory connections.

Rosenblatt used his perceptron model to address two questions. First, in what form is information stored, or remembered? Second, how does stored information influence recognition and behavior? His answers were as follows (Rosenblatt 1958):

> . . . the information is contained in connections or associations rather than topographic representations . . . since the stored information takes the form of new connections, or transmission channels in the nervous system (or the creation of conditions which are functionally equivalent to new connections), it follows that the new stimuli will make use of these new pathways which have been created, automatically activating the appropriate response without requiring any separate process for their recognition or identification.

The primary perceptron adaptation mechanism is self-organizing or self-associative in that the response that happens to become dominant is initially random. However, Rosenblatt also described systems in which training or "forced responses" occurred.

This paper laid the groundwork for both supervised and unsupervised training algorithms as they are seen today in back-propagation and Kohonen networks, respectively. The basic structures set forth by Rosenblatt are therefore alive and well, despite the critique by Minsky and Papert that is discussed later.

Rosenblatt also worked in the area of the recognition of sequences of patterns. His analyses showed that very long pattern sequences could be recalled if the number of neurons available was roughly equal to the number in the brain. The major quantitative results of his model for long-term sequential memory in the brain are summarized in Rosenblatt (1964).

Frank Rosenblatt died in a sailing accident on Chesapeake Bay in 1971 on his 43rd birthday. We can only speculate what further significant contributions he might have made had he lived longer.

The last stop in the Age of Camelot is with Bernard Widrow and Marcian Hoff. In 1960 they published a paper entitled "Adaptive Switching Circuits" that, particularly from an engineering standpoint, has become one of the most important papers on neural network technology (Widrow and Hoff 1960). Widrow and Hoff are the first engineers discussed in this history section. Not only did they design neural network implementations that they simulated on computers, they implemented their designs in hardware. And at least a couple of the lunch-box-sized machines they built "way back then" are still in working order!

Widrow and Hoff (1960) introduced a device called an *adaline* (for *ada*ptive *line*ar). Adaline consists of a single processing element with an arbitrary number of input elements that can take on values of plus or minus one and a bias element that is always plus one. Before being summed by a summing element, each input, including the bias, is modified by a unique weight that Widrow and Hoff call a "gain." (This name reflects their engineering background because the term *gain* refers to the amplification factor that an electronic signal undergoes when processed by an amplifier; it may be more descriptive of the function performed than the more common term *weight*.) Following the summer is a quantizer that has an output of plus one if the summer output, including the bias, is greater than zero, and an output of minus one for summer outputs less than or equal to zero.

What is particularly ingenious about the adaline is the adaptation algorithm. One of the main problems with perceptrons is the length of time it takes them to learn to classify patterns. The Widrow–Hoff algorithm yields adaptation that is faster and more accurate. The algorithm is a form of supervised adaptation that adjusts the weights (gains) according to the size of the error on the output of the summer (prior to the quantizer).

Widrow and Hoff showed that the way they adjust the weights minimizes the sum-squared error over all patterns in the training set. For that reason, the Widrow–Hoff method is also known as the least mean squares (LMS) algorithm. The error is the difference between what the output of the adaline should be and the output of the summer. The sum-squared error is obtained by measuring the error for each pattern presented to the adaline, squaring each value, and then summing all of the squared values.

Minimizing the sum-squared error involves an error reduction method called *gradient descent*, or *steepest descent*. Mathematically, it involves the partial derivatives of the error with respect to the weights. Widrow and Hoff showed that it isn't necessary to take the derivatives because they are proportional to the error (and its sign) and to the sign of the input.

They further showed that for n inputs, reducing the measured error of the summer by $1/n$ for each input does a good job of implementing gradient descent. Each weight is adjusted until the error is reduced by $1/n$ of the total error at the beginning. For example, if there are 12 input processing elements, each weight is adjusted to remove 1/12 of the total error.

This method provides for weight adjustment (adaptation) even when the output of the classifier is correct. For example, if the output of the summer is 0.5, the classifier output is 1.0. If the correct output is 1.0, there is still an error signal of 0.5 that is used to train the weights further. This is a significant improvement over the perceptron, which adjusts weights only when the classifier output is incorrect. That is one reason the adaptation of the adaline is faster and more accurate than that of the perceptron.

Widrow and Hoff's 1960 paper was prophetic, too. They suggested several practical implementations of their adaline: "If a computer were built of adaptive neurons, details of structure could be imparted by the designer by training (showing it examples of what he would like to do) rather than by direct designing."

An extension of the Widrow–Hoff adaptation algorithm is used today in back-propagation neural networks. In addition, their work in hardware implementation of neural network implementations heralded cutting-edge work in very large-scale integration (VLSI) by people such as Carver Mead and his colleagues at the California Institute of Technology (Mead 1989).

Widrow is the earliest significant contributor to neural network hardware system development who is still working in the area of neural networks. He and his students also did the earliest work known to the authors in biomedical applications of neural network tools. One of his doctoral students, Donald F. Specht (who later developed the probabilistic neural network paradigm), used an extension of the adaline, called an *adaptive polynomial threshold element*, to implement a vectorcardiographic diagnostic tool that used the polynomial discriminant method (Specht 1967, 1967a). Widrow and his colleagues later did pioneering work using the LMS adaptive algorithm for analyzing adult and fetal electrocardiogram signals (Widrow et al. 1975).

As the 1960s drew to a close, optimism was the order of the day. Many researchers were working in artificial intelligence (AI), both in the area exemplified by expert systems and in neural networks. Although many areas were still unexplored and many problems were unsolved, the general feeling was that the sky was the limit. Little did most folks know that, for neural networks, the sky was about to fall.

The Dark Age

In 1969 Marvin Minsky and Seymour Papert dropped a bombshell on the neural network community in the form of a book called *Perceptrons* (Minsky and Papert 1969). Although it could be argued that neural network development in the late 1960s had suffered from an overdose of hype and a paucity of performance, nearly all funding for neural networks (as well as for other computational intelligence concepts) dried up after the book was published. This was the beginning of the Dark Age.

Most of Minsky and Papert's book is about simple perceptrons, with only an input layer and an output layer (no hidden layer). Furthermore, neurons are threshold logic units, so only two states are allowed, on and off. The authors' analysis of simple perceptrons was generally correct, but even this part of their book has a disturbing undertone because of the authors' style of writing and because of what is *not* said. Their writing style is illustrated by statements such as "Most of this writing [about perceptrons] is without scientific value" and "It is therefore vacuous to cite a 'perceptron convergence theorem' as assurance that a learning process will eventually find a correct setting of its parameters (if one exists)" (Minsky and Papert 1969). Words and phrases such as "vacuous" and "without scientific value" project an attitude not likely to make friends and influence people. The book doesn't say much about perceptrons' good points; it isn't as much about what perceptrons *can* do as what they *can't* do.

The *coup de grace* came in the last chapter, where Minsky and Papert wrote, "[O]ur intuitive judgment [is] that the extension [to multilayer perceptrons with hidden layers] is sterile." This statement has proved to be incorrect and, in the opinions of some, a conscious "hatchet job" on a research area whose proponents were competing with Minsky, Papert, and their colleagues for funding.

Perhaps the most serious effect of the book is that it drove a wedge between the "traditional" AI folks (those who work with expert systems and symbolics) and the neural network people. This is particularly disturbing because it is becoming increasingly apparent that, at least in many areas, major breakthroughs in intelligent systems require a combination of approaches. The approaches of expert systems are being combined with neural networks, evolutionary computation, and fuzzy logic to form computational intelligence systems that are beginning to play an important role in complex systems such as those used for medical diagnosis, control systems, and financial analysis.

In the decade following the publication of Minsky and Papert's book, the number of researchers working in the neural network area dropped significantly. For those who remained, progress continued but in smaller steps. Now we look at the work of the Dark Age developers who have had a continuing impact on the field, particularly those whose contributions led to current techniques in neural network implementations.

Stephen Grossberg of the Center for Adaptive Systems at Boston University, the first Dark Age researcher discussed here, appeared on the neural network scene at about the same time as Minsky and Papert published their book. He became a productive, visible, and controversial personality in the field. His work is often abstract, theoretical, and mathematically dense. It is relatively difficult to read his papers because many of them refer to work described in several previous papers.

In his early work, Grossberg introduced several concepts that are used in a number of current neural network implementations. He and Gail Carpenter, his spouse, introduced and developed a network architecture known as adaptive resonance theory (ART). His early concepts include the "on-center off-surround" gain control system for a group of neurons. This basically says that if a PE in a population of PEs is strongly excited, the surrounding PEs will receive inhibition signals. This lateral inhibition idea is also used in other network implementations, such as Kohonen's self-organizing structures discussed later.

Grossberg also contributed much to the theories of network memories, that is, how patterns can stay active after inputs to the network have stopped. He wrote of short-term memory (STM) and long-term memory (LTM) mechanisms, how the former are related to neuron activation values and the latter to connection weights. Both activation values and weights decay with time, a feature called *forgetting*.

Activation values decay relatively quickly (short-term memory) whereas weights, having long-term memory, decay much more slowly.

Note that there is a basic difference between the Grossberg networks and the network structures discussed earlier. In the latter, the interconnecting weights are trained and then frozen, whereas Grossberg's patterns are presented to the networks to classify without supervised training. In previous networks, activation values of the PEs have no memory. The only thing determining the activation values is the pattern currently being presented to the network.

Grossberg gives PEs (or groups of them, called *cell populations*) short-term memory so that the current activation value depends on the previous one as well as on the average excitation of other connected populations. In accordance with on-center off-surround, Grossberg's earlier papers (Grossberg 1973) describe an inhibitory effect of activation values of connected populations.

He also wrote about a different kind of PE activation function (output versus input) than had been discussed earlier: a *sigmoid* function. A typical sigmoid response function, as described in Grossberg (1973), is illustrated in Figure 5.1. In this paper, he shows that signal enhancement and decreased sensitivity to noise can occur if the signals transmitted between cell populations are sigmoid functions of the populations' average activity levels. This sigmoid function differs in several respects from the one used with back-propagation networks described later. For one thing, it only plays an inhibitory role, even when it is used as part of the shunting self-excitation term for a population of PEs. For another, it is always nonnegative in Grossberg's 1973 implementation.

Another concept incorporated into Grossberg's network models that differs from those discussed previously is the adaptation algorithm. In models such as Widrow–Hoff and the back-propagation network, the training signal is proportional

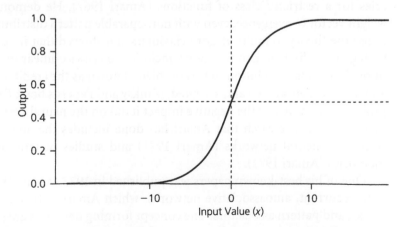

Figure 5.1 A sigmoidal activation function.

to the error in the output, that is, the difference between the desired and actual values. In Grossberg's models, adaptation is computed from the *sum* of the desired and actual values, represented in some of his models by input and learned feedback signals.

The adaptive resonance theory (ART) models developed by Grossberg and Carpenter incorporate most of the features described. There are several versions of the ART system, including ART1, ART2, and ART3. The ART network paradigms have been described as some of "the most complex neural networks ever invented" (Caudill 1989).

ART1 networks can process only binary input patterns. Almost all neural network applications require continuous-valued patterns, which have to be approximated (coded in binary) for input to ART1. ART2 networks are even more complicated than those of ART1 and can process discrete-valued input data. Until recently, many people have perceived the ART models as powerful research models rather than available neural network tools. Recently, however, several implementations of ART have been developed that are computationally efficient and feasible to run on PCs. Actually, these implementations are approximations of ART but are satisfactory for many applications.

Perhaps the most effective way to learn more about the ART2 and ART3 models is to study the collections of papers by Grossberg and Carpenter (Grossberg 1982, 1988). Carpenter and Grossberg have also published a readable article that is primarily focused on ART2 (Carpenter and Grossberg 1987b).

The Dark Age researcher discussed next is Shun-Ichi Amari, one of the most prominent researchers of artificial neural network theory. He began combining biological neural network activity and rigorous mathematical expertise in his studies of neural networks in the late 1960s.

One of Amari's earliest results was in the area of error correction adaptation, where he found a way to use a single hidden PE to form nonlinear decision boundaries for a restricted class of functions (Amari 1967). He demonstrated optimal weight vector convergence, even with nonseparable pattern distributions. He generalized the theory to multicategory classifiers and showed that it applies to the case with general discriminant functions, including piecewise-linear discriminant functions. Had Amari's solution to this problem, known as the credit assignment problem, been widely known and accepted, Minksy and Papert's book *Perceptrons* would probably not have had the negative impact it did on the neural network field. Other neural network research that Amari has done includes the analysis of randomly connected neural networks (Amari 1971) and studies of temporally associative memories (Amari 1972).

One of his best-known papers was published in 1977 (Amari 1977). It discusses both recurrent, autoassociative networks, which Amari calls *concept forming* networks, and pattern associators. The concept forming networks are precursors of the famous Hopfield networks discussed in the Renaissance section of this chapter.

An interesting feature of Amari's 1977 paper is his concept of *neuron pools*. Unlike most other researchers, Amari doesn't assume that the neuron is the fundamental element in neural networks. Rather, he uses the idea of small mutually connected groups of neurons, called neuron pools, as the fundamental units of his models.

In fact, there does not appear to be any reason why individual neurons should be considered the fundamental element. That is one reason why almost all researchers and developers today use terms such as processing element (PE), unit, processing unit, and neurode. The ability to assume a higher-level computing unit as the fundamental network computing element allows much more flexibility in network design and development.

In more recent work, Amari has extensively analyzed competitive adaptation, including that used in the self-organizing types of networks developed by Kohonen, described later. He is also well known for studies of the memory capacity of various kinds of networks.

In 1972, two researchers on different continents published similar neural network development results. One, Teuvo Kohonen of the Helsinki University of Technology in Finland, is an electrical engineer; the other, James Anderson, is a neurophysiologist and professor of psychology at Brown University in the United States. Although Kohonen called his neural network structure "associative memory" (Kohonen 1972) and Anderson named his "interactive memory" (Anderson 1972), their techniques in network architectures, adaptation algorithms, and transfer functions were almost identical. Despite the similarity of their results, the lists of references in the papers published by these two men do not contain a single item in common!

Kohonen is chosen as the focus here, partly because of the current implementations of his work in neural network implementations (discussed in detail in the next chapter) and partly because of his interest in applications such as pattern recognition and speech recognition. This is not to diminish in any way Anderson's work, which was and continues to be significant and relevant. In fact, a two-volume set edited by Anderson and Rosenfeld (1988) and by Anderson, Pellionisz, and Rosenfeld (1990) is arguably the best compilation of the significant early work in the neural network field. Each paper in the two volumes is prefaced by excellent introductory material that places the paper in context. Anderson has been interested more in physiological plausibility and models for his network structures and adaptation algorithms.

One of the most notable things about Kohonen's 1972 paper is the PE, or processing element, that he uses. It is linear and continuous-valued rather than the all-or-none binary model of McCulloch–Pitts and Widrow–Hoff. Not only is the output continuous valued, but so are the connection weights and input values. Remember that Widrow–Hoff used continuous values to calculate the error values, but the output of the PE was binary.

Also notable is Kohonen's use of networks with many simultaneously active input and output PEs, which are necessary when analyzing visual images or spectral speech information. Rather than have the output of the network represented by the activation of a single "winning" neurode or the activation level of a single multivalued PE, Kohonen uses activation patterns on a relatively large number of output PEs to represent the input classifications. This tends to make the network better able to generalize and less sensitive to noise.

Most notably, the paper lays the groundwork for a type of neural network very different from that evolved from the perceptron. The current version of the multilayer perceptron most commonly used is the back-propagation network, which is trained by giving it examples of correct classifications, an example of *supervised adaptation*. Most current versions of Kohonen's networks, often referred to as *self-organizing* networks, learn to classify without being taught. This is called *unsupervised adaptation* and can frequently be used to categorize information when we don't know what categories exist. It is also possible to combine Kohonen's unsupervised architectures with architectures such as back-propagation to do interesting and useful things.

The last researcher discussed in the review of the Dark Age is Kunihiko Fukushima of the NHK Broadcasting Science Research Laboratories in Tokyo. Fukushima has developed a number of neural network architectures and algorithms but is best known for the *neocognitron*. The neocognitron was briefly described first in English in a 1979 report, but the first thorough English-language description appeared in Fukushima (1980). Subsequent papers reported developments and refinements (Fukushima and Miyake 1982; Fukushima et al. 1983; Fukushima 1986).

The neocognitron is a model for a visual pattern recognition mechanism and is therefore concerned with biological plausibility. As stated by Fukushima, the goal of the work was "to synthesize a neural network model in order to endow it [with] an ability to [perform] pattern recognition like a human being." The network originally described is self-organized and thus able to learn without supervision.

Later versions of the model utilize supervised adaptation. Fukushima and colleagues (1983) admit that the supervised adaptation situation more nearly reflects "a standpoint of an engineering application to a design of a pattern recognizer rather than that of pure biological modeling." Because the network emulates the visual nervous system, starting with retinal images, each layer is two-dimensional. An input layer is followed by a number of modules connected in series. Each module consists of two layers, the first representing S-cells (the more simple visual cortex cells) and the second representing C-cells (the more complex visual cortex cells). Cell activations are nonnegative and continuous valued.

Weights from C-cells in one layer to S-cells in the next layer are modifiable, as are those from the input to the first S-cells. Weights within a layer, from S-cells to C-cells, are fixed. There are a number of "planes" within each layer. Each cell receives input from a fixed, relatively small region of the layer preceding it. By the time the output layer is reached, each output cell "sees" the entire input as a result of this telescoping effect of decreasing the number of cells in each plane with the depth into the network.

It is beyond the scope of this summary to describe the neocognitron fully, but it exhibits a number of interesting features. For example, the network response is not significantly affected by the position of the pattern in the input field. It also recognizes input correctly despite small changes in shape or size of the input pattern. Later versions cope even better with deformation and positional shift than early versions and, when presented with a complex pattern consisting of several characters, are able to pay selective attention to the characters one at a time, recognizing each in turn (Fukushima 1986).

A comprehensive version of the neocognitron has not been implemented to any significant degree on smaller computers such as PCs (although several of the concepts have appeared in current neural network implementations), probably because of the paradigm's complexity. For example, in the network described in Fukushima (1980) an input layer of 256 cells (16×16) was followed by three modules of 8,544, 2,400, and 120 cells, respectively. In addition to the complexity introduced by more than 11,000 PEs, the neocognitron has multiple feedforward paths and feedback loops, resulting in a computing complexity that is daunting.

One important thing that Fukushima figured out, however, was how to deal with adaptation of inner "hidden" cells (PEs) that are neither input nor output cells. He assumes not only that you know what your desired response is but also that you know what computational process needs to be followed stage by stage through the network to get that response. Knowing the computational process is possible only in certain well-defined cases, such as the one described by Fukushima in which the 10 digits, 0 to 9, were being recognized in handwritten form. Nevertheless, it was quite an accomplishment.

The Renaissance

Several publications appeared in the period from 1982 to 1986 that significantly furthered the state of neural network research. Several individuals were involved, one who published his first two landmark neural network papers by himself, and others who, in addition to their individual efforts, published as a group. We call these researchers the Renaissance men.

The individual who published by himself is John Hopfield of the California Institute of Technology. In the early 1980s, Hopfield published a paper that, according to many neural network researchers, played a more important role than any other single paper in reviving the field (Hopfield 1982). A number of factors were responsible for the impact of Hopfield's 1982 paper and his follow-up paper (Hopfield 1984). In addition to what he said, how he said it and his professional background are important. What he said is summarized later, but first let's examine his professional background and how he presented his findings.

Much of the significant work in neural networks during the Dark Age was done by biologists, psychologists, and other researchers who could be labeled "carbon-based." Hopfield is a well-respected physicist. One might say that he is a "silicon-based" researcher. In presenting his findings, he gathered a number of areas into a coherent whole. He identified network structures and algorithms that could be generalized and that had a high degree of robustness. Significantly, he pointed out throughout his papers that his ideas could be implemented in integrated circuitry, which is why we call him silicon-based. He presented his networks in a manner that was easy for engineers and computer scientists to understand, showing the similarities between his work and that of others.

Hopfield presented numerous lectures, all over the world, that convinced many researchers and developers to begin working in neural networks. According to Hecht-Nielsen (1990),

> By the beginning of 1986, approximately one-third of the people in the field had been brought in directly by Hopfield or by one of his earlier converts. Hopfield's work as a recruiter was perhaps the single most important contribution to the early growth of the revitalized field.

In summary, he got the attention of the technical world.

Hopfield didn't introduce many new ideas; he just put them together in new, creative, and brilliant ways. One new idea was his definition of the energy of a network. For a given state of the network, the energy is proportional to the overall sum of the products of each pair of node activation values (V_i, V_j) and the connection weight associated with them (W_{ij}); that is,

$$E = -0.5 \sum_{i,j; i \neq j} W_{ij} V_i V_j \qquad (W_{ii} = 0) \qquad \textbf{(5.1)}$$

In other words, he proved that the network has stable states.

Many of his ideas are incorporated into networks that we examine later in this chapter, but we don't present the Hopfield network in detail. Instead, we review the version of his network that uses binary processing elements (PEs) as presented in (Hopfield 1982).

The network Hopfield described in 1984 (Hopfield 1984) is similar except that it contains continuous-valued PEs with a sigmoidal nonlinearity. The same general mathematical method is used for computing network values in each case. Despite the continuous sigmoidal nonlinearity, inputs to the network must be expressed in binary form. This arises from the network equations (to be shown) and presents significant problems in using this version of the Hopfield net in many applications.

A very simple example of a Hopfield network (the original 1982 version) is illustrated in Figure 5.2. Each PE is binary; that is, it can take on only one of two values.

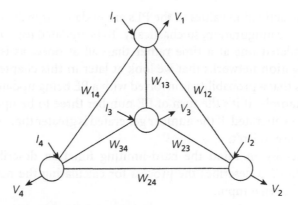

Figure 5.2 A simplified four-PE Hopfield network.

Hopfield used values of 1 and 0, but subsequently showed that values of 1 and –1 result in simplified mathematics. We use 1 and –1. The value that the PE assumes is governed by a *hard-limiting* function. By this we mean that if the net input to a PE is greater than or equal to some threshold value (usually defined to be 0), then the activation value is 1; otherwise, it is –1.

Before we review the operation of the network, two limitations of Hopfield networks should be mentioned. The first is that they can reliably store and recall only about 15 percent as many states as the network has PEs. For example, a network with 60 PEs can store about 9 states. A second limitation is that the patterns stored must be chosen so that the Hamming distance between two patterns is about 50 percent of the number of PEs. The Hamming distance between two binary patterns is the number of bits in which the values are different. For example, the patterns 1 1 1 1 1 and 1 –1 1 –1 1 have a Hamming distance of two.

From the first limitation, you can see that we're stretching things to say we can store much of anything in a four-PE network. We'll use the patterns 1 1 1 1 and –1 –1 –1 –1 as the two we'll store. We store the patterns by initializing (training) the interconnecting weights according to equation 5.2. The equation says that a weight is equal to the sum over all stored patterns of the product of the activation values of the PEs on each end of the connection:

$$W_{ij} = \sum_{patterns} V_i V_j \qquad (W_{ii} = 0) \qquad (5.2)$$

In our simple example, the sum over the two patterns of $V_i V_j$ for each weight is always $1 + 1 = 2$, so each weight in our trained network is 2. Now let's see how the network updates the activation values of the PEs, recovering complete patterns from partially incorrect ones.

The activation values of the PEs are updated asynchronously and, in Hopfield's original configuration, stochastically. To be updated *asynchronously* means that they are updated one at a time rather than all at once, as is the case with the back-propagation networks that we look at later in this chapter. Updating *stochastically* means that a probability is involved with a PE being updated at a given opportunity. For example, if it's the turn of PE number three to be updated, a random number [0, 1] is generated. If the number generated is greater than, say, 0.5, the PE is updated; otherwise, it isn't.

Keeping in mind the hard-limiting function described earlier, we find that equation 5.3 describes the process for calculating the net input to a PE, where I_i is the external input.

$$\text{Net input to PE } i = \sum_{i \neq j} W_{ij} V_j + I_i \tag{5.3}$$

The activation value of the PE will be 1 if the net input is greater than or equal to zero, and −1 otherwise. Let's look at how this network, trained to "remember" the two states 1 1 1 1 and −1 −1 −1 −1, deals with an "imperfect" input pattern.

We input a pattern of 1 1 1 −1, which has a Hamming distance of 1 from one of the two remembered states, and assume the four PEs now have these values. One way to think about this is to consider the weights W_{ij} set to 0 during the external input process. Then the activation state of each PE assumes whatever we input to it.

Now we asynchronously and stochastically update the activation states of all four PEs. If one of the PEs with a value of 1 is selected first, we calculate its new activation value. (External inputs are no longer being applied, so I_i is 0 for all PEs now.) Using equation 5.3, you can see that each of the three PEs with a value of 1 has the same net input whichever one is selected: 2(1) + 2(1) + 2(−1) = 2. Since 2 > 0, its activation value doesn't change.

When the PE with the activation value of −1 is selected and updated, its activation value is changed to 1 because the net input to it is 2(1) + 2(1) + 2(1) = 6. As soon as this happens, the pattern is stable, no matter how long you continue, because the net input of any PE selected is now greater than 0. We have thus successfully recovered one of the remembered states.

Similarly, you can see that the other remembered state is recovered if you start with any pattern with a Hamming distance of 1 from −1 −1 −1 −1, such as 1 −1 −1 −1. If you start with a pattern with a Hamming distance of 2 from each of the remembered states, the state recovered depends on which PE has its activation value updated first. That seems only fair because the test pattern is halfway between the two remembered states.

Although this is a simple example, the same principles apply to a large Hopfield network. You should be able to work out more useful examples for yourself with the information given.

Hopfield's work was noticed almost immediately by the semiconductor industry. Within three years of his 1984 paper, AT & T Bell Laboratories announced the first hardware neural networks on silicon chips, utilizing Hopfield's theories. Caltech colleague Carver Mead continued the innovations, fabricating hardware versions of the cochlea and retina.

Just prior to AT & T's announcement of the chips in 1986, the other Renaissance men, the Parallel Distributed Processing (PDP) Research Group, published their first two volumes (Rumelhart and McClelland 1986, McClelland and Rumelhart 1986). The third volume followed in two years (McClelland and Rumelhart 1988). Although it is difficult to pinpoint when work on these volumes began, a meeting organized by Hinton and Anderson in 1979 seems to have been the first meeting that involved a significant number of the PDP group. The Renaissance in neural networks, kindled by Hopfield, burst into flames with the release of their books. Sixteen researchers made up the PDP Research Group, and anywhere from one to four of them wrote each chapter in the first two PDP volumes. McClelland and Rumelhart edited the first two volumes and contributed to the third.

It is hard to overstate the effect these books had on neural network research and development. By late 1987, when one of the authors of this book [RE] bought his copy of volume 1, it was in its sixth printing. The software included with volume 3 sold more copies in 1988 than all other neural network software combined. What accounted for the unparalleled success of *Parallel Distributed Processing*? In one sentence: The books presented everything practical there was to know about neural networks in 1986 in an understandable, usable, and interesting way. In fact, 1986 seemed to mark the point at which a "critical mass" of neural network information became available.

Recall that neural network paradigms have three primary attributes: the architecture, the PE activation functions and attributes, and the adaptation algorithms. The PDP books presented a variety of these three items, building several network types as examples. The most read and quoted are probably in Chapters 1 to 4 and Chapter 8 in volume 1. Chapter 8 is entitled "Learning Internal Representations by Error Propagation" and contains the basic derivation of the back-propagation algorithm for multilayer perceptrons. It is one of the most quoted references in neural network literature. Other chapters also represent landmarks in neural network development, such as Chapter 7 on Boltzmann machines, written by Geoffrey Hinton of Carnegie-Mellon and Terry Sejnowski, then of Johns Hopkins University and now at the Salk Institute in San Diego. Hinton started out, with McClelland and Rumelhart, to be one of the editors of the books but decided to devote more of his time to the Boltzmann machine work.

Certainly one of the most significant contributions of the PDP volumes has been the derivation and subsequent popularization of the back-propagation adaptation algorithm for multilayer perceptrons, described in a landmark article in *Nature* at about the same time (Rumelhart et al. 1986). Other groups developed the basic back-propagation scheme in the late 1980s, including Paul Werbos and Dave Parker (Allman 1989).

We include in chapter 6 of this book an implementation of the back-propagation model for personal computers. Competitive adaptation is briefly reviewed before we present the Kohonen networks. We do not cover in any significant way a number of other models and mechanisms described by the PDP group, including interactive activation and competition, constraint satisfaction (including the Boltzmann machine), and the pattern associator.

The Age of Neoconnectionism

In about 1987 we moved into the Age of Neoconnectionism, named by Cowan and Sharp (1988). The field of neural networks and the development of neural network implementations for personal computers expanded almost unbelievably in the next decade. It was no longer feasible to assemble "all there is to know" about the current state of neural networks in one volume, or one set of volumes, as the PDP Research Group attempted to do in 1986–1988.

The first major conference on neural networks, the International Conference on Neural Networks, was held in San Diego in 1987, sponsored by the IEEE. This conference gave birth to both the IEEE Neural Networks Council (NNC) and the International Neural Networks Society (INNS). Robert Marks, then of the University of Washington, served as the first president of the IEEE NNC, and Steven Grossberg was the first INNS president. Marks also served as the founding editor-in-chief of *IEEE Transactions on Neural Networks*, arguably the most prestigious and widely read journal in the field. One of the authors [RE] served as the second president of the IEEE NNC. (In 2002 the IEEE Neural Networks Council became the IEEE Neural Networks Society, and it is now the IEEE Computelligence Society.)

Dozens of neural network paradigms, with hundreds of variations, were described in the literature. Because of the sheer volume of work being done by thousands of people, it is difficult to decide which individual researchers to highlight in the Age of Neoconnectionism. However, one new general class of networks was increasingly utilized. These networks, sometimes called "basis function" paradigms, include probabilistic neural networks and radial basis function networks. The person generally credited with having the most to do with the early development of probabilistic neural networks is Donald Specht, who published the first papers about them (Specht 1988, 1990) and continues to contribute significantly to the development of basis function paradigms.

In the decade from 1987 to 1997, the list of neural network applications expanded from biological and psychological uses to include uses as diverse as biomedical waveform classification, music composition, and prediction of commodity prices. Neural network development activity intensified worldwide. Another development occurred that is perhaps more important: the shift to PCs for neural network implementations. Personal computers had changed drastically since the introduction of the first Altairs and Apples. Their increased capabilities (speed, memory, mass storage, communications, and graphics) and reduced cost of personal computers made the implementation of useful and cost-effective neural network systems universally attractive. As of 1994, more than 50 million PCs were being sold annually worldwide (Gates 1995).

In 1994 the first IEEE World Congress on Computational Intelligence was held in Florida. For the first time, major conferences on neural networks, evolutionary computation, and fuzzy logic were held together. The boundaries between methodologies were beginning to erode.

The Age of Computational Intelligence

The second IEEE World Congress on Computational Intelligence was held in 1998 in Anchorage, Alaska. By this time, the boundaries between the three main areas of computational intelligence had eroded even more, and we choose this year as the beginning of the age of computational intelligence.

The third IEEE World Congress on Computational Intelligence in 2002 in Honolulu, Hawaii, was a gathering of engineers and scientists whose presentations and discussions were truly eclectic, and it was a celebration of the formation of the new IEEE Neural Networks Society.

In 2005 the IEEE approved the society's change of the name to properly reflect its fields of interest: The IEEE Computelligence Society. In 2006, the fourth IEEE World Congress on Computational Intelligence was held in Vancouver, British Columbia, Canada.

Hybrid systems are the order of the day. And if you want to keep up with the latest developments in neural networks, you have to skim the evolutionary computation and fuzzy logic journals because many, if not most, advances in computational intelligence cut across methodologies. There is no looking back!

What Neural Networks Are and Why They Are Useful

Neural networks are information processing systems. In general, they can be thought of as "black box" devices that accept inputs and produce outputs. In the simplest terms, neural networks map input vectors onto output vectors. Some of the operations that neural networks perform include the following.

Classification. An input pattern is passed to the network, and the network produces a representative class as output.

Pattern matching. An input pattern is passed to the network, and the network produces the corresponding output pattern that best matches the input pattern.

Pattern completion. An incomplete pattern is passed to the network, and the network produces an output pattern that has the missing pattern portions filled in.

Noise removal. A noise-corrupted input pattern is presented to the network, and the network removes some (or all) of the noise and produces a cleaner version of the input pattern as output.

Optimization. An input pattern representing the initial values for a specific optimization problem is presented to the network, and the network produces a set of variables that represent an acceptably optimized solution to the problem.

Control. An input pattern is presented that represents the current state of a controller and the desired response for it, and the network output is the command sequence that will create the desired response.

Simulation. An input pattern (or series of patterns) is presented that represents the current state vector (and possibly previous state vectors) of a system or time series. The trained network generates structured sequences or patterns that simulate behavior of the system with time.

Neural networks consist of processing elements and weighted connections. Figure 5.3 illustrates a typical neural network. Each layer in a neural network consists of a collection of processing elements. Each PE collects the values from all of its input connections, performs a predefined mathematical operation (such as a dot-product followed by a threshold), and produces a single output value. The neural network in Figure 5.3 has three layers: F_x, which consists of the PEs $\{x_1, x_2, x_3\}$; F_y, which consists of the PEs $\{y_1, y_2\}$; and F_z, which consists of the PEs $\{z_1, z_2, z_3\}$ (from left to right, respectively).

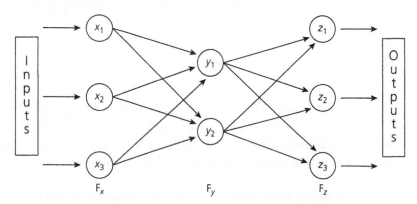

Figure 5.3 A typical neural network.

Processing elements are connected with weighted connections. In Figure 5.3 there is a weighted connection from every F_x PE to every F_y PE, and there is a weighted connection from every F_y PE to every F_z PE. Each weighted connection (referred to as either a connection or a weight; the terms are used interchangeably in this book) acts as both a label and a value. As an example, in Figure 5.3 the connection from the F_x PE x_1 to the F_y PE y_2 is the connection weight w_{21} (the connection from x_1 to y_2). Connection weights store the information, or knowledge, in a network. The values of the connection weights are often determined by a neural network adaptation procedure (although sometimes they are predefined and hardwired into the network). It is through the adjustment of the connection weights that the neural network is able to adapt. By performing the update operations for each PE when an input pattern is presented, the neural network is able to recall information.

There are several important features illustrated by the neural network shown in Figure 5.3 that apply to all neural networks:

- Each PE acts independently of all others; each PE's output relies only on its constantly available inputs from the abutting connections.

- Each PE relies only on local information; the information provided by the adjoining connections is all a PE needs to process. It does not need to know the state of any of the other PEs to which it does not have an explicit connection.

- The large number of connections provides redundancy and facilitates a distributed representation.

The first two features allow neural networks to operate efficiently in parallel. The last feature provides properly designed neural networks with fault-tolerance and generalization qualities that are very difficult to attain with most other computing systems.

In addition to these features, by properly arranging the topology of the networks, introducing a nonlinearity in the processing elements (i.e., adding a nonlinear threshold function), and using the appropriate adaptation rules, neural networks are able to "learn" arbitrary nonlinear mappings. This is a powerful attribute. There are three primary situations where neural networks are advantageous:

1. Situations where relatively few decisions are required from a massive amount of data (e.g., speech and image processing)

2. Situations where nonlinear mappings must be automatically acquired (e.g., loan evaluations and robotic control)

3. Situations where a near-optimal solution to a combinatorial optimization problem is required very quickly (e.g., job shop scheduling and telecommunication message routing)

A basic knowledge of neural networks requires an understanding of the nomenclature and a comprehension of the rudimentary mathematical concepts used to describe and analyze neural network processing. In a broad sense, neural networks comprise three principal elements needed to specify the network:

- *Topology*—how a neural network is organized into layers and how those layers are connected.
- *Adaptation*—how a network is configured to store information.
- *Recall*—how the stored information is retrieved from the network.

We describe each of these elements in detail after a discussion of connection weights, processing elements, and activation functions.

Neural Network Components and Terminology

Each neural network has at least two structural components: connection weights and processing elements. The combination of these components creates a neural network topology. A convenient analogy is the directed graph, where the edges are analogous to the connection weights and the nodes are analogous to the processing elements. In addition to connection weights and processing elements, processing element activation functions and input/output patterns are also basic components in the design, implementation, and use of neural networks. After a description of the terminology of neural networks, we examine each of these elements in turn.

Terminology

Neural network terminology remains varied, with standards yet to be adopted. The Standards Committee of the IEEE Neural Networks Council, now the IEEE Computational Intelligence Society, is actively involved in standardizing terminology and symbology (Eberhart 1990). We generally use terminology developed by the Standards Committee in this book. There are, however, exceptions. Therefore, for clarity, we explain the terminology as appropriate. Figure 5.4 shows an illustration of some of the terminology.

Input and output vectors (patterns) are denoted by subscripted capital letters from the beginning of the alphabet. The input patterns are denoted $A_k = a_{k1}$, $a_{k2}, \ldots, a_{kn})$; $k = 1, 2, \ldots, m$, and the output patterns as $B_k = (b_{k1}, b_{k2}, \ldots, b_{kp})$; $k = 1, 2, \ldots, m$. Note that the subscript k refers to a pattern and that there are m input patterns.

The processing elements (PEs) in a layer are denoted by the same subscripted variable. The collection of PEs in a layer form a vector, and these vectors are denoted

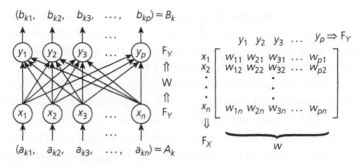

Figure 5.4 A network used to illustrate terminology.

by capital letters from the end of the alphabet. In most cases three layers of PEs are sufficient. The input layer of PEs is denoted $F_X = (x_1, x_2, \ldots, x_n)$, where each x_i receives input from the corresponding input pattern component a_{ki}. The next layer of PEs is the F_Y PEs, then the F_Z PEs (if either layer is necessary). If more than one inner (hidden) layer is required, they are designated F_{Y1}, F_{Y2}, and so on, moving from input to output.

The number of layers in a network is determined by its use. Using the network in Figure 5.4 as an example, the second layer of the network is the output layer; hence, the number of F_Y PEs must match the dimensionality of the output patterns. In this instance, the output layer is denoted $F_Y = (y_1, y_2, \ldots, y_p)$, where each y_j is correlated with the jth element of B_k. Connection weights are stored in weight matrices. Weight matrices are denoted by capital letters toward the end of the alphabet, typically U, V, and W. Referring to the example in Figure 5.4, this two-layer neural network requires one weight matrix to fully connect the layer of n F_X PEs to the layer of p F_Y PEs. The matrix in Figure 5.4 describes the full set of connection weights between F_X and F_Y, where the weight w_{ji} is the connection weight from the ith F_X PE, x_i, to the jth F_Y PE, y_j. For a two-layer network, the weight matrix is usually denoted by W. Additional layers and/or mean-variance weight configurations (discussed later) generally have weight matrices denoted by U and/or V.

Input and Output Patterns

Neural networks cannot operate without data. Some neural networks use only single patterns; others use pattern pairs. Note that the dimensionality of the input pattern is not necessarily the same as the output pattern. When a network uses only single patterns, it is defined as an *autoassociative* network. When a network uses pattern pairs, it is *heteroassociative*.

One of the key issues when applying neural networks is determining what the patterns should represent. For example, in speech recognition systems there are many types of features that can be employed, including linear predictive coding coefficients, Fourier spectra, histograms of threshold crossings, cross-correlation values, and others. The proper selection and representation of these features can greatly affect the performance of the network.

In some instances, feature representation as a pattern vector is constrained by the type of processing the neural network can perform. For example, some networks can process only binary data, such as the binary Hopfield network (Amari 1972; Hopfield 1982), binary adaptive resonance theory (Carpenter and Grossberg 1987a), and the brain-state-in-a-box (Anderson et al. 1977). Others can process real-valued data, including back-propagation (Parker 1982; Rumelhart et al. 1986; Werbos 1974) and learning vector quantization (Kohonen 1988). Creating the best possible set of features and properly representing those features is the crucial first step toward success in any neural network application. This task often takes a significant portion of the system development effort.

Network Weights

A neural network is equivalent to a directed graph (digraph). A digraph has edges (weights, or connections) between nodes (PEs) that allow information to flow in only one direction (the direction denoted by the arrow). Information flows through the digraph along the edges and is collected at the nodes. Within the digraph representation, connections serve a single purpose: They determine the direction of information flow.

Neural networks extend the digraph representation to include a weight with each edge (connection) that modulates the amount of signal passed from the output of one PE along the connection to the next PE. As an example, in Figure 5.4 the information flows from the F_X layer through the weighted connections, W, to the F_Y layer. For simplicity, a dual role for weights is used. A weight both defines the information flow through the network and modulates the amount of information passing between PEs.

The connection weights are adjusted during an adaptation process that captures information. Connection weights with positive values are excitatory connections. Those with negative values are inhibitory connections. A connection weight that has a zero value is the same as not having a connection present. By allowing only a subset of all the possible connections to have nonzero values, sparse connectivity between PEs can be simulated.

For reasons that will be discussed later, it is often desirable for a PE to have an internal bias value (threshold value). Figure 5.5(b) shows the PE y_j with three weights from F_X $\{w_{j1}, w_{j2}, w_{j3}\}$ and a bias value, b_j. It is convenient to consider this bias value as an extra weight, w_0, emanating from the F_X layer PE x_0, with the added constraint that x_0 is always equal to 1, as shown in Figure 5.5(b). This mathematically equivalent

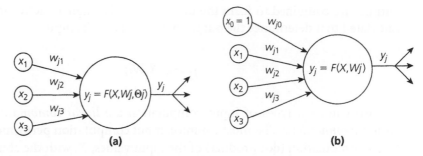

Figure 5.5 An illustration of PEs with internal (a) and external biases (b).

representation simplifies many discussions. We use this method of representing bias (threshold) values throughout this book.

Processing Elements

The processing element (PE) is the component of the neural network where computations are performed. Figure 5.5 illustrates the most common type of PE. A PE can have one input connection, as is the case when the PE is an input layer PE and it receives only one value from the corresponding component of the input pattern, or it can have several input weights, as is the case of the F_Y PEs shown in Figure 5.4 where there is a connection from every F_X PE to each F_Y PE. Each PE collects the information that has been sent down its abutting connections and produces a single output value. PEs possess two important qualities:

- PEs require only local information. All the information necessary for a PE to produce an output value is present at the inputs and resides within the PE. No other information about other values in the network is required.

- Each PE produces only one output value. This single output value either is propagated along the connections from the emitting PE to other receiving PEs or serves as an output from the network.

These two qualities facilitate neural networks' parallel operation. As is done with the weights, the value of the PE and its label are referred to synonymously. As an example, the jth F_Y PE in Figure 5.4 is y_j, and the output value of that PE is also y_j.

There are several mechanisms for computing the output of a processing element. The output value of the PE shown in Figure 5.5(b), y_j, is a function of the outputs of the preceding layer, $F_X = X = (x_1, x_2, \ldots, x_n)$ and the weights from F_X to y_j, $W_j = (w_{j1}, w_{j2}, \ldots, w_{jn})$. Mathematically, the output of this PE is a function of its inputs and its weights, as shown in equation 5.4. Actually, it is usually a function of a function. First, a calculation is performed to determine how the weights and previous outputs are combined to form the input to the PE. Then an activation function is calculated that determines the output of the PE given its input.

$$y_j = F(X, W_j) \qquad (5.4)$$

Two common types of input computation are *linear combination* and *mean-variance connections*. The most common input computation performed by a PE is a linear combination (dot product) of the input values, X, with the abutting connection weights, W_j, followed by an activation function (*cf.* Hecht-Nielsen 1990; Maren et al. 1990; Simpson 1990). Using the PE in Figure 5.5(b) as an example, the output y_j is computed using equation 5.5, where $W_j = (w_{j1}, w_{j2}, \ldots, w_{jn})$ and $f(.)$ is one of the activation functions described later in this chapter.

$$y_j = f\left(\sum_{i=0}^{n} x_i w_{ji} \right) = f(X \cdot W_j) \qquad (5.5)$$

The dot-product update has an appealing quality that is intrinsic to its computation. Looking at the relationship $A_k \cdot W_j = \cos(A_k, W_j)/\|A_k\| \, \|W_j\|$, we can see that the larger the dot-product (assuming fixed lengths A_k and W_j), the more similars the two vectors are. Hence, the dot-product can be viewed as a similarity measure. Note that if vectors X and W_j are of fixed length, maximizing their dot (inner) product is the same as minimizing their mean-square separations, since

$$\|X - W_j\|^2 = \|X\|^2 + \|W_j\|^2 - \text{two times the dot (inner) product.}$$

The second common type of input computation is mean-variance connections, which are used in instances where there are two weights connecting PE pairs instead of just one, as shown in Figure 5.6. One use of these dual weights is to allow one set of the abutting weights to represent the mean of a class, and the other the class variance (Lee and Kil 1989; Robinson et al. 1988). In this case, the output value of the PE depends on the inputs and both sets of weights, that is, $y_j = F(X, V_j, W_j)$, where the mean connections are represented by $W_j = (w_{j1}, w_{j2}, \ldots, w_{jn})$ and the variance connections $V_j = (v_{j1}, v_{j2}, \ldots, v_{jn})$ for the PE y_j.

Using this scheme, the activation function of y_j calculates the difference between the input, X, and the mean, W_j, divided by the variance, V_j, squaring the resulting quantity and passing this value through a Gaussian nonlinear function to produce the final output value, as shown in equation 5.6, where the Gaussian nonlinear function appears in equation 5.7.

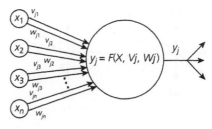

Figure 5.6   A PE with mean–variance connections.

$$y_j = g\left(\sum_{i=1}^{n} \left(\frac{w_{ji} - x_i}{v_{ji}} \right)^2 \right) \tag{5.6}$$

$$g(x) = \exp\left(\frac{-x^2}{2} \right) \tag{5.7}$$

Note that it is possible to remove one of the two connections in a mean-variance network, if the variance is known and stationary, by dividing by the variance prior to neural network processing. Gaussian nonlinear functions are described in the next section.

Processing Element Activation Functions

Processing element activation functions, also sometimes referred to as threshold functions or squashing functions, map a PE's (possibly) infinite domain to a pre-specified range. Although the possible number of activation functions is infinite, five are regularly employed by a majority of neural networks: (1) the linear function, (2) the step function, (3) the ramp function, (4) the sigmoid function, and (5) the Gaussian function. With the exception of the linear function, all of these functions introduce a nonlinearity into the network dynamics by bounding the output values within a fixed range. Each activation function is briefly described below and illustrated in Figure 5.7, parts (a) to (e).

The *linear activation function*, as in Figure 5.7(a), produces a linearly modulated output from the input x, as described by equation 5.8, where x ranges over the real numbers and α is a positive scalar. If $\alpha = 1$, it is equivalent to removing the activation function completely.

$$f(x) = \alpha x \tag{5.8}$$

The *step activation function*, as in Figure 5.7(b), produces only two values, β and $-\delta$. If the input to the activation function, x, equals or exceeds the threshold

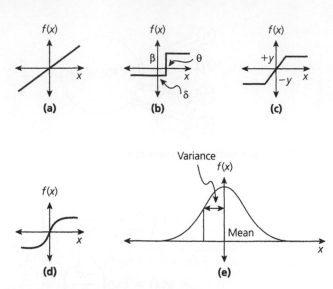

Figure 5.7 Five of the most common activation functions.

value θ, then the step activation function produces the value β; otherwise, it produces the value $-\delta$, where β and δ are positive scalars. This function is described mathematically in equation 5.9.

$$f(x) = \begin{cases} \beta & \text{if } x \geq \theta \\ -\delta & \text{if } x < \theta \end{cases} \qquad (5.9)$$

Typically the step activation function produces a binary value in response to the sign of the input, emitting +1 if x is positive and 0 if it is not. By making the assignments $\beta = 1, \delta = 0$, and $\theta = 0$, the step activation function becomes the binary step function of equation 5.10, which is common to neural networks such as the Hopfield neural network (Amari 1972; Hopfield 1982) and the bidirectional associative memory (Kosko 1988). A small variation of equation 5.10 is the bipolar activation function, which replaces the 0 output value with a -1. In punish–reward systems such as the associative reward–penalty paradigm (Barto 1985), the negative value is used to ensure changes where a 0 will not.

$$f(x) = \begin{cases} 1 & \text{if } x \geq 0 \\ 0 & \text{otherwise} \end{cases} \qquad (5.10)$$

The *ramp activation function*, as in Figure 5.7(c), is a combination of the linear and step activation functions. The ramp activation function places upper and lower bounds on the values that the function produces and allows a linear response between the bounds. These saturation points are symmetric around the origin and are discontinuous at the points of saturation. The ramp activation function is defined in equation 5.11, where γ is the saturation value for the function and the points $x = \gamma$ and $x = -\gamma$ are where the discontinuities in $f(.)$ exist.

$$f(x) = \begin{cases} \gamma & \text{if } x \geq \gamma \\ x & \text{if } |x| < \gamma \\ -\gamma & \text{if } x \leq -\gamma \end{cases} \tag{5.11}$$

The *sigmoid activation function*, as in Figure 5.7(d), is a continuous version of the ramp activation function. The sigmoid (*S*-shaped) function is a bounded, monotonic, nondecreasing function that provides a graded, nonlinear response within a prespecified range. The most common sigmoid function is the logistic function of equation 5.12, where $\alpha > 0$ (often $\alpha = 1$, which provides an output value from 0 to 1.

$$f(x) = \frac{1}{1 + e^{-\alpha x}} \tag{5.12}$$

This function is familiar to statistics (as the Gaussian distribution function), chemistry (describing catalytic reactions), and sociology (describing human population growth). Note that a relationship between equations 5.12 and 5.10 exists. When $\alpha = \infty$ in equation 5.12, the slope of the sigmoid function between 0 and 1 becomes infinitely steep and, in effect, becomes the step function described by equation 5.10. Two alternatives to the logistic sigmoid function are the hyperbolic tangent, $f(x) = \tanh(x)$, which ranges from -1 to 1, and the augmented ratio of squares described by equation 5.13, which ranges from 0 to 1.

$$f(x) = \begin{cases} \frac{x^2}{1+x^2} & \text{if } x > 0 \\ 0 & \text{otherwise} \end{cases} \tag{5.13}$$

The *Gaussian activation function*, as in Figure 5.7(e), is a radial function (symmetric about the origin) that requires a variance value greater than zero to shape the Gaussian function. In some networks the Gaussian function is used in conjunction with a dual set of connections, as described earlier by equation 5.6, and in other instances (Specht 1990) the variance is predefined. In the latter instance, the activation function is described by equation 5.14, where x is the mean and v is the predefined variance.

$$f(x) = \exp\left(\frac{-x^2}{v}\right) \tag{5.14}$$

Neural Network Topologies

The building blocks for neural networks have been described. Neural network topologies now evolve from the patterns, PEs, weights (weighted connections), and activation functions that have been described. Neural networks consist of one or more layers of PEs interconnected by weights. The arrangement of the PEs, weights, and patterns into a neural network is referred to as a topology. After we introduce some terminology, we describe two common neural network topologies.

Terminology

Neural networks are organized into *layers* of PEs. PEs within a layer are similar in two respects. First, the connections that feed the layer of PEs are from the same source. For example, the F_X layer of PEs in Figure 5.4 all receive their inputs from the input pattern, and the layer of F_Y PEs all receive their inputs from the F_X PEs. Second, the PEs in each layer use the same type of update dynamics. In other words, all the PEs use the same connection source(s) and destination(s) and the same type of activation function.

There are two types of weight that a neural network employs: *intralayer weights* and *interlayer weights*. Intralayer weights ("intra" is Latin for "within") are weights between PEs in the same layer. Interlayer weights ("inter" is Latin for "among") are weights between PEs in different layers. It is possible to have neural networks that consist of one or both types of weight.

When a neural network has connections that feed information in only one direction, from input to output without feedback pathways in the network, it is a *feedforward neural network*. If the network has any feedback paths, where feedback is defined as any path through the network that allows the same PE to be visited twice, then it is a *feedback neural network*. Thus, a network using PEs that have self-feedback loops is a feedback network.

Two-layer Networks

Two-layer neural networks consist of a layer of n F_X PEs fully interconnected to a layer of p F_Y PEs, as shown in Figure 5.8. The connections from the F_X to F_Y PEs

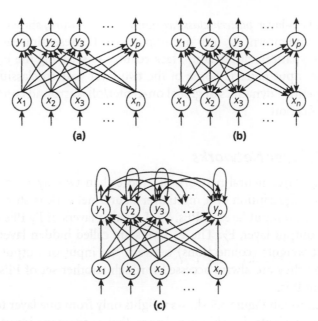

Figure 5.8 Two-layer neural networks.

form the n-by-p weight matrix W, where the entry w_{ji} represents the weight for the connection from the ith F_X PE, x_i, to the jth F_Y PE, y_j. There are three common types of two-layer neural network: feedforward pattern matchers, feedback pattern matchers, and feedforward pattern classifiers.

A two-layer *feedforward pattern matching neural network* maps the input patterns, A_k, to the most closely corresponding output patterns, B_k. The network shown in Figure 5.8(a) illustrates the topology of this feedforward network. The two-layer feedforward neural network accepts the input pattern A_k and produces an output pattern, $Y = (y_1, y_2, \ldots, y_p)$, that is the network's best estimate of the proper output given A_k as the input. An optimal mapping between the inputs and the outputs is one that always produces the correct response B_k when A_k is presented to the network, $k = 1, 2, \ldots, m$.

Most two-layer networks are concerned with finding the optimal linear mapping between the pattern pairs (A_k, B_k) (*cf.* Kohonen 1988; Widrow and Winter 1988), but there are other two-layer feedforward networks that work with nonlinear mappings by extending the input patterns to include multiplicative combinations of the original inputs (Maren et al. 1990; Pao 1989).

A two-layer *feedback pattern matching neural network*, shown in Figure 5.8(b), accepts inputs from either the F_X or F_Y layer, and produces the output for the other layer (Kosko 1988; Simpson 1990). An example of this kind of network is the bidirectional associative memory network (Kosko 1988).

A two-layer *pattern classification neural network*, shown in Figure 5.8(c), maps an input pattern, A_k, into one of p classes. Representing each class as a separate F_Y PE, the pattern classification task reduces to selecting the F_Y PE that best responds to the input pattern. Some of the two-layer pattern classification systems use the competitive dynamics of global on-center/off-surround connections to perform the classification.

Multilayer Networks

A multilayer neural network has more than two layers, possibly several more. A general description of a multilayer neural network is shown in Figure 5.9, where there is an input layer of PEs, F_X, L hidden layers of F_Y PEs (F_{Y1}, F_{Y2}, ., F_{YL}), and a final output layer, F_Z. The F_Y layers are called hidden layers because there are no direct weights (connections) between the input or output patterns to these PEs; rather, they are always accessed through another set of PEs such as the input and output PEs.

Although Figure 5.9 shows weights only from one layer to the next, it is possible to have weights that skip over layers, that connect the input PEs to the output PEs, or that connect PEs within the same layer. The added benefit of these weights is not generally understood, but some implementations use them.

Multilayer neural networks are used for pattern classification, pattern matching, and function approximation. By adding a continuously differentiable PE activation function, such as a Gaussian or sigmoid function, it is possible for the network to learn practically any nonlinear mapping to any desired degree of accuracy (White 1989).

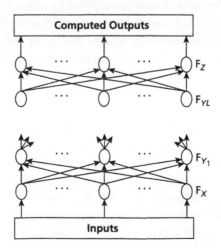

Figure 5.9 General form of a multilayer neural network.

The mechanism that allows such complex mappings to be developed is not fully understood for each type of multilayer neural network, but in general the network partitions the input space into regions, and a mapping from the partitioned regions to the next space is performed by the set of weights to the next layer of PEs, eventually producing an output response. This capability allows some very complex decision regions to be formed for classification and pattern matching problems, as well as for applications that require function approximation.

Several issues must be addressed when working with multilayer neural networks. How many layers are sufficient for a given problem? How many PEs are needed in each hidden layer? How much data is needed to produce a sufficient mapping from the input layer to the output layer?

Some of these issues have been addressed successfully. For example, several researchers have proved that three layers are sufficient to perform any nonlinear mapping (with the exception of a few remote pathological cases) to any desired degree of accuracy with only one layer of hidden PEs. See White (1989) for a review of this work. Although this is a very important result, it does not indicate the proper number of hidden layer PEs, or if the same solution can be obtained with more layers but fewer hidden PEs and weights overall. Note that throughout this book, the input is counted as a layer, so that a "three-layer" network has one hidden layer.

There are several ways that multilayer neural networks can have their weights adjusted to learn mappings. The most popular technique is the back-propagation algorithm (Parker 1982; Rumelhart et al. 1986; Werbos 1974) and its many variants (see Simpson 1990 for a list). Other multilayer networks include the neocognitron (Fukushima 1980), the probabilistic neural network (Specht 1990), the Boltzmann machine (Ackley et al. 1985), the Cauchy machine (Szu 1986), and radial basis function networks.

Neural Network Adaptation

Arguably the most appealing quality of neural networks is their ability to adapt. Adaptation in this context is defined as changes in connection weight values that result in the capture of information that can later be recalled. There are several procedures for changing the values of connection weights. After an introduction to some terminology, we describe two adaptation methods. For continuity of discussion, we describe the adaptation algorithms in pointwise notation (rather than vector notation). In addition, we describe the algorithms using discrete-time equations (rather than continuous time). The use of discrete-time equations makes them more accessible to computer simulations.

Terminology

As discussed in Chapter 2, adaptation can be classified into three categories: supervised, unsupervised, and reinforcement adaptation. We first focus on supervised and unsupervised adaptation. *Supervised adaptation* is a process that uses an external teacher and/or global information. The supervised adaptation algorithms discussed in the following sections include Hebbian, competitive, and error correction adaptation. Examples of supervised adaptation issues include deciding when to turn off the adaptation, deciding how long and how often to present each association for training, and supplying performance (error) information.

Supervised adaptation is further classified into two subcategories: structural and temporal. Structural adaptation is concerned with finding the best possible input-output relationship for each pattern pair. Examples include pattern matching and pattern classification. The majority of adaptation algorithms used in practical applications involve structural adaptation. Temporal adaptation is concerned with capturing a sequence of patterns necessary to achieve some final outcome. In temporal adaptation, the current response of the network depends on previous inputs and responses. In structural adaptation, there is no such dependence. Examples of temporal adaptation include prediction, simulation, and control. The primary example of supervised adaptation included in this book is the back-propagation neural network, for which an implementation is discussed in the next chapter.

Unsupervised adaptation, also referred to as self-organization, incorporates no external teacher or supervisor and relies only on local information during the entire adaptation process. Unsupervised adaptation algorithms perform clustering of the data. They organize presented data and discover its emergent collective properties. Examples of unsupervised adaptation that are discussed in this book include self-organizing feature maps and competitive adaptation. Implementations of the self-organizing feature map and learning vector quantization neural networks are discussed in the next chapter .

We next consider off-line and on-line adaptation. Most adaptation techniques can use off-line adaptation. When the entire pattern set is used to condition the weights prior to the use of the network, it is called *off-line adaptation*. For example, the back-propagation algorithm is used to adjust weights in multilayer neural networks, but it sometimes requires thousands of cycles through all the pattern pairs until the desired performance of the network has been achieved. Once the network is performing adequately, the weights are frozen and the resulting network is thereafter used in recall mode. Off-line adaptation systems have the intrinsic requirement that all the patterns be resident for training. Such a requirement does not make it possible to have new patterns automatically incorporated into the network as they occur; rather, these new patterns must be added to the entire set of patterns and the neural network must be retrained.

Not all neural networks perform off-line adaptation. Some networks can perform *on-line adaptation*, adding new information "on the fly" nondestructively. If a new pattern needs to be incorporated into the network's connections, it can be done immediately without loss of stored information. The advantage of off-line adaptation networks is that they usually provide superior solutions to difficult problems such as nonlinear classification, but on-line adaptation allows the neural network to adapt *in situ*. A challenge in the future of neural network computing is the development of adaptation techniques that provide high-performance on-line adaptation without high costs.

Hebbian Adaptation

The simplest form of adjusting weight values in a neural network is based on the correlation of PE activation values. The motivation for correlation-based adjustments has been attributed to Donald O. Hebb (1949), who hypothesized that the change in a synapse's efficacy (its ability to fire or, as we are simulating it in our neural networks, the connection weight) is prompted by a neuron's ability to produce an output signal. If a neuron, A, was active, and A's activity caused a connected neuron, B, to fire, then the efficacy of the synaptic connection between A and B should be increased. Hebb's work is discussed in the history section of this chapter.

This form of adaptation, now commonly referred to as basic Hebbian adaptation (or Hebbian learning), has been mathematically characterized as the correlation weight adjustment described in equation 5.15, where $i = 1, 2, \ldots, n$; $j = 1, 2, \ldots, p$; η is a constant that represents an adaptation rate; x_i is the value of the ith PE in the F_X layer of a two-layer network; y_j is the value of the jth F_Y PE; and the connection weight between the two PEs is w_{ji}.

$$w_{ji}^{\text{new}} = w_{ji}^{\text{old}} + \eta x_i y_j \tag{5.15}$$

In general, the values of the PEs can range over the real numbers, and the weights are unbounded. When the PE values and weights are unbounded, these two-layer neural networks are amenable to linear systems theory. Neural networks, such as the linear associative memory (Anderson 1970; Kohonen 1972), employ this type of adaptation and we can analyze the capabilities of these networks using linear systems theory. The number of patterns that a network trained using equation 5.15 with unbounded weights and connections can recognize is limited to the dimensionality of the input patterns (*cf.* Simpson 1990).

A special case of Hebbian adaptation is the *delta rule*, also sometimes called the *Widrow–Hoff rule* (Sutton and Barto 1981). It is called the delta rule because the amount of weight adjustment is proportional to the delta (the difference) between the target PE activation value provided by the "teacher" (b_{kj}) and the actual activation value calculated by the PE (y_{kj}). The delta rule is described in equation 5.16, where $\delta_{kj} \equiv b_{kj} - y_{kj}$, and η is the adaptation coefficient, which typically takes on values between 0 and 1. Since the subscript k denotes a pattern, and the subscript j in this case denotes an output PE, the value of delta calculated is for *one pattern* presented to *one PE*, and a_{ki} is the ith component of the kth input pattern. Implementation of the delta rule is discussed in the later section on multilayer error correction adaptation.

$$w_{ji}^{\text{new}} = w_{ji}^{\text{old}} + \eta \delta_{kj} a_{ki} \qquad (5.16)$$

Competitive Adaptation

Competitive adaptation (competitive learning), introduced by Grossberg (1970) and Von der Malsburg (1973), and extensively studied by Amari and Takeuchi (1978), Amari (1983), and Grossberg (1982), is a method of automatically creating classes for a set of input patterns. Competitive adaptation is a two-step procedure that couples the recall process with the adaptation process in a two-layer neural network. Each F_X PE represents a component of the input pattern, and each F_Y PE represents a class.

Step 1

Determine the winning F_Y PE. An input pattern, A_k, is passed through the connections from the input layer, F_X, to the output layer, F_Y, in a feedforward fashion using the dot-product update equation $y_j = \Sigma_{i=1}^{n} x_i w_{ji}$, where x_i is the ith PE in the input layer F_X, $i = 1, 2, \ldots, n$, y_j is the jth PE in the output layer F_Y, $j = 1, 2, \ldots, p$, and w_{ji} is the value of the connection weight between x_i and y_j. Each set of connections that abuts an F_Y PE, say y_j, is a reference vector $W_j = (w_{j1}, w_{j2}, \ldots, w_{jn})$ representing the class j. The reference vector, W_j, that is closest to the input, A_k, should provide the highest activation value.

If the input patterns A_k, $k = 1, 2, \ldots, m$ and the reference vectors W_j, $j = 1, 2, \ldots, p$ are normalized to Euclidean unit length, then the relationship of equation 5.17 holds, where the more similar A_k is to W_j, the closer the dot-product is to unity. The dot-product values, y_j, are used as the initial values for winner-take-all competitive interactions. The result of these interactions is identical to searching the F_Y PEs and finding the one with the largest dot-product value.

$$0 \le \left(y_j = A_k \bullet W_j = \sum_{i=1}^{n} a_{ki} w_{ji} \right) \le 1 \qquad (5.17)$$

Using equation 5.18, it is possible to find the F_Y PE with the highest dot-product value, called the winning PE. The reference vector associated with the winning PE is the winning reference vector.

$$y_j = \begin{cases} 1 \text{ if } y_j > y_k & \text{for all } j \neq k \\ 0 & \text{otherwise} \end{cases} \quad (5.18)$$

Step 2

Adjust the winning F_Y PE's weights. In competitive adaptation with winner-take-all dynamics like those described earlier, there is only one set of weights adjusted: those of the winning reference vector. The formula to adjust the winning reference vector and no others is equation 5.19, where $\alpha(t)$ is a nonzero, decreasing function of time. The result of this operation is the motion of the reference vector toward the input vector. Over many presentations of the data vectors [on the order of $O(n^3)$ (Hertz et al. 1990)], the reference vectors will become the centroids of data clusters (Kohonen 1986).

$$w_{ji}^{new} = w_{ji}^{old} + \alpha(t)y_j(a_{ki} - w_{ji}) \quad (5.19)$$

There have been several variations of this algorithm (*cf.* Simpson 1990), but one of the most important is the "conscience" mechanism (DeSieno 1988). By adding a conscience to each F_Y PE, it is only allowed to become a winner if it has won equiprobably. The equiprobable winning constraint improves both the quality of solution and the training time. Neural networks that employ competitive adaptation include learning vector quantization (Kohonen 1988), self-organizing feature maps (Kohonen 1988), adaptive resonance theory I (Carpenter and Grossberg 1987a), and adaptive resonance theory II (Carpenter and Grossberg 1987b). Implementations in the next chapter are devoted to the learning vector quantization paradigm, which includes a conscience mechanism, and to the self-organizing feature map.

Multilayer Error Correction Adaptation

Error correction adaptation (also called error correction learning) adjusts the connection weights between PEs in proportion to the difference between the desired and computed values of each output layer PE. Two-layer error correction adaptation is limited to capturing linear mappings between input and output patterns. Multilayer (> 2 layers) error correction adaptation is able to capture nonlinear mappings between the inputs and outputs.

A problem that once plagued error correction adaptation was its inability to extend adaptation beyond a two-layer network. Because it remained a two-layer adaptation rule, only linear mappings could be acquired. There were several attempts to extend the two-layer error correction adaptation algorithm to multiple layers, but the same problem kept arising: For how much of an output-layer PE error is each hidden-layer PE responsible? Using the three-layer neural network in Figure 5.10 to illustrate, the problem of multilayer adaptation (in this case, three-layer adaptation) is calculating the amount of error each hidden-layer PE, y_j, should be assigned for an output-layer PE's error. Note that the output layer of PEs has activation values $z_1, z_2, \ldots, z_q$, and that the weight matrix from the input layer to the hidden layer is denoted V.

This problem, called the credit assignment problem (Barto 1984; Minsky 1961), was solved through the realization that a continuously differentiable activation function for the hidden-layer PEs would allow the chain rule of partial differentiation to be used to calculate weight changes for any weight in the network. Using the three-layer network in Figure 5.10 to illustrate the multilayer error correction adaptation algorithm, the output error across all the F_Z PEs and for all m input patterns is found using the cost (error) function of equation 5.20.

$$E = 0.5 \sum_{k=1}^{m} \sum_{j=1}^{q} \left(b_{kj} - z_{kj} \right)^2 \tag{5.20}$$

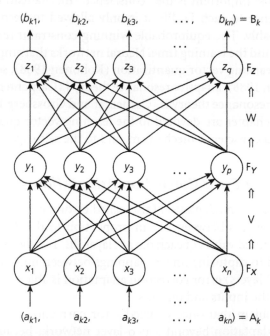

Figure 5.10 A network illustrating multilayer error correction adaptation.

The output of an F_Z PE for one pattern k, z_{kj}, is computed using equation 5.21, and the output of each F_Y (hidden-layer) PE for one pattern, y_{ki}, is computed using equation 5.22. The output layer thus comprises linear PEs, and $f_l(r_{kj})$ is a linear function. Since the hidden PE functions are nonlinear, $f_n(r_{ki})$ is a nonlinear function. Note that the subscript h is used for the input PE layer x. Since the input layer serves as just a pass-through layer, $a_{ki} = x_{kh}$. Also note from Figure 5.10 that there are p hidden PEs and q output PEs.

$$z_{kj} = \sum_{i=1}^{p} y_{ki}w_{ji} = f_l(r_{kj}), \quad \text{where } r_{kj} = \sum_{i=1}^{p} y_{ki}w_{ji} \tag{5.21}$$

$$y_{ki} = f_n\left(\sum_{h=1}^{n} a_{kh}v_{ih}\right) = f_n(r_{ki}), \quad \text{where } r_{ki} = \sum_{h=1}^{n} a_{kh}v_{ih} \tag{5.22}$$

The hidden-layer PE activation function is defined in equation 5.23. The hidden PE activation function is thus the sigmoid function, which is nonlinear, and $f_n(r_{ki})$ is a nonlinear function.

$$f_n(r_{ki}) = \frac{1}{1 + e^{-r_{ki}}} \tag{5.23}$$

The weight adjustments are performed by moving along the cost function in the opposite direction of the gradient to a minimum (where the minimum is considered to be the input-output mapping producing the smallest amount of total error). The connection weights between the F_Y and F_Z PEs are adjusted using the chain rule of partial differentiation, yielding equations 5.24(a) and (b).

$$\frac{\partial E_{kj}}{\partial w_{ji}} = \frac{\partial E_{kj}}{\partial z_{kj}} \frac{\partial z_{kj}}{\partial w_{ji}} \tag{5.24a}$$

$$\frac{\partial E_{kj}}{\partial w_{ji}} = \frac{\partial}{\partial z_{kj}} \left[\frac{1}{2}\left(b_{kj} - z_{kj}\right)^2\right] \frac{\partial}{\partial w_{ji}} \left[\sum_{i=1}^{p} w_{ji}y_{ki}\right]$$

$$= -(b_{kj} - z_{kj})y_{ki} \tag{5.24b}$$

$$= -\delta_{kj}y_{ki}$$

Next, the adjustments to the connection weights v between the input F_X and hidden F_Y PEs are calculated using the chain rule of partial differentiation. We define the error assigned to a hidden PE as $\delta_{ki} \equiv -\partial E_k / r_{ki}$, where r_{ki} is the net input to the hidden PE, thus yielding equation 5.25.

$$\frac{\partial E_k}{\partial v_{ih}} = \frac{\partial E_k}{\partial r_{ki}} \frac{\partial r_{ki}}{\partial v_{ih}} = -\delta_{ki} a_{kh} \tag{5.25}$$

The key is how to compute the ∂_{ki}'s for the hidden PEs. From equation 5.22, we see that $\partial y_{ki} / \partial r_{ki} = f_n'(r_{ki})$, or the derivative of the sigmoid activation function of the hidden PE. We now apply the chain rule again, as shown in equations 5.26(a) and (b), to arrive at a value for δ_{ki} in equation 5.26(c).

$$\delta_{ki} = -\frac{\partial E_k}{\partial r_{ki}} = -\frac{\partial E_k}{\partial y_{ki}} \frac{\partial y_{ki}}{\partial r_{ki}} = -\frac{\partial E_k}{\partial y_{ki}} f_n'(r_{ki}) \tag{5.26a}$$

but $$\frac{\partial E_k}{\partial y_{ki}} = \sum_j \frac{\partial E_k}{\partial r_{kj}} \frac{\partial r_{kj}}{\partial y_{ki}} = \sum_i \frac{\partial E_k}{\partial r_{kj}} \frac{\partial}{\partial y_{ki}} \left(\sum_i y_{ki} w_{ji} \right) = -\sum_j \delta_{kj} w_{ji} \tag{5.26b}$$

therefore $$\delta_{ki} = f_i'(r_{ki}) \sum_j \delta_{kj} w_{ji} \tag{5.26c}$$

But it is straightforward to show that $f_n'(r_{ki}) = \partial y_{ki} / \partial r_{ki} = y_{ki}(1 - y_{ki})$, so the error assigned to a hidden PE is given in equation 5.27. The calculation of the error assigned to an output PE with a sigmoid activation function is described in the later section on back-propagation.

$$\delta_{ki} = y_{ki}(1 - y_{ki}) \sum_j \delta_{kj} w_{ji} \tag{5.27}$$

The multilayer version of this algorithm is commonly referred to as the back-propagation of errors adaptation rule, or simply back-propagation. Using the chain rule, it is possible to calculate weight changes for an arbitrary number of layers. The number of iterations that must be performed for each pattern in the dataset is generally large, making this off-line adaptation algorithm relatively slow to train.

Although the cost function is computed with respect to only a single pattern for the single weight, it has been shown (Widrow and Hoff 1960) that the motion in the opposite direction of the error gradient for each pattern, when taken in aggregate, acts as a noisy gradient motion that still achieves the proper end result. Therefore, $\partial E_j / \partial w_{ji} = \sum_k (\partial E_{kj} / \partial w_{ji})$, which applies to one weight attached to one output PE, and the total error for an output PE is $E_j = \sum_k E_{kj}$. Analogous equations apply to hidden PEs.

Using equations 5.24(b) and 5.25, with the preceding relationships, the weight adjustment equations are given by equations 5.28 and 5.29, where α and β are positive, constant-valued adaptation rates that regulate the amount of adjustments made with each gradient move. In practice, α and β are usually identical and are set equal to an adaptation rate η that is uniform for all weight layers.

$$w_{ji}^{\text{new}} = w_{ji}^{\text{old}} - \alpha \frac{\partial E}{\partial w_{ji}} = w_{ji}^{\text{old}} + \alpha \sum_k \delta_{kj} y_{ki} \qquad (5.28)$$

$$v_{ih}^{\text{new}} = v_{ih}^{\text{old}} - \beta \frac{\partial E}{\partial v_{ih}} = v_{ih}^{\text{old}} + \beta \sum_k \delta_{ki} a_{kh} \qquad (5.29)$$

The back-propagation algorithm was introduced by Werbos (1974) and later independently rediscovered by Parker (1982) and Rumelhart, Hinton, and Williams (1986). The algorithm explanation presented here has been brief. There are several variations on the algorithm (*cf.* Simpson 1990), including alternative multilayer topologies, methods of improving the training time, methods for optimizing the number of hidden layers and the number of hidden-layer PEs in each hidden layer, and many more. Although many issues remain unresolved with the back-propagation of errors adaptation procedure, such as the proper number of training parameters, the existence of local minima during training, the relatively long training time, and the optimal number and configuration of hidden-layer PEs, the ability of this adaptation method to automatically capture nonlinear mappings remains a significant strength.

Summary of Adaptation Procedures

We have described two main classes of neural network adaptation algorithms: competitive adaptation and multilayer error correction adaptation (back-propagation). Now we briefly examine five attributes of these algorithms. This information is meant as a guide and is not intended to be a precise description of the qualities of each neural network.

Training time. How long does it take the adaptation algorithm to adequately capture information? Neither of the algorithms is fast. Competitive adaptation is usually described as slow and back-propagation as very slow.

Off-line/on-line. Competitive adaptation can be used either off-line or on-line; back-propagation is strictly an off-line algorithm.

Supervised/unsupervised. Back-propagation is a supervised adaptation procedure; competitive adaptation is unsupervised.

Linear/nonlinear. Back-propagation is capable of capturing nonlinear mappings; competitive adaptation is limited to linear mappings.

Storage capacity. Competitive adaptation is capable of fairly high information storage capacity relative to the number of weights in the network; back-propagation has a very high capacity.

Comparing Neural Networks and Other Information Processing Methods

Several information processing techniques have capabilities similar to the neural network adaptation algorithms described earlier. Despite the possibility of comparable solutions to a given problem, several additional aspects of a neural network solution are appealing, including fault tolerance through the large number of connections, parallel implementations that allow fast processing, and on-line adaptation that allows the networks to constantly change according to the needs of the environment. The following sections briefly describe some alternative methods of pattern recognition, clustering, control, and statistical analysis.

Stochastic Approximation

The method of stochastic approximation was first introduced by Robbins and Monro (1951) as a method for finding a mapping between inputs and outputs when the inputs and outputs are extremely noisy (i.e., they are stochastic variables). The stochastic approximation technique has been shown to be identical to the two-layer error correction algorithm (Kohonen 1988) and the multilayer error correction algorithm (White 1989) presented in previous sections.

Kalman Filters

A Kalman filter is a technique for estimating, or predicting, the next state of a system based on a moving average of measurements driven by additive white noise. The Kalman filter requires a model of the relationship between the inputs and the outputs to provide feedback that allows the system to continuously perform its estimation. Kalman filters are used primarily for control systems. Singhal and Wu (1989) have developed a method using a Kalman filter to train the weights of a multilayer neural network. Ruck and colleagues (1992) have shown that the back-propagation algorithm is a special case of the extended Kalman filter algorithm and have provided several comparative examples of the two training algorithms on a variety of datasets.

Linear and Nonlinear Regression

Linear regression is a technique for fitting a line to a set of data points such that the total distance between the line and the data points is minimized. This technique, used widely in statistics (Spiegel 1975), is similar to the two-layer error correction adaptation algorithm described previously.

Nonlinear regression is a technique for fitting curves (nonlinear surfaces) to data points. White (1990) points out that the activation function used in many error correction adaptation algorithms is a family of curves, and the adjustment of weights that minimizes the overall mean-squared error is equivalent to curve fitting. In this sense, the back-propagation algorithm described earlier is an example of an automatic nonlinear regression technique.

Correlation

Correlation is a method of comparing two patterns. One pattern is the template and the other is the input. The correlation between the two patterns is the dot-product. Correlation is used extensively in pattern recognition (Young and Fu 1986) and signal processing (Elliot 1987). In pattern recognition the templates and inputs are normalized, allowing the dot-product operation to provide similarities based on the angles between vectors. In signal processing, the correlation procedure is often used for comparing templates with a time series to determine when a specific sequence occurs (this technique is commonly referred to as cross-correlation or matched filters). The Hebbian adaptation techniques described earlier are correlation routines that store correlations in a matrix and compare the stored correlations with the input pattern using inner products.

Bayes Classification

The purpose of pattern classification is to determine to which class a given pattern belongs. If the class boundaries are not cleanly separated and tend to overlap, the classification system must find the boundary between the classes that minimizes the average misclassification (error). The smallest possible error (theoretically) is referred to as the Bayes error, and a classifier that provides the Bayes error is called a Bayes classifier (Fukunuga 1986). Two methods are often used for designing Bayes classifiers: the Parzen approach and k-nearest-neighbors. The Parzen approach uses a uniform kernel (typically the Gaussian function) to approximate the probability density function of the data. A neural network implementation of this approach is the probabilistic neural network mentioned previously (Specht 1990). The k-nearest-neighbors approach uses k vectors to approximate the underlying distribution of the data. The learning vector quantization network (Kohonen 1988) is similar to the k-nearest-neighbor approach.

Vector Quantization

The purpose of vector quantization is to produce a code from an n-dimensional input pattern. The code is passed across a channel and then used to reconstruct the original input with a minimum amount of distortion. Several techniques have been proposed to perform vector quantization (Gray 1984), with one of the most successful being the LBG algorithm (Linde et al. 1980). The learning vector quantization algorithm described earlier in this chapter is a method of developing a set of reference vectors from a dataset and is quite similar to the LBG algorithm. A comparison of these two techniques can be found in Ahalt et al. (1990).

Radial Basis Functions

A radial basis function is a function that is symmetric about a given mean (e.g., a Gaussian function). In pattern classification, a radial basis function is used in conjunction with a set of n-dimensional reference vectors, where each reference vector has a radial basis function that constrains its response. An input pattern is processed through the basis functions to produce an output response. The mean-variance connection topologies that employ the back-propagation algorithm (Lee and Kil 1989; Robinson et al. 1988) are methods of automatically producing the proper sets of basis functions (by adjustment of the variances) and their placement (by adjustment of their means).

Computational Intelligence

Neural networks are not the only method of adaptation that has been proposed for machines (although they are probably the most biologically related). Examples of other methods are evolutionary algorithms and fuzzy systems. Increasingly, engineers and computer scientists implementing applications are finding it useful to combine two or more of these machine adaptation techniques into an effective solution. This hybrid approach, which usually includes knowledge elements, has evolved into the field of computational intelligence, which is the focus of this book.

Preprocessing

In this section we describe the most important considerations in selecting and preparing data for training neural networks. Many of these considerations are also valid for other computational approaches.

Before data can be processed in a neural network, it must be prepared, using data editing tools and methods of data transfer, to get the data into the network. Generally, training sets, test sets, and validation sets must be selected from the available application data or obtained during a data gathering phase. Once a neural network has been trained, tested, and validated, it is put into production to process live data or to recall data directly from the application. Throughout the lifetime of the project, it is normally necessary to revisit the training and validation phases to ensure continued correct performance of the neural network. Proper selection and maintenance of the training and test sets are therefore an ongoing concern.

The training set data is almost never in a form that can be accepted directly by the neural network, and some form of normalization, scaling, or transformation must be done first.

Selecting Training, Test, and Validation Datasets

Selection and preparation of the training datasets, as well as the test and validation datasets, are crucial steps in successfully completing and deploying a project. If the datasets are selected or prepared improperly, the network will usually fail to train correctly or it might yield disappointing results during testing and production.

We first consider *training datasets*. All neural networks must be trained, tested, and validated before they can be reliably used to recall information. Neural networks that require off-line adaptation absolutely must be trained before they can be used; otherwise, they will be incapable of producing any results at all. At least a minimum level of training has to be completed first. Even neural networks employing on-line adaptation require preliminary training and test phases to validate their performance.

A neural net is trained with a training dataset, consisting of typical samples and patterns from the application data. The training set should be sufficiently representative of the patterns that the network is expected to encounter, once deployed in the application environment. The objective is to present sufficient examples of the application data so that the net adapts to recognize important features and also to generalize. Training patterns should cover the intended application data hyperspace reasonably well and especially should include patterns close to decision boundaries of the hyperspace. This will allow the net to be able to distinguish different pattern classes, even in cases where some samples fall close to the decision boundaries. If gross areas of the total data hyperspace are left out of the training set, the net is unlikely to recognize patterns that fall into those areas when put into production.

We now look at *test datasets*. The performance of a neural network is measured and evaluated using a test dataset, consisting of samples or patterns obtained using the procedures outlined for constructing the training set. The test set should be distinct from the training set; otherwise, testing will not reveal the true nature of the net's adaptation and generalization ability.

The normal procedure is to assemble and prepare a large dataset and then split it into training, test, and validation sets. Patterns can be selected randomly for each set; however, it is important that the training set be composed of samples that cover the range of expected patterns, as outlined earlier.

Once the training set has been composed, remaining patterns can be selected and placed in the test set and the validation set. The purpose of the test set is to evaluate net performance and determine how well the trained net is expected to perform in the production environment. Sometimes, when more training variety is sought, the training and test sets can be exchanged. That is, the original training set takes on the role of test set, while the original test set takes on the role of training set. For the training and test sets to be exchangeable in this way, it is necessary that both meet the criteria for selection of samples, described earlier. Each set should be similarly composed of representative samples from each class of data. Test sets generally should reflect the probability distribution of patterns expected in the running environment if it is known.

Once a neural network has been trained and tested, the performance is validated against an independent *validation dataset*, consisting of unused samples or patterns from the application data. The validation set should be distinct from, and independent of, both the training and test sets. It is important not to influence the method of training and testing through the use of the validation set (Masters 1993). Validation can also be used to determine when to stop training (when the error for the validation data hits a minimum) and/or to prune PEs from a network (Reed 1993).

The neural network, once trained and validated, can be used on-line to process real-time (live) patterns (real-time datasets) directly from the application environment. This processing primarily involves the multiplication of the input vectors by network weight vectors, which can often (usually) be done in real time, given the speed of today's microprocessors.

Preparing Data

The characteristics of the data determine how the neural net is structured and how data is presented to it. The data also needs to be compatible with the neural net, in terms of number of parameters (elements) and dynamic range.

Many neural nets and other computational intelligence tools require data to be *scaled* before it is presented. The raw data values are scaled so that they fall into a defined range acceptable to the neural network. Often, this will be the range 0 to 1 or, alternatively, -1 to $+1$. Scaling consists of applying a scale factor and an offset to each raw value. The scale factor and offset should be chosen such that they are applicable to training, test and validation sets, and live datasets. The factors should be the same in all cases so that data elements are not clipped and do not lose significant digits. This can occur if, for example, some large samples occur in one of the datasets and nowhere else. Equation 5.30 suggests a method for scaling a dataset.

$$A'_{ki} = \frac{(A_{ki} - A_{k\min})(\text{Hi} - \text{Lo})}{(A_{k\max} - A_{k\min})} + \text{Lo} \qquad (5.30)$$

Here, A'_{ki} is the ith element of the scaled input data vector; A_{ki} is the ith element of the raw data vector; $A_{k\min}$ is the minimum raw data value; $A_{k\max}$ is the maximum raw data value; $(A_{k\text{max}} - A_{k\text{min}})$ is the divisor, normalizing the raw input vector to the range 0–1; Hi is the highest desired input value; Lo is the lowest desired input value, defining the minimum value to be presented to the neural net; and (Hi − Lo) is the scale factor, mapping the raw data into the desired input range. For example, to scale raw data patterns in the range 0 to 1, set Hi = 1, and Lo = 0. To scale raw data patterns in the range −1 to +1, set Hi = 1, and Lo = −1.

Other neural networks, such as the LVQ-I network presented in the next chapter, require n-dimensional vector representations of the data rather than groups of independent values. The networks view the data as vectors in n-dimensional hyperspace. The data is *normalized* to unit length vectors, using equation 5.31.

$$A'_{ki} = \frac{A_{ki}}{\sqrt{\sum (A_{ki})^2}} \qquad (5.31)$$

Here, A'_{ki} is the ith element of the normalized input vector, A_{ki} is the ith element of the raw data vector, and $(\sum A_{ki}^2)^{1/2}$ is the length of the raw data vector. Dividing each element by the length of the original raw input vector gives a normalized vector of unit length, which is input to the network. A similar normalization step is often employed for weight vectors during training to ensure that they are also normalized. This is necessary for the Euclidean distance measure, which is used to determine the winner, to be valid. See Chapter 6 for more details on this aspect of normalization.

Normalization as described above, which is used to prepare data for presentation to the LVQ-I network, has its drawbacks. It requires that the length of input vectors be the same for all training and testing patterns, and therefore it loses information about the absolute magnitude of the parameters. Only relative magnitudes are retained. For example, the four-dimensional input vectors −1, 1, 2, 3 and −5, 5, 10, 15 will each be normalized to identical input vectors.

Z-axis normalization is an approach to solve this problem. Prior to carrying out z-axis normalization, each parameter must be scaled. For purposes of this discussion, assume each is individually scaled to the range $[-1, 1]$. This means, of course, that the minimum value for each parameter in the dataset is -1 and the maximum value for each parameter is 1. The Euclidean length L of the scaled input vector is $L = \left(\sum_{i=1}^{n} A_{ki}^2\right)^{1/2}$, where A_{ki} is the *scaled* input vector. Since each component is limited to a maximum absolute value of 1, the maximum Euclidean length for an n-dimensional vector is $\sqrt{n}$.

Z-axis normalization is similar to creating another dimension in the input data (Masters 1993). In the process, an additional input parameter, called a synthetic parameter, is created. The value of the synthetic parameter for each pattern is a function of the input parameters for that pattern.

The total length of the input vector with the synthetic parameter must, of course, still be 1. The z-axis normalization process is described by equations 5.32(a) and (b), where s is the synthetic variable.

$$A'_{ki} = \frac{A_{ki}}{\sqrt{n}} \qquad (5.32a)$$

$$s = \sqrt{1 - \frac{L^2}{n}} \qquad (5.32b)$$

Note that the absolute magnitude information regarding each parameter is preserved. Also note that the synthetic parameter becomes an additional input to the network, so that there are now $n + 1$ inputs instead of n.

To see how z-axis normalization works, consider a simple case where there are two (already scaled) four-dimensional input patterns: $-1, 1, -1, 1$ and $-0.6, 0.6, -0.6, 0.6$. They would, of course, normalize to identical input vectors using the method outlined in the previous section. Using z-axis normalization, the first pattern transforms into the input vector $-0.5, 0.5, -0.5, 0.5, 0$, where 0 is the value of the synthetic parameter. The second pattern ($L = 1.2$) transforms into $-0.3, 0.3, -0.3, 0.3, 0.8$, where $s = 0.8$.

The only cases where z-axis normalization is counterproductive are those in which a vast majority of individual parameter values stay at or near 0 for most patterns. In these cases, the synthetic parameter will consistently be the most significant component of the input vector. For many applications, however, including the preparation of inputs for the LVQ network, z-axis normalization can be beneficial.

The *presentation of patterns* is an important issue. The order in which patterns are presented to the network should be considered during the design and training phase of implementation. Patterns are presented to the network during training from the training sets constructed by the researcher or directly from the application environment, for recall. In the case of training, it is usually possible for the developer or researcher to control the order of presentation to optimize adaptation. However, in the case of recall, the order of presentation is usually controlled outside the neural network implementation and determined by the application environment.

During training, presentation order can dramatically affect the way adaptation is accomplished. If patterns are presented sequentially in the order they happen to occur in the training set, the network may be biased by the occurrence of samples early in the training set. This may prevent the net from being able to recognize subtle differences in later samples. Therefore, it is necessary to select patterns randomly from the training set, especially for networks employing on-line adaptation (that is, weight adaptation after every pattern presentation). For batch (off-line) adaptation, in which weights are adapted only at the end of each epoch, presentation order is not likely to have an effect. Another approach sometimes used is the shuffling of the data after each epoch (as opposed to random selection). The results of different training runs, each with randomly or sequentially selected patterns, should be compared for the effect of presentation order on the outcome of training.

Another important consideration in preparing data for training a neural network is the *addition of noise* to perturb the data. By adding noise (jitter) to the data, the result is a convolutional smoothing of the target (Reed, Marks, and Oh 1995). This is a technique that may be helpful when only a relatively small number of patterns are available for training the network; additional patterns may be generated by adding noise to existing patterns.

Postprocessing

This section describes the most common technique encountered in postprocessing the outputs of neural networks and other computational approaches: denormalization. Much of postprocessing is covered by the topics discussed in Chapter 10, Performance Metrics. This section concentrates on some of the basic concerns for obtaining the outputs in a usable form.

Denormalization of Output Data

Denormalization produces real-world output data from the internal form of the network or other computational tool. Denormalization is the reverse of the normalization procedure described earlier. The network typically produces output values in a limited range defined by the logistic or other activation function. These values bear little resemblance to the real-world values of the application environment, and steps should be taken to denormalize the data back to the original data domain. This procedure, suggested by equation 5.33, is analogous to that given in equation 5.30.

$$C'_{ki} = \frac{(C_{ki} - \text{Lo})(C_{kmax} - C_{kmin})}{(\text{Hi} - \text{Lo})} + C_{kmin} \qquad (5.33)$$

Here, C'_{ki} is the ith element of the real output vector; C_{ki} is the ith element of the raw net output vector; Lo is the minimum network activation value; Hi is the maximum network activation value; $(\text{Hi} - \text{Lo})$ is the divisor, normalizing the raw net output vector to the range 0–1; C_{kmax} is the upper limit of the output domain; C_{kmin} is the lower limit of the output domain; and $(C_{kmax} - C_{kmin})$ is the scale factor, mapping the net output into the desired output domain.

Summary

In this chapter we review the history of neural networks, discuss fundamental network elements and topology, and describe some of the main adaptation methodologies. We also describe data preprocessing and postprocessing approaches that should help you present input data to neural networks and obtain required results. And we compare neural network approaches and other information processing approaches.

The next chapter presents detailed implementation information for three neural network paradigms: learning vector quantization, self-organizing feature maps, and back-propagation. You will be able to apply the concepts discussed in this chapter.

Exercises

1. In a single-layer neural network with n processing elements (PEs), how many unique weights are possible if the only restriction is that no self-feedback connections are allowed? How many are possible if it is also specified that weights are symmetric, that is, $w_{ji} = w_{ij}$?

2. Show that a hidden layer doesn't change (improve) network performance if all PEs (hidden and output) have linear activation functions.

3. The sigmoid activation function is $1/(1 + e^{-input})$. Derive the first derivative of this function.

4. If one hidden layer of sigmoidal PEs can approximate any nonlinear function, why might we decide to use more than one?

5. What are the differences among supervised adaptation, unsupervised adaptation, and reinforcement adaptation?

6. Review White (1989). Summarize the reasoning behind the proof that one hidden layer is sufficient to approximate virtually any nonlinear function.

7. Prove the convergence of the binary Hopfield network.

8. Derive a back-propagation (BP) adaptation algorithm for a four-layer BP neural network. Assume the activation function of the hidden PEs is a sigmoid function as expressed by equation 5.23. The activation function of the output PEs is a linear function as expressed by equation 5.8 with $\alpha = 1$.

9. Assume we want to scale inputs to $[-1, 1]$ for z-axis normalization. One of the input parameters varies over all the patterns from -4.2 to $+10.0$. How would you scale this input? Why?

chapter
SIX

Neural Network Implementations

This chapter presents four neural network implementations: back-propagation neural networks, the learning vector quantizer, Kohonen's self-organizing feature map networks, and evolutionary multilayer perceptron neural networks. Executable code and source code for each implementation, together with other useful utilities, are available on the book's web site.

The source code is particularly useful for studying the implementation details of the neural network paradigms and if you wish to make changes to the code for your applications.

The source code is written in C and is being distributed as shareware. You are welcome to use it for classroom or personal learning in conjunction with the textbook at no cost. If you use it, either as is or with modification, for a project outside of your classroom (or learning on your own), please submit a payment in accordance with the shareware payment

instructions on the Internet site for the book.

The backpropagation source code for the neural network implementation is written to support the implementation of one or more hidden layers. The number of hidden layers and the number of PEs in each layer can be specified in the run file. The classification of Iris data is included as a benchmark problem to be solved.

The Iris dataset is a set of feature measurements for iris flowers popularized by Anderson (1935). It consists of 150 four-dimensional vectors representing 50 plants of each of three species: *Iris sectosa*, *Iris versicolor*, and *Iris virginica*:

$$x_i = (x_{i1}, x_{i2}, x_{i3}, x_{i4}), \quad i = 1, \dots, 150$$

where x_{i1} is the sepal length, x_{i2} is the sepal width, x_{i3} is the petal length, and x_{i4} is the petal width (Anderson 1935). All the attribute values have been scaled into real numbers in the range [0,1]. The problem here is to discriminate the species according to the feature vectors. This is a well-known three-class classification problem. Three of the 150 four-dimensional vectors are listed here as examples:

```
0.637500      0.437500      0.175000      0.025000      1    0    0
0.875000      0.400000      0.587500      0.175000      0    1    0
0.787500      0.412500      0.750000      0.312500      0    0    1
```

In each row, the first four elements correspond to the sepal length, sepal width, petal length, and petal width; the last three columns correspond to the three species, *Iris sectosa, Iris versicolor, and Iris virginica,* respectively. Value 0 means the feature vector doesn't belong to this class and value 1 means it does.

The back-propagation neural network is an example of supervised neural networks; the learning vector quantizer is implemented as an example of unsupervised neural networks.

The learning vector quantizer (LVQ), sometimes referred to as a Kohonen network, is probably second only to back-propagation in the number of applications for which it is being used. Kohonen networks (of which LVQ and self-organizing feature maps are examples) were originally described by Teuvo Kohonen of the Helsinki University of Technology in Finland.

Several versions of LVQ exist. The LVQ implementation included with this book and described in this chapter is discussed in the 1988 edition of Kohonen's book on self-organization and associative memory (Kohonen 1988). A good additional source is the tutorial given at the 1989 International Joint Conference on Neural Networks (Kohonen 1989). The book and tutorial also describe other versions of LVQ, as well as Kohonen's self-organizing feature map. Henceforth, the LVQ implementation presented in this book is referred to as LVQ-I. Another algorithm, LVQ-II, is briefly discussed later. The Roman numerals I and II are *not* synonymous with Kohonen's designations LVQ1 and LVQ2.

The LVQ-I and self-organizing feature map paradigms are more biologically oriented than the back-propagation model. One indication of this is that both networks learn without supervision. This roughly resembles learning in the neural cells of the brain in that nobody applies electronic stimuli to brain neurons to train them to, say, learn to walk or to speak. The self-organizing feature map—an extension of LVQ-I, described by Kohonen—bears some rough resemblance to the way areas of the brain are organized. ∎

Implementation Issues

This section discusses issues related to implementing neural networks on personal computers. The implementation issues are explained step by step, with detailed equations and explanations along the way. Some implementation issues, such as topology, are relevant to a variety of networks. Others are specific to a network type.

We describe the topologies of the neural network paradigms first. Then we described the ways input is presented to a neural network implementation. We also introduce normalization techniques and options.

We present equations describing the network training and operation. These equations are divided into two main categories: feedforward calculations and adaptation calculations.

Finally, we describe issues related to evolutionary neural networks.

Topology

All four of the neural networks implemented are layered networks. The back-propagation neural networks have more than two layers (at least one hidden layer), and the Kohonen networks have only two layers (no hidden layers).

The back-propagation network is described in terms of the *architecture* of the implementation. The term architecture, as applied to neural networks, has been used in different ways by various authors. Often its meaning has been taken to be basically equivalent to *topology*, that is, the pattern of PEs and interconnections, together with other attributes such as direction of data flow and PE activation functions.

We use the term *architecture* in this volume to mean the specifications sufficient for a neural network developer to build, train, test, and operate the network. The architecture is therefore not related to the details of the implementation but rather provides the complete specifications needed by someone for implementation.

A simple, three-layer back-propagation network is illustrated in Figure 6.1. This represents the network in detail, with each PE represented by a circle and each interconnection, with its associated weight, by an arrow. The PEs with the letter "b" inside are bias PEs.

We describe each network element a bit later. We also discuss the operation and training of the back-propagation network of Figure 6.1, with a description of what happens at each step. But first, we turn to presenting input to the network.

The LVQ-I and self-organizing feature map networks consist of a two-layer feedforward topology, where the input layer is fully connected to the output layer, as shown in Figure 6.2. The input PEs simply distribute the inputs to the output layer; the output PEs have linear activation functions.

Back-propagation Network Initialization and Normalization

Each neural network must be initialized first and the input data needs to be preprocessed. Different networks have different requirements for network initialization and input data preprocessing.

We first consider the back-propagation neural network. The left side of Figure 6.1 shows inputs to the input layer of the network, to a layer of PEs. The set of *n* inputs is presented to the network simultaneously. (However, when implemented on a Von Neumann computer, the network must process the data serially.)

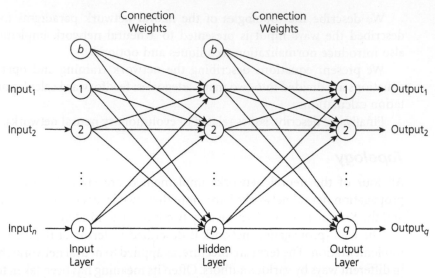

Figure 6.1 The back-propagation network structure.

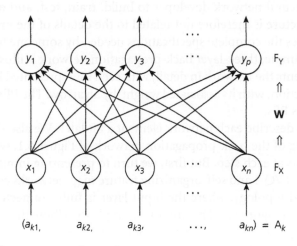

Figure 6.2 An LVQ-I Kohonen network topology.

These inputs may be a set of raw data, or a set of parameters, or whatever has been chosen to represent one single pattern of some kind. The way n, the number of inputs, is chosen depends on the kind of problem being solved and the way the data are represented.

To deal with a relatively small segment of a sampled raw voltage waveform, for example, one input PE may be assigned to each sampled value. On the other hand, to deal with a relatively large video image, a value averaged over several pixels may be presented to each PE. Another approach is to present calculated parameters to the input PE field.

Beware of the urge to "mix and match" input data in an attempt to reduce the number of input PEs. For example, generally resist the urge to combine parameters somehow before presentation to a PE. It will be a more efficient use of your and your computer's time if the network takes a little longer to train successfully than if it fails to train at all.

For the back-propagation implementation, each input can take on any real value between 0 and 1. That is, the input values are continuous and scaled between the values of 0 and 1. The fact that continuous-valued inputs can be used adds significant flexibility to the implementation.

Does the scaling between 0 and 1 constrain us in a significant way? Usually not. Whenever we deal with a computer system that is receiving input, we are limited by the size of numbers that can be processed.

As long as the resolution of the input data is not lost in the scaling process, the system will be able to get reasonable results. In the standard implementation of back-propagation, floating-point variables are used, called **float** in C. This type of variable is 32 bits long, using 24 bits for the value and 8 bits for the exponent. There is therefore a resolution of about one part in 16 million, or seven decimal places. So, if your data has seven or fewer significant digits, you'll be okay. Input data from a 16-bit analog-to-digital (A/D) converter requires a little less than five digits of resolution. Many applications seem to require only three to five digits of resolution.

Another approach is to use double-precision variables, which extend the resolution of computations considerably. This approach exacts a cost in performance as well as memory space. It is feasible to adopt this approach, however, given the gigahertz speed of personal computers and the gigabyte-sized RAMs available.

Scaling input patterns can actually provide a tool for preprocessing data in different way. The data can be scaled by considering all of the *n* inputs together, scaling each input channel separately, or scaling groups of channels in some way that makes sense. (*Input channel* means the stream of inputs to one input PE.) In some cases, the way chosen to scale inputs can affect the performance of the implementation, so this is one place to try different approaches.

If the input consists of raw data points, all channels are typically scaled together. If the input consists of calculated parameters, each channel may be scaled separately, or groups of channels representing similar parameters may be scaled together. For example, if input patterns consist of parameters that represent amplitudes and time intervals, then the amplitude channels might be scaled as a group and the time channels as a group.

Please note that so far we have talked only about scaling between values of 0 and 1. This is the most common type of scaling. However, for supervised adaptation, the scaling as well as the target values for network outputs are tied to the activation functions used in the network. Values of 0 and 1 are commonly used with a linear activation function. We often will scale from 0 to 1, and have output target values of 0 and 1, when the sigmoid function is used, but sometimes we will use values of 0.1 and 0.9 with this activation function. Often, we scale from −1 to 1, and use these as target values, when our network PEs have hyperbolic tangent activation functions.

This concludes our look at initialization and normalization for the back-propagation neural network.

Learning Vector Quantizer Network Initialization and Normalization

We now examine initialization and normalization for the learning vector quantizer neural network. At the bottom of Figure 6.2, a set of *n* inputs comes into the input layer of the network. The inputs are presented simultaneously, but bear in mind that most personal computer implementations simulate this network algorithm by processing the inputs serially.

The number of input processing elements selected depends, as in the case of the back-propagation network, on the problem to be solved. There is, however, a different emphasis than in back-propagation on how to think about the input and choose the number of input processing elements. It is more common to use "raw" data than precalculated parameters as inputs to the LVQ-I model. This is because one of the main accomplishments of LVQ-I is to cluster input data patterns into quasi-classes, thus reducing the dimensionality of the data. In other words, the LVQ-I model automatically parameterizes the data.

Another reason it is less common to use precalculated parameters is that most researchers working with LVQ-I normalize *each input vector*. With back-propagation, each individual input vector *component* is constrained to the range 0 to 1, without limiting the magnitude of the input vector, the square root of the sum of the squares of each input component.

For input to the LVQ-I network, parameterized inputs can be distorted by normalization in unpredictable ways. Carefully calculated parameters, perhaps "normalized" by constraining their values to lie between 0 and 1, can have their values changed in unforeseen ways during an input vector normalization process.

Several neural network researchers suggest that in some applications, input vectors do not necessarily have to be normalized. It is sometimes a good idea to try training with and without normalization and select the better method. Others argue that if input vectors are not normalized, then the Euclidean distance calculation cannot be used to select the "winning" processing element (Caudill 1989a).

There is general agreement on the need to initialize weight vectors by normalization. What isn't necessarily clear is the best way to do it. Typically, random values are first assigned to each weight. We might start with random values in the range ±0.3.

Some implementations choose values in the range 0 to 1. Other implementations generate initial weight vectors lying at random locations on the unit hypersphere.

The weight vector normalization procedure is done for all weights connected to a given output processing element, from all input processing elements. The most logical way to do this would seem to be to set the square root of the sum of the squares of the weights from all of the inputs to each output to the same value, presumably 1. The reason we say "would seem" and "presumably" is that various examples of Kohonen implementations have normalized weights in different ways.

Kohonen's ToPreM2 program uses a value of one-half times the sum of the squares of the weights, called the "squared norm" of the weights. Caudill, on the other hand, normalizes weight vectors in what appears to be a more logical way: dividing each weight vector component by the square root of the sum of the squares of all weight vector components (Caudill 1988). In this way, the total length of each weight vector from all inputs to a given output is 1. If w'_{ji} is the initial random weight generated in the interval from 0 to 1, then the normalized weight, w_{ji}, is given by equation 6.1.

$$w_{ji} = \frac{w'_{ji}}{\sqrt{\sum_{i=1}^{n} w'_{ji}{}^2}} \qquad (6.1)$$

Perhaps a two-dimensional geometric example of the process of initial normalization might make things clearer. In Figure 6.3(a), the circle has a radius of 1; it is what we call a unit circle. We show four unit-length two-dimensional weight vectors, w_1 through w_4, that have already been initialized randomly and normalized, perhaps using Caudill's method. They all terminate on the unit circle.

Now consider two inputs, i_1 and i_2 that have the values (2.0, 1.0) and (−0.5, −0.5), respectively. There are probably many more inputs, but we will consider just these two so that the explanation is clearer. Now, when these two inputs are normalized, they are modified so that they terminate on the unit circle, as shown in Figure 6.3(b). Note that the angles made with the axes stay the same; all we do is adjust their length to unit length.

Now we can see what we mean by "close to" in the sense of where the vectors terminate on the unit circle. The tip of w_1 is the closest weight vector tip to the tip of the normalized input $i_1{}^*$, and the tip of w_3 is closest to the tip of the normalized input $i_2{}^*$.

Feedforward Calculations for the Back-propagation Network

The feedforward calculations are used both in training (adaptation) operation mode and in testing or recall operation mode of the trained network. The feedforward

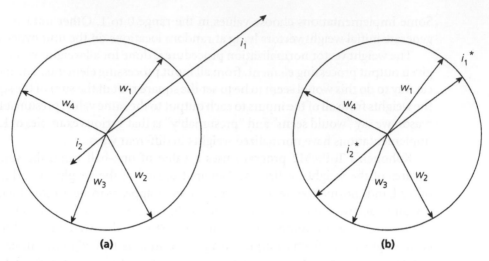

Figure 6.3 Weight vector and input vector initialization before (a) and after (b) input vector normalization.

calculation of one neural network generally is different from that of another network. We first consider the back-propagation network.

After the set of input patterns is scaled, what happens at the input layer? The input PEs simply distribute the signal along multiple paths to the hidden-layer PEs. The output of each input-layer PE is exactly equal to the input and is in the range of 0 to 1. (Another way of looking at the input layer is that it performs scaling, even though in most implementations this is done prior to presentation of the pattern to the network.)

Note that a *fully connected* feedforward topology is used. That is, each PE of the input layer is connected to every PE of the hidden layer. Likewise, each PE of the hidden layer is connected to every PE of the output layer.

Also note that each connection weight, and all data flow, goes from left to right in Figure 6.1. This is called a *feedforward* network. There are no feedback loops, even from a PE to itself, in a feedforward network. Almost all back-propagation implementations are feedforward.

For the remaining discussion on back-propagation networks in this chapter, unless otherwise stated, we assume that a sigmoid activation function is being used. Most back-propagation implementations today use the sigmoid function.

We present equations here that describe both the training (adaptation) and testing or recall modes of a back-propagation implementation. They are presented without derivations or proofs. This information can be found in Chapter 5, as well as in Rumelhart and McClelland (1986), where much of it is in Chapter 8, which focuses on internal representations.

The signal presented to a hidden layer PE in the network of Figure 6.1 due to one single connection is just the output value of the input PE (the same as the input of the input PE) times the value of the connection weight.

The activation of the ith F_Y (hidden) PE for a given input pattern k as a function of its input connections, is described in equation 6.2, where x_{kh} is the output of the F_X layer, v_{ih} the F_X to F_Y connection, and $f_{sig}(\cdot)$ the sigmoid function, described in Chapter 5. Note that h starts from 0, the bias PE.

$$y_{ki} = f_{sig}\left(\sum_{h=0}^{n} x_{kh}\, v_{ih}\right) \tag{6.2}$$

The nonlinear nature of the sigmoid transfer function plays an important role in the neural network's performance. Other functions can be used, as long as they are continuous and possess a derivative at all points. Functions such as the trigonometric sine and the hyperbolic tangent have been used, but the exploration of other transfer functions is beyond the scope of this book. For more information, refer to Rumelhart and McClelland (1986) and McClelland and Rumelhart (1988). (Note that the requirement that the function be continuously differentiable holds for the back-propagation learning algorithm, but that PE activations with hard [step] nonlinearities can be trained using random search techniques, simulated annealing, or evolutionary algorithms.)

The sigmoid (squashing) function can be viewed as performing a function similar to that of an analog electronic amplifier. The gain, or amplification, of the amplifier is analogous to the slope of the line, or the ratio of the change in output for a given change in input. The slope of the function (gain of the amplifier) is greatest for total (net) inputs near 0. This serves to mitigate problems caused by noise and by the possible dominating effects of large input signals.

Once the activations of all hidden-layer PEs have been calculated, the outputs of the F_Z layer are calculated in an analogous manner. The activation of the jth F_Z (output) PE as a function of its input connections is described in equation 6.3, where y_{ki} is the output of the F_Y (hidden) layer, and w_{ji} the F_Y to F_Z connection weight.

$$z_{kj} = f_n\left(\sum_{i=0}^{h} y_{ki}\, w_{ji}\right) \tag{6.3}$$

This set of feedforward calculations, resulting in the output state of the network (the set of activations of all output PEs), is carried out in exactly the same way during the training phase as during the testing phase. The test operational mode just involves presenting an input set to the input PEs and calculating the resulting output state in one forward pass.

Feedforward Calculations for the LVQ-I Net

As in the back-propagation neural network, the input PEs simply distribute the signal along multiple paths to the output layer PEs. The Euclidean distance between the input vector and the weight vectors associated with each output PE is first calculated according to equation 6.4. The Euclidean distance is the square root of the sum of the squares of the differences between each input vector component and its associated weight vector component. Since relative magnitudes are what is important, as is conserving computing time, square root calculations often are not done in software implementations. The output PE with the minimum Euclidean distance between the input vector and the weight vector associated with the output PE is the winner and represents the cluster or class to which the input vector belongs.

$$d_j = \sqrt{\sum_{i=1}^{n} \left(a_{ki} - w_{ji}\right)^2} \qquad (6.4)$$

Back-propagation Supervised Adaptation by Error Back-propagation

Adaptation calculations are applied only during training. Back-propagation is an example of a supervised adaptation model, while LVQ-I is a prime example of unsupervised adaptation. (LVQ-II is a supervised version of a Kohonen network.)

With supervised adaptation models, input patterns are presented with targets to the network, the targets being the desired output values for each input pattern. With unsupervised adaptation models, on the other hand, input patterns are presented without targets. The network adapts from the input patterns alone. In this section, we look at back-propagation supervised adaptation.

During the training phase, the feedforward output state calculation is combined with backward error propagation and weight adjustment calculations that represent the network's adaptation, or training. It is this adaptation process resulting from the back-propagation of errors, and how it is implemented, that is the "secret to the success" of the back-propagation implementation. Central to the concept of training a network is the definition of network error. A measure of how well a network is performing on the training set must be identified.

Rumelhart and McClelland (1986) define an error term that depends on the difference between the desired, or target, output value of an output PE, b_{kj}, and its actual value, z_{kj}. The error term is defined for a given pattern and summed over all output PEs for that pattern.

Equation 6.5 presents the definition of the error. The subscript k denotes that the value is for a given pattern. Note that the error calculation in the back-propagation training algorithm generally is implemented PE by PE over the entire set (epoch) of patterns, rather than on a pattern-by-pattern basis. The error is then summed over all PEs, giving a grand total for all PEs and all patterns.

Then the grand total is divided by the number of patterns, to give an "average sum-squared error" value. This makes sense because the number of patterns in our training set can vary, and we want some sort of standardized value that allows us to compare apples with apples, so to speak. And since the factor 0.5 is a constant, it is often deleted from the calculations. (The 0.5 *does*, however, allow "neat" differentiation that makes the math elsewhere easier. If not used, factors of two appear in other terms.)

$$E_k = 0.5 \sum_{j=1}^{q} \left(b_{kj} - z_{kj} \right)^2 \tag{6.5}$$

The goal of the adaptation process is to minimize this average sum-squared error over all training patterns. Figuring out how to minimize the error with respect to the hidden PEs was the key that opened up back-propagation models for widespread applications.

The derivation is not presented here. It can be found in a nonrigorous format in Chapter 5, or in Chapter 8 of Rumelhart and McClelland (1986). Even their derivation lacks absolute rigor, but reviewing it should provide an understanding of where the equations come from and help make you more comfortable with using them.

A quantity called the *error signal* δ_j, for sigmoid nonlinear output layer PEs, is defined in equation 6.6, where the term $z_{kj}(1 - z_{kj})$ represents the first derivative of the sigmoid function.

$$\partial_{kj} = z_{kj} \left(1 - z_{kj} \right) \left(b_{kj} - z_{kj} \right) \tag{6.6}$$

It is necessary to propagate this error value back and perform appropriate weight adjustments. There are two ways to do this:

On-line, or single-pattern, learning. Propagate the error back and adjust weights after each training pattern is presented to the network.

Off-line, or epoch, learning. Accumulate the δ's for each PE for the entire training set, add them together, and propagate the error back, based on the grand total δ.

The back-propagation algorithms in the implementation with this book are implemented using both off-line and on-line learning, with emphasis on off-line learning. In fact, Rumelhart and McClelland (1986) assumed that weight changes occur only after a complete cycle of pattern presentations. As they point out, it's all right to calculate weight changes after each pattern as long as the learning rate η is sufficiently small. It does, however, add significant computational overhead to do that, and it is desirable to speed up training whenever possible.

Before the weights can be updated, however, there must be something to update. That is, each weight must be initialized to some value. You can't just start out with all weights equal to 0 (or all equal to any single number, for that matter), or the network won't be trainable. The reason can be seen by studying the weight update equations presented next.

It is typical to initialize the weights in a back-propagation network to random values between 0.3 and −0.3. Picking random numbers over some range makes intuitive sense, and you can see how different weights go in different directions by doing this. But why pick −0.3 and 0.3 as the bounds? To be honest, there is no better reason than "it works." Most back-propagation implementations seem to train faster with these bounds than, say, 1 and −1. It may have something to do with the fact that the bounds of the PE activation values are 1 and −1. This makes the products of weights and activation values relatively small numbers. Therefore, if they start out "wrong," they can be adjusted quickly.

Neural network researchers have recommended a number of variations on the initial weight range. For example, Lee (1989) has shown that in some instances initializing the weights feeding the output layer to random values between 0.3 and −0.3, while initializing weights feeding the hidden layer to 0, speeds training. (Initializing all weights feeding the hidden layer to 0 is permissible, as long as the next layer up is initialized to random, nonzero values. This can be verified by working through the weight updating equations that follow.) In most cases, however, the random number initialization to values from −0.3 to 0.3 works well and is almost always a good place to start.

We now describe how to use δ_{kj} to update weights that feed the output layer, w_{ji}. To a first approximation, the updating of these weights is described by equation 6.7. Here, η (the lowercase Greek letter eta) is defined as the learning coefficient, with a value between 0 and 1.

$$w_{ji}^{\text{new}} = w_{ji}^{\text{old}} + \eta \sum_k \delta_{kj} y_{ki} \tag{6.7}$$

This kind of weight updating sometimes has a problem in that it gets caught in what are called "local energy minima." If you can visualize a bowl-shaped surface with a lot of little bumps and ridges in it, you can get an idea of the problem, at least in three dimensions.

The error minimization process is analogous to minimizing the energy of the position in the bumpy, ridge-lined bowl. Ideally, we'd like to move the position (perhaps marked by a very small ball bearing) to the bottom of the bowl, where the energy is minimum; this position is the globally optimal solution.

Depending on how much or how little the ball bearing can be moved at one time, however, it might get caught in some little depression or ridge that it can't get out of. This situation is most likely with small limits on each movement, which correspond to small values of η.

The situation can be helped by using the "momentum" of the ball bearing. Its momentum (previous movement) is taken into account by multiplying the previous weight change by a "momentum factor" that is labeled α, the lowercase Greek letter alpha. The momentum factor α can take on values between 0 and 1. Equation 6.8, which is just equation 6.7 with the momentum term added, becomes the equation actually used in the back-propagation implementation to update the weights feeding the output layer.

$$w_{ji}^{\text{new}} = w_{ji}^{\text{old}} + \eta \sum_k \delta_{kj} y_{ki} + \alpha \Delta w_{ji}^{\text{old}} \tag{6.8}$$

Watch out! We've just thrown another delta at you. This one, Δw^{old}, stands for the *previous weight change*. Stated in words, the new weight is equal to the old weight plus the weight change. The weight change consists of the δ error signal term and the α momentum factor term. The momentum term is the product of the momentum factor α and the *previous* weight change. The previous "movement" of the weight thus imparts "momentum" to the ball bearing (the weight), and it is much more likely to reach the globally optimum solution.

Keep in mind that there are "bias PEs," indicated by the letter "b" in Figure 6.1, which always have an output of 1. They serve as threshold units for the layers to which they are connected, and the weights from the bias PEs to each PE in the following layer are adjusted exactly like the other weights. In equation 6.8, then, for each of the output PEs, the subscript i takes on values from 0 to p, which is the number of hidden PEs. The 0th value is associated with the bias PE.

Now that we have the new values for the weights feeding the output PEs, we turn our attention to the hidden PEs. What is the error term for these units? It isn't as simple to figure this out as it was for the output PEs, where it could intuitively be reasoned that the error should be some function of the difference between the desired and the actual output.

We really have no idea what the value for a hidden PE "should" be. Again, refer to the derivation in *Chapter 5*, as well as to the one by Rumelhart and McClelland (1986). Both show that the error term for a hidden PE is given by equation 6.9, where the term $y_{ki}(1 - y_{ki})$ represents the first derivative of the sigmoid function.

$$\delta_{ki} = y_{ki}(1 - y_{ki}) \sum_{j=1}^{q} w_{ji} \delta_{kj} \tag{6.9}$$

The weight changes for the connections feeding the hidden layer from the input layer are now calculated in a manner analogous to those feeding the output layer, as shown in equation 6.10.

$$v_{ih}^{\text{new}} = v_{ih}^{\text{old}} + \eta \sum_k \delta_{ki} x_{kh} + \alpha \Delta v_{ih}^{\text{old}} \tag{6.10}$$

For each hidden PE, the subscript h takes on values of 0 to n, the number of input PEs. As before, the bias PEs are represented in the calculations by the 0th value.

We now have all of the equations (6.6, 6.8, 6.9, and 6.10) to implement back-propagation of errors and adjustment of weights for both groups of weights. First, the error terms are calculated for each output PE using equation 6.6, then for each hidden PE using equation 6.9 for each pattern in the training set. Then the error terms are summed after all patterns have been presented once, and the weight adjustments are calculated as in equations 6.8 and 6.10.

There are a few things to keep in mind.

- For updating using the off-line (epoch) mode, it is necessary, in equations 6.8 and 6.10, to sum over all patterns in the training set, whereas the δ's in equations 6.6 and 6.9 are calculated pattern by pattern.

- Although values for η and α can be assigned layer by layer, or even PE by PE, there is typically only one value selected for each in a given implementation. These values are often adjusted in the process of getting a network to successfully train, but once chosen are usually left alone.

- When δ's are calculated for the hidden layer in equation 6.9, the *old* (existing) weights (rather than new ones that might have been calculated from equation 6.8) from the hidden to the output layer are used in the equation. This is really only a potential problem if the weights are updated after each training pattern is presented. If epoch training is performed, weights aren't updated until all patterns have been presented, so there is no cause for worry.

LVQ Unsupervised Adaptation Calculations

The unsupervised adaptation process consists of presenting pattern vectors from the training set to the network one at a time. For each pattern presentation, select the winning processing element and adjust the weights of the winner.

The result of unsupervised adaptation is that the outputs of the network fall into class clusters reflecting the probability density of the input vectors. When the network has adapted, the output-layer processing elements represent pattern class clusters of the input pattern vectors. Note that the network isn't adapted in a supervised way by telling it what the "correct" answers are. The patterns are simply presented to the network repeatedly, and the network adapts by adjusting its weights so as to form pattern classes.

The winner is chosen by finding the PE with the minimum Euclidean distance between the input vector and the weight vectors associated with each output PE. The Euclidean distance is the square root of the sum of the squares of the differences between each input vector component and its associated weight vector component, as illustrated in equation 6.4. (See Chapter 10 for a discussion of other distance metrics.)

The winner for the particular iteration of an input pattern is the processing element with the smallest Euclidean distance. The calculation of this dimensionless Euclidean distance has meaning because the input and weight vectors are normalized before performing the calculations. The weights connected to the winner are then adjusted according to equation 6.11, where the learning coefficient η is a decreasing function of time. Note that equation 6.11 calculates the weight *change* that must be added to the weight.

$$\Delta w_{ji} = \eta(t)\left(a_{ki} - w_{ji}\right) \tag{6.11}$$

Equations 6.4 and 6.11 are calculated for each pattern presented to the network during adaptation. Presentations continue until the weight adjustments become acceptably small or a criterion for the maximum number of iterations is met.

Is it necessary to renormalize the weight vectors during or after training, given what was said about the validity of the dot product? No, not as long as the changes to the weight vector components carried out according to equation 6.11 are small enough. Keeping them small keeps the length of the weight vectors near 1 (near the surface of a unit hypersphere), and the dot product process remains valid.

Selection of training patterns for the LVQ-I network is the subject of much discussion in the literature (Kohonen 1988, 1989; Caudill 1989a). It is generally agreed that each category, or classification, to which the network is trained should be represented by "gold standard" examples (i.e., right down the center of the category space), as well as by examples near the decision surfaces with other categories. Experimentation is needed to determine the training vector requirements for a particular application.

The LVQ Supervised Adaptation Algorithm

The LVQ-II algorithm is a supervised adaptation extension of LVQ-I. The classifications of all patterns used for training must therefore be known. In implementing LVQ-II, assuming that the output PE layer has p PEs, the weights to these PEs should initially be set equal to p input patterns, such that the number of weights from each pattern class reflects the probability distribution of the classes. If there are c classes, and the distribution is unknown, then instantiate p/c weight vectors of each class.

The updating of weights is done with a reward–punish scheme: The weight of the winning PE is moved toward the pattern weight if the classification. Is correct and moved away if it is incorrect. Assume that the winning class is C_{win}. Then the winning PE's weight vector is adjusted according to equation 6.12. (Only the winning PE's weight vector is modified.)

$$w_{ji}^{\text{new}} = w_{ji}^{\text{old}} + \eta(t)(a_{kj} - w_{ji}) \quad \text{for } C_{\text{in}} = C_{\text{win}}$$
$$w_{ji}^{\text{new}} = w_{ji}^{\text{old}} - \eta(t)(a_{kj} - w_{ji}) \quad \text{for } C_{\text{in}} \neq C_{\text{win}}$$

$$(6.12)$$

This is a useful scheme when the classifications of the training patterns are known and it is desirable to reduce misclassifications. However, if classifications are known, a back-propagation network is generally a better pattern classifier, so an LVQ-II implementation is not included in this book. We include it here more for purposes of completeness.

Issues in Evolving Neural Networks

The neural network adaptation presented in the previous section is based on connection weight adaptation with fixed network architecture. Much of the time, it's hard to select the right network architecture for the application at hand. Both the network architecture and the connection weights need to be adapted simultaneously or sequentially.

Two of the general (nonevolutionary) approaches used to evolve network topology are *constructive* and *destructive* algorithms. A constructive algorithm starts with a minimal topology and evolves the appropriate topology by adding weights, PEs, and layers, as needed. The destructive approach starts with a large network and evolves the appropriate topology by removing weights, PEs, and/or layers.

In this chapter, we provide an implementation of a back-propagation neural network with an evolutionary algorithm (EA) using particle swarm optimization (PSO). EAs have been shown to be superior to these constructive and destructive approaches because of the large (often infinite) size, nondifferentiability, complexity, and multimodality of the search space (Yao 1995).

Evolutionary computation methodologies have generally been applied to three main attributes of neural networks: network connection weights, network architecture, and network learning algorithms. A fourth area, the evolution of inputs (finding the optimal set of inputs), has received a relatively minor amount of attention.

With respect to the architecture of a neural network, evolutionary algorithms have been applied to evolve the network weights, the network topology (structure), and the PE transfer function. Occasionally, they have been used for more than one purpose—for example, evolving the network weights and the structure simultaneously. Furthermore, evolutionary computing methodologies are sometimes used in combinations and sometimes with other methodologies. For example, it is possible for an EA such as a GA to find a set of weights in the global minimum's basin of attraction. A greedy local search algorithm can then be used to find the globally optimal neural network weight matrix (Yao 1995). A number of approaches have been used to encode the weights into the chromosome of a GA. Included are direct encoding schemes, in which each weight is explicitly represented in the chromosome, and indirect schemes, in which a compression scheme is used that requires an expansion of the chromosome to derive the individual weights. We cite a few specific examples of these approaches next. We chose them to be representative only; an exhaustive survey is beyond the scope of this book.

As early as 1968, Bremmermann, a pioneer in the evolutionary computation field, suggested in (Bremmermann 1968) that "we should be encouraged to try [evolutionary search] procedures on more complex problems, where no efficient algorithms are known (e.g., searching for strategies, optimizing 'weights' in a multilayer neural net, etc.)." Widespread efforts to evolve neural network parameters, however, did not occur until the popularization of the back-propagation algorithm.

One of the first published works that described use of a GA and included example applications was by Whitley (1989), in which a GA was used to learn the weights in a feedforward neural network. He applied the technique to relatively small problems, such as the exclusive—or (XOR). Also in 1989, Montana and Davis (1989) described the use of a GA to train a neural network of approximately 500 weights. It wasn't a "traditional" GA in that, instead of replacing the entire population each generation, only one or two individuals were produced, which then had to compete to be included in the new population. Also, network weights were represented by real, rather than binary, numbers. This type of implementation is known as a "steady-state" GA. Furthermore, Montana and Davis's paradigm included an option for improving population members using back-propagation. This was thus a truly hybrid approach. (This hill-climbing capability, however, did not result in better results than when using the GA alone.)

Another promising early result was that of Schaffer, Caruana, and Eshelman (1990), which demonstrated that an evolved neural network had better generalization performance than one designed by a human and trained with back-propagation. A number of similar papers were also published. The reported network training times were sometimes faster and sometimes slower than back-propagation but were generally not as fast as network training algorithms noted for their speed, such as quickprop.

Most of the work involving the evolution of network architecture has focused on the network topological structure. Relatively little has been done on the evolution of PE activation functions and even less on evolving topological structure and PE activation functions simultaneously.

Reduced (indirect) coding schemes have been developed in which parameters that specify the network topology are evolved. This approach often involves a discrete number (limited set) of architectures. Other times, the number of PEs and/or the number of hidden layers is encoded (Caudell 1990). These approaches result in chromosome discontinuities between any two network configurations.

Another approach is to evolve developmental rules used to construct the network topology. Kitano (1990) evolved a graph generation grammar, or rules for generating weight connection matrices. His grammar included rules for obtaining

2×2 matrices from 1×1 matrices, 4×4 matrices from 2×2 matrices, and so on, until a matrix of the size necessary to specify the weight connectivity for the network was obtained. Although Kitano reported better results than some direct encoding methods, his method is not very good at fine-tuning connections among single nodes.

Perhaps the first publication reporting the evolution of both network topology and PE activation functions using a GA was that of Stork and colleagues (1990). They were modeling a biological neuron in the tail-flip circuitry of a crayfish. Although the network had only seven PEs, the activation function evolved was the very complex Hodgkin–Huxley equation for neuronal activity. Chromosomes included coded specifications for neuron type, cell surface molecules, neurotransmitter type, synapse receptor types, cell channel densities, and other functional properties of the network.

Koza and Rice (1991) used the genetic programming paradigm to find both the weights and topology (number of layers, number of PEs per layer, and weight connectivity pattern) of a neural network. They encoded a tree structure of Lisp S-expressions in the chromosome. Special crossover and mutation operators were used that preserved the syntax. This may be the first published report of using genetic programming to evolve neural networks.

Some investigators have investigated the optimization of the EA operators used to evolve neural networks. Research work reported by Whitley, Dominic, and Das (1991) indicated that hill-climbing capabilities of GAs using real-valued encoding for the network weights were increased significantly by a combination of increasing the mutation rate, decreasing the crossover rate, and decreasing the population size. Convergence was faster, too, but the probability of obtaining a usable solution decreased by about 10 percent. It should be noted that "steady-state" GAs similar to those of Montana and Davis (1989) were used, resulting in relatively monotonic searches. This type of GA is referred to as a "genetic hill-climber" (Schaffer, Whitley, and Eshelman 1992). GAs have thus been designed that emphasize either global or local search. The trick, of course, is knowing which to use for a particular problem, or, perhaps more important, how and when to switch from one to the other when solving a problem.

Advantages and Disadvantages of Previous Evolutionary Approaches

In this section, we briefly summarize some of the advantages and disadvantages that have been discussed in the literature and that researchers have experienced with respect to using evolutionary computation techniques with artificial neural networks. The discussion is not meant to be thorough. Rather, we are highlighting the successes and examining issues that should be addressed in order to make progress. We do not review the advantages and disadvantages of neural networks and evolutionary algorithms individually. Such reviews appear in a number of places (Schaffer, Whitley, and Eshelman 1992; Yao 1995).

Let's first look at the advantages. Evolutionary algorithms can be used to adapt neural networks with nondifferentiable (even discontinuous) PE transfer functions. Step functions are an example. Additionally, not all of the transfer functions have to be identical in a network trained by an EA.

Evolutionary algorithms can also be used in cases where gradient or error information is not available (Schaffer, Whitley, and Eshelman 1992). (See, however, a statement from the same reference in the section below on disadvantages.) EAs can thus be applied to neural networks using many architectures and topologies. In addition to back-propagation, EAs have been applied to networks using a variety of learning algorithms, including reinforcement learning, recurrent learning, and higher order learning.

Evolutionary algorithms have the capability to perform a global search in the problem space.

The fitness of an architecture evolved by an EA can be defined in a way appropriate for the problem. For example, speed of learning, topological complexity, and performance on the test set can all be incorporated into the fitness function. Furthermore, the fitness function does not have to be continuous or differentiable.

Now, let's look at the disadvantages. Schaffer, Whitley, and Eshelman (1992) state that "Using a genetic algorithm as a replacement for back-propagation does not seem to be competitive with the best gradient methods (e.g., quickprop)." GAs are known to perform global search quite well but to be relatively inefficient in fine-tuned local search (Yao 1995).

Evolution of network topology is generally done in ways that result in discontinuities in the search space. Examples include removing and inserting connections (weights), discrete changes in connections (weights), from 1 to −1 for example, and removing and inserting PEs. These discontinuities usually require readaptation of the network. Since the adaptation of a back-propagation network is sensitive to the randomized initial weights, the fitness value used to measure the network's performance reflects noise as well as the network architecture. It is therefore usually necessary to adapt the network several times and compute an average fitness value, or partially adapt the network a number of times to get an indication of convergence rates. Either approach is computationally intensive.

Selection of a representation for the weights in a chromosome is often difficult. In addition to the basic decision whether to use binary or real representations, the ordering of the weights must be considered, especially if an EA that uses crossover or recombination is being used. For instance, should the heuristic (Yao 1995) that weights connecting into the same hidden PE be adjacent in the chromosome be implemented? If binary encoding is selected, which encoding method should be selected (uniform, Gray, exponential, etc.)? Once the representation is selected, the genetic operators (crossover, mutation, etc.) and their parameter values must be selected or, in many cases, developed. Often, operators are designed specifically for a problem.

If a real number representation for weights is used, a set of operators must be selected or developed. These must generally be tailored to the application. In addition, the criterion for selection must be specified.

Finally, a problem that has consistently been reported in the literature is the *permutation problem* (Yao 1995; Hancock 1992), also referred to as the *competing conventions problem* (Schaffer, Whitley, and Eshelman 1992) and the *isomorphism problem* (Hancock 1992). This situation arises whenever there exist multiple chromosome configurations that represent equivalent optimum solutions. These configurations are called *permutations* or *competing conventions*, and the error surfaces are multimodal. For example, two neural networks that have a different order to their hidden PEs (and thus have a different representation on the chromosome) but are otherwise identical are equivalent. In fact, any permutation of the hidden PEs produces an equivalent network in this case.

Hancock's work was limited to the specification of the network connectivity, not the weights associated with the connections. Nonetheless, he reported that "The most unexpected result here was that permutations are apparently more of a help than a hindrance" and that "It appears that, in practice, the permutation or competing conventions problem is not as severe as had been supposed" (Hancock 1992). We agree.

Evolving Neural Networks with Particle Swarm Optimization

The benefits of evolving attributes of neural networks are clear. Multilayer perceptrons (feedforward networks using the back-propagation algorithm as the learning algorithm) have been shown to be capable of being universal approximators (Hornick et al. 1989). The most common transfer function used is the sigmoidal function: output = $1/(1 + e^{-\text{input}})$. The idea of being able to automatically evolve a universal approximator is quite attractive, especially if it can be done as (or more) quickly than training the network with back-propagation.

One of the first uses of particle swarm optimization (PSO) was for evolving neural network weights. Eberhart, Simpson, and Dobbins (1996) reported using particle swarm optimization to replace the back-propagation learning algorithm in a multilayer perceptron.

The implementation reported in (Eberhart and Shi 1998) is the use of PSO to evolve the network weights and, indirectly, to evolve the structure. The methodology has the additional benefit of making the preprocessing (such as normalization or scaling) of input data unnecessary.

This is accomplished by evolving, in addition to the network weights, the slopes of the sigmoidal transfer functions of the hidden and output PEs of a feedforward network. In other words, if we now consider the transfer function to be output $= 1/(1 + e^{-k^*\text{input}})$, then we are evolving k in addition to evolving the weights. (The method is quite general and can be applied to other network topologies, such as recurrent networks, and to other transfer functions, such as radial basis functions.)

Slopes are allowed to be either positive or negative. The output of a transfer function with a negative slope is just one minus the output with a positive slope of the same absolute value. The effect of a transfer function with a negative slope is identical to that of a transfer function with a positive slope (with the same absolute value) if the signs of the input weights are reversed. There is thus no reason to constrain slopes to be positive, and by allowing them to take on negative values, the flexibility of the network evolution process is increased, resulting in faster convergence.

This method can be used to evolve the network structure indirectly. If the evolved slope is sufficiently small (the exact amount depends on the application), then the output is essentially constant regardless of the input. (In the case of the sigmoidal transfer function, the output would be 0.5, or very nearly so.) If the PE is in a hidden layer, it can therefore be removed. Its effect can be replicated by increasing the weights from the bias PE in that hidden layer to each of the PEs in the next layer by one-half the value of each weight from the PE being removed to the next-layer PEs. The method therefore can be used to prune PEs from the network, reducing network complexity.

Additionally, if the slope is sufficiently large (the exact amount depends on the application), then the sigmoid transfer function can be replaced by a step transfer function. A sigmoid with a large positive slope is thus replaced by a step transfer function that has an output of 0 for inputs less than or equal to 0, and 1 for positive inputs. A sigmoid with a large negative slope is replaced by a step function with an output of 1 for inputs less than or equal to 0, and 0 for positive inputs. Sigmoidal function PEs can thus evolve to be step function PEs, reducing the computational complexity of the network significantly.

Since the slopes can evolve to large values (relative to 1, which is the slope used in traditional back-propagation network transfer functions), input normalization or scaling is generally not needed. Since data preprocessing requires a significant amount of effort in most applications, this methodology can simplify the applications process and shorten development time.

Another feature of this methodology is the continuous nature of the PSO algorithm. Transfer function slopes are evolved in a continuous way; that is, slopes can vary continuously from large negative to large positive values. This results in an evolution of network structures that is also continuous. For example, as a hidden PE's transfer function slope approaches 0, it is replaced with revised connection weights from the bias PE; as the slope becomes very large, the sigmoidal PE is replaced by a threshold PE. No significant discontinuities exist in the evolutionary process such as those that plague other approaches to evolving network structures.

Back-propagation Implementation

This section discusses the back-propagation implementation. This is an implementation of a fully connected feedforward layered network. Connections exist only from the PEs in one layer to the PEs in the next layer. There are no feedback connections, even among PEs in the same layer. The number of hidden layers and number of PEs in each layer can be specified in a run file. For the basics of back-propagation neural networks, please refer to Chapter 5.

Programming a Back-propagation Neural Network

Figure 6.4 shows the state transition diagram used in the implementation of the back-propagation neural network discussed in this section. First we define some new data types in the next subsections.

We first look at general definitions for neural networks. In this section, some data types applicable to several neural network implementations in this book are defined as shown in Listing 6.1. In Listing 6.1 are the new enumeration data types. These definitions are also used in the implementations of other neural networks, in addition to the back-propagation neural network discussed in this section.

Listing 6.1 Enumeration data type definitions for neural networks.

```
/****************************************************************/
/* Enumerations                                                 */
/****************************************************************/
typedef enum NN_Operation_Mode_Type_Tag
{
    NN_TRAINING,
    NN_RECALL,
    NUM_BP_OPERATION_MODES
} NN_Operation_Mode_Type;

typedef enum NN_Function_Type_Tag
{
    NN_LINEAR_FUNCTION,
    NN_GAUSIAN_FUNCTION,
    NN_SIGMOID_FUNCTION,
    NUM_NN_FUNCTION_TYPES
} NN_Function_Type;

typedef enum NN_Layer_Type_Tag
{
    NN_INPUT_LAYER,
    NN_HIDDEN_LAYER,
    NN_OUTPUT_LAYER,
    NUM_NN_LAYERS
} NN_Layer_Type;
```

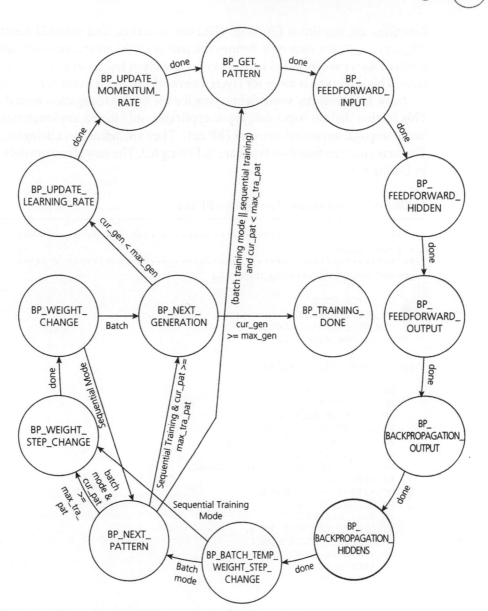

Figure 6.4 A back-propagation neural network state transition diagram in training mode.

The enumeration data type NN_Operation_Mode_Type defines the operation mode of the neural network. The neural network can be in training mode or in testing or recall mode. The data type NN_Function_Type defines the function types of the PE activation functions. Three kinds of activation functions are included. More can be included later if necessary. These three activation functions are the linear function, Gaussian function, and sigmoid function. The NN_Layer_Type data type defines the nature of the neural network layer. Three kinds of layers are included here. They are the input layer, hidden layer, and output layer. This data type is more for layered networks than for other types of networks.

Now, let's consider some definitions for the back-propagation neural network. This section defines some date types applicable only to the implementation of the back-propagation neural network (BP net). They are defined in Listings 6.2 and 6.3. The new enumeration data types are in Listing 6.2. The new structure data types are in Listing 6.3.

Listing 6.2 Enumeration data type for BP net.

```
/****************************************************************/
/* Enumerations                                                 */
/****************************************************************/
typedef enum BP_Training_Mode_Tag
{
    NN_BATCH_MODE,
    NN_SEQUENTIAL_MODE,
    NUM_NN_TRAINING_MODES
} BP_Training_Mode_Type;

typedef enum BP_State_Tag
{
    BP_GET_PATTERN,
    BP_FEEDFORWARD_INPUT,
    BP_FEEDFORWARD_HIDDEN,
    BP_FEEDFORWARD_OUTPUT,
    BP_BACK_PROPAGATION_OUTPUT,
    BP_BACK_PROPAGATION_HIDDENS,
    BP_BATCH_TEMP_WEIGHT_STEP_CHANGE,
    BP_NEXT_PATTERN,
    BP_WEIGHT_STEP_CHANGE,
    BP_WEIGHT_CHANGE,
    BP_NEXT_GENERATION,
    BP_UPDATE_LEARNING_RATE,
    BP_UPDATE_MOMENTUM_RATE,
    BP_TRAINING_DONE,
    BP_RECALL_DONE,
    NUM_BP_STATES
} BP_State_Type;
```

The enumeration data type BP_Training_Mode_Type specifies the training mode for the back-propagation implementation. It can be either in batch training mode (off-line adaptation) or in sequential training mode (on-line adaptation). The data type BP_State_Type defines all the states in the back-propagation state machine. There are fifteen states, each with a corresponding state handling routine.

Listing 6.3 Structure data type definitions for BP net.

```
/*****************************************************************/
/* Structures                                                    */
/*****************************************************************/
typedef struct Neuron_Type_Tag
{

    NN_Function_Type         neuron_function; // neuron function
    float                    in;              // neuron input
    float                    out;             // neuron output
    FVECTOR                  w;
                             // connection weights from the previous layers
    double                   error;           // error of neuron's output
    FVECTOR                  delta_w;         // step change of weights
    FVECTOR                  temp_delta_w;    // temp. step change of weights

} Neuron_Type;

typedef struct NN_Layer_Arch_Type_Tag
{

    int                      size;       // number of neurons in the layer
    Neuron_Type              *neurons;   // pointer to the array of neurons
    NN_Layer_Type            layer_type;

} NN_Layer_Arch_Type;

typedef struct BP_Arch_Type_Tag
{

    int              size;           // number of layers
    NN_Layer_Arch_Type *layers;      // pointer to the layers
    int              *hidden_number;

} BP_Arch_Type;

typedef struct BP_Env_Type_Tag
{

    NN_Operation_Mode_Type operation_mode; // training or recall
    BP_Training_Mode_Type train_mode;    // training mode if in training
    float                 alpha;         // learning rate   0.075
    float                 gama;          // momentum rate   0.15
    float                 criterion; // error criterion for termination
    int                   max_gen;   // maximum number of generations
    int                   cur_gen;   // current generation index
    int               max_tra_pat;   // total number of training patterns
    int                   cur_pat;   // current training pattern index
} BP_Env_Type;

typedef struct BP_Type_Tag
{

    BP_Arch_Type             arch;
    BP_Env_Type              env;
```

```
    double                mse;              // mean squared error
} BP_Type;


typedef struct BP_Pattern_Set_Type_Tag
{
    int                 size;             // number of patterns
    int                 dim_in;           // input dimension
    int                 dim_out;          // output dimension
    FMATRIX             patterns; // pointer to the array of in/outpatterns
} BP_Pattern_Set_Type;
```

The structure data type `Neuron_Type` defines the parameters of the network's PEs (neurons)—the basic building components of the neural network. It consists of an activation function (`NN_Function_Type`), input (`float`), output (`float`), connection weights to a PE (`FVECTOR`), error (`double`), step change of weights (`FVECTOR`), and temporary step change of weights (`FVECTOR`). The last three are included for the purpose of training, especially when used in a back-propagation neural network. The `NN_Layer_Arch_Type` defines the architecture of the neural network layer. It consists of a layer type (`NN_Layer_Type`), a pointer to the PEs (`Neuron_Type`) in the layer, and the number of PEs in the layer (`int`). (Note that in the code PEs are referred to as neurons.)

The structure data type `BP_Arch_Type` defines the architecture of the back-propagation neural network. The component `size` (`int`) specifies the number of layers in the network; the component `layers` (`NN_Layer_Arch_Type *`) is a pointer to the layers; and the component `hidden_number` (`int *`) is a pointer to the number of PEs in hidden layers.

The `BP_Env_Type` defines all of the environment parameters for running the back-propagation implementation. They are operation mode (`operation_mode`), training mode (`train_mode`), learning rate (`alpha`), momentum (`gama`), training error criterion for termination (`criterion`), maximum number of generations (`max_gen`), current generation index (`cur_gen`), total number of training patterns (`max_tra_pat`), and current training pattern index (`cur_pat`).

The `BP_Type` defines a `struct` data type, which specifies the back-propagation neural network. It includes BP architecture data (`arch`), BP environment data (`env`), and mean squared error (`mse`).

The `BP_Pattern_Set_Type` defines the set of patterns that are fed to the BP net. It consists of number of patterns (`size`), input dimension (`dim_in`), output dimension (`dim_out`), and a pointer to the array of input/output pairs of patterns (`patterns`).

The *main()* routine is shown in Listing 6.4. It is kept as simple as possible to make the back-propagation module as independent as possible. In the `BP_Start_Up()` routine, all the necessary parameters for running the back-propagation implementation are read from the input (run) file; the dynamic data storage variables are allocated memory space and initialized. In the BP_Clean_Up() routine, the results are stored in an output file and the memory space previously allocated is de-allocated. The BP_Main_Loop() routine is the core of the back-propagation implementation, where the state machine is run.

Listing 6.4 Back-propagation `main()` routine.

```
void main (int argc, char *argv[])
{
    int idx_i;

    // check command line
    if (argc != 2)
    {
        printf("Usage: exe_file run_file");
        exit(1);
    }

    main_start_up(argv[1]);
    BP_Main_Loop();
    main_clean_up();
}

static void main_start_up (char *dataFile)
{
    BP_Start_Up(dataFile);
}

static void main_clean_up (void)
{
    BP_Clean_Up();
}
```

We now consider the *BP_Main_Loop()* routine. Before running the BP_Main_Loop() routine, several BP module scope variables are defined as follows:

```
static BP_Type              bp;
static BP_Pattern_Set_Type  patset;
static BP_State_Type        bp_cur_state;
```

These three variables are defined as static to prevent them from being accidentally changed by outside modules. The variable bp has information related to the back-propagation net during the run.

The variable patset stores all the input/output pairs of patterns. The variable bp_cur_state records the current state of the back-propagation state machine. When the BP_Main_Loop() routine is running, it keeps calling the current state's handling routine through bp_state_handler (bp_cur_state), where the current state performs its action until it is transitioned to another state. The BP_Main_Loop() keeps running until its current state is transitioned to either the state `BP_TRAINING_DONE` when BP is in the training operation mode or to the state `BP_RECALL_DONE` when BP is in the recall/test operation mode.

```
void BP_Main_Loop (void)
{
    BOOLEAN running;

    running = TRUE;
    while (running)
    {
        if ((bp_cur_state == BP_TRAINING_DONE) || (bp_cur_state ==
                                        BP_RECALL_DONE))
        {
            running = FALSE;
        }
        bp_state_handler(bp_cur_state);
    }
}
```

The Back-propagation State Handling Routines

We now examine the BP state handling routines. The most important part of the BP state machine is its state handler, which is shown in Listing 6.5. As shown in the listing, which state handler routine is called is based on the current BP state.

Listing 6.5 Main part of the BP state machine.

```
static void bp_state_handler (int state_index)
{
    switch (state_index)
    {
        case BP_GET_PATTERN:
            bp_get_pattern();
            break;
        case BP_FEEDFORWARD_INPUT:
            bp_feedforward_input();
            break;
        case BP_FEEDFORWARD_HIDDEN:
            bp_feedforward_hidden();
            break;
        case BP_FEEDFORWARD_OUTPUT:
            bp_feedforward_output();
            break;
        case BP_BACK_PROPAGATION_OUTPUT:
            bp_back_propagation_output();
            break;
        case BP_BACK_PROPAGATION_HIDDENS:
            bp_back_propagation_hiddens();
            break;
        case BP_BATCH_TEMP_WEIGHT_STEP_CHANGE:
            bp_batch_temp_weight_step_change();
            break;
        case BP_NEXT_PATTERN:
```

```
          bp_next_pattern();
          break;
     case BP_WEIGHT_STEP_CHANGE:
          bp_weight_step_change();
          break;
     case BP_WEIGHT_CHANGE:
          bp_weight_change();
          break;
     case BP_NEXT_GENERATION:
          bp_next_generation();
          break;
     case BP_UPDATE_LEARNING_RATE:
          bp_update_learning_rate();
          break;
     case BP_UPDATE_MOMENTUM_RATE:
          bp_update_momentum_rate();
          break;
     case BP_TRAINING_DONE:
          bp_training_done();
          break;
     case BP_RECALL_DONE:
          bp_recall_done();
          break;
     default:
          break;
     }
}
```

In the BP_GET_PATTERN state, the portion of the current pattern specified by bp.env.cur_pat is copied to the input PEs in the input layer and to the target output; then the current state is transitioned to the state BP_FEEDFORWARD_INPUT. The state handler routine is shown here.

```
static void bp_get_pattern (void)
{
     int idx;

     for (idx = 0; idx < (bp.arch.layers[0].size); idx++)
     {
          bp.arch.layers[0].neurons[idx].in =
                    patset.patterns[bp.env.cur_pat][idx];
     }
     for (idx = 0; idx < patset.dim_out; idx++)
     {
          target_out[idx] = patset.patterns[bp.env.cur_pat]
                              [patset.dim_in + idx];
     }
     bp_cur_state = BP_FEEDFORWARD_INPUT;
}
```

In the BP_FEEDFORWARD_INPUT state, the output of the input layer is calculated. Normally, the input layer is treated only as a path to the hidden layer. The output of each PE in the input layer is equal to the input of the same PE. Certainly, a different type of activation function can be used for the PEs in the input layer, and some data preprocessing can be encoded into the activation function of the PEs in the input layer. Here, in our implementation, the data preprocessing is done outside of the neural network implementation and the input layer is a linear layer featured as an input path to the hidden layer. The current state transitions to the state BP_FEEDFORWARD_HIDDEN. The state handler routine is shown here.

```
static void bp_feedforward_input(void)
{
    int idx;

    for (idx = 0; idx < (bp.arch.layers[0].size); idx++)
    {
        bp.arch.layers[0].neurons[idx].out =
            bp.arch.layers[0].neurons[idx].in;
    }
    bp_cur_state = BP_FEEDFORWARD_HIDDEN;
}
```

In the BP_FEEDFORWARD_HIDDEN state, the outputs of PEs in the hidden layer(s) are calculated. If there is more than one hidden layer, the outputs of the PEs in the first hidden layer are first calculated, then the second hidden layer, until all the hidden layer outputs have been calculated. In the calculation of the output of a PE, first the net input to the PE is calculated; then the output is calculated by calling the function activate_function(net_input, function_type). Normally, in a back-propagation network, the activation function for PEs in the hidden layer is the sigmoid function. The current state transitions to the state BP_FEEDFORWARD_OUTPUT. The state handler routine is shown here.

```
static void bp_feedforward_hidden (void)
{
    int idx, idx_prev,idx_cur;
    float sum;

    for (idx = 1; idx < (bp.arch.size - 1); idx++)
    {   // loop through the hidden layers

        for (idx_cur = 0; idx_cur < (bp.arch.layers[idx].size); idx_cur++)
        {   // loop through the neurons of the current hidden layer
            sum = 0.0;
            for ( idx_prev = 0; idx_prev < (bp.arch.layers
                                        [idx - 1].size);idx_prev++)
        {   // loop through the outputs of the previous layer
            sum += (bp.arch.layers[idx - 1].neurons[idx_prev].out) *
                    (bp.arch.layers[idx].neurons[idx_cur].w[idx_prev]);
        }
        sum += (bp.arch.layers[idx].neurons[idx_cur].
                w[bp.arch.layers[idx - 1].size]);
        bp.arch.layers[idx].neurons[idx_cur].in = sum;
        bp.arch.layers[idx].neurons[idx_cur].out =
                    activate_function(sum,bp.arch.layers[idx].
                    neurons[idx_cur].neuron_function);
```

```
        }
    }
    bp_cur_state = BP_FEEDFORWARD_OUTPUT;
}
```

In the BP_FEEDFORWARD_OUTPUT state, the outputs of PEs in the output layer are calculated. The calculation procedure is the same as that in hidden layers. The current state transitions to the state BP_BACK_PROPAGATION_OUTPUT if the operation mode is NN_TRAINING; otherwise, it transitions to the state BP_NEXT_PATTERN to test the next pattern. The state handler routine is shown here.

```
static void bp_feedforward_output (void)
{
    int idx_out, idx_prev;
    float sum;

    for (idx_out = 0; idx_out < (bp.arch.layers[bp.arch.size - 1].size);
                    idx_out++)

    {   // loop through the neurons of the output layer
        sum = 0.0;

        for (idx_prev = 0; idx_prev < (bp.arch.layers
                        [bp.arch.size - 2].size);idx_prev++)
        {   // loop through the outputs of the previous layer
            sum += (bp.arch.layers[bp.arch.size - 2].neurons
                    [idx_prev].out) * (bp.arch.layers[bp.arch.size - 1].
                    neurons[idx_out].w[idx_prev]);
        }
        sum +=(bp.arch.layers[bp.arch.size - 1].neurons[idx_out].
                w[bp.arch.layers[bp.arch.size - 2].size]);
                bp.arch.layers[bp.arch.size - 1].neurons[idx_out].in=sum;
                bp.arch.layers[bp.arch.size - 1].neurons[idx_out].out =
                    activate_function(sum,bp.arch.layers[bp.arch.size - 1].
                    neurons[idx_out].neuron_function);

    }
    if (bp.env.operation_mode == NN_RECALL)
    {
        print_recall_result();
    }
    if (bp.env.operation_mode == NN_TRAINING)
    {
        bp_cur_state = BP_BACK_PROPAGATION_OUTPUT;
    }
    else
    {   // recall
        bp_cur_state = BP_NEXT_PATTERN;
    }
}
```

In the BP_BACK_PROPAGATION_OUTPUT state, the errors of the PEs in the output layer are calculated for the current training pattern. The calculation depends on the type of activation function of the output PEs. For a back-propagation network, the activation function is usually a linear function or one of several S-shaped functions. The mean-square error is also accumulated for this training pattern.

The current state transitions to the state BP_BACK_PROPAGATION_HIDDENS. Following is the state handler routine.

```
static void bp_back_propagation_output (void)
{
    lint idx;
    double tempA,tempB;

    for (idx = 0; idx < (bp.arch.layers[bp.arch.size - 1].size); idx++)
    {
        tempA = (target_out[idx] - bp.arch.layers[bp.arch.size - 1].
                                        neurons[idx].out);
        switch (bp.arch.layers[bp.arch.size - 1].neurons[idx]
                                                .neuron_function)
        {
          case NN_LINEAR_FUNCTION:
             bp.arch.layers[bp.arch.size - 1].neurons[idx].error =
                                                          tempA;
           break;
          case NN_GAUSIAN_FUNCTION:
            printf("BP net can't have Gaussian Neurons, exit\n");
            exit(1);
            break;
          default:   // NN_SIGMOID_FUNCTION
            tempB = (bp.arch.layers[bp.arch.size - 1].neurons[idx].out) *
                (1.0 - (bp.arch.layers[bp.arch.size - 1]
                         .neurons[idx].out));
            bp.arch.layers[bp.arch.size - 1].neurons[idx].error =
                                                  tempA * tempB;
            break;
        }
        bp.mse += (tempA * tempA);
    }
    bp_cur_state = BP_BACK_PROPAGATION_HIDDENS;
}
```

In the BP_BACK_PROPAGATION_HIDDENS state, the errors of the PEs in all hidden layers are calculated. The errors are calculated backward, from the last hidden layer to the first hidden layer. Since only one kind of S-shaped function, the sigmoid function, is included in the enumeration data type NN_Function_Type, the calculation is hard-coded into the function that is below. If more S-shaped functions are included later, then either an if–else statement or a switch statement should be used. The current state transitions to the state BP_BATCH_TEMP_WEIGHT_STEP_CHANGE. The state handler routine is shown here.

```
static void bp_back_propagation_hiddens (void)
{
    int idx_1, idx_cn, idx_nn;
```

```
double tempA, sum;

for (idx_l = bp.arch.size - 2; idx_l > 0; idx_l--)
{    // loop through all the hidden layers
    for (idx_cn = 0; idx_cn < (bp.arch.layers[idx_l].size); idx_cn++)
    {    // loop through all the neurons in the current hidden layer
        sum = 0.0;
        for (idx_nn = 0; idx_nn < (bp.arch.layers[idx_l + 1].size);
                        idx_nn++)
        {    // loop through the next layer's neurons
            sum += (bp.arch.layers[idx_l + 1].neurons[idx_nn].error) *
                   (bp.arch.layers[idx_l + 1].neurons[idx_nn]
                                            .w[idx_cn]);
        }
        tempA = bp.arch.layers[idx_l].neurons[idx_cn].out *
                (1.0 - (bp.arch.layers[idx_l].neurons[idx_cn].out));
        bp.arch.layers[idx_l].neurons[idx_cn].error = sum * tempA;
    }
}
bp_cur_state = BP_BATCH_TEMP_WEIGHT_STEP_CHANGE;
}
```

In the `BP_BATCH_TEMP_WEIGHT_STEP_CHANGE` state, the temporary connection weight incremental changes are calculated. This state is added for the purpose of batch mode training. If only the sequential training mode is used, this state is unnecessary. The calculation is based on equation 6.8. The current state transitions either to the state `BP_NEXT_PATTERN` if batch mode training is being used or to the state `BP_WEIGHT_STEP_CHANGE` if sequential mode training is being used. The state handler routine is listed here.

```
static void bp_batch_temp_weight_step_change (void)
{
    int idx_layer, idx_cn, idx_pn;
    double tempA;

    for (idx_layer = bp.arch.size - 1; idx_layer > 0; idx_layer--)
    {    // loop through layers
        for (idx_cn = 0; idx_cn < (bp.arch.layers[idx_layer].size);
                                                        idx_cn++)
        {    // loop through neurons in the current layer
            for (idx_pn = 0; idx_pn < (bp.arch.layers[idx_layer - 1].size);
                            idx_pn++)
            {    // loop through neurons in the previous layer
                tempA = bp.arch.layers[idx_layer].neurons[idx_cn].error *
                        bp.arch.layers[idx_layer - 1].neurons[idx_pn].out;
                tempA *= bp.env.eta;
                bp.arch.layers[idx_layer].neurons[idx_cn]
                        .temp_delta_w[idx_pn] += tempA;
            }
            bp.arch.layers[idx_layer].neurons[idx_cn].temp_delta_w[bp.arch
                    .layers[idx_layer - 1].size] += bp.env.eta *
                        bp.arch.layers[idx_layer].neurons[idx_cn].error;
        }
    }
```

```
      if (bp.env.train_mode == NN_BATCH_MODE)
      {
          bp_cur_state = BP_NEXT_PATTERN;
      }
      else
      {
          bp_cur_state = BP_WEIGHT_STEP_CHANGE;
      }
  }
```

The BP_NEXT_PATTERN state is used to determine which state to transition to according to back-propagation network environment information. First, the current training pattern index is increased by one.

If the back-propagation net is in training operation mode and the training mode is batch mode training, then the current training pattern index is compared with the maximum number of training patterns. If the current training pattern index is less than the maximum number of training patterns, the current state transitions to the state BP_GET_PATTERN; otherwise, it transitions to the state BP_WEIGHT_STEP_CHANGE.

If the back-propagation net is in the training operation mode and the training mode is sequential training, then if the current training pattern index is less than the maximum number of training patterns, the current state transitions to the state BP_GET_PATTERN. Otherwise, it transitions to the state BP_NEXT_GENERATION.

If the back-propagation net is in recall/testing operation mode, then the current training pattern index is compared with the maximum number of patterns. If the current training pattern index is less than the maximum number of patterns, the current state transitions to the state BP_GET_PATTERN; otherwise, it transitions to the state BP_RECALL_DONE. The state handler routine is listed here.

```
static void bp_next_pattern (void)
{
    bp.env.cur_pat++;
    if (bp.env.operation_mode == NN_TRAINING)
    {
        if (bp.env.train_mode == NN_BATCH_MODE)
        {
            if (bp.env.cur_pat < bp.env.max_tra_pat)
            {
                bp_cur_state = BP_GET_PATTERN;
            }
            else
            {
                bp_cur_state = BP_WEIGHT_STEP_CHANGE;
            }
        }
        else    // sequential learning
        {
            if (bp.env.cur_pat < bp.env.max_tra_pat)
```

```
            {
                bp_cur_state = BP_GET_PATTERN;
            }
            else
            {
                bp_cur_state = BP_NEXT_GENERATION;
            }
        }
    }
    else  // recall
    {

        if (bp.env.cur_pat < patset.size)
        {
            bp_cur_state = BP_GET_PATTERN;
        }
        else
        {
            bp_cur_state = BP_RECALL_DONE;
        }
    }
}
```

In the BP_WEIGHT_STEP_CHANGE state, the connection weight step changes
are calculated according to equation 6.8, and the temporary connection weight step
changes are cleared. The current state transitions to the state BP_WEIGHT_CHANGE.
The state handler routine is listed next.

```
static void bp_weight_step_change (void)
{
    int idx_layer, idx_cn, idx_pn;

    for (idx_layer = 1; idx_layer < (bp.arch.size); idx_layer++)
    {   // loop through the layers
        for (idx_cn = 0; idx_cn < (bp.arch.layers[idx_layer].size);
            idx_cn++)
        {   // loop through the neurons in the current layer
            for (idx_pn = 0; idx_pn <= (bp.arch.layers[idx_layer-1].size);
                idx_pn++)
            {// loop through the connection weights of the current neurons
                bp.arch.layers[idx_layer].neurons[idx_cn].delta_w[idx_pn]*=
                                                    bp.env.alpha;
                bp.arch.layers[idx_layer].neurons[idx_cn].delta_w[idx_pn]
                        +=(bp.arch.layers[idx_layer].neurons[idx_cn]
                                .temp_delta_w[idx_pn]);
                bp.arch.layers[idx_layer].neurons[idx_cn]
                        .temp_delta_w[idx_pn] = 0.0;
            }
        }
    }
    bp_cur_state = BP_WEIGHT_CHANGE;
}
```

In the BP_WEIGHT_CHANGE state, the connection weight changes are
calculated according to equation 6.8. The current state transitions to the state

BP_NEXT_GENERATION if in batch mode training; otherwise, to the state BP_NEXT_PATTERN. The state handler routine is shown next.

```
static void bp_weight_change (void)
{
    int idx_layer, idx_cn, idx_pn;

    for (idx_layer = 1; idx_layer < (bp.arch.size); idx_layer++)
    {   // loop through the layers
        for (idx_cn = 0; idx_cn < (bp.arch.layers[idx_layer].size);
                        idx_cn++)
        {   // loop through the neurons in the current layer
            for (idx_pn = 0;idx_pn <= (bp.arch.layers[idx_layer - 1].size);
                        idx_pn++)       .
            { // loop through the connection weights of the current neurons
                bp.arch.layers[idx_layer].neurons[idx_cn]
                    .w[idx_pn] += bp.arch.layers[idx_layer].neurons[idx_cn]
                                    .delta_w[idx_pn];
            }
        }
    }

    if (bp.env.train_mode == NN_BATCH_MODE)
    {
        bp_cur_state =  BP_NEXT_GENERATION;
    }
    else
    {
        bp_cur_state =  BP_NEXT_PATTERN;
    }
}
```

In the BP_NEXT_GENERATION state, the errors of all PEs in the network are first cleared for the next generation; then the mean-squared error is calculated by dividing the accumulated mean-squared error by the total number of training patterns. The current generation index is increased by 1 and compared with the maximum number of generations. If the current generation number is less than the maximum number of generations, the mean-squared error is cleared and the state transitions to the state BP_UPDATE_LEARNING_RATE; otherwise, the current state transitions to the state BP_TRAINING_DONE.

```
static void bp_next_generation (void)
{
    int idx_layer, idx_cn;

    for (idx_layer = 0; idx_layer < (bp.arch.size); idx_layer++)
    {   // loop through the layers
        for (idx_cn = 0; idx_cn < (bp.arch.layers[idx_layer].size);
                                                    idx_cn++)
        {   // loop through the neurons in the current layer
            // clear the error
            bp.arch.layers[idx_layer].neurons[idx_cn].error = 0.0;
        }
    }
```

```
bp.mse /= bp.env.max_tra_pat;

if ((++bp.env.cur_gen) < bp.env.max_gen) // add error criterion later
{
    bp.mse = 0.0; //clear mean squared error
    bp_cur_state = BP_UPDATE_LEARNING_RATE;
}
else
{
    bp_cur_state = BP_TRAINING_DONE;
}
}
```

In the two states, BP_UPDATE_LEARNING_RATE and BP_UPDATE_ MOMENTUM_RATE, if a dynamic learning rate and/or momentum rate are used, then the new learning rate and momentum rate are updated. In our implementation, rates are fixed. Therefore, these two state handler routines do nothing except transition the current state to state BP_UPDATE_MOMENTUM_RATE and state BP_GET_PATTERN, respectively.

In the two states BP_TRAINING_DONE and BP_RECALL_DONE, the postprocessing of data or results is performed. In the current implementation, nothing is performed in either state.

Running the Back-propagation Implementation

To run the back-propagation neural network implementation requires the executable file bp.exe and an associated run file, for example, iris_bp.run. To run the implementation from within the directory containing bp.exe and iris_bp.run, at the DOS system prompt type bp iris_bp.run.

The contents of the iris_bp.run file, an example of a run file for a back-propagation network with one hidden layer, are listed here:

```
0
0
0.075
0.15
0.01
10000
99

3
4
150
4
3
iris.dat
```

The first entry (0) is for specifying the network operation mode, 0 for training and 1 for recall or testing. The second entry (0) tells which training mode is going to be used if the operation mode is the training mode (0); otherwise, the value is ignored. 0 specifies batch mode training and 1 specifies sequential mode training. The third value (0.075) and the fourth value (0.15) are the learning rate and momentum rate, respectively.

The next value, 0.01, is the error termination criterion. In the current implementation, the only termination criterion is the maximum number of generations. Implementing the error termination criterion is left as an exercise at the end of this chapter.

The next value (10000) is the maximum number of generations followed by the total number of training patterns (99). Note that the Iris dataset has 150 patterns; here we are using 99 of them for training.

Following the total number of training patterns are the number of layers (3), the number of PEs in the hidden layer (4), the total number of patterns (150), the dimension of the input (4), the dimension of the output (3), and the filename of the data file (iris.dat) where the patterns are stored. Note that this run file (with three layers) is valid for a network with one hidden layer.

For a network with two hidden layers, see the contents of the iris_bp2.run file, listed next.

```
0
0
0.075
0.15
0.01
10000
99

4
4
3
150
4
3
iris.dat
```

In this example, following the total number of training patterns are the number of layers (4), the number of PEs in the first hidden layer (4), the number of PEs in the second hidden layer (3), the total number of patterns (150), the dimension of the input (4), the dimension of the output (3), and the filename of the data file (iris.dat) where the patterns are stored.

Following the training of the network, the results, which include the weights of the trained network and the final mean-squared error for the training pattern set, are in file BP_RES.TXT. After you run the test patterns, a summary of the test results appears in BP_TEST.TXT, and a pattern-by-pattern listing of the target values versus output values for the Iris dataset appears in irisres.txt. Note that the weights of the trained network are the essential output of this training step.

The Kohonen Network Implementations

In this section, we first present an implementation of another common neural network paradigm, the learning vector quantizer (LVQ), sometimes referred to as a Kohonen network. We then discuss the implementation of Kohonen's self-organizing feature map network, which is an extension of LVQ.

Programming the Learning Vector Quantizer

Figure 6.5 shows the state transition diagram for the implementation of the learning vector quantizer discussed in this section. First we define some new data types.

We now present LVQ network definitions. This section defines some data types applicable only to the implementation of the LVQ network. The general definitions previously discussed in the General Definitions for Neural Networks subsection of the Back-propagation Implementation section are still valid here. The new data types are shown in Listings 6.6 and 6.7. The new enumeration data types are in Listing 6.6, and the new structure data types appear in Listing 6.7.

Listing 6.6 Enumeration data types for the LVQ network.

```
/****************************************************************/
/* Enumerations                                                 */
/****************************************************************/
typedef enum LVQ_Training_Mode_Tag
{
  LVQ_RANDOM_MODE,
  LVQ_SEQUENTIAL_MODE,
  NUM_LVQ_TRAINING_MODES
} LVQ_Training_Mode_Type;

typedef enum LVQ_State_Tag
{
  LVQ_GET_PATTERN,
  LVQ_WEIGHT_NORMALIZATION,
  LVQ_FEEDFORWARD_INPUT,
  LVQ_FEEDFORWARD_OUTPUT,
  LVQ_WINNING_NEURON,
  LVQ_WEIGHT_STEP_CHANGE,
  LVQ_WEIGHT_CHANGE,
  LVQ_NEXT_PATTERN,
  LVQ_NEXT_ITERATION,
  LVQ_UPDATE_LEARNING_RATE,
  LVQ_UPDATE_CONSCIENCE_FACTOR,
  LVQ_TRAINING_DONE,
  LVQ_RECALL_DONE,
  NUM_LVQ_STATES
} LVQ_State_Type;
```

```
typedef enum LVQ_Conscience_Type_Tag
{
  LVQ_NO_CONSCIENCE,
  LVQ_CONSCIENCE,
  NUM_LVQ_CONSCIENCE
} LVQ_Conscience_Type;
```

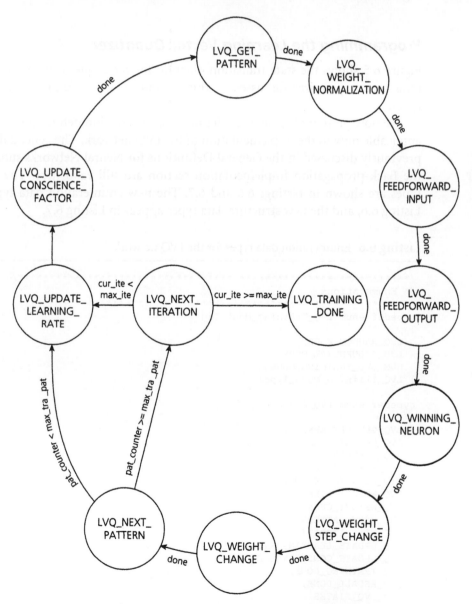

Figure 6.5 A state diagram of the LVQ network in training operation mode.

The enumeration data type LVQ_Training_Mode_Type defines two training modes: LVQ_RANDOM_MODE and LVQ_SEQUENTIAL_MODE. In LVQ_RANDOM_MODE training mode, the training pattern is randomly selected from the training pattern set and presented to the LVQ network; in LVQ_SEQUENTIAL_MODE training mode, the training pattern is selected in the order of the patterns in the training pattern set and presented to the network.

The data type LVQ_State_Type defines all the states in the LVQ state machine. There are a total of 13 states, each of which has a corresponding state handling routine. The states transition to each other according to the state transition diagram, as shown in Figure 6.5.

The data type LVQ_Conscience_Type defines two conditions: LVQ_NO_CONSCIENCE and LVQ_CONSCIENCE. These two conditions, as explained in the subsection describing the LVQ_UPDATE_CONSCIENCE_FACTOR state, specify how the LVQ adapts with or without a conscience.

Listing 6.7 Structure data types for the LVQ network.

```
/***************************************************************/
/* Structures                                                  */
/***************************************************************/
typedef struct Neuron_Type_Tag
{

  NN_Function_Type       neuron_function;   // neuron function
  float                  in;                // neuron input
  float                  out;               // neuron output
  FVECTOR                w;             // weights from the previous layers
  FVECTOR                delta_w;           // step change of weights
  float                  c_f;               // conscience factor
  float                  b_v;               // bias value
  int                    w_s;        // winner status, y in equation

} Neuron_Type;

typedef struct NN_Layer_Arch_Type_Tag
{

  int                    size;       // number of neurons in the layer
  Neuron_Type            *neurons;    // pointer to the neurons
  NN_Layer_Type          layer_type;
} NN_Layer_Arch_Type;

typedef struct LVQ_Arch_Type_Tag
{

  int                    size;           // number of layers
  NN_Layer_Arch_Type     *layers;        // pointer to the layers
} LVQ_Arch_Type;
```

```
typedef struct LVQ_Env_Type_Tag
{
  NN_Operation_Mode_Type operation_mode;   // training or recall
  LVQ_Training_Mode_Type train_mode;       // training mode
  float                  eta;              // learning rate
  float                  gama;             // bias factor
  float                  beta;             //
  float                  shrink;           // (eta) shrinking coefficient
  float                  criterion;        // criterion for termination
  int                    max_ite;          // maximum number of iterations
  int                    cur_ite;          // current iteration index
  int                    max_tra_pat;      // total number of training patterns
  int                    cur_pat;          // current training pattern index
  int                    pat_counter;
  LVQ_Conscience_Type    conscience;       // 0: no conscience, 1: conscience
  int                    winner;           // index of winning neuron
  int                    no_clusters;      // number of clusters
} LVQ_Env_Type;

typedef struct LVQ_Type_Tag
{
  LVQ_Arch_Type          arch;
  LVQ_Env_Type           env;
} LVQ_Type;

typedef struct LVQ_Pattern_Set_Type_Tag
{
  int                    size;             // number of patterns
  int                    dim_in;           // input dimension
  int                    dim_out;          // output dimension
  FMATRIX                patterns;         // pointer to the array of patterns
} LVQ_Pattern_Set_Type;
```

The structure data types for the LVQ network are shown in Listing 6.7. The structure data type Neuron_Type defines PEs (neurons)—the basic building components for the LVQ implementation. It is similar to the definition of PEs in the back-propagation implementation. They share several identical elements and have their own unique elements, which are put there for the purpose of the corresponding learning algorithms' implementation. In a more organized way (left as a exercise), the common elements can be put together alone and defined as a data type Neuron_Type, and the unique elements in each network can be defined as data types BP_Neuron_Type and LVQ_Neuron_Type, as shown in Listing 6.8. Other data types will then use BP_Neuron_Type and LVQ_Neuron_Type instead of Neuron_Type.

The structure date type LVQ_Env_Type defines the environment parameters for running the LVQ network in a manner similar to the BP implementation. It includes operation mode (operation_mode), training mode (train_mode),

Listing 6.8 Alternative way to define the neuron (PE) data type.

```
typedef struct Neuron_Type_Tag
{
  NN_Function_Type        neuron_function;    // neuron function
  float                   in;                 // neuron input
  float                   out;                // neuron output
  FVECTOR                 w;          // weights from the previous layers
  FVECTOR                 delta_w;            // step change of weights
} Neuron_Type;

typedef struct BP_Neuron_Type_Tag
{
  Neuron_Type             neuron;             // basic neuron data type
  FVECTOR                 temp_delta_w; // temp. step change of weights
} Neuron_Type;

 typedef struct LVQ_Neuron_Type_Tag
{
  Neuron_Type             neuron;             // basic neuron data type
  float                   c_f;                // conscience factor
  float                   b_v;                // bias value
  int                     w_s;            // winner status, y in equation
} LVQ_Neuron_Type;
```

learning rate (`eta`), bias factor (`gama`), constant value beta (`beta`), learning rate shrinking rate (`shrink`), training criterion for termination (`criterion`), maximum number of iterations (`max_ite`), current iteration index (`cur_ite`), total number of training patterns (`max_tra_pat`), current pattern index (`cur_pat`), pattern learned counter within the current iteration (`pat_counter`), flag for whether conscience is used (`conscience`), index of current winning neuron (`winner`), and number of clusters (`no_clusters`). Note that the number of clusters is the number of output PEs.

The definition of structure date types `NN_Layer_Arch_Type`, `LVQ_Arch_Type`, `LVQ_Type`, and `LVQ_Pattern_Set_Type` are the same as defined in the BP implementation except that the mean-squared error (`mse`) and hidden layers are not included in the data type definitions since LVQ is a two-layered network and no error back-propagation-like learning algorithm is used.

The `main()` routine is shown in Listing 6.9. As in the back-propagation implementation, it is kept as simple as possible to make the LVQ module as independent as possible. In the `LVQ_Start_Up()` routine, all the necessary parameters for running the LVQ implementation are read from the input file, and the dynamic data storage variables are allocated memory space and initialized. In the `LVQ_Clean_Up()` routine, the results are stored in a output file and the memory space previously allocated is de-allocated. The `LVQ_Main_Loop()` routine is the primary part of the LVQ implementation.

Listing 6.9 LVQ `main()` routine.

```
void main (int argc, char *argv[])
{
    // check command line
    if (argc != 2)
    {
        printf("Usage: exe_file run_file");
        exit(1);
    }

    main_start_up(argv[1]);
    LVQ_Main_Loop();
    main_clean_up();
}

static void main_start_up (char *dataFile)
{
    LVQ_Start_Up(dataFile);
}

static void main_clean_up (void)
{
    LVQ_Clean_Up();
}
```

We now consider the `LVQ_Main_Loop()` routine. Before running this routine, we define several LVQ file scope variables.

```
static LVQ_Type              lvq;
static LVQ_Pattern_Set_Type  patset;
static LVQ_State_Type        lvq_cur_state;
```

As in the back-propagation implementation, these three variables are defined as `static` to prevent them from accidentally being changed by outside modules. The variable `lvq` stores information related to the LVQ net during the run. The variable `patset` stores all the input/output pairs of patterns. The variable `lvq_cur_state` records the current state of the LVQ state machine. When the `LVQ_Main_Loop()` routine is running, it calls the current state's handling routine through `lvq_state_handler(lvq_cur_state)`, where the current state performs its action until it is transitioned to another state. The `lvq_Main_Loop()` keeps running until its current state is transitioned to the state `LVQ_TRAINING_DONE` when the LVQ net is in training operation mode or the state `LVQ_RECALL_DONE` when the LVQ net is in recall/test operation mode. The `LVQ_Main_Loop()` routine is listed here.

```
void LVQ_Main_Loop (void)
{
    BOOLEAN running;

    running = TRUE;
```

```
    while (running)
    {
        if ((lvq_cur_state == LVQ_TRAINING_DONE) ||
            (lvq_cur_state == LVQ_RECALL_DONE))
        {
            running = FALSE;
        }
        lvq_state_handler(lvq_cur_state);
    }
}
```

LVQ State Handling Routines

We now examine the LVQ state handling routines. As in the BP implementation, the most important part of the LVQ state machine is its state handler, which is shown in Listing 6.10. The state handler calls its current state's handling routine until the current state is transitioned to a new state, where the new state's handling routine is called by the state machine.

Listing 6.10 Main part of the LVQ state machine.

```
static void lvq_state_handler (int state_index)
{
    switch (state_index)
    {
        case LVQ_GET_PATTERN:
            lvq_get_pattern();
            break;
        case LVQ_WEIGHT_NORMALIZATION:
            lvq_weight_normalization();
            break;
        case LVQ_FEEDFORWARD_INPUT:
            lvq_feedforward_input();
            break;
        case LVQ_FEEDFORWARD_OUTPUT:
            lvq_feedforward_output();
            break;
        case LVQ_WINNING_NEURON:
            lvq_winning_neuron();
            break;
        case LVQ_WEIGHT_STEP_CHANGE:
            lvq_weight_step_change();
            break;
        case LVQ_WEIGHT_CHANGE:
            lvq_weight_change();
            break;
        case LVQ_NEXT_PATTERN:
            lvq_next_pattern();
            break;
        case LVQ_NEXT_ITERATION:
            lvq_next_iteration();
            break;
        case LVQ_UPDATE_LEARNING_RATE:
            lvq_update_learning_rate();
            break;
```

```
            case LVQ_UPDATE_CONSCIENCE_FACTOR:
                lvq_update_conscience_factor();
                break;
            case LVQ_TRAINING_DONE:
                lvq_training_done();
                break;
            case LVQ_RECALL_DONE:
                lvq_recall_done();
                break;
            default:
                break;
        }
    }
```

In the LVQ_GET_PATTERN state, the current pattern portion specified by lvq.env.cur_pat is copied to the input PEs in the input layer and to the target output; then the current state transitions to the state LVQ_WEIGHT_ NORMALIZATION if the operation mode is NN_TRAINING mode; otherwise, it transitions to the state LVQ_FEEDFORWARD_INPUT. The state handling routine is shown here.

```
static void lvq_get_pattern (void)
{
    int idx;

    for (idx = 0; idx < (lvq.arch.layers[0].size); idx++)
    {
        lvq.arch.layers[0].neurons[idx].in = patset.patterns
                        [lvq.env.cur_pat][idx];
    }
    for (idx = 0; idx < patset.dim_out; idx++)
    {
        target_out[idx] = patset.patterns[lvq.env.cur_pat]
                        [patset.dim_in + idx];
    }
    if (lvq.env.operation_mode == NN_TRAINING)
    {
        lvq_cur_state = LVQ_WEIGHT_NORMALIZATION;
    }
    else
    {
        lvq_cur_state = LVQ_FEEDFORWARD_INPUT;
    }
}
```

In the LVQ_WEIGHT_NORMALIZATION state, the weight vector is normalized according to equation 6.1. The if statement if(sum > 0.0) is added to avoid the rare situation where all the weights connected to output neurons are 0s. The current state transitions to the state LVQ_FEEDFORWARD_INPUT. The state handling routine is shown here.

```
static void lvq_weight_normalization (void)
{
    int idx_cn, idx_pn;
    double sum;
    float temp_f;

    for (idx_cn = 0; idx_cn < (lvq.arch.layers[1].size) ; idx_cn++)
    {   // loop through neurons in the output layer
        sum = 0.0;
        for (idx_pn = 0; idx_pn < (lvq.arch.layers[0].size) ; idx_pn++)
        {   // loop through all the weights connected to this neuron
            sum += lvq.arch.layers[1].neurons[idx_cn].w[idx_pn] *
                    lvq.arch.layers[1].neurons[idx_cn].w[idx_pn];
        }
        sum = sqrt(sum);
        if (sum > 0.0)
        {
            for (idx_pn = 0; idx_pn < (lvq.arch.layers[0].size) ; idx_pn++)
            {   // loop through all the weights connected to this neuron
                temp_f = lvq.arch.layers[1].neurons[idx_cn].w[idx_pn]/sum;
                lvq.arch.layers[1].neurons[idx_cn].w[idx_pn] = temp_f;
            }
        }
    }
    lvq_cur_state = LVQ_FEEDFORWARD_INPUT;
}
```

In the `LVQ_FEEDFORWARD_INPUT` state, the output of the input layer is calculated. As in the back-propagation implementation, the input layer is treated as only a path to the next layer (the output layer). The output of each input PE equals its input. The current state transitions to the state `LVQ_FEEDFORWARD_OUTPUT`. The state handling routine is shown here.

```
static void lvq_feedforward_input(void)
{
    int idx;

    for (idx = 0; idx < (lvq.arch.layers[0].size); idx++)
    {
        lvq.arch.layers[0].neurons[idx].out = lvq.arch.layers[0]
                                            .neurons[idx].in;
    }
    lvq_cur_state = LVQ_FEEDFORWARD_OUTPUT;
}
```

In the `LVQ_FEEDFORWARD_OUTPUT` state, the Euclidean distance between the input vector and the weight vector for each output PE (neuron) is first calculated according to equation 6.4. Then the output of each output PE is calculated, which is equal to the its Euclidean distance since the output PEs have a linear activation function. The current state transitions to the state `LVQ_WINNING_NEURON`. The state handling routine is shown here.

```
static void lvq_feedforward_output (void)
{
    int idx_out, idx_prev;
    double sum, temp_f;

    for (idx_out = 0; idx_out < (lvq.arch.layers[1].size); idx_out++)
    {   // loop through the neurons of the output layer
        sum = 0.0;
        for (idx_prev = 0; idx_prev < (lvq.arch.layers[0].size);
                                      idx_prev++)
        {   // loop through the neurons of the input layer
            temp_f = (lvq.arch.layers[0].neurons[idx_prev].out -
                    lvq.arch.layers[1].neurons[idx_out].w[idx_prev]);
            sum += (temp_f * temp_f);
        }
        temp_f = sqrt(sum);
        lvq.arch.layers[1].neurons[idx_out].in = temp_f;
        lvq.arch.layers[1].neurons[idx_out].out =  activate_function(
            temp_f,lvq.arch.layers[1].neurons[idx_out].neuron_function);
    }
    lvq_cur_state = LVQ_WINNING_NEURON;
}
```

In the LVQ_WINNING_NEURON state, the new winning PE for the current input pattern is determined. The last and new winning neurons' winning statuses are updated. The current state transitions to the state LVQ_WEIGHT_STEP_CHANGE if it is in training operation mode; otherwise, it transitions to the state LVQ_NEXT_PATTERN and the recall/test result is recorded. The state handling routine is shown here.

```
static void lvq_winning_neuron (void)
{
    int idx, temp_w;
    float min_v = 1000.0;

    for (idx = 0; idx < (lvq.arch.layers[1].size); idx++)
    {   // loop through the neurons in output layer
        if ((lvq.arch.layers[1].neurons[idx].out -
            lvq.arch.layers[1].neurons[idx].b_v) < min_v)
        {
            min_v = lvq.arch.layers[1].neurons[idx].out -
                    lvq.arch.layers[1].neurons[idx].b_v;
            temp_w = idx;
        }
    }
    lvq.arch.layers[1].neurons[lvq.env.winner].w_s = 0;
    lvq.env.winner = temp_w;
    lvq.arch.layers[1].neurons[lvq.env.winner].w_s = 1;

    if (lvq.env.operation_mode == NN_TRAINING)
    {
        lvq_cur_state = LVQ_WEIGHT_STEP_CHANGE;
    }
    else
    {   // recall
```

```
        update_recall_result();
        lvq_cur_state = LVQ_NEXT_PATTERN;
    }
}
```

In the `LVQ_WEIGHT_STEP_CHANGE` state, the winning neuron's weight change increments are calculated according to equation 6.11. The state transitions to the state `LVQ_WEIGHT_CHANGE`. The state handling routine is shown here.

```
static void lvq_weight_step_change (void)
{
    int idx_pn;

    for (idx_pn = 0; idx_pn < (lvq.arch.layers[0].size) ; idx_pn++)
    {   // loop through the connect weights of the current neurons
        lvq.arch.layers[1].neurons[lvq.env.winner].delta_w[idx_pn] =
                    lvq.arch.layers[0].neurons[idx_pn].out -
                    lvq.arch.layers[1].neurons[lvq.env.winner].w[idx_pn];
        lvq.arch.layers[1].neurons[lvq.env.winner].delta_w[idx_pn] *=
                    lvq.env.eta;
    }
    lvq_cur_state = LVQ_WEIGHT_CHANGE;
}
```

In the `LVQ_WEIGHT_CHANGE` state, the winning neuron's weights are updated by adding its newly calculated weight change increments. The state transitions to the state `LVQ_NEXT_PATTERN`. The state handling routine is shown here.

```
static void lvq_weight_change (void)
{
    int idx_pn;

    for (idx_pn = 0; idx_pn < (lvq.arch.layers[0].size) ; idx_pn++)
    {   // loop through the connect weights of the current neurons
        lvq.arch.layers[1].neurons[lvq.env.winner].w[idx_pn] +=
            lvq.arch.layers[1].neurons[lvq.env.winner].delta_w[idx_pn];
    }
    lvq_cur_state =  LVQ_NEXT_PATTERN;
}
```

The `LVQ_NEXT_PATTERN` state is used to determine which state is the next state according to the LVQ network environment information.

If the LVQ is in training operation mode, first the next input pattern is selected. If it is in random training mode, an input pattern is randomly selected from the training pattern set. Otherwise, the next pattern in the training pattern set is selected, or the first pattern is selected if it is at the end of the training pattern set. The pattern counter is then increased by one. If it is less than the total number of training patterns, the current state transitions to the `LVQ_UPDATE_LEARNING_RATE`. Otherwise, it transitions to the state `LVQ_NEXT_ITERATION`.

If the LVQ is in recall operation mode, the current pattern index is increased by one. If the current pattern index is less than the total number of training patterns, the current state transitions to the state LVQ_GET_PATTERN; otherwise, it transitions to the state LVQ_RECALL_DONE. The state handling routine is shown here.

```
static void lvq_next_pattern (void)
{
    if (lvq.env.operation_mode == NN_TRAINING)
    {
        if (lvq.env.train_mode == LVQ_RANDOM_MODE)
        {   // random training
            lvq.env.cur_pat = rand()%(lvq.env.max_tra_pat);
        }
        else
        {   // sequential training
            if (++lvq.env.cur_pat >= lvq.env.max_tra_pat)
            {
                lvq.env.cur_pat = 0;
            }
        }
        if ((++lvq.env.pat_counter) <lvq.env.max_tra_pat)
        {   // add other termination criterion here
            lvq_cur_state = LVQ_UPDATE_LEARNING_RATE;
        }
        else
        {
            lvq_cur_state = LVQ_NEXT_ITERATION;
        }
    }
    else // recall
    {
        if ((++lvq.env.cur_pat) < patset.size)
        {
            lvq_cur_state = LVQ_GET_PATTERN;
        }
        else
        {
            lvq_cur_state = LVQ_RECALL_DONE;
        }
    }
}
```

In the LVQ_NEXT_ITERATION state, the current iteration index is increased by one. If the index is less than the maximum number of iterations, the current state transitions to the state LVQ_UPDATE_LEARNING_RATE; otherwise, it transitions to the state LVQ_TRAINING_DONE. The state handling routine is shown here.

```
static void lvq_next_iteration (void)
{
    lvq.env.pat_counter = 0;
    if ((++lvq.env.cur_ite) < lvq.env.max_ite)
    {   // add other termination criterion here
        lvq_cur_state = LVQ_UPDATE_LEARNING_RATE;
    }
```

```
    else
    {
        lvq.env.pat_counter = 0;
        lvq_cur_state = LVQ_TRAINING_DONE;
    }
}
```

In the `LVQ_UPDATE_LEARNING_RATE` state, the new learning rate $\eta(t)$ decreases over time. In this implementation, $\eta(t)$ is shrinking over time (number of patterns presented to the LVQ network) and is calculated according to equation 6.13.

$$\eta(t + 1) = \eta(t) \times \mu$$
$$\eta(0) = \eta_0$$
(6.13)

where both η_0 and μ are positive constants. Other decreasing functions of time can also be used as functions to update learning rate $\eta(t)$, which is left as a exercise for the student.

The current state transitions to the state `LVQ_UPDATE_CONSCIENCE_FACTOR`. The state handling routine is shown here.

```
static void lvq_update_learning_rate (void)
{
    lvq.env.eta *= lvq.env.shrink;
    lvq_cur_state = LVQ_UPDATE_CONSCIENCE_FACTOR;
}
```

In the `LVQ_UPDATE_CONSCIENCE_FACTOR` state, a "conscience" is added into the network if a network conscience is specified in the input file. We now explain what a conscience is and why it is often necessary for an LVQ network to incorporate a conscience.

Optimally, in an LVQ network with n output PEs, each PE should represent (should have been the winner for) exactly $1/n$ of the training patterns. Given a network free to train constrained only by equation 6.11, however, it is not likely that this evenly distributed representation will occur. It is especially unlikely to occur if the distribution of the (randomized) initial weights does not match the probability distribution of the pattern set used for training very well. The following example should help you visualize this situation.

Consider a case of three-dimensional pattern vectors that all terminate on the surface of a sphere. Assume that the pattern vectors are fairly evenly distributed over the sphere's surface. Further assume that the weight vectors are initialized so that all but one terminate in, and are fairly evenly distributed over, one hemisphere; the last weight vector is alone near the center of the other hemisphere. The lone weight vector will thus be the "winner" for far more of the patterns than any other weight vector; it will "dance" around its hemisphere trying to represent far more than its share of patterns, and it will end up not representing them well at all. What is needed is some mechanism that "punishes" the lone weight for winning too often and moves other weight vectors into the lone weight's hemisphere.

A method to accomplish this was developed by DeSieno (1988). He describes the method as adding a *conscience* to the network. First, for a given input pattern, the Euclidean distance as described in equation 6.4 is calculated for each output PE. Normally, the PE with the minimum distance would be declared the winner, and the weights abutting it would be updated according to equation 6.11. Before a winner is declared, however, the following calculations are made.

Before starting the training, a conscience factor f_j is defined for each output PE, and each is initialized to the value $1/n$, where n is the number of output PEs. Each time a pattern is presented to the network, the winning PE is selected according to equation 6.14(a), where b_j is a bias value calculated for each output PE according to equation 6.14(b). (When training starts, each bias value is 0.) The "bias factor" γ in equation 6.14(b) is usually set to a value of approximately 10.

Only the single winning PE selected in equation 6.14(a) has its weights updated according to equation 6.11. Following the winning PE's weight updates, all PEs have their conscience factors updated according to equation 6.14(c), where β is a constant typically valued at about 0.0001.

$$y_j^{winner} = 1 \quad \text{for} \quad \min(d_j - b_j), \qquad y_j = 0 \quad \text{for all other PEs} \quad \text{(a)}$$

$$b_j = \gamma\left(\frac{1}{n} - f_j\right) \qquad \qquad \text{(b)} \qquad \textbf{(6.14)}$$

$$f_j^{new} = f_j^{old} + \beta\left(y_j - f_j^{old}\right) \qquad \text{(c)}$$

A brief example may clarify how the conscience works. Consider a network with 10 output PEs. The initial values of all f_j's are thus 0.1. When the very first training pattern is presented to the network, the PE with the weight vector closest to the pattern (minimum Euclidean distance) is the winner and has its weights updated (all b_j's are 0 at this point). All output PEs then have their conscience factors updated. For the winning PE, the new value of f_j is $[0.1 + 0.0001(1.0 - 0.1)] = 0.10009$; for all other PEs, the new conscience factor is $0.1 - 0.00001 = 0.09999$. The value of b_j for the winner is now -0.0009; its value is 0.0001 for all other PEs. When the second pattern is presented, the previous winner's Euclidean distance is thus penalized by having 0.0009 added to it; all others are enhanced by having 0.0001 subtracted from them. Frequent winners will have negative b_j's, infrequent winners will have positive b_j's, and the result will be a good model of the probability density function of the input patterns.

The constant β should be picked so that the conscience factors f_j do not reflect random fluctuations in the data. The bias factor γ determines the distance a losing

PE can move in order to enter the solution. A bias factor of 0 corresponds to a "plain vanilla" Kohonen LVQ.

The `LVQ_UPDATE_CONSCIENCE_FACTOR` state transitions to the state `LVQ_GET_PATTERN`. The state handling routine is shown here.

```
static void lvq_update_conscience_factor (void)
{
    int idx;
    float temp_f;
    if (lvq.env.conscience == LVQ_CONSCIENCE)
    {
        for (idx = 0; idx < (lvq.arch.layers[1].size); idx++)
        {   // loop through the neurons in output layer
            temp_f   = lvq.arch.layers[1].neurons[idx].c_f;
            lvq.arch.layers[1].neurons[idx].c_f = temp_f + lvq.env.beta *
                (lvq.arch.layers[1].neurons[idx].w_s - temp_f);
            lvq.arch.layers[1].neurons[idx].b_v = lvq.env.gama *
                (1.0/lvq.env.no_clusters - lvq.arch.layers[1]
                                           .neurons[idx].c_f);
        }
    }
    lvq_cur_state = LVQ_GET_PATTERN;
}
```

We now examine the states `LVQ_TRAINING_DONE` and `LVQ_RECALL_DONE`. As in the back-propagation implementation, in these two states the post-processing of the data or results can be performed. In our current implementation, the `lvq_weight_normalization()` routine is called in the state `LVQ_TRAINING_DONE`'s handling routine.

Running the LVQ Implementation

To run the learning vector quantizer implementation requires the executable file `lvq.exe` and an associated run file, for example, `iris_lvq.run`. To run the implementation from within the directory containing `lvq.exe` and `iris_lvq.run`, at the DOS system prompt type: `lvq iris_lvq.run`.

The contents of the `iris_lvq.run` run file are shown in Listing 6.11.

Listing 6.11 Run file `iris_lvq.run`.

```
0
0
0.3
0.999
10
0.0001
0.001
500
```

```
99
1
6

150
4
3
iris.dat
```

The file contains specifications for a run. The file specifies operation mode (0) (0 is training, 1 is testing), training mode (0) (0 is random pattern selection, 1 is sequential), learning rate (0.3), learning rate shrinking coefficient (0.999), bias factor (10), beta (0.0001), training termination criterion (0.001), maximum number of iterations (500), total number of training patterns (99), network conscience status (1), maximum number of clusters (6), total number of patterns in the training file (150), dimension of pattern input (4), dimension of pattern output (3), and pattern data filename (iris.dat) from which the patterns are read.

At the end of the run, two output files are obtained. The file LVQ_RES.txt contains the weights for the LVQ network. The file LVQ_TEST.TXT contains a summary of the results. The summary table lists how many patterns from each class were put into each cluster.

Programming the Self-organizing Feature Map

The self-organizing feature map neural network is an extension of the learning vector quantizer. In this section, we discuss the implementation of the self-organizing feature map (SOFM), starting with an introduction to SOFM concepts.

The self-organizing feature map neural network, like LVQ networks, was developed by Teuvo Kohonen (1982a, 1982b) of the Helsinki University of Technology. Self-organizing feature maps pick up where LVQ-I, as described earlier in this chapter, leaves off. All of the features of LVQ-I, including the conscience, are incorporated into self-organizing feature maps. In addition, the adaptation procedure used by SOFMs incorporates what is called a *neighborhood*. In order to discuss neighborhoods and how they are used, we introduce the notion of a *PE slab*, which examines topology and notation for the network.

To facilitate understanding the adaptation process of a self-organizing feature map network, we implement the concept of a slab in the context of neural networks. Slabs can simplify network diagrams because groups of PEs can be represented by one symbol.

Functionally, a slab of PEs is a collection of PEs with similar attributes and a defined (and fixed) topology. These attributes include such things as activation function, learning coefficient, and, if applicable, momentum factor. (Some attributes have meaning only for certain types of network.) In addition, all PEs in a given slab

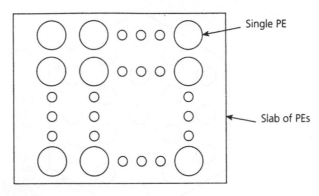

Single PE

Slab of PEs

Figure 6.6 A rectangular slab of PEs.

receive their inputs from the same source(s) (slab(s) and/or input pattern) and send their outputs to the same destination(s) (slab(s) and/or output pattern).

The main difference between a layer of PEs and a slab of PEs is that topology plays an important role in a slab. In PE layers, PEs can be moved around if their weights (and inputs or outputs, if applicable) are moved with them. This is not the case with slabs. While there usually are no connections among PEs in a slab, their topological relationships are important, and operations are carried out that depend on that topology. We suggest that the term *slab* be used only when these topologically dependent operations are present.

Figure 6.6 illustrates the concept of a slab. In the figure, the PEs are arranged in a rectangular pattern. The geometrical arrangement of PEs in a slab can vary and depends on the application. (Most implementations of slabs are two-dimensional; the word *slab* implies a flat structure, such as a thick plate or slice.) In the self-organizing feature map, a rectangular array is usually used to depict the PEs in the input slab and is often used for the output slab as well. Another arrangement, the hexagonal array (Figure 6.7), is also sometimes used to represent the output slab in the self-organization model. The geometry chosen to represent the output slab determines the configuration of the neighborhood of each PE, a subject we address later.

A simple illustration of a self-organizing feature map appears in Figure 6.8. We use essentially the same notation as we used for the LVQ-I network, except for the input and output slabs.

The two-dimensional slab configuration makes it desirable, in some cases, to use double subscripts for PEs and for the input and output vectors. We use the single subscript version in this section, primarily for simplicity.

A learning coefficient that is defined later is represented by the lowercase Greek letter η (eta). A few words of caution are appropriate here. This learning coefficient isn't exactly the same as the one for the back-propagation implementation.

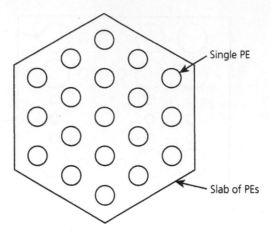

Figure 6.7 A slab of PEs in a hexagonal array.

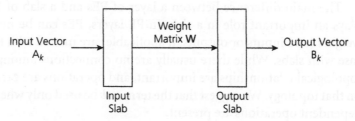

Figure 6.8 Self-organizing feature map network model.

(We discuss that later.) Also, Kohonen used the lowercase Greek letter α (alpha) for his learning coefficient. We chose η for consistency with the back-propagation implementation. When you see η in this book in connection with neural networks, you know that it's a learning coefficient, and when you see α, you know it's a momentum term.

Let's look at network initialization and input. On the left of Figure 6.8 a set of inputs comes into the input slab of the network. As is the case with the LVQ-I paradigm, you are more likely to use raw data and less likely to use precalculated parameters as inputs to a self-organizing feature map. As with LVQ-I, most people working with SOFM usually normalize each entire input vector (see equation 6.1). Be careful of destroying useful information in the normalization process; you may want to consider using the z-axis normalization process described in Chapter 5.

There is general agreement about the need to initialize the SOFM weight vectors by normalization. What isn't necessarily clear is the best way to do it. First, random values are assigned to each weight. One common approach is to initially assign random weight values between 0.4 and 0.6. However, if you refer to the initial illustration of Figure 5.16 in Kohonen (1988), you see that he initialized his network weights to values between 0.45 and 0.55. If you look at the Pascal code for a program called ToPreM2, which he published with his 1989 tutorial notes (Kohonen 1989), you find each weight initialized to a random value between 0.4 and 0.6. Meanwhile, in Caudill (1989a) initial weight vectors are generated that lie at random locations on the unit circle, in accordance with equation 6.1.

The *adaptation process* for SOFM is quite similar to that for LVQ-I. The winning PE is selected based on the minimum Euclidean distance between the input and weight vectors using equation 6.4. The update of the weight vectors, however, is different from the update in LVQ-I and involves a concept known as a neighborhood. Weight adjustments are made using a PE neighborhood that shrinks over time and a learning coefficient that also decreases with time. The result is that the values of the weights form clusters that reflect the probability density of the input vectors. When the network has self-organized and training is complete, PEs that are topologically near each other react similarly to similar input patterns.

The neighborhood is the portion of the output slab (the PEs) within a specified topological radius of a given winning PE. We must first define the initial size of the neighborhood. All PEs in the neighborhood of the winning PE have their weights adjusted. Each iteration of a complete training pattern dataset is a discrete step in time, or epoch. Thus, the first epoch is at t_0, the next at t_1, and so on. In a rectangular output slab, the topology of the PEs may (or may not, depending on the user) wrap around left to right and top to bottom.

For the moment let us suppose that the PE in the center of the slab illustrated in Figure 6.6 is the winner. For the first group of iterations (epochs), the neighborhood of the winning PE is relatively large, perhaps large enough to cover most or all of the output slab. For example, in Figure 6.7 the initial neighborhood may consist of the winning PE and the 18 PEs surrounding it. After further iterations, the neighborhood is decreased in size. This smaller neighborhood could consist, in our example, of the winning PE plus the six PEs immediately surrounding it. Finally, after another set of iterations, the neighborhood could shrink to include only the winning PE. The number of iterations between changes in neighborhood size varies appreciably with the application but is often in the range of a few hundred to a few thousand.

Now that you know how to decrease the size of the neighborhood with time, what do you do with the weights of the PEs inside the neighborhood? (Remember that the weights of the PEs outside the neighborhood are not changed.) Figure 6.9 illustrates three approaches to weight adjustment. To implement these functions, imagine that the PE slab is significantly larger than those of Figures 6.6 and 6.7, so that the initial neighborhoods can be eight to ten PEs in diameter.

Figure 6.9(a) illustrates the "Mexican hat" function described by Kohonen (1988). The largest weight adjustment, which is positive, occurs for the winning PE. Somewhat smaller positive changes are made to adjacent PEs, and still smaller changes to PE weights adjacent and just outside of these, and so on, until at some distance r_0

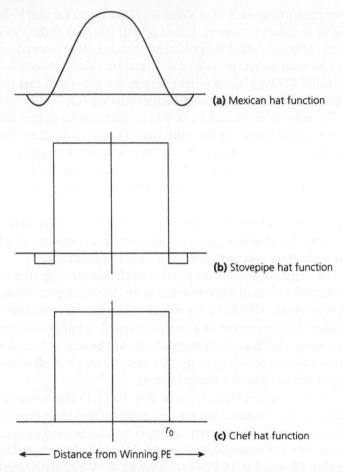

(a) Mexican hat function

(b) Stovepipe hat function

r_0 **(c)** Chef hat function

◄──── Distance from Winning PE ────►

Figure 6.9 Magnitude of weight correction versus distance from winning PE in a self-organizing feature map.

the weight adjustments go to 0. The weight changes then become slightly negative for a while, finally becoming 0.

The shape of the Mexican hat function is reminiscent of the on-center off-surround excitation pattern observed in some biological systems and implemented by Grossberg (1973) in his gain control system for a PE group (see the section in the history of neural networks of Chapter 5). Although the Mexican hat function may exhibit biological plausibility, it adds computational complexity to a set of calculations that is usually performed thousands of times while training a SOFM. Therefore, most applications of SOFMs have used simplified functions.

In the "stovepipe hat" function of Figure 6.9(b), identical positive weight changes are made to all PEs within a radius of r_0 of the winning PE, and identical negative weight changes are made to PEs at a slightly larger radius. Taking the simplification even further, we arrive at the "chef hat" function, shown in Figure 6.9(c), in which only identical positive weight changes are made to those PEs within the r_0 radius. This simple method is often used in implementations of the SOFM network (Kohonen 1988).

In addition to reducing computational complexity, the chef hat function is used for a practical reason. If we assume r_0 is about three times as large as the region of negative reinforcement beyond it, as in Figure 6.9(a and b), then there won't be any negative reinforcement for neighborhoods less than nine PEs across. For a neighborhood nine PEs across, the winning PE and three PEs on each side will receive positive weight reinforcement, while one PE on each side (and four PEs away) will receive negative reinforcement. As soon as the neighborhood shrinks to five across, all in the neighborhood will receive positive reinforcement. In the authors' experience, we have seldom worked with output slabs larger than five across, and never larger than eight across, so it is rare that we start with neighborhood larger than five across.

In summary, training consists of finding the winning PE according to the minimum Euclidean distance method (perhaps including the effects of a conscience), as in LVQ-I, and then updating the PE weights in the neighborhood according to equation 6.15. Note that this equation is identical to that for weight updating for LVQ-I with the addition of the neighborhood function $n(t)$. In the simplest version (most often implemented) $n(t)$ is 1.0 within the chef hat neighborhood and 0.0 outside the neighborhood, and the neighborhood size shrinks over time.

$$w_{ji}(t+1) = w_{ji}(t) + n(t)\eta(t)(\alpha_{ki} - w_{ji}) \qquad (6.15)$$

Iterations continue until the corrections in equation 6.15 become acceptably small or the specified maximum number of iterations is reached. As with LVQ-I, it is not necessary to renormalize the weight vectors during or after training as long as the changes to the weight vector components carried out according to equation 6.15 are small enough. Keeping them small keeps the weight vector near the surface of the unit hypersphere and the dot-product remains valid. See the discussion of the selection of training patterns for the LVQ-I paradigm; similar guidance should be followed for SOFM. Also remember that the same conscience mechanism as that for LVQ-I should be implemented for SOFM.

Let's now examine *SOFM data type definitions*. SOFM is an extension of LVQ. Thus the data types defined for the LVQ implementation are utilized here with minor changes and different names—for example, `LVQ_Type` is renamed `SOFM_Type`. Since in the SOFM a neighborhood concept is incorporated and is the main difference between LVQ and SOFM, the neighborhood concept is programmed into the SOFM implementation. For SOFM, for visualization, the output slab is most often two-dimensional; the neighborhood is therefore two-dimensional. The PEs (neurons), at least in the output slab, use double subscripts. Certainly, one- or three-dimensional output slabs can also be used. If the output slab is one-dimensional, the source code for LVQ implementation, except the routines for updating weights, can be used here, where now all the PEs within the neighborhood of the winning PE, instead of only the winning PE as in LVQ, have their weights updated. Actually, this can also be true even for a two- or three-dimensional output slab, but it involves some conversion routines from one-dimensional subscript expression to double or triple subscripts and from double or triple subscripts to one-dimensional subscripts. In our implementation, the common two-dimensional slab and double subscripts are used. Therefore, minor changes to the LVQ implementation are required for the SOFM implementation. The new data types are listed in Listing 6.12 for convenience.

Listing 6.12 Data type definitions for SOFM.

```
/******************************************************************/
/* Enumerations                                                   */
/******************************************************************/
typedef enum SOFM_Training_Mode_Tag
{
  SOFM_RANDOM_MODE,
  SOFM_SEQUENTIAL_MODE,
  NUM_SOFM_TRAINING_MODES
} SOFM_Training_Mode_Type;

typedef enum SOFM_State_Tag
{
  SOFM_GET_PATTERN,
  SOFM_WEIGHT_NORMALIZATION,
  SOFM_FEEDFORWARD_INPUT,
  SOFM_FEEDFORWARD_OUTPUT,
  SOFM_WINNING_NEURON,
  SOFM_UPDATE_NEIGHBORHOOD,
  SOFM_WEIGHT_CHANGE,
  SOFM_NEXT_PATTERN,
  SOFM_NEXT_ITERATION,
  SOFM_UPDATE_LEARNING_RATE,
  SOFM_UPDATE_CONSCIENCE_FACTOR,
  SOFM_TRAINING_DONE,
  SOFM_RECALL_DONE,
  NUM_SOFM_STATES
} SOFM_State_Type;

typedef enum SOFM_Conscience_Type_Tag
{
  SOFM_NO_CONSCIENCE,
  SOFM_CONSCIENCE,
  NUM_SOFM_CONSCIENCE
} SOFM_Conscience_Type;

typedef enum Neighbor_Function_Type_Tag
```

```
{
  CHEF_HAT,
  MEXICAN_HAT,
  STOVEPIPE_HAT,
  NUM_NEIGHBOR_FUNC
} Neighbor_Function_Type;

/***************************************************************/
/* Structures                                                  */
/***************************************************************/
typedef struct SOFM_2D_Size_Type_Tag
{         // rectangular
  int    width;
  int    height;
} SOFM_2D_Size_Type;

typedef struct Neuron_Type_Tag
{
  NN_Function_Type        neuron_function;
  float                   in;
  float                   out;
  FVECTOR                 w;
  FVECTOR                 delta_w;
  float                   c_f;
  float                   b_v;
  int                     w_s;
} Neuron_Type;

typedef struct NN_Layer_Arch_Type_Tag
{
  SOFM_2D_Size_Type       size;
  Neuron_Type             **neurons;
  NN_Layer_Type           slab_type;
} NN_Slab_Arch_Type;

typedef struct SOFM_Arch_Type_Tag
{
  int                     size;
  NN_Slab_Arch_Type       *slabs;
} SOFM_Arch_Type;

typedef struct SOFM_Env_Type_Tag
{
  NN_Operation_Mode_Type  operation_mode;
  SOFM_Training_Mode_Type train_mode;
  float                   eta;
  float                   gama;
  float                   beta;
  float                   shrink;
  float                   criterion;
  int                     max_ite;
  int                     cur_ite;
  int                     max_tra_pat;
  int                     cur_pat;
  int                     pat_counter;
```

```
  SOFM_Conscience_Type       conscience;
  SOFM_2D_Size_Type          winner;
  SOFM_2D_Size_Type          neighbor;
  SOFM_2D_Size_Type          cur_neighbor;
  Neighbor_Function_Type     neighbor_function;
} SOFM_Env_Type;

typedef struct SOFM_Type_Tag
{
  SOFM_Arch_Type             arch;
  SOFM_Env_Type              env;
} SOFM_Type;

typedef struct SOFM_Pattern_Set_Type_Tag
{
  int                        size;
  int                        dim_in;
  int                        dim_out;
  FMATRIX                    patterns;
} SOFM_Pattern_Set_Type;
```

As shown in Listing 6.12, most data types are the same as those in the LVQ implementation except for having different names, but there are some differences. A new state SOFM_UPDATE_NEIGHBORHOOD is added into SOFM_State_Type, and two states for weight changes are merged into one state SOFM_WEIGHT_CHANGE.

A new struct data type SOFM_2D_Size_Type is defined to record the two-dimensional object. Another new data type Neighbor_Function_Type is defined to enumerate the neighborhood function types. The name of the element neurons in NN_Slab_Arch_Type is a double pointer, instead of a pointer, to Neuron_type. The name of the element layer_type has been changed to slab_type to reflect the slab concept. The same is true for element slabs in SOFM_Arch_Type.

In the data type SOFM_Env_Type, the element no_clusters is removed, the element winner's data type int is replaced with data type SOFM_2D_Size_Type, and the new elements neighbor, cur_neighbor, and neighbor_function are added. The SOFM_2D_Size_Type neighbor records the initial neighborhood size, the cur_neighbor records the current neighborhood size, and the Neighbor_Function_Type neighbor_function stores which neighborhood function is being used.

There are a few programming differences between SOFM and LVQ. Most of the SOFM implementation is similar to the LVQ implementation except that double subscripts represent the PEs where LVQ uses single subscripts. The main difference is that a new state SOFM_UPDATE_NEIGHBORHOOD is added to update the neighborhood size, and the state handling routine for state SOFM_WEIGHT_CHANGE has to be significantly modified to reflect that all the PEs within the neighborhood of the winning PE are required to update their weights; in LVQ only the winning PE must update its weight.

In the SOFM_UPDATE_NEIGHBORHOOD state, the neighborhood size is updated. The variable ite_per_update_neighbor.height records the rate at which neighborhood size is decreased. Both dimensions of the neighborhood size are updated. The current state transitions to the state SOFM_WEIGHT_CHANGE. The state handling routine is shown here.

```
static void sofm_update_neighborhood (void)
{
    static int temp_c;

    temp_c = sofm.env.cur_ite/ite_per_update_neighbor.height;
    sofm.env.cur_neighbor.height =  sofm.env.neighbor.height - temp_c;

    temp_c = sofm.env.cur_ite/ite_per_update_neighbor.width;
    sofm.env.cur_neighbor.width =  sofm.env.neighbor.width - temp_c;

    if (sofm.env.cur_neighbor.height < 0)
    {
        sofm.env.cur_neighbor.height = 0;
    }
    if (sofm.env.cur_neighbor.width < 0)
    {
        sofm.env.cur_neighbor.width = 0;
    }

    sofm_cur_state = SOFM_WEIGHT_CHANGE;
}
```

In the SOFM_WEIGHT_CHANGE state, all the PEs within the neighborhood of the wining PE have their weights updated. When considering the neighborhood, the PEs' subscripts are wrapped around; the PEs on one side of a boundary are topological neighbors to the PEs on the other side of the boundary. The neighbor_func() routine is called to get the neighborhood weight value. The current state transitions to the state SOFM_NEXT_PATTERN. The state handling routine is shown here.

```
static void sofm_weight_change (void)
{
    int idx_pn, idx_h, idx_w;
    int n_h,n_w;

    for (idx_pn = 0; idx_pn < (sofm.arch.slabs[0].size.width) ; idx_pn++)
    {   // loop through the connect weights of the current neurons
        for (idx_h = -(sofm.env.cur_neighbor.height); idx_h <=
                    (sofm.env.cur_neighbor.height) ; idx_h++)
        {
            n_h = sofm.env.winner.height + idx_h;

            if (n_h < 0)
            {
                n_h += sofm.arch.slabs[1].size.height;
```

```
            }
            else if (n_h >= sofm.arch.slabs[1].size.height)
            {
                n_h -= sofm.arch.slabs[1].size.height;
            }
            for (idx_w = -(sofm.env.cur_neighbor.width); idx_w <=
                            (sofm.env.cur_neighbor.width) ; idx_w++)
            {
                n_w = sofm.env.winner.width  + idx_w;

                if (n_w < 0)
                {
                    n_w += sofm.arch.slabs[1].size.width;
                }
                else if (n_w >= sofm.arch.slabs[1].size.width)
                {
                    n_w -= sofm.arch.slabs[1].size.width;
                }
                sofm.arch.slabs[1].neurons[n_h][n_w].delta_w[idx_pn] =
                        sofm.arch.slabs[0].neurons[0][idx_pn].out -
                        sofm.arch.slabs[1].neurons[n_h][n_w].w[idx_pn];
                sofm.arch.slabs[1].neurons[n_h][n_w].delta_w[idx_pn] *=
                        (sofm.env.eta * neighbor_func(idx_h,idx_w));;

                sofm.arch.slabs[1].neurons[n_h][n_w].w[idx_pn] +=
                        sofm.arch.slabs[1].neurons[n_h][n_w].delta_w[idx_pn];
            }
        }
    }
    sofm_cur_state = SOFM_NEXT_PATTERN;
}

static float neighbor_func (int height, int width)
{
    int temp_i;
    float result;

    temp_i = (height > width)?height:width;
    switch (sofm.env.neighbor_function)
    {
        case CHEF_HAT:
          result = chef_hat(temp_i);
          break;
        case MEXICAN_HAT:
          result = mexican_hat(temp_i);
          break;
        case STOVEPIPE_HAT:
          result = stovepipe_hat(temp_i);
          break;
        default:
          printf("need to specify neighborhood function\n");
          exit(1);
          break;
    }
    return(result);
}
```

Running the SOFM Implementation

To run the self-organizing feature map implementation requires the executable file `sofm.exe` and an associated run file, for example, `iris_sof.run`. To run the implementation from within the directory containing `sofm.exe` and `iris_sof.run`, at the DOS system prompt type `sofm iris_sof.run`.

The content of an `iris_sof.run` run file is shown in Listing 6.13.

Listing 6.13 The run file `iris_sof.run`.

```
0
0
0.3
0.999
10
0.0001
0.001
500
99
1
1
1
4
4
0

150
4
3
iris.dat
```

The file contains specifications for a run. It specifies operation mode (0), training mode (0), learning rate (0.3), learning rate shrinking coefficient (0.999), bias factor (10), beta (0.0001), training termination criterion (0.001), maximum number of iterations (500), number of patterns used for training (99), network conscience status (1), initial width of neighborhood size (1), initial height of neighborhood size (1), width of output slab (4), height of output slab (4), neighborhood function type (0), total number of patterns in pattern file (150), dimension of pattern input (4), dimension of pattern output (3), and pattern data filename of (iris.dat) from which the patterns are read. In our implementation, the only neighborhood function type available is 0, a chef hat function. Implementation of other neighborhood types is left as an exercise for the reader.

Two output files are generated for each run. One is SOFM_RES.TXT, which contains the weights for the SOFM network. The other is SOFM_TES.TXT, which is a summary table listing the number of patterns of each input class assigned to each output PE in the output slab.

Evolutionary Back-propagation Network Implementation

The implementation of the evolutionary back-propagation network discussed in this section applies particle swarm optimization to evolve network weights. The slope of sigmoid function of each neuron can easily be added to go through evolution, as discussed previously, which is left as an exercise. A review of techniques used to evolve neural networks can be found in Eberhart and Shi (1998).

Programming the Evolutionary Back-propagation Network

To implement the evolutionary back-propagation network, we simply merge the particle swarm optimization implementation and the back-propagation implementations with some minor changes. The BP network gets its connecting weights from a PSO individual and runs under recall operation mode, which, in turn, feeds its performance back to PSO as the fitness of that PSO individual. To the data type `Evaluate_Function_Type` on the PSO side, a new element `BP` is added to reflect that a BP net is being evolved. In addition, some new functions have to be added to act as interfaces between the PSO implementation and the BP implementation, and the `main()` function must be modified accordingly.

The `main()` routine is shown in Listing 6.14. It differs from both the PSO and BP implementations in that now both the PSO and BP startup routines and cleanup routines are included instead of only one, as in either implementation alone, but only the `PSO_Main_Loop()` is included since the BP network is treated as an application problem for PSO to solve. The `BP_Main_Loop()` routine is called only when an individual of the PSO needs to be evaluated.

Listing 6.14 The `main()` routine of evolutionary BP net.

```
void main (int argc, char *argv[])
{
    // check command line
    if (argc != 3)
    {
        printf("Usage: exe_file pso_run_file bp_run_file\n");
        exit(1);
    }

    // initialize
    main_start_up(argv[1],argv[2]);
    PSO_Main_Loop();
    main_clean_up();
}
static void main_start_up (char *psoDataFile,char *bpDataFile)
{
    BP_Start_Up(bpDataFile);
    PSO_Start_Up(psoDataFile);
}

static void main_clean_up (void)
```

```
{
    PSO_Clean_Up();
    BP_Clean_Up();
}
```

Now we discuss *interface routines*. To initialize the PSO, the length of an individual particle is calculated by calling the `BP_Get_PSO_Dimension()` routine, which returns the number of connection weights (including the biases) in the BP net to be evolved. The `BP_Get_PSO_Dimension()` routine is shown in Listing 6.15.

Listing 6.15 The `BP_Get_PSO_Dimension()` routine.

```
int BP_Get_PSO_Dimension (void)
{
    int idx_l;
    pso_dimension = 0;

    for (idx_l = 0; idx_l < (bp.arch.size - 1); idx_l++)
    {
        pso_dimension +=
            ((bp.arch.layers[idx_l].size + 1) * bp.arch.layers
                [idx_l + 1].size);
    }
    return(pso_dimension);
}
```

Since the BP element is added into data type `Evaluate_Function_Type`'s definition, the `evaluate_function()` routine should add a corresponding case to handle the evaluation of the BP net. In the modified `evaluate_functions()` routine shown in Listing 6.16, only the new case is shown. To evaluate the current individual, which is a representation of the weights of a BP network, the individual is first transformed to the connection weights of a BP net by calling `BP_Weights_From_PSO(current_individual)`; then the routine `BP_Main_Loop()` is called to evaluate the BP net. The routine is the same as that in the BP implementation except that here it returns a float value, which records the number of patterns the BP net being evaluated recognizes correctly.

Listing 6.16 The `evaluate_Functions()` routine.

```
static void evaluate_functions (int fun_type)
{
    switch (fun_type)
    {
        .
        .
        .
        case BP_MIN:
```

```
            BP_Weights_From_PSO(psos[cur_pso].
                    position_values[psos[cur_pso].popu_index]);
            psos[cur_pso].eva_fun_value = BP_Main_Loop();
            break;
        default:
            break;
    }
}

void BP_Weights_From_PSO (float *vec)
{   int idx_layer, idx_cn, idx_pn;
    int counter = 0;

    for (idx_layer = 1; idx_layer < (bp.arch.size) ; idx_layer++)
    {   // loop through the layers
        for (idx_cn = 0; idx_cn < (bp.arch.layers[idx_layer].size) ;
                    idx_cn++)
        {   // loop through the neurons in the current layer
            for (idx_pn = 0; idx_pn <= (bp.arch.layers[idx_layer - 1]
                        .size) ; idx_pn++)
            {   // loop through the connect weights of the current neurons
                bp.arch.layers[idx_layer].neurons[idx_cn].w[idx_pn] =
                        vec[counter++];
            }
        }
    }
    if (counter != pso_dimension)
    {
        printf("not match in BP_Weights_From_PSO routine 1 \n");
        exit(1);
    }
}
```

Running the Evolutionary Back-propagation Network

To run the evolutionary BP network implementation requires the executable file pso_nn.exe and *two* associated run files, for example, pso.run and bp.run. The two run files specify the information required for running the PSO part and the BP part of the evolutionary BP network, respectively. To run the implementation from within the directory containing pso_nn.exe, pso.run, and bp.run, at the DOS system prompt type pso_nn pso.run bp.run.

The pso.run file is the same format as the run file for running a single PSO in the PSO implementation except that the length of the PSO individual is not specified in the run file, but rather is obtained from the BP module by calling BP_Get_PSO_Dimension() as discussed in the preceding section on interface routines. Note that the optimization type should be set to "maximize," since we are trying to maximize the number of correct classifications. Also note that the evaluation function will be a unique code for calling BP weights from within the PSO application. The bp.run file is shorter than the run file for running the entire BP implementation since the BP is run in the recall operation mode only. Therefore, the parameters related to the network training don't need to be specified in the run file. The content of a `bp.run` file for the Iris dataset is shown in Listing 6.17.

Listing 6.17 The `bp.run` file.

```
3
4
150
4
3
iris.dat
```

The first entry (3) specifies the number of layers in the BP net to be evolved, followed by the number of PEs (neurons) in each hidden layer (4). The third entry (150) specifies the number of patterns involved in the evaluation of the BP net. The next two values (4 and 3) specify the input and output dimensions of each pattern, respectively. The last entry (`iris.dat`) provides the name of the pattern data file where the patterns are obtained.

Summary

In this chapter, we look at implementation issues for several types of neural network. We then discuss four network implementations: back-propagation, learning vector quantization, self-organizing feature maps, and evolutionary back-propagation. The code for all of these implementations is on the web site for the book. The source code is distributed as shareware.

In the next chapter, we continue our journey through the primary concepts of computational intelligence by looking at fuzzy logic history, concepts, and paradigms.

Exercises

1. In back-propagation networks, why should we use PEs with biases in the hidden and output layers? Why choose nonlinear functions as activation functions?

2. During back-propagation network training, is it generally desirable to train the network to have as small a sum-squared error as possible on the training patterns? Why?

3. It is usually recommended to scale or preprocess the input values prior to presentation to a neural network. List some reasons for doing this. List some ways to do this.

4. Compare the LVQ-I , LVQ-II, and SOFM network paradigms. What are the similarities? What are the differences? Why might you choose to use SOFM rather than LVQ-I?

5. List the attributes necessary to specify a back-propagation neural network implementation. Repeat for an evolutionary back-propagation implementation.

6. List the attributes necessary to specify a learning vector quantizer neural network implementation. Repeat for a self-organizing feature map implementation.

7. Add an error termination criterion into the back-propagation implementation so that the BP training can be terminated based on either maximum number of generations or the error termination criterion.

8. Using `BP_Neuron_Type` as the definition for the PE (neuron) in the back-propagation network, make necessary changes to other data types, and specify the corresponding changes that should be made in the source code.

9. Assume that the activation function for PEs in the hidden and output layers of the back-propagation implementation is the hyperbolic tangent function. Specify the changes that should be made in the source code.

10. In the state `BP_FEEDFORWARD_HIDDEN`, all hidden layers are calculated in one cycle of the state machine. Modify the code so that only one hidden layer is calculated in one cycle.

11. In the state `BP_FEEDFORWARD_OUTPUT`, modify the state handling routine so that calculations for only one output PE are done for each cycle of the state machine.

12. Define one or two decreasing functions of time for updating the learning rate $\eta(t)$ and make corresponding changes in the `lvq_update_learning_rate()` routine. Compile and run the LVQ and compare the performance with the original version.

13. Modify the LVQ source code for the implementation of a SOFM with a one-dimensional output slab.

14. Based on the implementation from exercise 8, implement the SOFM with a two-dimensional output slab.

15. Modify the evolutionary back-propagation implementation so that it also evolves the slope of the sigmoid function.

16. Run the back-propagation implementation on the web site using the run files provided for training and testing on the Iris dataset. Keeping everything else

constant in the run files, try training for 10,000, 1,000, and 100 iterations. Discuss your results with respect to both training and testing.

17. Run the learning vector quantization implementation on the web site using the run files provided. Vary the number of clusters specified. Try 6 clusters as specified in the run file on the Web; then try 3 clusters, then try 9 clusters. Discuss your results. Which number of clusters would you select for this problem? Why?

chapter
seven

Fuzzy Systems Concepts and Paradigms

This chapter presents the computational intelligence component methodology that is known as *fuzzy logic*. Fuzzy logic provides a general concept for description and measurement. Most fuzzy logic systems encode human reasoning into a program to make decisions or control machinery. Fuzzy logic is most widely used to control dynamical systems, such as equipment that must adjust to constantly changing conditions. The concept, or perhaps we could say the *philosophy*, of fuzzy logic can be as abstract as any body of thought or it can be as down to earth as common sense. The present chapter discusses fuzzy sets and approximate reasoning, and the next presents an implementation of a fuzzy-logic system. We begin with a brief history of the field that focuses on some of the people who made significant contributions. ■

History

There are those who would argue that a discussion of the history of fuzzy logic should start with an examination of the life of Gautama Buddha, born about 563 BC. Indeed, Buddhism often describes things in shades of gray and embraces what Westerners would consider contradictions, or paradoxes. Everything exists and interacts in a continuum (Goddard 1970). The statement "X is not-X" is accepted by most Buddhists and rejected by almost all Westerners.

By contrast, Western scientific and mathematical thought has been shaped by the logic of Aristotle, born approximately 200 years after Gautama Buddha. Aristotle's logic is the "crisp logic" of either–or, true or false, 1 or 0. Truth is all or nothing, absolutely true or absolutely false, with no middle ground possible. Aristotle's logic has ruled Western thought for more than two millennia.

Probability is then overlaid on Aristotle's logic, supporting it and making it more reasonable and workable. Although the axioms of probability spring, as do all axioms, from assumptions rather than being derived from general theory, Westerners have built mathematics and science around it.

Aristotelian logic and probability have ingrained Westerners with much resistance to the concepts surrounding fuzzy logic and approximate reasoning, while the same concepts have been embraced by scientists, engineers, and mathematicians in the East. For a more detailed discussion of the differences between Eastern and Western approaches, see Kosko (1993).

With Western cultural resistance to the idea of fuzziness or approximate reasoning established, we begin our history of the development of fuzzy logic with a Polish mathematician. Jan Lukasiewicz was born in 1878 and taught at the University of Warsaw before fleeing to Germany and Ireland as a result of World War II. He first published a short paper on three-valued logic in 1920. He expanded his foundation to include logic with an arbitrary number of values in a book originally published in Poland in 1923 (Lukasiewicz 1963). In discussing the values of truth assigned to statements, he said:

> In this way we should obtain a bundle of many-valued logics: a three-valued logic, a four-valued logic, etc., and finally a logic of infinitely many values. Symbols other than "0" and "1" used in the proofs of independence would thus correspond to the various degrees of truth of sentences in logics with the corresponding numbers of values.

In the same book, he also established that every theorem of three-valued logic is also a theorem of two-valued logic (but not vice versa), and therefore that "three-valued logic is a proper part of two-valued logic." Jan Lukasiewicz thus developed the structure of fuzzy sets and established their relationship to traditional logic.

Following Lukasiewicz's pioneering work, such luminaries as Kurt Gödel and John Von Neumann developed multivalued logics of their own. There can, in fact, be many multivalued logic schemes.

The next stop along the fuzzy logic history track is with quantum philosopher Max Black, who taught at Cornell for his entire career. He recognized that a continuum implies vagueness and that vagueness has degrees. In a now famous paper, he described quasi-fuzzy sets (Black 1937). He used as an example objects that more or less resembled chairs. He recognized that a number could be assigned to each object based on the degree to which it was perceived to be a chair. At this point, however, he took a different tack than would be taken by today's fuzzy logicians: Black assigned to "degree" the percentage of people (as would be obtained in a poll) who would label the object a chair. Thus, his work, if it had been widely recognized and accepted, might have altered the development of fuzzy logic as we know it.

When electronic computers came into existence in the mid-twentieth century, it was immediately apparent that, besides doing numerical calculations, these machines could be used to manipulate symbols: They should be able to perform logical reasoning.

It almost immediately turned out, however, that computers did not live up to expectations. They could fairly easily accomplish the logical operations of complicated deductive arguments, and they could even find solutions to difficult logical puzzles. Although computers only became widely available in the 1950s, by the mid-1950s Newell and Simon (1956) had already written a program that could prove mathematical theorems—even discovering proofs that had eluded human thinkers.

But these "brilliant" machines weren't very good at solving *real* problems, problems having to do with real people and real business, and things with moving parts. It seemed that no matter how many variables were added to the decision process, there was always something else. Systems didn't work the same when they were hot, or cold, or stressed, or dirty, or cranky, or in the light or in the dark, or when two things went wrong at the same time. There was always something else. The problem was that the computer was unable to make accurate inferences. It couldn't very well tell what would happen given some preconditions, no matter how precisely specified they were. It remained for the man we discuss next to set it straight.

Lotfi A. Zadeh is certainly the single most significant developer and champion of fuzzy logic theory and applications. Born in 1921 in Baku in Soviet Azerbaijan, he came to the United States as a graduate student at the Massachusetts Institute of Technology in 1944, where he received a master's degree in electrical engineering in 1946. He then went to Columbia University, where he earned his Ph.D. in 1949. A year later, he co-published with his thesis advisor, John Ragazzini, a paper entitled, "An Extension of Wiener's Theory of Prediction," an analysis of time series prediction that Zadeh cites as his first significant technical contribution (Perry 1995).

In 1954 Zadeh published a paper entitled "System Theory," which was the foundation for a new field of the same name that is still active. Fuzzy logic theory, in fact, seems to have evolved out of his work in the area of complex systems. He moved to the University of California at Berkeley in 1959 and has been there ever since, except for a short time at IBM. He apparently first conceived of some of the basic ideas of fuzzy quantities in about 1961, when he suggested in a paper that a new approach was needed that involved "fuzzy" mathematics.

His landmark paper that launched the field, entitled "Fuzzy Sets," was written in late 1964 and published the next year (Zadeh 1965). By the time the paper was published, Zadeh was well known for his text on linear systems theory, published in 1963, which was used as a textbook in many universities. One of the amazing things about the paper is its comprehensiveness. In effect, Zadeh's paper gave birth to a relatively mature paradigm. Everything that is needed to apply fuzzy logic is in the original paper (although the paper doesn't contain the term "fuzzy logic").

Zadeh's key concept is that of membership values. A membership value measures the degree or extent to which an object meets vague and/or imprecise properties. These membership values are defined over the universe of discourse by a *membership function*, which is the fuzzy set. Zadeh also defined what have become known as the "classical" operations for fuzzy sets, which comprise all the mathematical tools necessary to apply them.

Zadeh immediately became a tireless spokesperson for the nascent field. In the beginning, his job was difficult. He was often harshly criticized, both verbally and in writing. For example, in 1972 R. E. Kalman said (Perry 1995): "Fuzzification is a kind of scientific permissiveness; it tends to result in socially appealing slogans unaccompanied by the discipline of hard scientific work."

But Zadeh always stands up for what he believes and endures criticism with patience and grace. He has, of course, prevailed. Among his numerous awards, he was the recipient in 1995 of the IEEE Medal of Honor, the highest award the Institute of Electrical and Electronics Engineers can bestow. He thereby joins the ranks of such Medal of Honor awardees as Alexander Graham Bell and Thomas A. Edison.

It was the early 1970s before someone articulated the first fuzzy control strategy implementing Zadeh's concepts. Working at London University in 1973, Ebrahim Mamdani and one of his graduate students, Sedrak Assilian, designed and built a fuzzy controller for a small steam plant consisting of a boiler and an engine. They implemented a 24-rule fuzzy control system that used fuzzy membership functions for pressure error and the change in pressure error to control the change in the heat. The entire control system was designed over one weekend (McNeill and Freiberger 1993) and the results published two years later (Mamdani and Assilian 1975). This work, while only a laboratory-based development, was an important milestone in that it demonstrated that Zadeh's ideas could be reduced to practice.

Also in the early 1970s, Hans Zimmerman became active in fuzzy logic at the University of Aachen in Germany. He founded the first European working group on fuzzy logic in 1975. He also co-founded and became the first editor of *Fuzzy Sets and Systems*, the first important journal in the field, in 1978. In June 1984, as a result of a conference in Hawaii, Zimmerman helped create the International Fuzzy Systems Association (IFSA) and became its first president.

In France, Didier Dubois and Henri Prade became charter members of the European working group. With computer science and mathematical backgrounds, they went back to first principles to develop the mathematical foundations of fuzzy operators. They also developed families of operators and co-authored a textbook on fuzzy logic (Dubois and Prade 1980). Prade was instrumental in founding a fuzzy logic institute in France.

Meanwhile, in the United States two important contributors in the early years (1965–1975) were King Sun Fu at Purdue University and Azriel Rosenfeld at the University of Maryland. Their impact was significant partly because both were already well known professionally, and both encouraged students to do fuzzy sets work. Fu, who was the founding president of the North American Fuzzy Information Processing Society (Bezdek and Pal 1992), published one of the earliest papers on fuzzy pattern recognition with his student Bill Wee (Wee and Fu 1969). Wee is believed to have written the first Ph.D. dissertation on fuzzy pattern recognition (Wee 1967). It is hard to judge the importance of Fu and Rosenfeld because at the time Zadeh was enduring considerable ridicule, and these two individuals were insightful enough to understand fuzzy logic's potential.

Two other important early contributors in the United States were Enrique Ruspini of the Artificial Intelligence Center at SRI International and James Bezdek of the University of West Florida.

Ruspini was born in Buenos Aires, Argentina, and received his Ph.D. from the University of California at Los Angeles in 1977. He derived significant theoretical underpinnings of fuzzy logic and wrote the first paper on fuzzy clustering (Ruspini 1969). His clustering methodology used fuzzy partitions, and similarity was measured using membership values (Ruspini 1970).

Bezdek received his Ph.D. in applied mathematics from Cornell University in 1973 and later served as director of the Information Processing Laboratory at the Boeing Electronics High Technology Center. He developed fuzzy pattern recognition algorithms, introduced the fuzzy c-means clustering algorithms, and was one of the first to recognize the importance of, and develop applications of, combinations of fuzzy logic and neural networks (Bezdek and Harris 1978; Bezdek 1981).

Bezdek and Ruspini have been active in fuzzy logic professional society activities. Among other activities, Bezdek chaired the IFSA meeting in Hawaii out of which the society was born, served as the second president of both IFSA and the North American Fuzzy Information Processing Society (NAFIPS), and was the founding editor-in-chief of the *IEEE Transactions on Fuzzy Systems*. Bezdek and Ruspini served as chairs of the first and second FUZZ/IEEE international conferences (IEEE international conferences on fuzzy systems), respectively.

The first industrial application of fuzzy control was developed in the late 1970s by L. P. Holmblad and J.-J. Ostergaard, two engineers living in Denmark (Sugeno 1985). Their first control system was for a cement kiln, and it was followed by additional similar systems in Sweden and other countries (McNeill and Thro 1994).

After a few successful applications in the 1970s, fuzzy logic entered what is considered its dark age in the 1980s, especially in the United States. Funding in the United States was largely allocated to development of expert systems and other traditional artificial intelligence (AI) projects. That distinctively irreverent word, "fuzzy," seemed to make engineers, computer scientists, and, more significantly, funding agency program managers think that the method was somehow inadequate for "serious" projects; it became the kiss of death for research proposals.

Then, as has happened with a number of other American innovations, fuzzy logic really caught on in Japan; the Japanese, calling it *faaji*, began using fuzzy logic for everything from vacuum cleaners, cameras, and elevators to robots. The activity in Japan, however, had begun in the early 1970s; practical applications proliferated there earlier because of the continuity of activity (funding support) compared with the United States and Europe. We begin our look at Japan with an early Japanese researcher, Michio Sugeno.

Sugeno received his undergraduate degree in 1962 from the University of Tokyo. He joined the Tokyo Institute of Technology in 1965, where he began working with Toshiro Terano in the control engineering department. In 1972 Terano formed a fuzzy systems working group, with Sugeno as secretary. In 1974 Sugeno developed a fuzzy measure theory for his Ph.D. dissertation. He then spent eight months in England with Mamdani and eight months in France before going back to Japan in 1977. He was convinced that the way to stimulate interest and activity in fuzzy logic was to develop a successful application. In 1978, therefore, he began working on fuzzy control systems and in 1983 implemented one for a water purification plant owned by Fuji Electric Company. It was the first commercial application of fuzzy logic in Japan.

The first consumer product to utilize fuzzy technology was a shower head that used fuzzy circuitry to control the water temperature, produced in Japan in 1987 by Matsushita Electric. Perhaps the most visible early fuzzy application also occurred in Japan in 1987. Engineers at the Hitachi Systems Development Laboratory, Shoji Miyamoto and Seiji Yasunobu, developed a fuzzy control system for the subway system in Sendai. Later in 1987 a landmark conference was held in Tokyo. At this meeting, T. Yamakawa demonstrated an application of fuzzy control to the "inverted pendulum" system using a set of fuzzy logic chips (Kecman 2001). It is believed by many that the second annual International Fuzzy Systems Association (IFSA) conference was a turning point for the technology.

In 1989 Terano was named director of the Laboratory for International Fuzzy Engineering Research (LIFE) in Yokohama, and Sugeno was named its "leading advisor." LIFE quickly became a center for leading-edge fuzzy technology development.

As we enter the new millennium, a growing number of concepts, paradigms, and implementations are being fuzzified. In the words of Klir and Yuan (1995), perhaps the most important thing being gained through this fuzzification is "a methodology for exploiting the tolerance for imprecision."

Fuzzy Sets and Fuzzy Logic

It is hardly an exaggeration to say that Lotfi Zadeh single-handedly conceptualized many of the important developments in the field. Though fuzzy logic was first greeted with skepticism, it has since become widely accepted by engineers and computer scientists and is becoming common in applications in many diverse fields.

Previous theories of logic had assumed that the rules of reasoning were clear and that they could be expressed in words or mathematical symbols. Then one only had to introduce some premises, follow the rules, and the conclusions would be produced automatically. But Zadeh noted that this "first-order logic" was insufficient for solving real problems. Almost all of human reasoning, he argued, is *imprecise*. The amazing process called "common sense," which humans are very good at, was too hard for computers because it is fundamentally imprecise.

In the remainder of this chapter, we introduce some of the basic concepts of fuzzy logic knowledge engineering. We begin with a brief discussion of Zadeh's theory of fuzzy sets, especially comparing the theory to previously existing theories of binary logic. Next we discuss "approximate reasoning," that is, how inferences are made from fuzzy sets. In the final sections we review some of the issues and applications of fuzzy logic. In the next chapter, implementations of fuzzy logic demonstrate how fuzzy systems are created.

Logic, Fuzzy and Otherwise

Fuzzy logic comprises *fuzzy sets*, which are a way of representing nonstatistical uncertainty, and *approximate reasoning*, which includes the operations used to make inferences in fuzzy logic. Traditional Aristotelian logic is two-valued in both facts and operations. Thus, in two-valued logic a statement is either true or false; it implies another statement or it doesn't. A traditional logic program does one thing if statement X is true and another thing if it's false. These kinds of rules, technically called *production rules*, are often referred to as "if–then" rules because they're expressed in the form "if A, then B." Of course, they can be more complicated than that, for instance:

- If A and B, then C.
- If A and not-B, then C.

- If A or B, then not-C.
- If (((not-A) or B) and not-C) or D, then E.

For more on traditional binary logic processing, a good reference is Patrick Henry Winston's (1984) *Artificial Intelligence*, especially Chapter 7, "Logic and Theorem Proving," which clearly lays out the principles of inference in traditional artificial intelligence.

One of Zadeh's insights was that in the real world we often encounter degrees of truth, phenomena that are "sort of A" or "mostly B" or "very C." A, B, and C are not entirely true or false, or perfect members of a set or category. Consequently, a rule such as "If it's cloudy, then it will rain" simply doesn't work in the real world. Sometimes—*most* of the time—it's partly cloudy, or kind of cloudy, or maybe it's entirely cloudy, but the clouds are wisps of puff that couldn't produce rain no matter what. Real things occur *by degree.* Cloudiness can range from "not cloudy at all" to "completely cloudy." In fuzzy set theory, the sky is a member of the set "cloudy skies" by degree; the statement "The sky is cloudy" can vary in its degree of truth on a scale from 0 to 1. This introduces the concept of *fuzziness*, which Bellman and Zadeh (1970) defined as "a type of imprecision which is associated with . . . classes in which there is no sharp transition from membership to non-membership."

Not only are there degrees of cloudiness, but rain also occurs by degree. It might rain just a little bit, or it might rain a lot. So in the real-world application, it would not make much sense—that is, *common* sense—to assign a value of 0 or 1 to cloudiness and then try to estimate the 1/0, yes/no, true/false answer to whether rain will fall. But that is how traditional logic would attempt to answer the question. Fuzzy logic goes about it in a different way.

Fuzziness Is Not Probability

Criticisms of fuzzy logic are often based on confusion between the concepts of fuzziness and probability. Each morning the weather forecaster tells us the probability of rain for that day, based on a kind of if–then reasoning like that given earlier but, of course, taking into account a number of variables. Probability is a number from 0 to 1 that expresses the certainty that an event will occur. If probability = 0.0, then we are certain that the event will not occur. If it is 1.0, we are certain that it will occur (or that it has already occurred). Returning to the weather example, note that forecasters usually don't say *how much* rain will fall: Occurrence itself is either 0 or 1, a binary variable, at least when the meteorologist says it.

One important difference is that probability is meaningful only for things that haven't happened yet. Once the event occurs, probability evaporates (it becomes 1 or 0). The credibility of weather forecasters would decrease if they announced the probability of it raining yesterday! Yet it is meaningful, and in fact it does happen, for the announcer to talk about the *severity* of yesterday's weather. With pictures of torn-off roofs and downed power lines, they inform the audience that the storm was a "real bad one," or "yesterday was a beautiful day, if you're a duck." These are ways of saying that, as storms go, this was a *real* storm: Its membership in the set "storms" was very high. Probability is meaningless, but fuzzy set membership continues after the event.

Other important differences exist between fuzzy logic and probability. Probability is based on a closed world model in which it is assumed that everything is known: Fuzzy logic is not based on that model and makes no such assumption. Probability is based on frequency (Bayesian on subjectivity); fuzzy logic and crisp logic state objective descriptions/measures. Probability requires independence of variables; fuzzy logic has no such requirement. In probability, absence of a fact implies knowledge; in fuzzy logic, it does not.

This discussion isn't meant to imply that probability is useless. Probability is appropriate for randomly governed occurrences. If, when solving a problem, everything needed to calculate probabilities is available and valid, design of a probabilistic system may be a good idea. On the other hand, the more complex a system is, and the more it involves intelligent behavior (defined in Chapter 2), the more likely it is that fuzzy logic will be a good approach. We continue our examination of this approach with a discussion of the theory of fuzzy sets.

The Theory of Fuzzy Sets

Zadeh's fuzzy logic can be seen as an extension of set theory. In classical set theory, an element is either a member of a set or it is not. In a Venn diagram (Figure 7.1), we can see that part of the universe exists inside the circle that represents a set and some of it exists outside that circle. We have never seen a Venn diagram where, if a set was represented by a red circle, some parts of it were pink and some parts were dark scarlet. In two-valued logic, it's either red or it's not.

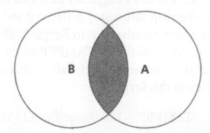

Figure 7.1 The shaded area represents the intersection of sets A and B in traditional binary set theory. Fuzzy set theory would allow areas of the Venn diagram to be darker or lighter shades of gray.

In fuzzy logic, set membership occurs by degree. Suppose we want to talk about the set "tall men." Professional basketball player Shaquille O'Neal is 2.16 meters (7 feet 1 inch) tall. By any standard, in any country in the world, "Shaq" is a member of the set "tall men." On the other hand, another basketball player, Travis Best is "only" 1.80 meters (5 feet 11 inches) tall. This is about the average height for an American male (1.78 meters, or 5 feet 10 inches), but it is definitely not tall for an American male professional basketball player. In our unscientific survey of six U.S. National Basketball Association teams (Indiana Pacers, Los Angeles Lakers, Atlanta Hawks, Boston Celtics, Detroit Pistons, and Utah Jazz), we didn't find anyone playing at the time this chapter was written shorter than 1.80 meters. (There were altogether three players on the six teams 1.80 meters tall.)

This exercise points out something to which you must pay attention when discussing fuzzy sets: It is important to define the set carefully, including specifying over which domain a set is defined. So let's recast our set as "tall American male professional basketball players," or TAMPBP, over the domain "American male professional basketball players." Thus, using traditional, two-valued logic, with a universe consisting of these two individuals, we would assert:

$$TAMPBP = \{Shaquille\ O'Neal\}\ and\ Not\text{-}TAMPBP = \{Travis\ Best\}$$

Given the extremes of these two players, this set assignment would be fine for some things. But that's a mighty small universe, two guys. What if we encounter someone like Reggie Miller of the Pacers, who is 2.01 meters (6 feet 7 inches)? That's pretty tall, but not extraordinary for a pro basketball player, especially next to someone like O'Neal. At first glance, we might be inclined to put Miller into the TAMPBP set, but closer inspection of the height distribution of his Pacer teammates reveals that nine of them are taller than he is and only four are shorter. So which set does he go into?

The fuzzy solution is to assign degrees of set membership to everyone. We might say that Shaquille O'Neal's set membership is 1.0; that is, he is entirely a member of the set TAMPBP. Travis Best gives us a little trouble: He isn't tall for a professional basketball player, but in certain company he might stand head and shoulders above the others. He's not a 0, so we might say he is a member of the set TAMPBP to degree 0.1. (All set membership values stay between 0 and 1.) Suddenly it is not too hard to see how we can assign membership to Reggie Miller. He is "pretty" tall; perhaps we will say he is a member of the set TAMPBP to the degree 0.6. (And notice how we were able to translate the term "pretty tall" into a set membership value.) The fuzzy set can be written in this form:

$$TAMPBP = 1.0/\ Shaquille,\ 0.1/\ Travis, 0.6\ /\ Reggie$$

where the first term is the name of the set, and the terms on the right side of the equals sign name elements of the set with their set membership value, separated by a slash.

In the developing field of fuzzy logic, however, notation is still not completely standardized; there are other ways to represent degrees of membership in fuzzy sets. Perhaps the most common, and the one we will use throughout the remainder of the book, is a representation of the form $\mu_A(x) = m$, which states that the membership value of x in the fuzzy set A is m, where $0 \leq m \leq 1$. The example of *TAMPBP* can therefore be written in the form $\mu_{TAMPBP}(Shaquille) = 1.0$, $\mu_{TAMPBP}(Travis) = 0.1$, and so forth.

Now any statements about "tall American male professional basketball players" can be applied to anyone. Suppose someone proposed the statement "Only tall American male professional basketball players are outstanding at making basketball slam dunks." (For those readers unfamiliar with basketball, a *slam dunk* is a basketball goal worth two points that is made by a player who jumps high enough to carry the basketball sufficiently above the rim of the goal so that the ball is physically and forcefully pushed downward through the goal.) With two-valued logic, we would have inferred that Shaquille O'Neal was outstanding at slam dunks in basketball and that Travis Best was not, since he's not a member of the set TAMPBP. What would we do, though, with Reggie Miller? We wouldn't know if we could infer anything about his ability to make basketball shots since we don't even know if he belongs to the set, and we are only allowed those two choices.

With fuzzy logic, though, we are able to make an inference. We infer that to the degree that the statement is true, Shaquille is outstanding at slam dunks, Travis is not outstanding at slam dunks, and Reggie is fairly (about halfway) outstanding at slam dunks. Thus we are able to reason by degree, applying logical operations to fuzzy sets. The operations are discussed later, in the section titled "Approximate Reasoning."

Fuzzy Set Membership Functions

One thing that is immediately obvious is that there is a kind of "shape" to the set TAMPBP if we graph it over the variable *American male professional basketball players' height*. Men whose height is under 1.75 meters have zero membership; then the degree of membership increases with their height, as shown in Figure 7.2(a), until we reach a height, about 2.15 meters, above which everybody has membership = 1.0. Thus, set membership rises with height from 0 until it reaches the maximum.

A fuzzy set on a numeric variable such as height or temperature is represented by a *fuzzy membership function*. Figure 7.2(b) illustrates one way to draw a fuzzy membership function for the linguistic variable *warm*. It is this function that *is* the fuzzy set. The function can be linear, either descending or ascending; it can be normal, bell-shaped, or triangular; it can be an S-shaped (sigmoid or logistic) function; it can be arbitrary or irregular; it can have plateaus or "shoulders," as in the preceding example of TAMPBP. It is customary for the highest part (maximum value) of the function to be set to 1.0: This is called *normalization* of the function. Without normalization, the effect of a fuzzy set tends to be watered down and weak.

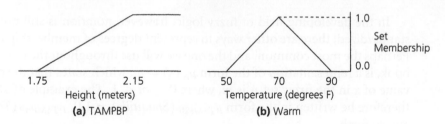

(a) TAMPBP
(b) Warm

Figure 7.2 Two kinds of fuzzy membership function.

Graphs, as in Figure 7.2, are one way to specify membership functions. Another way is to specify enough of the membership function points to allow someone to graph them. A common way to do this is illustrated for the fuzzy sets TAMPBP and Warm of Figure 7.2 as follows:

$$TAMPBP = \left\{ \frac{0}{1.75} + \frac{0.50}{1.95} + \frac{1}{2.15} \right\}$$

$$Warm = \left\{ \frac{0}{50} + \frac{0.50}{60} + \frac{1}{70} + \frac{0.50}{80} + \frac{0}{90} \right\}$$

Note that in this type of specification the plus signs do not represent addition but rather the aggregation or collection of representative domain points. Also note that the horizontal lines do not represent division but are delimiters, with the membership value above the line associated with the domain point below the line. This kind of fuzzy set representation is most often used for triangular fuzzy sets (consisting of only straight lines).

Now let's consider another fuzzy set. We want to buy a high-speed cable modem for our computer at a fair price. Below "fair price," we expect that the quality of the product will decline, and above "fair price," we feel we are spending money needlessly. The fuzzy set "fair price," then, must be defined for cost in such a way that it drops off below (as TAMPBP did), and also drops off above, some point, which for this particular product is around $80.00 (membership = 1.0). If the cable modem were being sold for less than $60.00, we would suspect it to be inferior ("fair price" membership $\cong 0.0$), and if the price were above $100.00 we would feel we were being cheated (also "fair price" membership $\cong 0.0$). Thus, the set membership function can be represented as $\mu_{FAIR\_PRICE}(p) = e^{-(p-80)^2/50}$, where p is the price in dollars, which resembles the normal distribution seen in probability theory. Because of the computational costs of this curvilinear function, many fuzzy logic applications use a triangular approximation for functions of this type, as shown in Figure 7.2(b) for the fuzzy set "warm." It turns out that the trade-off in terms of performance usually is small compared to the savings in computation.

There are, of course, infinitely many shapes of set membership functions. A membership function for "short American male pro basketball players (SAMPBP)," for instance, might have the same shape as one for TAMPBP, but reach a plateau on the left. Medium-height players, MAMPBP, might drop off on both sides, but with a plateau in the middle for some small range of heights. Further, as we will see, fuzzy sets can be combined to form sets like "medium or tall," "short or tall and not medium," and so on. These new sets can have complex set membership functions.

As we will see when we work with complete fuzzy systems, the dynamic range of a variable such as height or temperature is usually covered by several fuzzy sets. *Cold*, *warm*, and *hot* comprise one choice for three fuzzy sets to cover the temperature domain, for example. The number of fuzzy sets chosen is problem dependent, but often the number is three or five, and almost always it is an odd number (perhaps so that the exact middle of the dynamic range has a membership value of 1.0 in one of the membership functions).

Linguistic Variables

One of the most exciting things about fuzzy logic is its ability to translate ordinary language into logical or numerical statements. It accomplishes this by use of the concept of the *linguistic variable*. Zadeh has devoted much of his writing to this concept. He defines a linguistic variable as "a variable whose values are words or sentences in a natural or artificial language" (Zadeh 1975). These are contrasted with numeric variables. For instance, instead of talking about "tall American male professional basketball players" in the previous example, we could have stated the rule in an equation relating the independent variable *height* to the dependent variable *ability to make basketball slam dunks*. (We would probably have had to use a nonlinear function, such as logistic "squashing," to keep the result in the [0,1] range.)

This kind of formula might work, and it would take into account the differences in height and their effect on some consequent variable. There are advantages, though, to encoding the statements using linguistic variables, especially when effects are not linearly related to causes, as in a curvilinear membership function such as that for "fair price." Many engineering control applications that were previously implemented using precise and complex equations been improved significantly by using the simpler, flexible rules of fuzzy logic.

According to Zadeh, a label such as "tall" is really a *linguistic value* for the numeric variable *height*. We could have said that Shaquille O'Neal was 2.16 meters tall, and by that we would have gained precision, but we would have eroded our ability to reason about other tall basketball players. The very imprecision of linguistic variables makes them useful for reasoning.

There are three main categories of linguistic variable: *quantification terms, usuality terms*, and *likelihood terms*. Examples of quantification terms are *all, most, many, about half, few*, and *no*. Examples of usuality terms are *always, frequently, often*, *occasionally, seldom,* and *never.* Likelihood terms include *certain, likely, possible, uncertain, unlikely,* and *certainly not.*

Linguistic Hedges

An important aspect of linguistic variables is that they can modify or qualify one another. Consider, for instance, the word "very." A "very tall" man is taller, in general, than a "tall" one. In other words, "very" modifies tall by shifting it *up* on the scale of height. But look what it does to "short": A very short man is shorter than a short man, so "very" shifts short *down* on the scale of height. Linguistic variables that change the shape or position of a membership function are called *linguistic hedges* (Zadeh 1972).

There are many linguistic hedges, some more clearly understood than others. For instance, "sort of" is perceived by some to shift values in the other direction from "very": a man who is "sort of short" is likely to be taller than a man who is "short," and a man who is "sort of tall" could be perceived shorter than a "tall" man. Others think of "sort of" as a synonym for words that are *centered* on the concept. It is therefore important to be careful in the use of linguistic hedges and to define them clearly.

Besides moving the center of a linguistic variable up and down on the underlying numeric variable, linguistic hedges can affect the width of the graph of the linguistic variable's membership function. An easy example is that of "medium-height" men. "Sort of medium," assumes a function similar to that of medium, but it's wider at the peak. "Sort of medium" includes both shorter and taller men than "medium" by itself. On the other hand, "very medium" is narrower than "medium." We expect someone who is very, very medium in height to be exactly the average.

Some common kinds of linguistic hedges are ones that

- intensify a fuzzy set (very, extremely).
- dilute a fuzzy set (about, somewhat, sort of, generally).
- express probabilities (probably, not very likely).
- approximate a scalar or single number (exactly).
- express vague quantities (many, most, seldom).

The richness of human language suggests that there can be very many kinds of linguistic hedges. Just as we are able to insinuate unstated facts in subtle ways through skillful use of language, fuzzy set memberships can be rather tricky to implement. On the other hand, the richness of language, operated upon with a tool as versatile as the concept of the linguistic variable, results in a very powerful instrument for modeling complex systems.

Some conventions have arisen for the programming of linguistic hedges in fuzzy systems. For example, Zadeh (1975) has suggested that the linguistic hedge "very" is a mathematical square. If a room has, for instance, 0.50 membership in the set "warm," it would have 0.25 membership in the set "very warm." It is not until membership in warm = 1.0 that the element is equivalently a member of very warm. On the other hand, the linguistic hedge "somewhat" can be implemented by taking the square root of a membership function; thus, a room that is 0.81 "warm" (to make an easy example) would be 0.9 "somewhat warm." This operation generally causes a variable's membership in the "somewhat" set to be slightly higher than in the fuzzy set without "somewhat." Thus, if we ordinarily say a room is "warm," we would likely say that calling it "somewhat warm" is an understatement.

Linguistic hedges such as "very" that reduce the membership values for values other than 1.0 are called *concentrations*, and those such as "somewhat" that increase the membership values for values other than 1.0 are called *dilations* (Zadeh 1972).

Another linguistic hedge concept is called *intensification*, which is a kind of combination of concentration and dilation. For original membership values between 0.5 and 1.0, membership values are increased, and original membership values between 0.0 and 0.5 are decreased. The original version of intensification proposed by Zadeh (1972) appears in equation 7.1. Other versions are, of course, possible.

$$a_{\text{intensified}} = \begin{array}{ll} 2\mu_a{}^2(x) & \text{for } 0 \leq \mu_a(x) \leq 0.5 \\ 1 - 2\left[1 - \mu_a(x)\right]^2 & \text{for } 0.5 \leq \mu_a(x) \leq 1.0 \end{array} \tag{7.1}$$

Intensification increases the differentiation between set elements with membership greater than 0.5 and those with less than 0.5 membership. We invoke this concept by saying that something is *intensely a*.

Approximate Reasoning

Reasoning in fuzzy systems involves logic. Many relations and operations used in fuzzy reasoning have evolved from familiar Boolean algebra (cf. Kennedy 1973) and have familiar names, such as AND, OR, and NOT. However, if something's membership in fuzzy set A = 0.8 and in fuzzy set B = 0.2, how much is it a member of the union, the set made up of A OR B? Fuzzy logic requires new definitions for these concepts.

Paradoxes in Fuzzy Logic

Fuzzy logic solves paradoxes that are irresolvable in traditional binary logic. Popular writers are in the habit of expressing the difference between fuzzy logic and binary logic as if it were the same as the difference between Eastern and Western philosophy. Perhaps they're essentially correct, but it seems fair to point out that Western thinkers have always been fascinated with paradoxes.

Consider the oft-quoted "Cretan paradox," in which a person from Crete says, "All Cretans are liars." The paradox is that if the statement is true, then the speaker himself is lying and so the statement must be false. Ironically, many examples cited by writers to demonstrate that "Western thought" is uncomfortable with paradoxes have actually been created by mainstream Western thinkers! The Cretan paradox is not known as the Tokyo, Bombay, or Beijing paradox. In fact, "Western thought" at least since the time of the Greeks has been fascinated by paradoxes even if they have been excluded from the branch of philosophy known as logic.

Aristotelian logic includes rules that forbid a statement's being true and not-true at the same time (though Aristotle himself acknowledged that one statement could be "truer" than another). The two relevant axioms are the Law of Noncontradiction and the Law of the Excluded Middle. These "laws" are not relevant to the operations of fuzzy logic, and it is worthwhile here to consider the reasons for this.

The Law of Noncontradiction states that the intersection of a set with its complement results in an empty or null set. *Intersection* in binary logic means that the AND operator, that is, the intersection of A and B, contains all the elements that are members of set A AND members of set B. In a Venn diagram, this is where two circles overlap. The intersection of a set with its complement, then, is the set that contains all members of A *AND* all members of not-A. Impossible, you say? In traditional logic, yes, it's impossible; but in fuzzy logic, it's not a problem. We look out our window and see several clouds in a blue sky. Is today a member of the set "cloudy days"? Technically, yes, it is. It does have clouds. Is it a member of the set "not cloudy days?" Well, yes, it really isn't *that* cloudy; it's mostly sunny. So if A = "cloudy days," today is a member of A and not-A. *In real life*, the Law of Noncontradiction is broken constantly.

The Law of the Excluded Middle states that the union of a set with its complement results in a universal set of the underlying domain. A set made up of all elements that are either members of A *or* are members of not-A, in binary logic, should include the universe. Everything either is A or is not A, either a statement is true or it's not true. Where the Law of Noncontradiction asserts that a statement can't be true and false at the same time, the Law of the Excluded Middle asserts, beyond that, that a statement must be either true or false. In a Venn diagram, a point is either inside or outside a circle. This law fades away to insignificance in fuzzy logic.

Equality of Fuzzy Sets

In traditional binary logic, two sets containing the same elements are equal: $\{a, d, g\}$ equals $\{a, d, g\}$. That is really a pretty easy concept to grasp, but what does it mean for two fuzzy sets to be equal? Let us say there are two fuzzy sets, X and Y, and each is defined on a universe of three discrete values: a, d, and g. For fuzzy set X, a has a 0.1 membership, d has a 0.6 membership, and g has a 0.8 membership. For fuzzy set Y, on the other hand, a's membership is 0.9, d's is 0.7, and g's is 0.8.

Stated in a notation we introduced earlier:

$$X = \left\{ \frac{0.1}{a} + \frac{0.6}{d} + \frac{0.8}{g} \right\}$$

$$Y = \left\{ \frac{0.9}{a} + \frac{0.7}{d} + \frac{0.8}{g} \right\}$$

Are these fuzzy sets equal? No.

By equality, we are saying that two sets are *the same*. While it may be that sets X and Y are rather similar to one another, they are not the same. In fuzzy logic, two sets are considered equal if and only if they have identical set membership values on identical domains. For continuous domains, the graphs of the fuzzy sets lie on top of one another.

Containment

In crisp logic, a set A is considered a subset of another set B if and only if all elements in A are also in B. Thus, no apples are included in the set "oranges," but the sets "apples" and "oranges" are subsets of the set "fruit." These sets are clear.

Now consider the fuzzy sets X and Y defined above. Our goal is to determine whether X is a subset of (is contained in) Y. This is a way of asking whether each element's membership in Y is greater than or equal to its membership in X. Comparing the individuals' memberships in the two sets, we see that all membership values in Y are greater than or equal to corresponding membership values in X, and therefore X is contained in Y. If we were to, say, change d's membership in Y to 0.4, then X would no longer be contained in Y.

Thus, containment in fuzzy logic means that membership values for all elements in a subset are less than or equal to the membership values of those same elements in the superset. In many cases containment is seen when a linguistic variable is added to modify an existing set: Very tall men is contained in tall men, hot engines is contained in somewhat hot engines, and so on.

NOT: The Complement of a Fuzzy Set

In binary logic, the complement of a set is simply the set of all the elements that are not in that set. The complement of A is not-A. This is obviously not so easy when sets are fuzzy. If everyone has *some* degree of membership in the set of middle-aged people, how would we define the set of *not*-middle-aged people?

The answer is that everyone also has some degree of membership in the set of not-middle-aged people. Suppose we say that "middle-aged" (M) has a triangular membership function:

$$M = \left\{ \frac{0}{20} + \frac{1}{45} + \frac{0}{70} \right\}$$

Randy is 50 years old, and we have assigned him degree of membership 0.8 in the set of middle-aged people. The solution is to say that Randy's membership in the set "not-middle-aged" ($\widetilde{M}$) is 1 minus 0.8 = 0.2. He is 80 percent a member, so he is 20 percent *not* a member. In general, then, the value of the complement of a membership value is (1 − the membership value):

$$\widetilde{M} = \left\{ \frac{1}{20} + \frac{0}{45} + \frac{1}{70} \right\}$$

Using our earlier examples of fuzzy sets X and Y:

$$\widetilde{X} = \left\{ \frac{0.9}{a} + \frac{0.4}{d} + \frac{0.2}{g} \right\}$$

$$\widetilde{Y} = \left\{ \frac{0.1}{a} + \frac{0.3}{d} + \frac{0.2}{g} \right\}$$

Now we can see why the Law of the Excluded Middle is not appropriate in fuzzy logic. That law states that something must be *either* A *or* not-A. The violation of this Aristotelian law of logic is the lifeblood of fuzzy logic. Of course, says Lotfi Zadeh, every statement is both true and not-true—reality flourishes on ambiguity.

AND: The Intersection of Fuzzy Sets

Fuzzy logic's ability to remain unflustered by paradoxes results from the flexibility of fuzzy sets. Something can be true and not-true because it's not entirely true or false. In binary logic, as mentioned earlier, the *intersection* of two sets contains elements that are contained in both sets: The intersection of A and B contains those elements that are in A AND in B. If things can be members of sets by degree, however, it is not immediately intuitively obvious how to define the intersection of sets. A couple of guidelines exist, however.

First, we need to be able to apply the intersection operator (also the union operator, discussed later) in a pairwise fashion irrespective of the order. Second, for a particular element, a decrease in the membership value of that element in either fuzzy set can't lead to an increase in the intersection of the two sets. These properties are known as associativity and monotonicity, respectively.

In usual practice, the *weakest* membership determines the degree of membership in the intersection of two or more fuzzy sets. Zadeh's intersection operation in fuzzy logic is simply to take the minimum set membership. For instance, if an item has 0.5 membership in set A, 0.9 membership in set B, and 0.2 membership in set C, then its membership in A AND B AND C is defined as 0.2, the minimum membership value.

Referring back to fuzzy sets X and Y, their intersection is

$$X \cap Y = \left\{ \frac{0.1}{a} + \frac{0.6}{d} + \frac{0.8}{g} \right\}.$$

Note that since X is contained in Y ($X \subset Y$), the intersection is just the original fuzzy set X.

To provide other examples, let's define fuzzy set Z on the same universe of three discrete values (a, d, and g) as fuzzy sets X and Y, as follows:

$$Z = \left\{ \frac{0.3}{a} + \frac{0.4}{d} + \frac{0.9}{g} \right\}$$

Now,

$$X \cap Z = \left\{ \frac{0.1}{a} + \frac{0.4}{d} + \frac{0.8}{g} \right\}$$

$$Y \cap Z = \left\{ \frac{0.3}{a} + \frac{0.4}{d} + \frac{0.8}{g} \right\}$$

We can see that the Law of Noncontradiction has become moot. Something can be A and not-A at the same time; the fuzzy intersection of A and not-A is not empty or null. Using the previously defined fuzzy set X as an example,

$$X \cap \tilde{X} = \left\{ \frac{0.1}{a} + \frac{0.4}{d} + \frac{0.2}{g} \right\}.$$

OR: The Union of Fuzzy Sets

The union of two sets in crisp set theory is made up of all the elements that are either in one set or in the other, or both. The union of A and B includes everything that is a member of A OR a member of B. In a Venn diagram with two circles drawn in it, the union of the two sets is everything contained in both circles. (Note that the Exclusive–OR, or XOR, set contains elements that are in one set, or circle, or the other, but not in both. The overlap of two circles is excluded.)

The union operator is just the opposite of the intersection operator. In usual practice, the *strongest* membership determines the degree of membership in the union of two or more fuzzy sets. Zadeh's union operation in fuzzy logic is to take the maximum set membership. For instance, if an item has 0.5 membership in set A, 0.9 membership in set B, and 0.2 membership in set C, then its membership in A OR B OR C is defined as 0.9, the maximum membership value.

Using fuzzy sets X and Z, X OR Z is

$$X \cup Z = \left\{ \frac{0.3}{a} + \frac{0.6}{d} + \frac{0.9}{g} \right\}.$$

Summary of Fuzzy Relations and Operators

If $\mu_A(x)$ and $\mu_B(x)$ represent the degrees to which x is a member of fuzzy sets A and B, respectively, and the sets have common domains, then the following are the basic relations of fuzzy sets:

Equality $A = B$ iff all $\mu_A[x] = \mu_B[x]$

Containment $A \subset B$ iff all $\mu_A[x] \leq \mu_B[x]$

The following are the basic operations on fuzzy sets:

Intersection $\mu_{A \cap B}(x) = \min(\mu_A[x], \mu_B[x])$

Union $\mu_{A \cup B}(x) = \max(\mu_A[x], \mu_B[x])$

Complement $\mu_{\tilde{A}}(x) = 1 - \mu_A[x]$

Compensatory Operators

Note that there are alternative fuzzy operators to those we have defined; the choice needs to be made carefully, depending on the particular situation. Compensatory operators are alternatives to the set operations such as intersection and union defined by Zadeh. Experience with numerous fuzzy system applications has demonstrated the need for these operators, particularly for the fuzzy intersection operator most commonly used in the antecedent (if) portion of fuzzy rules. The operators are called compensatory because they provide less strict (softer) relationships than Zadeh's original operators. Note, however, that they still must comply with the properties of associativity and monotonicity described earlier.

With Zadeh's intersection operator, the truth level for the entire antecedent is controlled by the minimum membership value. For example, for the rule "If A and B and C and D, then Q," if the membership values for A through D are 0.9, 0.7, 0.8, and 0.2, respectively, then the truth level of the expression is 0.2. In practical applications, the effect of this is often too extreme in terms of its effect on the fuzzy system.

A number of compensatory operators have been defined. Some of them involve only relatively simple arithmetic transformations, and others require more complicated functional transformations. A complete review of compensatory operators is beyond the scope of this book; we refer you to sources such as (Cox 1994) and (Von Altrock 1997).

These operators attempt to answer the question "How much of an increase in one parameter can compensate for a lower value in another?" There is no pat answer to this question, and sometimes it doesn't have an answer. A sailboat needs at least one sail and one rudder. Two sails do not compensate for no rudder; and two rudders can't compensate for no sails. But in many cases, a compensatory operator makes sense.

We limit our discussion to two compensatory operators: the *mean operator* and the *gamma operator*. The former is a simple arithmetic operator; the latter is more complex. We suggest that you use these operators with caution. It is a good idea in most cases to start out with Zadeh's original operators, incorporating compensatory operators only if needed; and, if needed, start with a relatively simple one, such as the mean operator.

The intersection of two fuzzy sets is usually defined as the minimum set membership value, but with the mean operator it is defined as the average (mean) of the various set membership values. Thus, for our previous example for which the antecedent terms have truth values of 0.9, 0.7, 0.8, and 0.2, the truth level of the expression using the mean operator is 0.65 (rather than 0.20). Referring to the previously defined fuzzy sets X, Y, and Z, we can see that

$$X \cap Y \cap Z_{\mathrm{mean}} = \left\{ \frac{0.43}{a} + \frac{0.57}{d} + \frac{0.83}{g} \right\}$$

In our fuzzy rule system implementation, which we discuss in the next chapter and is provided on the book's web site, we implement the mean operator as well as the traditional Zadeh intersection (min) operator.

The more complex gamma operator was developed by Zimmerman and Zysno (1980, 1983). They report that it represents, or mimics, the human decision process more faithfully than Zadeh's min/max operators used for intersection and union. The gamma operator is defined as follows:

$$\mu_{\mathrm{gamma}} = \left[\prod_{i=1}^{m} \mu_i \right]^{(1-\gamma)} \cdot \left[1 - \prod_{i=1}^{m} (1 - \mu_i) \right]^{\gamma}$$

where $0 \leq \gamma \leq 1$ and m is the number of fuzzy membership values.

The determination of the best value for gamma in a particular situation can be complicated and is beyond the scope of this book (see Von Altrock 1997 for a step-by-step process). In practice, most folks end up with a value between 0.2 and 0.4 for gamma. We suggest that you try an initial value of 0.25 or 0.30 and adjust up or down by 0.05 until you get the best system performance you can. As an example of a result obtained with the gamma operator, consider the case for which $\gamma = 0.3$, $\mu_1(x) = 0.3$, and $\mu_2(x) = 0.8$. Then $\gamma(\mu_1, \mu_2) = 0.35$. You may want to work out other examples for yourself.

Fuzzy Rules

Fuzzy rules, like the if–then rules in a traditional rule (or expert) system, have an antecedent part and a consequent part. There are several forms of fuzzy rules used in the literature. Usually, they share the same form for the antecedent part but have different expressions for the consequent part. Two of the most common fuzzy rules are the Mamdani-type fuzzy rule (Mamdani and Assilian 1975) and the TSK model (Takagi and Sugeno 1985; Sugeno and Kang 1986). Mamdami and Assilian employed rules in which the consequent is another fuzzy variable, while Takagi and colleagues used rules whose consequent is a polynomial function of the inputs (TSK model). The following two rules represent the generic expressions of the two forms of rules, respectively.

If X_1 is A_1 and . . . and X_n is A_n then Y is B_j

If X_1 is A_1 and . . . and X_n is A_n then $Y = p_0 + p_1 X_1 + \cdots + p_n X_n$

where $X_1, . . . , Xn$ are fuzzy input variables. A_i represents one of the fuzzy sets defined over the domain of the fuzzy variables X_i. Y is a fuzzy output variable, B_j is one of the fuzzy sets defined over the domain of variable Y, and $p_0, . . . , p_n$ are parameters.

In addition to these two forms of rules, there is a rule form especially designed for classification (Ishibuchi et al. 1995):

If X_1 is A_1 and . . . and X_n is A_n, then Y is class i with confidence degree $= CD_i$.

By default, the fuzzy rules discussed in this chapter are of the Mamdani-type. The TSK model is described in the later section of this chapter entitled The Takagi-Sugeno-Kang Method. For details on the third form of fuzzy rules, please refer to Ishibuchi et al. (1995) or other references.

Fuzzification

Given the fuzzy operators we have described, we can make significant progress toward constructing a workable fuzzy system. The first step is to learn how to combine antecedent sets, that is, the sets on the "if" side of a rule, using the operators just given; this step is called *fuzzification*. Next we will discuss how fuzzy rules fire in parallel. Then we'll figure out how to get the combined sets to produce an output that can be used to make an inference or control a system; this step is called *defuzzification*. Throughout this process we'll use a simplified example of a gas flow regulator for a furnace. The furnace may be used to heat air (more common in the United States) or to heat water that passes through radiators (more common in Europe).

Suppose that a set of fuzzy if–then rules has been written to control the gas flow for the furnace. (Increasing the gas flow, of course, increases the energy available to heat the building, and vice versa.) These rules could include such input parameters as indoor temperature, outdoor temperature, and change in indoor temperature over the past five minutes. Each input parameter would, of course, have fuzzy membership functions defined over its domain. (We recognize that a real controller of this type would almost certainly have more than three input parameters.) Our output parameter is the change in gas flow to the furnace.

For purposes of our furnace example, we define the following parameters and fuzzy sets:

For input parameters, we use those listed above, abbreviated to *InTemp*, *OutTemp*, and *DeltaInTemp*. Our output parameter is called *FlowChange*. The fuzzy sets are all triangular membership functions.

For the *InTemp* parameter, we define three fuzzy sets: *cool*, *comfortable*, and *too_warm*.

For *OutTemp*, we define five fuzzy sets: *very_cold*, *chilly*, *warm*, *very_warm*, and *hot*.

For *DeltaInTemp*, we define five fuzzy sets: *large_negative*, *small_negative*, *near_zero*, *small_positive*, and *large_positive*.

For *FlowChange*, we define five fuzzy sets: *decrease_greatly*, *decrease_small*, *no_change*, *increase_small*, and *increase_greatly*.

Note that you don't have to use the same number of membership functions for each parameter; the number selected depends on a variety of things such as the resolution needed for that parameter.

We don't concern ourselves with the details of all of the membership functions for all of the parameters here; we consider just enough of them to build a few rules. Following are a few possible rules:

Rule 1: If *InTemp* is *comfortable* and *DeltaInTemp* is *near_zero*, then *FlowChange* is *no_change*.

Rule 2: If *OutTemp* is *chilly* and *DeltaInTemp* is *small_negative*, then *FlowChange* is *increase_small*.

Rule 3: If *InTemp* is *too_warm* and *DeltaInTemp* is *large_positive*, then *FlowChange* is *decrease_greatly*.

Rule 4: If *InTemp* is *cool* and *DeltaInTemp* is *near_zero*, then *FlowChange* is *increase_small*.

There may be a dozen or more rules in an actual system, but we'll consider only these four. Now, we have to know what the membership functions used in these four rules are before we can put them into action. Again, we look only at those we need for the four rules. (Temperatures and changes in temperatures are in degrees Fahrenheit.)

For *InTemp, comfortable* $= \{\frac{0}{60} + \frac{1}{70} + \frac{0}{80}\}$. Just as a review, this is a triangular membership function with a membership value of 0.0 at 60 degrees, 1.0 at 70 degrees, and 0.0 at 80 degrees. So the membership values at both 65 and 75 degrees are 0.5.

For *InTemp, too_warm* $= \{\frac{0}{70} + \frac{1}{80} + \frac{1}{90}\}$. This is called a "right-triangular" membership function with a membership value of 0.0 at 70 degrees and 1.0 at 80 degrees and above.

In an analogous manner, for *InTemp, cool* $= \{\frac{1}{50} + \frac{1}{60} + \frac{0}{70}\}$. This is a "left-triangular" membership function with a membership value of 0.0 at 70 degrees, and 1.0 at 60 degrees and below.

For *DeltaInTemp*:

$$small\_negative = \left\{ \frac{0}{-4} + \frac{1}{-2} + \frac{0}{0} \right\}$$

$$near\_zero = \left\{ \frac{0}{-2} + \frac{1}{0} + \frac{0}{+2} \right\}$$

$$large\_positive = \left\{ \frac{0}{2} + \frac{1}{4} + \frac{1}{6} \right\}$$

For *OutTemp*:

$$chilly = \left\{ \frac{0}{30} + \frac{1}{50} + \frac{0}{70} \right\}$$

Note that we've defined only those fuzzy sets we need to implement our four rules.

We'll look at the details of the output parameter fuzzy sets later. For now, let's pick a set of input parameters and fuzzify them. Let's assume that the indoor temperature is 67.5 degrees, the change in indoor temperature over the past five minutes is −1.6 degrees, and the outdoor temperature is 52 degrees. We now determine the resulting membership values for the fuzzy sets in our four rules.

For *InTemp*, $\mu_{cool}(67.5) = 0.25$, $\mu_{comfortable}(67.5)$
$= 0.75$, and $\mu_{too\_warm}(67.5) = 0.0$.

For *DeltaInTemp*, $\mu_{small\_negative}(-1.6) = 0.8$, $\mu_{near\_zero}(-1.6)$
$= 0.2$, and $\mu_{large\_positive}(-1.6) = 0.0$.

For *OutTemp*, $\mu_{chilly}(52) = 0.9$.

Remember that Zadeh's method for the AND process, which we use here, is to take the minimum of the values in the antecedent.

For Rule 1, we obtain $0.75 \cap 0.20 = 0.20 = \mu_{no\_change}$ for our output *FlowChange*.

For Rule 2, we have $0.9 \cap 0.8 = 0.8 = \mu_{increase\_small}$ for *FlowChange*.

For Rule 3 we get $0.0 \cap 0.0 = 0.0 = \mu_{decrease\_greatly}$ for *FlowChange*, which means that rule 3 does not produce any output. Rule 3 is said to have fired but not to have been activated.

For Rule 4 we get $0.25 \cap 0.2 = 0.2 = \mu_{increase\_small}$ for *FlowChange*.

Note that rules 2 and 4 result in the activation of the *increase_small* fuzzy set.

Fuzzy Rules Fire in Parallel

So far, it has not been very hard to determine the set membership of various aspects of the furnace parameters and the consequences implied by the fuzzy sets. In this simple example, it is important to notice that all the rules were fired but only three out of four rules were activated, whether they were relevant (produced output) or not: Fuzzy rules fire in parallel. Of course, on a sequential "Von Neumann" computer, the parallelism is simulated by evaluating the rules in series and then executing an action based on the result.

This parallelism entails quite a different approach from that of other control methods. For instance, in traditional AI systems, decisions are made sequentially, one after the other, and if the process runs into a dead end it backs out again or starts over, depending on what kind of algorithm (i.e., "depth first," "breadth first") is being used.

When equations are used to make decisions, numeric variables must be defined precisely, and the decision is a function of those precise numbers. Forming rules using vague linguistic variables is often much more efficient for the task. Fuzzy logic evaluates an entire group of expressions and then makes a decision based on the set of evaluations.

For our furnace gas flow controller with the input parameters given in the previous section, assume that only rules 1, 2, and 4 among all the fuzzy rules are activated, then only two out of five fuzzy sets defined over the output variable domain are activated. The fuzzy set *no_change* is activated by rule 1, and the fuzzy set *increase_small* is activated by rules 2 and 4 with two different activation levels (membership values). Usually, especially when the number of fuzzy rules in the rule set is large, several fuzzy sets will be activated by several fuzzy rules with different activation levels. The activation levels for all activated fuzzy sets are combined to obtain the membership value for this fuzzy set.

Remember that Zadeh's method for the OR process, which we use here, is to take the maximum of the membership values produced for each fuzzy set of the output variable in the consequent part by all the rules. So for the output fuzzy set *no_change*, we obtain membership value 0.2. For fuzzy set *increase_small*, we get $0.2 \cup 0.8 = 0.8 = \mu_{increase\_small}$. For the other three fuzzy sets, we get membership values of 0.

Defuzzification

Note that the rules for our furnace gas flow controller relate to the *change* in the gas flow, not to its absolute quantity. The output (control) parameter is accordingly defined as *flow change* in cubic meters per minute, as illustrated in Figure 7.3. Note that five fuzzy membership functions are defined over the flow change domain.

We have created a set of triangular membership functions that are positioned over different portions of the output variable domain (the change of gas flow rate). Specific values must be assigned to the domain range because defuzzification must yield one precise value for the output variable (or, in the case of more than one output variable, a precise value for each).

As can be seen, the *no_change* (NC) membership function is centered at 0 change and has left and right boundaries at −1 cubic meter per minute (CMM) change in gas flow and 1 CMM, respectively. The *increase_slightly* (IS) membership function is centered at 1 CMM change and has boundaries at 0 and 2 CMM. The *increase_greatly* (IG) membership function is centered at 2 CMM change with a left boundary at 1 CMM. It then has a constant membership value of 1 from 2 CMM to the upper limit of the dynamic range of the *change_in_flow,* specified as 3 CMM flow change. The left side of the graph of membership functions is symmetric, specifying values for decreasing flow: *decrease_slightly* (DS) and *decrease_greatly* (DG). For this example, a minimum flow increment (or decrement) of 0.1 CMM is specified. A *discrete domain* for flow change is thus defined with 61 possible values (including 0).

Now suppose that the input parameters are as given in the previous section on fuzzification. We have shown that the *if* parts of the if–then rules produce the

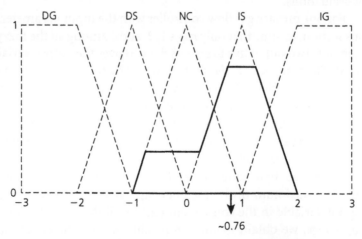

Figure 7.3 Defuzzification of the furnace gas flow example.   DG, decrease greatly; DS, decrease slightly; NC, no change; IS, increase slightly; IG, increase greatly.

following *FlowChange* fuzzy set membership values: $\mu_{IS} = 0.8$, $\mu_{NC} = 0.2$, and the three other memberships = 0.0. (One of the rules fired but didn't produce an output.)

Clearly the membership values suggest increasing the gas flow somewhat, but how much? The final step is to get a nonfuzzy number or *scalar* out of our fuzzy logic system in order to precisely control the gas flow by increasing or decreasing it. The process of translating the output of the fuzzy rules into a scalar (a precise change in gas flow, in this case) is called *defuzzification*.

There are a number of methods for defuzzification. Here we illustrate one called the *clipped center of gravity* approach. Numerical values associated with the antecedent linguistic variables (the *if* parts of the if–then rules) can be thought of as chopping off the set membership functions of the consequent (output) linguistic variables in Figure 7.3. In accordance with the *FlowChange* membership values listed above, then, we "chop off" *increase_small* (IS) at its 0.8 level and *no_change* (NC) at its 0.2 level. Chopping off the tops results in trapezoidal shapes. The other three fuzzy memberships are chopped off at 0, so they have no effect (in many fuzzy systems, *most* output fuzzy memberships produce zero effect).

The most common way to derive a scalar from these functions is called the *clipped center of gravity*, or *centroid*, method: The idea is to find the "center of gravity" of the composite output membership function (the overlapping trapezoids), draw a vertical line from that point to the numeric variable, and use the numeric value found there to control the system or define a conclusion.

If we represent the membership of element x_i in fuzzy set A as $\mu_A[x_i]$ and the *i*th value of the underlying numeric variable as x_i, then equation 7.2 describes centroid defuzzification. Note that the output variable *FlowChange* in our example is defined over a discrete domain with 61 possible values. In the cases where the output variable is defined over a continuous domain, the summations in equation 7.2 are replaced with integrals.

$$Output = \frac{\sum_i x_i \mu(x_i)}{\sum_i \mu(x_i)} \tag{7.2}$$

There are several ways to perform centroid defuzzification. One method allows the membership functions to overlap (cover one another), as seen in Figure 7.3. Each area of overlap is used only once. The center of gravity then defines a point on the numeric variable. This method, which is frequently used in fuzzy applications, yields a value of about 0.76 CMM increase in flow that should occur in the case illustrated in Figure 7.3.

Another method *adds* the set membership functions where they overlap. An area is counted (weighted) twice if it is part of that triangular area common to two membership functions that will be defuzzified. In Figure 7.3 the triangular area common to the IS and NC membership functions below the membership value of 0.2 would be counted (weighted) twice. It has been argued that this guarantees that each *if* variable has an effect on the *then* variable, as set memberships are not covered by one another.

In this simple example, the only output variable is the change in gas flow. In the later section on fuzzy control, we discuss the implementation of fuzzy logic in more realistic systems with multiple inputs and outputs.

Other Defuzzification Methods

There are other methods of defuzzification besides the centroid method, to be adapted to the particular situation in which they are being used. Defuzzification takes the outputs of all the fuzzy rules, maps them onto a numeric variable, and produces a scalar, or real nonfuzzy number, which can be used to define the conclusion of an argument, suggest changes in a dynamic system, or run a control device.

A detailed discussion of these methods is beyond the scope of this book. We examine only three: the *max-membership* method, the *mean-max membership* method, and the *center-of-maximum* method. For more information about options for defuzzification, see a fuzzy logic textbook such as Ross (1995). The names of the methods may seem confusing to you; they are to us, too. In fact, it seems that many of the names are interchangeable. So it may be helpful to remember what they do and how they do it, rather than what they're called.

Each method we discuss in this section is very simple. Each also uses a simplified representation of the output similar to Figure 7.4.

The max-membership method is very simple and somewhat inexact. In this method, the centroid of the fuzzy membership function with the highest value is used for the defuzzified output scalar. In our furnace example, the centroid of the highest membership value (0.8) is at 1.0, so the output is set to 1.0 CMM flow change. This is significantly different from the value of 0.76 CMM obtained by the centroid method.

Each of the remaining two methods projects the output for each membership function that is not 0 onto one point on the output domain. In the case of membership functions with a peak, the point coincides with the location of the peak. For a membership function with a flat top (the maximum membership is a plateau), the location coincides with the median value of the plateau projected down onto the domain axis.

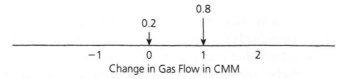

Figure 7.4 Simplified representation of output for gas furnace example.

In our example, the two values on the domain axis, x_1 and x_2, are 0 and 1, and the corresponding membership values, $\mu(x_1)$ *and* $\mu(x_2)$, are 0.2 and 0.8, corresponding to the clipped values of the fuzzy sets NC and IS.

The mean-max membership method (also called the *middle-of-maximum* method) simply averages the values on the domain axis (Ross 1995). So the output for our furnace gas example is $(x_1 + x_2)/2 = 0.5$ CMM. Like the max-membership method, this value is significantly different from the value of 0.76 obtained by the center of gravity method, and it may not be sufficiently representative for many applications. On the other hand, it is extremely simple and fast to calculate.

The center-of-maximum method (Von Altrock 1997) seems to us to be more representative of the clipped output membership functions. The activated membership functions are represented by arrows, the length of which correspond to the (clipped) membership values, as in Figure 7.4. These are treated as weights pushing down on the dynamic range axis, and the "best compromise" position that balances the weights is chosen as the output. In our case, that occurs at point 0.8. Since in our example the interval between x_1 and x_2 is 1.0, the calculation is $0.2 * x_{out} = 0.8 * (1.0 - x_{out})$, and $x_{out} = 0.8$. This method produces an output value close to that produced by the centroid method (0.76) and is fast to calculate. It seems like a reasonable choice for many practical applications.

In the fuzzy rule system implementation described in the next chapter, we have included three types of defuzzification: the *center of gravity without overlap*, *center of gravity with overlap*, and *max-membership* methods. You might want to implement the center-of-maximum (or some other) method on your own.

Measures of Fuzziness

Now that we've discussed the process of running a fuzzy system, let's consider fuzziness metrics that help us answer the question "How fuzzy is it?" In this section, we discuss quantitative measures of fuzziness for discrete fuzzy sets. Measures of fuzziness are metrics of fuzzy uncertainty, which is that type of uncertainty that arises from linguistic imprecision or vagueness. Stated another way, measures of fuzziness estimate the *average* ambiguity in fuzzy sets in some well-defined sense (Pal and Bezdek 1994). Ambiguity is the degree or extent to which an element belongs to a fuzzy set. One measure of ambiguity is entropy.

Set membership functions describe the degree to which an element is a member of a set. Thus, a fuzzy membership value near 0 or near 1 represents an item that would be considered *not-in* or *in* the corresponding crisp set. For example, in the set "fish,"

$$\mu_{fish}(\text{bass}) = 1.0, \mu_{fish}(\text{goldfish}) = 1.0, \mu_{fish}(\text{seahorse}) = 0.8, \mu_{fish}(\text{whale}) = 0.0$$

we can say with some certainty that a crisp set, "fish," would contain {bass, goldfish}, and that "not-fish" would contain {whale}. We may need to consult a zoology text before deciding that seahorses are indeed a kind of fish, thus pushing its "fish" set membership toward 1.0.

On the other hand, a set such as "flowers,"

$$\mu_{flowers}(\text{rose}) = 1.0, \mu_{flowers}(\text{dogwood}) = 0.5, \mu_{flowers}(\text{bread}) = 0.0$$

presents the problematic case of the dogwood, whose "flower" is actually an ornate ring of white or pink leaves.

It is meaningful, then, to state that classification of roses and bread as flowers is more certain than classification of dogwoods. The set of fuzzy membership values "flowers" is fuzzier than the set "fish." Fuzzy logic needs a measure of the fuzziness of sets, or the uncertainty of set membership values, in order to completely describe the relationships of elements to sets and sets to one another.

Entropy is a measure of the disorganization of a physical or informational system, which is presumed to be constantly increasing as systems wear down, run down, and deteriorate. Even though the universe appears to be an orderly arrangement of planets circling stars and stars clustering in galaxies, according to commonly accepted theories of the universe, we may be sure that eventually all the planets will fall from their orbits and all the stars will burn up and collapse into a dark heap: This is a great source of pleasure for cynics and misanthropes. Everyone's desk, on its own, tends to get messy. Entropy always tends to increase. Entropy is also used in information theory as a measure of information in a message or bit string. High uncertainty corresponds to high entropy.

Because entropy is a measure of ambiguity, the concept of entropy is relevant to a discussion of fuzziness. A set with membership values near 0 and 1 can be used with a degree of certainty that correlates with the extremity of memberships. On the other hand, operations involving sets whose elements are not clearly "in" or "out" of the set present problems: The uncertainty, or entropy, of those sets seems to escalate as the sets are combined, until the outcome is entirely unpredictable and meaningless. From a strictly geometrical perspective (Kosko 1994), fuzzy entropy is thus maximum at the center of the hypercube defined by the fuzzy membership values defined in the fuzzy set.

Numerous measures of fuzziness have been proposed. Many of them are discussed in Pal and Bezdek (1994). These measures are based on things such as the distance from a set of fuzzy membership values to the nearest crisp set and the distance between a set of fuzzy membership values and its complement.

A number of attributes exist that seem to make sense for any definition of fuzziness. For example, since the ambiguity of any crisp set is 0, its fuzziness should also be 0. And since maximum ambiguity occurs for a 0.5 membership value, the set S with maximum fuzziness is one for which $\mu_S(x) = 0.5 \; \forall \; x$. As membership values move away from 0.5 toward 0 or 1, ambiguity (and therefore fuzziness) decreases.

One way of describing decreasing ambiguity is to define a *sharpened* set. A set S^* is said to be a sharpened version of S when $\mu_{s^*}(x) \leq \mu_s(x)$ if $\mu_s(x) \leq 0.5$, and $\mu_{s^*}(x) \geq \mu_s(x)$ if $\mu_s(x) \geq 0.5$. Since a sharpened set is less ambiguous, it also has a lower fuzziness.

Another attribute is that the fuzziness of a set and its complement should be the same. There is equal ambiguity in "tall" and "not-tall," for example.

Partially based on these attributes, a number of requirements, or conditions, have been developed that measures of fuzziness should satisfy. We use the word "should" because various authors do not agree on the minimum requirements. Five requirements proposed by Ebanks (1983) are listed below. The first three were originally suggested by DeLuca and Termini (1972). A sixth was also proposed by Ebanks, but it is generally not considered because of its difficulty of interpretation (Pal and Bezdek 1994). In the following requirements P1 to P5, A and B are fuzzy sets over a domain X, and $H(A)$ and $H(B)$ are fuzziness measures for the sets.

P1, sharpness: $H(A) = 0$ if A is a crisp set; that is, $\mu_A(x) = 0$ or $1 \; \forall \; x \in X$.

P2, maximality: $H(A)$ is maximum for $\mu_A(x) = 0.5 \; \forall \; x \in X$.

P3, resolution: $H(A) \geq H(A^*)$, where A^* is a sharpened version of A.

P4, symmetry: $H(A) = H(1-A)$, where $\mu_{1-A}(x) = 1 - \mu_A(x) \; \forall \; x \in X$.

P5, valuation: $H(A{\cup}B) + H(A{\cap}B) = H(A) + H(B)$.

As stated earlier, authors disagree about which of the conditions are sufficient for a fuzziness measure. For example, Yager and Filev (1994) believe that the first three (P1–P3) are sufficient, while Pal and Bezdek (1994) assert that all five (P1–P5) are required.

The first four seem intuitive relative to the fifth. P5 derives from crisp sets, where the number of elements in the union of two sets plus the number in their intersection equals the sum of the number of elements in each set. It is not clear that this condition is necessary for all fuzzy applications. The three measures of fuzziness discussed next adhere at least to P1 to P4, and two of them adhere to all five requirements.

The first fuzziness measure presented is that developed by DeLuca and Termini (1972). Their entropy measure, H_{DT}, is of the same form as Shannon's entropy measure. Equation 7.3 presents the measure, where K is a constant of normalization. This fuzziness measure adheres to all five conditions (P1–P5).

$$H_{DT}(A) = -K \sum_{i=1}^{n} \left(\mu_i \, log\mu_i + (1 - \mu_i) \, log\,(1 - \mu_i) \right) \qquad (7.3)$$

Remember that we are working with discrete fuzzy sets, so each n value of the subscript i corresponds to one of the n discrete values of x over the domain X.

The second fuzziness measure was developed by Pal and Pal (1989). It is based on a measure they developed for probabilistic entropy that incorporates an exponential gain function. Equation 7.4 presents the Pal and Pal entropy measure H_{PP}, where $e = 2.718. . .$, and K is again a normalization constant, which, when set properly, allows H_{PP} to satisfy all five conditions P1 to P5.

$$H_{PP}(A) = K \sum_{i=1}^{n} \mu_i e^{(1-\mu_i)} + (1 - \mu_i)\, e^{\mu_i} \tag{7.4}$$

The third fuzziness measure was developed by Kosko (1986). This measure requires the definition of the distance $d_q(A, A_{near})$ between a fuzzy set A and the crisp set A_{near} nearest to A, and the distance $d_q(A, A_{far})$ between A and the crisp set A_{far} farthest from A.

Membership values for A_{near} and A_{far} are

$$\mu_{Anear}(x) = \begin{cases} 1 & \text{if } \mu_A(x) \geq 0.5 \\ 0 & \text{otherwise} \end{cases}$$

$$\mu_{Afar}(x) = \begin{cases} 1 & \text{if } \mu_A(x) \leq 0.5 \\ 0 & \text{otherwise} \end{cases}$$

Now,

$$d_q(A, A_{near}) = \left[\sum_{i=1}^{n} \left| \mu_{A,i} - \mu_{Anear,i} \right|^q \right]^{1/q} \quad \text{and}$$

$$d_q(A, A_{far}) = \left[\sum_{i=1}^{n} \left| \mu_{A,i} - \mu_{Afar,i} \right|^q \right]^{1/q}$$

The distances are called the *linear (Hamming)* or *quadratic (Euclidean)* distances for $q = 1$ or 2, respectively.

The entropy measure defined by Kosko, H_K, is the ratio of the distance between a fuzzy set A and A_{near} to the distance between A and A_{far}, as illustrated in equation 7.5. Either the Hamming or the Euclidean distances may be used (the same value of q must be used in the numerator and denominator). H_K satisfies conditions P1 to P4, but doesn't always satisfy P5.

$$H_K(q, A) = \frac{d_q(A, A_{near})}{d_q(A, A_{far})} \tag{7.5}$$

Note that for practical systems, H_{DT} and H_{PP} are often normalized so that they produce values between 0 and 1; H_K is inherently normalized. Also note that higher values of fuzziness are not necessarily "better" in an application. Remember that maximum fuzziness is represented by a membership function with a membership value of 0.5 over its entire domain (which is almost certainly useless).

Fuzziness measures are often used to measure the relative fuzziness of various models, selecting the model to "harden" that is least fuzzy. For example, in the case of cluster validity functions, the partition of the data that has the minimum fuzziness is chosen as "best."

If one of the three measures of fuzziness described here doesn't meet your needs in an application, refer to Pal and Bezdek (1994) for others you can evaluate. Or you can create your own.

Now that we've completed our initial look at approximate reasoning, including an example of the process of fuzzification, fuzzy rule firing, and defuzzification, and our look at measures of fuzziness, let's review an example a common application of fuzzy logic: fuzzy control.

Developing a Fuzzy Controller

Fuzzy logic is studied by researchers in many fields, including not only engineering and computer science but also psychology, business and management, linguistics, philosophy, and mathematics. Not surprisingly, developments in the field have been diverse in their interpretation and applications, ranging from the ethereally philosophical to nuts-and-bolts arguments about the best way to defuzzify a particular system. The topics introduced in this section have implications for a wide range of fuzzy implementations.

One of the largest applications of fuzzy logic is in the area of control engineering. The use of fuzzy logic for control was first presented by Mamdani and his colleagues in the early 1970s (Mamdani and Assilian 1975) and grew to the point that there were thousands of industrial applications of this technology by the mid-1990s (Hirota 1995).

Why Fuzzy Control

There are several reasons why fuzzy control has gained such popularity. From an operational perspective, fuzzy controllers provide a systematic and efficient framework for incorporating linguistic information from human experts. Fuzzy control is a nonparametric approach that does not require a mathematical model of the system under control. Fuzzy control also produces nonlinear controllers, which extend their utility to a wide range of applications.

From a practical perspective, assuming you have sufficient knowledge about system behavior, fuzzy controllers are relatively easy to design, making them less expensive than alternative approaches. In addition, fuzzy controller concepts are relatively easy to understand because they are based on rules and their interactions.

A Fuzzy Controller

One general approach to fuzzy control is shown in Figure 7.5. The system being controlled, the plant, has its state changed by inputs. The change in the plant's state produces a different plant response (output). The fuzzy controller's job is to provide a set of inputs that produce the desirable output from the system. The fuzzy controller interacts with the plant through an *action interface* (defuzzifier) for plant inputs and a *condition interface* (fuzzifier) that accepts plant outputs.

A rule base defines the actions of the fuzzy controller. There are five steps in constructing this fuzzy rule base:

1. Identify and name the input variables and their ranges.
2. Identify and name the output variables and their ranges.
3. Define a set of fuzzy membership functions for each input and each output variable.
4. Construct the rule base that will govern the controller's operation.
5. Determine how the control actions will be combined to form the executed action.

This rule base construction process is illustrated in the next section with an idealized problem. In this example we use an approach that was pioneered by Mamdani

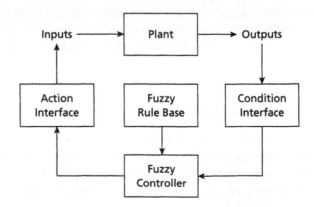

Figure 7.5 Fuzzy controller overview.

(Mamdani and Assiliani 1975). We use an approach developed by Takagi and Sugeno (1985) later.

Building a Mamdani-type Fuzzy Controller

To illustrate the construction of a rule base, we use the problem of controlling the speed of a train. The objective of the controller is to smoothly slow and stop a train that is traveling at any speed and is any distance from the station.

Step 1: Identify and name the input linguistic variables and their numerical ranges

Two input variables have been identified: train speed and distance to the station. There are five ranges of speed:

Table 7.1 Speed (km/hr)

Linguistic range	Low	High
Fast	26.5	70
Medium fast	6.5	46.5
Slow	2.5	10.5
Very slow	1	4
Stopped	0	2

There are also five ranges of distance:

Table 7.2 Distance (meters)

Linguistic range	Low	High
Far	1,500	∞
Medium far	100	3,000
Near	3	200
Very near	1	5
At	0	2

Step 2: Identify and name the linguistic output variables and their numerical ranges

There are two output variables that have been identified: train throttle and train brake. There are five ranges of throttle (%):

Table 7.3 Throttle

Linguistic range	Low (%)	High (%)
Full	60	100
Medium	20	80
Slight	3	30
Very slight	1	5
No	0	2

There are also five ranges of brake (%):

Table 7.4 Brake

Linguistic range	Low (%)	High (%)
Full	98	100
Medium	95	99
Slight	70	97
Very slight	20	80
No	0	40

Step 3: Define a set of fuzzy membership functions for each input variable

In this example, we use triangular (including left- and right-triangular) membership functions. Each range of input and output variables is defined to associate with a fuzzy set that has the same name as the range. Therefore, there are five fuzzy sets defined for each input and output variable. The low and high values of each range are used to define its associated fuzzy set's triangular membership functions. The membership functions for speed and distance are shown in Figures 7.6 and 7.7, respectively. The membership functions for throttle and brake are shown in Figures 7.8 and 7.9, respectively. Note that the height of each function is 1.0 and the function bounds do not exceed the high and low ranges listed above for each range. Note also that the horizontal scales are not linear. They are drawn so that they fit on the page, but emphasize those portions with which we are most concerned in our example.

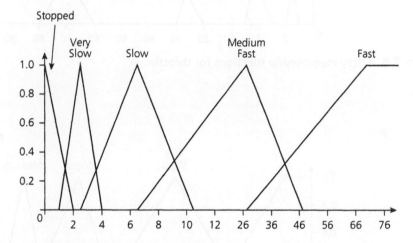

Figure 7.6 Fuzzy membership functions for speed.

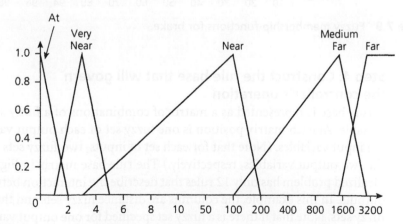

Figure 7.7 Fuzzy membership functions for distance.

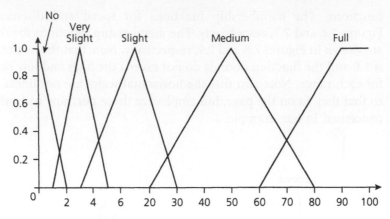

Figure 7.8 Fuzzy membership functions for throttle.

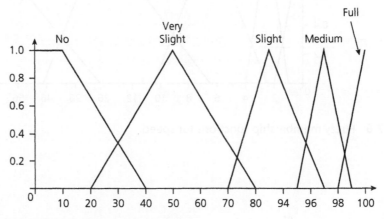

Figure 7.9 Fuzzy membership functions for brake.

Step 4: Construct the rule base that will govern the controller's operation

A rule base is represented as a matrix of combinations of a fuzzy set of each input variable. At each matrix position is one fuzzy set of each output variable related to the input variables. (Note that for each set of inputs, two fuzzy sets are specified for the two output variables, respectively.) The rule base matrix in Figure 7.10 for our idealized problem has only 12 rules that describe the interaction between inputs and outputs. In this example, the columns are distance fuzzy sets and the rows are speed fuzzy sets. Note that if there is a fuzzy set specified for one output variable, all output variables must have fuzzy sets specified.

	At	Very Near	Near	Medium Far	Far
Stopped	Full Brake No Throttle	Full Brake VS Throttle			
Very Slow	Full Brake No Throttle	Medium Brake VS Throttle	Slow Brake VS Throttle		
Slow	Full Brake No Throttle	Medium Brake VS Throttle	VS Brake Slow Throttle		
Medium Fast				VS Brake Medium Throttle	No Brake Full Throttle
Fast				VS Brake Medium Throttle	No Brake Full Throttle

Figure 7.10 Fuzzy rule base matrix.

Each entry in the rule base is defined by ANDing the inputs to produce individual output responses. As an example, the shaded matrix entry in Figure 7.10 means

IF (speed) IS (stopped) AND IF (distance) IS (at)

THEN (full brake) AND (no throttle)

Each of the matrix entries uses the same rule combination process.

Step 5: Determine how the control actions will be combined to form the executed action at the action interface

To illustrate how the control actions are combined to produce the executed action at the action interface, consider the inputs

$$\text{speed} = 3\text{km/hr}$$

$$\text{distance} = 1.8 \text{ m}$$

The first step is to determine which membership functions are activated and to what degree. Four fuzzy sets are activated: the distance fuzzy sets *At* and *Very Near* and the speed fuzzy sets *Very Slow* and *Slow*. The membership of the speed of 3 km/hr for the fuzzy set *Very Slow* is 0.667 and the membership of 3 km/hr for the fuzzy set *Slow* is 0.125. Mathematically these are denoted as

$$\mu_{Very\ Slow}(3) = 0.667$$

$$\mu_{Slow}(3) = 0.125$$

These membership function values are graphically illustrated in Figure 7.11.

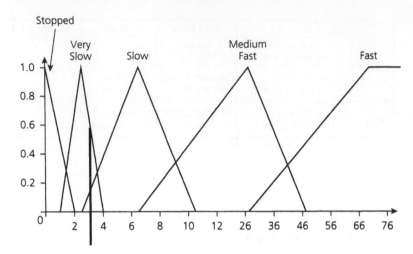

Figure 7.11 A speed of 3 km/hr activates two fuzzy membership functions, *Very Slow* and *Slow*.

Similarly, the membership values for the distance of 1.8 m in the fuzzy sets for *At* and *Very Near* are

$$\mu_{Very\ Near}(1.8) = 0.4$$

$$\mu_{At}(1.8) = 0.1$$

These fuzzy membership values are shown in Figure 7.12. This results in four rules firing in the rule base matrix, as shown in Figure 7.13 (rule numbers, arbitrarily assigned, are shown in the lower right corner of the matrix entry).

Next, we combine the membership values using the AND (min) operator for each rule combination:

Rule 1: $\mu_{Very\ Slow}$ AND $\mu_{At} = \mu_{Very\ Slow \cap At} = \min(0.667, 0.1) = 0.1$

Rule 2: μ_{Slow} AND $\mu_{At} = \mu_{Slow \cap At} = \min(0.125, 0.1) = 0.1$

Rule 3: $\mu_{Very\ Slow}$ AND $\mu_{Very\ Near} = \mu_{Very\ Slow \cap Very\ Near} = \min(0.667, 0.4) = 0.4$

Rule 4: μ_{Slow} AND $\mu_{Very\ Near} = \mu_{Slow \cap Very\ Near} = \min(0.125, 0.4) = 0.125$

The values 0.1, 0.1, 0.4, and 0.125 are the *firing strengths* of rules 1 through 4, respectively, for the input (3, 1.8).

Let's compute the output value for *Brake* first. We determine the membership value for each fuzzy set of the output variable *Brake*. Rules 1 and 2 are associated with the fuzzy set *Full Brake*. Rules 3 and 4 are associated with the fuzzy set *Medium Brake*. The fuzzy set *Full Brake* is activated with membership values 0.1 and 0.1. The fuzzy set *Medium Brake* is activated with membership values 0.4 and 0.125. Therefore, the fuzzy set *Full Brake* has membership value 0.1 and the fuzzy set *Medium Brake* has

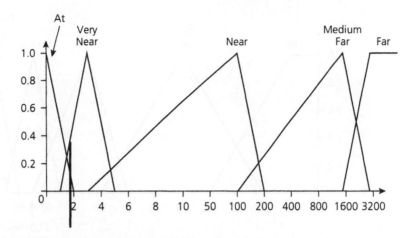

Figure 7.12 A distance of 1.8 m activates two fuzzy sets, *At* and *Very Near*, with membership values of 0.1 and 0.4, respectively.

	At	**Very Near**	**Near**	**Medium Far**	**Far**
Stopped	Full Brake No Throttle	Full Brake VS Throttle			
Very Slow (VS)	Full Brake No Throttle ₁	Medium Brake VS Throttle ₃	Slow Brake VS Throttle		i
Slow	Full Brake No Throttle ₂	Medium Brake VS Throttle ₄	VS Brake Slow Throttle		
Medium Fast				VS Brake Medium Throttle	No Brake Full Throttle
Fast				VS Brake Medium Throttle	No Brake Full Throttle

Figure 7.13 Four rules are activated with the inputs speed = 3 and distance = 1.5.

membership value 0.4 by taking the maximum of the two activated membership values for each fuzzy set, respectively.

The centroid defuzzification with overlap, described earlier, is used here to obtain the output value. The resulting centroid is shown in Figure 7.14. The horizontal coordinate of the centroid along the *x*-axis yields an output value of 97.01 percent application of the brake.

The same methodology is used to determine the output value for the percentage of throttle, which is left as an exercise (Exercise 5) for the student. The construction of the fuzzy controller is now complete.

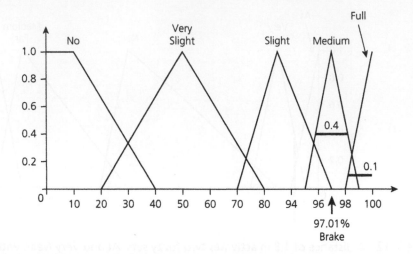

Figure 7.14 Extrapolation of the centroid to the percentage of brake.

Fuzzy Controller Operation

During operation, input values are continually sampled and presented to the fuzzy controller. The fuzzy controller then repeats the process described earlier in step 5:

- Determine the fuzzy membership values activated by the inputs (illustrated by Figures 7.11 and 7.12).

- Determine which rules are activated in the rule base matrix (illustrated by Figure 7.13).

- Combine the membership values for the activated rules using the AND operator (illustrated by computing rules 1 through 4).

- Combine the activated membership values for each fuzzy set of an output variable.

- Use centroid defuzzification to determine the value for each output variable (illustrated by Figure 7.14).

Takagi–Sugeno–Kang Method

Another methodology for modeling and control is the Takagi–Sugeno–Kang (TSK) fuzzy reasoning method (Sugeno and Kang 1986; Takagi and Sugeno 1985), which yields Quasilinear Fuzzy Models (Yager and Filev 1994). The main difference between the TSK method and that of Mamdani is that rather than having a fuzzy consequent, each rule's consequent is a mathematical function. This function calculates an output value as a function of one or more of the set of input variables;

some or all of these same input variables are used in the fuzzy antecedents of the rules. As developed by Takagi, Sugeno, and Kang, the function is affine (the output is a linear plus a constant function of the inputs), but the method has been extended to nonlinear functions.

The general form of a fuzzy rule in a TSK model, then, is

$$
\text{If } x_1 \text{ is } S_1 \text{ and }, \ldots, \text{ and } x_k \text{ is } S_k \text{ then } y = u(x_1, \ldots, x_k) = a_0 + a_1 x_1 \\
+ a_2 x_2 + \cdots + a_k x_k \tag{7.6}
$$

where y is the consequent (output) variable whose value is inferred, each x_i is an input variable (an antecedent) that may also appear in the consequent part of the rule, each S_i is a fuzzy set represented by a membership function, and $u(x_1, \ldots, x_k)$ is a specified function, $u : \mathcal{R}^k \to \mathcal{R}$. *Linear membership functions* over each input variable are linear functions that monotonically increase (or decrease) over their domain. Linear membership functions were used by Takagi and Sugeno, but their method is routinely used with other kinds of membership functions, including sigmoidal and Gaussian.

Variables that are not input variables (x_{k+1}, etc.) that are important for obtaining the output estimation can also be included in the consequent (conclusion) function on the right of equation 7.6. For example, in our furnace gas flow example discussed earlier, we might add the current (total) gas flow (*CurFlow*) as a variable to be included in the consequent function.

A complete model, or system, then, is defined by n fuzzy rules R_i for $i = 1, \ldots, n$, as follows:

$$
\text{If } x_{1i} \text{ is } S_{1i} \text{ and }, \ldots, \text{ and } x_{ki} \text{ is } S_{ki}, \text{then } y_i = u_i(x_{1i}, \ldots, x_{ki})
$$

Calculating the output of the system involves finding the intersection, usually the minimum or product, of the fuzzy membership values of the antecedents. That is,

$$
\alpha(y_i) = \min \{\mu_{S1i}(x_{1i}), \ldots, \mu_{Ski}(x_{ki})\} \text{ or}
$$
$$
\alpha(y_i) = \Pi \{\mu_{S1i}(x_{1i}), \ldots, \mu_{Ski}(x_{ki})\}
$$

where $\alpha(y_i)$ is the firing strength, or truth (membership) value, of rule i.

Then the system output y resulting from all n rules is calculated as shown in equation 7.7

$$
y = \sum_{i=1}^{n} \frac{\alpha(y_i) \, y_i}{\sum_{j=1}^{n} \alpha(y_j)} = \sum_{i=1}^{n} \frac{\alpha(y_i)}{\sum_{j=1}^{n} \alpha(y_j)} u_i(x_{1i}, \ldots, x_{ki}) \tag{7.7}
$$

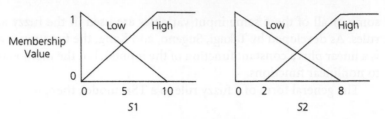

Figure 7.15 Fuzzy membership functions for the Takagi–Sugeno–Kang example.

The system output y is thus a weighted average of the individual subsystem outputs y_i.

The following simple example illustrates implementation of the Takagi–Sugeno–Kang method. Assume that we have a system with fuzzy membership functions over the input domains, as shown in Figure 7.15. Also assume that there are two rules, as follows:

Rule 1: If u_1 is $S1\_low$ and u_2 is $S2\_low$, then $y_1 = 0.5u_1 + 0.2u_2$

Rule 2: If u_1 is $S1\_high$ and u_2 is $S2\_high$, then $y_2 = u_1 + u_2$

Now suppose that $u_1 = 8$ and $u_2 = 4$. Then $\mu_{S1\_low}(u_1) = 0.2$ and $\mu_{S2\_low}(u_2) = 0.5$, so the first rule results in $\alpha(y_1) = 0.2$. Likewise, since $\mu_{S1\_high}(u_1) = 0.8$, and $\mu_{S2\_high}(u_2) = 0.33$, the second rule results in $\alpha(y_2) = 0.33$.

Since $y_1 = 4.8$ and $y_2 = 12$, the crisp output value inferred by the two rules is

$$y = \frac{0.2(4.8) + 0.33(12)}{0.2 + 0.33} \cong 9.36$$

The determination of system structure and parameters is discussed in detail in Takagi and Sugeno (1985). Methods for determination of the parameters $a_0, a_1, \ldots,$ for the consequent function (see equation 7.6), for example, include the least mean squares technique. Data taken during successful operation by a skilled operator can be used to develop the "learning model" for the parameters. With respect to this learning model, Terano, Asai, and Sugeno (1989) say, "It is not too much to say that it is indispensable." System structure design and parameter identification can also be accomplished using evolutionary computing methods similar to those described in Chapter 8 for the evolutionary fuzzy rule system.

The TSK method is particularly useful for modeling very complex systems. The method's fuzzy techniques facilitate the decomposition of the state spaces of these systems into relatively simple subsystems. The TSK methodology is used to smoothly interpolate system dynamics among the multiple regions to which an operating point may belong.

The TSK method allows objective system performance data, in the form of either system equations or actual operating data, to be explicitly incorporated into the system model. This can be done while incorporating expert knowledge in the formulation of the fuzzy rules.

Summary

Evolutionary computation and neural networks are attempts to mimic or simulate emergent natural processes that have proved effective information-processing methods "in the wild." Logic, on the other hand, is an artificial method devised by humans. Although one could argue that the *capacity* for reasoning evolved through natural adaptation, it is clear that the calculus of symbolic logic has only been invented through millennia of investigation, and only in certain societies on earth. More likely one would say that what has evolved is actually the ability to use language, which is primarily communicative but can be exploited to encode inferential relations among symbols.

Western society has always trusted that Aristotelian logic would eventually be used to explain all kinds of causal and implicative relations. But with the invention of fast electronic computers, it became apparent very quickly that binary logic was adequate for explaining *very few* real-world logical relations. It was too precise, especially in assuming that objects in the world really do belong to crisp taxonomic classes.

Zadeh's revolution, however, has opened the possibility that reasoning can explain a great amount about the world, with some fundamental adjustments. First, the distinction between *A* and *not-A* has been weakened, so that an element can belong to a set (class or category) and also *not* belong to that set. The element can even belong to a set and to its opposite.

Second, in fuzzy expert systems all rules fire at once, at least theoretically. Practically, this means that the system always produces an answer. Traditional expert systems can get "stuck," a situation that arises from the rules firing sequentially, when the answer to a question leads to a condition from which it is not possible to proceed. The importance of this aspect of the fuzzy revolution can hardly be overstated. Fuzzy logic asks all the questions simultaneously and blends the answers in parallel to form an answer from the whole.

This parallelism constitutes a step back from the artificiality of binary logic, toward the more natural implementation of massive neural parallelism. If the computational intelligence perspective is seen as a tendency to focus on the *emergence* of solutions within a computer program, as opposed to the *imposition* of solutions through rules and constraints, then fuzzy logic belongs here. A strength of the fuzzy method is that the rules encoded in a fuzzy system allow unanticipated solutions; solutions can emerge that were not imposed by a knowledge engineer or programmer. This is computational intelligence.

Exercises

1. Given that we are working with the domain of "age" of a population of people, define a set of fuzzy membership functions over the domain that might be appropriate for use by an insurance company determining risk of Alzheimer's disease, which affects mainly older people. Repeat the exercise for use by a medical organization for diagnosing appendicitis, which is assumed for this exercise to affect people regardless of age. Justify the number and distribution of fuzzy sets.

2. Fuzzy sets V and W are defined on the same universe of five individuals as follows:

$$V = \left\{ \frac{1.0}{q} + \frac{0.8}{r} + \frac{0.6}{s} + \frac{0.20}{t} + \frac{0}{u} \right\}$$

$$W = \left\{ \frac{1.0}{q} + \frac{0.6}{r} + \frac{0.45}{s} + \frac{0.15}{t} + \frac{0}{u} \right\}$$

For V and W, find: (a) $V \cap W$, (b) $V \cup W$, (c) $\widetilde{V}$, (d) $\widetilde{W}$, (e) $\widetilde{V} \cap W$, (f) $V \cup \widetilde{W}$.

3. For each of the three measures of fuzziness defined in the chapter (equations 7.2, 7.3, and 7.4), calculate the fuzzy entropy of one of the fuzzy membership functions you defined in exercise 1. (Remember that the membership function is defined over the entire age domain.)

4. Using the fuzzy membership functions defined in the chapter for the slowing of a train near a station, determine the percent of braking applied when the train is moving 3 km/hr and is 8 m from the station.

5. Determine the percent of throttle applied for the conditions described in exercise 4.

6. Use the centroid with overlap defuzzification method to calculate the output value of the output variable *FlowChange* as shown in Figure 7.3.

7. Implement the center of maximum method of defuzzification in the fuzzy source code.

8. What are the advantages of using fuzzy controllers?

9. Following the five steps discussed in this chapter, design a fuzzy room temperature controller.

chapter
eight

Fuzzy Systems Implementations

In the last chapter, we discussed the basic concepts of fuzzy logic and fuzzy systems. Now we are ready to apply what we learned. This chapter presents two implementations of fuzzy systems: fuzzy rule systems and evolutionary fuzzy rule systems. First, we discuss common issues, such as how to represent fuzzy rules, related to fuzzy rule system and evolutionary fuzzy rule system implementations. Then we provide the detailed descriptions of the system implementations. The executable code and source code are available at the book's web site.

Similarly to previous chapters on implementation (Chapters 4 and 6), we have included code listings such as class definitions and operator definitions. If you are not interested in the details of programming, you may want to skim these listings, noting what is included and what is accomplished by the code in each listing.

The source code is being distributed as *shareware*. You are welcome to download it and use it for classroom or personal learning experiences in conjunction with the textbook at no cost. If you use it, either as is or with modification, for a project outside of your classroom (or learning on your own), please submit a payment in accordance with the shareware payment instructions on the Internet site for the book. ▪

Implementation Issues

Before we get to the specific implementations, it is a good idea to address the main issues common to the implementations of fuzzy rule systems and evolutionary fuzzy rule systems. We do that in this section. These issues include the representation of fuzzy rules, evolutionary design of fuzzy rule systems, and the programming language to be used for implementations of fuzzy systems.

Fuzzy Rule Representation

In this chapter, a fuzzy rule system with Mamdani-type fuzzy rules is implemented. (Mamdani fuzzy systems are described in Chapter 7.) Theoretically, each fuzzy variable can have any number of fuzzy sets, but 3, 5, 7, or 9 fuzzy sets are common for each fuzzy variable. (An odd number of fuzzy sets is almost always used. There seems to be no particular reason for this other than the resulting symmetry about the center of the variable range.) Each fuzzy rule can be easily described in linguistic terms. For example, a one-input–one-output fuzzy rule can be described as

```
if input is Low, then output is Medium
```

This linguistic representation is favored by human beings but not by digital computers, which use numbers as the medium for computation. To represent the language of a computer better, in the following implementation numbers represent the fuzzy rules. For example, for a fuzzy variable with 3 fuzzy sets (Low, Medium, High), four integer numbers (0,1,2,3) can be used to represent these fuzzy sets: 0 represents don't care, and 1, 2, and 3 represent Low, Medium, and High, respectively. For a fuzzy variable with 5 fuzzy sets (Very Low, Low, Medium, High, Very High), six numbers (0,1,2,3,4,5) can be used to represent these fuzzy sets: 0 again represents don't care and 1, 2, 3, 4, and 5 represent Very Low, Low, Medium, High, Very High, respectively. With this in mind, the above one-input–one-output rule can be represented as 1 2, assuming that three fuzzy sets exist for each variable.

For a fuzzy rule with the modifier not before its fuzzy set, the rule can be numerically represented by adding a minus sign (–) before the corresponding number. For example, if the above rule is changed to

```
if input is not Low, then output is Medium
```

its numerical representation is accordingly changed to –1 2.

To illustrate further, here are two fuzzy rules for a two-input–one-output fuzzy rule system, with each fuzzy variable having three fuzzy sets:

```
if input_1 is not Low, and input_2 is High, then output is Medium
if input_2 is Low, then output is High
```

These two rules can be represented numerically as -1 3 2 and 0 1 3 (remember that 0 means "don't care").

Evolutionary Design of a Fuzzy Rule System

One common approach to designing fuzzy rule systems uses human experts' experience and a trial-and-error approach. This may work well for some simple applications, especially with only a few variables. When human expertise is not available and/or the system is complicated, however, automated approaches are preferable for developing fuzzy rule systems.

A straightforward approach is to use clustering algorithms to divide the problem space into many subspaces with or without overlaps. Each subspace is transformed into a rule by mapping its center according to the definitions of fuzzy variables. The obtained rules are generally adjusted by, for example, tuning the membership functions or selecting fuzzification and defuzzification methods.

In this chapter, we describe an implementation of an evolutionary fuzzy system using a genetic algorithm (GA). The design of a fuzzy rule system can be looked at as a search problem in a multidimensional space that is infinitely large, nondifferentiable, complex, noisy, multimodal, and deceptive (Shi, Eberhart, and Chen 1999). Evolutionary algorithms have been shown to be superior to traditional design approaches in finding optimal and near-optimal solutions in this complex high-dimensional search space.

To design fuzzy rule systems using GAs, several issues need to be addressed, as follows:

- What parts of the system are being evolved?
- How are system elements best represented?
- How should the population be initialized?
- How are individual fitnesses evaluated?
- What genetic operators should be used?

We now look at each of these issues in turn.

The first issue is to decide *what parts of the system are being evolved.* The performance of a fuzzy rule system is completely determined by its fuzzy rules and membership functions, and its fuzzification and defuzzification approaches. Which of these parts are to be evolved depends on the problem to be solved. Each part can be evolved with other parts fixed, or a combination of several parts, or even the whole system, can be evolved simultaneously. In our implementation, we focus on the evolution of the fuzzy rule set (including the number of rules in the fuzzy rule set) and the membership functions (including the membership function location and the membership function type—for example, triangle, sigmoid, etc.).

The next issue to consider is *how to represent the system elements*. Similar to evolutionary neural networks, the fuzzy rule system to be evolved needs to be represented as individuals for an evolutionary algorithm to work on. Various representations can be used. Binary representations were originally used in genetic algorithms. It is natural to represent fuzzy rules using binary strings. For a fuzzy variable with three fuzzy sets (`Low`, `Medium`, and `High`), a string of three bits can be used to represent which fuzzy set(s) is (are) included in the rule. For example, `101` means that the `Low` and `High` fuzzy sets for this fuzzy variable are included but the `Medium` fuzzy set is not. For a fuzzy system with two input fuzzy variables and one output fuzzy variable, if each variable has three fuzzy sets, then a binary string of the nine bits `101 001 100` represents the fuzzy rule: `if input one is Low or High and input two is High, then the output is Low`.

A feature of this representation is that it can represent rules with the OR operation. Another way to represent the fuzzy rules is through using 1 and 0 to represent whether a fuzzy rule exists or not. This approach can only represent AND operations among the variables in the antecedent part. For example, for the above fuzzy system, the total number of possible fuzzy rules is $3 \times 3 \times 3 = 27$, so a binary string of 27 bits can completely represent the fuzzy rule set with the position index of the bit representing the content of the rule and the position value 0 or 1 representing whether this rule exists or not.

Fuzzy membership functions can also be represented by binary bits. For example, each parameter of a membership function can be represented by a string of binary bits, say 7 bits (Karr and Gentry 1993). The disadvantage of this kind of representation is that the length of the chromosome will be extremely long when the number of variables and the number of fuzzy sets for each variable are large. Also, inaccuracy is brought in when binary strings represent the real-valued parameters of the membership functions. The advantage of the binary representation is its simplicity and generality.

For the representation of fuzzy rules, perhaps a more natural way is to use integer representation. For the above fuzzy rule system, the number of possible combinations of the antecedent part is $3 \times 3 = 9$, then, provided that integers $\{0,1,2,3\}$ are used to represent symbols $\{$`don't care`, `Low`, `Medium`, `High`$\}$, a string of 9 integers can be used to completely represent the fuzzy rule set with the position index representing the antecedent part and the position integer value representing the consequent part (Hwang and Thompson 1994). The real-valued parameters of fuzzy membership functions can also be represented by integers but, as with binary representations, inaccuracies are introduced (Shi, Eberhart, and Chen 1999). The advantage of this kind of representation is that the length of the chromosome is reduced compared with that of the binary representation.

To overcome the inaccuracy introduced by binary and integer representations for encoding the real-valued parameters of the membership functions, a real-valued representation can be used (Herrera, Lozano, and Verdegay 1995). The use of a real-valued representation makes it possible to use large domains (even unknown domains) for the variables, which is difficult to achieve with binary and integer representations. The disadvantage of this representation is that the fuzzy rules can't be represented easily. So it is better to use real-valued representations when only fuzzy membership functions are to be evolved.

Another issue is *how to initialize the population*. Generally, the population is randomly initialized. Each possible individual is given the same priority. But for some applications, existing experience and knowledge may be helpful in the automatic design of the fuzzy rule system. This kind of experience and knowledge can be incorporated into the initialization of the population. The drawback is that this experience and knowledge may quickly become dominant in the population and therefore trap the system in a local optimum. If sufficient computation time is allowed, the authors always try to run evolutionary fuzzy rule systems with completely random initializations.

The next issue to consider is *how to evaluate the fitness of an individual*. The method used to evaluate the fitness of an individual depends on the problem to be solved and your objective. Having a good evaluation function for the fuzzy rule system can make it easier for the GA to evolve a good fuzzy rule system more efficiently and effectively.

For classification problems, it is natural to choose the number of correctly and/or wrongly classified training patterns as fitness. Other common fitness functions are the mean-square error (or absolute difference error) function if you prefer your system to have a bigger tolerance, and the relative difference error function if you prefer your system to have similar accuracy for any target output value. Other requirements for the system can also be encoded into the fitness function. For example, if a simple system is preferred, then a measure of the complexity of the fuzzy system (such as the number of rules evolved) should be included in the fitness function. Performance metrics for computational intelligence systems are discussed in Chapter 10.

The final issue we consider is *the selection of the genetic operators to be used*. What kind of genetic operators to adopt depends on the representation approach. For a binary representation, the genetic operators have been studied extensively and applied. Some widely used operators can be adopted without modification. For integer and real-valued representations, some new operators or modifications of existing operators generally are recommended. For example, for an integer representation of a fuzzy rule system (Shi, Eberhart, and Chen 1999), a position-based mutation operator is used because each element in an individual represents a different integer range.

An Object-oriented Language: C++

In the previous implementations, we used `struct` in C to group related data variables and `typedef` to define new data types. A new data type can be looked at as an object, which is accessible in its own module. All the modules are designed to be as independent as possible. Therefore, each module can be as reusable as possible. Programming is focused on the newly defined objects. The programming can be considered object-based programming but not strictly object-oriented programming.

To make the source code more reuseable, C++ is used in the implementations discussed in this chapter and the next. C++ is a language designed to be object oriented like Java and Smalltalk. It can be considered as an extension of the C language. Almost all the features in C can be used in C++, and C++ has its own features—for example, *data abstraction*, *inheritance*, and *dynamic binding*. (Please refer to a C++ programming book for details.) Certainly, to some extent, C can also be programmed to have these features, but it is not designed to have them. C++ is not perfect, but it is a useful and practical language for real-world problem solving. Please note: we are not here to argue which language is better.

Fuzzy Rule System Implementation

Now that we've looked at some of the issues related to implementation, this section discusses the implementation of a fuzzy rule system. We focus on the use of the implementation for classification. The implementation is a flexible tool that is capable of solving a wide variety of classification and diagnostic problems.

Programming Fuzzy Rule Systems

In contrast to the previous implementations in this book, the implementation of fuzzy rule systems and all other implementations to be discussed are written in C++. In C, a `struct` data structure is defined to include all the related data and even some methods (functions); in C++, a new class is defined that binds the data and methods together. The new classes to be defined in this section for the implementation of fuzzy rule systems are shown in Figure 8.1. The class `FuzzyMember` is the fundamental class, which defines an object class of membership function associated with a fuzzy set. The class `FuzzyVariable` defines an object class of fuzzy variable, which consists of several fuzzy sets (`FuzzyMembers`). The class `FuzzyRule` defines an object class of fuzzy rule, which is composed of `FuzzyVariable` classes and an integer vector class, which is a template class of `vector`. The class `FuzzyRuleSet` defines an object class of fuzzy rule set, which is composed of `FuzzyRule` classes.

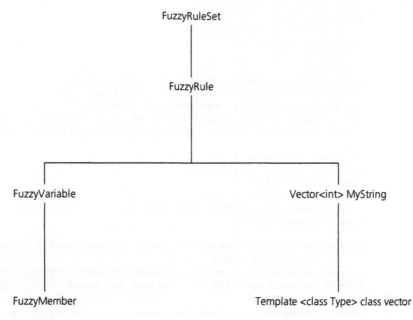

Figure 8.1 Class tree in the implementation of the fuzzy rule system.

First, let us start with a discussion of the classes. The class *vector* is defined as a template class (`template <class Type>`) so that one class definition can be used for the declaration of different kinds of vector. For example, integer vector `vect_i` and float vector `vect_f` can be declared as

```
vector<int>     vect_i;
vector<float>   vect_f;
```

The class `vector` is shown in Listing 8.1. The `vector` class has two private data members. The `row (int)` defines the length of the vector, and the `arr (Type)` defines a pointer to the vector of data with type `Type`. The descriptor "private" protects these two data members from being accessed by other classes directly. Private

Listing 8.1 Definition of template class `vector`.

```
template <class Type>
class vector
{
  private:
    int    row;
    Type *arr;
  public:
    //constructors
    vector():row(0),arr(0) {}
```

```
    vector(int a);
    vector(const vector<Type>& a);
    vector(int a,Type* b);
    ~vector(){delete []arr;}
    //operators
    vector<Type>& operator =(const vector<Type>& a);
    vector<Type>& operator +=(const vector<Type>& a);
    int operator !=(const vector<Type>& a) const;
    int operator <(const vector<Type>& a) const {return (row<a.row);}
    Type& operator [] (int i) const {assert(i>=0&&i<row); return arr[i];}

    //member functions
    int len() const {return row;}
    Type sum() const;
    int maximum_index() const;
    vector<Type>& changeSize(const int& a);
    Type minimum() const;

    friend vector<Type> operator |(const vector<Type>& a, const
        vector<Type>& b);
    friend istream& operator >> (istream& is,vector<Type>& a);
    friend ostream& operator << (ostream& os, const vector<Type>& a);
};
```

data members can be accessed from outside of the class only through the class's public methods (functions).

The public constructors provide ways to declare vectors. For example, vector<int> vect_i declares an integer vector with zero elements; vector<float> vect_f(2) declares a float type vector of length 2; vector<float> vect_f_2(vect_f) declares a new float type vector that is a copy of float type vector vect_f.

The public operators define overloaded operators for the operation of vectors. For example, assume that v1, v2 are two float type vectors with the same length. Then v1 = v2 copies v2 to v1; v2 += v1 means that v1 and v2 are first added and then the summation is assigned to v2; and v2 != v1 returns 0 if v2 equals v1; otherwise, it returns 1.

The public member methods provide ways to operate on the data members of the class. The len() method returns the length of the vector; the sum() method returns the summation of all the vector elements; the maximum_index() method returns the index of the vector element that has the maximum value; and the minimum() method returns the minimum value of vector elements.

The friend operators << and >> provide methods for vector input and output. For example, assume that inDataFile is an opened object with data type ifstream and vect_f is of vector<float> data type; then inDataFile >> vect_f will input data from inDataFile to vect_f.

The class Mystring is shown in Listing 8.2. It has three private data members. Data member stringSize defines the length of the string, stringPtr is a

Fuzzy Rule System Implementation

Listing 8.2 Definition of class `MyString`.

```cpp
class MyString
{
  private:
    int    stringSize;
    char *stringPtr;
    int    currentPosition;

  public:
    //constructors
    MyString():stringSize(0),stringPtr(0),currentPosition(0) {}
    MyString(int a);
    MyString(char * str);
    MyString(const MyString& a);

    //destructor
    ~MyString() {delete []stringPtr;}

    //member functions
    int get_stringSize() const {return stringSize;}
    int get_currentPosition() const {return currentPosition;}
    char* get_stringPtr() const {return stringPtr;}
    MyString& change_stringSize(const int& a);
    MyString& change_currentPosition(const int& a);
    MyString& change_stringContent(char *str);
    int findNextF(char ch) const;
    int findNextB(char ch) const;
    int totalNumberF(char ch) const;
    int totalNumberB(char ch) const;
    MyString get_subString(const int& a);    //a: size of subString
                                             //from current position

    // operators
    char& operator [] (int i) const;
    MyString& operator =(const MyString& a);
    int operator ==(const MyString& a) const;

    //friend I/O operators
    friend ostream& operator <<(ostream& os, const MyString& a);
    friend istream& operator >>(istream& is, MyString& a);
};
```

pointer to the string, and `currentPosition` is the index of the character within the string being manipulated.

The public constructors provide ways to declare a `MyString` type variable. For example, `Mystring s1` declares an empty `Mystring` variable `s1`; `Mystring s2(3)` declares a `Mystring` variable `s2` with length 3; `Mystring s3("Triangle")` declares a `Mystring` variable `s3` that has length 8 and `stringPtr` pointing to a memory space (8 bytes total) with the values "Triangle" stored in them; `Mystring s4(s3)` declares a `Mystring` variable `s4` that is a copy of `s3`.

The public `get_stringSize()`, `get_currentPosition()`, and `get_stringPtr()` member methods provide interfaces to obtain the private data members from the outside the `Mystring` class.

The public `change_stringSize()`, `change_currentPosition()`, and `change_stringContent()` member methods provide interfaces to modify the `Mystring` class private data members from outside `Mystring` class.

The public method `findNextF(char ch)` provides a way to find the next character ch in the `Mystring` variable starting from the `currentPosition` to the end; the method `findNextB(char ch)` provides a way to find the next character ch going backward from the `currentPosition` to the beginning of the string; the method `totalNumberF(char ch)` obtains the total number of char ch in the string from the `currentPosition` to the end; the method `totalNumberB(char ch)` obtains the total number of char ch in the string from the `currentPosition` backward to the beginning; the method `get_subString(n)` returns a new `Mystring` data structure with length n and its `stringPtr` pointing to a string that has n characters copied from the original string starting from the `currentPosition`.

The public operator `[]` provides a way to obtain a character from a `Mystring` variable. For example, assume s1 is a `Mystring` variable with `length 10`; then `s1[2]` returns the third character in the string pointed to by `stringPtr`. The public operator = assigns one `Mystring` variable to another one. For example, `s2 = s1` means that the `Mystring` variable s1 is assigned (copied) to the `Mystring` variable s2. The operator `==` compares two `Mystring` variables. It returns 1 (true) if the two are equal; otherwise, it returns 0 (false).

The friend operators `<<` and `>>` provide ways for getting input and output for the `Mystring` variable, respectively.

The *class FuzzyMember* is shown in Listing 8.3. FuzzyMember provides a way to declare and manipulate a data type variable for a membership function.

Listing 8.3 Definition of class `FuzzyMember`.

```
Class FuzzyMember
{
  private:
    float      startPoint;
    float      endpoint;
    char       *functionType;

  public:
    //constructor
    FuzzyMember():startPoint(0),endpoint(0),functionType(0) {}
    FuzzyMember(float a,float b, char *str);
    FuzzyMember(const FuzzyMember& a);
```

```
//destructor
~FuzzyMember(){delete []functionType;}

//member function
float memberFunction(const float& a) const;
float not(const float& a) const;
vector<float> membership2input(const float& a) const;
float get_startPoint() const {return startPoint;}
float get_endpoint() const {return endpoint;}
char* get_functionType() const {return functionType;}
int member_flag(const float& a) const;
int setTypeFlag() const;

FuzzyMember& change_member(const float& a,const float& b,char *str);

vector<float> centroid(const float& a,const float& b) const;

//operators
FuzzyMember& operator =(const FuzzyMember& a);
int operator ==(const FuzzyMember& a) const;
int operator < (const FuzzyMember& a) const;
    //the FuzzyMember is left of a);
int operator > (const FuzzyMember& a) const;
    //the FuzzyMember is right of a);

//friend operator I/O
friend istream& operator >> (istream& is,FuzzyMember& a);
friend ostream& operator << (ostream& os,const FuzzyMember& a);
};
```

Since a membership function is tightly associated with a fuzzy set, we use a membership function and a fuzzy set interchangeably. In the implementation, six functions are adopted as candidate choices for membership functions. These six functions are `left_triangle`, `right_triangle`, `triangle`, `Gaussian`, `sigmoid`, and `reverse_sigmoid`. Other definitions are possible, of course, but the authors have found these to be sufficient for a variety of problems. The definitions of these functions are shown in Figure 8.2. From the definitions, it can be seen that each membership function is determined by three values: the `start_point` x_1, the `end_point` x_2, and the function type (one of the six defined functions shown in Figure 8.2).

The class `FuzzyMember` has three private data members. They are the `float` type variables `startPoint` and `endPoint`, which correspond to the `start_point` x_1 and the `end_point` x_2, respectively, and a `char` pointer `function Type`, which points to a string of characters to specify which of the six possible functions it is. The `functionType` variable records the exact name of the membership function. For example, if the membership function is a triangle function, then the `functionType` points to the string of characters `"Triangle"`. An alternative way is to define an enumeration data type, say `Member_Function_Type`,

Left triangle membership function:

$$f_{left\_triangle} = \begin{cases} 1 & \text{if } x < x_1 \\ \dfrac{x_2 - x}{x_2 - x_1} & \text{if } x_1 \le x \le x_2 \\ 0 & \text{if } x > x_2 \end{cases}$$

Right triangle membership function:

$$f_{right\_triangle} = \begin{cases} 0 & \text{if } x < x_1 \\ \dfrac{x - x_1}{x_2 - x_1} & \text{if } x_1 \le x \le x_2 \\ 1 & \text{if } x > x_2 \end{cases}$$

Triangle membership function:

$$f_{triangle}(x) = \begin{cases} 0 & \text{if } x < x_1 \\ 2\dfrac{x - x_1}{x_2 - x_1} & \text{if } x_1 \le x \le \dfrac{x_2 + x_1}{2} \\ 2\dfrac{x_2 - x}{x_2 - x_1} & \text{if } \dfrac{x_2 + x_1}{2} < x \le x_2 \\ 0 & \text{if } x > x_2 \end{cases}$$

Gaussian membership function:

$$f_{Gaussian}(x) = e^{-0.5y^2} \quad \text{where } y = \dfrac{8(x - x_1)}{x_2 - x_1} - 4$$

Sigmoid membership function:

$$f_{sigmoid}(x) = \dfrac{1}{1 + e^{(-y+6)}} \quad \text{where } y = \dfrac{12(x - x_1)}{x_2 - x_1}$$

Reverse sigmoid membership function:

$$f_{reverse\_sigmoid}(x) = 1 - f_{sigmoid}(x)$$

Figure 8.2 Definitions of the six membership functions.

which includes all six functions, and replace the char `*functionType` with `Member_Function_Type function_type`. This could be a better way from the perspective of good programming practice, but it makes the rule file less readable. The rule file specifies the fuzzy rule system and is read in to define it. The details of the rule file will be explained later.

The public constructors provide ways for declaring `FuzzyMember` variables. For example, `FuzzyMember f1` declares an empty variable; `FuzzyMember f2(1.0,2.5, "Triangle")` declares a `FuzzyMember` variable `f2` that has `startPoint` equal to `1.0`, `endPoint` equal to `2.5`, and the `functionType` is `"Triangle"` function; `FuzzyMember f3(f2)` declares a `FuzzyMember` variable `f3` that is a copy of `f2`.

The public member methods `get_startPoint()`, `get_endPoint()`, and `get_functionType()` are methods to obtain private data member values from outside the class. The method `member_flag(f_v)` determines whether `float` value `f_v` is within the dynamic range of the membership function. It returns `1` if it is; otherwise, it returns `0`. The `setTypeFlag()` method returns which of the six defined functions is the membership function. Magic numbers `1` through `6` have been used to encode the six functions. As mentioned, an enumeration data type `Member_Function_Type` should be defined to eliminate the magic numbers in the source code as much as possible. This is left as an exercise for readers.

The `change_member(const float& a, const float& b, char *str)` public method provides a way to modify the membership function in which the `startPoint` is changed to be `float` value a, the `endPoint` is changed to be b, and the new `functionType` is changed to be `str`.

The public method `memberFunction(const float& f_v)` calculates the membership value with which the input value `f_v` belongs to the fuzzy set. The method is shown in Listing 8.4 for clarification. Please note that the magic

Listing 8.4 Implementation of method `memberFunction()`.

```
float FuzzyMember::memberFunction(const float& a) const
{
    float tmp;

    switch(this->setTypeFlag())
    {
        case 1:
          tmp=LeftTriangle(a,startPoint,endPoint);
          break;
        case 2:
          tmp=RightTriangle(a,startPoint,endPoint);
          break;
        case 3:
          tmp=Triangle(a,startPoint,endPoint);
          break;
        case 4:
```

```
        tmp=Sigmoid(a,startPoint,endPoint);
        break;
    case 5:
        tmp=reverseSigmoid(a,startPoint,endPoint);
        break;
    case 6:
        tmp=Gaussian(a,startPoint,endPoint);
        break;
        default:
        cout<<"unknown fuzzySet type"<<endl;
        exit(1);
    }
    return tmp;
}
```

numbers should be replaced by the corresponding elements included in the data type `Member_Function_Type` if it is defined.

The public method `membership2input(const float& m_v)` returns two values that, when applied to the membership function as input, have their membership values set to be m_v. The method `not(const float& f_v)` returns the membership value with which input f_v does not belong to this fuzzy set. The method `centroid(const float& m_v, const float& s_s)` calculates the `centroid` of the membership function by giving the membership value m_v and step size value s_s. The smaller the step size value is, the more accurate the `centroid` calculation is.

The public overloaded operators =, ==, <, and > provide ways to operate on `FuzzyMember` variables intuitively. For example, f_m1 = f_m2 assigns `FuzzyMember` variable f_m2 to `FuzzyMember` variable f_m1; f_m1 == f_m2 compares f_m1 with f_m2; it returns 1 if f_m1 equals f_m2; otherwise, it returns 0; f_m1 < f_m2 checks whether f_m1 is on the left side of f_m2. If it is, it returns 1; otherwise, it returns 0; accordingly, f_m1 > f_m2 checks whether f_m1 is on the right side of f_m2. For illustration, the definition of one of the public `operators ==` is shown in Listing 8.5.

Listing 8.5 Definition of public operator == in class `FuzzyMember`.

```
int FuzzyMember::operator ==(const FuzzyMember& a) const
{
    int tmp=1;
    if ((&a)==this) return 1;

    MyString str1(functionType);
    MyString str2(a.functionType);
    if (str1==str2)
    {
        if (startPoint !=a.startPoint)
            tmp=0;
```

```
          if (endPoint !=a.endPoint)
              tmp=0;
    }
    else
        return 0;

    return tmp;
}
```

The friend operators << and >> provide ways for input and output of FuzzyMember variables, respectively.

The class *FuzzyVariable* defines a new data type for fuzzy variables, as shown in Listing 8.6. The FuzzyVariable data type has five private data members. The data member setSize(int) records the number of fuzzy sets defined/included

Listing 8.6 Definition of class FuzzyVariable.

```
class FuzzyVariable
{
 private:
   int       setSize;
   float      startPoint;
   float      endpoint;
   char      *variableName;
   FuzzyMember *fuzzySet;

 public:
   //constructors
   FuzzyVariable():setSize(0),startPoint(0),endpoint(0),
           variableName(0),fuzzySet(0){}
   FuzzyVariable(int a,float b,float c);
   FuzzyVariable(int a,float b,float c,char *str);
   FuzzyVariable(const FuzzyVariable& a);

   //destructor
   ~FuzzyVariable(){delete []fuzzySet;delete []variableName;}

   //member functions
   FuzzyVariable& standardVariable();
   char* get_variableName() const {return variableName;}
   int get_setSize() const {return setSize;}
   float get_startPoint() const {return startPoint;}
   float get_endPoint() const {return endPoint;}
   FuzzyVariable& change_setSize(const int& a);
   FuzzyVariable& change_startPoint(const float& a);
   FuzzyVariable& change_endPoint(const float& a);
   FuzzyVariable& change_variableName(char *str);
   char* setMeaning(const int& a,const int& b) const;
   vector<int> setFireFlag(const float& a) const ;
   float output(const float& a,const int& b) const;
   float defuzzifyMax(const int& a,const vector<float>& b) const;
   int defuzzyMax_index(const int& a,const vector<float>& b) const;
```

```
    float defuzzyCentroid_add(const int& a,const vector<float>& b) const;
    float defuzzyCentroid(const int& a,const vector<float>& b) const;

    //operators
    FuzzyMember& operator [] (int i) const;
    FuzzyVariable& operator =(const FuzzyVariable& a);

    //friend operator I/O
    friend istream& operator >> (istream& is,FuzzyVariable& a);
    friend ostream& operator << (ostream& os,const FuzzyVariable& a);
};
```

in this fuzzy variable; data member fuzzySet (FuzzyMember*) is a pointer to the setSize number of fuzzy membership functions; data members startPoint (float) and endPoint (float) define the dynamic range of this fuzzy variable; the variableName (char *) stores the name of the fuzzy variable. It makes much more sense to use the char * data type than that in the FuzzyMember class for data member functionType since the number of possible variable names is unlimited, and actually they can be anything. The purpose of data member variableName is to provide the user with the capability to get a verbal description of the fuzzy rules.

The public constructors provide ways to declare the FuzzyVariable variables. For example, FuzzyVariable f_v1 declares an empty FuzzyVariable type variable f_v1; FuzzyVariable f_v2(3, -1.0, 2.3) declares a FuzzyVariable variable f_v2 that has 3 (setSize) fuzzy sets and its start point and end point values are -1.0 (startPoint) and 2.3 (endPoint), respectively; FuzzyVariable f_v3(3, -1.0, 2.3, "temperature") declares a FuzzyVariable variable f_v3 almost the same as f_v2 except that it has a variable name temperature (variableName); FuzzyVariable f_v4(f_v3) declares a FuzzyVariable variable f_v4 that is a copy of f_v3.

The get_variableName(), get_setSize(), get_startPoint(), and get_endPoint() public methods return the variableName, setSize, startPoint, and endPoint, respectively. The public methods change_setSize(const int& a), change_startPoint (const float& a), change_endPoint(const float& a), and change_variableName (char *str) set the setSize, startPoint, endPoint, and variableName, to new values, respectively.

The public method standardVariable() provides a way to define the setSize number of fuzzy sets over the variable's dynamic range (from startPoint to endPoint) uniformly.

The public method setMeaning() provides a way to get the verbal meaning for a fuzzy set. For example, for a variable with 3 fuzzy sets, the fuzzy sets have verbal descriptions Low, Medium, and High. The purpose of this method is to convert fuzzy rules represented by numbers to fuzzy rules described by verbal descriptions for users. This is explained later. It is not involved in the mathematical operations of the fuzzy rule system.

The public method `setFireFlag(const float& f_v)` checks which fuzzy sets are activated by the input value `f_v`. Since the fuzzy sets are overlapped, more than one fuzzy set for a given input value will generally be activated. That is what makes the fuzzy rule system powerful.

The public method `output(const float& f_i, const int& s_i)` returns the membership value for fuzzy set `s_i` with input value `f_i`.

The `defuzzifyMax()`, `defuzzyCentroid()`, and `defuzzy Centroid_add()` public methods provide three ways to defuzzify. The `defuzzifyMax()` returns the median value of the range of the fuzzy set, the index of which is the largest fuzzy set activated (having membership value > 0). The `defuzzyCentroid()` returns the centroid value of all the fuzzy sets activated. The `defuzzyCentroid_add()` is the same as the `defuzzyCentroid()` except that the overlapped areas are involved in the calculation as many times as the number of activated fuzzy sets overlapped in this area. For details of these three methods, please refer to Chapter 7.

The `operator []` provides a way to get an indexed `FuzzyMember` member from the `FuzzyVariable` variable. For example, if `f_v` is a `FuzzyVariable` type variable with three fuzzy sets, `f_v[1]` returns the second `FuzzyMember` type data `fuzzySet[1]`. The `operator =` assigns one `FuzzyVariable` variable to another `FuzzyVariable` variable.

The friend operators `<<` and `>>` provide ways for getting input and output for `FuzzyVariable` variables, respectively.

The class *FuzzyRule* is shown in Listing 8.7. `FuzzyRule` has seven private data members. The `variableSize (int)` records the number of input

Listing 8.7 Definition of class `FuzzyRule`.

```
class FuzzyRule
{
  private:
    int           variableSize;    //number of variables in a rule
    int           outputSize;      //number of outputs in a rule
    vector<int>   inputSetFlag;    //which set is activated for each variable
    vector<int>   outputSetFlag;   //which set is activated for each variable;


    FuzzyVariable *inputVariable;    //pointers to the input variables
    FuzzyVariable *outputVariable;   //pointers to the output variables
    char          *ruleContent;

  public:
    FuzzyRule():variableSize(0),outputSize(0),ruleContent(0),
              inputVariable(0),outputVariable(0)
```

```
    {
        vector<int> vec;
        inputSetFlag=vec;
        outputSetFlag=vec;
    }
    FuzzyRule(int a,int b,vector<int> c,vector<int> d);
    FuzzyRule(int a,int b,vector<int> c,vector<int> d,char* str);

    FuzzyRule(const FuzzyRule& a);

    ~FuzzyRule(){delete []ruleContent;
    delete []inputVariable;delete []outputVariable;}

    //member functions
    int get_variableSize() const {return variableSize;}
    int get_outputSize() const {return outputSize;}
    vector<int> get_inputSetFlag()const {return inputSetFlag;}
    vector<int> get_outputSetFlag() const {return outputSetFlag;}
    char* get_ruleContent() const {return ruleContent;}

    FuzzyRule& change_inputSetFlag(const vector<int>& a);
    FuzzyRule& change_outputSetFlag(const vector<int>& a);
    FuzzyRule& change_variableSize(const int& a);
    FuzzyRule& change_outputSize(const int& a);
    FuzzyRule& change_ruleContent(char* str);
    FuzzyRule& form_ruleContent();

    FuzzyRule& change_outputVariable(const FuzzyVariable& a,const int& b);
        //both outputVariable change to a
    int checkRuleActive(const vector<float>& a) const;
        //check whether this rule is activated via input a or not
    vector<float> FuzzyOutput(const vector<float>& a) const;
        //calculate the fuzzy output vector
    vector<float> FuzzyOutput_average(const vector<float>& a) const;
    FuzzyVariable& get_outputVariable(const int& a) const;
    vector<int> formRange(const int& a) const;
        //a: maximum rules; get possible maximum fuzzy set no. for each
                variable

    //operator
    FuzzyVariable& operator [] (int I) const;
    FuzzyRule& operator =(const FuzzyRule& a);

    //I/O operators
    friend istream& operator >>(istream& is, FuzzyRule& a);
    friend ostream& operator <<(ostream& os,const FuzzyRule& a);
};
```

variables in the antecedent (if) part of a fuzzy rule; the outputSize (int) records the number of output variables in the consequent (then) part of a fuzzy rule; the inputVariable (FuzzyVariable*) is a pointer pointing to the variableSize number of input fuzzy variables; the outputVariable

(FuzzyVariable*) is a pointer pointing to the outputSize number of output fuzzy variables; the inputSetFlag (vector<int>) records which fuzzy set for each input fuzzy variable is involved in the fuzzy rule.

For example, inputSetFlag[0] = 1 means that the first fuzzy set of the first input variable is involved in this rule. Assume that the first variable temperature has three fuzzy sets (Low, Medium, and High); then the fuzzy rule involved could be if temperature is Low,..., ..., then .... The outputSetFlag records which fuzzy set for each output fuzzy variable has been activated if the fuzzy rule is fired by the current input; the ruleContent(char*), like variableName in FuzzyVariable, is used to record the fuzzy rule in words instead of numbers to enhance the readability of fuzzy rules.

The public constructors provide ways to declare the FuzzyRule variables. For example, assume that the fuzzy rule has two inputs and one output and each variable has three fuzzy sets (Low, Medium, and High). Further assume that vec_1 is a vector<int> type vector with length 2 and the two elements are 1 (Low) and 2 (Medium); vect_2 is also a vector<int> type vector with length 1 and the one element is 3 (High). Then FuzzyRule f_r1 declares an empty FuzzyRule variable f_r1; FuzzyRule f_r2(2, 1, vec_1, vec_2) declares a FuzzyRule variable f_r2 and this rule, in verbal description, is if input_1 is Low, input_2 is Medium, then output_1 is High. The FuzzyRule f_r3(f_r2) declares a FuzzyRule variable f_r3 that is a copy of variable f_r2.

The get_variableSize(), get_outputSize(), get_inputSetFlag(), get_outputSetFlag(), and get_ruleContent() public methods provide ways to obtain variableSize, outputSize, inputSetFlag, outputSetFlag, and ruleContent, respectively, from outside the FuzzyRule class. The public methods change_variableSize(), change_ outputSize(), change_inputSetFlag(), change_output SetFlag(), and change_ruleContent() provide ways to change variableSize, outputSize, inputSetFlag, outputSetFlag, and ruleContent, respectively, from outside the FuzzyRule class. The public method form_ruleContent() is used to form the verbal description (ruleContent) of the fuzzy rule from its vector<int> inputSetFlag, outputSetFlag. The public method get_ outputVariable(const int& idx) returns the outputVariable[idx] to provide a way to obtain the output variable from outside the class.

The checkRuleActive(const vector<float>& vec_in) public method checks whether the fuzzy rule is fired by the input vec_in. For the fuzzy set of each variable involved in this rule, it checks to see whether this fuzzy set is activated by the corresponding input. More than one fuzzy set can be activated, but we only need to check whether the fuzzy set involved in the rule is activated. If the variable `i` is not involved in the rule (`inputSetFlag[i]==0`), then no check is required for this variable. The rule is fired if all the variables involved in the rule are activated by the input. The method returns `1` if the rule is fired; otherwise, it returns `0`. For clarification, this method is shown in Listing 8.8.

Listing 8.8 Implementation of method `checkRuleActive()` in class `FuzzyRule`.

```
int FuzzyRule::checkRuleActive(const vector<float>& a) const
{//check whether this has been activated
    assert(a.len()==variableSize);

    vector<int>* vec;
    vec= new vector<int>[variableSize];

    int sum=0;
    for (int i=0;i<variableSize;i++)
    {
        if (inputSetFlag[i]==0)
            sum++;
        else
        {
            vec[i]=inputVariable[i].setFireFlag(a[i]);
            int ind=abs(inputSetFlag[i])-1;
            if (vec[i][ind]==1)
                sum++;
        }
    }

    delete []vec;
    if (sum==variableSize)
        return 1;

    else
        return 0;
}
```

The public methods `FuzzyOutput(const vector<float>& a)` and `FuzzyOutput_average(const vector<float>& a)` provide ways to obtain the membership values for the output variables when input `a` is presented to the rule. The `FuzzyOutput()` method takes the minimum values of the membership values of all activated fuzzy variables as the activation strength of its `if` part, and the `FuzzyOutput_average()` method takes the average of the membership values of all activated fuzzy variables as the activation strength of its `if` part. If an output variable has a modifier `not` before it, its membership value is calculated by subtracting the activation strength from `1.0`; otherwise, its membership value is equal to the activation strength. For clarification, the method `FuzzyOutput()` is shown in Listing 8.9.

Listing 8.9 Implementation of method `FuzzyOutput()` in class `FuzzyRule`.

```cpp
vector<float> FuzzyRule::FuzzyOutput(const vector<float>& a) const
{
    //check the input dimension
    assert(a.len()==variableSize);
    //check whether the rule is activated
    if (checkRuleActive(a) !=1)
    {
        fprintf(stderr,"try to use unactivated rule\n");
        exit(1);
    }
    float min=1.0,tmp;
    for (int i=0;i<variableSize;i++)
    {
        if (inputSetFlag[i]!=0)
        {
            tmp=inputVariable[i].output(a[i],inputSetFlag[i]);
            if (min>tmp)
                min=tmp;           //get the minimum value
        }
    }
    vector<float> tmpout(outputSize);
    for (i=0;i<outputSize;i++)
    {
        if (outputSetFlag[i] ==0)
            tmpout[i]=0.0;
        else
        {
            if (outputSetFlag[i]>0)
                tmpout[i]=min;
            else
            {
                if (min>=0.9999)
                    tmpout[i]=0.0001;
                else
                    tmpout[i]=1-min;
            }
        }
    }
    return tmpout;
}
```

The public operator `[]` provides a way to return an indexed input fuzzy variable. For example, `f_r3[1]` returns the second input `FuzzyVariable`, `inputVariable[1]` of the `FuzzyRule` variable `f_r3`. The public operator `=` provides a way to copy one `FuzzyRule` variable to another `FuzzyRule` variable. The friend operators `<<` and `>>` provide ways to input and output `FuzzyRule` variables, respectively.

The class *FuzzyRuleSet* is shown in Listing 8.10. It has two private data members. The member `ruleSetSize` (int) stores the number of fuzzy rules in the fuzzy rule set of the fuzzy rule system. The member `rules` (`FuzzyRule*`) is a pointer pointing to the set of fuzzy rules.

Listing 8.10 Definition of class `FuzzyRuleSet`.

```
class FuzzyRuleSet
{
  private:
    int          ruleSetSize;   //how many rules in the set
    FuzzyRule *rules;           //pointers to the fuzzy rule set

  public:
    FuzzyRuleSet():ruleSetSize(0),rules(0) {}
    FuzzyRuleSet(int a);
    FuzzyRuleSet(int a, FuzzyRule *b);
    FuzzyRuleSet(const FuzzyRuleSet& a);

    ~FuzzyRuleSet() {delete []rules;}

    //member functions
    int get_ruleSetSize() const {return ruleSetSize;}
    FuzzyRuleSet& addRuleB(const FuzzyRule& a,const int& b);
          //add rule a at position b
    FuzzyRuleSet& addRule(const FuzzyRule& a);
          //add rule a at the end of set
    FuzzyRuleSet& deleteRule(const int& a);
          //delete the 'a'th rule
    vector< vector<float> > fuzzyOutputValue_max(const vector<float>& a,
                          const int& b) const;
    vector< vector<float> > fuzzyOutputValue_add(const vector<float>& a,
                          const int& b) const;
            //a:input vector,
            //b: mode for antecedent-0:min 1:aver,
    vector<float> defuzzify(const vector< vector<float> >& a,
                          const int& b) const;
            //b: mode for defuzzyfy-0:max 1:centroid without overlap
            //2: with overlap;
            //a: fuzzy output values
    vector<float> output(const vector<float>& a, const int& b,
                          const int& c, const int& d) const;
            //a: input  b:add/max c:min/aver d:max/without/with overlap
            //return the value after defuzzify

    vector<float> output_new(const vector<float>& a, const int& b,
                    const int& c,const int& d) const;

    FuzzyVariable& get_outputVariable(const int& a) const;

    int checkRuleSetFired(const vector<float>& a) const;
            //check this rule set is fired or not due to 'a'

    //operators
    FuzzyRule& operator [](int I) const;
    FuzzyRuleSet& operator =(const FuzzyRuleSet& a);

    //I/O operators
```

```
        friend istream& operator>>(istream& is, FuzzyRuleSet& a);
        friend ostream& operator<<(ostream& os, const FuzzyRuleSet& a);
};
```

The public constructors provide ways to declare `FuzzyRuleSet` variables. For example, `FuzzyRuleSet f_r_s1` declares an empty fuzzy rule set; `FuzzyRuleSet f_r_s2(3, f_r)` declares a fuzzy rule set with three fuzzy rules, and the three fuzzy rules are obtained from the `FuzzyRule` pointer `f_r`, which points to a memory space where it has more than three `FuzzyRule` data stored. `FuzzyRuleSet f_r_s3(f_r_s2)` declares a `FuzzyRuleSet` variable `f_r_s3` that is a copy of variable `f_r_s2`.

The public method `get_ruleSet_Size()` provides an interface to obtain the number of rules in the rule set from outside the class.

The public method `addRule(const FuzzyRule& f_r)` adds a new `FuzzyRule f_r` at the end of the fuzzy rule set. The public method `addRuleB (const FuzzyRule& f_r, const int& idx)` inserts a new `FuzzyRule f_r` at position `idx`, which must be within the range `[0, ruleSetSize]`. The public method `deleteRule(const int& idx)` deletes the fuzzy rule `idx` from the fuzzy rule set.

The public method `checkRuleSetFired(const vector<float>& a)` returns the number of rules fired in the fuzzy rule set when presented with input a.

The operator `[]` provides a way to obtain an indexed fuzzy rule from the fuzzy rule set. For example, `rules[2]` returns the third rule in the rule set. The operator = assigns one `FuzzyRuleSet` variable to another `FuzzyRuleSet` variable.

The public methods `vector< vector<float> > fuzzyOutputValue_max(const vector<float>& in, const int& a_s)` and `vector < vector<float> > fuzzyOutputValue_add (const vector<float>& in, const int& a_s)` return the output membership values of all output variables. The float vector `in` is the input to the fuzzy rule system, and the integer `a_s` indicates which method is used to calculate the activation strength value of the antecedent part. If `a_s` is 0, `FuzzyOutput()` defined in the `FuzzyRule` class (minimum approach) is called; if `a_s` is 1 `FuzzyOutput_average` defined in the `FuzzyRule` class (average approach) is called.

An enumeration data type can be defined to avoid magic numbers with respect to `a_s`. This is left as an exercise for the reader. The `fuzzyOutputValue_max()` calculates the output values by taking maximum activation strength out of all fired fuzzy rules for each fuzzy variable. The method `fuzzyOutputValue_add()` calculates the output values by adding together the activation strength values of all fired rules for each variable. If the summation is greater than 1, then it is assigned to

be 1 since membership values are limited to [0,1]. For clarification, the method
fuzzyOutputValue_max() is shown in Listing 8.11.

Listing 8.11 Implementation of method fuzzyOutputValue_max() in class
FuzzyRuleSet.

```
Vector< vector<float> >
FuzzyRuleSet::fuzzyOutputValue_max(const vector<float>& a,
       const int& b) const
{
    if (a.len() !=rules[0].get_variableSize())
    {
        fprintf(stderr,"input dim doesn't match
          the inputVariable no. of the rule");
        exit(1);
    }
    int outVarDim=rules[0].get_outputSize();
    vector< vector<float> > result(outVarDim);
    vector<int> varDim(outVarDim);
    for (int i=0;i<outVarDim;i++)
    {
        varDim[i]=rules[0].get_outputVariable(i).get_setSize();
        result[i].changeSize(varDim[i]);
    }

    //initialization of result
    for (i=0;i<outVarDim;i++)
        for (int j=0;j<varDim[i];j++)
            result[i][j]=0;

    vector<float> tmpres(outVarDim);
    for (i=0;i<ruleSetSize;i++)
    {
        int ter=rules[i].checkRuleActive(a);
        if (ter==1)
        {
            vector<int> tmpvec=rules[i].get_outputSetFlag();
            if (b==1)
                tmpres=rules[i].FuzzyOutput_average(a);
            else
                tmpres=rules[i].FuzzyOutput(a);

            for (int j=0;j<outVarDim;j++)
            {
                if (tmpvec[j] !=0)
                    result[j][abs(tmpvec[j])-1] =
                        max(result[j][abs(tmpvec[j])-1],tmpres[j]);
            }
        }
    }
    return result;
}
```

The `vector<float> defuzzify(const vector< vector<float> > & m_o, const int& d_a)` public method provides a way to defuzzify output variables. The variable `m_o` is the returned variable from `fuzzyOutputValue_max()` or `fuzzyOutputValue_add()`. The integer `d_a` indicates which defuzzification approach described in the `FuzzyVariable` class is called. For clarification, the `defuzzify()` method is shown in Listing 8.12.

Listing 8.12 Implementation of method `defuzzify()` in class `FuzzyRuleSet`.

```
vector<float>
FuzzyRuleSet::defuzzify(const vector< vector<float> >& a,
                const int& b) const
{
    //get output variables in a rule
    int outVarDim=rules[0].get_outputSize();
    vector<float> tmp(outVarDim);
    vector<int> varDim(outVarDim);

    for (int i=0;i<outVarDim;i++)
    {
        //fuzzy set no. in output variable i
        varDim[i]=this->get_outputVariable(i).get_setSize();
        //defuzzify for output variable i

        if (b==0)
            tmp[i]=this->get_outputVariable(i).defuzzifyMax
                (varDim[i],a[i]);
        else if (b==1)
            tmp[i]=this->get_outputVariable(i).defuzzyCentroid
                (varDim[i],a[i]);
        else
            tmp[i]=this->get_outputVariable(i).
                defuzzyCentroid_add(varDim[i],a[i]);
    }
    return tmp;
}
```

The method `vector<float> output(const vector<float>& a, const int& b, const int& c, const int& d)` provides a one-step approach to calculate the output from the input. This method combines the methods discussed earlier to obtain the output from the input within one method, where vector `a` is the input, integer `b` is the selection of the approaches for calculating activation strength, integer `c` is the selection of the way to calculate the membership values for the output variables, and integer `d` is the choice for defuzzifying the output variables to obtain the output values for each output variable. As mentioned, it would be better if integers `b`, `c`, and `d` had enumeration data types defined for them to avoid using the magic numbers in the source code. For clarification, Listing 8.13 shows the `output()` method in the `FuzzyRuleSet` class.

Listing 8.13 Implementation of method `output ()` in class `FuzzyRuleSet`.

```
vector<float> FuzzyRuleSet::output(const vector<float>& a, const int& b,
            const int& c,const int& d) const
{            //a: input  b:add/max c:min/aver d:max/without/with overlap
             // return the value after defuzzify
    if (a.len() !=rules[0].get_variableSize())
    {
        fprintf(stderr,"input dim doesn't match
            the inputVariable no. of the rule");
        exit(1);
    }

    int outVarDim=rules[0].get_outputSize();
       //outputVariable no.in rules
    vector< vector<float> > result(outVarDim);

    vector<int> varDim(outVarDim);

    for (int i=0;i<outVarDim;i++)
    {
        varDim[i]=rules[0].get_outputVariable(i).get_setSize();
        result[i].changeSize(varDim[i]);
    } //allocate memory for result

    if (b==1)
        result=this->fuzzyOutputValue_max(a,c);
    else
        result= this->fuzzyOutputValue_add(a,c);

    vector<float> tmp(outVarDim);
    tmp=this->defuzzify(result,d);

    return tmp;
}
```

The friend operators << and >> provide mechanisms for input and output, respectively, of `FuzzyRuleSet` variables. The methods are shown in Listing 8.14 for clarification. By using the operators << and >>, the fuzzy rule set can be read in from a rule file or written to a rule file, respectively. These operations will be made more clear in the discussion of the `main ()` function, shown in Listing 8.15.

Listing 8.14 Definition of operators << and >> in `FuzzyRuleSet` class.

```
istream& operator>>(istream& is, FuzzyRuleSet& a)
{
    is>>a.ruleSetSize;
    if (a.rules !=0)
        delete []a.rules;
    a.rules =new FuzzyRule[a.ruleSetSize];
    is>>a.rules[0];
    vector<int> vecin(a.rules[0].get_variableSize());
    vector<int> vecout(a.rules[0].get_outputSize());
```

```
    for (int i=1;i<a.ruleSetSize;i++)
    {
        a.rules[i]=a.rules[0];
        is>>vecin;
        a.rules[i].change_inputSetFlag(vecin);
        is>>vecout;
        a.rules[i].change_outputSetFlag(vecout);
        a.rules[i].form_ruleContent();
    }
    return is;
}

ostream& operator<<(ostream& os, const FuzzyRuleSet& a)
{
    assert(a.ruleSetSize !=0);
    os<<a.ruleSetSize<<endl;
    os<<a[0];

    for (int i=1;i<a.ruleSetSize;i++)
        os<<(a[i].get_inputSetFlag()|a[i].get_outputSetFlag());
    return os;
}
```

Listing 8.15 Implementation of main().

```
void main(int argc,char *argv[])
{
    extern void fl(char *);
    if (argc !=2)
    {
        fprintf(stderr,"usuage: fl run_file_name\n");
        exit(1);
    }
    fl(argv[1]);
}
```

Next, we discuss the main() and fl() routines. The main() routine does nothing except call the fl() routine shown in Listing 8.16. In the fl() routine, first the read_fl_runfile() routine, shown in Listing 8.17, is called to read in the following parameters: the name of file where the fuzzy rules are stored (ruleInName), the name of file where the data patterns to be classified are stored

Listing 8.16 Implementation of fl().

```
void fl (char *dataFile)
{
    read_fl_runfile(dataFile);
    read_fl_rulefile();
    write_fl_rules();
```

```
ifstream dFile;
dFile.open(dataFileName,ios::in);
if (!dFile)
{
    cerr<<"can't open file "<<dataFileName<<" for input"<<endl;
    exit(1);
}

int indim,outdim; //input dim and output dim
dFile>>indim>>outdim;
vector<float> invec(indim);
vector<int>   outvec(outdim);
vector<int>   classN(outdim);  //store class no. for each output
dFile>>classN;

int outVarDim=ruleSet[0].get_outputSize();
if (outdim !=outVarDim)
{
    cout<<"dim of data outputs isn't equal to dim of
            output variables in rules"<<endl;
    exit(1);
}

ofstream rFile;
rFile.open(resultFileName,ios::out);
if (!rFile)
{
    cerr<<"can't open file " <<resultFileName<< " for output\n"<<endl;
    exit(1);
}

rFile<<"index\t"<<"Wrong?\t"<<"Target\t"<<"Obtained"<<endl;

int in_order=0;
int misclassify=0;
vector<int> cla(outVarDim);
vector<float> tmp(outVarDim);

while (dFile>>invec)
{
    dFile>>outvec;
    in_order++;
    rFile<<in_order<<"\t";
    if (ruleSet.checkRuleSetFired(invec)==1)
    {
        tmp=ruleSet.output(invec,ruleEffectFlag,fuzzyFlag,defuzzyFlag);

        //get output class
        for (int idx=0;idx<outVarDim;idx++)
                cla[idx]=(int)(tmp[idx]*classN[idx]);

        //output data dim equal to outputVariable dim
        if (cla !=outvec)
        {
            rFile<<"wrong\t";
            misclassify++;
        }
```

```
                else
                    rFile<<"\t";

                rFile<<(outvec|cla);
        }
        else
        {
            rFile<<"rule set not fired"<<endl;
            misclassify++;
        }
    }
    dFile.close();

    rFile<<"total misclassification is  :"<<misclassify<<endl;
    rFile.close();
}
```

Listing 8.17 Implementation of read_fl_runfile().

```
static void read_fl_runfile (char *dataFile)
{
    int true;
    char Msg[NAME_MAX];
    strcpy(Msg,"edit ");
    strcat(Msg,dataFile);

    ifstream runFile;
    do
    {
        runFile.open(dataFile,ios::in);
        if (!runFile)
        {
            cerr<<"can't open file "<<dataFile<<" for input"<<endl;
            exit(1);
        }
        runFile>>ruleInName>>dataFileName>>ruleName>>resultFileName;
        runFile>>fuzzyFlag>>defuzzyFlag>>ruleEffectFlag;
        runFile.close();
        cout<<ruleInName<<endl;
        cout<<dataFileName<<endl;
        cout<<ruleName<<endl;
        cout<<resultFileName<<endl;
        cout<<fuzzyFlag<<"  0:minimum  1:average"<<endl;
        cout<<defuzzyFlag<<" 0:maximum  1:without overlap 2:with
                overlap"<<endl;
        cout<<ruleEffectFlag<<
                "1: maximum of output values from each rule 0:add"<<endl;
        cout<<" (C)ontinue, (Q)uit, (M)odify runfile ";
        char condition;
        cin>>condition;
        switch(condition)
        {
            case 'c': true=0;
```

```
                    break;
            case 'C': true=0;
                break;
            case 'q': exit(1);
            case 'Q': exit(1);
            case 'm': true=1;
                system(Msg);
                break;
            case 'M': true=1;
                system(Msg);
                break;
            default:
                true=1;
                break;
        }
    } while (true==1);
}
```

(dataFileName), the name of file where the verbal descriptions of the fuzzy rules are written (ruleName), the name of file where the classification results will be stored (resultFileName), the choice of reasoning approaches (fuzzyFlag), the choice of defuzzification approaches (defuzzyFlag), and the choice of rule output combination approaches (ruleEffectFlag). The do-while loop is for the user to view and modify the contents of the run file.

Second, the read_fl_rulefile() routine, shown in Listing 8.18, is called to read in the fuzzy rule set from the rule file (ruleInName). It is as simple as iFile>>ruleSet, where iFile is an object of ifstream class and ruleSet is an object of FuzzyRuleSet class.

Then the write_fl_rules() routine, shown in Listing 8.19, is called to generate a verbal description of the fuzzy rule set and write the verbal rules to an output file (ruleName).

Listing 8.18 Implementation of read_fl_rulefile().

```
static void read_fl_rulefile (void)
{
    // FuzzyRule
    ifstream iFile;
    iFile.open(ruleInName,ios::in);
    if (!iFile)
    {
        cerr<<"can't open file "<<ruleInName<<" for input"<<endl;
        exit(1);
    }
    iFile>>ruleSet;
    iFile.close();
}
```

Listing 8.19 Implementation of `write_fl_rules()`.

```
static void write_fl_rules (void)
{
    //output formed rules
    ofstream oFile;
    oFile.open(ruleName,ios::out);
    if (!oFile)
    {
        cerr<<"can't open file "<<ruleName<<" for output"<<endl;
        exit(1);
    }
    for (int i=0;i<ruleSet.get_ruleSetSize();i++)
        oFile<<i<<"th rule: "<<ruleSet[i].get_ruleContent()<<endl;
    oFile.close();
}
```

Finally, each input/output pattern pair is read in. The input `invec` is then checked to see what can be fired within the rule set by performing the `ruleSet.checkRuleSetFired(invec)` routine. If the rule set is fired, then the output of the fuzzy rules under the input `invec` is obtained by calling the `ruleSet.output(invec,ruleEffectFlag,fuzzyFlag,defuzzyFlag)` routine. The output values are then converted to the class to which each output variable belongs. The classification result is finally recorded into an output file (`resultFileName`). This process is repeated until all the input/output pairs in the data pattern file have been read in and classified.

All the routines discussed are here for clarification. (See Listings 8.15, 8.16, 8.17, 8.18, and 8.19.)

Running the Fuzzy Rule System

The fuzzy rule system implementation is a flexible tool that is capable of solving a wide variety of classification and diagnostic problems. It utilizes user-defined triangular and/or nonlinear membership functions. The executable code for the system is in the file `fl.exe`, and the specifications of files and other parameters appear in a run file, `filename.run`. To run the system, at the system prompt type `fl filename.run`, making sure that the run file is in the same directory as the executable.

To begin to understand how the system functions, we examine the contents of the run file. We use the Iris dataset, described at the beginning of Chapter 6 (Anderson 1935; Fisher 1936). A typical run file for the Iris dataset example is as follows:

```
iris.rul
iris.dat
rules.out
```

```
results.out
1
1
0
```

Two of the files contain input information for the system and must be present at run time. They are `iris.rul` and `iris.dat`. Two files are output at the end of a run. They are `rules.out` and `results.out`. Following the list of files are three input parameters: The first specifies how the antecedents of rules are handled, and the second and third affect how defuzzification is accomplished.

The first input file (the second file in the list) is `iris.dat`, the input data file. A fuzzy rule system can be developed to classify or diagnose practically any data. The data file contains values for input variables and associated output variable(s). The first line of the data file contains the number of input variables (4) and the number of output variables (1) in the data file followed by the number of classes (3) to which the data can belong. Any number of input and output variables can be used. The remaining lines of the data file contain input/output patterns: Inputs followed by one or more outputs. Each output specifies the classification or diagnosis for the corresponding inputs. This file is similar to the data files used by the neural networks discussed earlier in this book except that here only one output variable specifies the class to which this data pattern belongs. Following are the first four lines of the fuzzy logic system data file (on the book's web site) for the Iris dataset. The output variable in this file is 0, 1, or 2, which, depending on the Iris class, indicates that this data pattern belongs to class 1, 2, or 3, respectively.

```
4 1 3
0.6375 0.4375 0.1750 0.0250 0
0.8750 0.4000 0.5875 0.1750 1
0.7875 0.4125 0.7500 0.3125 2
...
```

The first file listed in the run file list, `iris.rul`, called the "rules file," contains the fuzzy rules and the definitions for the fuzzy membership functions for both the input and output variables. It is necessary to understand the contents of the rules file thoroughly in order to use the fuzzy rule system successfully. Conversely, knowing all about the rules file provides an understanding of how the fuzzy rule system works. Because of its central importance to the fuzzy rule system, the complete listing of a rules file for classifying the Iris dataset appears as Listing 8.20.

Listing 8.20 Example of a rules file for the fuzzy rule system.

```
16
4 1

sepalLength 3 0.4 1.0
        reverseSigmoid 0.4 0.8
        Gaussian 0.4 1.0
```

```
        Sigmoid 0.6 1.0

sepalWidth 3 0.0 0.6
        leftTriangle 0.0 0.3
        Triangle 0.15 0.45
        rightTriangle 0.3 0.6

petalLength 3 0.0 1.0
        leftTriangle 0.0 0.4
        Triangle 0.2 0.7
        rightTriangle 0.4 1.0

petalWidth 3 0.0 0.4
        leftTriangle 0.0 0.2
        Triangle 0.1 0.3
        rightTriangle 0.2 0.4

output 3 0.0 1.0
        reverseSigmoid 0.0 0.4
        Gaussian 0.3 0.7
        rightTriangle 0.5 1.0

2   1   2   2   1
3   3   3   3   3
1   3   1   1   1
1   1   2   2   3
2   1   3   3   3
1   3   1   1   1
2   2   3   3   2
3   1   3   3   3
1   3   1   1   1
3   2   3   2   2
2   1   2   2   2
1   2   1   1   1
2   2   3   3   3
3   2   3   3   3
1   1   1   1   1
1   1   2   2   2
```

The first line in the rules file contains the number of rules listed in the file, in this case 16. The next line contains the number of input fuzzy variables followed by the number of output fuzzy variables, in this case 4 and 1, respectively. Note that there is only one fuzzy output variable, while there are three classifications in the dataset. Each classification has been mapped to one fuzzy set on the domain of the output variable.

Next, the fuzzy sets for all input and output variables are defined. In accordance with the second line of the rules file, we define 4 input and 1 output fuzzy variable. The next line, sepalLength 3 0.4 1.0, defines the first fuzzy input variable's name as *sepalLength*, specifies the variable's domain to have three fuzzy sets, and defines the variable's dynamic range (domain) to be 0.4 to 1.0. The variable name is chosen by the user, as is the number of fuzzy sets in the variable's domain.

The numbers 0.4 and 1.0 define the dynamic range of the input variable; they specify where the leftmost fuzzy membership function assumes a value of 1 and the rightmost assumes a value of 1, respectively. They are generally equal to (and at least related to) the variable's minimum and maximum values, respectively, in the dataset. Because three fuzzy sets have been specified, the next three lines in the rules file each define one fuzzy set for the variable sepalLength.

Two main kinds of membership function are available: nonlinear and linear. The variable sepalLength is represented by the nonlinear fuzzy membership functions reverseSigmoid, Gaussian, and Sigmoid (it could also be represented by linear functions).

The second fuzzy input variable is named sepalWidth and also has three fuzzy membership functions specified. Note that sepal width's dynamic range is from 0.0 to 0.6. This time, the family of linear membership functions is specified.

From Listing 8.20, we can see that the other two fuzzy input variables, petalLength and petalWidth, use three linear (triangular) membership functions each, defined over their respective dynamic ranges. Depending on the problem being solved, the number of membership functions defined for each variable can vary, and all variables do not have to have the same number of functions. For example, for some particular problem, one input variable might have three fuzzy membership functions defined over its domain, while another has five, and still another has seven.

We are now ready to examine the output of our fuzzy rule system. From the rules file, we see that the output variable is named output and is defined by three fuzzy membership functions over the domain [0,1]. We have thus chosen, in this case, to represent each of the three output classifications with one fuzzy membership function (a fuzzy set) over the domain of one output variable. It can be seen from the definitions of the three fuzzy sets constituting the output that we can "mix and match" linear and nonlinear fuzzy membership functions. The membership functions representing classes 1 and 2 are nonlinear (reverse sigmoid and Gaussian, respectively), while class 3 is represented by a linear membership function (right triangle).

The next line, 2 1 2 2 1, is the first rule in the fuzzy rule set. Based on the fuzzy set definitions, we see that the rule states, "If sepal length is medium and sepal width is low and petal length is medium and petal width is medium, then output is low (output is class 1 of 3)." Finally, the remaining fuzzy rules are listed. Their meanings are also clear from the definitions listed above them. In this case, an additional 15 rules are listed. The maximum absolute value that any rule variable can assume is the number of fuzzy membership functions defined over that variable's domain.

Note that there are three occurrences of the same rule: 1 3 1 1 1 (if sepal length is low and sepal width is high and petal length is low and petal width is low, then class is low: class 1 of 3). The reason for this is explained later in the discussion of the Iris dataset application. Also note that there are three sets of rules with "conflicts." One example is rule 1: 2 1 2 2 1, and rule 11: 2 1 2 2 2. These two rules have the same antecedents but different consequents. For the same conditions, rule 1 says the output class is low (class 1 of 3), while rule 11 says that it is medium (class 2 of 3). Such conflicts are "legal" in fuzzy rule systems; they are, in fact, not unusual. Such conflicts, of course, are not permissible in traditional rule systems.

In the case of multiple occurrences of the same rule, all but one can be eliminated. This is permissible because of the kinds of defuzzification defined with this rule system. Even with the overlap version of defuzzification selected, overlap *within* a membership function is ignored. By eliminating two of the three 1 3 1 1 1 rules, we are left with 14 rules.

It is acceptable to use a zero (0) at any antecedent location in a rule. A zero signifies that the corresponding antecedent is ignored. Some situations may call for writing a rule with a 0 at one or more locations. Another way to use a 0 is illustrated by the rule set in Listing 8.20. Rules 3, 12, and 15 are 1 3 1 1 1, 1 2 1 1 1, and 1 1 1 1 1, respectively. These three rules can be collapsed into one rule: 1 0 1 1 1. Likewise, rules 2, 8, and 14 can be collapsed into 3 0 3 3 3. We are now left with only the 10 rules in Listing 8.21.

Listing 8.21 Final minimal rule set for Iris dataset classification.

```
2  1  2  2  1
3  0  3  3  3
1  0  1  1  1
1  1  2  2  3
2  1  3  3  3
2  2  3  3  2
3  2  3  2  2
2  1  2  2  2
2  2  3  3  3
1  1  2  2  2
```

It is also acceptable to use negative integers in rules. Thus, −2 would mean "not medium" in this case. Negative numbers can be used for either antecedents or consequents. Thus, 1 −2 3 2 −1 would represent "If low and not medium and high and medium, then not low." Care should be exercised when collapsing rules, however. It might be tempting to collapse 1 1 2 2 2 and 1 1 2 2 3 into 1 1 2 2 −1, but this would not give the same results because of the way negatives are defuzzified. A negative such as −2 (not 2) is defuzzified as the fuzzy complement: $\mu_x(2) = 1 - \mu_x(-2)$.

It is possible to have more than one output fuzzy variable. The fuzzy sets for each output variable, of course, must be defined in the rules file. Each rule must specify the antecedents and consequents for each input and output variable. So, if we have four fuzzy input variables and two fuzzy output variables, a rule might be 1 2 3 2 0 1. This would mean that we "don't care" about the first of the two outputs, but the rule fires the fuzzy set corresponding to "1" in the second output. A rule can fire more than one output simultaneously, but the defuzzification of each output variable is done independently in this implementation. Rules 1 2 3 2 0 1 and 1 2 3 2 1 0 can thus be collapsed into the single rule 1 2 3 2 1 1.

We now discuss the output files. Two of the filenames in the run file refer to output files that are written on completion of a program run. The third file listed in the run file, rules.out, is the *rule output* file, which contains a list of the rules in words. For example, the fifth rule, which is listed in the rules file as 2 1 3 3 3, is written out in the rule output file as if_sepalLength_is_Medium_and_ sepalWidth_is_Low_and_petalLength_is_High_and_petalWidth_ is_High_then_output_is_High.

It is easier to write the rules using numbers (typographical errors are much less likely), but it is helpful to have a written listing of the rules so that they can be checked for accuracy.

The other output file, the *results file* results.out, contains a listing of the correct classifications for the input patterns in the data file, with a listing of the classification made by the fuzzy rule system. Errors are identified, and an error total appears at the end of the list.

Three input parameters follow the list of files in the run file. The first specifies how the antecedents of rules are handled, and the second and third specify how defuzzification is to be done.

The first input parameter is the *averaging flag*. When it is set to 0, the AND statements in the antecedents are treated as is usual in fuzzy logic systems: The minimum membership value is output. When the averaging flag is set to 1, the *average* of the membership values ANDed together is output. In the case of the Iris dataset example, the average of the four fuzzy membership values is used.

The second input parameter is the *defuzzification parameter*. It can take one of three possible values: 0, 1, or 2. When it is 0, the centroid of the fuzzy membership function with the highest value is used for the defuzzified output scalar. When it is 1, the "no overlap" method of defuzzification is used. When it is 2, the overlap of different membership functions is included in the centroid calculation (the overlap within a membership function is not considered). See Chapter 7 for more information on defuzzification.

The third input parameter is the *summation flag*. Its value specifies how output fuzzy membership values are formed *prior to defuzzification*. In other words, this flag takes effect before the defuzzification parameter, discussed previously, does. If the summation flag is set to 1, and a number of rules fire the same output fuzzy membership function, the *maximum value* caused by any *one* rule is selected as the value to be passed on to the defuzzification step. For example, if a triangular membership function is fired and the maximum value arising from any single rule is 0.5, then the triangular function is truncated at the 0.5 level, and the resulting trapezoidal shape participates in defuzzification.

If the summation flag is set to 0, the sum of *all* values caused by the rules firing (up to a maximum summed value of 1) is computed as the value to be passed to defuzzification. For example, if three rules fire that activate a particular output fuzzy membership function with the values of 0.3, 0.5, and 0.1, respectively, then the membership value established for defuzzification is 0.5 if the summation flag is 1 and 0.9 if the flag is set to 0. As another example, if three rules fire, each activating a certain output fuzzy membership function at the 0.5 level, then its membership value is set to 0 .5 if the flag is set to 1. If the flag is set to 0, the membership value is set to 1.

It can be seen that this option amounts to something between a "no overlap" situation and a "full overlap" case (not available in this fuzzy expert system implementation), where overlap is computed even within a membership function.

Iris Dataset Application

The fuzzy rule system implemented in the book has been used to build a classifier for the Iris dataset, as can be seen from the run file discussed previously. Several of the system's special features were used. In this section, we summarize the application.

Among the first issues that must be resolved when developing a fuzzy rule system for classification are how to formulate the rules and how to define the fuzzy membership functions. Examining the data in the data file reveals that the dynamic ranges of the four input variables are 0.53 to 0.98, 0.25 to 0.45, 0.13 to 0.82, and 0 .01 to 0.31, respectively. It would have been possible to scale these values so that each range was [0,1], but it is sometimes desirable to be able to work with data just the way we get them. Therefore, the data were not scaled, but the domains of the fuzzy membership functions were adjusted to reflect the dynamic ranges. Thus, the domain of sepal length was set to [0.4,1.0], sepal width to [0.0,0.6], petal length to [0.0,1.0], and petal width to [0.0,0.4]. These values are listed in the rules file. Initially, three triangular membership functions were defined over each input and output variable domain. Although the domain location and membership type were in some cases adjusted during system development, the final system configuration comprises three fuzzy membership functions for each fuzzy input and output variable.

The formulation of rules from raw data can be problematic for any rule system, fuzzy or crisp. How, then, were the fuzzy rules formulated? It would be possible, at least theoretically, to form a fuzzy rule from each pattern. Such an approach would be tedious at best and, with a pattern file of any significant size, infeasible. It was decided in this case to use an LVQ neural network to cluster the Iris data and to use the weight vector (centroid) for each cluster to form a fuzzy rule.

Since the number of clusters formed is a user-defined parameter (see the discussion of LVQ in Chapter 6), the user can specify the number of fuzzy rules for the system. The number of clusters was set to 16, which resulted in the 16 rules listed in the rules file (refer to Listing 8.20). Recall that three rules in Listing 8.20 are identical; this reflects three clusters generating identical rules. All three rules were left in the list for completeness. Having identical rules in the rule set does not affect the scalar output for any of the defuzzification techniques used in the fuzzy expert system described here, unless the summation flag is set to 0, which may or may not affect the results. The duplicate rules should generally be removed to conserve computing time.

Each cluster center (input) vector was fuzzified using the membership functions, then (since the averaging flag was set to 1) the average of the four fuzzy membership values was used for activating the output variable fuzzy set. The summation flag was set to 0, so that the contributions from all rules that fired were summed (to a maximum value of 1) to determine the value to be defuzzified for each variable. The specific output fuzzy set used was, of course, that corresponding to the classification in the data file for each pattern. The defuzzification parameter was set to 1, resulting in the "no overlap" method of defuzzification.

Good results were obtained by using nonlinear functions for classes 1 and 2 and a triangular function for class 3. The triangular membership function has the effect of emphasizing class 3 values near the class 2 boundary—a feature that facilitates the system performance demonstrated.

After the adjustments just described are made, the fuzzy rule system is able to classify all but 7 of the 150 Iris dataset patterns correctly. This is acceptable performance for this dataset, matching the performance by some neural network classifiers. It exceeds the performance of other rule systems known to the authors except for the system described below that classifies all but 4 patterns correctly. Other system parameter combinations also gave good results. For example, with the summation flag set to 0, the same result (7 mistakes) was obtained using only linear (triangular) membership functions.

The adjustments of fuzzy membership types and locations on the domain axis were done manually by the authors. An evolutionary algorithm can be employed instead, and it is discussed in the next section. As the automated system is now envisioned, the pattern set will be presented to an LVQ neural net or a GA. The LVQ net or GA will be told how many patterns with how many inputs and outputs are present, and the maximum number of clusters will be specified. A fuzzy rule system will either be developed using each cluster centroid from the LVQ to form a fuzzy rule or will use rules evolved by a GA, after defining fuzzy membership functions over the domains of the fuzzy input and output variables. Fuzzy membership functions can also be evolved using evolutionary algorithms. Membership functions can be evolved much like a neural network.

In summary, all that will need to be specified are the numbers of patterns, inputs and outputs; the number of clusters; (perhaps) the number of membership functions for each fuzzy variable; and the level of system performance that is acceptable.

An LVQ neural network or GA, fuzzy rule system, and evolutionary algorithm will do the rest. All of it. And by keeping track of which fuzzy rules fired for any decision and what the contribution of each was, an explanation facility can be provided as well.

The "next step" on the path to a completely automated classification tool is described in the next section. An implementation comprising a GA preprocessing (rule and membership function evolution) system and a fuzzy rule system classifier is described that can evolve a fuzzy rule set of only *four rules* that classifies the Fisher Iris dataset with only 4 out of 150 misclassifications. The software for this system is available on the book's web site.

Evolving Fuzzy Rule Systems

This section discusses the implementation of an evolutionary fuzzy rule system. An integer version of a genetic algorithm is implemented to evolve the fuzzy rule system. The links between the two systems presented in this chapter are the representation and the fitness. By representation, we mean the part of a fuzzy system that is encoded into the individual of the genetic algorithm; by fitness, we mean how to evaluate each individual in the population. This evaluation involves decoding each individual into a fuzzy rule system and then using this system on the problem to be solved to see how well this fuzzy system works for solving the problem. In our implementation, both the fuzzy rule set and the fuzzy membership functions can be evolved. The primary reason we use an integer representation of a genetic algorithm is that we used integers to represent the fuzzy rules and types of membership functions in the implementation of our fuzzy rule system in the previous section.

Programming the Evolutionary Fuzzy Rule System

To implement the evolutionary fuzzy rule system, we have to implement both the fuzzy rule system and an evolutionary algorithm (a genetic algorithm here). The fuzzy rule system implemented in the previous section will be adopted here. Since an integer version of the genetic algorithm is used here, we will focus on the implementation of the genetic algorithm in C++. The genetic operators are quite similar to those in the binary version of the genetic algorithm discussed in the Chapter 4 except for the mutation operator, which is explained later in this section.

As in evolutionary neural networks, the individual representation of the evolutionary fuzzy rule system serves as the bridge between the genetic algorithm and the fuzzy rule system to be evolved. On the genetic algorithm side, the individual represents the parts of the fuzzy system to be designed (adapted). It can theoretically be any part of, or the entire, fuzzy rule system. On the fuzzy system side, each GA individual is decoded into a fuzzy rule system. The fuzzy system is then presented with training patterns (the Iris dataset in our implementation) to be evaluated. The evaluation is then fed back to the genetic algorithm as the fitness of the individual.

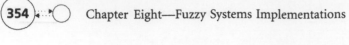

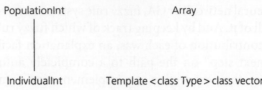

Figure 8.3 Class tree in the implementation of the genetic algorithm.

In the following discussion, we discuss the individual representation first, followed by a discussion of the C++ classes defined in the implementation. The new classes to be defined in this section for the implementation of the GA are shown in Figure 8.3. The class `IndividualInt` is the fundamental class, which defines an object class of individual integer representation in the genetic algorithm. The class `PopulationInt` defines an object class of population in the genetic algorithm, which consists of a set of `IndividualInt` classes.

For our discussion of the individual representation, assume that we are designing a fuzzy system with four input variables and one output variable, and that each variable has three fuzzy sets representing the linguistic descriptions `low`, `medium`, and `high`. As in the implementation of the fuzzy rule system, the three fuzzy sets are represented by the integers 1 to 3. The integer 0 represents the absence of a fuzzy set. The minus sign, –, encodes the modifier `not`. Therefore, a fuzzy rule can be completely encoded by five integers. For example, the rule `if input_1 is not low, input_2 is not medium, and input_4 is high, then output is high` can be encoded as `-1 -2 0 3 3`. If the rule set contains 20 rules, then an integer string of length 100 (5 × 20) can represent the rule set completely. (We may not use all 20 rules. That is dealt with later.)

A membership function as explained before is completely determined by three values: the `start_point` x_1, the `end_point` x_2, and its function type value. In the implementation of our fuzzy rule system, a total of six types of function (defined in the preceding section) are defined to be possible candidates for the membership functions. As discussed previously, each is represented by an integer from 1 to 6. In order to have a homogeneous chromosome, integers are chosen to represent the `start_point` x_1 and the `end_point` x_2 instead of real values. Assume for the variable x that its dynamic range is $[a, b]$ and that it has n fuzzy sets. If the fuzzy membership functions are distributed over the range with halfway overlap, as shown in Figure 8.4, then the center point c_i ($i = 1, \ldots, n$) of the ith membership function is located at

$$c_i = a + i^* \ step \quad i = 1, \cdots, n, \ \text{where} \quad step = \frac{b - a}{n + 1}$$

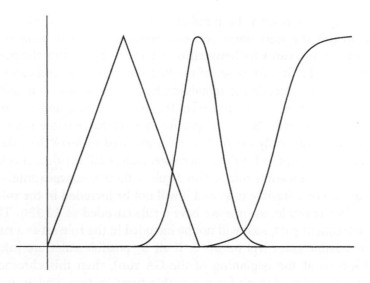

Figure 8.4 Three overlapping membership functions.

We constrain the `start_point` x_1^i of the *i*th membership function to vary only between c_{i-1} and c_i, and the `end_point` x_2^i of the *i*th membership function can vary only between c_i and c_{i+1}. Assume an integer s ($s = 0, \ldots, 10$) is used to "tune" x_1^i and x_2^i; then x_1^i and x_2^i can be calculated from the integer s using the following formula:

$$x_1^i = i * step - \frac{step * (10 + s_{i1})}{2 * 10} + a$$

$$x_2^i = i * step + \frac{step * (10 + s_{i2})}{2 * 10} + a \qquad\qquad i = 1, \cdots, n$$

For an unknown fuzzy system, we generally have little or no idea how many rules should be included in the rule set before the system is designed. A maximum acceptable number can be guessed and/or given, however. Within the maximum number constraint, the number of fuzzy rules in the rule set can also be evolved. Assume for our example system that the maximum acceptable number is 20; then if both fuzzy rule set and membership functions (shape and type) are to be evolved, the total length (in integers) of the chromosome representing the system is

$$1 + 5 * (3 * (2 + 1)) + 5 * 20 = 1\,46$$

and the system can be represented as

$$s_1\ s_2\ s_3\ s_4\ \cdots\cdots\ s_{14}\ s_{15}\ s_{16}\ s_{17}\ \cdots\cdots\cdots\ s_{46}\ s_{47}$$

$$s_{48}\ s_{49}\ s_{50}\ s_{51}\ \cdots\cdots\ s_{142}\ s_{143}\ s_{144}\ s_{145}\ s_{146}$$

where s_1 represents the number of rules varying between 1 and 20, s_2 and s_3 represent the start point and end point for the first fuzzy set of the first input variable and can vary between 0 and 10, s_4 represents the membership function type for the first fuzzy set of the first input variable and can vary between 1 and 6, s_5 to s_{46} encode the remaining fuzzy membership functions (start point, end point, type), s_{47} to s_{51} represent the first fuzzy rule, and s_{142} to s_{146} represent the last possible rule. Since s_1 specifies how many possible rules are encoded in the chromosome, only the first s_1 rules are used to form the rule set, but every rule may or may not be feasible. Therefore, each possible rule is checked to see whether it represents a feasible rule or not. A rule without a nonzero antecedent or consequent part is not a feasible rule, and it will not be included in the rule set.

For example, assume we have a rule encoded as 12320. This has no nonzero consequent part, so it will not be included in the rule set as a rule, and the number of feasible rules will be s_1-1. If all s_1 possible rules are infeasible (this mostly happens at the beginning of the GA run), then this chromosome contains no feasible rules, doesn't form a usable fuzzy system, and is assigned a very small (around 0.0001) positive random value as its fitness value. If the fuzzy rule set contains feasible fuzzy rules, the individual is decoded into a fuzzy rule system, which is then presented with the testing patterns to obtain the fitness for this individual.

The class array is defined to handle a two-dimensional array. The class array is shown in Listing 8.22. It has three private elements: the number of rows (int row), the number of columns (int col), and a float pointer to the array (float* arr).

The public constructors provide ways to declare array-type variables. For example, array a1 declares an empty array variable a1; array a2(2,3)

Listing 8.22 Definition of class array.

```
class array
{
  private:
    int    row;
    int    col;
    float* arr;
  public:
    array():row(0),col(0),arr(0) {}
    array(int a,int b);
    array(const array& a);
    ~array(){delete []arr;}

    array& operator =(const array& a);
    array& operator =(const float& a);
    array& operator =(const vector<float>& a);
    float* operator [] (int i) const;
```

```
int len() const {return row;}
int wid() const {return col;}
float* poi() const {return arr;}
vector<int> max_index() const;
float sum() const;
array noise(const float& a,const float& b) const;
array square() const;
array t() const;
array map(float (*f)(float)) const;

//arithmetic operation
array& operator +=(const array& a);
array& operator -=(const array& a);
array& operator *=(const array& a);
array& operator *=(const float& a);

friend array  operator * (const float& a, const array& b);
friend array  operator * (const array& a, const float& b);
friend array  operator * (const array& a, const array& b);
friend array  operator % (const array& a,const array& b);
friend array  operator + (const array& a, const array& b);
friend array  operator - (const array& a, const array& b);
friend array  operator - (const float& a,const array& b);
friend array  operator - (const array& a, const float& b);
friend istream& operator >> (istream& is,array& a);
friend ostream& operator << (ostream& os,const array& a);
};
```

---

declares an `array` variable a2 with 2 rows and 3 columns and all elements ($2 \times 3 = 6$) initialized to be zeros; `array s3(s2)` declares an `array` variable s3, which is a copy of `array` variable s2.

The public member functions `len()`, `wid()`, and `poi()` provide an interface to obtain the private data members `row`, `col` and `arr`, respectively, from outside of the `array` class.

The public member function `max_index()` returns the index of the element that has the maximum value among all `array` elements. The member function `sum()` returns the summation of all element values. The member function `noise(a,b)` returns an array with each of its elements having a random value with the range [b, b+a]. The member function `square()` returns a new `array` with each new element equal to the square of its corresponding old element. The member function `t()` returns a new `array` that is a transposition of the original `array`. The member function `map(float (*f)(float))` returns a new `array` with each element equal to the return value of function `f(x)`, where x is the corresponding element in the original `array`.

The public operator `= (const array& a)` returns a new `array` that is a copy of the original one. The public `operator = (const float& a)` returns a new `array`, each element of which equals `float` value a. The public

`operator = (const vector<float>& a)` **converts** `(vector<float> a)`
into an `array` variable with one column and the number of rows equal to the
length of the vector a.

The public operators +=, −=, *= , +, −, *, and % provide operations for
the array variables. For example, assume `a(r,c)` represents an `array` variable
a with `row = r` and `col = c`. Then we can have `array` operations such as
`a1(2,3) += a2(2,3)`; `a1(2,3) *= a2(3,2)`; `a1(2,3) = a2(2,3) + s3(2,3)`; and `a1(2,3) = a4(2,4) * a5(4,3)`.

The friend operators << and >> provide methods for input and output, respectively, of an array variable.

The class `IndividualInt` is shown in Listing 8.23. This class is defined for the
individual of the integer version of the genetic algorithm. All the data variables related

Listing 8.23 Definition of class `IndividualInt`.

```
class IndividualInt
{
  private:
    int length;        //length of the individual
    int* ptr;          //pointer to the individual
    float m_rate;      //mutation rate
  public:
    IndividualInt():length(0),ptr(0),m_rate(0) {}
    IndividualInt(int a,float b);
    IndividualInt(int a,int* b,float c);
    IndividualInt(vector<int> a, float b);
    IndividualInt(const IndividualInt& a);

    ~IndividualInt() {delete []ptr;}

    //member function
    int get_length() const {return length;}
    float get_mrate() const {return m_rate;}
    IndividualInt& change_mrate(const float& a);
    IndividualInt& change_length(const int& a);
    IndividualInt& initialize(const int& a,const int& b);
    IndividualInt& initialize_range(const IndividualInt& a);
    IndividualInt& initialize_range_RM(const IndividualInt& a);
    IndividualInt& initialize_range_RMT(const IndividualInt& a);
    FuzzyRuleSet formRuleSet(const FuzzyRule& a) const;
    FuzzyRuleSet formRuleSet_RM(const FuzzyRule& a,const
            IndividualInt& b) const;
    FuzzyRuleSet formRuleSet_RMT(const FuzzyRule& a,const
            IndividualInt& b) const;
    float fitness(const FuzzyRule& a, const array& b,const
            vector<int>& cn, const int&c, const int& d, const int&e) const;
    float fitness_RM(const FuzzyRule& a, const array& b,const
            vector<int>& cn, const int&c, const int& d, const int& e, const
            IndividualInt& f) const;
    float fitness_RMT(const FuzzyRule& a, const array& b,const
            vector<int>& cn, const int&c, const int& d, const int& e, const
            IndividualInt& f) const;
```

```
    IndividualInt& mutate_one(const IndividualInt& a);
    IndividualInt& mutate_one_RM(const IndividualInt& a);
    IndividualInt& mutate_one_RMT(const IndividualInt& a);

    friend void crossoverOP(IndividualInt& a, IndividualInt& b);
    friend void crossoverTP(IndividualInt& a, IndividualInt& b);
    friend void crossoverUniform(IndividualInt& a, IndividualInt& b);

    //operators
    int& operator [] (int i) const;
    IndividualInt& operator =(const IndividualInt& a);

    //I/O operators
    friend istream& operator >>(istream& is, IndividualInt& a);
    friend ostream& operator <<(ostream& os, const IndividualInt& a);
};
```

to the individuals and all the functions performed on the individuals are bound here and defined in the class `IndividualInt`.

The class `IndividualInt` has three private data members. The data member `length` (`int`) records the length of the individual. The integer pointer `ptr` points to the individual. The data member `m_rate` (`float`) records the mutation rate for the individual. Other parameters can be put here, for example, the crossover rate, but we prefer to put the crossover rate at the population level since it involves two individuals instead of one, as is the case for mutation.

Public constructors provide ways to declare an `IndividualInt` variable. For example, `IndividualInt i1` declares an empty `IndividualInt` variable `i1`; `IndividualInt i2(4,0.1)` declares an `IndividualInt` variable `i2` with a length of 4 and the `m_rate` of `0.1`; and `IndividualInt i3(i2)` declares an `IndividualInt` variable `i3` that is a copy of `IndividualInt` variable `i2`. Assume `v1` is a class `vector<float>` variable with 5 elements; then `IndividualInt i4(v1, 0.05)` declares an `IndividualInt` variable `i4` that has a `length` of 5, with 5 elements copied from the variable `v1` and `m_rate` of `0.05`.

The public `operator []` provides a way to access an element. The public `operator =` provides a way to copy one `IndividualInt` variable to another.

The public member functions `get_length()` and `get_mrate()` provide ways to obtain `length` and `m_rate` from outside the `IndividualInt` variable. The public member functions `change_length()` and `change_mrate()` provide ways to change the `length` and `m_rate` from outside the `IndividualInt` variable.

As mentioned previously, the implementation can be used to evolve the fuzzy rule set and fuzzy membership functions. In the following discussion, if a function's name has the extension _RM, it means that both the rule set and the membership function's shape are evolved. If its name has extension _RMT, it means that the rule set together with the membership functions' shape and type are evolved; if its name does not has these extensions, it means that only the rule set is evolved.

The public member function `initialize()` initializes each individual uniformly, randomly for all its elements. The member functions `initialize_range()`, `initialize_range_RM()`, and `initialize_range_RMT()` initialize the individuals according to an `IndividualInt` variable `range`. Each element in the individual may have a different range. For example, if one variable has five fuzzy sets, then its corresponding elements in the individual representation have the integer range {0, 1, 2, 3, 4, 5}; if another variable has three fuzzy sets, then the integer range will be {0, 1, 2, 3}. For the function types, since six functions are implemented in the fuzzy rule system, the integer range for the function type element has the integer range {1, 2, 3, 4, 5, 6}. The `IndividualInt` variable `range` is built to record the dynamic integer ranges for each element. This is extremely useful for initialization of the individuals and the mutation operation since an element can't have an integer value out of its range. For example, if an element for function type has a value of 8, then the corresponding fuzzy system will issue a error since it can't find the right membership function to obtain a membership value.

The public member functions `formRuleSet()`, `formRuleSet_RM()`, and `formRuleSet_RMT()` return a fuzzy rule system by constructing the fuzzy rule system from the individual.

The public member functions `mutate_one()`, `mutate_one_RM()`, and `mutate_one_RMT()` perform mutation on the individual. Each element is randomly chosen to undergo mutation according to the mutation rate (`m_rate`). If this element is selected for mutation, its integer value is increased or decreased by one randomly. If the mutated value is out of range, it is wrapped around. For example, for an element representing a fuzzy variable with 5 fuzzy sets, if its current value is 5, then increasing by one means its mutated value will be −5 (the `not` modifier is implemented here). For an element representing a function type, if its current value is 1, decreasing by one means the mutated value will be 6 (remember that the function type can't be 0).

The public functions `fitness()`, `fitness_RM()`, and `fitness_RMT()` provide ways to evaluate the individual. Each first decodes the individual into a fuzzy rule system, then runs the fuzzy system to get the fitness value.

The `crossoverOP()`, `crossoverTP()`, and `crossoverUniform()` friend functions perform one-point, two-point, and uniform crossover operations, respectively.

The friend operators << and >> provide methods for input and output, respectively, of `IndividualInt` variables.

The class `PopulationInt` is shown in Listing 8.24. It is defined for the population of the integer version of the genetic algorithm. It has five private data

Listing 8.24 Definition of class `PopulationInt`.

```cpp
class PopulationInt
{
  private:
    int length;          //population size
    int width;           //individual length
    IndividualInt* ptr;  //pointer to the individual
    float c_rate;        //crossover rate
    float m_rate;        //mutation rate

  public:
    PopulationInt():length(0),width(0),ptr(0),c_rate(0),m_rate(0) {}
    PopulationInt(int a,int b);
    PopulationInt(int a,int b,float c,float d);
    PopulationInt(const PopulationInt& a);

    //member function
    int get_length() const {return length;}
    int get_width() const {return width;}
    float get_crate() const {return c_rate;}
    float get_mrate() const {return m_rate;}
    PopulationInt& change_crate(const float& a)
        {assert(a>=0&&a<=1); c_rate=a; return *this; }
    PopulationInt& change_mrate(const float& a);
    PopulationInt& initialize_range(const IndividualInt& a);
        //a: rule range, for evolving rule set only
    PopulationInt& initialize_range_RM(const IndividualInt& a);
        //a: rule range, for evolving rule set and tuning membership
            functions
    PopulationInt& initialize_range_RMT(const IndividualInt& a);
        //a: rule range, for evolving rule set and tuning membership
            functions
    PopulationInt& mutate_one(const IndividualInt& a,const int& b);
        //a: rule range  b: best fitness index
        //for rule set only
    PopulationInt& mutate_one_RM(const IndividualInt& a,const int& b);
        //a: rule range  b: best fitness index
        //for rule set and membership functions
    PopulationInt& mutate_one_RMT(const IndividualInt& a,const int& b);
        //a: rule range  b: best fitness index
        //for rule set and membership functions and type
    PopulationInt& crossover(const int& a, const int& b);
        //a: crossover flag
        //0:uniform 1:one point 2: two point b: best individual index
    PopulationInt& selection(const vector<float>& a,const int& b,
            const int& c);
        //a: fitness vector b: best individ. index c: shift flag
            (1: yes, 0: no)
    vector<float> fitness(const FuzzyRule& a,const array& b,const
        vector<int>& cn,
        const int& c,const int& d,const int&e) const;
        //a:base rule, b:input array c:ruleEffectFlag
        //d:fuzzyFlag e:defuzzyFlag cn:class no. for output
        //for evolving rule set only
    vector<float> fitness_RM(const FuzzyRule& a,const array& b,
```

```
                const vector<int>& cn,
                const int& c, const int& d, const int& e, const IndividualInt& f)
                        const;
                //a:base rule, b:input array  c:ruleEffectFlag
                //d:fuzzyFlag e:defuzzyFlag cn:class no. for output
                //f: range individual
                //for evolving rule set and membership functions
             vector<float> fitness_RMT(const FuzzyRule& a, const array& b,
                const vector<int>& cn, const int& c, const int& d, const int& e,
                const IndividualInt& f) const;
                //a:base rule, b:input array  c:ruleEffectFlag
                //d:fuzzyFlag e:defuzzyFlag cn:class no. for output
                //f: range individual
                //for evolving rule set and membership functions

             //operators
             IndividualInt& operator [] (int i) const
                {assert(i>=0&&i<length); return ptr[i];}

             //I/O operators
             friend ostream& operator<<(ostream& os, const PopulationInt& a);
             friend istream& operator>>(istream& is, PopulationInt& a);
    };
```

members: the population size (int length), the length of the individual (int width), the population-level crossover rate (float c_rate), the population-level mutation rate (m_rate), and the pointer to the individuals (IndividualInt* ptr). The purpose of defining the mutation rate in both class IndividualInt and class PopulationInt is to have the capability to implement a genetic algorithm with one unique mutation rate for the whole population, or to give each individual its own mutation rate.

The public constructors provide ways to declare the PopulationInt type variable. For example, PopulationInt p1 declares an empty PopulationInt variable p1; PopulationInt p2(20,30) declares a PopulationInt variable p2 with population size 20 and individual length 30; PopulationInt p3(20,30,0.7,0.1) declares a PopulationInt variable p3 with population size 20, individual length 30, crossover rate 0.7, and mutation rate 0.1. PopulationInt p4(p3) declares a PopulationInt variable p4 that is a copy of PopulationInt variable p3.

The public member functions get_length(), get_width(), get_crate(), and get_mrate() provide ways to access the private data members from outside the PopulationInt variable. The public member functions change_crate() and change_mrate() provide ways to change the crossover rate and mutation rate from outside the PopulationInt variable.

The public member functions initialize_range(), initialize_range_RM(), and initialize_range_RMT() provide ways to initialize the population by calling its individuals' initialization routines accordingly.

The public member functions `mutate_one()`, `mutate_one_RM()`, and `mutate_one_RMT()` provide ways to perform mutation over the population by calling each individual's mutation routine accordingly.

The public member function `crossover(const int& co_type, const int& best_index)` performs a crossover operation on the population according to the crossover rate. The best individual with index `best_index` will not undergo the crossover operation. The type of crossover operation is based on the crossover operation type `co_type` (one-point, two-point or uniform crossover). The crossover operation is similar to that in the binary GA implementation discussed in Chapter 4. The public member `selection()` performs selection on the population and is similar to that in the binary GA implementation discussed in Chapter 4.

The public functions `fitness()`, `fitness_RM()`, and `fitness_RMT()` return fitness vectors of all individuals by calling their corresponding individual's fitness routine. The public `operator []` provides a way to access its element (`IndividualInt`).

The friend operators `<<` and `>>` provide methods for input and output, respectively, of the `PopulationInt` variable.

We now examine the `main()` and `ga()` routines. The `main()` routine does nothing except implement the choice of system you want to run—the fuzzy rule system or the evolving fuzzy rule system. The `main()` routine is shown in Listing 8.25 for clearness. It firsts reads in the run files for both the fuzzy rule system and the genetic algorithm and then provides you with an option. The fuzzy rule system will be run if you input "c" or "C." The genetic algorithm will be run if you input "g" or "G."

Listing 8.25 The `main()` routine.

```
void main(int argc,char *argv[])
{
    char gaName[80],fileName[80];
    char Msg[80];
    char condition;
    int true=1;

    ifstream runFile;
    runFile.open(argv[1],ios::in);
    if (!runFile)
    {
        cerr<<"can't open file "<<argv[1]<<" for input"<<endl;
        exit(1);
    }
    runFile>>gaName>>flName;
    runFile.close();

    do
    {
```

```
        clrscr();
        cout<<"G: generating rules"<<endl;
        cout<<"C: classification"<<endl;
        cout<<"other Keys: quit"<<endl;
        cout<<"your choice? ";
        cin>>condition;
        switch(condition)
        {
            case 'g':
            case 'G':
                ga(gaName);
                break;
            case 'c':
            case 'C':
                fl(flName);
                break;
            default:
                true=0;
        }
    } while (true==1);
}
```

The fuzzy rule system is used to test the fuzzy system designed by the genetic algorithm. It is the same as the one previously discussed in the section on the implementation of the fuzzy rule system. If you choose to run the genetic algorithm, it calls the ga(ga_run_file_name) routine. The ga() routine is the core part of the implementation of the evolutionary fuzzy rule system. The ga() routine is shown in Listing 8.26. First, several variables are defined at the file level in which the ga() routine is defined.

```
FuzzyRule    baseRule;
vector<int> rangeint;
PopulationInt popu;
vector<float> fitvec;
int        inLen,outLen;
array        arrayPat;
vector<int>  classN;
```

The FuzzyRule variable baseRule is defined to store the rule specification—that is, the format of a fuzzy rule in the fuzzy rule system to be evolved. The vector<int> variable rangeint stores the vector of range values for each element in the individual representation. The PopulationInt variable popu stores the population of the genetic algorithm. The vector<float> variable fitvec records the fitness values of the individuals. The int variables inLen, outLen store the numbers of input and output dimensions, respectively. The array variable arrayPat stores the training/testing patterns. The vector<int> variable classN stores the number of classes for each output variable.

Listing 8.26 Definition of the ga() routine.

```
void ga(char *dataFile)
{
    read_ga_runfile(dataFile);
    read_fuzzy_base_rule();
    read_ga_training_patterns();
    form_range_vector();
    IndividualInt range(rangeint,0);
    int tmplen = get_population_length();
    update_popu(p_size,tmplen,c_rate,m_rate);
    popu_initialize(range);
    fitvec.changeSize(p_size);

    int bestfit;
    for (int idx = 0;idx < generation;idx++)
    {
        calculate_fitness(range);
        bestfit=fitvec.maximum_index();
        if (fitvec[bestfit]>criterion)
            break;

        if (idx != (generation -1))
        {   //not the last generation
            popu.selection(fitvec,bestfit,shift); //1:sfite
            popu.crossover(flag_c,bestfit);
            popu_mutate(range,bestfit);
        }
    }
    write_ga_fuzzy_rules(idx, range, bestfit);
}
```

The ga() routine first reads in parameters from the input files and initializes all the file level variables to prepare for running the GA. The read_ga_runfile() reads in the parameters from the GA run file. The read_fuzzy_base_rule() routine reads in the variable baseRule from the base rule file specified in the run file. The read_ga_training_pattern() routine reads in the training patterns from the pattern data file specified in the run file. The form_range_vector() routine forms the variable rangeint, which is used to declare the IndividualInt variable range. The get_population_length() routine is called to calculate the length of the population depending on what elements of the fuzzy rule system are to be evolved. The variable popu is rescaled by calling the update_popu() routine. The rescaled variable popu is then initialized by calling popu.initialize() followed by rescaling the variable fitvec by calling fitvec.changeSize().

In each generation, the GA first calculates individual fitnesses by calling the calculate_fitness() routine; then the selection, crossover, and mutation operations are performed in sequence by calling popu.selection(), popu.crossover(), and popu_mutate(), respectively. This process is repeated until either the termination criterion has been met (`fitvec[bestfit]>criterion`, where `bestfit` is the index of the individual with the best fitness value obtained by calling `fitvec.maximum_index()`) or the maximum number of generations, specified in the GA run file, has been reached.

Finally, the fuzzy rule system decoded from the best individual is written to the output rule file specified in the GA run file by calling the `write_ga_fuzzy_rules()` routine.

Running the Evolutionary Fuzzy Rule System

To run the program, within the appropriate subdirectory, enter

```
flga flga.run
```

The main run file `flga.run` contains only two items: the name of the GA run file and the name of the fuzzy rule system run file. An example of the contents of the main run file is

```
ga.run
fl.run
```

As indicated by the listing of two additional run files within the main run file, the evolutionary fuzzy rule system is run in two stages. The first stage, using a GA, generates (evolves) the rules (and perhaps the membership functions) to be used by the fuzzy rule system. The second, using the fuzzy rule system, classifies the patterns in a pattern file using the fuzzy rules (and perhaps the membership functions) stored in a rules file.

When the `flga.exe` program is run, you are given the choice of generating (evolving) rules, classifying patterns, or modifying the run file. If you choose to modify the run file by typing m, the DOS text editor is called, allowing you to make changes in the main run file.

If you choose to generate (evolve) a rule set by typing g, a set of rules will be evolved using the contents of the GA run file `ga.run`. An example of this run file appears in Listing 8.27.

Listing 8.27 Example of run file for rule generation (evolution).

```
iris.dat
base.rul
result_4.rul

1
2
0.75
0.01

0
300
```

```
50
20
10

150
0.965
1
1
1
```

The first entry in this run file is the *GA input data* file, in this case `iris.dat`. The GA data file is in a format similar to that used previously for the fuzzy rule system. The first two lines are

```
4 1 3
.6375 .4375 .1750 .0250 0
```

The first line in the GA input data file specifies the number of inputs, outputs, and classes. The second line is the first pattern in the file with its output classification. These two lines are followed by the remaining patterns in the pattern file with their classifications.

The second file in the GA run file is the *rule specification* file, in this case `base.rul`. A typical rule specification file for evolving rules to classify the Iris dataset appears in Listing 8.28.

The first line in the rule specification file defines the number of fuzzy input variables (4) and fuzzy output variable(s) (1). Then the domain and fuzzy sets for each

---

Listing 8.28 Example of a rule specification file for evolving rules.

```
4 1
sepalLength 3 0.4 1.0
        leftTriangle 0.4 0.8
        Triangle 0.5 0.9
        rightTriangle 0.6 1.0

sepalWidth 3 0.0 0.6
        leftTriangle 0.0 0.3
        Triangle 0.15 0.45
        rightTriangle 0.3 0.6

petalLength 3 0.0 1.0
        leftTriangle 0.0 0.4
        Triangle 0.2 0.7
        rightTriangle 0.4 1.0

petalWidth 3 0.0 0.4
        leftTriangle 0.0 0.2
        Triangle 0.1 0.3
        rightTriangle 0.2 0.4
```

```
output 3 0.0 1.0
        leftTriangle 0.0 0.4
        Triangle 0.3 0.7
        rightTriangle 0.5 1.0
 1 1 1 1 1
```

fuzzy variable are defined, in the same way described in the description of the fuzzy rule system implementation. The final line in the file comprises a "template," or example, for a rule. In this case, with four inputs and one output, any five digits can appear, such as 0 0 0 0 0 or 1 2 3 2 1.

The third file in the GA run file is the *output rule* file, in this case result_4.rul. This file is the main product of running the rule generation (evolution) stage of the evolutionary fuzzy rule system. A listing of result_4.rul appears as Listing 8.29, which is the result of an actual rule generation run for evolving a rule set only.

Listing 8.29 Example of an output rule file from rule generation (evolution) stage.

```
4
4 1
sepalLength 3 0.4 1.0
        leftTriangle 0.4 0.8
        Triangle 0.5 0.9
        rightTriangle 0.6 1.0

sepalWidth 3 0.0 0.6
        leftTriangle 0.0 0.3
        Triangle 0.15 0.45
        rightTriangle 0.3 0.6

petalLength 3 0.0 1.0
        leftTriangle 0.0 0.4
        Triangle 0.2 0.7
        rightTriangle 0.4 1.0

petalWidth 3 0.0 0.4
        leftTriangle 0.0 0.2
        Triangle 0.1 0.3
        rightTriangle 0.2 0.4

output  3 0.0 1.0
        leftTriangle 0.0 0.4
        Triangle 0.3 0.7
        rightTriangle 0.5 1.0
  1  0 -1 -1 -1
 -2 -1 -1 -1 -2
 -3 -2  2  0  2
  3  0  3 -3 -3
 generation: 42
 fitness=0.973333
```

The first line in the file contains the number 4, which indicates that the system found a rule set comprising just four rules that classifies the Iris dataset. We will see how well the evolved rules work when we run the classification stage of the evolutionary fuzzy rule system. The next line (4 1) confirms that four input fuzzy variables and one output were used. The domain and fuzzy sets for each variable are then listed, and they are the same as in the rule specification file since only the fuzzy rule set is specified to be evolved here (this is explained later).

Next, the rules are listed. Note that negative integers appear. The evolved rules can contain integers, positive or negative, with the maximum absolute value equal to the number of fuzzy sets specified for each variable. Also note that the only rule relating to (firing) classification number 1 has a negative consequent (−1). This is also true for classification number 3. This is "legal" because of the way defuzzification is done: The fuzzy complement of the fuzzy value for consequent 1 is defuzzified when this rule is fired. The last items in the output rule file in Listing 8.29 are the generation at which the rule list was evolved and the fitness value. We see that in this case the rule set listed in the file evolved in the 42nd generation. The fitness value indicates that only 4 errors were made out of the 150 training patterns.

Going back to the GA run file (Listing 8.27), we see a list of parameter values after the name of the GA adaptation rule file. The first value (1) is the value of the *fitness shift* flag. When set to 1, all fitness values are shifted so that the minimum value is 0.1; the `min_value` to `max_value` fitness range is preserved. The next value (2) specifies that two-point crossover be used. The next two values (.75 and .01) are the crossover and mutation rates, respectively.

The next value (0) specifies which part of the fuzzy rule system is to be evolved. If it is 0, only the fuzzy rule set is evolved; if it is 1, the fuzzy rule set plus the membership function's `start_points` and `end_points` are evolved while the membership function's types are fixed; if it is 2, the membership function's types also undergo evolution.

The next value (300) is the maximum number of generations to be allowed, while the population size is set at 50. Next, the maximum allowable number of rules is specified (20), followed by number of divisions (10) for each membership function's start point and end point. The number of divisions defines the range for the membership function's start point and end points. Next is the number of patterns in the input data file to use for rule generation (150). Next, the acceptable fitness value to terminate the run (.965) appears. Note that achievement of this fitness value for the Iris dataset requires that no more than 5 errors be made for 150 patterns. All of the parameters (except for the maximum number of rules allowed and the number of divisions) are discussed in detail in the GA section of Chapter 4.

The last three parameters in the GA run file are related to the fuzzy rule system. The first (1) is the value of the averaging flag. When the averaging flag is set to 1, the average of the membership values ANDed together is output. The second (1) is the defuzzification parameter. When it is 1, the "no overlap" method of defuzzification is used. Third is the summation flag (1). Its value specifies how output fuzzy membership values are formed *prior to defuzzification*. When the summation flag is set to 1, the maximum value caused by any one rule firing is the value passed to defuzzification. These parameters are discussed in detail in the discussion of the fuzzy rule system implementation.

The rule generation stage of the evolutionary fuzzy expert system is now complete. You are next given the opportunity to run the classification stage by typing c. If you choose to classify a pattern set according to a rule set previously generated, the contents of the FL run file fl.run will be used. An example of this run file appears in Listing 8.30.

Listing 8.30 Example of a fuzzy logic run file for the evolutionary fuzzy expert system.

```
result.rul
iris.dat
iris.out
result_4.out
1
1
1
```

Four file names and three parameters appear in this run file. The first two files contain input necessary to run the classification stage, and the last two comprise the output. The first file listed is the *rule* file, which will be used by the fuzzy rule system to classify the patterns. The contents of this file, the output rule file from the GA stage, are discussed above. The second file listed is the fuzzy logic input data file. It is identical in format and contents to the GA input data file, described above.

The third file listed is the *rule output* file, which contains a list of the rules in words, in this case iris.out. Since the rule set produced by the rule generation stage was listed only in numbers in result.rul, it is helpful to have this listing, which can be more easily understood. The fourth file is the *output file*, result.out. It contains a listing of the correct classifications for the input patterns in the data file, with a listing of the classification made by the fuzzy expert system. Errors are identified, and an error total appears at the end of the list.

The results file result_4.out, by using the fuzzy rule system shown in Listing 8.29, contains the listing for the Iris dataset, showing that the evolutionary fuzzy rule system made only 4 errors out of 150 patterns classified. This is a very good result, given that only four rules were needed! Two of the errors were misclassifications, and two, for patterns 84 and 135, state rule set not fired. This indicates that for those two input patterns, none of the rules was fired.

The three parameters listed at the end of the file are the averaging flag, the defuzzification parameter, and the summation flag. When the averaging flag is set to 1, the average of the input membership values ANDed together is output. When the defuzzification parameter is 1, the "no overlap" method of defuzzification is used. When the summation flag is set to 1, the maximum value caused by any one rule firing is the value passed to defuzzification. These three parameters are the same as those used in the rule generation stage.

The evolutionary fuzzy rule system is a powerful tool for evolving rules and developing a fuzzy rule system for classification and/or diagnosis. You should now be able to use the software at the book's web site to solve real-world applications. We encourage you to experiment with the membership functions, and so on, to gain a deeper understanding of the potentials for the software.

Summary

In this chapter, we look at implementation issues for fuzzy rule systems, including fuzzy rule representation, the evolutionary design of a fuzzy rule system, and the programming language to be used. We then discuss two fuzzy system implementations: a fuzzy rule system and an evolutionary fuzzy rule system. The code for these implementations is on the web site for the book. The source code is distributed as shareware, with conditions as discussed on the web site.

In the next chapter, we discuss implementations of computational intelligence systems. By using both an evolutionary algorithm and fuzzy logic, the evolutionary fuzzy rule system of this chapter is a kind of computational intelligence system, so it provides a bridge to the subject matter of the next chapter.

Exercises

1. For a two-input, two-output fuzzy system, assume each variable has three fuzzy sets and encode the following rule in a string of bits: If Input_1 is Medium and Input_2 is High, then Output_1 is High and Output_2 is Low.

2. Define an enumeration data type for the membership functions used in the implementation, and illustrate what other changes should be made accordingly.

3. Define an enumeration data type for the methods to calculate the activation strength of the if part for each rule, and specify the corresponding changes.

4. Redefine the *FuzzyMember* class so that it can be used to represent more general forms of membership functions such as an asymmetrical triangular function.

5. Run the evolutionary fuzzy rule system software on the Iris data using three membership functions for each input variable. Use all 150 patterns to develop

the system. Evolve only the rule system. Set the acceptable performance to 0.949, which allows six errors out of the 150-pattern Iris dataset.

6. Define five membership functions for each input variable and repeat exercise 3. Describe the differences in the results.

7. Repeat exercise 5, evolving both the rule set and the start and end points of each membership function.

8. Repeat exercise 5, evolving everything: the rule set, the start and end points of each membership function, and the membership function types.

9. Repeat exercises 5 and 6, but use only 100 patterns to develop the fuzzy rules; then test (classify) all 150 patterns. Describe the differences in the results.

chapter
nine

Computational Intelligence Implementations

Chapter 2 discussed the basic concepts of computational intelligence. In subsequent chapters we presented the three constituent methodologies of computational intelligence with implementations for each. We introduced combinations of the methods in the preceding chapters, such as the evolutionary fuzzy rule system in Chapter 8, that are examples of computational intelligence.

This chapter discusses some of the issues related to implementations of computational intelligence. We discuss issues related to fuzzy evolutionary fuzzy rule system implementations. We present an additional implementation of computational intelligence: a fuzzy evolutionary fuzzy rule system. We provide detailed descriptions of the system implementation. (The executable code and source code are

available at the book's web site.) We then look at the big picture and consider how we go about choosing the best tool(s) for a practical problem. We look at the strengths and weaknesses of each methodology and discuss some practical considerations. Finally, we examine a sample application of computational intelligence for data mining. This example shows how the various methodologies of computational intelligence can be combined, and even intertwined.

Similarly to previous chapters on implementation (Chapters 4, 6, and 8), we have included code listings such as class definitions and operator definitions. If you are not interested in the details of programming, you may want to skim these listings, noting what is included and what is accomplished by the code in each listing. ∎

Implementation Issues

Computational intelligence has three core components: artificial neural networks, evolutionary computation algorithms, and fuzzy logic systems. Combinations of these three components and/or other components comprise a computational intelligence system. For example, a back-propagation neural network combined with a global search algorithm such as a genetic algorithm is a computational intelligence system. The neural network is first adapted by the genetic algorithm to find a near-optimum global solution, which can then be used as a starting point for the back-propagation learning algorithm to fine-tune the solution.

Several implementations discussed in previous chapters are examples of computational intelligence systems. The evolutionary back-propagation neural network in Chapter 6 is the combination of a back-propagation neural network and the particle swarm optimization algorithm. The evolutionary fuzzy rule system in Chapter 8 is a combination of a fuzzy rule system and a genetic algorithm. The main issue in implementing computational intelligence is how to combine core components to solve problems efficiently and effectively. In this chapter, we illustrate common issues related to implementing computational intelligence systems with an example of an implementation of a fuzzy evolutionary fuzzy rule system.

The fuzzy evolutionary fuzzy rule system is developed based on the evolutionary fuzzy rule system discussed in Chapter 8. We use an additional fuzzy system in the evolutionary fuzzy rule system to adapt the parameters of the genetic algorithm while the GA is evolving the fuzzy system for problem solving.

The relationships between the genetic algorithm and the fuzzy rule system in the evolutionary fuzzy rule system are shown in Figure 9.1. The individual representation of the genetic algorithm represents the fuzzy rule system to be evolved, which is decoded into a fuzzy rule system for evaluation. The decoded system performs on the training patterns to measure the system's performance, which is then fed back to

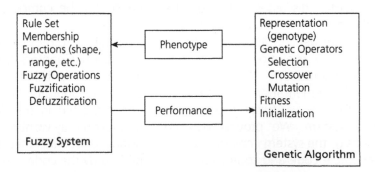

Figure 9.1 Relationships between the genetic algorithm and the fuzzy system in the evolutionary fuzzy rule system.

the genetic algorithm to determine the fitness of the individual. These relationships are described and discussed in Chapter 8. In this section, we focus on using a fuzzy rule system to adjust the parameters of the genetic algorithm.

Adaptation of Genetic Algorithms

The genetic algorithm in the evolutionary fuzzy rule system as discussed in Chapter 8 is a static genetic algorithm; that is, its parameters are fixed during the course of running the GA. The performance of a genetic algorithm depends on the relationship between exploration and exploitation, that is, the selection of its parameters. For example, the crossover operation facilitates exploration (global search) and the mutation operation facilitates exploitation (local search). A global search is generally favored at the beginning of the search process, and a local search is favored at the end. A simple and straightforward approach is to use crossover with a relatively large crossover rate and mutation with a relatively small mutation rate at the beginning of the search process. The crossover (mutation) rate is then linearly decreased (increased) over the course of the search process. This strategy can frequently result in getting caught in local optima. Ideally, the crossover and mutation rate should be nonlinearly, dynamically adjusted to avoid local optima while retaining the ability to fine-tune the near-global optimum resolution.

The adjustment (adaptation) of a genetic algorithm can occur on four levels: environment, population, individual, and component (Shi 2000). In environment-level adaptation, the environment itself is changed over the course of the search process, and the fitness function, which measures how well an individual fits into the environment, is adapted to reflect the altered environment.

Most adaptation is performed by adjusting parameters at the population level. For example, if a particular crossover (mutation) rate is used over the entire population, then this crossover (mutation) rate is a candidate to undergo adaptation. In some implementations each individual has its own mutation rate, so the adaptation of the mutation rate is performed at the individual level. In Bäck (1992), the adaptation is performed at the component (element) level. Each element in each individual is associated with a mutation rate that is encoded into the individual representation to undergo evolution.

Fuzzy Adaptation

Little is known about the operation (search) process of genetic algorithms, which is highly nonlinear and complicated. It is very difficult, if not impossible, to mathematically model this process so that the parameters of genetic algorithms can be dynamically set to obtain an optimal search process. Fortunately, genetic algorithms have been extensively studied and reported in the literature. In addition, a lot of experience has been accumulated and some linguistic understanding of the relationships between the search process and the GA parameters is available. This understanding and experience make fuzzy systems good candidates for dynamically setting the parameters of genetic algorithms.

The main idea is to design a fuzzy rule system with its inputs based on the performance measurements of the search process and its outputs being the parameters of the genetic algorithms. The fuzzy rule system adjusts the parameters of the genetic algorithm (output) based on the current performance measurements of the genetic algorithm. The relationships between the fuzzy rule system and the genetic algorithm are shown in Figure 9.2. The fuzzy rule system obtains input (the performance measurements) from the genetic algorithm and feeds back output (new parameter values) to the genetic algorithm.

The output from the fuzzy system can be parameters being adapted or changes to the parameters being adapted. The parameters normally include the crossover and mutation rates, but other parameters of genetic algorithms are also sometimes used. The adaptation is usually conducted at the population level because of the significant increase in computation cost at the individual level or component level.

The input to the fuzzy rule system is based on the performance measurements, which can reflect the parameters of the genetic algorithm directly or indirectly. Some common measurements are the measurement of the population diversity, the variance of the fitness of all of the individuals, the best performance in the current generation, and the measurement of premature convergence.

When should fuzzy adaptation be used? When a fuzzy rule system is used to adapt the parameters of the genetic algorithm, the genetic algorithm, generally speaking, can have better performance. Does this mean we should always use a fuzzy rule system (or other adaptive approaches) to adjust parameters of the genetic algorithm? Not necessarily. When a genetic algorithm used to search for a solution that is time critical and/or the computation cost of the evaluation of individuals is at the same magnitude as the computation cost of the fuzzy rule system, it is better not to use

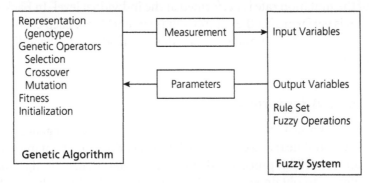

Figure 9.2 Relationship between the fuzzy system and the genetic algorithm in fuzzy adaption.

a fuzzy rule system to adjust the parameters of a genetic algorithm. Fixed parameters or a simple and fast parameter adjustment approach should be adopted instead. When the computation cost of the evaluation of individuals is much higher than that of a fuzzy rule system, however, we suggest that you develop a fuzzy rule system or other adaptive approach to dynamically adjust the parameters of the genetic algorithm.

Knowledge Elicitation

Fuzzy rules such as those listed in the next section flow from heuristics developed from the authors' experience with genetic algorithm implementations. For example, our experience with genetic algorithms indicates that when the fitness is low, such as occurs at the beginning of the run, lower mutation rates and higher crossover rates are productive. Conversely, if the fitness has not changed for a long time and the variance of the fitness values is low (a condition that often occurs near the end of a run), then a higher mutation rate and lower crossover rate are usually helpful.

This leads us to a general subject related to traditional expert system development known as knowledge acquisition and its most important area: *knowledge elicitation*. The term is usually used to describe the process of extracting knowledge from human experts for use in traditional AI-based expert systems. A detailed treatment of knowledge elicitation, or knowledge acquisition, is beyond the scope of this book. The reader is referred to sources such as Brachman and Levesque (2004).

Without going into details, it is accurate to characterize knowledge elicitation as difficult, time-consuming, complex, and expensive. It involves finding one or more experts with the required domain knowledge who are willing and able to share their relevant knowledge (and who are willing to do this for the amount of money you have in your budget). It is a complex and iterative process of interviews and knowledge model development.

By this point in the book, it should be clear that the ability to evolve major portions of fuzzy expert systems, such as fuzzy rule sets and fuzzy membership functions, generally makes knowledge elicitation in the traditional sense unnecessary. It is necessary only to identify those input parameters that appear to be important in the determination of the system output(s). Although some system knowledge may be needed to do this, it can be done with little or no involvement of a domain expert.

We do not contend that knowledge elicitation is never needed. Sometimes, as is the case in the formulation of the fuzzy rules in the next section, it can facilitate improved system performance. Much of the time, however, computational intelligence applications can be developed without it (or with only a small amount of it), resulting in cost savings and significantly accelerating successful system implementation.

Fuzzy Evolutionary Fuzzy Rule System Implementation

This section discusses the implementation of a fuzzy evolutionary fuzzy rule system, which is similar to the implementation of the evolutionary fuzzy rule system discussed in Chapter 8. The main difference with the previous system is that a predesigned fuzzy rule system is added to the system to dynamically tune the crossover and mutation rates of the genetic algorithm over the course of running the genetic algorithm. The purpose is to achieve a better balanced global and local search ability and a more effective search process.

The source code for the implementation is written in C++ and is being distributed as shareware. You are welcome to use it for classroom or personal learning experiences in conjunction with the textbook at no cost. If you use it, either as is or with modification, for a project outside of your classroom (or learning on your own), please send us payment in accordance with the shareware payment instructions on the web site for the book.

Programming the Fuzzy Evolutionary Fuzzy Rule System

The ga() routine contains the only difference between the implementation of the fuzzy evolutionary fuzzy rule system and that of the evolutionary fuzzy rule system discussed in Chapter 8. The new ga() routine is shown in Listing 9.1, in which the differences are in bold type for clarity.

Listing 9.1 The ga() routine in the fuzzy evolutionary fuzzy rule system implementation.

```
void ga(char *dataFile)
{
    read_ga_runfile(dataFile);

    read_adapt_rule();
    vector<float> vecin_m(adaptRuleSet[0].get_variableSize());
    vector<float> vecout_m(adaptRuleSet[0].get_outputSize());

    read_fuzzy_base_rule();
    read_ga_training_patterns();
    form_range_vector();
    IndividualInt range(rangeint,0);
    int tmplen = get_population_length();
    update_popu(p_size,tmplen,c_rate,m_rate);
    popu_initialize(range);
    fitvec.changeSize(p_size);
    float prebest=0.1;
    float nu=0.0;
    float var;
    float mrate=m_rate;
    float crate=c_rate;

    int bestfit;
    for (int idx=0;i<generation;i++)
```

```
      {
          calculate_fitness(range);
          bestfit=fitvec.maximum_index();
          var=variance(fitvec,aver);
          if (fitvec[bestfit]>criterion)
            break;

          if (idx != (generation -1))
          {   //not the last generation
            popu.selection(fitvec,bestfit,shift);
            if (m_flag==1)
            {    //change mutate/crossover rate
              if (fitvec[bestfit]==prebest)
                nu +=1.0;
              else
                nu=0.0;
              vecin_m[0]=fitvec[bestfit];
              vecin_m[1]=nu;
              vecin_m[2]=var;
              vecout_m = adaptRuleSet.output(vecin_m,0,1,1);
              mrate=vecout_m[0];
              crate=vecout_m[1];
              prebest=fitvec[bestfit];
              popu.change_mrate(mrate);
              popu.change_crate(crate);
            }
              popu.crossover(flag_c,bestfit);
              popu_mutate(range,bestfit);
          }
      }
      write_ga_fuzzy_rules(idx,range,bestfit);
  }
```

In addition to the file-level variables declared in the evolutionary fuzzy rule system implementation, a new file-level `FuzzyRuleSet` variable, `adaptRuleSet`, is defined to store the fuzzy rule system that is used to adapt the crossover and mutation rates. The `read_adapt_rule()` routine is called to read in the `FuzzyRuleSet` variable `adaptRuleSet`. One example of the adaptive fuzzy rule system is shown in Listing 9.2. It has three input variables, two output variables,

Listing 9.2 A fuzzy rule system for genetic algorithm adaptation.

```
8
3 2
Fitness 3 0.0 1.0
        leftTriangle 0.0 0.7
        Triangle 0.5 0.9
        rightTriangle 0.7 1.0

Number  3 0 20
        leftTriangle 0 6
        Triangle 3 9
```

```
        rightTriangle 6 12

Variance 3 0.0 0.2
        leftTriangle 0.0 0.12
        Triangle 0.1 0.14
        rightTriangle 0.12 0.2

Mrate 3 0.005 0.1
        leftTriangle 0.005 0.015
        Triangle 0.01 0.02
        rightTriangle 0.015      0.1

Crate 3 0.4 0.9
        leftTriangle 0.48 0.65
        Triangle 0.55 0.75
        rightTriangle 0.65 0.83

1 0 0 1 3
2 1 0 1 3
2 2 0 2 2
0 3 2 3 1
3 1 0 1 3
3 2 0 2 2
0 3 1 3 1
0 3 3 1 3
```

and eight fuzzy rules. The three input variables are the best fitness of the current generation, the number of generations that the best fitness has not improved, and the variance of all the individuals' fitnesses in the current generation. The two output variables are the new mutation and crossover rates. The linguistic descriptions of these eight rules follow.

- If Fitness is Low, then Mrate is Low and Crate is High.
- If Fitness is Medium and Number is Low, then Mrate is Low and Crate is High.
- If Fitness is Medium and Number is Medium, then Mrate is Medium and Crate is Medium.
- If Number is High and Variance is Medium, then Mrate is High and Crate is Low.
- If Fitness is High and Number is Low, then Mrate is Low and Crate is High.
- If Fitness is High and Number is Medium, then Mrate is Medium and Crate is Medium.
- If Number is High and Variance is Low, then Mrate is High and Crate is Low.
- If Number is High and Variance is High, then Mrate is Low and Crate is Low.

Two `vector<float>` variables, `vectin_m` and `vectout_m`, are declared to store the input and output variables of the fuzzy rule system, respectively. Five `float`-type variables are declared to store the best fitness of the previous generation (`prebest`), the number of generations that the best fitness has not improved (`nu`), the variance of the fitnesses (`var`), the new mutation rate (`mrate`), and the new crossover rate (`crate`).

The mutation and crossover rates are adjusted before calling `popu.crossover()` and `popu.mutate()` to perform crossover and mutation operations. The `m_flag` is first checked to see whether it is TRUE or FALSE. The `m_flag` is read in from the run file (see next section). When `m_flag` is TRUE, the crossover and mutation rates are dynamically adjusted by applying the fuzzy rule system. When `m_flag` is FALSE, the fuzzy evolutionary fuzzy rule system is the same as the evolutionary fuzzy rule system discussed in Chapter 8.

When `m_flag` is TRUE, `prebest` is compared with the best fitness in the current generation. If they are equal, the variable `nu` is increased by 1; otherwise, `nu` is set to 0. Then the best fitness, `nu` and `var` are fed into the fuzzy rule system, and the output values of the fuzzy rule system are assigned as the new mutation and crossover rates. The `popu.change_mrate()` and `popu.change_crate()` are called to change the population's mutation and crossover rates, respectively.

Running the Fuzzy Evolutionary Fuzzy Rule System

To run the program, at the DOS prompt within the appropriate subdirectory, enter

```
flgafs flgafs.run
```

The main run file `flgafs.run` contains only two items: the names of the GA run file and the fuzzy rule system run file. An example of the contents of the main run file is

```
ga.run
fl.run
```

The `fl.run` file is the same as that in the evolutionary fuzzy rule system, and the `ga.run` file is almost the same as that in the evolutionary fuzzy rule system except that two lines have been added. For illustration, the new `ga.run` file is shown in Listing 9.3. The fourth line contains a file name, `ga_adapt.rul`, from which the fuzzy rule system for adapting GA parameters is to be read. The contents of the `ga_adapt.rul` file provided with this software are shown in Listing 9.2. The ninth line in Listing 9.3 contains an integer number, 1. It is a flag that tells whether the fuzzy adaptation is to be used or not, as explained in the last section (`m_flag`). The other contents of the `ga.run` file are described in detail in Chapter 8.

Listing 9.3 Example of a run file for rule generation (evolution).

```
iris.dat
base.rul
result.rul
ga_adapt.rul

1
2
0.75
0.01
1

2
1000
50
20
10

100
0.99
1
1
1
```

Choosing the Best Tools

The main concepts discussed in this book (evolutionary computation, neural networks, and fuzzy logic) can be used individually or in combination to solve a wide array of problems. We have given you only the basic information on each concept and only a few examples of how to combine them into powerful computational intelligence tools. More information exists in other references, as do more examples of computational intelligence. And we are sure that our readers will develop many more exciting implementations and applications.

At this point, we believe it is helpful to step back and look at the big picture. What are the strengths and weaknesses of various approaches that might influence your choice of computational intelligence tool(s) for a particular problem? What practical issues associated with the problem environment might influence your choices?

Strengths and Weaknesses

We have discussed strengths and weaknesses of various tools throughout the book. Here we summarize some of the most general concepts.

First, consider the individual concepts, or methodologies, and how to choose one. All else being equal, in what cases would we choose to use a neural network versus a fuzzy system for a diagnostic system, for example? One important factor is the quantity of (presumably high-quality) data available. If a copious amount of data that permeates the problem space is provided, we would be inclined to train or evolve a neural network. If only a relatively small dataset is available, or the data don't cover the problem space to well, it may be better to develop or evolve a fuzzy rule-based system.

A fuzzy system may also be indicated if a significant portion of our data is linguistic or imprecise. Fuzzy sets allow us to quantify uncertainty.

Another factor that can influence our choice of approach is data representation. For example, if we have an existing dataset for an optimization system we are developing, and the data are in binary format, a genetic algorithm may be a reasonable approach. We developed one logistics planning system for which we wanted to apply particle swarm optimization, but we couldn't figure out how to represent the data so that we could use PSO effectively. The problem lent itself to a genetic algorithm representation, so we used a GA.

What we've said so far primarily applies to choosing an individual methodology. But this book is mainly about computational intelligence. So what about those hybrid (computational intelligence) tools that allow us to exploit the strengths of the individual tools to solve problems that are intractable (or at least very difficult) for any individual approach?

As we stated at the beginning of the book, our view is that computational intelligence is built on a foundation of evolutionary computation. We may choose an evolutionary computation tool such as particle swarm optimization for an application and use it essentially by itself. But when we include a neural network or fuzzy logic, there is almost always an evolutionary computation component. When we use a neural network, we usually evolve the network weights and sometimes the network structure. When we use fuzzy logic, we usually evolve the rules and sometimes the membership functions.

Whenever feasible, we compare two or more approaches and choose the one that gives us the best performance. Although it is true that we have played significant roles with Jim Kennedy in developing particle swarm optimization, we try never to bias our viewpoint in favor of PSO or any other approach. The best solution to a problem usually depends on the problem.

Modeling and Optimization

Many applications, such as system identification, can be handled as black-box systems: A group of inputs is sent into the box and responses are expected as results. In order to solve such a problem, two main steps need to be taken. First, we need to establish a model based on the knowledge we have to map the inputs to the outputs; this is modeling. Second, we need to adapt the model to tune the outputs' response to the inputs; this is optimization.

There are many traditional methods to model various simple or complex, linear or nonlinear, continuous or discrete systems. A variety of parameter estimation techniques have been developed and discussed in the literature. Computational intelligence tools can be applied to both steps to facilitate the problem-solving process. Artificial neural networks (ANNs) and fuzzy systems are particularly suitable in the modeling process, and evolutionary algorithms are often used in the optimization process.

Fuzzy systems and ANNs provide alternative solutions to model and identify systems. In traditional methods, accurate models must be provided to identify a system. Furthermore, it is hard to estimate the parameters if the system is highly nonlinear. However, for many complex problems, such as chemical reactions and biomedical applications, it is nearly impossible to specify an accurate link between the inputs and the outputs. Computational intelligence tools may be the only tools currently available.

Fuzzy systems and ANNs have advantages and disadvantages. ANNs are suitable for problems with large-scale and well-distributed patterns; fuzzy systems work better when the patterns are not as large or have an uneven distribution. Incomplete and imprecise domain knowledge can also be integrated into fuzzy systems, but ANNs do not need any domain knowledge.

Artificial neural networks are fast and simple to implement if sufficient datasets are provided. However, it's hard to explain the meaning of neural networks and extract domain knowledge from the network structure and weights. On the other hand, fuzzy systems consist of a set of fuzzy rules obtained through domain experts or from raw data by using an automatic rule generation method such as an evolutionary algorithm and an artificial neural network. These fuzzy rules generated from raw data represent domain knowledge. These automatic rule generation methods can be particularly useful approaches for data mining or knowledge discovery.

Evolutionary algorithms (EAs) are optimization techniques. They can be used not only in evolving neural networks or fuzzy systems but also in optimizing parameter sets. The advantages are that they do not need any domain knowledge to do the optimization, and they can handle nonlinear, nondifferentiable, noncontinuous, and large complex systems well. The trade-off is that EAs aren't guaranteed to obtain the best (optimal) solution, only a sufficient one.

Practical Issues

In an ideal world, you would be able to choose the computational tool for your problem with total objectivity by selecting the tool most likely to give you the best solution. We do not, however, live in an ideal world. Every project has time, resource, and budget constraints.

It is very unlikely that you will have the luxury of developing the best tool possible (assuming you think you know what that is). In most cases, you will develop what we call *sufficient* solutions. Recall that earlier in the book we defined a sufficient solution as one that is good enough, fast enough, and cheap enough.

There will even be times when your customer practically dictates how you should solve the problem. As an example, one of the authors worked on a project to develop a diagnostic system for an automotive electrical system application. There was a very large amount of data, and a neural network-based system seemed to be the most promising approach. The sponsor, however, insisted that the diagnostic system be rule-based, in part so that the explanation facility (see Chapter 11) would be an inherent part of the system. We thus were persuaded to use a fuzzy rule-based system, even though a neural network would probably have performed a little better. On the other side of that coin, in an application for another commercial sponsor, we had a fair amount of data but were leaning toward evolving a fuzzy rule-based system, minimizing the number of rules as part of our fitness function. In this case, the sponsor persuaded us to adapt a neural network because of the relatively lower cost of implementing the trained network weight matrix on the custom chip being developed for the system. The overall system manufacturing cost thus drove our development approach.

If we develop a sufficient solution using good engineering practices and our customer is happy, we've done our job!

Applying Computational Intelligence to Data Mining

This section presents an example of applying computational intelligence methodologies to data mining. The example illustrates how the various methodologies of computational intelligence can be combined and even intertwined.

Data mining is the process of using computational algorithms to process large databases to find useful patterns and relationships. Traditional computational tools include clustering, classification, and rule mining. Data mining is also commonly referred to as knowledge discovery in databases (KDD). A comprehensive treatment of data mining is beyond the scope of this book. You are referred to books focused on data mining such as Han and Kamber (2006).

Software that simply rearranges data in a database isn't doing data mining. Data mining is used to find previously unrecognized patterns or relationships among the data that are useful. Depending on the application, the object of data mining may include reducing cost, improving performance, and predicting behavior or trends. An example of data mining is the detailed analysis of sales data by a large discount store chain such as Wal-Mart to discover geographical patterns in customers' buying habits.

In the remainder of this section, we outline one approach using multiple computational intelligence methodologies for a data mining system that deals with real-time analysis of a large stream of textual data.

An Example Data Mining System

In working with a huge amount of streaming textual data, the example system described here could discover and display related entities and patterns as they appear over time. It could establish associations across textual reports from multiple sources. Therefore, in addition to "mining" clusters, the proposed system could discover linked activity networks over time, then display the data to analysts using state-of-the-art visualization techniques.

The fitness of the system can be dynamic and knowledge driven, and cluster membership could imply fitness relations within hyperplanes that adapt with time. The example system could discover and follow the faint trails of data that lead to meaningful spatio-temporal clusters.

The system we have designed incorporates the three main constituent methodologies of computational intelligence: evolutionary computation, neural networks, and fuzzy logic. At the core of the system are clustering and classification models, such as neural networks, that use both supervised and unsupervised algorithms. These models can be evolved using particle swarm optimization (PSO), which is capable of handling multimodal, multiple-constraint, nonlinear problems in complex and changing environments.

Wrapped around the system's core is a fuzzy logic shell. The fuzzy rules, membership function shapes, and fuzzy set locations in the problem domain can be evolved using evolutionary computation techniques such as genetic algorithms and PSO. This fuzzy shell handles user preferences and rules at the macro level. The system is thus capable of adapting to individual users over time. Figure 9.3 illustrates the components of the system.

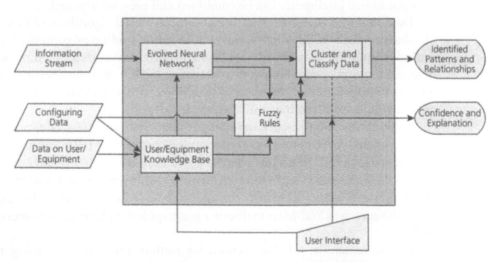

Figure 9.3 Diagram of the computational intelligence data mining system.

As indicated on the system output, it is important to provide users with an "explanation facility" for this system and to indicate the confidence level of the outputs. The hybrid nature and the complexity of the system make traditional explanation facilities impossible. However, recently developed techniques using evolutionary computation described in this book can be used to develop such a facility. This facility is also very important in that it would be usable as a prediction system to identify and predict new (previously unseen) combinations of parameters and events that might be expected to be indicators of interest.

Summary

In this chapter, we discuss common implementation issues for fuzzy evolutionary fuzzy rule systems. We describe the implementation of the fuzzy evolutionary fuzzy rule system. In the system, a genetic algorithm is used to design the fuzzy rule system for solving problems, and another fuzzy rule system is employed to adapt the genetic algorithm. The relationships among them are shown in Figure 9.4. "How much fuzzification is enough?" It would be conceivable to evolve everything we fuzzify and to fuzzify everything we evolve, *ad infinitum*. The optimal extent (depth) of evolution and fuzzification is almost certainly problem-specific and is highly dependent on what computation cost we can afford. Next, we look at some issues related to picking the best tool(s) for a particular job. We discuss both individual methodologies and computational intelligence approaches. Finally, we examine an example of the computational intelligence approach to data mining.

In the next chapter we examine methods to measure how well our systems perform. The performance metrics described in the chapter can be used in applications both inside and outside the computational intelligence field.

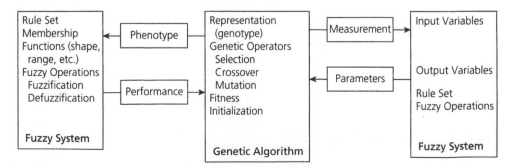

Figure 9.4 Relationships among fuzzy systems and genetic algorithms in the fuzzy evolutionary fuzzy rule system.

Exercises

1. List two parameters that can be adapted to improve a GA's performance at the levels of environment, population, individual, and component.

2. Compare the strengths and weaknesses of the four levels of adaptation of genetic algorithms: environment, population, individual, and component.

3. Briefly describe how to use a fuzzy system to adapt the parameters you listed in Exercise 1.

4. If you are asked to use a fuzzy system to adapt the PSO in the implementation of the evolutionary neural network discussed in Chapter 6, what will be the input and output of the fuzzy system?

5. Run both the evolutionary fuzzy rule system (m_flag = 0) and the fuzzy evolutionary fuzzy rule system (m_flag = 1), and compare the results.

6. Modify the fuzzy rule system in Listing 9.2, and run the software again to see whether you can obtain better results.

7. How generally applicable is the system diagram of Figure 9.3 to other applications such as analysis of large video data streams? Identify another application area, and draw a diagram analogous to Figure 9.3 for that application.

chapter
ten

Performance Metrics

The first nine chapters of this book focused on computational intelligence concepts, paradigms, and implementations. We showed you how to design, develop, and test your systems. But how, exactly, do you measure how well your system is working?

Measuring how well a system is performing is relatively straightforward sometimes. We simply specify the percentage of correct answers in a test or operational situation and compare that with the specification that was established beforehand. Another common approach is to measure a system's performance with respect to some specified tolerance. The situation is seldom this simple, however, when we must measure the performance of computational intelligence implementations and compare different system configurations.

In this chapter, we examine some issues related to measuring how well a computational intelligence implementation is doing. Unfortunately, this subject has not been discussed extensively in the literature, so in some cases we adapted performance measurement techniques that have been applied in related areas.

We first discuss general issues that cut across performance metrics. These issues include the selection of gold standards; partitioning patterns for training, testing, and validation; cross validation; the use and interpretation of fitness functions; and the use of statistical tools.

The performance measures that are discussed include the relatively simple measure of the percent correct, average sumsquared error, absolute error, normalized error, evolutionary algorithm effectiveness, the Mann–Whitney U statistic, receiver operating characteristic (ROC) curve measurements, measurements based on ROC curve parameters (recall, precision, sensitivity, specificity, etc.), confusion matrices, cost functions, and the chi-square goodness-of-fit metric.

The measure chosen depends on the type of system and on other, somewhat more loosely defined parameters, such as the level of technical sophistication of the system's end user.

General Issues

In this section, we discuss a number of general issues related to measuring the performance of computational intelligence implementations. We call them "general" because these issues arise for more than just a single specific performance metric. We present issues that relate only to a single performance metric in the section where that metric is discussed.

Examples of general issues are specifying the sizes and numbers of iterations for training datasets, and the selection of test datasets, for neural networks. Other examples are the selection of the "gold standards" against which performance is measured, and the role the decision threshold level of a processing element in a neural network can play in determining system performance. Additional issues include fitness and fitness functions and the use of parametric and nonparametric statistics. These are issues that must be addressed regardless of whether the performance metric is percent correct or some other metric such as normalized error.

We first examine the issues of selecting gold standards, selecting test sets, and selecting training sets for those implementations, such as neural networks, that require them.

Selecting Gold Standards

At least two issues are associated with the selection of gold standards, for both training sets and testing sets. The first is the classification itself, and the second is the selection of a representative pattern set. A third issue to be addressed, which encompasses the first two, is selecting the person(s) or process used to designate the gold standards.

Relative to the first issue, in a classification problem it is sometimes straightforward to specify the classification of the items, or patterns, in the training and testing sets. For example, if the computational intelligence implementation is being used to classify printed versions of individual letters of the alphabet, such as A, B, and C, there should be no disagreement about which letter is which. On the other hand, some classification tasks can be more difficult. For example, in the classification of biopotential waveforms, such as electrocardiograms and electroencephalograms, the interpretation of waveforms can be a matter of opinion among experts. For example, in the case of a neural network system to detect epileptiform spikes described in Eberhart and Dobbins (1990), and summarized as a case study in Chapter 12 of this book, the average overlap in identification of individual spike waveforms was only about 60 percent between any two of the six neurologists who evaluated the data records.

It is therefore important to obtain agreement beforehand on the classification process and the classifications themselves, and to state both clearly when presenting any performance measurement results. In this step, it is extremely important to get the active participation of the end users of the system (such as the neurologists in the case just mentioned).

Given that classifications can be made and agreed to, the next job is usually the selection of the "representative examples" for the training and testing sets, if required. This is an area in which much development work is currently being done. It is possible to state guidelines, but few hard rules exist.

The examples selected for the training and testing sets, in addition to being agreed to by the experts as representatives of the class, must be appropriately distributed over the class being represented. That is, the examples should not all be ideal, or textbook, examples of the pattern class, with pattern vectors "right down the middle" of the classification. Rather, they should include patterns that, though clearly belonging to the identified class, are somewhat borderline, having attributes that place them near a decision hypersurface with another class or classes. This is particularly important for cases, such as biopotential waveform analysis, in which human perception is involved and opinions, though generally in agreement, may vary from expert to expert. Kohonen (1988, 1989) and Rumelhart and McClelland (1986) have discussed and demonstrated the need for using training/testing patterns near decision boundaries. Their work provides an excellent resource for more information on this aspect of pattern selection.

The selection of the person(s) or process used to identify the gold standard training and testing cases is very important. Too often, engineers and programmers working on a project take it upon themselves to do this identification. This should be avoided. It is important to involve the end users of the system in this process. Although the engineers and programmers can provide the end users with information regarding the technical constraints within which the system must operate, it should be left to the users, as much as possible, to provide the case data selection, or at least the process for the selection. This is particularly important in areas such as biomedical engineering: Medicine must drive engineering, not the other way around.

Involving users in the selection of the gold standard data does not relieve the engineer or programmer of all responsibility for this data. The quality of the data, including potential problems such as noisy data and missing data elements and how those will be handled, must be worked out and agreed to by all interested parties.

Partitioning the Patterns for Training, Testing, and Validation

It is generally not acceptable to test a computational intelligence implementation with the same set of patterns used to train it. A portion of the patterns is used for training, and the remainder, often chosen randomly, is used for testing. Taking this one step further, a project sponsor may withhold a portion of the datasets to be used for testing after the system is proclaimed to meet specifications. These datasets are sometimes referred to as validation datasets. So some datasets have been divided into three portions—training, testing, and validation. This idea of testing a system on data it has not previously seen is the basis for *cross validation*, discussed later, although cross validation involves more than just dividing patterns into training and testing portions.

Furthermore, it is frequently a good idea to rotate training and testing cases through all available cases. That is, a given set of cases can be selected for training one time and a different set another time. Likewise, different cases can be used for testing at different times. It is desirable to examine the performance of a computational intelligence implementation with these changes, if possible. This approach begins to look something like cross validation.

When training some neural networks, especially back-propagation networks, it is often a good idea to select a training set with about the same number of patterns for each classification. That is, if the network has three output processing elements (PEs), each of which becomes active for a particular pattern classification, it is probably a good idea to have a training pattern set with about one-third of the patterns from each classification. This is, for some people, counterintuitive.

A more intuitive argument is that the numerical distribution of patterns should reflect the probability distribution of the classes. For example, if we are training a neural network implementation with two output PEs and if one of the classes appears in the real world 20 percent of the time, then it would make sense to some people to draw 20 percent of the training cases from this class (and 80 percent from the other class).

Better network performance often results, however, if, in the case just described, approximately 50 percent of the training patterns are selected from each class, regardless of the probability distribution. In fact, the authors have seen cases in which allocating the percentage of classes of training patterns according to probability distributions has resulted in a failure to train the network.

Cross Validation

Cross validation is a method that allows us to estimate how well a system will perform on data it has not seen previously (during training). It thus predicts how well the system can generalize.

Cross validation starts by partitioning a dataset into subsets for training, testing, and perhaps validation. Just holding out a subset for testing, by itself, does not comprise cross validation since none of the data are "crossed over" (described later). There are two main types of cross validation, although the second is just a special case of the first: k-fold cross validation and leave-one-out cross validation.

For *k*-fold cross validation, the dataset is partitioned into *k* subsets. In an iterative process, one of the *k* subsets is used for testing and the remaining *k* − 1 subsets are used for training. This is repeated *k* times until all *k* subsets have been used once for testing. The results from the *k* iterations can then be averaged or combined in some other way to provide an error estimate. The variance of the result decreases as *k* increases.

Leave-one-out cross validation takes *k*-fold cross validation to the limit by iteratively using a single pattern as the test set. Thus, *k* is the total number of patterns in the dataset, and each pattern is used exactly once as the test set. Leave-one-out cross validation is computationally intensive for large datasets.

How *k* is chosen is more of an art than a science, and it depends on the nature of the problem. In the authors' experience, if the total number of patterns is less than 100 or so, leave-one-out cross validation is probably worth the effort. In very large datasets comprising thousands of patterns, a value of *k* between 10 and 100 is a good place to start.

Note that the cross validation process is applicable across a variety of performance metrics. It can be applied, for example, to neural networks using a percent correct metric as well as to fuzzy controllers using an absolute error metric.

Fitness and Fitness Functions

The fitness of a solution is a numeric value that provides an indication of how well the solution meets the objective(s) of the problem. The concept of fitness is central to evolutionary computation (EC) methodology (discussed in Chapters 3 and 4).

The concept of fitness is applied over a broad spectrum of EC problems. At one end of the spectrum are benchmark problems such as the Rastrigin function for which an equation exists and the location of the global optimum is known. Fitness in such cases is a function of the error with respect to the global optimum. The highest fitness is known and is often zero. A solution that is closer to the global optimum has a smaller error and a higher fitness than a solution farther away.

At the other end of the spectrum are problems for which the global optimum is unknown. It may not even be known whether or not a global optimum exists, and, if it does, whether there are multiple global optima. Most examples of this type of problem are *NP-hard* and the fitness score is a function of the system output(s). Furthermore, the fitness score may be a weighted function of output parameters. An example is a logistics scheduling problem, where the numbers and types of items delivered, the time windows of the deliveries, and priority scores may all be weighted and incorporated into fitness values.

Note that use of the concept of fitness should not be limited to EC implementations. If percent correct is being used to measure the fitness of a neural network output, then percent correct measurements over a number of cases may be considered as fitness values (higher is better). If a fuzzy logic control system output is measured over a number of cases, the output error measurements (number of degrees deviation from a thermostat setting, for example) may be treated as fitness values (lower is better).

Recall the three spaces of adaptation discussed in Chapter 2: input parameter space, system output space, and fitness space. System output space is the space defined by the dynamic range(s) of the output variable(s). The fitness space is the space we use to define the "goodness" of the solutions in the output space. We often scale fitness to values between 0 and 1, with either 0 or 1 being the optimal value, depending on whether we are minimizing or maximizing. Thus, system output and fitness generally do not coincide.

Furthermore, the numerical value of fitness rarely has meaning. We nearly always use fitness values to rank solutions. A system configuration with a fitness value of 0.980 is rarely exactly twice as good as a system configuration with a fitness value of 0.490. We simply have a rank-ordered list of how good a solution is relative to other solutions.

It is common practice to vary parameters such as crossover rate in a GA and attempt to see what value produces a better system. We may, for example, run the GA ten times with one crossover rate and ten times with another crossover rate. Due to the stochastic nature of the algorithm, we may very well get a different fitness value each time, although it is possible that a few may be identical due to the precision of our computer.

How do we determine which system configuration is better? If all of the fitness values for one crossover rate are better than those for another crossover rate, the situation is clear: Use the system configuration that consistently produces the better fitness values. However, the situation is seldom so simple. Especially in the later stages of system development, when we are fine-tuning parameters to maximize system performance, we may have situations that are hard to analyze and interpret.

Parametric and Nonparametric Statistics

For analysis and interpretation, we turn to the field of statistics. We need to be very careful how we use statistics, however. In this section we summarize this approach and provide the justification for using nonparametric (also sometimes referred to as "distribution-free") statistics tools rather than those of parametric statistics. The discussion in this section ignores many issues and details related to the field of statistics. We encourage you to refer to a text on probability and statistics to fill in the gaps. An excellent book written for engineers and scientists is Ross (2004).

Performance metrics measure how well (or poorly) your system is performing. What the performance metrics do *not* tell you is whether differences in system performance as reflected in fitness values are statistically significant. Inferential statistics tools can be used to assess statistical significance. However, we must be very cautious about which tools we use.

You have probably taken a statistics course (or have studied it on your own) during your educational process. It is likely that you studied parametric statistics tools (such as the Student's *t*-test and the analysis of variance) almost exclusively. For results to be valid using parametric statistics tools, however, the underlying distribution of data must be normal, or exponential, or of some other specified form.

The datasets we deal with in computational intelligence, such as lists of fitnesses, usually do not conform to any particular type of distribution. They may be anything. Most of the time they are just lists of real numbers.

This is where nonparametric statistics come in. They do not assume that the data are in any particular parametric form. Any nonparametric tool can thus be applied without regard to the data distribution form. We discuss two nonparametric statistics tools in this chapter: the Mann–Whitney U test and the chi-square test. The Mann–Whitney U test provides a powerful tool for analyzing the performance of evolutionary algorithms. It is both useful and easy to use. The chi-square test can be applied to the analysis of structured sequences or patterns by systems adapted to examples. An example is a system that simulates some process, such as a biological process, that can be described statistically.

To learn more about nonparametric statistics, we suggest you refer to the book that most people consider the foundation book in the field, Siegel (1956). This book is both comprehensive and easy to read.

Now that we've covered general issues related to performance metrics, we will discuss some specific examples. They are not discussed in any particular order.

Percent Correct

Because it is, at least on the face of it, the simplest, we describe first the measurement of computational intelligence system performance by determining the percent correct obtained in a particular situation. This is simply the percentage of all answers that were judged to be correct according to some gold standard. A value for percent correct is obtained for training, testing, and validation. It should be noted that, for some applications, the concept of percent correct is not particularly useful, such as in the composition of music and in the simulation of a system; other measures, or metrics, are then used.

Once one has made the selection of training/testing patterns, the selection of representative samples, and the selection by expert end users of the process to be used in designating the gold standards, the calculation of percent correct is relatively straightforward. There is still, however, the issue of how to interpret the different values of percent correct obtained for the testing and training sets. (We discuss the issue of interpreting error values for training and testing elsewhere in this book, but we emphasize here that it is important to use different sets of cases (patterns) for training and testing.)

Note that neural network implementations often establish ranges within which answers are considered correct. For example, if the output can vary from 0 to 1, then any output in the range 0.8 to 1.0 might be considered as a 1 and any output in the range of 0.0–0.2 might be taken as a 0. In a more extreme case, anything above 0.5 may be considered a 1 and anything <= 0.5 a 0. Manipulating the percent correct metric like this introduces subjectivity, but makes it more useful in a practical sense, since we are almost never able to train a network to exactly the target values (and if we did, it would be seriously overtrained and unable to generalize).

Percent correct has limitations as a performance metric, as is illustrated by the following example. Suppose that out of a group of 100 stocks, a computational intelligence tool accurately predicted 90 percent of the time last month which stocks would outperform the Dow Jones average on a percentage basis. Stocks that did less well than the Dow Jones average were predicted with 60 percent accuracy. This month, only 85 percent of the stocks outperforming the Dow Jones average were accurately predicted and only 55 percent of the stocks that did less well than the Dow Jones average were accurately predicted. Overall ability to predict, however, improved.

To see how this is possible, suppose that half of the stocks last month were in each of the two categories. The overall performance was thus (90 * 0.50) + (60 * 0.50) = 75 percent correct. Further suppose that this month 70 percent of the stocks outperformed the Dow Jones average. The performance was thus (85 * 0.70) + (55 * 0.30) = 76 percent correct. Overall predictive accuracy therefore increased, even though the predictive accuracy on the individual metrics decreased. Part of this seeming contradiction results because the proportions of instances of the categories (i.e., those that outperformed the Dow Jones average) were unequal in the two months.

The example shows that percent correct can be misleading if it is the only method of evaluating performance. In the example, we might have chosen a computational intelligence system trained on the second set of data over one trained on the first set, even though the two systems may have been identical. The following sections describe performance metrics that can be used in place of, or in addition to, percent correct.

Average Sum-squared Error

As is discussed in Chapter 6, the goal of neural network adaptation when using the back-propagation algorithm is to minimize the *average sum-squared error*. The average sum-squared error is obtained by computing the difference between the output value that an output PE is supposed to have for a pattern k, called b_{kj}, and the value the PE actually has as a result of the feedforward calculations, called z_{kj}. This difference is squared, and then the sum of the squares is taken over all output

PEs. Finally, the calculation is repeated for each pattern in the testing or training set, as applicable. The grand total sum over all PEs and all patterns, multiplied by 0.5, is the *total error E_t*, as given in equation 10.1.

$$E_t = 0.5 \sum_k \sum_j \left(b_{kj} - z_{kj} \right)^2 \qquad (10.1)$$

The total error is then divided by the number of patterns to yield the average sum-squared error.

There are a few things relative to average sum-squared error that are worth considering. They relate to being able to compare results. First, the original definition of average sum-squared error made by Rumelhart and McClelland (1986) includes the multiplier 0.5, as discussed in Chapter 6. Many implementations ignore this factor of 0.5 (it reduces calculation time to eliminate it), but it is important to be aware of how the error term is calculated in your neural network implementation and in any one with which results are being compared.

Second, the error term is summed over all output PEs. This is also the way it is defined by Rumelhart and McClelland (1986). A potential problem is that if you happen to be using various network configurations with different numbers of output PEs, the average sum-squared error may not accurately reflect the performance of the network.

It is possible, for example, to train a network with one output PE to a given error, then find that the error increases when essentially the same net with several output PEs is trained. The performance of the network as measured by percent correct may have increased at the same time as the average sum-squared error (per pattern) increased. It is therefore important to keep in mind that average sum-squared error, as it was originally defined, means that it is averaged by dividing by the number of patterns in the training or test set, not that it is averaged on a per-PE basis. It will probably be desirable, for many applications, to compute the error per PE by dividing the average sum-squared error (per pattern) by the number of output PEs. This metric is called the *average per PE sum-squared error*.

Because the average per PE sum-squared error is often used in conjunction with the neural network back-propagation algorithm, when used as a performance metric it is frequently used with a back-propagation implementation. There is no reason, however, why it can't be used with other CI paradigm implementations, such as learning vector quantization and fuzzy expert systems, as long as the correct values of the outputs are known.

It should be cautioned that the average sum-squared error measure (whether per pattern or per PE and per pattern) may not adequately measure the network performance in some instances. For example, depending on the threshold value selected in a back-propagation model, the average sum-squared error may not accurately reflect the performance of the neural network implementation.

The *threshold value* is the number, between 0 and 1 for a sigmoid activation function in a back-propagation implementation, above which an output PE is considered to be on and below which it is off. The most common value selected for the threshold is 0.5, but a different value, such as 0.7 or 0.8, may be more appropriate for some applications.

Following are two cases for which the values of the average (per pattern) sum-squared error are somewhat misleading. Assume that there is only one output PE (so the error is also a per PE error), ten patterns in the set, and a threshold value of 0.5. Also assume that for five of the patterns the output PE should be *on* and for the other five it should be *off*.

If the values of the output PE for the *on* patterns are always 0.6 and always 0.4 for the *off* patterns (the error is always 0.4), then, with the threshold value of 0.5, the network is classifying all ten patterns correctly and is thus performing perfectly, based on percent correct. The average per pattern (and per PE) sum-squared error is [10(0.16)]/10, or 0.16.

Now consider a case in which the output PE has a value of 0.9 for all *on* patterns and 0.1 for all *off* patterns except two, for which it has a value of 0.6. Thus it is getting eight of the ten patterns correct, so it is 80 percent correct, which is less than the previous case. The average sum-squared error, however, is [8(0.01) + 2(0.36)]/10 = 0.08, only one-half of the value in the previous example in which the network exhibited perfect performance.

For cases in which the threshold is a value such as 0.5, it may be more appropriate to calculate the average sum-squared error based on values (or a single value) other than 0 and 1. With a threshold of 0.5, for example, it may be more meaningful to calculate an error value only for those PEs that are on the incorrect side of the threshold and to use the threshold as the desired value.

In the first of these two examples, then, this threshold-based average sum-squared error is 0, whereas in the second case it is [2(0.01)]/10, or 0.002. This method of error calculation seems to provide a more realistic picture of the network performance in these examples.

Absolute Error

For many people, average sum-squared error has little meaning at an intuitive level. Seldom, if ever, are errors measured and then squared to help a human understand a system's performance.

A more intuitive error measure is the *absolute error*. One metric incorporating the absolute error that is often used is *mean absolute error*, defined in equation 10.2 on a per PE per pattern basis, where m is the number of patterns and q is the number of output PEs. Another metric using absolute error is the *maximum absolute error*, which is just the maximum value of absolute error for any single pattern in the test set. As can be seen, absolute error is analogous to sum-squared error, with the absolute value of the error replacing the sum-squared term.

$$E_{ma} = \frac{1}{mq} \sum_{k=1}^{m} \sum_{j=1}^{q} |b_{kj} - y_{kj}| \tag{10.2}$$

Normalized Error

A problem with the average per PE sum-squared error is that it is corrupted by the target variances of the output PEs. It is therefore desirable to have some error metric that is independent of these variances.

For those of you who are not statisticians and, like the authors, have forgotten most of what little statistics you ever knew, a brief discussion of variance may be helpful. For more information, refer to a book on statistics, such as the ones by Armitage and Berry (1987) and Ross (2004).

Variance is the average of the squared deviations from the mean. It is often referred to as the *mean square*. Two slightly different versions of variance exist: the population variance and the sample variance. Although there is sometimes disagreement about which should be used in descriptive statistics, the authors have chosen to work with the population variance. In practical applications of neural network tools, there is very little difference between them.

The population (target) variance for a single output PE z_j is represented as σ_j^2, and the equation for the target variance is given in equation 10.3, where μ_j is the population (target) mean, or the average of a given output PE's *target* values for all of the patterns, and m is the number of patterns. The standard deviation, by the way, is just the square root of the variance, or the *root mean square* (rms); therefore, the standard (target) deviation for a single output PE is represented as σ_j.

$$\sigma_j^2 = \frac{\sum\limits_{k=1}^{m} \left(b_{kj} - \mu_j\right)^2}{m} \tag{10.3}$$

An error measure that removes the effects of target variance and yields an error value between 0 and 1 for all networks regardless of configuration was developed by Pineda (1988). This error measure involves the calculation of a quantity defined in equation 10.4 that Pineda calls E_{mean}, which is the sum of squared deviations of the target values about the target mean. Note that for a given training pattern dataset or test pattern dataset, E_{mean} remains constant.

$$E_{\text{mean}} = 0.5 \sum_k \sum_j \left(b_{kj} - \mu_j\right)^2 \qquad \textbf{(10.4)}$$

Now, the *normalized error*, E_n, (see equation 10.5) is defined as the total error E_t (defined in equation 10.1) divided by E_{mean} (defined in equation 10.4).

$$E_n = \frac{E_t}{E_{\text{mean}}} \qquad \textbf{(10.5)}$$

As Pineda explains, E_n is particularly useful for back-propagation neural networks because regardless of network topology or the particular application, a back-propagation network learns relatively easily the pattern represented by the average target values of the output PEs. This is sort of a "worst case," in which the network is "guessing" the correct output to be the average target value and results in a value of $E_n = 1$. As the patterns are learned, the normalized error value moves toward 0. The speed of movement depends on the network architecture and the application.

A word of caution is appropriate here. Think about what would happen if you had an output PE in your network that never changed value. Every target value would be equal to the mean value μ_j, and E_{mean} would be 0, making the normalized error "artificially" larger. This situation isn't as farfetched as it may seem. On more than one occasion, the authors have trained a network with several output PEs using only a partial training set (i.e., one that didn't contain one or more of the output classifications). For the missing classifications, of course, the corresponding output PE values were 0. We suggest that you remove PEs that don't change value.

One way to look at the normalized error is that it reflects the proportion of the output variance that is due to error rather than the architecture (including the initial random weight values) of the network itself. Overall, it is believed that this error measure may be, in many cases, the most useful one for back-propagation neural network implementations.

Evolutionary Algorithm Effectiveness Metrics

Two metrics for the effectiveness of genetic algorithms (GAs) were described by De Jong (1975). These metrics, however, are appropriate for any evolutionary computation implementation that "evolves" a population of solutions. De Jong named these metrics *off-line performance* and *on-line performance*.

When an evolutionary computation system (or any other optimizer) is being run off-line, many system configurations can be evaluated (the fitness calculated) and the best configuration selected. For on-line work, however, configurations must be evaluated in real time, and therefore the usual goal is to develop an acceptable solution as soon as possible.

The on-line performance, which measures the ongoing performance of a system configuration, is defined in equation 10.6, where $\overline{f_s(g)}$ is the average population fitness for a system configuration s during generation g, and G is the number (index) of the latest generation.

$$p_s^{\text{online}} = \frac{1}{G} \sum_{g=1}^{G} \overline{f_s(g)} \tag{10.6}$$

The off-line performance measures convergence of the algorithm and is defined in equation 10.7, where $f_s^*(g)$ is the best fitness of any population member in generation g for system configuration s. Off-line (convergence) performance is thus the average of the best fitness values from each generation up to the present.

$$p_s^{\text{offline}} = \frac{1}{G} \sum_{g=1}^{G} f_s^*(g) \tag{10.7}$$

Mann–Whitney U Test

The Mann–Whitney U test is a useful and easy-to-use tool for analyzing the performance of evolutionary algorithms. It is reported to have been developed independently by Mann and Whitney (1947) and by Wilcoxon (1945). It is thus variously referred to as the Mann–Whitney–Wilcoxon test or the Wilcoxon rank-sum text.

The test evaluates whether the medians of two samples of data are the same. The *null hypothesis* is that the medians are equal, and the two samples have the same distribution (Siegel 1956). The samples must comprise *ordinal* or continuous measurements so that it is possible to say which of two measurements is greater.

The number of measurements in each of the two samples, n_1 and n_2, need not be the same. Also, results with significance at the 0.05 level (and sometimes even at the 0.01 level) can often be obtained with values of n_1 and n_2 of 10 or fewer, thus making the test easier to use than tools that require more measurements in order to achieve useful significance levels.

In this section, we describe how to calculate U when n_1 and n_2 are each less than 20. With larger values for n_1 and n_2, Mann and Whitney (1947) demonstrated that the sampling distribution of U approaches a normal distribution. It is unlikely that you will need to calculate U for large values of n_1 and n_2, but if you do, please refer to a text describing the Mann–Whitney U test such as Siegel (1956).

We will illustrate the calculation and interpretation of U two ways. The first method is quick and direct and should provide you with an understanding of the U statistic. The second uses a formula and will probably be your method of choice when using a computer. (Most statistical packages for PCs include the Mann–Whitney U test.)

We consider two samples of best fitness values obtained when running an evolutionary algorithm with two configurations. Assume that we are running a minimization problem, with an optimum of 0.0. One or more algorithm parameters are different for each of the two runs. (Perhaps we have changed the crossover and mutation rates for a GA or altered the inertia weight for a swarm.) We call the configurations, and the samples reflecting those configurations, A and B, where B is our "baseline" configuration. Say that we make five runs with configuration A and obtain best fitness values of 0.079, 0.062, 0.073, 0.047, and 0.085. With configuration B our best fitness values are 0.102, 0.069, 0.055, and 0.049. The values for n_1 and n_2 are thus 5 and 4, respectively.

First, we arrange these measurements in the order of fitness, keeping track of which belong to A and which to B:

0.047	0.049	0.055	0.062	0.069	0.073	0.079	0.085	0.102
A	B	B	A	B	A	A	A	B

We now have a list ranked by fitness, with better fitness values to the left in the table. The simple and direct method of calculating U is to count the number of A entries that are better than (to the left of) each of the B entries. We thereby obtain a value of U of $1 + 1 + 2 + 5 = 9$.

You can also calculate the number of B entries that are better than each of the A entries and obtain an answer of $0 + 2 + 3 + 3 + 3 = 11$. Let's call this result U'. The statistic U is the smaller of these two possible calculations. If you are not sure whether you've done it the right way, it is helpful to know that U and U' are related as follows: $U = n_1 n_2 - U'$ Remember, always choose the smaller of the two.

To calculate U using a formula, we first arrange the measurements as before. Recall that in the preceding table the ranks go from 1 to 9 as you go from left to right. We first add up all of the ranks for one of the samples. For A, this sum of ranks is $1 + 4 + 6 + 7 + 8 = 26$. Since this sum of ranks is associated with n_1, we call it R_1. The total sum of all ranks is $N(N + 1) / 2$, where $N = n_1 + n_2$, so we can calculate the sum of ranks for B as $45 - 26 = 19$, which we call R_2. (You can also calculate it as we did for A: For B, the sum of ranks is $2 + 3 + 5 + 9 = 19$.)

We then calculate U as the smaller of the values obtained as in equations 10.8 and 10.9.

$$U = n_1 n_2 + \frac{n_1 (n_1 + 1)}{2} - R_1 \qquad (10.8)$$

or, alternatively,

$$U = n_1 n_2 + \frac{n_2 (n_2 + 1)}{2} - R_2 \qquad (10.9)$$

Using equation 10.8, we obtain a value for U of $20 + 15 - 26 = 9$. Using equation 10.9, we calculate U as $20 + 10 - 19 = 11$. These are the same values we obtained by the direct method. We assign the lesser value of 9 to U.

We now determine whether or not the null hypothesis is rejected at some significance level by referring to a table of critical values of U for the combination of n_1 and n_2. In Table 10.1, if a calculated U for a pair of samples of sizes n_1 and n_2 is less than or equal to the value given in the table, then the null hypothesis may be rejected at a significance level of 0.05 for a one-tailed test. (This test is usually configured so that the region of rejection is one-tailed and comprises all values of U sufficiently small that the probability of their occurrence under the null hypothesis is less than or equal to the significance level.)

In the case we just calculated, the entry in the table for n_1 of 5 and n_2 of 4 is 2, so the null hypothesis is not rejected. That means that we cannot say that one configuration produces fitness values that are significantly higher than the other.

Table 10.1 Critical Values of the Mann–Whitney U
for Small Values of n_1 and n_2

n_1 \\ n_2	3	4	5	6	7	8	9	10
3	0	0	1	2	2	3	4	4
4	0	1	2	3	4	5	6	7
5	1	2	4	5	6	8	9	11
6	2	3	5	7	8	10	12	14
7	2	4	6	8	11	13	15	17
8	3	5	8	10	13	15	18	20
9	4	6	9	12	15	18	21	24
10	4	7	11	14	17	20	24	27

In our test case, even though one of the runs using configuration A had the highest fitness of the nine runs, we cannot say that configuration A is significantly better than our baseline configuration B to a significance level of 0.05.

Now, let's test another configuration of the EC tool. Let's call this configuration C. As before, we make five runs using configuration C and compare the fitness values with the four baseline cases using configuration B. Ignoring the specific fitness values for purposes of this illustration (since the rank is all that matters), we obtain:

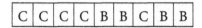

Using the simple and direct method of calculating U, we count the number of C entries that are better than (to the left of) each of the B entries. We thereby obtain a value of U of $4 + 4 + 5 + 5 = 18$. Counting the number of B entries that are better than each C entry, we obtain an answer of $0 + 0 + 0 + 0 + 2 = 2$. Therefore, U has the lesser value of 2. The same answer can be obtained using equations 10.8 and 10.9. In this case, since the value of U is less than or equal to the value in Table 10.1, we can say that our new configuration C is statistically better than our baseline configuration B, and the null hypothesis is rejected at the 0.05 level.

Note that Table 10.1 is only a partial table of critical values of the Mann–Whitney U and is valid only for one-tailed tests at the significance level of 0.05. Tables that are valid for values of n_1 and n_2 up to 20, for other significance levels and for two-tailed tests are available in statistics texts and on the Internet by searching for "Mann–Whitney U test." Remember to refer to a statistics text such as Siegel (1956) if you want to use n_1 or n_2 of more than 20, at which point the sampling distribution of U is rapidly approaching the normal distribution.

The Mann–Whitney U test is a powerful tool for evaluating EC implementations. It is, of course, also applicable to the analyses of neural network, fuzzy system, and computational intelligence systems using a wide variety of fitness measures such as percent correct and normalized error.

Receiver Operating Characteristic Curves

Another way to measure the performance of a computational intelligence system is with receiver operating characteristic (ROC) curves. For some generalized applications, these curves are called relative operating characteristic curves. The use of these curves dates back to the 1940s for both electronic communications systems and the field of psychology. More recently, the use of ROC curves has been described as useful for measuring the performance of diagnostic systems, including those that use expert systems and neural networks (Adlassnig and Scheithauer 1989; Centor and Keightley 1989; Green and Swets 1966; Hanley and McNeil 1983; McClish 1987; Meistrell and Spackman 1989; Swets 1964, 1988).

ROC curves provide a means to quantify the accuracy of an automated diagnostic or classification system by comparing the decisions or classifications of the system, such as one that contains a neural network implementation, with a "gold standard." ROC curves are particularly valuable tools when they are used with neural network and other computational intelligence systems because the results are not sensitive to the probability distribution of training or testing cases (patterns) or to decision bias.

The curves can be generated and compared qualitatively with little regard for their statistical attributes. The use and interpretation of these statistical attributes have, however, become increasingly popular. For example, the calculation of (and understanding the meaning of) the area under the ROC curve has become a common way of evaluating system performance.

An ROC curve is generated for, and reflects, the system's performance for one given result such as a particular diagnosis or classification. It indicates how well the system did, compared with a gold standard, in making a given diagnosis or a given decision. The ROC curve thus represents the performance of one output PE in a neural network application or one diagnosis or classification in a fuzzy expert system. The discussion that follows focuses on the use of a one-PE curve, but the use for multiple-output PE cases is reviewed in the literature (Hanley and McNeil 1983; McClish 1987).

For a given decision, indicated, for example, by a given output PE in a neural network implementation, four possible alternatives exist. These are illustrated in Table 10.2, which shows the contingency matrix used in the definition and computation of ROC curves.

The first alternative is a true positive decision (TP), in which the positive diagnosis of the system coincides with a positive diagnosis according to the gold standard. For example, the system may have identified a tumor that was also identified by an oncologist. The second is a false positive decision (FP), in which the system made a positive diagnosis that was not included in the gold standard; this would mean that the system identified a tissue mass as a tumor, but the oncologist did not. The third possibility is a false negative decision (FN), in which the gold standard made a positive diagnosis that was not made by the system. This

Table 10.2 Contingency Matrix Used in ROC Curve Definition

		System Diagnosis	
		Positive	**Negative**
Gold Standard Diagnosis	**Positive**	TP (true positive)	TN (false negative)
	Negative	EP (false positive)	TN (true negative)

is analogous to the oncologist identifying a tissue mass as a tumor when the system failed to do so. The fourth possibility is a true negative decision (TN), in which both the gold standard and the system indicate the absence of a positive diagnosis (neither the oncologist nor the system identified the tissue mass as a tumor).

The ROC curve makes use of two ratios involving these four possible decisions. The first ratio is TP/(TP + FN), which is generally called the *true positive ratio*; it is also called, for some applications, the *sensitivity*. The second ratio is FP/(FP + TN), generally called the *false positive ratio*. Because the ratio TN/(FP + TN), generally called the *true negative ratio*, is also called the *specificity*, it follows that the false positive ratio is the same thing as (1 − specificity). Sensitivity and specificity are discussed in more detail later.

The ROC curve is a plot of the true positive ratio versus the false positive ratio. When applied to the performance of neural network implementations, the curve is usually obtained by plotting points for various values of the PE threshold, then connecting the points with either line segments or a smooth curve. A typical way to proceed is to plot points for a number of PE threshold values, for example, 0.1, 0.2, . . . , 0.9. To plot the points for the true positive ratio versus false positive ratio, each of the four possible decisions in the contingency matrix must be calculated for each chosen value of the PE threshold.

Another way to plot the ROC curve is to use actual output PE values obtained for a training or test set. A given output PE is typically trained to respond with either a 1 or a 0, depending on the input pattern. When the set of patterns is actually presented to the network, whether it is the last iteration for the training dataset or the one and only iteration for the test set, the PE typically responds with outputs close to but not equal to 1 or 0 for most patterns. A few patterns may result in values scattered in between.

The process is to use the output values, rather than the fixed values, of the PE threshold as the "break points" for calculating the ROC curve. Again, the values for each of the four possible decisions must be calculated for each value of the output PE.

Figure 10.1 illustrates a hypothetical case involving two configurations of a neural network implementation that result in the two ROC curves shown. The curve representing the configuration of NN2 reflects better overall system performance than that of NN1. The dotted line drawn along the major diagonal where the true positive and false positive ratios are equal represents the situation in which no discrimination exists. In other words, a system can achieve this performance solely by chance. When the curve follows the left vertical and upper horizontal axes, the system is discriminating perfectly. In this case, for all values of the false positive ratio, the true positive ratio is one.

From this brief discussion, it is evident that the ROC curve has two attributes: It always lies above the major diagonal, and it is always monotonically increasing in value from left to right. This discussion also implies that a single-value performance measure of a system might be obtained by measuring the area under the ROC

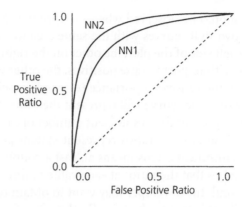

Figure 10.1 Examples of ROC curves.

curve. This is, in fact, the preferred measure of system performance using the ROC curve.

Note that the total area of the graph is one square unit, and the area under the ROC curve is just the proportion of the entire graph lying beneath the curve. Also note that the area under the curve is always between 0.5, the area under the diagonal when no discrimination exists, and 1.0, the area corresponding to perfect performance.

There are two main ways to calculate the area under the ROC curve. One is to generate a smooth curve through the points and calculate the area under it. An easier way is to connect the points with straight-line segments and calculate the area under it using the *trapezoidal rule*. The trapezoidal rule simply means taking the average of two adjacent values of the true positive ratio (*y*-axis values) and multiplying by the corresponding false positive ratio interval along the *x*-axis, then adding all of these individual segment areas together to obtain the total area.

It should be obvious that an ROC curve requires some minimum number of points if a reasonably smooth curve is to be plotted or if the area under a curve constructed of straight-line segments between adjacent points is to have meaning. Generally speaking, an absolute minimum of 5 points should be used to construct a smooth curve, and 9 or 10 will give a reasonably fine-grained structure from which to calculate an area from straight-line segments.

The information represented by an ROC curve can be used in a number of ways. For example, the shape of the curve can indicate the sensitivity of the system performance to the threshold value. As another example, the shape of and area under the ROC curve may reflect changes in network parameters (such as *eta* and *alpha* in a back-propagation network) or adaptation regimens (such as the number of training epochs) more sensitively than other performance measures such as percent correct.

Caution should be observed when interpreting ROC curves. For example, it is possible for two ROC curves with the same area to intersect (one will have higher values on the left side of the plot, the other on the right). One will thus exhibit better performance with respect to false positives, the other with respect to false negatives. Depending on the relative importance (or cost) associated with each of these error types, one or the other curve will represent the more desirable system.

Also, it is important that a sufficient number of cases be analyzed so that the true positive and false positive ratios represent system performance over the range of operating environments. This means at least a couple of things. First, enough cases should be used so that the ratios at each value of threshold chosen to plot the curve are valid. Second, the developer may want to obtain data from the system at points not necessarily of interest otherwise (in the case of a neural network, for example, threshold values near 0.5).

Networks typically are trained to values of 1 and 0. In a well-performing network with just one or two output PEs, then, not many, if any, cases will be available that result in output activation values around 0.5. Techniques involving network inversion, or evolutionary, computation tools (described Chapter 9), can be used to obtain such cases. In systems with numerous output classes or diagnoses, it is more likely that cases resulting in activation values around 0.5 for most of the output PEs will exist.

Other parameters and measurements associated with the ROC curve might prove useful in some applications. The standard error, for example, can help in assessing the reliability of the calculation of the area. The discussion of these items is beyond the scope of this book, but a number of references are available that will assist in further pursuit of the subject (Hanley and McNeil 1982, 1983; McClish 1987; Meistrell and Spackman 1989).

Note that ROC curves and their associated contingency matrices do not take into account the prior probabilities of the event and nonevent (or class and nonclass) represented by the output PE. Prior probabilities do, however, enter into the calculations for the confusion matrix, discussed later.

Recall and Precision

Several ways of looking at the performance of a neural network or other computational intelligence system use the four possible decisions defined in the contingency table (refer to Table 10.1) and in the definition of ROC curves. One way is the use of metrics that have been familiar in the fields of expert systems and databases: recall and precision (Saito and Nakano 1988; Stanfill and Kahle 1986).

Recall is the number of positive diagnoses correctly made by the system divided by the total number of positive diagnoses made by the gold standard. Recall is sometimes called the *probability of detection*. This is defined in the discussion on ROC curves as the true positive ratio and provides an indication of the relative number of false negatives.

Precision is the number of positive diagnoses correctly made by the system divided by the total number of positive diagnoses made by the system. In the parlance of Table 10.1, this is TP/(TP + FP), and it provides an indication of the magnitude of false positives.

Recall and precision are just another way of looking at the four quantities in the contingency matrix; they "cut" the data in a different way than the sensitivity and specificity parameters do. Which metric is most appropriate depends heavily on the application and end users. Eberhart and Dobbins (1990) found that recall and precision were a metric of choice when developing an epileptiform spike detection system for use by neurologists (summarized in Chapter 12). In that application, the number of true negatives had relatively little meaning, and the precision metric provided more meaningful information than specificity.

Other ROC-related Measures

In this section, we summarize four performance metrics derived from the contingency table (Table 10.1) that can often be more informative for characterizing network performance than percent correct and that are easy to compute.

Sensitivity, or the *probability of detection* [TP/(TP + FN)], is the likelihood that an event will be detected, given that it is present. It is likely to be especially important when it is critical that an event be detected. For example, the detection of AIDS is important because its consequences are severe.

Specificity, or the *true negative rate* [TN/(TN + FP)], is the likelihood that the absence of an event will be detected, given that it is absent. For example, the absence of a "blip" on a radar screen is likely to be an important event: perhaps a downed airplane.

Positive predictive value, [TP/(TP + FP)], is the likelihood that a signal of an event is associated with the event, given that a signal occurred. This is an especially important statistic when it is imperative that a signal be attended to. For example, neurology staff always pay attention to a signal spike in an EEG, especially if the spike has a high probability of being associated with the corresponding signal of interest.

False alarm rate, or the *probability of false alarm* [FP/(FP + TN)] = [1 − specificity], is the likelihood that a signal is detected (falsely), given that a nontarget event occurred. It is easy to see where the name came from.

Accuracy, [(TP + TN)/(TN + FP + FN + TP)], indicates the probability of a correct classification. It is the estimate of percent correct for a system.

Other ROC-related measures are especially useful when dealing with "unbalanced data." For example, there may be very few cases of a rare disease in a large database of medical symptoms and diagnoses. It is still important to achieve a high accuracy on the diagnosis of this rare disease. Another example is correctly predicting loan defaults. Two metrics used for unbalanced data in situations such as this are the *geometric mean (G-mean)* developed by Kubat (1998) and the *F-measure* developed by Lewis and Gale (1994). They are defined in equations 10.10, 10.11, and 10.12, where *PD* is probability of detection, *PR* is precision, and *SP* is specificity.

$$G\text{-mean}_1 = sqrt\,(PD^*PR) \tag{10.10}$$

$$G\text{-mean}_2 = sqrt\,(PD^*SP) \tag{10.11}$$

$$F\text{-measure} = [(\beta^2 + 1)\,{}^*PR^*PD]\,/\,(\beta^{2*}PR + PD) \tag{10.12}$$

In the calculation of *F*-measure, β can be any nonnegative value, and it manipulates the weights assigned to *PD* and *PR*. If β is 1, which is a typical case, equal weights result. The relative weights of *PD* and *PR* are problem-specific and should be determined on a case-by-case basis.

Each of the ROC-related statistics described here can be computed at each output location in a multiple-output neural network or other computational intelligence system. If the outputs are mutually exclusive, the criterion for correctness is based on the winning PE having the largest value, not on its merely being above 0.5. If the output PEs are not mutually exclusive, then a criterion of 0.5 can be used.

Examples of the former, with mutually exclusive categories, might be mammal, fish, or bird. In such a case, only one can be considered correct. An example of categorizations that are not mutually exclusive are output PEs that indicate the presence of properties: warm-bloodedness, breathes air, and so on. Assuming in both cases that the input vector is a list of primitive features for an animal, the latter case clearly could contain instances of multiple correct categories (many animals are cold-blooded and breathe air).

Confusion Matrices

An ROC curve (calculated from a contingency matrix) is useful when examining the performance of a single output PE, or any other computational intelligence system with one output. An analogous performance metric that is useful when a system has multiple output classes represented by multiple PEs is the *confusion matrix*.

For a system comprising n classes, an $n \times n$ matrix is constructed. The rows, designated by the subscript i, reflect the "gold standard" classification. The columns, designated by the subscript j, reflect the classifications as made by the computational intelligence system (which could be a neural network with multiple outputs). The entry in each position of the matrix represents the total count (total number of instances, each represented by a pattern) of the situation that occurred in the test set represented by that position.

The positions along the main diagonal of the matrix are those instances that were correctly classified; for example, s_{33} is the number of instances of the third class that were correctly classified. The positions off the diagonal represent errors: s_{ij} $(i \neq j)$ is the number of instances of the class i that were misclassified as belonging to class j.

Sometimes a column is added onto the right side of the matrix that represents instances that could not be classified according to system decision criteria. For the remainder of this discussion, however, it is assumed that an $n \times n$ matrix is used.

There are several ways to use information in a confusion matrix. In any case, the matrix is prepared by first performing calculations row by row (one "gold standard" class at a time). The first step in interpreting the matrix is to calculate each "class confusion" by dividing each matrix entry by the total count of instances in its row (gold standard class). The numbers in each row now add to 1.0. Note that the contingency matrix used to calculate the ROC curve is just a class confusion matrix with $n = 2$.

The resulting *class confusion matrix* can now be used to calculate an average percent correct for the system by adding all of the entries on the main diagonal of the matrix and dividing the result by the number of classes. Note that this may not be a "true" percent correct unless all classes have the same prior probabilities, but it can be a useful measure, particularly if no more information is available.

In order to further use the matrix for calculating cost information, it is necessary to know the prior probability of each class. Each element in the class confusion matrix is then multiplied by the prior probability for the class represented by the row where the element is located. Each value in the matrix represents a probability of occurrence: The sum of all matrix values is now 1.0.

The last step in interpreting the confusion matrix is to multiply each element in the matrix by its cost. It is often assumed that correct classifications (on the main diagonal) have associated costs of 0. It is necessary to know the cost of *each* type of misclassification *accurately* in order to make the best use of a confusion matrix. It is sufficient for many purposes if the cost ratios among all of the misclassifications are known. The total cost is then calculated by summing all of the individual costs. Note that subjective measures of cost, such as pain incurred because of a mistaken medical diagnosis, are not acceptable for inputs to the confusion matrix. The results are very sensitive to both prior probabilities and costs.

Let's work through an example of a confusion matrix. We'll assume that we have a medical diagnostic system with three possible diagnoses: A, B, and C. We have trained a back-propagation neural network with 50 cases of each diagnosis. (We often use about the same number of each output class, diagnosis in this case, to train a network, as discussed in the first part of this chapter.) We know from an extensive database of case histories that the prior probabilities of the three classes are 0.60, 0.30, and 0.10, respectively.

We next use 50 cases of each diagnosis (that were *not* used in training) to test the system. It may or may not be realistic to expect that we will have 50 test cases for each diagnosis. (Keep in mind that the probability of diagnosis C is only 10 percent. If we need 50 cases of C for training and 50 for testing, that implies that we have about 1,000 cases from which to draw data. If, for example, we have only about 800 cases, we could end up with only about 30 cases of C for testing.) The results are depicted in Table 10.3, where the gold standards are represented by the rows. Then the class confusion matrix is formed by dividing each entry by the total number of instances in its row as in Table 10.4.

We now multiply each element in Table 10.4 by the prior probability for each class, resulting in the final confusion matrix of Table 10.5. Each element in the matrix is now the probability for each application of the diagnosis tool of that outcome.

Before we go on to calculate costs (and inject some reality into this example), let's look at what we have so far. We have a diagnostic system that performs with an accuracy of 82.8 percent (the sum of the main diagonal values). On the surface, it appears that we are doing pretty well with respect to the third diagnosis, C.

Table 10.3   Test Results for Medical Diagnostic Example

		CI System Diagnoses		
		A	**B**	**C**
Gold Standard Diagnoses	**A**	40	8	2
	B	6	42	2
	C	1	1	48

Table 10.4   Class Confusion Matrix for Medical Diagnostic Example

		CI System Diagnoses		
		A	**B**	**C**
Gold Standard Diagnoses	**A**	0.80	0.16	0.04
	B	0.12	0.84	0.04
	C	0.02	0.02	0.96

Table 10.5 Final Confusion Matrix for Medical Diagnostic Example

		CI System Diagnoses		
		A	**B**	**C**
Gold Standard Diagnoses	**A**	0.480	0.096	0.024
	B	0.036	0.252	0.012
	C	0.002	0.002	0.096

However, now is when we inject reality. The medical diagnosis represented by A is a condition that can be cured by an over-the-counter drug available at any drugstore that costs, say, $10. Medical diagnosis B is a more serious medical problem that requires aggressive treatment with a prescription antibiotic that costs, say, $100. Condition C is a very serious condition that requires hospitalization and surgery, with a total cost of $5,000. And, by the way, if condition C is not diagnosed *right now*, the patient has only a 20-percent chance of survival. Although it is impossible to assign a dollar value to a human life, let's say that the average insurance policy of these patients is $100,000, and use that value, crass as it may appear. That means that each misdiagnosed condition C will result in an average cost of $80,000 (80 percent chance of death times $100,000 life insurance policy). We ignore the millions of dollars for which the hospital or clinic may be sued by a malpractice attorney.

We stated previously that it is often assumed that correct classifications have zero cost, but it should also be apparent by now that the costs of the *correct* diagnoses in this example are not zero; they are $10, $100, and $5,000 for A, B, and C, respectively. A diagnosis of A as B will cost $100 (misdiagnosis) plus $10 (eventually a correct diagnosis). Our cost of a diagnosis of B as A will be $10 (incorrect diagnosis) plus $100 (eventually a correct diagnosis). Likewise, a misdiagnosis of B as C is assumed to cost $5,000 (misdiagnosis) plus $100 (correct diagnosis) plus a very angry patient (no cost assigned). And so on. Our final cost matrix is in Table 10.6.

Table 10.6 Final Cost Matrix for Example Problem

		CI System Diagnoses		
		A	**B**	**C**
Gold Standard Diagnoses	**A**	4.80	10.56	120.24
	B	3.96	25.20	61.20
	C	160.02	160.20	480.00

The figures in Table 10.6 tell us that the average estimated cost of each application of the diagnostic system is \$1,026.18. There are two main ways to reduce this average estimated cost. The first is to reduce the costs for the treatments of the three conditions. We probably have little or no control over those costs, however. The most obvious way to reduce costs is to lower the costs of missed diagnoses, and the most obvious place to start is with the misdiagnoses of condition C.

The cost calculations from confusion matrices can be used in a variety of ways to fine-tune a computational intelligence system. For example, a system can first be trained and tested using whatever methodologies are appropriate. For example, a neural network–based diagnostic system is trained for the best performance on the test set. Then, the threshold levels of the output PEs, or membership functions of fuzzy sets, or whatever, can be adjusted by calculating the costs associated with a variety of choices, choosing the combination that produces the lowest system cost. If there is only one, or only a few PEs or membership functions, simple iterative procedures can be used. If there are numerous outputs or functions, an evolutionary computation tool can be used to find the best (lowest cost) combination. If appropriate cost information is not available, the system can still be tuned so as to minimize the off-diagonal numbers, the sum of which represents the percent incorrect.

Chi-square Test

At least one of the preceding performance metrics will probably be useful whenever the supposed results are known. For example, in a pattern classification situation, if the "gold-plated" classification is known in each case, it's relatively easy to tell how well the system is doing its job. Depending on the specific application, the percent correct, recall and precision, or some other measure can be calculated. What should be done, however, if the "right" answers are unknown? This situation isn't as far-fetched as it might seem at first glance.

An example is one of the main areas of application of neural networks described in Chapter 1. The fourth area described is different from the other four in that no classification is involved. Instead, it involves the generation of structured sequences or patterns from a network trained to examples. The composition of music, based on training to a given music style, is an example of this area. Another example is the simulation of some process, such as a biological process, that can be described statistically. In this general class of applications, the expected specific result of each case may not be known, but an idea probably exists of what the statistical distribution of results should look like. A useful measurement tool we can use in many such cases is the *chi-square test*.

The chi-square test examines the frequency distribution of all of the categories (or answers or classifications) that it is possible to obtain from a particular network system. That is, it looks at how often each category is expected to occur versus how often it actually occurs. The expected frequency of occurrence for a particular category is defined as E, and the actual (observed) frequency of occurrence for that category as O. Categories may be on a nominal, ordinal, or interval scale, but they must be mutually exclusive and collectively exhaustive (Roscoe 1969).

The activation values of output PEs don't directly enter into the chi-square test. Only the frequencies of occurrence of the output classes do. Of course, the chosen threshold value plays a role in the selection of the winning output pattern, so the output values play an indirect role. The values themselves, however, don't enter into the chi-square calculation.

The chi-square test is used to determine whether a given set of output categories, when compared with an expected distribution, has a variance from probability or a predefined expectation greater than would be expected by chance alone. It should be noted that the chi-square test assumes normally distributed data. If the data are not normally distributed, performance may not be acceptable. Equation 10.13 presents the chi-square calculation, where n is the number of categories.

$$\chi^2 = \sum_{i=1}^{n} \frac{(O_i - E_i)^2}{E_i} \qquad (10.13)$$

The calculation and interpretation of the chi-square test are now outlined. For a detailed explanation, refer to any reputable book on statistics such as Armitage and Berry (1987), Moore (2001), and Ross (2004).

Remember that the focus is on the frequency distribution of the output patterns. If there are four output PEs in a neural network application, and the PE with the largest activation (output) indicates the output classification ("winner take all"), then $n = 4$, and the calculation is relatively straightforward.

Assume that in any test set of 50 patterns, the expected frequency distribution of classifications is 5, 10, 15, and 20, respectively, for PEs 1 to 4. Suppose that for one 50-pattern test set, the frequency distribution obtained is 6, 10, 14, and 20 for PEs 1 to 4, respectively. Then chi-square for this first test set, as calculated by equation 10.13, is 0.267. Suppose that for a second test set, a distribution of 2, 15, 8, and 25 for PEs 1 to 4, respectively, is obtained. Chi-square for this second test set, calculated by equation 10.13, is 8.82.

Now that values have been calculated, a determination must be made as to how many degrees of freedom the system has, which corresponds to the number of frequency distribution values required to uniquely determine the entire set of values, given that the total number of tests is known. In the example case, if the frequencies of occurrence are known for any three of the four output PEs, we can calculate the fourth, given that the total number is known. Thus, there are three degrees of freedom. (In general, if there are n output PEs, each representing exactly one possible classification, then we can say that there are $n-1$ degrees of freedom.

Or, if there are m classifications in a fuzzy expert system, there are $m - 1$ degrees of freedom.)

The next step is to refer to chi-square distribution tables that you can find in a statistics textbook or a collection of statistical tables. Along the row corresponding to three degrees of freedom, under the probability of 0.950 is the value 0.352; under the probability of 0.050 is the value 7.81. The results for the two test sets can now be interpreted.

For the first test set, the *hypothesis of no difference* (sometimes called the *null hypothesis*) between the expected and obtained distributions is sustained at the 0.95 level. Stated another way, no significant difference between the two distributions exists with a probability exceeding 95 percent. (It is more than 95 percent probable that the differences are due solely to chance.)

For the second test set, the null hypothesis is rejected at the 0.05 level. In other words, there is a greater difference between the two distributions than would have been expected by chance, with a probability of less than 5 percent that the difference was due to chance.

Another way to interpret the results is by using a spreadsheet application such as Microsoft Excel. To find the probability that the null hypothesis is sustained or rejected, use the Excel command =CHIDIST(x^2, df), where x^2 is the calculated chi-square value and *df* is the degrees of freedom. In our example, entering =CHIDIST(0.267, 3) yields an answer of 0.966, and entering =CHIDIST (8.92, 3) yields an answer of 0.030. Using the spreadsheet software thus gives us more precise answers. We now can say that for the first test set the null hypothesis is sustained at the 0.966 level, and in the second test set the null hypothesis is rejected at the 0.030 level.

We can use another command in Excel to generate the chi-square values given a probability p and the degrees of freedom *df*. The command is =CHIINV(p, df). So, for example, if we enter =CHIINV(0.95, 3), we obtain the value 0.352, the value we saw in the chi-square table. You can thus build your own chi-square table for particular ranges of p and *df* that are of interest to you.

Now that the chi-square test and its use have been reviewed, a few comments are appropriate. First, note that the chi-square test measures the performance of the entire system at once, that is, all of the output PEs in the case of a neural network implementation. Remember that the ROC curve is designed to analyze one output PE at a time. The other side of that coin, however, is that it is necessary (for chi-square) to determine exactly how many output combinations are possible.

For example, in a music composition situation, it could be that there are 20 output PEs: 14 that represent note values such as C and F# and 6 that represent duration times such as quarter notes and half notes. In this case, there would be up to $14 \times 6 = 84$ possible combinations. In the expected distribution, there may be fewer than 84 if some combinations don't occur. It will be necessary to decide how to handle these combinations with zero expected frequencies, if they are obtained, because it would be necessary to divide by 0 if the chi-square test were strictly applied. It is also difficult to find chi-square tables with more than about 30 or 40 degrees of freedom.

In general, a good guideline is that you should use the chi-square test only when 20 percent or fewer of the expected counts are < 5 and all individual expected counts are at least 1 (Moore 2001).

It should be obvious that, when using a computational intelligence system for modeling or simulation, the goal is for the chi-square test to yield the smallest value feasible. In other words, the goal is for the differences between the modeled and the modeling systems' outputs to be so small that they are attributed to chance.

It would not be surprising if new learning algorithms were developed for neural networks that replaced the back-propagation algorithm for modeling and simulation applications. These algorithms could be based on minimizing of chi-square values for the network as a whole rather than minimizing error values summed over individual PEs. For other computational intelligence tools that use a single, overall performance figure as a training (or testing) metric, such as simulators based on fuzzy logic or a prediction system based on a reinforcement learning neural network, the chi-square test could be the metric of choice.

Summary

In this chapter, we look at a variety of ways to measure the performance of a computational intelligence system, ranging from cases where we can assign specific costs to missed classifications and know the prior probabilities of each class (confusion matrixes) to cases where we don't have any training data and only a general idea of what to expect from a system (chi-square goodness of fit). In the next chapter we consider ways to analyze and explain a system's behavior, including explanation facilities that show the user what the system is doing.

Exercises

1. We have developed a diagnostic system with three possible diagnoses, Q, R, and S, that are equally probable (0.333 each). Assume that the costs associated with the three diagnoses are x, $2x$, and $5x$, respectively, and that the raw cost matrix comprises the base costs on the diagonal and the sum of the row and column values for off-diagonal values, as illustrated in Table 10.7. (For example, Q misdiagnosed as S costs $x + 5x$, and so on.) Actually, the cost of condition S is $10x$, but we are reimbursed 50 percent of the cost by Medicare, so *our* cost is $5x$, and Table 10.7 is valid. Assume that, despite the cost differences in diagnosing the conditions, each diagnosis represents a relatively mild problem and none is more health-threatening than any other; that is, none is more serious than a common cold.

Table 10.7 Raw Cost Matrix for Exercise 10.1

		CI System Diagnoses		
		Q	**R**	**S**
	Q	x	$3x$	$6x$
Gold Standard Diagnoses	**R**	$3x$	$2x$	$7x$
	S	$6x$	$7x$	$5x$

Table 10.8 System I Results for Exercise 10.1

		CI System I Diagnoses		
		Q	**R**	**S**
	Q	36	3	1
Gold Standard Diagnoses	**R**	2	37	1
	S	3	2	35

Table 10.9 System II Results for Exercise 10.1

		CI System II Diagnoses		
		Q	**R**	**S**
	Q	30	10	0
Gold Standard Diagnoses	**R**	8	37	0
	S	1	0	39

Further assume that we have trained two computational intelligence diagnostic systems, I and II, and the results are evaluated using the 40 cases of each diagnosis we have for testing with the results, as shown in Tables 10.8 and 10.9.

How many patients are misdiagnosed in each case? Purely based on cost, which of the two systems should be used? Assuming x is $20, what are the estimated cost savings in 1,000 cases?

Now assume that the federal government announces that it will stop reimbursing us for S, so that our cost for correctly diagnosing S suddenly doubles to $10x$. (Off-diagonal costs must be adjusted accordingly as well.) From a cost perspective, which diagnostic system should we use now? Why? Comment on this method of selecting the diagnostic system.

2. For a pattern set we are using to train a neural network, one-half of the target values are 1 and one-half are 0. Calculate E_{mean}. What happens to E_{mean} if targets of 0.9 and 0.1 are used instead of 1 and 0, respectively?

3. Train a neural network on the Iris dataset using the back-propagation implementation (see Chapter 6). Plot an ROC curve for each of the three output PEs, using at least 10 values for the threshold value. Discuss your results.

4. Given the following set of targets and outputs, calculate the average sum-squared error and the normalized error.

Target	Output
1	.90
1	.87
1	.79
1	.89
1	.88
0	.12
0	.11
0	.21
0	.13
0	.10

Repeat your calculations, assuming that the targets were 0.9 and 0.1 instead of 1 and 0, respectively, and the outputs were the same.

5. We are developing a simulation of the game of baseball. We want to measure how well our system simulates the margin of victory. In general, we like the margin of victory to be 1, 2, or 3 runs. A 4-run game isn't too bad, but games with margins of 5 or more runs are okay once in a while but aren't very interesting. So, after consulting baseball statistics to see what the margin of victory was in American and National League playoff games, we decide that we'd like the distribution of the margin of victory of games played by our system to be as shown on the "Ideal" row in the following table. We develop two versions of the simulator and play 100 games with each system. The margins of victory from our simulations are shown on the lines for System 1 and System 2.

Margin of victory	1	2	3	4	>=5
Ideal number of games	25	30	20	15	10
System 1 number of games	28	29	21	14	8
System 2 number of games	24	27	21	17	11

Use the chi-square metric to analyze the two systems. At what level does each of them sustain the null hypothesis? Which one would you choose? Why? Is there a problem with using chi-square for this analysis? If so, what is it?

6. Use k-fold cross validation to analyze the Iris dataset. Using 3-fold and 10-fold approaches, partition the dataset into 3 and 10 subsets, respectively. What results for training and testing are obtained with each approach? What significant differences do you see? For this dataset, what maximum value of k would you recommend? Why?

7. Use PSO to evolve the weights for different configurations of neural networks that classify the Iris dataset. Use the Mann–Whitney U test to evaluate the configurations. Find two configurations for which the null hypothesis is not rejected and two for which it is rejected at the 0.05 level. Limit the values of n_1 and n_2 to 10 or less so that you can use Table 10.1, but justify your choices of n_1 and n_2. *Hint:* You may want to make the network perform terribly on purpose in order to make it easier to reject the null hypothesis.

chapter
eleven

Analysis and Explanation

The previous chapter discussed performance metrics: ways to measure how *well* a system performs. This chapter presents analysis and explanation tools that can be used to explain *how* computational intelligence systems do what they do. Only a few are discussed; it is beyond the scope of this book to deal with the subject in detail.

We first discuss sensitivity analysis. We describe a few practical and useful approaches that assess relative significance of system inputs. Next we discuss Hinton diagrams, used with neural networks to analyze patterns of connection weights.

Then we discuss explanation facilities. We review the explanation facility's differences and similarities in requirements for symbolic and numeric systems; then we discuss neural networks, fuzzy systems, and evolutionary computation tools for explanation facilities with a focus on evolutionary computation tools.

Applications of evolutionary computation paradigms are playing increasingly important roles in explanation facilities. Until now, these applications have been primarily in the area of artificial neural network diagnostic systems. This section explores the application of evolutionary computation to explanation facilities, both in numeric-based systems such as artificial neural networks and in symbolic-based applications such as expert systems. We will suggest ways in which more traditional approaches used in knowledge-based systems can be combined with evolutionary computation tools to produce improved explanation facilities for hybrid and computational intelligence systems.

In the last section of this chapter, we present a software implementation of an analysis and explanation tool: an evolutionary computation explanation facility tool.

This implementation appears on the book's web site and is distributed as shareware in accordance with the information on the web site.

Techniques have been developed to extract rules from neural networks (e.g., Craven 1993). We do not cover these techniques in this book. Instead, we focus on directly evolving fuzzy expert systems, as discussed in Chapters 7, 8, and 9.

Sensitivity Analysis

Various definitions of sensitivity exist. In the previous chapter, which focuses on performance metrics, sensitivity is defined within the context of the ROC curve as true positive divided by true positive plus false negative [TP/(TP + FN)], which is also called the *true positive ratio*.

In this chapter, which deals with analyzing how computational intelligence systems work, sensitivity analysis provides one method for evaluating the relative importance of system inputs. A basic premise is that the significance of an input can be evaluated by measuring the effect it has on the output(s).

This information can be applied in a couple of main ways. One is during the development of the system, when it is important to know which inputs are important and should be retained and which are redundant or insignificant and should be removed. An example of this approach is the system developed to predict the bioactivities of molecules based on a set of descriptive features by Embrechts and colleagues (2002). Another is used after the system is developed, when sensitivity analysis of a system model or simulator can tell us what parameters are most significantly contributing to an output we want to minimize (such as cost) or maximize (such as profit). For example, see Guo and Uhrig (1992), who used sensitivity analysis to identify significant parameters relative to the thermal performance of a nuclear power plant.

There are a variety of ways to measure sensitivity. Many of them involve clamping or otherwise controlling one input at a time while looking at the effects on the output values or system error. Many pitfalls exist in using these techniques. A few, however, can be useful when used in the correct way. We first describe one approach, called *relation factors*.

Relation Factors

Relation factors reflect the strength of the relationships between individual inputs and individual outputs of a computational intelligence system. They are discussed in detail in the context of a neural network diagnostic system by Saito and Nakano (1988), but they are also applicable to other system configurations. They could probably also be called "causal factors." Relation factors can sometimes represent information similar to rules in expert systems. Two kinds of relation factor used to analyze system performance are described in this section. We refer to them as relation factor one and relation factor two.

Relation factor one is the effect of a given system input on a given output when all other inputs are constrained to be constant, usually 0. For example, for a back-propagation neural network, the effect is calculated by subtracting the value of a given output PE with all other inputs set to a constant value, say, 0, from its value with the one specified input set to 1. For a fuzzy system, the input to be tested is varied between the minimum and maximum of its dynamic range, while all other inputs are set to the minimum values of their dynamic ranges. With i inputs and o outputs, there are a total of i times o relation factors one. In some systems, it may be valid to clamp the "other" inputs to the midpoint of the input range rather than to 0. This would, for instance, clamp the other inputs to 0.5 in the case of a standard back-propagation neural network, and to the input value corresponding to the maximum value of the middle membership function for an expert system. (If the membership function is trapezoidal, the input value corresponding to the middle value of the maximum membership can be used.)

Relation factor two takes into account the fact that the effect of a given input on a given output differs with varying input value combinations (input patterns). Relation factor two measures the average effect of a given input on a given output over a set of input patterns.

For the set of patterns, relation factor two is calculated as follows. First, calculate the change in an output's value when a given input is switched over its entire range while all other inputs hold the value defined by the first input pattern. Examples are to switch from 0 to 1 for a neural network input, or from the minimum to the maximum value of the dynamic range for a fuzzy system. For the same input, repeat the calculation for each pattern in the pattern set. Then add all of the changes together and divide by the number of patterns. This yields a value for relation factor two for a given input-output pair. Now repeat the process for each remaining input. Then repeat the process for each output. Again, there are i times o relation factors two.

An example of using relation factors can occur when working with a partial set of inputs, and it is desired that the system be somewhat "intelligent" about what input it requests next. For example, for working with a medical diagnostic system to distinguish between two illnesses, a variation of the relation factor method can be used to decide which medical symptom to enter next.

Just present the partial set of symptoms obtained thus far to the system and switch each of the remaining inputs, one by one, over its range (0 to 1 for a neural network, or over the input's dynamic range for a fuzzy system, for example). The input that causes the largest differential to occur between the two diagnoses can correspond to the symptom entered next into the system.

Next we review a sensitivity analysis and network-pruning process developed by Zurada and colleagues (1994), which we call the Zurada sensitivity analysis.

Zurada Sensitivity Analysis

Before we review the analysis process, let's recall some of the terminology related to neural networks that we introduced in Chapter 5. Remember that input patterns are denoted $A_k = (a_{k1}, a_{k2}, ..., a_{kn})$; $k = 1, 2, ..., m$, and the output (target) patterns as $B_k = (b_{k1}, b_{k2}, ..., b_{kp})$; $k = 1, 2, ..., m$. Note that the subscript k refers to a pattern, there are m input patterns, and there are p outputs. The input layer of PEs is denoted $F_X = (x_1, x_2, ..., x_n)$, where each x_i receives input from the corresponding input pattern component a_{ki}, and $i = 1, 2, ..., n$. Also remember that the trained output of an F_Z PE for one pattern k is z_{kj}.

For any training pattern k, Zurada and colleagues (1994) define the sensitivity of a trained output z_{kj} with respect to an input a_{ki} as $S_{ji}^{(k)} = \frac{\partial z_{kj}}{\partial a_{ki}}$. Thus, a sensitivity matrix $S^{(k)}$ is associated with each complete training pattern k, and we must calculate the sensitivity matrix for each input of the m patterns. Once that has been done, Zurada and colleagues define three sensitivity measures over the complete training pattern set.

The *mean square average sensitivity* matrix S_{avg} is defined as

$$ S_{ji,\,avg} = \sqrt{\frac{\sum_{k=1}^{m} \left[S_{ji}^{(k)} \right]^2}{m}} \qquad (11.1) $$

The *absolute value average sensitivity* matrix S_{abs} is defined as

$$ S_{ji,\,abs} = \frac{\sum_{k=1}^{m} \left| S_{ji}^{(k)} \right|}{m} \qquad (11.2) $$

The *maximum sensitivity* matrix S_{max} is defined as

$$ S_{ji,\,max} = \max_{k=1,\,...,\,m} \left\{ S_{ji}^{(k)} \right\} \qquad (11.3) $$

Note that the inputs and outputs must be scaled to the same range for valid comparisons to be made.

This method is computationally intensive, requiring that a sensitivity matrix be calculated for each pattern. There are ways to implement the "spirit" of the Zurada process using fewer calculations. One such method that the authors find useful is described by Embrechts and colleagues (2002). To implement this method, first select the median (or calculate the mean) value for each input parameter over the pattern set. Next hold all input values at their medians (means) except one. Now measure the output(s) while varying the selected input over its dynamic range. Although it would be ideal to vary the selected input continuously, the output can be measured for a number of discrete values. Embrechts and colleagues measured the output for 13 discrete values of the input. You may select a number other than 13, based on your problem.

An input parameter's sensitivity with respect to an output is the maximum minus the minimum for that output over the discrete values of the input. We now have an estimated sensitivity for each input–output pair. Let's call this estimated sensitivity $S_{ji,e}$. Following a process analogous to equations 11.1 through 11.3, we can calculate a sensitivity for each input $S_{i,e}$ in one of three ways.

The *mean square average estimated sensitivity* $S_{i,eav}$ is defined as

$$S_{i,eav} = \sqrt{\frac{\sum_{j=1}^{p} [S_{ji,e}]^2}{p}} \tag{11.4}$$

The *absolute value average estimated sensitivity* $S_{i,eab}$ is defined as

$$S_{i,eab} = \frac{\sum_{j=1}^{p} |S_{ji,e}|}{p} \tag{11.5}$$

The *maximum estimated sensitivity* $S_{i,emx}$ is defined as

$$S_{i,emx} = \max_{j=1,\dots,p} \left\{ S_{ji,e} \right\} \tag{11.6}$$

Once the sensitivity is calculated for each input, the list of sensitivities can be rank-ordered. The rank-ordered information can be used in a couple of ways. First, and simplest, is to delete the input with the lowest sensitivity and try to train the network again. If you get sufficiently good test results (and they may even be a little better), then you know that you can remove that input parameter.

A more scientific way to proceed is to use an additional random variable as an additional input when training the network. Then any input with sensitivity less that that for the input representing the random variable can safely be removed, usually one at a time starting with the variable with lowest sensitivity. (Also, of course, remove the random variable input.) Using successive training/testing iterations to remove these inputs with lowest sensitivities is described as "strip mining" by Embrechts and colleagues (2002).

The following list summarizes the process of sensitivity analysis and pruning of inputs we have just described.

1. Train the neural network on the training set with one additional input representing a random variable.

2. Calculate all input–output sensitivity estimates using the clamping and discrete values method outlined here, followed by equation 11.4, 11.5, or 11.6.

3. Remove the random input.

4. Remove the input with the lowest sensitivity.

5. Retrain/retest the network with the pruned input set.

6. As long as results are acceptable, repeat steps 4 and 5 until all inputs with sensitivities lower than the random input are removed.

Removing inputs with little or no relevance to the performance of the system can improve system performance, both in terms of accuracy and in terms of ability to generalize.

The same general approach can be adapted for fuzzy systems. The number of discrete values should be chosen so that the fuzzy membership functions are properly activated, and remember to scale the inputs and outputs to the same range.

Evolutionary Computation Sensitivity Analysis

Evolutionary computation has been applied to many areas. Sensitivity analysis related to the applications of evolutionary computation is sometimes focused on the problem and/or solution domain, which is beyond of the scope of this book. In this section, we briefly discuss sensitivity analysis focused on the evolutionary computation method itself.

The parameters of evolutionary algorithms play an important role in their search capability. The sensitivity of an evolutionary algorithm with respect to its parameters is critical to its performance and, therefore, its successful applications. Using this approach, we consider the parameters of an evolutionary algorithm as the input values to the sensitivity analysis, and its performance values as the output values. The sensitivity analysis approaches discussed in previous sections such as relation factors one and two can be used here. For most evolutionary algorithms, the output values can include parameters such as fitness value, convergence rate, and the maximum generation required to reach a good enough solution.

The input values may be different for different algorithms. For example, for genetic algorithms, the input values can be mutation rate, crossover rate, population size, and so on. For particle swarm optimization algorithms, the input values can be inertia weight w, the cognitive and social coefficients c_1 and c_2, and so on.

A straightforward way to conduct the sensitivity analysis on the input–output pair is through experiments (Beielstein et al. 2002). The experimental results can be plotted for graphical visualization. We hope this will provide insights into how the algorithm's parameters can be tuned for best overall performance.

Hinton Diagrams

Extreme care must be taken when interpreting the values of weights in a neural network. Just because a weight is large doesn't mean that the processing element (PE) on the input side of it is particularly important. A high input-to-hidden weight doesn't necessarily make that input PE any more important than others; perhaps the magnitude of that input is always very small or the effect always gets canceled out in some way. Likewise, a small weight doesn't always denote an insignificant input; perhaps the value gets augmented from other inputs. For example, suppose a network system is designed to predict a person's ability to play basketball. Suppose that among the inputs are height and athletic ability. Neither alone is nearly as important an indicator as the two together.

It is still sometimes worthwhile to examine the weight matrices in a neural network system. Since networks typically have a large number of connections, it can be difficult to display these in a meaningful and useful way.

Perhaps the most obvious way is to display an array of numbers representing the weights. This can be done by examining on-screen or printing out the weights file for a network. This is usually not a very useful technique, however (though we have to make do with it if nothing better is available), because humans are not particularly good at working with lots of numbers or perceiving patterns and trends in data.

A better way to represent network weight matrices is with graphics. A method developed by Geoffrey Hinton, called a Hinton diagram (McClelland and Rumelhart 1986; Rumelhart and McClelland 1986), graphically shows the magnitudes of connection weights to or from a neural network layer. One method of implementation uses blue rectangles (or squares) to represent positive weights and red to depict negative weights. The size of the rectangle (or square) is proportional to the magnitude of a weight.

Figure 11.1 shows a Hinton diagram with lightly shaded rectangles denoting positive weights; dark ones are negative. This figure displays the weights for a feed-forward neural network with one hidden layer and with nine input, four hidden, and two output PEs. In the figure, input-to-hidden weights are shown at the top and hidden-to-output are at the bottom. A bias weight is the leftmost value in each row. The top row of the top block of weights depicts the magnitude of weights from the input PEs (bias first) to the first hidden PE. The second from the top row of the top block depicts weight magnitudes from the input PEs to the second hidden PE, and so on. Likewise, the top row of the bottom weight block depicts weights

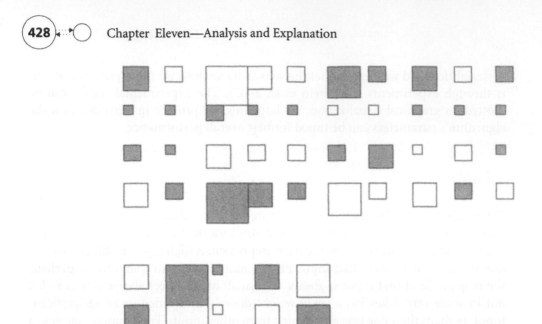

Figure 11.1 Hinton diagram for a 9–4–2 feedforward neural network.

from the hidden PEs (bias first) to the first output PE. This diagram represents the weights of one of the networks developed to detect electroencephalogram spikes, as described in one of the case studies in Chapter 12 on this book's web site.

There are several variations of this scheme. Activation values as well as weights can be displayed, for example. Different geometric representations can be used to display multiple layers and their interconnections. For large networks, it may be possible to display only a part of a layer at a time.

The Hinton diagram can be displayed continually as the network runs and can be refreshed each iteration. This may not be a good idea in a production system, however, because the display may take significant processing time away from the network. Also, it is not very useful if the network is iterating rapidly because changes may happen too fast for a human observer to follow. In that case, it may be better to display the weights once every fixed number of iterations or to suspend the network while the "frozen" state is examined. Another option is to have no real-time display but to examine the state after the network has finished training.

The authors sometimes use diagrams such as that in Figure 11.1 to provide guidance for "pruning" trained networks. For example, in the figure, nearly identical weight patterns from hidden to outputs indicate that fewer than four hidden PEs are required. Indeed, the network represented by the figure works just as well with three.

Computational Intelligence Tools for Explanation Facilities

End users have traditionally wanted, and in some cases demanded, to know how experts arrive at conclusions or recommendations. When computer systems are involved, users tend toward the "demand" end of the spectrum. Computer system utilities designed to make classification and/or diagnostic decisions or recommendations understandable to users, often by citing reasons why these decisions or recommendations were made, are frequently called *explanation facilities*.

Explanation facilities must perform similar functions regardless of the computational paradigm(s) at the heart of the system. The user seldom knows, and rarely cares, whether the system is using a knowledge base, a neural network, a Bayesian classifier, another paradigm, or some combination of paradigms. They just want to know how the classification or recommendation was derived, and they want to be provided this information in a way that is understandable and helpful.

In this section, we briefly review the design and implementation of explanation facilities. We assume that you are familiar with explanation facilities implemented for expert systems; we describe the implementation of facilities for neural network-based systems in somewhat more detail. We also describe two evolutionary computation tools that can be used to build explanation facility components. We explore explanation facility requirements of hybrid systems and computational intelligence systems and discuss various approaches.

Explanation Facility Requirements

Explanation is a complex form of interaction, or communication, between and/or among humans. It is a communication skill related to humans' ability to reason. It is not well understood.

Requirements, or specifications, for explanation facilities vary somewhat according to the application and with the situation. To illustrate this, consider the following definitions. *Webster's Ninth New Collegiate Dictionary* (1991) states that "explanation" means "the act or process of explaining" or "something that explains." The same source offers three definitions of "explain": "**1 a:** to make known; **b:** to make plain or understandable; **2:** to give the reason for or cause of; **3:** to show the logical development or relationships of."

The computational system itself usually fulfills definition 1a by "making known" the classification or diagnosis. One or more of the other three definitions (1b, 2, and 3) are generally relevant to explanation facility attributes. Interaction with the explanation facility may be initiated by the user or by the computer system, or perhaps a mixture of both depending on the situation.

Why use an explanation facility? The most commonly stated answer is that it can, upon demand, provide reasons why the system arrived at a particular conclusion. The explanation facility can thus provide justification for classification or diagnostic recommendations. Explanation facilities were originally developed for expert systems, however, to provide debugging tools for design engineers (Martin and Oxman 1988).

Other roles played by explanation facilities include providing information to the user about the knowledge domain covered by the system and about system limitations. They may also provide clarification and/or a meaning for something.

All of the preceding justifications for explanation facilities seem to add up to just one word: *trust*. The system user needs to trust that the system is providing the "correct" (from the user's perspective) diagnosis or recommendation, given the available information.

Assuming that we have determined the need for an explanation facility, how do we go about designing it? The design and implementation of an explanation facility, whether for a neural network or for a knowledge base, is closely tied to the design and implementation of the user interface. The explanation facility, therefore, must be designed to match the user's level of expertise. It should be kept in mind that novice users tend not to use an explanation facility (Harmon and Sawyer 1990), so user tutorials and user help facilities should include explanation facility information.

Information presented by the facility should use terminology that can be understood by the user. This is probably *not* the same terminology used by experts or by system designers.

If possible, the technical level of explanation should be adjusted to the user's level of expertise. It may be necessary to query the user for his or her level of expertise at the beginning of each session.

Let's briefly consider the functions of an explanation facility. An explanation facility typically allows a system's user to ask why and/or how certain results were obtained. Further, some explanation facilities allow queries as to why a certain question was asked of the user or why certain different results were not obtained. "Trace" capabilities that allow stepping through the session one inference at a time are sometimes available in the case of knowledge bases, but they are more likely to be used for debugging by knowledge engineers than by end users (Lucas and van der Gaag 1991).

As good as explanation facilities can be, many users resist their use. This resistance is due in part to actual or perceived shortcomings with explanation facilities, and as system designers we need to be aware of some of these potential shortcomings.

Although some believe a list of rules is an adequate explanation facility for many rule-based systems, most people do not think about sequential rule firing when assigning a classification or making a "human" decision. For example, when asked if an object we are holding in our hand is a pencil or a pen, we don't mentally review a rule list associated with the attributes of a pencil with those associated with a pen. Instead, we mentally compare the overall pattern (perception) of the object in our hand with examples of pencils and pens we have previously experienced and choose the classification closest to the "quintessential" examples with which we are familiar.

Furthermore, starting with a (possibly incomplete) set of inputs, which may be a mixture of binary and analog values, the typical explanation facility for a backward chaining expert system does not provide details on the decision hypersurface location. For instance, it doesn't specify which inputs would need to change, and by what amount, in order to change the classification in a certain way. This is, however, the way humans often relate to classification: A physician often thinks about the way in which signs and symptoms would have to change to arrive at a specific (different) diagnosis.

Neural Network Explanation

Some neural network explanation facilities provide the "best" examples of the various classes. They also can provide information on the location of the decision hypersurface, providing information on what input to request next or how much to change certain inputs to arrive at a different decision.

For neural network systems, the "best" examples of the various classes are known as codebook vectors, or quintessential examples, for each classification or diagnosis. The term *codebook vector* refers to an input pattern that generates a maximum or nearly maximum activation value for a given output processing element (classification) of a neural network. These codebook vectors can be retrieved from examples stored or can be generated on-line if, for example, the user is looking for a codebook vector within a specified Euclidean distance in hyperspace of the input pattern. Information is also available regarding the decision hypersurface (sometimes called the differential diagnosis), which is the hypersurface that defines the boundary between any two classifications. For example, the distance to the decision hypersurface can be provided with either a complete or a partial set of inputs present. In this way, the user can determine which inputs would need to be changed, and by how much, for the classification or diagnosis to change in a specified way.

Explanation facilities have also been developed for hybrid systems. An example is the neural network expert system called MACIE, which stands for a MAtrix Controlled Inference Engine. Stephen Gallant developed the original version of MACIE in the mid-1980s and used the term "matrix controlled" because neural networks were somewhat out of vogue at the time (Gallant 1993). When asked why it requests a certain value, MACIE gives explanations relative to the goal variable with the highest likelihood, listing the effect (positive or negative) on intermediate variables. MACIE evolved into a commercial product that was released in the early 1990s.

The situation with respect to neural networks is complicated by the fact that explanation facilities are more readily applied to some neural network paradigms than to others. For example, neural networks using radial basis functions or other mathematically related paradigms are considered by some to be more amenable to explanation facility implementation (than, say, multilayer perceptrons) because of their nearest-neighbor attributes (Simpson and Brotherton 1995).

Many explanation facilities for neural networks have shortcomings as well. When a loan application is denied because of the recommendation of a neural network–based system, for example, it may not be sufficient to cite examples of codebook vectors or distances to decision hypersurfaces. The user may demand to know the rules, or guidelines, that were violated and led to the denial of credit.

Fuzzy Expert System Explanation

For fuzzy expert systems, the explanation facility can list all rules that contributed to the classification or recommendation, ranked according to the significance of their contribution. Depending on the extent to which the solution is supported by the fuzzy rules, a degree of certainty can be assigned to the solution. The facility can also indicate where in the domain of the solution variable (low, medium, etc.) the solution is located (Cox 1994).

Building explanation facilities for forward chaining or fuzzy expert systems is particularly difficult because of their parallel nature. Many rules (fuzzy rules, in the case of fuzzy expert systems), acting in parallel, often combine to contribute to the result. Unlike backward chaining expert systems, then, it is not possible to explain a specific system action by tracing a crisp sequence of rules. In fact, the explanation facility portion of a fuzzy expert system may contain some of the most complex code in the system (Cox 1994).

Evolutionary Computation Tools for Explanation

Evolutionary computation consists of machine learning optimization and classification paradigms that are roughly based on evolution mechanisms such as biological genetics and natural selection. Previously in this book, we examined five main areas of the evolutionary computation field: genetic algorithms, evolutionary programming, genetic programming, particle swarm optimization, and evolution strategies.

Genetic programming evolves and obtains a mathematical formula or logical function from the input and output datasets. The solutions that are evolved themselves provide explanations of how the results can be obtained through the formula or function from the input data. Therefore, unlike the other evolutionary algorithms, a genetic programming system can, to some extent, provide solutions with some explanation capability.

In the remainder of this section, we focus on the design and search capability of evolutionary algorithms to develop explanation facilities that are not part of any explanation capability the systems themselves can provide. We thus focus on using the other four areas of evolutionary computation: genetic algorithms, particle swarm optimization, evolutionary programming, and evolution strategies. For a discussion of all five evolutionary computation areas, refer to Chapter 3.

To illustrate the use of evolutionary computation tools in developing components of an explanation facility for a neural network, consider one of the network's output processing elements. Higher values of this output processing element (close to 1) indicate the existence of some classification, condition, or decision C, and lower activation values (close to 0) represent $\bar{C}$.

To obtain codebook vectors for C, the trained neural network is used as the fitness function for the evolutionary computation tool. The fitness value returned by the evolutionary computation tool's evaluation function (in this case, the feedforward neural network calculation) is equal to the processing element activation value for C. Thus, the evolutionary computation tool is *maximizing* the processing element activation, or finding input patterns with very high output values. For networks with more than one output, a high fitness means that high values for the class C PE must be accompanied by values near 0 for all other output class PEs.

Codebook vectors for $\bar{C}$ are obtained by *minimizing* the processing element activation (finding input patterns that result in an output close to 0). The decision hypersurface is explored by fixing the processing element output value at the value that represents the boundary between two classes (often 0.5) and using the evolutionary computation tool to find input patterns that minimize the difference between the processing element output and the class boundary value. Different regions of the decision hypersurface can be explored in a number of ways, for instance by varying the random number seed used by the evolutionary computation tool.

Components of neural network explanation facilities have been developed using genetic algorithms. Results are reported in Eberhart and Dobbins (1991) and Eberhart (1992). When a genetic algorithm (GA) or other evolutionary computation tool is used, the decision hypersurface can be explored, and additional codebook vectors obtained, by using rank-ordering when assigning fitness values, in addition to varying the random number seed. Rank ordering causes fitness values to be distributed uniformly over a defined interval, such as 0 to 1, instead of being allowed to cluster near the top of the range, as often happens otherwise.

It has been demonstrated that other evolutionary computation tools can be used in building explanation facilities. A particle swarm optimizer has been shown to produce results similar to the genetic algorithm (Kennedy and Eberhart 1995).

Evolutionary computation tools can also be used to build explanation facility components for fuzzy expert systems, in a manner analogous to the method used for neural networks. In this case, the fitness value to be maximized is the closeness to a specific membership value for an output parameter of the fuzzy expert system. The expert system itself serves as the fitness function.

As we have pointed out throughout this book, the component paradigm tools of a computational intelligence system often become inseparable and indistinguishable. In other words, for the user, each tool loses its individual identity. This makes the design and implementation of an explanation facility significantly more complex.

As we stated at the beginning of this section, the user seldom knows, and rarely cares, what paradigms are being used in a diagnostic or classification tool. It is therefore important that the explanation facility be useful and consistent across computational modules. Some of this consistency can be implemented via an intelligent user interface design. Much of it, however, must be provided for in the basic design of the system.

Consider, for example, the diagnostic system depicted in Figure 11.2. This could be, for example, a medical diagnostic system with three main modules: perhaps one for abdominal disorders, one for chest pain, and one for ocular complaints. The user must be able to query the explanation facility and receive information that is useful and understandable, regardless of the situation. And the "look and feel" of the system should be as consistent as feasible.

If the user is making a diagnosis that uses Module 1, the explanation facility may retrieve codebook vectors that were generated using an evolutionary algorithm, then use the output of the module to trigger a rule-based explanation. If the differential diagnosis (distance to the decision hypersurface) is requested, the explanation facility can invoke an evolutionary algorithm to calculate what input symptoms must change, and by how much. These altered inputs can also be used to generate a neural net output that triggers a rule-based explanation using the shell.

A particle swarm optimizer might be used to generate codebook vectors and decision hypersurface information for Module 3, which uses fuzzy logic. The fuzzy outputs of the fuzzy logic diagnostic system would be defuzzified and used as inputs for the shell.

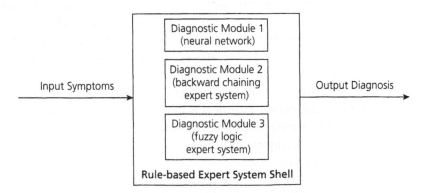

Figure 11.2 Modular medical diagnostic system.

For either Module 1 or Module 3, the previously described analysis tools known as relation factors can be invoked to provide information on the sensitivity of the diagnosis to each individual input. For example, with the remainder of the inputs held at values representing the current input pattern, each input can individually be varied over its range (from 0 to 1, for example) while looking at the effect on the output. This technique can be used to determine which input could have the most significant impact on the diagnosis; it can also be used to select the next question to be asked.

For Module 2, which uses a conventional backward chaining expert system, a standard rule-based explanation could be incorporated. In addition, however, it may be desirable to include a sensitivity measure based on relation factors. This measure could be implemented with a genetic algorithm or particle swarm optimizer. Because outputs are typically not responsive to continuous changes in inputs, however, some limitations on the resolution of relation factors exist. Since outputs are discontinuous, small changes in inputs may result in large output class differences.

An Example Neural Network Explanation Facility

A rudimentary example of an explanation facility for a neural network using particle swarm optimization is available on this book's web site. The filename for the application is nnexp.exe. The source code is written in C and compiled using Borland C++ Version 4.5. The source code is being distributed as *shareware*. You are welcome to use it for classroom or personal learning experiences in conjunction with the textbook at no cost, as discussed on the book's web site.

Using the Iris dataset as an example, we will step through the use of this explanation facility software. You can use it with any back-propagation neural network weight file obtained from the back-propagation neural network software provided with this book.

You need to specify the names of the run files. As in the evolutionary neural network implementation in Chapter 6, two run files (for example, bp.run and pso.run) are specified for the BP net and the PSO, respectively. To run the implementation from within the directory containing nnexp.exe, bp.run, and pso.run, at the system prompt type: nnexp bp.run pso.run.

The file pso.run is the same as that in the evolutionary neural network implementation in Chapter 6 except that the evaluation function type value is 18 instead of 17 (line 5) and the optimization type is minimization (0) instead of maximization (1) (line 4). See Chapter 6 for explanations of the other inputs. Listed here are the contents of pso.run:

```
1
0
1
0
18
```

```
1
1
0.0
1.0
0.5
1.0
1000
30
0.9
0
```

Within the back-propagation run file (bp.run), you specify the name of the neural network weight file along with the number of layers, the number of hidden PEs in each hidden layer, and the number of inputs and outputs for the network. In our example, the name of the weight file is iris.wts and the network has three layers (one hidden layer), four hidden PEs in the hidden layer, and four inputs and three outputs.

You next need to tell the program what you're looking for. For example, if you are looking for "quintessential" examples of output class 1 of 3, then you might specify 1 0 0 as the target. However, since numbers 1 and 0 are saturation values of the activation function, we specify the target values as 0.9 0.1 0.1 instead of 1 0 0 in the run file. (If you want to explore the decision hypersurface between classes 1 and 2, you specify 0.5 0.5 0.1 as the target.) Next you specify the sum-squared error you are willing to accept for the best particle. The maximum number of iterations for the PSO to run if that error is not achieved is specified in the file pso.run. In our example, we choose 0.011 and 1000 (see pso.run), respectively. Finally, specify the name of the output file; in our case we chose irisexp.out.

Listed here are the contents of bp.run:

```
iris.wts
3
4
4
3
0.9 0.1 0.1
0.011
irisexp.out
```

The program uses particle swarm optimization to "reverse-engineer" the neural network, finding the best examples it can of the target. The application uses a standard particle swarm with 30 particles, including an inertia weight (see Chapters 3 and 4).

In this case, the format of the output file is input1 input2 input3 input4 target values (0.9 0.1 0.1) error. Since there are 30 particles, there are 30 lines of output. You are most interested in those lines that have the smallest value for the error. In the example case, if the input error criterion is met, there will be at least one line with an error value less than 0.011. Depending on your problem, you may be interested only in the best particle, but you will probably be interested in all of them with sufficiently low error values, say, less than 0.013 or 0.015 in our example case.

In one of our runs, we obtained the following line of output representing the lowest error:

```
0.186070   0.373782   0.297252   0.154958   0.900000   0.100000   0.100000
      0.010015
```

What does the output tell us? In this case, it says that a quintessential example (codebook vector) for classification 1 is $(0.186070, 0.373782, 0.297252, 0.154958)$. Other vectors nearly as good are $(0.345683, 0.098616, 0.179630, 0.081630,$ and $0.341431, 0.685645, 0.394660, 0.132066)$. Recall that each of these inputs represents, one of the four attributes of an iris flower: sepal length, sepal width, petal length, and petal width. Also recall that we are classifying each pattern as belonging to one of the three species of iris flower: *Iris sectosa, Iris versicolor*, and *Iris virginica*. Remember that we normalized the raw measurement data for presentation to the neural network. If we convert the numbers in the codebook vector back to raw measurements in centimeters, the four numbers we obtain are the dimensions of the sepal length, sepal width, petal length, and petal width for a "quintessential" example of an *Iris sectosa* flower.

Now, if we use $0.5 \ 0.5 \ 0.1$ instead of $0.9 \ 0.1 \ 0.1$ as our target, we'll get examples of input patterns that are very near the decision hypersurface (the differential diagnosis) for the dataset, in this case, the decision hypersurface between classes 1 and 2. The output provides examples of patterns that cannot be classified as either class 1 or class 2 (*Iris sectosa* or *Iris versicolor*) by our system or, presumably, by an expert.

Summary

Sensitivity analyses are important for determining how various inputs contribute to the output(s) of a system. They can be used during the system design phase to prune inputs that are irrelevant to the system output(s). We present different approaches to sensitivity analysis, including an approach featuring relation factors and a sensitivity analysis methodology described by Zurada and colleagues. Explanation facilities are relatively common for traditional expert systems. Recently, using evolutionary computation tools such as genetic algorithms and particle swarm optimization, explanation facilities have been constructed for neural network systems. Hybrid diagnostic and classification systems incorporating a number of paradigms require explanation facilities that are useful, understandable, and consistent. These explanation facilities can be developed using a hybrid of rule-based and evolutionary computation tools. We provide an example of an explanation facility for a neural network, using the Iris dataset as an example. In the next (and last) chapter, which is on the book's web site, we tie together the concepts, paradigms, and implementations we've examined so far in the book into illustrative case studies.

Exercises

1. Run the example software to obtain codebook vectors for each class of iris flower in the Iris dataset. Discuss your results.

2. Run the example software to explore the decision hypersurface between each pair of classes. Discuss your results.

3. Specify a method for calculating relation factor one for a fuzzy rule-based system.

4. Assume that you are implementing in the C language the method discussed in this chapter for calculating the Zurada sensitivity two for an m-input, n-output system. Draw the flowchart for your implementation.

5. Design and run experiments using PSO to plot relationships between the PSO's parameter (or input) values and its performance (or output) values.

6. Propose an alternative way to display the information contained in a Hinton diagram.

7. Using the Zurada sensitivity process, calculate the *mean square average estimated sensitivity* $S_{i,eav}$ for each input of the Iris dataset. What do these sensitivities tell you?

8. Specify several possible codebook vectors for fuzzy expert systems.

Bibliography

Ackley, D., G. Hinton, and T. Sejnowski. 1985. A learning algorithm for Boltzmann machines. *Cognitive Science*, **9**:147–169.

Adlassnig, K. P., and W. Scheithauer. 1989. Performance evaluation of medical expert systems using ROC curves. *Computers and Biomedical Research*, **22**:297–313.

Ahalt, S., A. Krishnamurthy, P. Chen, and D. Melton. 1990. Competitive learning algorithms for vector quantization. *Neural Networks*, **3**:277–290.

Allman, W. F. 1989. *Inside the Neural Network Revolution*. New York: Bantam Books.

Amari, S.-I. 1967. A theory of adaptive pattern classifiers. *IEEE Transactions on Electronic Computers*, **EC16**:299–307.

———. 1971. Characteristics of randomly connected threshold-elements networks and network systems. *Proceedings of the IEEE*, **59**(1):35–47.

———. 1972. Learning patterns and pattern sequences by self-organizing nets of threshold elements. *IEEE Transactions on Computers*, **C21**:1197–1206.

———. 1977. Neural theory of association and concept formation. *Biological Cybernetics*, **26**:175–185.

———. 1983. Field theory of self-organizing neural nets. *IEEE Transactions on Systems, Man and Cybernetics*, **SMC-13**:741–748.

Amari, S.-I., and M. Takeuchi. 1978. Mathematical theory on formation of category detecting nerve cells. *Biological Cybernetics*, **29**:127–136.

Anderberg, M. R. 1973. *Cluster Analysis for Applications*. New York: Academic Press.

Anderson, E. 1935. The IRISes of the Gaspe peninsula. *Bulletin of the American IRIS Society*, **59**:2–5.

Anderson, J. A. 1972. A simple neural network generating on interactive memory. *Mathematical Biosciences*, **14**:197–220.

Anderson, J. A., and E. Rosenfeld, Eds. 1988. *Neurocomputing: Foundations of Research*. Cambridge, MA: MIT Press.

Anderson, J. A., A. Pellionisz, and E. Rosenfeld, Eds. 1990. *Neurocomputing 2: Directions for Research*. Cambridge, MA: MIT Press.

Anderson, J. A., J. Silverstein, S. Ritz, and R. Jones. 1977. Distinctive features, categorical perception, and probability learning: Some applications of a neural model. *Psychological Review*, **84**:413–451.

Armitage, P., and G. Berry. 1987. *Statistical Methods in Medical Research*, 2nd ed. Oxford, UK: Blackwell Scientific Publications.

Ashby, W. R. 1945. The physical origin of adaptation by trial and error. *Journal of General Psychology*, **32**:24.

Ashby, W. R. 1947. Principles of the self-organizing dynamic system. *Journal of General Psychology,* **37**:125.

Axelrod, R. 1980. Effective choice in the Prisoner's Dilemma. *Journal of Conflict Resolution,* **24**:3–25.

———. 1984. *The Evolution of Cooperation.* New York: Basic Books.

Bäck, T. 1992. Self-adaptation in genetic algorithms. In F. J. Varela and P. Bourgine, Eds. *Proceedings of the First European Conference on Artificial Life.* Cambridge, MA: MIT Press, 263–271.

———. 1995. Generalized convergence models for tournament and (mu, lambda) selection. *Proceedings of the Sixth International Conference on Genetic Algorithms.* San Francisco: Morgan Kaufmann, 2–7.

Bäck, T., and H.-P. Schwefel. 1993. An overview of evolutionary algorithms for parameter optimization. *Evolutionary Computation,* **1**(1):1–23.

Bagley, J. D. 1967. The behavior of adaptive systems which employ genetic and correlation algorithms. Ph.D. Dissertation, The University of Michigan, Ann Arbor, MI.

Baker, J. A. 1987. Reducing bias and inefficiency in the selection algorithm. *Proceedings of the Second International Conference on Genetic Algorithms: Genetic Algorithms and Their Applications.* Hillsdale, NJ: Lawrence Erlbaum Associates.

Barto, A. 1984. Simulation experiments with goal-seeking adaptive elements. Technical Report AFWAL-TR-84-1022, Air Force Wright Aeronautical Laboratory, Wright Patterson AFB, OH.

———. 1985. Learning by statistical cooperation of self-interested neuron-like computing units. *Human Neurobiology,* **4**:229–256.

Beielstein, T., K. E. Parsopoulos, and M. N. Vrahatis. 2002. Tuning PSO parameters through sensitivity analysis. Technical Report of the Collaborative Research Center 531, Computational Intelligence CI–124/02, University of Dortmund.

Bellman, R. 1957. *Dynamic Programming.* Princeton, NJ: Princeton University Press.

Bellman, R. E., and L. A. Zadeh. 1970. Decision-making in a fuzzy environment. *Management Science,* **17**:141–164.

Bentley, P. J., and D. W. Corne, Eds. 2002. *Creative Evolutionary Systems.* San Francisco: Morgan Kaufmann.

Bezdek, J. C. 1981. *Pattern Recognition with Fuzzy Objective Function Algorithms.* New York: Plenum Press.

———. 1992. On the relationship between neural networks, pattern recognition and intelligence. *International Journal of Approximate Reasoning,* **6**(2):85–107.

———. 1994. What is computational intelligence? In *Computational Intelligence: Imitating Life,* J. Zurada, R. Marks, and C. Robinson, Eds. Piscataway, NJ: IEEE Press, 1–12.

———. 1998. Computational intelligence defined—by everyone! In O. Kaynak, L. A. Zadeh, B. Türkşen, and I. J. Rudas, Eds. *Computational Intelligence: Soft Computing and Fuzzy-Neuro Integration with Applications.* Berlin: Springer-Verlag, 10–37.

Bezdek, J. C., and J. Harris 1978. Fuzzy partitions and relations: an axiomatic basis for clustering. *Fuzzy Sets and Systems,* **1**:112–127.

Bezdek, J. C., and S. K. Pal. 1992. *Fuzzy Models for Pattern Recognition: Methods that Search for Structure in Data.* Piscataway, NJ: IEEE Press, 413–414.

Black, M. 1937. Vagueness: an exercise in logical analysis. *Philosophy of Science,* **4**:427–455.

Bonabeau, E., M. Dorigo, and G. Theraulaz. 1999. *Swarm Intelligence.* New York: Oxford University Press.

Brachman, R. J., and H. J. Levesque. 2004. *Knowledge Representation and Reasoning,* San Francisco: Morgan Kaufmann.

Bremmermann, H. J. 1968. Numerical optimization procedures derived from biological evolution processes. In *Cybernetic Problems in Bionics,* H. L. Oestreicher and D. R. Moore, Eds. New York: Gordon and Breach, 597–616.

Bruns, R. 1993. Direct chromosome representation and advanced genetic operators for production scheduling. *Proceedings 5th International Conference on Genetic Algorithms.* San Mateo, CA: Morgan Kaufmann.

Bryson, A. E., and Y.-C. Ho 1975. *Applied Optimal Control.* New York: John Wiley.

Carpenter, G. A., and S. A. Grossberg. 1987a. A massively parallel architecture for a self-organizing neural pattern recognition machine. *Computer Vision, Graphics, and Image Understanding,* **37**:54–115.

———. 1987b. ART2: self-organization of stable category recognition codes for analog input patterns. *Applied Optics,* **26**(23):4919–4930.

Caudell, T. P. 1990. Parametric connectivity: feasibility of learning in constrained weight space. *Proceedings of the IEEE International Joint Conference on Neural Networks.* Hillsdale, NJ: Lawrence Erlbaum, **I**:667–675.

Caudill, M. 1988. Neural networks primer: Part IV. *AI Expert,* **3**(8):61–67.

———. 1989. Neural network primer: Part VIII. *AI Expert,* **4**(8):61–67.

———. 1989a. *Naturally Intelligent Systems.* Cambridge, MA: MIT Press.

Centor, R. M., and G. E. Keightley. 1989. Receiver operating characteristics (ROC) curve area analysis using the ROC analyzer. *Proceedings of the Thirteenth Annual Symposium on Computer Applications in Medical Care,* 222–226.

Clerc, M. 1999. The swarm and the queen: towards a deterministic and adaptive particle swarm optimization. *Proceedings of the 1999 Congress on Evolutionary Computation,* Washington, DC. Piscataway, NJ: IEEE Service Center, 1951–1957.

Cowan, J. D., and D. H. Sharp. 1988. Neural nets and artificial intelligence. *Daedalus,* **117**(1): 85–121.

Cox, E. 1994. *The Fuzzy Systems Handbook.* Boston: Academic Press, 130–158, 278–281.

Craven, M. W., and J. W. Shavlik. 1993. Learning symbolic rules using artificial neural networks. *Proceedings of the Tenth International Conference on Machine Learning,* 73–80.

Davis, L., Ed. 1991. *Handbook of Genetic Algorithms.* New York: Van Nostrand Reinhold.

De Jong, K. A. 1975. An analysis of the behavior of a class of genetic adaptive systems. Ph.D. Dissertation, The University of Michigan, Ann Arbor, MI.

DeLuca, A., and S. Termini. 1972. A definition of nonprobabilistic entropy in the setting of fuzzy sets theory. *Information and Control,* (20):301–312.

DeSieno, D. 1988. Adding a conscience to competitive learning. *Proceedings of the International Conference on Neural Networks.* Piscataway, NJ: IEEE Service Center, **1**:117–124.

Dimopoulos, C., and A. M. S. Zalzala. 2000. Recent developments in evolutionary computation for manufacturing optimization: problems, solutions and comparisons. *IEEE Transactions on Evolutionary Computation,* **4**(2):93–113.

Dubois, D., and H. Prade. 1980. *Fuzzy Sets and Systems: Theory and Applications.* New York: Academic Press.

Dyson, G. B. 1997. *Darwin among the Machines.* Reading, MA: Perseus Books.

Ebanks, B. R. 1983. On measures of fuzziness and their representations. *Journal of Math. Analysis and Applications*, (94):24–37.

Eberhart, R. C. 1990. Standardization of neural network terminology. *IEEE Transactions on Neural Networks*, 1:244–245.

———. 1992. The role of genetic algorithms in neural network query-based learning and explanation facilities. In L. D. Whitley and J. D. Schaffer, Eds. *COGANN-92: International Workshop on Combinations of Genetic Algorithms and Neural Networks.* Los Alamitos, CA: IEEE Computer Society Press, 169–183.

Eberhart, R. C., and R. W. Dobbins, Eds. 1990. *Neural Network PC Tools: A Practical Guide.* San Diego: Academic Press.

———. 1991. Designing neural network explanation facilities using genetic algorithms. *Proceedings of the IEEE International Joint Conference on Neural Networks.* Piscataway, NJ: IEEE Service Center, 1758–1763.

Eberhart, R. C., R. W. Dobbins, and W. R. S. Webber. 1989. CaseNet: A neural network tool for EEG waveform classification. *Proceedings of the IEEE Symposium on Computer Based Medical Systems*, Minneapolis, MN. Piscataway, NJ: IEEE Service Center.

Eberhart, R. C., and J. Kennedy. 1995. A new optimizer using particle swarm theory. *Proceedings of the Sixth International Symposium on Micro Machine and Human Science*, Nagoya, Japan. Piscataway, NJ: IEEE Service Center, 39–43.

Eberhart, R. C., and Y. Shi. 1998. Evolving artificial neural networks. *Proceedings of the 1998 International Conference on Neural Networks and Brain*, Beijing, P.R.C., PL5–PL13.

———. 2001. Tracking and optimizing dynamic systems with particle swarms. *Proceedings of the Congress on Evolutionary Computation 2001*, Seoul, Korea. Piscataway, NJ: IEEE Service Center.

Eberhart, R. C., P. K. Simpson, and R. W. Dobbins. 1996. *Computational Intelligence PC Tools.* Boston: Academic Press.

Elliot, D., Ed. 1987. *Handbook of Digital Signal Processing.* San Diego: Academic Press.

Embrechts, M. J., F. Arciniegas, M. Ozdemir, M. Momma, C. M. Breneman, L. Lockwood, K. P. Bennett, and R. H. Kewley. 2002. Stripmining for molecules. *Proceedings of the IEEE World Congress on Computational Intelligence.* Piscataway, NJ: IEEE Service Center.

Fang, H. L., D. Corne, and P. Ross. 1996. A genetic algorithm for job-shop problems with various schedule quality criteria. In *Evolutionary Computation AISB Workshop, Selected Papers*, T. C. Fogarty, Ed. Berlin, Germany: Springer-Verlag, 39–49.

Farley, B. G. 1960. Self-organizing models for learned perception. In M. C. Yovits and S. Cameron, Eds. *Self-Organizing Systems: Proceedings of an Interdisciplinary Conference,* 5 and 6 May, 1959. Oxford, UK: Pergamon Press, 7–30.

Farley, B. G., and W. A. Clark. 1954. Simulation of self-organizing systems by digital computer. *Transactions of IRE*, **PGIT-4**:76–84.

Fisher, R. A. 1936. The use of multiple measurements in taxonomic problems. *Annals of Eugenics*, 7:179–188.

Fogel, D. B. 1990. A brief history of simulated evolution. Technical report, ORINCON Corporation, San Diego.

————. 1991. *System Identification Through Simulated Evolution: A Machine Learning Approach to Modeling.* Needham Heights, MA: Ginn Press.

————. 1995. *Evolutionary Computation: Toward a New Philosophy of Machine Intelligence.* Piscataway, NJ: IEEE Press.

————. 2000. What is evolutionary computation? *IEEE Spectrum*, 37(2).

Fogel, L. J. 1994. Evolutionary programming in perspective: the top-down view. In J. M. Zurada, R. J. Marks II, and C. J. Robinson, Eds. *Computational Intelligence: Imitating Life.* Piscataway, NJ: IEEE Press, 135–146.

Fogel, L. J., A. J. Owens, and M. J. Walsh. 1966. *Artificial Intelligence through Simulated Evolution.* New York: John Wiley.

Fraser, A. S. 1957. Simulation of genetic systems by automatic digital computers. *Australian Journal of Biological Science*, 10:484–499.

————. 1960. Simulation of genetic systems by automatic digital computers: 5-linkage, dominance and epistasis. In O. Kempthorne, Ed. *Biometrical Genetics.* New York: Macmillan, 70–83.

————. 1962. Simulation of genetic systems. *Journal of Theoretical Biology*, 2:329–346.

Friedberg, R. M. 1958. A learning machine: Part I. *IBM Journal of Research and Development*, 2:2–13.

Friedberg, R. M., B. Dunham, and J. H. North. 1959. A learning machine: Part II. *IBM Journal of Research and Development*, 3:282–287.

Fukunuga, K. 1986. Statistical pattern classification. In T. Young and K. Fu, Eds. *Handbook of Pattern Recognition and Image Processing.* San Diego: Academic Press, 3–32.

Fukushima, K. 1980. Neocognitron: a self-organizing neural network model for a mechanism of pattern recognition unaffected by shift in position. *Biological Cybernetics*, 36:193–202.

————. 1986. A neural network model for selective attention in visual pattern recognition. *Biological Cybernetics*, 55:5–15.

Fukushima, K., and S. Miyake. 1982. Neocognitron: a new algorithm for pattern recognition tolerant of deformations and shifts in position. *Pattern Recognition*, 15:455–469.

Fukushima, K., S. Miyake, and T. Ito. 1983. Neocognitron: a neural network model for a mechanism of visual pattern recognition. *IEEE Transactions on Systems, Man and Cybernetics*, SMC-13:826–834.

Gallant, S. J. 1993. *Neural Network Learning and Expert Systems.* Cambridge, MA: MIT Press.

Gates, W. 1995. *The Road Ahead.* New York: Viking Penguin.

Goddard, D., Ed. 1970. *A Buddhist Bible.* Boston: Beacon Press.

Goldberg, D. E. 1983. Computer-aided gas pipeline operation using genetic algorithms and rule learning (doctoral dissertation, University of Michigan). *Dissertation Abstracts International*, 44(10), 3174B.

————. 1987. Computer-aided pipeline operation using genetic algorithms and rule learning. Part I: Genetic algorithms in pipeline optimization. *Engineering with Computers*, 3:35–45.

————. 1989. *Genetic Algorithms in Search, Optimization, and Machine Learning.* Reading, MA: Addison-Wesley.

Gray, F. 1953. Pulse code communication. United States Patent Number 2,632,058, March 17.

Gray, R. 1984. Vector quantization. *IEEE ASSP Magazine,* **1**(2):4–29.

Green, D. M., and J. A. Swets. 1966. *Signal Detection Theory and Psychophysics.* New York: Wiley.

Grefenstette, J. J. 1984a. GENESIS: A system for using genetic search procedures. *Proceedings of the 1984 Conference on Intelligent Systems and Machines,* 161–165.

————. 1984b. A user's guide to GENESIS. Technical Report CS-84-11, Computer Science Dept., Vanderbilt University, Nashville.

————., Ed. 1985. *Proceedings of an International Conference on Genetic Algorithms and Their Applications.* Hillsdale, NJ: Lawrence Erlbaum Associates.

Grossberg, S. A. 1970. Neural pattern discrimination. *Journal of Theoretical Biology,* **27**: 291–337.

————. 1973. Contour enhancement, short term memory, and constancies in reverberating neural networks. *Studies in Applied Mathematics,* **52**(3):213–257.

————. 1982. *Studies of Mind and Brain.* Dordrecht, Holland: Reidel Press.

————. 1988. *Neural Networks and Natural Intelligence.* Cambridge, MA: MIT Press.

Guo, Z., and R. E. Uhrig. 1992. Sensitivity analysis and applications to nuclear power plant. *Proceedings of the 1992 IEEE International Joint Conference on Neural Networks.* Piscataway, NJ: IEEE Service Center, **2**:453–458.

Haldane, J. B. S. 1990. *The Causes of Evolution.* Princeton, NJ: Princeton University Press.

Han, J., and M. Kamber. 2006. *Data Mining: Concepts and Techniques.* San Francisco: Morgan Kaufmann.

Hancock, P. J. B. 1992. Genetic algorithms and permutation problems: a comparison of recombination operators for neural net structure specification. In L. D. Whitley and J. D. Schaffer, Eds. *COGANN-92: International Workshop on Combinations of Genetic Algorithms and Neural Networks.* Los Alamitos, CA: IEEE Computer Society Press, 108–122.

Hanley, J. A., and B. J. McNeil. 1982. The meaning and use of the area under a receiver operating characteristic (ROC) curve. *Radiology,* **143**:29–36.

————. 1983. A method of comparing the areas under receiving operating characteristic curves derived from the same cases. *Radiology,* **148**:839–843.

Harmon, P., and B. Sawyer. 1990. *Creating Expert Systems for Business and Industry.* New York: John Wiley.

Haupt, R., and S. Haupt. 1998. *Practical Genetic Algorithms.* New York: John Wiley.

Hebb, D. O. 1949. *The Organization of Behavior.* New York: John Wiley.

Hecht-Nielsen, R. 1990. *Neurocomputing.* Reading, MA: Addison-Wesley.

Herrera, F., M. Lozano, and J. L. Verdegay. 1995. The use of fuzzy connectives to design real-coded genetic algorithms. *Mathware & Soft Computing,* **1**(3):239–251.

Hertz, J., et al. 1990. *Introduction to the Theory of Neural Computation.* Reading, MA: Addison-Wesley.

Hirota, K. 1995. History of industrial applications of fuzzy logic in Japan. In J. Yen, R. Langari, and L. Zadeh, Eds. *Industrial Applications of Fuzzy Logic and Intelligent Systems*, Piscataway, NJ: IEEE Press.

Holland, J. H. 1962. Outline for a logical theory of adaptive systems. *Journal of the Association for Computing Machinery*, 3:297–314.

———. 1992 (orig. ed. 1975). *Adaptation in Natural and Artificial Systems*. Cambridge, MA: MIT Press.

Holland, J. H., and J. S. Reitman. 1978. Cognitive systems based on adaptive algorithms. In D. A. Waterman and F. Hayers-Roth, Eds. *Pattern-Directed Inference Systems*. New York: Academic Press.

Hopfield, J. J. 1982. Neural networks and physical systems with emergent collective computational abilities. *Proceedings of the National Academy of Sciences*, 79:2554–2558.

———. 1984. Neurons with graded response have collective computational properties like those of two-state neurons. *Proceedings of the National Academy of Sciences*, 81:3088–3092.

Hornick, K., M. Stinchcombe, and H. White. 1989. Multilayer feedforward neural networks are universal approximators. *Neural Networks*, II:359–366.

Hwang, W. R., and W. E. Thompson. 1994. Design of intelligent fuzzy logic controllers using genetic algorithms. *Proceedings of the 1994 IEEE International Conference on Fuzzy Systems*. Piscataway, NJ: IEEE Press, 1383–1388.

IEEE Neural Networks Council. 1995. Glossary of fuzzy logic terms (working draft). Piscataway, NJ: IEEE Standing Committee on Standards.

———. 1996. Glossary of evolutionary computation terms (working draft). Piscataway, NJ: IEEE Standing Committee on Standards.

Ishibuchi, H., K. Nozaki, N. Yamamoto, and H. Tanaka. 1995. Selecting fuzzy if–then rules for classification problems using genetic algorithms. *IEEE Transactions on Fuzzy Systems*, 3.

James, W. 1890. *Psychology (Briefer Course)*. New York: Holt.

Kandel, E. R., J. H. Schwartz, and T. M. Jessell. 2000. *Principles of Neural Science*, 4th ed. New York: McGraw-Hill.

Karr, C. L. 1991a. Genetic algorithms for fuzzy controllers. *AI Expert*, 6(2):26–33.

———. 1991b. Applying genetics to fuzzy logic. *AI Expert*, 6(3):38–43.

Karr, C. L., and E. J. Gentry. 1993. Fuzzy control of pH using genetic algorithms. *IEEE Transactions on Fuzzy Systems*, 1(1):46–53.

Kauffman, S. A. 1993. *The Origins of Order*. New York: Oxford University Press.

———. 1995. *At Home in the Universe*. New York: Oxford University Press.

Kecman, V. 2001. *Learning and Soft Computing*. Cambridge, MA: MIT Press.

Kennedy, J. 1998. Thinking is social: experiments with the adaptive culture model. *Journal of Conflict Resolution*, 42:56–76.

Kennedy, J., and R. C. Eberhart. 1995. Particle swarm optimization. *Proceedings of the IEEE International Conference on Neural Networks*, Perth, Australia. Piscataway, NJ: IEEE Service Center, IV:1942–1948.

———. 1999. The particle swarm: social adaptation in information processing systems. In D. Corne, M. Dorigo, and F. Glover, Eds. *New Ideas in Optimization*. London: McGraw-Hill.

Kennedy, J., R. C. Eberhart, and Y. Shi. 2001. *Swarm Intelligence*. San Francisco: Morgan Kaufmann.

Kennedy, J. F. 1973. Boolean algebra and computer switching. *Radio-Electronics,* **44**(7): 23–25, 68.

Kitano, H. 1990. Designing neural network using genetic algorithm with graph generation system. *Complex Systems,* **4**:461–476.

Kleyn, P. A. 1963. Conceptual design of self-organizing machines. In J. E. Garvey, Ed. *Self-Organizing Systems 1963*. ACR-96, Office of Naval Research, Washington, DC: U.S. Government Printing Office, 52–64.

Klir, G. J., and T. A. Folger. 1988. *Fuzzy Sets, Uncertainty, and Information*. Englewood Cliffs, NJ: Prentice Hall.

Klir, G. J, and B. Yuan. 1995. *Fuzzy Sets and Fuzzy Logic: Theory and Applications*. Upper Saddle River, NJ: Prentice Hall.

Kohonen, T. 1972. Correlation matrix memories. *IEEE Transactions on Computers,* **C21**(4): 353–359.

———. 1982a. A simple paradigm for the self-organized formation of structured feature maps. In *Competition and Cooperation in Neural Nets* (Lecture Notes in Biomathematics), **45**, Berlin: Springer-Verlag.

———. 1982b. Self-organized formation of topologically correct feature maps. *Biological Cybernetics,* **43**:59–69.

———. 1986. Learning vector quantization for pattern recognition. Technical Report No. TKK-F-A601, Helsinki University of Technology, Finland.

———. 1988. *Self-Organization and Associative Memory,* 2nd ed. Berlin: Springer-Verlag.

———. 1989. Tutorial: Self-organizing feature maps. *IEEE International Joint Conference on Neural Networks*, Washington, DC. Piscataway, NJ: IEEE Service Center.

Kosko, B. 1986. Fuzzy entropy and conditioning. *Information Science,* **40**:165–174.

———. 1988. Bidirectional associative memories. *IEEE Transactions on Systems, Man and Cybernetics,* **SMC-18**:42–60.

———. 1993. *Fuzzy Thinking: The New Science of Fuzzy Logic*. New York: Hyperion.

Koza, J. R. 1992. *Genetic Programming: On the Programming of Computers by Means of Natural Selection*. Cambridge, MA: MIT Press.

Koza, J. R., and J. P. Rice. 1991. Genetic generation of both the weights and architecture for a neural network. *IEEE International Joint Conference on Neural Networks*. Piscataway, NJ: IEEE Press, **II**:397–404.

Koza, J. R. and M. A. Keane. 1990. Cart centering and broom balancing by genetically breeding populations of control strategy programs. *Proceedings of the International Joint Conference on Neural Networks*. Hillsdale, NJ: Lawrence Erlbaum Associates, 198–201.

Kubat, M., R. C. Holte, and S. Matwin. 1998. Machine learning for the detection of oil spills in satellite radar images, *Machine Learning,* **30**(2–3):195–215.

Latané, B. 1981. The psychology of social impact. *American Psychologist,* **36**:343–356.

Lee, D. G., Jr. 1989. Preliminary results of applying neural networks to ship image recognition. *Proceedings of the International Joint Conference on Neural Networks.* Piscataway, NJ: IEEE Service Center, **II**:576.

Lee, S., and R. Kil. 1989. Bidirectional continuous associator based on Gaussian potential function network. *Proceedings of the International Joint Conference on Neural Networks.* Piscataway, NJ: IEEE Service Center, **1**:45–54.

Lewis, D., and W. Gale. 1994. A sequential algorithm for training text classifiers. *Annual ACM Conference on Research and Development in Information Retrieval, the 17th Annual International ACM SIGIR Conference on Research and Development in Information Retrieval.* New York: Springer-Verlag, 3–12.

Levy, S. 1992. *Artificial Life.* New York: Random House.

Liepins, G. E., and W. D. Potter. 1991. A genetic algorithm approach to multiple-fault diagnosis. In L. Davis, Ed. *Handbook of Genetic Algorithms.* New York: Van Nostrand Reinhold.

Linde, Y., A. Buzo, and R. M. Gray. 1980. An algorithm for vector quantizer design. *IEEE Transactions on Communications,* **28**(1):84–95.

Lucas, P., and L. van der Gaag. 1991. *Principles of Expert Systems.* Wokingham, UK: Addison-Wesley.

Lukasiewicz, J. 1963. *Elements of Mathematical Logic.* [Original title: *Elementy logiki matematycznej.*] New York: Macmillan.

Mamdani, E., and S. Assilian. 1975. An experiment in linguistic synthesis with a fuzzy logic controller. *International Journal of Man-Machine Studies,* **7**(1):1–13.

Mange, E. A., and A. P. Mange. 1998. *Basic Human Genetics.* Sunderland, MA: Sinauer Associates.

Mann, H. B., and D. R. Whitney. 1947. On a test of whether one of 2 random variables is stochastically larger than the other. *Annals of Mathematical Statistics,* **18**:50–60.

Maren, A., C. Harston, and R. Pap. 1990. *Handbook of Neural Computing Applications.* San Diego: Academic Press.

Marks, R. 1993. Intelligence: computational versus artificial. *IEEE Transactions on Neural Networks,* **4**(5):737–739.

Martin, J., and S. Oxman. 1988. *Building Expert Systems.* Englewood Cliffs, NJ: Prentice Hall.

Masters, T. 1993. *Practical Neural Network Recipes in C++.* San Diego: Academic Press.

McClelland, J. L., and D. E. Rumelhart. 1986. *Parallel Distributed Processing: Explorations in the Microstructure of Cognition, Vol. 2: Psychological and Biological Models.* Cambridge, MA: MIT Press.

———. 1988. *Explorations in Parallel Distributed Processing: A Handbook of Models, Programs, and Exercises.* Cambridge, MA: MIT Press.

McClish, D. K. 1987. Comparing the areas under more than two independent ROC curves. *Medical Decision Making,* **7**:149–155.

McCulloch, W. C., and W. Pitts. 1943. A logical calculus of the ideas immanent in nervous activity. *Bulletin of Mathematical Biophysics,* **5**:115–133.

McKee, J. K. 2000. *The Riddled Chain: Change, Coincidence, and Chaos in Human Evolution.* Piscataway, NJ: Rutgers University Press.

McNeill, D., and P. Freiberger. 1993. *Fuzzy Logic.* New York: Simon and Schuster.

McNeill, F. M., and E. Thro. 1994. *Fuzzy Logic: A Practical Approach*. Boston: Academic Press.

Mead, C. 1989. *Analog VLSI and Neural Systems*. Reading, MA: Addison-Wesley.

Meistrell, M. L., and K. A. Spackman. 1989. Evaluation of neural network performance by receiver operating characteristic analysis: examples from the biotechnology domain. *Proceedings of the Thirteenth Annual Symposium on Computer Applications in Medical Care*, 295–301.

Michalewicz, Z., and M. Michalewicz. 1995. Pro-life versus pro-choice strategies in evolutionary computation techniques. In M. Palaniswami, Y. Attikiouzel, R. Marks, D. Fogel, and T. Fukuda, Eds. *Computational Intelligence: A Dynamic System Perspective*. Piscataway, NJ: IEEE Press, 137–151.

Michalewicz, Z., J. D. Schaffer, H.-P. Schwefel, D. B. Fogel, and H. Kitano, Eds. 1994. *Proceedings of the First IEEE Conference on Evolutionary Computation*. Piscataway, NJ: IEEE Service Center.

Michalewicz, Z., and Schoenauer, M. 1996. Evolutionary algorithms for constrained parameter optimization problems. *Evolutionary Computation*, 1(4):1–32.

Minsky, M. 1961. Steps toward AI. *Proceedings of the IRE*, **49**:5–30.

Minsky, M., and S. Papert. 1969. *Perceptrons*. Cambridge, MA: MIT Press.

Mish, F. C., Ed. 2001. *Merriam-Webster's Collegiate Dictionary*. Springfield, MA: G. & C. Merriam Co.

Mitchell, M. 1996. *An Introduction to Genetic Algorithms*. Cambridge, MA: MIT Press.

Montana, D. J. 1991. Automated parameter tuning for interpretation of synthetic images. In L. Davis, Ed. *Handbook of Genetic Algorithms*. New York: Van Nostrand Reinhold.

Montana, D. J., and L. Davis. 1989. Training feedforward neural networks using genetic algorithms. *Proceedings of the Eleventh Annual Joint Conference on Artificial Intelligence*. San Mateo: Morgan Kaufmann, 762–767.

Newell, A., and D. S. Moore. 2001. *Statistics: Concepts and Controversies*. New York: Freeman, 475.

Newell, A., and H. A. Simon. 1956. The logic theory machine: a complete information processing system. *Transactions on Information Theory (Institute of Radio Engineers)*, **IT-2**:61–79.

Nilsson, N. J. 1998. *Artificial Intelligence: A New Synthesis*. San Francisco: Morgan Kaufmann.

Pal, N. R., and J. C. Bezdek. 1994. Measuring fuzzy uncertainty. *IEEE Transactions on Fuzzy Systems*, **2**(2):107–118.

Pal, N. R., and S. K. Pal. 1989. Object-background segmentation using new definitions of entropy. *IEEE Proceedings*, **136**(2):284–295.

Pao, Y. 1989. Adaptive Pattern Recognition and Neural Networks. Reading, MA: Addison-Wesley.

Parker, D. 1982. Learning logic. Invention report 581–64, Department of Electrical Engineering, Stanford University, Stanford.

Pedrycz, W. 1998. *Computational Intelligence: An Introduction*. Boca Raton, FL: CRC Press.

Perry, T. S. 1995. Lotfi A. Zadeh. *IEEE Spectrum*, **32**(6):32–35.

Pineda, F. J. 1988. Dynamics and architecture for neural computation. *Journal of Complexity*, **4**:216–245.

Pinedo, M. 1995. *Scheduling: Theory, Algorithms and Systems*. Englewood Cliffs, NJ: Prentice-Hall.

Principe, J. C, N. R. Euliano, and W. C. Lefebvre. 2000. *Neural and Adaptive Systems: Fundamentals Through Simulations*. New York: John Wiley.

Rechenberg, I. 1965. Cybernetic solution path of an experimental problem. Royal Aircraft Establishment, library translation 1122, Farnborough, Hants, U.K.

———. 1973. *Evolutionsstrategie: Optimierung technischer Systeme nach Prinzipien der biologischen Evolution*. Stuttgart, Germany: Frommann-Holzboog Verlag.

———. 1994. Evolution strategy. In J. Zurada, R. Marks, II, and C. Robinson, Eds. *Computational Intelligence—Imitating Life*. Piscataway, NJ: IEEE Press, 147–159.

Reed, R. 1993. Pruning algorithms—a survey. *IEEE Transactions on Neural Networks*, **4**:740–747.

Reed, R., R. J. Marks II, and S. Oh. 1995. Similarities of error regularization, sigmoid gain scaling, target smoothing, and training with jitter. *IEEE Transactions on Neural Networks*, **6**:529–538.

Robbins, H., and S. Monro. 1951. A stochastic approximation method. *Annals of Mathematical Statistics*, **22**:400–407.

Robinson, A., M. Niranjan, and F. Fallside. 1988. Generalizing the nodes of the error propagation network. Cambridge University Engineering Department Technical Report CUED/F-INENG/TR.25, Cambridge, U.K.

Roscoe, J. T. 1969. *Fundamental Research Statistics*. New York: Holt, Rinehart, and Winston, 190–191.

Rosenblatt, F. 1958. The perceptron: a probabilistic model for information storage and organization in the brain. *Psychological Review*, **65**:386–408.

———. 1962. *Principles of Neurodynamics*. Washington, DC: Spartan Books.

———. 1964. A model for experiential storage in neural networks. In J. T. Tou and R. H. Wilcox, Eds. *Computer and Information Sciences: Collected Papers in Learning, Adaptation and Control in Information Systems*. Washington, DC: Spartan Books.

Ross, S. M. 2004. *Introduction to Probability and Statistics for Engineers and Scientists*. San Diego: Elsevier/Academic Press.

Ross, T. J. 1995. *Fuzzy Logic with Engineering Applications*. New York: McGraw-Hill, 134–146.

Ruck, D., S. Rogers, M. Kabrisky, P. Maybeck, and M. Oxley. 1992. Comparative analysis of backpropagation and the extended Kalman filter for training multilayer perceptrons. *IEEE Transactions on Pattern Analysis Machine Intelligence*, **14**(6):686–691.

Rumelhart, D. E., G. E. Hinton, and R. J. Williams. 1986. Learning representations by backpropagating errors. *Nature*, **323**(9):533–536.

Rumelhart, D. E., and J. L. McClelland. 1986. *Parallel Distributed Processing: Explorations in the Microstructure of Cognition, Vol. 1: Foundations*. Cambridge, MA: MIT Press.

Ruspini, E. H. 1969. A new approach to clustering. *Information and Control* 15(1):22–32.

———. 1973. New experimental results in fuzzy clustering. *Information Sciences* 6:273–284.

Saito, K., and R. Nakano. 1988. Medical diagnostic expert system based on PDP model. *Proceedings IEEE International Conference on Neural Networks*. San Diego, **I**:255–262.

Schaffer, J. D. 1984. Some experiments in machine learning using vector evaluated genetic algorithms. Unpublished doctoral dissertation, Vanderbilt University, Nashville.

Schaffer, J. D., R. A. Caruana, and L. J. Eshelman. 1990. Using genetic search to exploit the emergent behavior of neural networks. In S. Forrest, Ed. *Emergent Computation*. Amsterdam: North Holland, 1990, 244–248.

Schaffer, J. D., L. D. Whitley, and L. J. Eshelman. 1992. Combinations of genetic algorithms and neural networks: a survey of the state of the art. In L. D. Whitley and J. D. Schaffer, Eds. *COGANN-92: International Workshop on Combinations of Genetic Algorithms and Neural Networks*. Los Alamitos, CA: IEEE Computer Society Press, 1–37.

Schwefel, H.-P. 1965. Kybernetische Evolution als Strategie der experimentellen Forschung in der Stromungstechnik. Diploma thesis, Technical University of Berlin, Germany.

———. 1994. On the evolution of evolutionary computation. In J. M. Zurada, R. J. Marks II, and C. J. Robinson, Eds. *Computational Intelligence: Imitating Life*. Piscataway, NJ: IEEE Press.

Shi, Y. 2000. Fuzzy adaptive evolutionary computation: a review. *Proceedings of the Fourth World Multiconference on Systemics, Cybernetics and Informatics*, Orlando, July 23–26.

Shi, Y., and R. C. Eberhart. 1998a. Parameter selection in particle swarm optimization. In *Evolutionary Programming VII: Proceedings EP98*. New York: Springer-Verlag, 591–600.

———. 1998b. A modified particle swarm optimizer. *Proceedings of the IEEE International Conference on Evolutionary Computation*, 69–73. Piscataway, NJ: IEEE Press.

———. 2000. Experimental study of particle swarm optimization. *Proceedings SCI2000 Conference*, Orlando.

Shi, Y., R. C. Eberhart, and Y. Chen. 1999. Implementation of evolutionary fuzzy system. *IEEE Transactions on Fuzzy Systems*, Piscataway, NJ: IEEE Press.

Shi, Y., and Krohling, R. A. 2002. Co-evolutionary particle swarm optimization to solve min–max problems. *Proceedings of the 2002 Congress on Evolutionary Computation*, Honolulu, HI, Piscataway, NJ: IEEE Press.

Siegel, S. 1956. *Nonparametric Statistics for the Behavioral Sciences*. New York: McGraw-Hill.

Simpson, P. K. 1990. *Artificial Neural Systems: Foundations, Paradigms, Applications and Implementations*. Elmsford, NY: Pergamon Press.

Simpson, P. K., and T. Brotherton. 1995. Fuzzy neural network machine prognosis. *Proceedings of Aerosense '95: Applications of Fuzzy Logic Technology II*, SPIE–The International Society for Optical Engineering, Bellingham, WA, **2493**:21–27.

Singhal, S., and L. Wu. 1989. Training multi-layer perceptrons with the extended Kalman algorithm. In D. Touretzky, Ed. *Advances in Neural Information Processing Systems*. San Mateo, CA: Kaufmann Publishing.

Smith, S. F. 1980. A learning system based on genetic adaptive algorithms. Unpublished doctoral dissertation, University of Pittsburgh, Pittsburgh.

Specht, D. F. 1967. Vectorcardiographic diagnosis using the polynomial discriminant method of pattern recognition. *IEEE Transactions on Biomedical Engineering*, **BME-14** (2):90–95.

———. 1967a. Generation of polynomial discriminant functions for pattern recognition. *IEEE Transactions. on Electronic Computers*, **EC-16**(3):308–319.

———. 1988. Probabilistic neural networks for classification, mapping or associative memory. *Proceedings of the IEEE International Conference on Neural Networks*, **1**:525–532.

———. 1990. Probabilistic neural networks. *Neural Networks,* **3**(1):109–118.

Spiegel, M. 1975. *Schaum's Outline of Theory and Problems of Probability and Statistics.* New York: McGraw-Hill.

Stanfill, C., and B. Kahle. 1986. Parallel free-text search on the connection machine system. *CACM,* **29**(12):1229–1239.

Stork, D. G., S. Walker, M. Burns, and B. Jackson. 1990. Preadaptation in neural circuits. *Proceedings of the International Joint Conference on Neural Networks.* Hillsdale, NJ: Lawrence Erlbaum Associates, **I**:202–205.

Stubbs, D. 1988. Neurocomputers. *M. D. Computing,* **5**(3):14–24.

Sugeno, M. 1985. *Industrial Applications of Fuzzy Control.* New York: North-Holland.

Sugeno, M., and G. T. Kang. 1986. Fuzzy modeling and control of multilayer incinerator. *Fuzzy Sets and Systems,* **18**:329–346.

Sutton, R., and A. Barto. 1981. Toward a modern theory of adaptive networks: expectation and prediction. *Psychology Review,* **88**:135–171.

Swets, J. A., Ed. 1964. *Signal Detection and Recognition by Human Observers.* New York: John Wiley.

———. 1988. Measuring the accuracy of diagnostic systems. *Science,* **240**:1285–1293.

Syswerda, G. 1989. Uniform crossover in genetic algorithms. In J. D. Schaffer, Ed. *Proceedings of the Third International Conference on Genetic Algorithms.* San Mateo, CA: Morgan Kaufmann.

———. 1991. Schedule optimization using genetic algorithms. In *Handbook of Genetic Algorithms,* L. Davis, Ed., New York: Van Nostrand Reinhold.

Syswerda, G., and J. Palmucci. 1991. The application of genetic algorithms to resource scheduling. *Proceedings Fourth International Conference on Genetic Algorithms.* San Mateo, CA: Morgan Kaufmann.

Szu, H. 1986. Fast simulated annealing. In J. Denker, Ed. *AIP Conference Proceedings 151: Neural Networks for Computing.* New York: American Institute of Physics, 420–425.

Tahk, M. J., and Sun, B.-C. 2000. Coevolutionary augmented Lagrangian methods for constrained optimization. *IEEE Transactions on Evolutionary Computation,* (4)2: 114–124.

Takagi, T., and M. Sugeno. 1985. Fuzzy identification of systems and its applications to modeling and control. *IEEE Transactions on Systems, Man, and Cybernetics,* **SMC-15**(1): 116–132.

Terano, T., K. Asai, and M. Sugeno. 1989. *Applied Fuzzy Systems.* Cambridge, MA: AP Professional, 71–85.

Thrift, P. 1991. Fuzzy logic synthesis with genetic algorithms. *Proceedings of the International Conference on Genetic Algorithms.* San Mateo, CA: Morgan Kaufmann, 509–513.

Turing, A. M. 1937. On computable numbers, with an application to the Entscheidungsproblem. *Proceedings of the London Mathematical Society (serv. 2),* **42**:230–265; correction **43**:544–546.

Von Altrock, C. 1997. *Fuzzy Logic and NeuroFuzzy Applications in Business and Finance.* Upper Saddle River, NJ: Prentice Hall PTR.

Von der Malsberg, C. 1973. Self-organization of orientation sensitive cells in the striate cortex. *Kybernetik,* **14**:85–100.

Webber, W. R. S. 1988. JHH EMU spike viewer manual. Baltimore: The Johns Hopkins Hospital Department of Neurology.

Webber, W. R. S., B. Litt, K. Wilson, and R. P. Lesser, Eds. 1994. Practical detection of epileptiform discharges in the EEG using an artificial neural network: a comparison of raw and parameterized data. *Electroencephalography and Clinical Neurophysiology*, **91**: 194–204.

Wee, W. G. 1967. On generalizations of adaptive algorithms and application of the fuzzy sets concept to pattern classification. Ph.D. dissertation, Purdue University, West Lafayette, IN.

Wee, W. G., and K. S. Fu. 1969. A formulation of fuzzy automata and its application as a model of learning systems. *IEEE Transactions on Systems, Science. and Cybernetics*, **SSC-5**:215–223.

Werbos, P. 1974. Beyond regression. Ph.D. dissertation, Harvard University, Cambridge, MA.

White, H. 1989. Learning in neural networks: A statistical perspective. *Neural Computation*, **1**:425–464.

White, H. 1990. Neural network learning and statistics. *AI Expert*, Fall issue.

Whitley, D. 1989. Applying genetic algorithms to neural network learning. *Proceedings of the Seventh Conference of the Society of Artificial Intelligence and Simulation of Behavior*. Sussex, England: Pitman Publishing, 137–144.

Whitley, D., S. Dominic, and R. Das. 1991. Genetic reinforcement learning with multilayer neural networks. In R. K. Belew and L. B. Booker, Eds. *Proceedings of the Fourth International Conference on Genetic Algorithms*. San Mateo, CA: Morgan Kaufmann, 562–569.

Widrow, B., and M. E. Hoff. 1960. Adaptive switching circuits. *1960 IRE WESCON Convention Record: Part 4, Computers: Man-Machine Systems*, Los Angeles, 96–104.

Widrow, B., and R. Winter. 1988. Neural nets for adaptive filtering and adaptive pattern recognition. *IEEE Computer Magazine*, March:25–39.

Widrow, B., J. R. Glover, Jr., J. M. McCool, J. Kaunitz, C. S. Williams, R. H. Hearn, J. R. Zeidler, E. Dong, Jr., and R. C. Goodlin. 1975. Adaptive noise cancelling: principles and applications. *Proceedings of IEEE*, 63(12):1692–1716.

Wilcoxon, F. 1945. Individual comparisons by ranking methods. *Biometrics Bulletin*, 1:80–83.

Winston, P. H. 1984. *Artificial Intelligence*. Reading, MA: Addison-Wesley.

Wolfram, S. 1994. *Cellular Automata and Complexity*. Reading, MA: Addison-Wesley.

Yager, R. R., and D. P. Filev. 1994. *Essentials of Fuzzy Modeling and Control*. New York: John Wiley.

Yao, X. 1995. Evolutionary artificial neural networks. In A. Kent and J. G. Williams, Eds. *Encyclopedia of Computer Science and Technology*. New York: Marcel Dekker.

Young, T., and K. Fu, Eds. 1986. *Handbook of Pattern Recognition and Image Processing*. San Diego: Academic Press.

Yovits, M. C., and S. Cameron, Eds. 1960. *Self-Organizing Systems*. New York: Pergamon Press.

Zadeh, L. A. 1965. Fuzzy sets. *Information and Control*, **8**:338–353.

———. 1972. A fuzzy-set-theoretic interpretation of linguistic hedges. *Journal of Cybernetics*, **2**(2):4–34.

———. 1975. The concept of a linguistic variable and its application to approximate reasoning, Parts 1 and 2. *Information Sciences*, **8**:199–249, 301–357.

———. 1994. Soft computing and fuzzy logic. *IEEE Software* (November):48–56.

————. 1998. Roles of soft computing and fuzzy logic in the conception, design and deployment of information/intelligent systems. In O. Kaynak, L. A. Zadeh, B. Türkşen, and I. J. Rudas, Eds. *Computational Intelligence: Soft Computing and Fuzzy-Neuro Integration with Applications.* Berlin: Springer-Verlag, 10–37.

Zimmerman, H.-J., and P. Zysno. 1980. Latent connections in human decision making. *Fuzzy Sets and Systems*, **4**:37–51.

————. 1983. Decision analysis and evaluations by hierarchical aggregation of information. *Fuzzy Sets and Systems*, **10**:243–266.

Zurada, J. M., A. Malinowski, and I. Cloete. 1994. Sensitivity analysis for minimization of input dimension for feedforward neural networks. *Proceedings of the IEEE International Symposium on Circuits and Systems*, London.

Index

About the Authors

Russell C. Eberhart is professor of electrical and computer engineering at the Purdue School of Engineering and Technology, Indiana University Purdue University Indianapolis (IUPUI). He is also vice president of Computelligence LLC in Indianapolis, Indiana. He received his Ph.D. from Kansas State University in electrical engineering. He is coeditor of a book on neural networks, and coauthor of *Computational Intelligence PC Tools* (Academic Press, 1996). Russ is coauthor of a book with Jim Kennedy and Yuhui Shi entitled *Swarm Intelligence* (Morgan Kaufmann/Academic Press, 2001). He was awarded the IEEE Third Millennium Medal. In 2001, he became a Fellow of the IEEE, and in 2002 he became a Fellow of the American Institute for Medical and Biological Engineering.

Yuhui Shi is an applied specialist for Electronic Data Systems, Inc. He received his Ph.D. in electrical engineering in 1992 from Southeast University in China. He has been actively involved in organizing several IEEE conferences related to computational intelligence. Yuhui is an associate editor of the *IEEE Transactions on Evolutionary Computation*, and an adjunct faculty member of the Department of Radio Engineering, Southeast University, and the Department of Electrical and Computer Engineering, Indiana University Purdue University Indianapolis.